THE SEA OF GLASS

A CLEAR UNDERSTANDING OF THE SCRIPTURES IN SPIRITUAL TERMS: SELF-CONTROL, SELF-LEARNING, AND SELF-UNDERSTANDING

ROGER AKERLEY

First Edition

Fulton Books
Meadville, PA

Published by Fulton Books 2022

ISBN 979-8-88505-113-2 (paperback)
ISBN 979-8-88505-114-9 (digital)

Printed in the United States of America

ACKNOWLEDGEMENT

First, and foremost, I wish to thank the Almighty God for inspiring me to write this book.

Second, my grandson, Austin Akerley, for explaining how to use the technology to make writing my book look easy. His patience for this old man is inspiring. What a fine young man he is. Thank you, Austin!

Thirdly, Michael Wojculewicz, for his assistance with the editing of this book.

And last, but not least, Rita Paradis Thibeault, my personal secretary and partner in life.

INTRODUCTION

There is no subject or part of life that can be lived or endured to any amount of success without a proper understanding of that subject. The subject of the Lord, the soul, and life itself is no exception. If anyone wishes to learn the word of the one true God with the desire of living with him in the real kingdom of Heaven, both the physical and the spiritual parts of life are to be accepted as different sides of the one true understanding of life as it was created to be. Simply put, the same common sense that is needed to explain any physical subject in life is also the key to understanding in spirit. Yet for thousands of years the accepted authorities on spirituality, organized religion, have been falsely preaching the opposite.

The intention of this book is simply to inform mankind of our beliefs. The knowledge we have gained using the above-mentioned common-sense approach. It is a knowledge that we believe anyone can achieve. Our view is that the understanding of the truth of the spirit is achieved and accepted or rejected inside each one of us individually with no one in between any person and the Lord. This book serves as a starting point of spiritual knowledge. A basic explanation of the simple truth of life as a means to point the reader in the proper direction. The reader should work directly with the Lord with the goal of eventually outgrowing even this book as they develop their own personal understanding of life as it was created to be lived.

CONTENTS

THE OLD TESTAMENT

To begin this book, I will begin with the Book of Genesis and the seven days of the creation. Try to understand the *power* of the Book of Genesis. To do this, you must first come to realize that the book we call the Bible is a *spiritual* book, *not* a book about the *physical* part of life. Since the body dies but the spirit lives forever, it only makes sense that the laws contained in the Bible, which the Lord tells us are "everlasting laws" would be meant for the *everlasting* part of life, i.e., the *spirit*, *not* the body. This means that as you read the teachings of the Lord, you have to understand that *he* is talking about a *spiritual* Adam and Eve, a *spiritual* Garden of Eden, a *spiritual* serpent, and so on. And since *all* spirits are *one* spirit, these events happen *inside* every one of us. The names and places are not historical events that happened thousands of years ago in another part of the world in past generations. They are "spiritual" events that are *present* in our lives for *all* generations. It is the *only* way the scriptures make complete sense and can be realistically understood and lived.

Now we come to the creation of Adam and Eve in the understanding of the seven days of the creation. What was created in the Book of Genesis happened over a period of six thousand years because each thousand years is *one day* in terms of the Creation. During the last millennium, we have lived seven lives in each thousand years that the Lord counts in the setting up of the forty lives that we have "lived in the wilderness" where a human being could *not* understand that the Lord *is* God. Hence, we now come to understand the *power* of what God *is* in the *spiritual* understanding.

You must come to understand the *power* that God had to establish this Creation in five days and, during the last one thousand years, transformed this created man to the *modern man.* We have to understand that God has used this last one thousand years to create mankind and make us human beings "immortal in spirit" where an individual comes to understand the *power* of his Creation. We are living in the seventh day, the day of rest, on which the Lord must bring the modern man to understand the *value* of the "real" Kingdom of God and to understand that God is *not* a magician. He creates, in time, in that we are in *one power under God.* Each of us was created with all the hardships of mankind and through war and peace, where human beings are created by the *grace of intelligence.* Now we must come to understand each thousand years that it took to bring mankind to his creation.

Try to understand the animal that God created six thousand years ago that we call mankind and bring that animal to *this* creation *now* in the glory of heaven, where human beings come to understand his own creation and the *power* of the wisdom of the wise—where we come from and where we are going on the *seventh* day of the Lord that we *just started* in the seven days of the Creation. We must come to understand that this Creation is the *power* that we, as human beings, are created from. Also, the *value in our spiritual power* to understand the Lord our God. This Creation is the *power of intelligence* to *understand.* Since mankind was only created in the last thousand years, trying to understand the Creation of the animal into a man to complete the wisdom of the wise is what we are living in the creation of human knowledge. We must bring to our attention *all* things created by God in the last thousand years, where there was war after war, destruction after destruction or human beings being asked to be placed in different wars to build his intelligence by the suffering of the great sacrifices of war. Try to understand that in *all* wars, man has learned from his mistakes, and in every single battle of intelligence, man has stood in *front* of his deeds to glorify the day of his Creation.

Next, we come to Adam and Eve in the battle of the understanding of life by a group of people that the Lord has chosen to bring the *reality* of all *true light*. God's love *is* the *light*, and he gives his power to have light on earth in the *power of human thinking*. God sends the light to a group of men that he chose to bring this light to mankind. We come to the light of heaven, where we will come to understand life on Earth. God created this group of men in *his wisdom* and sent to them the *purpose* and the *glory* of his great kingdom.

Adam represents the "spirit," and Eve represents the "mind." Every one of us has *both* a spirit and a mind. The glory of having a spirit and a mind means that we must come to understand where we are going and what to do to get to this place where a human being must be born again in his soul. The place where he must defeat the animal that's in his mind in order to accomplish the *spiritual* understanding that he was created to live by. Now let's understand *God*, our *spiritual mind*, and the *glorifying power* of this *wisdom*. The Lord has created the spirit to understand what a human being is in this spiritual power. Each person must receive this spiritual birth of human thinking *inside* their soul.

Adam and Eve had two sons, Cain and Abel. These two brothers are children of this spiritual understanding of the Scriptures. You know that Cain killed his brother, Abel, because of *jealousy*. Cain stands for "wrong" and Abel stands for "right over wrong." They both brought offerings to the Lord, but the Lord only looked with favor upon Abel's offering. This means that in the kingdom of the Lord, *right* will be *above wrong*. Cain became angry that his brother was chosen and not him, so he attacked Abel and killed him. The descendants of wrong, which is Cain, are going to be part of what was created in *wrong over right*, wherein human beings (because Abel was killed) must first understand the Scriptures in wrong *before* he can understand right, and this is where the power of the Lord comes in. The power of wrong over right must come to be *first* in human understanding. Because what happened in the beginning must be brought to *this* day, where a human being must be in "wrong" in order to receive "right," this is the part of the Creation of the Lord, who made man in his own image.

Now you have all the false prophets of religion who are teaching people to worship others and not God alone. The Catholic Church teaches the Scriptures in *physical*, not spiritual, terms. They have daily worshipping of the birth and the life of Jesus that is *wrong over right*. In their teaching of falsehood, they are bringing people to the "cave" of falsehood where they have to attend mass on Sunday. Their church is nothing more than a cave where there is *no* spiritual understanding. Understand well that you must have the *birth* of the Spirit to understand the Almighty God. None of these organized religions that I have ever listened to has understood the *spiritual* birth of intelligence. If they did, they would have transferred all their talk of the Scriptures to the spiritual understanding, where human beings must understand *every single word* of the Scriptures in the spiritual, *not* the physical, understanding.

We must take the physical part *out* of the Scriptures so we can have a new birth of intelligence when we read the Bible. I don't think I have ever heard a single Catholic priest talk of this spiritual part of the Scriptures, and in any of the falsehood of Christianity, I have found *not* a single clergyman who has acknowledged this *spiritual* part. There is, in my belief, none of them who can understand the power of the Scriptures we are going to. God *is* the Truth and *not* a human being of flesh. If you need to understand God and pray to God, you *cannot* pray to a *man*. If you do as the Christians and the Catholics do, you are praying to a *false god*. These people are placing all of their understanding into the *physical* part of Jesus, and they don't understand the One "True" God. The parables of Jesus are the words of God and *not* the physical part of Jesus. I accept the parables of Jesus as the son of God, but I do *not* accept the physical life of a man as the son of God. If you pray to Jesus, you are praying to a false god, and you'll never understand the Scriptures, and if you don't understand the scriptures, you'll *never* be part of the Kingdom of God.

All the false teachings that say Jesus saves people are *wrong*, and that is why we will have to go through wrong *before* we can understand what is right. The "truth" is *right over wrong*. You must come to understand that you were wrong to worship Jesus because you have to be wrong *before* you can be right, and you have to learn right over wrong because wrong comes *first* over right. You have to understand the glory of intelligence where wrong is the descendant of right, and that is why the descendants of Cain is where you took off in the wrongdoing of prejudice. The son of Cain is *bigotry*—the son of Cain and all the falsehood of the sons of Cain where a man must receive the birth of the spirit inside his soul. You must keep away from *all* false religion because their arrogance will never come to understand and accept the truth because they believe in wrong over right.

Next, we come to the understanding of Noah and the great flood. Each one of us must "build" an "Ark" inside our heart. An Ark of the Covenant Laws of God is where your ship of human understanding will not sink to the bottom of the water and you will not drown in the misunderstanding of the Scriptures.

You must come to understand the Ark of the Covenant Laws of the Lord your God with all your soul. You must build this ark with the Holy Laws that come from the burning bush in the understanding of the Law where you can *see* the face of God in the middle of all the lies of the world.

A *Covenant* is what comes from the Lord in the spiritual value of a human being on the covenant laws that will keep you on the ship of the Ark that lives inside you and the love of *all* mankind. Understand well that you must transfer every human thought to a "feeling" inside your spirit to understand this powerful Covenant that you made with the Lord. After many days on the ship of the Covenant of the Lord, meaning for the lifetime in the desert of human understanding, you come to rest your ship on the glory of land. The ship rests in reality inside a human heart where you can feel and understand the truth about your lost soul. The soul comes to life for standing on solid ground with the *true* Laws of God. This is the Covenant between God and Noah inside *all* men.

Now we come to understand the "golden table" with the power to grasp how *all* these religions separate themselves from the truth. Understand that it is the mind of mankind that forms religion according to their weak female mind inside each of us for the period of forty lifetimes on earth before the Lord opens the door of heaven for people to understand what the Promised Land really is. No one can break the Seal that God has placed on the Scriptures because man has to learn from wrong to right in the power of himself to receive right over wrong and that the first will be last and the last will be first in the teaching of the Lord. Each person comes in wrong to accomplish right in his spirit and has to live in the desert for forty years—that is forty *lifetimes*. This is what I call the *mystery of life*, where a human being has to be taught by wrong in order to be right.

This is how the human race has to learn to understand the Lord your God. Everyone who is called to the understanding must come to the gates of hell first, where human beings have to suffer and go through the great persecution of the Lord. You *cannot* learn without the sacrifice of life, and you cannot live without understanding wrong over right in the birth of intelligence. That is why the Lord your God sent you into misery in order for you to *gain* this intelligence and the wisdom of the wise. You had a mission of sacrifice over *all* wrong in this process called *learning*. In your sacrifice, you were asked to start in the land where the descendants of Cain will bring you in order to *receive* the Kingdom of God. That is why God made false religion, to fool the minds of men so that they can learn from wrong to be right in the Kingdom of God by worshiping the Almighty God and live in the Kingdom of Intelligence, where human beings will worship the Lord and *his* Creation for the rest of eternity.

We come to the Tower of Babel, where men were placed in many different religions, where they could *not* understand *anything* in perfect form in the wisdom that made no sense whatsoever. In these false religions, no one can understand each other because the Lord made the Tower of Babel to reach the port of confusion in the land of the misguided. *Each* religion preaches *different* doctrines, and each doctrine forms *lies* and *total stupidity* in the ignorance of mankind. Try to understand *any* organized religion and you will come up empty in the word of the Lord. The confusion of stupidity does *not* make sense to anybody because these false religions made it so that you have to worship a man as the Lord your God. Each religion was born in lies by the confusion of physical value over spiritual value. This physical part of a human being is *not* mentioned in the Scriptures. This confused the false prophets of the earth where they had ministries of all kinds given to them by the hand of man. They called themselves priests, rabbis, ministers, teachers, etc., who preached and confused *everybody* on Earth.

They made it impossible to *really* understand the *true* Laws of God. All these false religions in the Tower of Babel made up what they could out of the Scriptures because remember that Jacob's son Dan is *your* affiliation with God. *Everybody* wants to believe in God, but the false prophets, who were created by God to confuse the world, made up everything that they could pull out of the Scriptures to preach how to love Jesus and worship an "idol man" before the Lord.

Remember that the scriptures were written for spiritual value, and these false religions could *not* understand this, so they made up what they could for the value of the introduction of their lies. They fed the people in the physical sense with what they could find in the Bible to prove their point of lying to the people. God did *not* choose these people to form any religion outside the spiritual understanding of the Lord. In many ways, the Lord *planned* to fool the world of man. When you learn the truth after forty lifetimes on earth, you have come to learn from wrong in order to cross over. The Lord brings you to this day where he has to destroy false religion and bring *true* religion for the human race. This will separate the goats from the sheep. Those who cannot be proven right through the teaching of the truth will come to live with their falsehood, and those who accept the truth will live forever. I just want to warn you ahead of time that whoever decides *not* to follow the power to understand the truth of life will *not* gain life, and whoever didn't know before but accepts the truth now will gain life.

Now we come to understand the power where the teaching of the Lord comes alive inside you. Be aware, however, that if you become angry with the Lord because you are full of pride and arrogance, then your pride and arrogance will *not* save you and you *will* lose your soul. You will not be able to stay in heaven because the Lord of Justice has put inside of you the root of your destiny—you are going to be on the side of the goat and push people around with your falsehood.

Next, we come to understand Abraham, Isaac, and Jacob. Abraham represents the truth, Isaac represents reality, and Jacob represents common sense. Make sure that you do not look at the image of man here. Instead, you must understand this in spiritual terms. When I say that Abraham is the truth, try to understand that there are three persons in God: truth, reality, and common sense. Also, you must understand the Lord to be what he is. God is really in the feelings of human understanding, where we feel what is inside us: the Temple of the Lord. The calling of Abraham by the Lord must be understood by the human race to mean that God called him to make sense in the understanding of this great spiritual value, where human beings come to understand that God has chosen them for a special understanding of the Scriptures. In this understanding of the Lord and the Scriptures, Abraham is the truth, Isaac is the reality, and Jacob is common sense, so you have the truth, reality, and common sense of the Lord. This is why you *must* believe that God is truth.

Now we come to the Covenant of God with Abraham. In truth, this is the power to understand the Lord where a human being inside himself comes to understand the great glory of God. To understand the Scriptures, you must understand the voice that is inside your soul. When the Lord speaks to you, he tells you the things he wants you to do. You must believe that this is the voice of the Lord. If you understand that voice inside you, speak to that voice and the voice will answer you because this is the voice of the Lord. Most people don't realize that their conscience is the voice of the Lord inside them. Your conscience tells you not to do something or to do it. If you listen to the bad choices of your mind and you think that you have to go to church to receive the Lord, this is *false* because your mind has overpowered your Spirit. You listened to your *mind* and then you go to church.

Try *not* to learn from false prophets and other people who know *far less* than you do. Make an effort to understand the *power* of your spiritual voice inside your soul and do things where you will benefit the most. If you listen to your mind on spiritual matters, you're listening to the part that is too weak to understand in spiritual terms. If you listen to your own feelings instead, this will be the voice of God that tells you the *truth*. Then and only then will you not be a slave to any religion. Understand that God *is* the voice in your soul, and when you speak to that voice, you will receive an answer and will know what to do. You won't need to be a slave to any false religion of the earth.

If you believe that the pope, archbishop, bishop, priest, or minister knows better than your conscience, you are wrong. If you listen to the voice of your heart, you will come to understand the Lord your God inside your soul; you will understand the truth, and you will be able to live *in* the truth.

But if you listen to laws made by men, you will most certainly lose your soul.

Try to understand these laws and do a lot better than you have done so far. The pope makes laws according to his mind, the weaker part of a human being. If you listen to these rules and laws of the mind that make no sense whatsoever and you obey them, you will be placed on the road to hell. You will suffer greatly for obeying these laws of worthless value that has nothing to do with your spiritual understanding. Your spirit will fall in the dark value, and you will think that heaven is what false religion claims it is.

Make a covenant of rules and laws with the *Lord* himself that makes sense inside your spirit. Do *not* practice any law or rule that comes from a worthless church or house of worship that man has created for himself. You must come to understand the *real* laws of God inside you match your spiritual understanding. When you come to worship the Lord your God with all your soul, make sure that you understand these laws and rules with your own heart and not with the heart of the false prophet. This is your covenant with the Lord.

Next, we come to the birth of Isaac, meaning the birth of reality. In the word of man, reality has brought the human race to the point where one understands the *value* of reality. The human race lives in a world of make-believe because this is what religion has taught the world to understand. All the generations of people have learned, through organized religion, is to believe in the world of make-believe. This is where human beings believe that God is a magician of superstitious value and that he can change anything in the creation as he pleases. God is a Creator that creates through time, and through that time, he creates just like a man builds a house. You cannot build a house with the split-second motion of your hand like a magician, and God *cannot* create anything with a split-second motion of his hand and do magical tricks in the sky.

Do understand, however, that God is not just a magician who does as he pleases. The Creation of man and animals took thousands of years to come to the point of the present day. Human beings were created through hardship, war, destruction, pain, and suffering. God did *not* do this in a split-second. It took the Lord God to send man through all the suffering and persecution to bring mankind to where it is now.

Now we come to those who don't accept the values of the Lord. A human being comes from an animal who lives in *justice*, and when he cannot find that justice, he must struggle and fight for the value that *all* men are created with: justice, fairness and unity with the Lord. You must come to understand the laws of God that he brings to you in reality so you will be able to live with your brother in the value of brotherhood according to the laws and the scales of justice. Isaac, the son of Abraham, brings the birds of reality to mankind where a man must bring his own value to the table of brotherhood. No man is allowed to use this justice over others—it has to become the justice of reality for *all* men. If you come into the teaching of the Lord, you *must learn* the value of the laws of God inside your soul. The *only* place that you will find this value is in your own heart.

Next, we come to understand Jacob, the son of Isaac and grandson of Abraham. Try to understand that Jacob and Esau were both born from the line of Abraham where a human being comes to understand the truth, common sense, and reality to complete the understanding of the Lord. You must understand the Lord from the father, Abraham (truth), to the son, Isaac (common sense), and then to Jacob (reality)—the same common sense that Jesus used in his parables—it *is* the Word of God that was revealed the through the lessons of Abraham, Isaac, and Jacob.

You also have a physical teaching here representing a spiritual truth. Esau and Jacob were brothers who were also twins which, in spirit, means close to one another. Esau represents laziness, and Jacob represents ambition. What this means is that they represent two different sides of the *same* teaching. They were born at the same time, but Esau was born first with Jacob holding onto Esau's heel. This is how we know that they are close to each other in wisdom. The firstborn son is the one to receive the birthright—this means the one to assume leadership of the family upon the passing of the father. Esau being born first is why we always first consider being lazy before we get things done. But Jacob got his brother to give him the birthright. So even though we first want to be lazy, it is ambition that will ultimately be in charge. Understand that laziness is born before ambition in your physical life. You must control both your laziness and your ambition. You must use Jacob (your ambition) to learn as much as you can because Esau (your laziness) will always be there to try to defeat your ambition for the reason that Jacob received the blessing, even though he was *not* born first. This means that you have to work with ambition to defeat your laziness even though it is not the first thought in your mind.

Let's look further at Jacob, son of Isaac, and understand your common sense. Inside each one of us, there is a Jacob that lives in the "feelings" of receiving the blessing of the Lord. We have to come in this knowledge that brings common sense to *all* reality because both the father (Isaac) and the son (Jacob) is inside each one of us. Try to understand that your common sense comes from the blessing of the Lord, and when you receive the blessing of your Father in heaven, you receive the blessing of your Father where you come to understand your weakness before your strength and spiritual value. This is why Esau was born first.

Try to comprehend the value of the firstborn over the second born. What this means is that inside you, you will *always* have your *first* feelings in the firstborn son, meaning the first idea over the second idea, because this is the way you learn in human value. You *always* have to start understanding everything after you have received the true blessing from your Father in heaven. That is the way the Lord has created life to be, and that is the way you will always learn. Because Esau was born first and Jacob was born second, the blessing of the father will come second. I bring this teaching to you in the value of your false religion so that you can understand the value of falsehood. Now understand the great power of the truth, that lies will always be easier to learn. This is the way you will understand first and second. When it makes sense to you, the truth will be *first* because of Jacob's blessing from Isaac. This is how it works in all intelligence and why the children of God will come to understand the common sense of their intelligence.

The only way to *truly* understand the Scriptures, as well as life itself, is through *ambition*. This means that it is impossible to gain the victory of life by sitting back and doing nothing. Anyone who believes that by simply believing in Jesus gains you the victory of life is believing in laziness, and laziness only keeps you ignorant. Understand well that this is the story of the human race. Whatever was lived then must be lived today in our lives. We have a split in human feelings where we cannot agree with each other, so you have to split the brothers apart to send one on the other side and one must stay and build his life according to what he believes.

This is where a human being comes to know the power that God has given them to understand the truth. The common sense of truth will represent the family of Jacob and the common sense of intelligence. Esau, on the other side, is the spirit that does *not* see wisdom in the same fashion. Try to understand here the value of the power of life. This value states that when we feel different about something in the Scriptures, it is the biggest feeling of separation that the world can endure. You must understand that the split of intelligence between ambition and laziness becomes the greatest split of the power of human thinking. This is where some people work to understand life and the Scriptures, and others don't think they need to learn anything in spiritual value.

You have inside your soul the need to understand life and the glory to receive life everlasting. You have the ambition side of the spirit to tell you the events of your life that have been created in learning. On the other side, you have laziness that tells people that you don't need to learn anything. You just want to live in the same values that you always have as long as you have fun. You live your life according to your *own* understanding of the Scriptures. You don't mind being where you are and what you are, and you don't have to learn anything above what you know now. You have to *work* to gain wisdom, and you must choose to understand and love *both* sons because they are part of the human race that God has created.

Esau comes with an army of four hundred excuses why he cannot learn. He doesn't want to change anything that he believes in, even though life everlasting is given to the one who understands the truth. The spirit of human thinking is the life inside us. It is what we live and learn in the value of what is right and what is wrong. You must understand that many human beings have *not* learned anything about right and wrong in this life according to their feelings. They feel nothing for the value of spiritual value. They live according to what they have learned so far and don't care about the rest.

We come to understand the battle between common sense and ignorance in the value of Jacob wrestling with the man in the value of the spirit. This is where the power to understand comes to a split. Jacob, our common sense, wrestles against falsehood. Here you must understand the spiritual value of trying to gain wisdom through a struggle between common sense and what makes *no* sense.

Here, I must tell you about the battle of false religion versus the religion of common sense. This is where a human being must fight to keep his senses going toward the value of common sense. God allowed mankind to form falsehood, and from that, false religion was born where people would believe in the ignorant understanding that Jesus is the son of God. Man has raised these false beliefs to the highest point almost to being God Almighty because they believe in the physical part of the Scriptures and cannot understand the way God has written *both* the Old and New Testaments.

Some people only look at the physical part of life to understand the Lord their God. They think that they are good enough to enter the Kingdom of God only by what they believe in the physical part of their understanding. God created wisdom to be understood by mankind, and he brought man to the understanding of the Scriptures. You have to go deep into the spiritual part of yourself to understand the Scriptures that were written for your spiritual value. You have to struggle to know the common sense of mankind to bring the truth to the light of the lampstand.

A human being has two parts to himself. He has a physical side, and then he needs to learn the spiritual value in what was "written in spirit." You must know *both* sides if you are to understand life itself. If you throw all of your energy on your physical side, then you may have gained wealth on that side, but it will be at the expense of your spiritual side. How can you be free if you only struggle for the wealth of the earth and not the wealth of the spirit also? If you only understand one side, you will not be able to break free from your struggle because you placed all your eggs on the same side. You need to eat the living bead of life inside your spirit to understand your outer life so the struggle between common sense and the physical part of a human being is *not* the same law. You must understand that the struggle of life is to understand justice, fairness, and unity. Every island and every mountain will be moved from its place, so understand well that the laws of your physical part are not the same laws that you must live through in the understanding of the struggle of common sense against man. In one value inside a man, with the split of intelligence, you can understand the two sides of the struggle where one side makes sense to you in the physical part of life and the other side makes sense to you in the spiritual part.

The same goes for your spiritual self. If you place all your eggs in the same value in spirit, you will neglect your physical side. Then you will be poor and unable to accomplish your honesty in the value of the struggle. You must fight to gain the wealth on both sides in order to be free in what you are to understand. You are not allowed to go to your physical side more than your spiritual side and live against true freedom in the heart that God has created for us. Understand well that the "new" heart comes in the value and the struggle on *both* sides of the issue. The new heart lives in the knowledge that you were created with the balance of power that lives in your split heart. This is the struggle of Esau and Jacob.

This is where you take the two sides and *unite* them inside your own spirit to make your faith in human thinking. Try to understand and accept the two sides of the value, both in spirit and in your physical part. Understand clearly that the struggle inside your spiritual value becomes very strong inside you and you begin to understand life in the new fashion where you live in your spiritual part as well as your physical part. This is how the wisdom of the Lord comes on both sides of the scroll of the Scriptures, who are 95 percent spirit and only 5 percent physical.

If you are in a struggle to understand, you must figure out why you have failed so hard to understand in the false religion of the earth, where you were crucified by false religion in your learning. Now understand that this struggle for human beings has a split between your heart and your physical understanding. You have to sort them out in the value of the heaven over your physical part. You must come to understand the value of your spirit and place it above your physical part so you will be able to understand the change of the Law that I will bring you in the spirit.

Understanding the power of the struggle that the Lord will send to you is not going to be easy because Esau inside you will try to hold on to what you have gathered so far. To win the battle, you have to change and bring your "stiff neck" onto the side of the spirit. You must come to understand Jacob (common sense) and Esau (the wild side) of the physical part of life. Jacob meets Esau in the value of brotherhood, where both sides agree so they can get along with the power of God's great glory. You must meet your brother in the struggle of life—where life must be life and death must be death, where one side understands life and the other side has no purpose to understand life.

It is a part of life that each man must struggle to understand the other side so you can have *both* sides. When you read the Scriptures, don't grieve for the physical part because this is the Book of the Spirit, and you must understand in your spiritual heart that life has to meet at the center of *both* physical and spiritual in the value of the center of common sense. You must come to the power of loving each other, and you must come to love your brother on the opposite side of your understanding to meet each other in life. You must understand that life exists on both sides and both sides must be understood in truth.

You cannot live your life only in spiritual value with no value for your physical side. Try to accept your physical as well as your spiritual side.

You must come to understand that *both* values are important, but you cannot use your physical side to understand your spiritual side nor can you use your spiritual side to understand the physical side—you have to live in *both* sides in order to understand the two sides of the scroll in truth. Understand the descendants of Esau is where the part of your spiritual side comes to life in a loss in the wilderness. This is where people come to the understanding of the happiness of your physical side and try to find happiness in their physical value of the earth. You must live on *both* sides of the Scroll to meet in the center of your happiness where you are on the side of the Lord God inside of you. Then you must accomplish your physical needs and place the two together to accomplish your happiness in which you were created to be.

Now we come to the understanding of Jacob and his descendants in common sense. The children of common sense are the twelve sons of Jacob—the twelve main "verbs" of the Creation. Try to understand that the first son of Jacob is Reuben, meaning "faith." Faith is your firstborn son inside your soul, so faith becomes a way of life—it is *not* just a way of thinking. After you have accomplished this faith in your heart, you will begin to understand the Lord, who teaches you the way of your heart and brings the value of what makes sense. Remember that your Father is common sense, and when you have faith in common sense, you bring the above knowledge inside yourself so you can come to understand faith in the Almighty God—the God of Creation—and you must hold these feelings to that faith for Life Everlasting.

The second son of Jacob is Simeon, meaning "understanding," where you come to understand what is *in* your soul. Understanding is the second son of common sense where you develop this understanding of common sense with your intelligence. See the Lord inside the great power of your common sense. Understand well that your second son gives you the power to create and accomplish the great technology of your soul, where your second son is a gift to you in the value of yourself to God, where *all* the wisdom of the wise comes from.

Verb number three is *love.* Levi is the third son born to Jacob in your common sense. Levi is the priesthood inside each one of us to understand the value of all brotherhood that lives in an honest understanding where you love people of *all* races and colors created by the Lord your God—people who live beside you anywhere on earth. To understand Levi, you must love every single human being on the face of this earth. Love is more than just verbs blowing in the wind. Love is your salvation. Love *saves* your soul and brings you to the Kingdom of God. This is how important love is. Understanding love in your heart is the way to the Kingdom of God—you *cannot* enter the Kingdom of God outside of love. You have to be within the boundaries of loving *all* human beings and *all* animals on the face of this earth. You must love the truth in front of all lies, and you must love the power that makes you wise in the teaching of intelligence. Love is one of the *greatest* sacrifices on earth, and this is why so many people just cannot love people. The great power of a human being is to understand love and to live in love.

Love is like a verb in your heart that you come to understand that anyone or anything has a value. You have this value to choose and to accept others in love *or* to turn your heart upside down and create hate instead of love because your Levi is the power of the twelve sons of Jacob. When you come to understand all that is written in the Scriptures, you will come to see the greatness and the power of love, and that is your Levi, the son of Jacob.

The fourth son of Jacob is Judah, meaning the power of speech in the speaking of words to one another. Speech is also the fourth verb in human understanding. This is where you transfer your intelligence to others in the *magnificent* way of understanding each other. The power to understand the speechmaker is to understand the translation between mind and spirit and the transfer of this knowledge to others in feelings. This is where *you* come in. Before you translate everything that you *think* and *feel* to what people are, you must understand this is a *verb* in the Creation of mankind. This is where you can explain the power of all your feelings and all your thoughts to other people.

The verbs of the Creation are created in *all* human deeds, where a man's deeds are his own creation. These verbs tell you how to do things in all that we are created to be in the power to the soul of human intelligence—your deeds become your verbs. The Lord created and blessed Jacob with verbs in the birth of his sons and this is how we come to function in the creation.

Man must understand that the creation of verbs by the Lord gives us the value of understanding where your speech becomes the power of your own creation. This makes you create and gain knowledge with the Creation of the Lord. Your speech translates your thoughts and feelings in the power that you bring to one another by explaining the creation of your own dreams or when people understand what you mean by that speech.

It is hard to explain the power of translation between the mind and spirit, where a human being comes to understand the spiritual value of the dream, meaning what you know. If other people are not born in spiritual value, it is because their feelings and mind have to be addressed in a different fashion of human understanding. This is why God has written the Bible in the way that he did. You have to receive that birth of speechmaking and transfer the reality of the fantasy into words where you understand the power of the Lord inside yourself.

Now we come to the understating of Dan, the fifth son of Jacob and the first son of Bilhah. Bilhah was the servant of the slave girl, Rachel, Jacob's second wife. Dan represents your belief in the Lord. Since Rachel is a slave girl, this means that you have to become a slave to understand that you are affiliated with the Lord. You cannot escape believing in God because the Lord made Dan the first son of the slave girl. You will be a slave, and you will know in your thoughts that the Lord God of Israel takes the biggest man who claims to know the Lord to be a man of no understanding of God because that man is lying in the value of truth. Also, because *no* man on earth can create what God has created, you must *not* believe in the God of the Christians, Catholics, and all false religions.

You have to believe that the Creation was accomplished in seven days. Because you lived in the time of the Creation and you were a part of this Creation, you have to believe that there must be a Creator that looks like a divine being above you. You have to understand that to have supreme power in the teaching of the Lord, you must understand the supreme power above yourself. God *is* the truth, and the truth makes sense to those who live with intelligence. Try to understand that the supreme value of intelligence *will* make you understand that there is something above yourself that must be respected in all value. If you say you don't believe in God, then you must prove, without doubt, that you are above yourself. If you *can* prove that you are above yourself in the sacrifice of understanding, then you understand *nothing* because the value of God is with you no matter if you believe it or not. You cannot live in any intelligence unless you value the supreme power of intelligence.

The next son is Naphtali, the sixth son of Jacob. He is the second son of Bilhah who was the servant of the slave girl Rachel, Jacob's second wife and also the wife that Jacob loved the most. You have to understand the servant of the slave girl giving birth to our understanding of government. Mankind needs the value in our physical being to create intelligent control of the human race. You must have government and the established government in each country of the world. Without government, there would be no control of our physical being. This is why God gave his son to mankind (in the physical sense of controlling each other) where government must be truthful in the justice of *all* mankind. Otherwise, government would *not* survive very long.

Government is the establishment through the Bill of Rights, in human form, in order to rule over the physical world. Government rules with the value of the Court of Justice where a man cannot be without justice. This has to be presented in the value that all men are created equal. This must be brought to the understanding that it *has* to be fair in the unity of *all* the laws of value in the Constitution of Justice. Just like everywhere else, the life of the mind has to do with what lies in your courtroom that prevents justice. The holy justice of the soul is to be exhibited in the *soul* of man. You must come to understand the value of the truth in our court, where human beings must practice the dedication of justice so *all* men are treated with justice and fairness. The son of Jacob, the verb of intelligence, tell us that you have the right to form government and your court system... but you have to use total justice, total fairness, and total unity with *all* men. All men deserve to live in justice, and no man deserves to be accused unfairly and unjustly. Remember that the Lord gave the power to man to create his own intelligence in the courtroom of justice. But man *cannot* proceed with injustice when human beings come to live in the heart of the Lord because the Lord himself brings justice to *all* men.

With the power to perceive justice for all mankind, you have gained the power to administer justice to all men in the wisdom of the wise given to us to understand what is "fair and just" in the court of the Lord. If one man administers false justice in this courtroom, he must pay the difference between the reality of justice in the fair value where all men must be treated with the value of God. *No* human being should be placed in prison for life in an unfair court without justice because the hand of the Lord will punish those who place judgment against justice.

Now we come to the second slave girl in the understanding of the sons of Jacob. Leah is the older sister of Rachel, and Leah gave her slave girl, Zilpah, to Jacob. He slept with Zilpah, and she became pregnant and gave birth to Gad—the understanding of wealth but not money itself. Gad is the *seventh* son of Jacob. I want to say that money is the value of dealing fairly with each other in justice. Remember that we all become slaves to money on earth because it was born from the slave girl. You must come to understand that every man must be a slave to money because every feeling of money inside of us has to be lived in justice, fairness, and unity.

You must always have justice, fairness, and unity with the four sons of the slave girls because it is *very important* that you bring love into all your verbs. Each verb has a purpose in the creation of life to understand the value of money. Money was created to deal in fairness and justice with each other so you must understand that these things are related. Love is where you cannot use money against people or to deprive people of the necessities of life. Money is a tool to deal with each other. It's not money that is evil...it is the human heart that makes money evil when you use it to do wrong to others. Money is a value that is born inside of us and is created to deal with each other. It is *not* okay for a human being to use money to hurt people.

You must understand that this is not a question of rich and poor here. It's a question of justice and fairness that lives inside of us for the purpose that a human being must be fair to all others. What a man owns is *not* the greatest value. Rather, what he does in justice and fairness is the *greatest value of all.* This is because the Lord is watching each one of us, and He has the power to make life miserable for anyone who "misuses" the value of money over people. Understand that your brother is *equal* to you and he must be brought to the value of justice, fairness, and unity. It is from the same slave girl because business and money are brothers in the same slavery. The labor of all men has to be brought to the place of one's value where you must bring this understanding to the power of God's side. This is where a man brings the fruits of his labor to be valued by his Master in the equal share of life.

Now we go to the second son of the slave girl of Leah. Asher is the eighth son of Jacob. Here, you have the verb of business. This is where you see that in money and business, you have to labor in the business to make money. This means that you do not get anything for nothing. To be successful at business, just like any subject of life, you must work hard. Asher is the son of a slave girl, so this means that we are a slave to the way business works in reality. The rule of business states that nothing is merely handed to you. You must work hard and sacrifice to be successful. This has always been the way business works, and this rule has never changed. This is what being a slave to business means. You cannot change the rules of business just to fit your laziness, ignorance, etc. The brotherhood in slavery of business is where one person must work hard to create a paycheck and must be treated fairly in justice by whoever hires him to perform at a high labor to make business. This is indeed a brotherhood because neither the boss nor the employee is above the other. Both share an *equal* responsibility in its successful operation, and each should view each other in justice and fairness as necessary to the whole. You cannot think that you can get away with anything without justice on both sides just because one side can cheat the other. If you are a laborer and you decrease performance on the job, the master makes no money. This is also true if you are the owner of that company. Pay equal value for another man's labor.

Next, we go to the son of Leah, the first wife of Jacob and the wife Jacob loved the least. It is hard to understand that to be loved the least and to give more sons to Jacob, you need to be appreciated and loved. Here we have Issachar, the fifth son of Leah. This is where life becomes a gamble in human living. You must take chances in life to accomplish the impossible, and you must bring those chances to the Lord.

The power of taking a chance for the better side of life, even when all the odds are against you, is very holy if done in the true understanding of life. Just take a chance and create what you must do in the verbs of your birth to accomplish God's words in all this power.

This leads to an understanding of life where the human being must gamble in what is real and can be trusted in the heart. A human being must come to understand the value of gambling as a part of life in the service of the Lord. Therefore, you should make your life where you present yourself to the Lord with your loving power of creating value against all odds. This is where the Lord sends your soul to the winning side of your dream, and when there is loss in your soul, it is also on the winning side.

Now we come to Zebulun, the tenth son of Jacob, where life becomes a fight between the glories of the victory of heaven and the evil of the world. You must fight in the goodness of your heart where your accomplishments will be in the understanding of the Lord. The fight must be brought to the attention of wisdom. You must struggle to understand the Lord your God because *he* hides from people when you gain a little bit of knowledge and *he* wants you to work harder at it.

When you try to understand the Scriptures or anything in this world, it becomes a "struggle" in the value of intelligence in your common sense. Always try to make sense so your reward will be great in heaven because the Lord will be on your side. When you try to do what is right in the justice of all mankind, you *must* struggle to find the right way to understand the truth.

Now you come to Joseph, the first son of Rachel and the wife that Jacob loved the most because of her beauty and attractiveness. You must understand that Jacob is common sense. When you use common sense to understand life in truth, you always succeed in creating great dreams, plenty of wisdom, and deep technology. With the understanding of life in truth, human beings will use *all* means possible to make life easier for anyone in the dream of the dreamer.

Joseph, the dreamer, is Jacob's eleventh son and represents the value of intelligence, which is technology. Joseph was sold into slavery in the land of Egypt by his jealous brothers because they considered him to be stupid because of his spiritual understanding. They felt that they had to get rid of him and sell him into slavery because they didn't like his dream that brings the spirit above your understanding. Joseph had no choice but to accept his brothers' will. The power of slavery is when you believe that the Lord your God is only temporary in the struggle for life everlasting. We have to follow our destiny wherever it leads, and sometimes your destiny brings you to a loss of your freedom. But it's only temporary when you believe in the Lord your God. The Lord will send you to such an unfair destiny for where you are going in the dream of your life. You will have to struggle to make sure that your faith is strong in the value of the Lord. If you follow your destiny fairly, you will come out ahead in your struggle when justice comes because the Lord is fair with each one of us. Try to understand that fairness leads you to a better life and these struggles give you new opportunities in life. You must come to understand that when you reach a low point in your life with the struggles inside of you, you come to visit the power of the Lord to resist the temptation of losing your soul. This is because you believe that you were treated unfairly. Remember that the struggle of life comes in the value of where you were sent by your brothers who think they understand life better than you. When you enter into slavery, be *proud* that the Lord sent you in the struggle against the will of your brothers who did not understand *your* value. Always remember that the Lord sent you in your destiny for making you better and stronger in his value.

The story of Joseph and his brothers is the story that all mankind must come to live in the struggle of who you are in the family of man. Where you were sent to be is what makes your struggle to understand the fairness of the Lord and when people think they got rid of you. This is where the struggle begins and where the dreamer will come to be at the end of human dignity. This is where a man comes ahead when he was sent behind, and this requires the power to prove that he was right in the struggle of life. You will recall that the dreamer is in charge of all technology in what man creates. Without the dreamer you cannot have great technology, but the one who dreams inside his soul puts two and two together. His dream usually comes with the perfect dimension of the struggle of technology where mankind comes to advance himself in the dream of those who believe in the dream of life.

Joseph dreams, not because he is smarter than his brothers but because the Lord sends the dream of value inside his soul so he can tell his brothers. This is so the world can come to understand that a dream in God's word is the reality of life. God is *not* flesh, and he can only send what he has, which are dreams. In the reality of spiritual understanding, mankind can only understand God through his dreams. That's what God *is* in the value of the soul of mankind where the understanding of this great power exists. The dream is God inside the voice in your soul. Your physical needs are brought to you in the understanding of your mind, and this brings to you a different value than the dream of your soul. Be grateful and believe in the dream of the dreamer. Every great believer in God is a dreamer. Try to understand the dream of reality with the wisdom that comes inside of you to reveal the dream of the Scriptures that God has created for us to understand his might. This is what we are and what we will be in the power of the struggle of life.

This is the great birth of intelligence in true wisdom where mankind can travel in the power invented by both the mind of man and the soul of the dream of the dreamer. This is what the son of

Jacob, the verb of intelligence, means. Intelligence born by men in the spirit of Joseph, who once was sold into slavery because man could not understand, will eventually see this intelligence and the future to come. Are you beginning to see the power of the twelve verbs, meaning the twelve sons of Jacob? You must understand that these verbs were created for making life easier by the will of the wisdom of the wise *and* must be respected by those who don't understand the wisdom of the dreamer. In God, we have the power to understand the wisdom of the Lord and accept it so your life and the life of your brothers will be much easier to live with on this earth. I am writing this book with a word processor on the computer so I can make life easier for people in my *own* dream. This is what the dream of the dreamer stands for. This is who we are.

This means that technology, in all its forms, is mainly used to make money when the main goal of technology should have been the benefit and betterment of mankind. Try to comprehend that your brothers will misunderstand the power of your deeds because of their arrogance. You must come to understand that people will sell you into slavery because they think you have no value in intelligence. But Joseph was the son who was favored by his father. His brothers hated him because they thought that he was only trying to gain his father's blessing since Jacob loved him the most. They were jealous because *intelligent things* were coming from the dreams of Joseph. This means that in the life of brotherhood, there will always be jealousy between brothers against the one who is wiser than the others, against the one chosen to do great things. This is because the brothers, in life, cannot grasp that there are those who receive the *real* wisdom from the Lord that no one else can. Jealousy sets in, and then evil follows in the heart of your brothers. Next thing you know, evil deeds are done against you and they think that they can sell their brother into slavery. Jealousy has *always* been a great sin in the heart of mankind because it makes you do "unclean" things. Try to "straighten out" your heart and learn the wisdom that some people receive greater gifts than you. When you live with your brothers, always try to understand that the value of the wiser one comes before you and that there's nothing you can do to gain his wisdom or to be better than him. Don't be like the brothers of Joseph who sold him into slavery. Joseph going to Egypt meant that vengeance against his brothers would eventually be fulfilled.

Understand that the power to interpret dreams is given to one who is humble in the understanding of the Lord. This is where a human being sees things that other people cannot, and they bring the interpretation to declare what the dream means in the understanding of life. Understand well that if God gave you the dream of a dreamer, then your dreams are holy and must be respected as holy because the heart of the humble man only sees what the Lord reveals to him. Thus, your dreams are holy in the sight of the Lord but not in the sight of your brothers. In human understanding, one man sees things differently than others because the Lord has *blessed* that man with the way of understanding with the Lord your God. If you sell your brother in the land of slavery, in time, you will have to be a slave to that person. When you come to understand the power to reach the goal of human intelligence you will come to visit the brotherhood of reality, where you will see the difference between true wisdom and arrogance that caused you to sell your brother into slavery. Clearly understand that your brother, no matter what you think of him, is *still* your brother, and sometimes he sees things that is higher in knowledge than you.

Don't be skeptical of this knowledge because this knowledge will come to save you in the loss of your soul. Love the brotherhood that you live in by the power of the Lord your God, for God will come to give you the freedom of your soul. You must try to understand and not rebel against your brother because you *think* that you are better than him. Try to understand that brotherhood means *unity* inside each man. Unity is the third angel of love where you will come to understand the value of the dreams of the dreamer.

Let me give you an example: If your brother invented the telephone or the engine of the car that will replace the horse, don't be skeptical about what other people dream. Try to encourage that person to bring his dreams to a higher value where mankind will come to learn this higher value. This is where we will get to live in the intelligence of the wise. True wisdom will eventually come to understand that this is where a human being can cross the boundaries of an animal in knowledge—where we come to understand the dream of the dreamer that creates all physical gadgets that is usable by mankind to understand the fulfillment of his dream.

God's dreams tell us ahead of time what will happen to this world. Therefore, we must try to understand that as your blowing winds of intelligence go one way in the intelligence of the animal human being, the dream of the dreamer brings you higher where you come to the understanding of the dreamer, and you become the future in what we call progress in human thinking. You must follow across the intelligence of the dreamer to understand where we go in life, from one side to the other, where wisdom becomes the value of the future and where the dream of the dreamer comes to be reality in human existence. You can accomplish more with the wisdom of the wise and make life easier for yourself. This is what was created to be a good idea because you have dreamed of it in a better way of understanding life and spirit and in your physical hardships.

This is the understanding of Joseph, the son of Jacob, who dreams and makes technology in the advancement of mankind. You must come to understand the dream of the dreamer that manifests itself in the heart of humanity. One person, under the dream of the dreamer, can feed millions of people with one strong dream. This dream can take intelligence to the *highest* point, where life will become better and easier as a result of your hard labor. This will change over to the intelligence of a machine to do this work because someone before you saw what this machine could do. You should *not* be jealous of the intelligence of others.

Before AD 1830, all the power was performed by animals. Everything in man's way of living was either pulled by man or by an animal. The power of man and beast was the only power on earth. Then mankind dreamed of an engine to work using the power of steam. Now the power of an animal would be changed to the power of intelligence and the dream of the dreamer. If you put two and two together, you have reality, and in your dream to live together in your soul, you begin to *believe* the power of the dream of Joseph, the son of Jacob.

You can't take the spiritual part out of life, and you have to understand that inside of you, is the dream of intelligence that creates common sense within you. God is "spirit" in the dream of intelligence, and you must struggle to understand what you cannot see yet still believe in the value that brings mankind to the level of the intelligence that the Lord stands for. Take the power of the dreamer out of life and you don't have the spiritual value in this power that we believe in. You also will not have the truth that you could not see in your physical form but that you can feel in your spiritual dream of reality. A *dreamer* obeys the Lord his God. The one who thinks that the dream of the dreamer is nothing more than the figment of the imagination *cannot* come to understand this dream.

Life comes from the dream because God is spiritual and the dream is spiritual. You cannot make a "god" of *flesh* out of the God of spirit. No matter how much you try, you cannot bring God above the dream of life unless you *accept* the dream of life. Also understand that if you believe in the God of flesh like Christianity does and you believe that the life of Jesus is God, then you break the boundaries of the dream of the dreamer and you end up bringing the physical to the only values that you can understand! God is spirit…and a spirit is a dream that lives inside our soul to give us knowledge of life itself.

Come to understand that the power of the spiritual value is what you will gain to live in the new heart of the New Jerusalem that is coming to mankind. Here, I am talking about the *real* knowledge of the New Jerusalem where mankind will be able to understand *both* sides of the scroll because the new scroll is visible and can be seen on both sides in truth. You must understand Joseph and the value of his dream because it happened exactly the way he dreamed it. Mankind has to understand wrong in their physical value *before* they can come and live in the New Jerusalem of this great teaching that God has sent to you.

Now we come to Benjamin, the twelfth son of Jacob and the last son of Rachel, the wife that Jacob loved the most. Since Benjamin is the son of Rachel, you must understand that if Jacob is the history of the Scriptures, this tells you that he loves one woman more than the other. This means the mind will love the verbs that come from them more than others, and therefore, mankind will do the same. Benjamin is the power to understand the glory of competition between men. Look at sports. People go crazy about sports. They love sports above everything else. You see people spending all kinds of money to go and watch the competition of men because it's a great thing to watch athletes compete with each other in the value that is in the hearts of mankind—to see who is *best* at something in competition. You must try to understand the verb of competition. It could be in sports, or it could be in fighting with one another. It could be in *anything* where you would compete such as in politics among other things.

Competition is part of the value of mankind. This is where human beings place an interest in the power to understand between a winner and a loser—the glory of victory and the agony of defeat—where one side must take power over the other side. I have explained power in the way that I understand it in the wisdom that the Lord has given me to understand.

To summarize what we have learned about the lives of the twelve sons of Jacob is to understand how to live with each other in the family of mankind—you must understand jealousy, hate, and bigotry on one side and love on the other side. First, you start with Reuben, your faith. Reuben is the firstborn son of Jacob. You must hold your faith to the understanding where you believe in brotherhood and the laws of faith first, before all else, in order to believe in the one true God. Try to hear the Lord in your faith so you can come to understand how to live with other people. I am not asking you to be perfect because no one will ever be perfect. But in faith, you must hold on to understand the Lord your God.

Learn these twelve verbs that are the sons of Jacob. The first four sons of Leah were born to make you understand all the sons in the creation of the spirit of man.

Twelve different brothers live inside you. The first four sons of Leah are your understanding of the Assembly of Living that God has created in the understanding of brotherhood with each other—faith, understanding, love, and speech. The next four sons are born of slave girls. They represent our slavery to government, money, technology, and wisdom, where you must be a slave to the four-winged creature from the Book of Revelation that got its place in front of the Throne of God and the Lamb of God. This is where the great persecution was given to those who received power over the beasts and became the prosecutor where they decided the destiny of others.

To begin the understanding of the great persecution that got us through, you must look at those four creatures in the living truth to see the power to restore mankind and bring man out of slavery in the land of Egypt. This is the power to understand that the twelve tribes of Israel are within us and must be fulfilled in the justice of the Lord. This is where a human being will be counted as an equal to *all* others in the brotherhood of mankind, where the twelve tribes of the understanding of mankind become the power to love one another.

However, you must understand the power of the creation that God has made a human being in his *own* image. If you truly love God, you have to love your brother in the unity of love, the justice of love, and the fairness of love because those are the three angels of love that come from our Levi, the son of Jacob, meaning the sons of common sense. You must come to believe the twelve verbs that God has created for us so we can come to understand the high points of this heavenly knowledge.

There is no higher knowledge in this world than where human beings can come to understand the Lord your God. You must understand the highest wisdom of God and take hold of that wisdom. Try to understand that the wisdom of the creation of the twelve tribes is that they were all human_beings. This means that all brothers are created equal in value.

The salvation of man that comes from beliefs such as Christianity and Catholicism, where you are saved by Jesus, is a *big lie* that brings people to believe in the free victory in the Kingdom of God. This is *not true*. You are *not* saved by any one person. You must come to understand that you are saved *only* by the feelings of brotherhood of those who went through the great persecution. These feelings were persecuted because man believed these people were *not* equal to them, and this is where people live in the great sin of arrogance. This is where you lose your own soul with your own arrogance of thinking that you are better than everybody else.

Remember that the Bible is a *spiritual* book, and the only way you can understand this spiritual book is to understand the spirit. Arrogant thinking is the way to *lose* your soul. The way to understand scripture and life itself is *not* by worshiping Jesus as the son of God or even by worshipping God himself according to the ideas of false religion. To practice the true religion of the soul, you must practice the "real" religion of brotherhood where you love your brothers as yourself and loving God in the highest wisdom of his existence. You do *not* save your soul by going to church on Sunday and listening to false prophets who tell you nothing but lies because they do not understand the Kingdom of God.

The Kingdom of Brotherhood is both the key to opening the door of heaven as well as the key to opening your heart into the Kingdom of God. God will open the door of brotherhood and bring to our attention that human beings must come to understand that the least regarded person in your life has to become the most important brother to love. You must love the man who did the *worst crime* and has *failed* in every possible way if you wish to understand the Lord and his law. Brotherhood comes in the value of humanity where *all human beings are in equal value.* This means that the *last* man needs to come *first* in what your feelings expect of him. In brotherhood, a weak man is, in the value of his soul, equal to you. One must understand that the weak soul is just as important as the righteous.

If you look at a person in the courtroom who has been found guilty of a crime that is despicable to others, that person, in his soul, is more important than *all* the righteous of the world. This is because it is the *soul* that has failed righteousness in his heart. Here you must recognize the Laws of God in that person's heart because it is not when you did everything right that you should be appreciated but when you did wrong that must be recognized in the hearts of human feelings. That person is sorry for what he has done, and his wrong cannot constitute right. However, the value of his crime can because, in the constitution of wrong, the only power that works is to feel regret for what you have done.

In the soul of the righteous who believe they are right all the time, there is no regret, and there is no sacrifice of wrongdoing. But in the soul of someone who has committed the worst crime and regrets the belief that brought them to do such a crime, this is where the Lord God of heaven is. The constitution of judgment in the value of right over wrong is accepted in heaven with the power to constitute justice, fairness, and unity in the understanding of mankind. This is where man must come to understand the *real* constitution of all men in the right to be wrong as well as the wrong to be right. You must come to constitute what you think in the law and match this with the poor soul who has committed the worst crime and who has to be separated from society for a period where he can find himself in the luxury of being right or wrong.

Now we go into the lives of the sons of Jacob. This is to understand how to live with each other in the family of mankind. To understand life with the sons of Jacob, you must understand jealousy, hate, and bigotry on one side and the understanding of love on the other side. First, you start with Reuben, your faith. Reuben is the firstborn son of Jacob. You must hold your faith to the understanding where you believe in brotherhood and the Laws of Faith first before all else in order to believe in the *one true god*. Try to hear the Lord in your faith so you can come to understand how to live with other people. I'm not asking you to be perfect because *no one will ever be perfect.* But in *faith*, you must hold on to understand the Lord your God.

The second son of Jacob is Simeon. The second verb of the family of Jacob is to understand, where you must learn everything that you possibly can learn from the Lord your God. Do *not* learn from the false prophet because the false prophet can teach you *nothing*. That is the Law and the verbs of learning. *You must learn from the voice of the Lord that is inside you, and when you do, you will learn to get along with all men in the brotherhood of mankind.*

The third son of Jacob is Levi, and you must come to understand this value. *Love* is the verb of Levi, and you must learn to love and to learn the power that God has made love to be in brotherhood. Love has a second power because love is a verb and each verb was created from the Lord. You must understand love in the divine nature that it was created for. Love is not to be on one side or the other. It must be affiliated with God. And it is the power to understand the brotherhood of all others in the value where you *cannot* judge others. You cannot find others guilty by the laws of your own mind. You cannot displace the values of others in the power that the earth is giving you, and you cannot trade in love like you trade in business or with money.

You must understand love as one of the greatest glories that God ever created. Understand that love brings you to the full power of justice, fairness, and unity—the three angels of God and of love. You must make sure that in your love you have justice, you are fair to other people, and you try to *unite* the brotherhood of man. Mankind must go to the side of common sense to find love and the power of the Lord where your priesthood and the determination of brotherhood are. In the exchange of love, you must bring your sacrifice to the value where you have to suffer to consider the exchange of love fairly and in justice, even if you have to sacrifice your own self in front of the Laws of God.

You must consider the value of others when you come to understand what love is. If love does not hurt in the sacrifice, it's *not* true love. Love is the greatest sacrifice on earth because *love hurts*. It is not like the Christians or the Catholics who proclaim what love is. Love is the beginning of your_firstborn in the value that you bring about the meaning of all sacrifice. It is not like the love of Christianity where you only love the people in your church or in your congregation. I tell you, in truth, that the most worthless love is when you only love those who love you. Even the pagans of this world only love someone that loves them.

When I say love is a sacrifice, I mean that it comes in pain and suffering. That is what you must do for others. If you only make sacrifices to those that you approve of, then you don't understand the sacrifice of love because love is a sacrifice of giving birth in feelings that a human being must feel for others. Try to protect other people in your feelings where the Lord lives with the true power of love.

When you see a man and he says to you that he loves his neighbor, he just means that he loves the people around him who believe as he does. But the love of the Lord comes in the *brotherhood of all nations*. All countries, all faiths and religions, and all mankind must unite before the Lord in your *own* heart. This is where a man feels for all the suffering of the world and tries to change it by explaining "true love" to others. Saying "I love you" to others is very easy, but try to accept their pain and suffering because of the mixed-up feelings of intelligence inside the hearts of those who cannot love you.

You must be within the Lord's domain to understand that the purpose of love is to bring people to justice in the fair way of understanding unity. True love has *never* been understood in the mind of man because most men understand love as loving a certain person because they are good people. You must love those that irritate you. You must come to understand the Creation with love because we are all created in *equal* fashion, where human beings must come to the feelings where right must be accomplished against *all* wrong to create love and work to bring love to the highest balcony of heaven. You must find love and wisdom but not merely in the thinking of your mind. The real understanding of love is, in reality, where a man gives up all that he knows and loves and starts over in the *brotherhood* of all men where he lives in the power of being a simple human being. This is where love becomes simple and honest in the fairness of justice and unites people with all the glory of heaven.

Now we come to Judah, the fourth son of Jacob and Leah. Judah is the power to speak and introduce your ideas to others, and as the speechmaker, you must have the intention to tell the truth at all gathering of human understanding. You must claim the value of speech to bring the truth to the surface of all reason, where human beings must claim the power to know the glorious understanding of truth. This is where human beings learn the truth and then speak the truth in the value where there are no lies in that which you speak. *You cannot bring anything to the attention of others that is not the truth*. You must *never* speak against the power that created you because you are *one* in the Lord your God with all others.

If you say something untrue to somebody else, you *defile* the value of life, where a human being must not lie to gain favor over others. The verb of Judah, the son of Jacob, *forbids* you to say anything that may fool other people. You will be responsible for what you have said to others because God will *not* accept your ignorance.

Whatever you say in vain against the truth, you must bring the power of your wrong against others in the eyes of the Lord. Until you come to repent your ignorance, things will *not* go well for you in your life.

If you say to others that they are *not allowed* to make love to anyone unless they are married, then you have to remain without love yourself. This is just an example of the Lord punishing you. When you say something untrue in the name of the Lord, you must be punished on the reverse side of what you have said that is untrue. What you say to others will happen to you because you are the liar. Remember, that God is about *feelings*, so if you feel like making love to someone, then this is indeed *holy* in the eyes of the Lord.

Now we come to the understanding of Dan, the first son of Bilhah, the slave girl of Rachel. Rachel is the wife whom Jacob loved the most. When I say "the wife that Jacob loved the most," I mean she represents the family of the Scriptures—the family of God's people that reality loves the most. Understand that the tribe of Dan in the Bible is the affiliation with God. In other words, there is everlasting understanding of God by mankind. Anyone who lives in this world and says that there is no God is *incorrect* because *we were created by God.* Therefore, we have an *affiliation* with God that cannot be denied by any person or individual.

In Dan, you must understand that God is real because he lives in your soul. You could not function without the reality of a higher power. That higher power is the divine God. This is the separation of the people who understand truth and the people who read the Scriptures like little locusts by jumping from one place to another but don't understand much at all of the truth. Let me tell you in truth that God is real, and if you don't believe me, then look in your soul and see that there's room for something above yourself to find in the reason of all intelligence. Understand well that the four verbs of the two slave girls are your affiliation with religion, your affiliation with government, your affiliation with money, and your affiliation with business. These four sons are born of slave girls. This means that you are a *slave* to these four-winged creatures that control the whole world in physical value.

Now we come to understand Jacob and his brother Esau. You must understand that they are twin brothers, which in spirit means "close to each other." Jacob is ambition, and Esau is laziness. They had to be split because of the injustice made by Jacob to receive the blessing of their father, Isaac. Esau was born first, with Jacob holding onto Esau's heel. This is how we know that they are close to each other in wisdom. The firstborn son is the one to receive the *birthright*—this means the one to assume leadership of the family upon the passing of the father. Esau being born first is why we always first consider being lazy before we get things done. But Jacob got his brother to give him the birthright. So even though we first want to be lazy, it is ambition that will ultimately be in charge.

The only way to truly understand the Scriptures as well as life itself is through ambition. This means that it is *impossible* to gain the victory of life by sitting back and doing nothing. Anyone who believes that by simply believing in Jesus gains you the victory of life is believing in laziness, and laziness only keeps you ignorant. Understand well that this story is the story of the human race. Whatever was lived then must be lived today in our lives. We have a split in human feelings where we cannot agree with each other, so you have to split the brothers apart to send one on one side, and the other must stay and build his life according to what he believes.

This is where a human being comes to know the power that God has given them to understand truth. The common sense of truth will represent the family of Jacob and the common sense of intelligence. Esau, on the other side, is the spirit that does *not* see wisdom in the same fashion. Try to understand the value here of the power of life. This value states that when we feel different about something in the Scriptures, it is the biggest feeling of separation that the world can endure. You must understand that the split of intelligence between ambition and laziness becomes the greatest split of the power of human thinking. This is where some people work to understand life and the Scriptures, and others don't think they need to learn anything in spiritual value.

You have inside your soul the need to understand life and the glory to receive life everlasting. On one side, you just want to live your life and you don't want to be bothered with anything that you do *not* understand. You have the ambition side of the spirit to tell you the events of your life that have been created in learning, and on the other side, you have laziness that tells people that you don't need to learn anything. You just want to live in the same values that you always have as long as you have fun. You live your life according to your own understanding of the scriptures. You don't mind being where you are, who you are, and you don't have to learn anything above what you know now. You have to work to gain wisdom, and you have to understand and love both sons because they are part of the human race that God has created.

Esau comes with an army of four hundred excuses why he cannot learn. He doesn't want to change anything that he believes in, even though life everlasting is given to the one who understands in truth. The spirit of human thinking is the life inside of us. It is what we live and learn in the value of what is right and what is wrong. You must understand that many human beings have not learned anything about right and wrong in this life according to their feelings. They feel nothing for the value of spiritual value—they live according to what they have learned so far and don't care about the rest.

Now we come to understand the battle between common sense and ignorance in the value of Jacob wrestling with the man in the value of your spirit. This is where the power to understand comes to a split. Jacob, our common sense, wrestles against falsehood. Here, you must understand the spiritual value of trying to gain wisdom through a struggle between common sense and what makes no sense.

Here I must tell you about the battle of false religion versus the religion of common sense. This is where a human being must fight to keep his senses going toward the value of *all* common sense. God allowed mankind to form falsehood, and from this falsehood was born false religion, where people would believe in the ignorant understanding that Jesus is the son of God. Man has raised these false beliefs to the highest point almost to being God Almighty because they believe in the physical part of the Scriptures and cannot understand the way God has written both the Old and the New testaments.

Some people only look at the physical part of life to understand the Lord their God. They think that they're good enough to enter the Kingdom of God only by what they believe in the physical part of their understanding. God created wisdom to be understood by mankind, and He brought man to the understanding of the scriptures. You have to go *deep* into the spiritual part of yourself to understand the Scriptures that were written for your spiritual value. You have to make a *great effort* to know the common sense of mankind to bring the truth to the light of the lampstand. A human being has two parts to himself—he has a physical need and then must learn the spiritual value in what was written in spirit. You need to eat the living bread of life inside your spirit to understand your outer life, so the struggle between common sense and the physical part of a human being is not the same law. Every island and mountain will be moved from its place, so understand that the laws of your physical part are not the same laws that you must live through in the understanding of the struggle of common sense against man. In one value inside of a man with the split of intelligence, you can understand the two sides of the struggle where one side makes sense to you in the physical part of life and the other side makes no sense to you in the spiritual part.

This is where you take the two sides and unite them inside your *own* spirit to make your faith in human thinking. Try to understand and accept the two sides of the value both in spirit and in your physical part. Perfectly understand that the struggle inside your spiritual value becomes very strong and you begin to understand life in the new fashion where you live in your spiritual part as well as your physical part. This is how the wisdom of the Lord comes on both sides of the Scroll of the Scriptures, which is 95 percent spirit and only 5 percent physical. If you are in the struggle to understand, then you must come to be thoroughly familiar as to why you have failed so hard to understand in the false religion of the earth, where you were crucified by false religion in your learning. Now grasp that the struggle for human beings has a split between your heart and your physical understanding, and you have to sort them out in the value of the heaven over your physical part. You must come to understand the value of your spirit and place it *above* your physical part so you will be able to comprehend the change of the law that I will bring you in the spirit.

Understanding the power of the struggle that the Lord will send to you is not going to be easy because Esau inside you will try to hold on to what you have gathered so far. To win the battle, you have to change and bring your "stiff neck" onto the side of the spirit. You must come to understand Jacob, the common sense, and Esau, the wild side of the physical part of life. Jacob meets Esau in the value of brotherhood where both sides agree so they can get along with the power of God's great glory. You must meet your brother in the struggle of life, where life must be life and death—where one side understands life and the other side has no purpose to understand life.

It is a part of life that each man has to struggle to understand the other side so you can have both sides inside each man. When you read the Scriptures, don't grieve for the physical part because this is the book of the spirit, and you must understand in your spiritual heart that life has to meet at the center of *both* physical and spiritual in the value of the center of common sense. You must come to the power of loving each other, and you must come to love your brother on the opposite side of your understanding to meet each other in life. You *must* understand here that life exists on both sides, and both sides must be understood in truth. You cannot live your life only in spiritual value, with no value for your physical side. Try to accept your physical side as well as your spiritual side. You must come to understand that both values are important, but you *cannot* use your physical side to understand your spiritual side, nor can you use your spiritual side to understand the physical. You have to live in *both* sides in order to understand both sides of the Scroll in truth. Now we come to understand the now, we come to understand the descendants of Esau where the part of your spiritual side comes to life in a *loss in the wilderness*. This is where people come to the understanding of the happiness of your physical side and try to find happiness in their physical value of the earth. Understand that you have to live on *both* sides of the Scroll to meet in the *center* of your happiness, where you are on the side of the Lord God inside you. Then you must accomplish your physical needs and place the two together to accomplish your happiness in which you were created to be. You must come to understand that God gave you two sides of life—a physical side and a spiritual side. You must know *both* sides if you are to understand life itself. If you throw all your energy on your physical side, then you may have gained wealth on that side, but it will be at the expense of your spiritual side. Understand well that the struggle of life is to understand justice, fairness, and unity. You must accomplish in your soul the struggle of understanding before anything else so you can come to set yourself free in the struggle of life. How can you be free if you only struggle for the wealth of the earth and not the wealth of the spirit also? If you only understand one side, you will not be able to break free from your struggle because you placed all your eggs on the same side. You must come to understand that you made yourself a slave to this value, and you cannot complete the struggle of life without the knowledge of both sides of life inside you—the same goes for your spiritual self. If you place all your eggs in the same value in spirit, you will neglect your physical side. Then you will be poor and unable to accomplish your honesty in the values of the struggle. You must fight to gain the wealth on both sides in order to be free in what you are to understand. You are *not allowed* to go to your physical side more than your spiritual side and live against true freedom in the heart that God has created for us. Completely understand that the new heart comes in the value through the struggle on *both* sides of the issue. The new heart lives in the knowledge that you were created with the balance of power that lives in your split heart. This is the struggle of Esau and Jacob.

Now we come to understand the dreams of Joseph and what happened to the world of men. Try to understand what the Scriptures tell us about men selling their brother into slavery. They consider him to be stupid because of his spiritual understanding. You feel that you must get rid of him and sell him into slavery because you don't like his dream that brings the spirit above your understanding. You believe that you must sell him into slavery to accomplish what you think is right over what he thinks is right. It has always been a struggle in mankind to decide that people who dream of something, are either crazy or stupid only because they gain favor above you. This is why there's always a struggle between brothers where we *must learn the truth*.

Understand well that life comes from the dream because God is spiritual and the dream is spiritual. You *cannot* make a *god of flesh* out of the God of spirit. No matter how much you try, you cannot bring God above the dream of life unless you accept the dream of life. Understand that if you believe in the God of flesh like Christianity does and you believe that the life of Jesus is God, then you break the boundaries of the dream of the dreamer and you end up bringing the physical part to the only values that you can understand. Believe that God is spirit and spirit is a dream that lives inside of our soul to give us knowledge of life itself.

You can't take the spiritual part out of life, and you have to understand that inside of you is the dream of intelligence that creates common sense within you. Understand that God is spirit in the dream of intelligence, and you must struggle to understand what you cannot see yet still believe in the value that brings mankind to the level of intelligence that the Lord stands for. Take the power of the dreamer out of life, and you won't have the spiritual value in this power that we believe in. You also will not have the truth that you could not see in your physical form but you can feel in your spiritual dream of reality. Truly believe that a dreamer *obeys* the Lord, his God. The one who thinks that the dream of the dreamer is nothing more than the figment of their imagination *cannot* come to understand this dream. You must come to understand what is spirit and what is flesh. You must come to understand that the power of the spiritual value is what you will *gain* to live in the new heart of the New Jerusalem that is coming to mankind. Here, I'm talking about the *real* knowledge of the New Jerusalem, where mankind will be able to understand *both* sides of the scroll. This is because the new Scroll will be visible on both sides and will be seen in truth. You must understand Joseph and the value of his dream because it happens exactly the way we have dreamed it. Mankind has to understand wrong in their physical value before they can come and live in the New Jerusalem of this great teaching that God sent you to understand.

Joseph dreams, not because he is smarter than his brothers but because the Lord sends the dream of value inside his soul so he can tell his brothers. This is so the world can come to understand that a dream, in God's word, is the reality of life. God is not flesh, and he can only send what he has, which are dreams. In the reality of spiritual understanding, mankind can only understand God through his dreams. This is what God *is* in the value of the soul of mankind, where the understanding of this great power exists. The dream is God inside the voice in your soul. Your physical needs are brought to you in the understanding of your mind, and this brings to you a different value than the dream of your soul. Be *grateful* and *believe* in the dream of the dreamer. *Every great believer in God is a dreamer.* Try to understand the dream of reality with the wisdom that comes inside you to reveal the dream of the Scriptures that God has created for us to understand his might. This is who we are and what we will be in the power of the struggle of life.

Joseph is sold into slavery by the jealousy of his brothers, but the power of slavery, when you believe in the Lord your God, is only *temporary* in the struggle for life everlasting. God *is* the *truth* in the dream of the dreamer. We have to follow our destiny wherever it leads us, and sometimes, your destiny brings you to a loss of your freedom, but it is only temporary when you believe in the Lord your God. Understand well that the Lord will send you to such an unfair destiny for where you are going in the dream of your life and for using your struggle to make sure that your faith is strong in the value of the Lord.

God is the dream, and he will advance those who advance him in truth. The person who has the right idea about life must be brought forth to the struggle of the dream of God. If a human being dreams of bringing mankind to a higher common sense of intelligence, then he has to go inside his dream to reveal it to mankind. This is because the church struggles to understand that the Lord God called us to live in our spirit, and he introduces us to the value of intelligence where human beings come to be born in the flesh and then struggle to be born in spirit.

Judah is the fourth son of Jacob and Leah. Judah is the power of speech that makes man dedicated to the understanding of life. Understand well the angel of technology, the power to speak, and to understand how to speak to people, much like the man who takes the microphone in his hand and tries to teach the spiritual understanding of the Scriptures without understanding a single clue of the Scriptures.

You must come to understand the power where mankind could not understand the scriptures because God has sealed the Scriptures from understanding because of man's arrogance. A man comes and says "Listen to me," and he opens his mouth without speaking one single word of truth, and his son became very wicked because he learned lies from his father. So the Lord said "I'm going to kill them." It's not the killing of the flesh here but the killing of the spirit because the grandson of the verb of technology in the tribe of Judah has failed to understand the Word of God. Instead of worshiping God, they worshipped Jesus—a man who was a servant of God but *not* God. They missed the point and they wore a cross tied around their necks—meaning they missed the point because they did not understand the spiritual power of the Scriptures and created a teaching of the mind with their value.

I think the worst son of technology is the Catholic Church. This is why the Book of Revelation puts the Catholic Church as the "great prostitute" of mankind. The Catholic Church has all these false teachings on the life of Jesus from his birth, to his ministry, to his crucifixion. The life of Jesus and his crucifixion are part of the Lamb of God because of his suffering, but understand that he was *not the only man* on earth who suffered for the sins of all those who went through the great persecution that the Lord created on mankind for salvation. Everybody else on earth has suffered greatly because of this great prostitute, and the world has failed to understand this point. Wearing a cross around your neck does not make you part of the salvation of the Lord.

Understand the suffering of the children of God, where a man was brought to a foreign continent and became a slave in the land of the people who persecuted him. The Indian in the United States who had to go through the great persecution because they were not *recognized* by_the "civilized" people as brothers. The blacks were also heavily persecuted by the hand of the unjust. Also, the Jewish people at the hand of the Nazis, where millions of people were executed unfairly. This has to be written in the Book for justice. All those who forgot the value and did not recognize their brother in brotherhood must be brought to the Throne of the Lord on this most valuable day of the Seven Days of the Creation.

Every man who has used other people in injustice so painful and so cruel in the heart of mankind must recognize their brother and the slavery that they sent their brother into. Anyone who is guilty of the persecution of man *must lay down his life in front of the Lord to pay for the value of his sins.* The persecution of Cain over Abel happens because man was taught to hurt people since they couldn't find any value or recognize their brother in the teaching of life. Understand and remember well that these things happen on earth because the heart of Cain was *interrupted by cruelty.* Whoever was a descendent of Judah and the verb of technology must come to pay equal in value on their *own* spirit. If you did not recognize your brother before, then how can you recognize your brother on this day of the Sabbath that the Lord planned for you from the very beginning of the Creation?

All preachers and priests of the false church and ministers of the false word of God will *fall backward* in their teaching to people the value of no purpose in the persecution of others. You must come to understand your guilt by the verb and words you lost in the Tribe of Israel because you preach and teach everything that was *wrong.* Even though you had the Bible to back you up, you did not listen to the voice of the Lord in your heart. You brought upon the world the *greatest disaster of falsehood* the world has ever seen before now. This is because you have lied in front of others by telling them that the Lord has chosen you, and then you turned around and preached what you yourself did *not* understand. All the people who brought falsehood to mankind must *learn* on this day the value of the chair they are sitting in. You must be brought in justice to the teaching where a human being has to pay the equal value of what he took from others to enter the kingdom of God. This is the justice of the Lord.

Grasp and understand the adultery of false religion where one person thinks he is right in what he believes, but he does not do the will of the Lord. Remember that you went to school in the ministry of falsehood where you have to determine truth over lies. You knew in your heart that the religion itself did *not* stand up to your common sense but you went along anyway. *That makes you guilty of wrongdoing.* Try to understand the words of the prophets that were written in the Bible. You read about their teachings in the night and you knew that there was something wrong because it didn't make sense, and if it doesn't make sense, you should have *known* that it was wrong. You knew inside your heart that you did *not* understand the Scriptures.

By trying to figure out what the Scriptures meant, you closed the Bible so many times. Then you turned around and lied to your brother day and night, especially you Catholic priests. You knew how corrupt the Catholic Church was, but you chose to ignore it because you had a nice meal inside of you and did not want to bother to find the truth. Remember that the value of your life was handpicked by those who listen to you, the same people that you have fooled in so many ways. As we come to understand Joseph being sold to the caravan, you must come to understand that the sons of Jacob are very important here. You have Ruben, which is faith, who did *not* want his brothers to kill Joseph. Then you have Judah who took Joseph and made him a prisoner.

First try to understand Joseph's dreams where he told his brothers that one day, they would have to bow down to him. When you understand the verb, you understand that Joseph is the angel of technology. Joseph was born to Jacob when Jacob was very old. This means that mankind will come to experience in the time we live now with *all* the technology that came out. Everybody asked about being bound to technology because this is what our lifestyle is. The gadgets that make life easier for us now have always been a point of jealousy. When someone comes along with the right ideas about something, the non-believers always seem to find a way to put that person's idea down or say that he makes no sense at all. But the dreamer understands the value of it. The people of the world *cannot* see the future, so they don't understand what the idea does.

Now you can understand that Joseph is the dreamer, and he is the understanding that his brothers cannot understand. It has always been like that in every dimension of the world of mankind. You must come to understand that new ideas and new technology always attacks the mind that cannot understand it, and the mind goes against these ideas and tries to kill them. When the car took over for the horse, there was great complaints about that contraption and people who did not believe in it. But cars made it all the way to modern times. The truth is that Joseph, the angel of technology, will come to be king in the world, but nobody could see it before it happens. It's the same thing as the story of Joseph inside the spirit of mankind. You understand things that your brothers could not even comprehend. Your brothers become jealous because they cannot understand as their minds and souls were too small to understand the future.

Joseph brought a dream that all his brothers would fall on their knees to his wisdom, and that's the way the life of brotherhood works. You cannot prove on the day of your dream that your dream is true and fair, but to the dreamer, the power to understand comes first. And whoever brings it down, must be made a fool of in the world of men. If you cannot see the future, you should keep your mouth shut, say nothing, and think nothing until you see the reason of those who dreams of the future. Understand the power of the future that comes before you in the land of wisdom. Try to understand the way it works in the world of brotherhood and the family of Jacob and his sons. This is the way it's always going to work because the idea here is the intelligence of the smart man who sees the future and understands the value even after he has been persecuted. You must understand that not all brothers are as intelligent as the dreamer. Man will *always* have to bow down, in false understanding, to the dreamer, and the truth will win the battle of the dreamer.

Now we come to the understanding that the dreamer was sold into slavery to the caravan and brought to Egypt where the dreamer made his way through hardship to gain the prosperity of his dream in the land of higher technology. Now you see that the story of Jacob and his sons is the story of the family of man. This is the way it works in the intelligence of the family of man. It is the same story because life is lived through jealousy, hardship, and the pursuit of happiness. Those who dream_the big dreams come to accomplish great things through the criticism of others who cannot understand the value of technology. Now we live in a world of technology where the gadgets of the dreamer are all around us, every day, in the wonder of all mankind. We see how this technology works, and we accept it without criticism.

Now it's a new world that God has built for us. If Joseph had not been sold into slavery in the land of Egypt, he never would have been the second in charge in the land of Egypt and his brothers could never have understood the dream. Technology will win the battle as it does every single time that wisdom becomes more powerful than ignorance. Understand that *every* name in the Bible is a word that has to be changed into the wisdom of the spirit so you can come to understand that a name is a *verb* and must be understood as a verb in order to understand the Bible. This is because the Bible was written by the hand of God in the spirituality of verbs, meaning of deeds done in the action of its purpose.

We live in a time where the human mind and spirit has not really been born in the spiritual value because the weakness that man possesses stops him from crossing over to a spiritual understanding. The Scriptures tell you here that *false religion* is in slavery by trying to tell you that what they understood was a big lie. The understanding of the Bible and the theology of the Scriptures can only come to your faith by God and God alone. Your divine understanding of all Scriptures that was written for life on earth comes in the dream of he who lives the dream himself to understand the value of God's purpose in mankind. To receive the understanding of the theology of the Scriptures, you must come to bring to light *all* the keywords of the Scriptures.

I wish I had enough time in my old age to explain every keyword of the Scriptures, but I must jump over part of it because of the time that I have. I tell you that I have to leave the plowing of the Scriptures' side of the field for the people that will come after me and dream the dream of the dreamer to bring the whole world to its knees in fulfillment of the dream. God gave me a purpose: to bring the Scriptures to a *great value* where mankind can open its heart in the spiritual matter and read the Scriptures with the keywords and gain the understanding of life by worshiping the Lord, your God. *No one* can understand the Scriptures unless he worships the Lord his God and stops worshiping in false religion.

The whole Bible was written on the fact that you cannot worship people. If you do, you commit a great sin against the Lord. Christianity and the Catholic Church worships Jesus and the life of Jesus in front of the Lord. That is why they never understood a single word in the Scriptures. To them, the Scriptures is just a riddle of words that makes no sense. But I tell you that in the Scriptures, you have thousands and thousands of keywords that brings us to understand the Kingdom of God. You must worship the one true God of the creation and stop worshiping the false prophet. Stop placing Jesus in *front* of God. Stop worshipping Popes and people that the Catholic Church calls "saints" through their ignorance of mankind. The idea that the church calls people saints is *not* true and will *never* be true, so forget about the stupidity that the Catholic Pope brings value in front of God. This is something that *cannot* be tolerated by the intelligence of a human being.

I condemn the stupidity of bringing man *above* himself and the belief that anyone who does *any* good deed is a saint in the false value of lies. The sacrifice of these people is a worthless sacrifice of the physical side of their life. Remember that God is spirit and spirit alone. If you want to be called great, you must come in the greatness that God has placed *inside* you, not on the *outside* of your physical self, where you have only accomplished physical deeds to help your brother and nothing in the value of heaven. In order to be great, you must sacrifice yourself in learning so you can help your brother in spiritual value.

This is where a human being will become wise enough in the will of God to become a better man and take care of himself. Do not feed them physical food, but feed them a "spiritual" value where he will learn to take himself to the higher level. He will not starve anymore in his physical body because he has learned to understand the value of his spirit. Doing this is so that each man has the power to take care of himself like the Lord gives the power to the birds and animals in the wild to take care of themselves. However, man does not need anyone to bring them physical food. But they do need someone to bring *spiritual* food to change the hearts of these people in the value of heaven. Anyone who works for the value of his spirit will receive from the Lord the power and the strength to take care of himself, both physically and in spirit.

Do not call man saints because they have accomplished nothing. They have wasted their life learning nothing. They just try to make themselves look good in front of other people, where their deed was only in the plowing of the earth and did not accomplish anything in heaven. If man calls another man *saint*, it is because he has lost his own soul in the value of the earth and his physical needs.

Now we come to *Pharaoh's dreams*. This is where his dreams will come to the interpretation by Joseph, who would be the one to understand the dreams and bring them to a human value. This is where you will be able to understand the famine that was about to come on the world and help the king of Egypt to save the physical part of the children of Egypt. The wisdom of the wise comes from the dream because God *is* the dream. Try to understand that God sends *his* dream inside people. Be well aware that we are men in our physical side but also men in our spiritual side. We come inside the dream of reality to bring the world of mankind to the value of human pain. This will bring about the power to become a better world and to make men free of their ignorance. Where the impossible once was in the dream, it now becomes reality to work inside us and to create new ideas and a new way of thinking. What was left behind by the people who worship in ignorance must now be embraced.

You have to *step up* to a higher value when you hear the truth ring the bell of knowledge. This is where you come to be wiser and continue being wiser in the wisdom of the wise. Understand well the power of progress where human beings used to believe in lies and now believes in the higher step, where he can make a difference with the dream that was placed inside him. Your spirit has a higher value in the divine knowledge of the creation and must be brought up, one step at a time, where the value of your divine power comes alive when the Lord starts dreaming inside your soul. Then your spirit will be with the spirit of the Lord.

When you become part of the spirit of the Lord, you can do *amazing* things so the world can progress in value. You cannot do these things just for yourself. In the progress of the value of mankind, you will accomplish great deeds because, in the verb of your soul, you have higher steps to climb until you come to the divine power of the Lord. When you cross over to your spiritual value by understanding all that was written for you and what you are in God, then you trust where you step in the value above to bring the famine of man to an end.

To bring humanity to the power of its Creator, remember that *life is a dream*. You must bring the dream to the *highest* value, where you will bring mankind out of the great famine of spiritual value that we are experiencing in the world at this time. After the life of Jesus, the false prophet stopped learning. In the city where God was condemned, the curtain ripped down to the floor and was never repaired by the hand that succeeded in the understanding of the parables. What man learned in the past two thousand years was just the replica of life because man has failed to understand in the value of heaven.

All who came and tried in their false ministry accomplished *absolutely nothing* and wasted two thousand years of preaching the gospel of Jesus. Today, we must accept the value of the Old Testament and understand that the false prophets of the earth told people that we didn't need the Old Testament and that Jesus brought a new covenant to mankind. They all said, "You have to believe in Jesus in order to be saved. Place all your faith in Jesus and you will be safe from the anger of the Lord." This is the *great mystery* in the Scriptures because Jesus was just a man like the rest of us. The dream of Joseph can come alive in our divine knowledge that God will bring inside you with the same understanding that Jesus understood two thousand years ago. Always understand that the parables of Jesus were given to him by the Lord your God, and without the Lord, Jesus could *not* bring those parables to a clear understanding of our soul.

Now we come to the great famine where people were starving and where, in the teaching of Nostradamus of the great famine, they came over to the land where man will eat other men in the greatest famine the world has ever seen. The greatest famine of all time is where the abundance of the world brings forth a spiritual famine by the false prophet ruling the earth with falsehood and no one has anything to eat in the kingdom of God.

The teaching that no one seems to understand is the *Tower of Babel.* This is where a human is being asked to believe in other human beings and to eat from what they have to offer even though it's the *poison* of the spirit of humanity. They formed religion in the physical value and taught nothing about changing the nouns into spiritual verbs that understand that this world *cannot survive* without the spirit of God. There is *no one* that I can see on this earth that understands enough about the Lord to feed anyone because *they do not understand the power.*

Then you have religions full of idols and the worshiping of idols in front of the Lord. This is where you analyze people in front of the Lord because they have no value in the spirit that creates the fruit of the spirit. In other words, a man worships the Lord in the value of idols, when *all* the prophets of the Bible specifically told you that you should *not* worship idols. You must worship in brotherhood where you feel for your brothers in the great persecution of the human race. Do *not* worship where you live in wealth and do not care for the people who live in poverty and you have no feeling for the people who are being treated unfairly. *Do not believe that the kingdom of God is free.* Do not believe like the people who think they are going to be first to understand the kingdom of God because they were first to receive the good life and believe that the Lord will give them a free state of value in the kingdom of God.

You must understand that those who live in the famine of falsehood will bring falsehood on themselves. This was meant to be. The first will be last because they were eating good in the famine while everybody else was starving in the loss of their soul where the human race comes to understand God and the value of what they have accomplished in the great famine. They ate well, and so they did not try to develop the spiritual power to understand what was right and what was wrong. They must look at themselves in the middle of the famine and see where they stand.

Now Joseph is placed in charge of the complete stores of food and grain in the land of Egypt. This is where you will live in abundance in the land of Egypt, while your brothers, in the land of Canaan, are starving and have to go buy grain from Egypt. The brotherhood, in the land of Canaan, is starving because they forgot to understand the true God of the Creation, where the power to reason came in their physical deeds, and they could not understand the power that the world is experiencing right now where the famine is so great that people have to go and worship other people in spirit because they have lost their soul.

You must worship the Lord your God *in your soul* for all the greatness that we have come to be. This is the value of bringing the great famine in the land to the spiritual value. When the families get worse in the land of Canaan, they have to go to Egypt to buy food so they can survive and live where starvation does not consume them. This famine is to prove to the world that you must *always* worship the Lord your God with all your soul so you can survive the day of the Lord and enter the Kingdom of God by the door of brotherhood, where the key will open the door for whoever knocks. Do understand that the Kingdom of God is not free by believing in Jesus by the door of the false prophet. You must understand that the key to "open" the door is through the brotherhood of reality, where you understand truth in the wisdom of the wise. This is where a human being finds the pursuit of happiness.

Now we come to understand the power where your brothers come to the land of Egypt to buy food and grain so they will not starve in the middle of this great famine that we live in. The world has left the center of intelligence to believe in false gods. They have failed to understand the land of Canaan, where you only worship *one* God in the understanding of life. This is where man made himself a god out of the golden calf of Jesus. When you worship outside the truth, you lose the faith in the one *true* God, and you starve to death when you worship a false god. That is why you have such a great famine in the land of Canaan—because you did *not* trust in the Lord your God with the faith of the wisdom in which you were created. For some reason, in the middle of the stream, you changed your horse and got it wrong.

Unless you come back to the *one real God* of the Creation, you will be starving in the land of Canaan where you should have all the food you need in the understanding by worshiping one true God. People, in general, don't like to worship God. They cannot understand that God is the dream. In the common sense of intelligence, you have to place your trust in the Lord your God and there will be great wisdom coming to you. If you place your trust in the one true God, you will not starve in the middle of the great famine. If you worship a false god, you will be greatly punished and you will have to be hungry in a fruitful land that you left behind to follow the false gods of Christianity and the Catholic Church. All the religions of the world will not bring you to the truth because they *don't have the truth to give*. You have to go, on Sunday morning, in their "cave of darkness" that they call your church. But that is a *big* lie—that is *not* the truth.

Now the brothers of Joseph go to the land of Egypt to buy grain. Joseph recognizes his brothers, but they did not recognize him as their brother that they had sold into slavery. When you do something wrong to someone, you do not remember what you did because you are dressed like an Egyptian. The brothers thought that Joseph was just a "big wheel" who was in charge. Joseph didn't say anything and sold them some food to prevent them from starving. In the wisdom of his physical mind, Joseph wanted to get back at them for selling him into slavery, but his patience and honesty wanted to find out how his father was doing, if he was still alive, and if they had any other siblings. And if they had other siblings, perhaps on their next trip into Egypt, they could bring their brother, Benjamin. When something happens between brothers, there are little feelings of pain left over from the terrible ordeal that happens, and it is only human to feel that way. Understand that the power of reason comes from these feelings.

Next, we come to "The Understanding of the Cupbearer and the Baker." Become *thoroughly* familiar with the meaning of the dream that the Lord sent on earth to make us understand who will be accepted and who will not be accepted. Here, you have the story of a human being who holds the cup and one who bakes the bread. You see the difference between the one who filled your cup with the understanding of the Scriptures and the one who just bakes the bread. Both of them are to be put in prison for doing wrong to the King of Egypt—the one who holds the cup is the one who tries to understand the Scriptures, and the one who bakes the bread is the one who tells you what to do. One of them must be killed and his head must be cut off because the bread maker tries to *control* people.

God's word is the bread of life and the wine is the understanding, so you must come to understand that the wine is more important than the bread. In the way organized religion works, they try to make you understand the word of God just be baking and eating bread alone. They tell you that you don't have to understand what is in the cup of the consecration. The blood is more significant than the bread because the bread, unless you reverse the understanding of spiritual value, is worth nothing.

Take this story and try to fully understand its meaning. When you do understand the purpose of it, you become more in tune with the knowledge of God's word. Try to understand that what happened in the land of Egypt at the time of the Book of Genesis has to be what the world will come to be in organized religion. The false prophet will try to bake bread without the knowledge of this understanding—they are just talking in riddles and don't have a clue of what it means. But if you drink the wine—the blood of the understanding in your soul—then you know the truth because blood means life in the value of the Scriptures.

You have to understand in order to teach what is right and what is wrong. Most people try to teach what they *think* is right and cannot understand anything in the Scriptures. If you try to tell them something about the Scriptures, they laugh at you and think that you're crazy, but the Lord is the Lord in the value of the blood, meaning the understanding of reality. Just try to understand the story here in your spiritual value and you will see the difference and the understanding of the Lord that comes in his dream to feed the human race with the reality of truth. This is a story that happened to Joseph, and when you don't truly understand it, then it has no meaning. But when you understand that Joseph is the angel of the dream of the dreamer and God is a dream, you will begin to understand. To understand God, you have to understand his dream so you can understand what God is talking about in the reality of the baker and the cupbearer. It is a simple story, and all the false prophets of the world have gone over it without a clue of what it means.

Many people have read that story because it is one of the famous stories of the Bible. The Bible is the most read book in the world, yet no one has understood what it *really* means. No one can be wise unless they understand the dream of the dreamer, and they pray to God to give them the understanding of the dream, where they can hold the cup of the truth that will give them life everlasting.

Now we come to understand the "great power" of the brothers of Joseph returning back to Egypt for their second trip to buy grain so they would have food to eat and not starve to death. Understand here that Egypt is the book of the false prophet of the earth, where food is needed so you will not starve. False religion in the land of Egypt is brought to the mind of mankind, where humans believe that they are saved by Jesus just by believing in Jesus. Salvation without sacrifice is *not* true salvation because true salvation comes in the sacrifice of learning.

If you cannot understand the dream that is in the Bible, then you cannot enter God's kingdom because the teaching of brotherhood must be understood on earth by those who want salvation and harvest the land of the Kingdom of God. This is where human beings seek and increase their knowledge to understand that life is a dream because our Father of Wisdom is a dreamer of truth over lies where human beings are caught in the struggle of right over wrong. This is where man lives and takes the gamble of life over death in the struggle to understand. One side of the scroll is the side of the blood and the other side is the side of bread. You must determine for yourself the power of what it means so you can come to understand the other side of the Scroll, which is the power of the wisdom of the wise.

We now come to understand the dream of the King of Egypt, where Joseph became second-in-command to the king. Whoever understands the Scriptures is second-in-charge in the kingdom of human intelligence. This is because, once you understand the Scriptures, you have the power over the authority of man to understand wisdom. You will gain the power from the Lord your God to bring together the understanding of Joseph's brothers returning to the land of Canaan, where Joseph has mercy on them so they will not starve. Understand that we live in this time of great famine where, in the land of Canaan, people are starving with the falsehood of the false prophet. *No one* can produce any value in what was written in the Old Testament because they were burned by all the lies of the world.

Know that the brothers of Joseph came and kneeled in front of him, begging to buy food so they would not starve. This time, they brought their younger brother because Joseph told them to bring Benjamin so he can meet him. Joseph then had their grain sacks filled with grain and their silver returned to them. He had his servant place a silver cup, his personal cup, in the grain sack of Benjamin. Try to understand that Benjamin here is the angel of competition. Since Benjamin was born by Rachel, the wife that Jacob loved the most because she was beautiful, this meant that Benjamin will be loved by the world of men in sports and all kinds of competition.

The competition will be accepted as the cup of the covenant, and every winner will receive the cup and a trophy for their accomplishments in the waiting power of the struggle where the physical part of men will be rewarded. They will make a lot of money and will be treated like heroes because the physical part of their association with life will be greatly rewarded with cups and trophies of all kinds. Their achievements will be the gift of the love of the beauty of Rachel, the wife that Jacob loved the most.

Understand that Jacob here is the angel of common sense and Joseph is the son of his father where common sense and all struggles are appreciated by the physical side of mankind. You now see where the power of God is because the truth is also God. Whoever would choose to live in the dream and the truth will be greatly rewarded, even in your physical value where heaven stands between reality and lies. Believe that your physical side is real. It lives in the value where the physical part of your deeds must be appreciated by the power of the struggle between the agony of defeat to the glory of winning in the heart of mankind.

The great power of the struggle is spiritual because you determine between the loser and winner, where the goal of being on the winning side wins the trophy of his struggle in the value of the heart of a human being. Now you have the competition of *all* struggles in life. Whether it is in sports, business, or money, you must be put on the winning side, where your feats bring you to the value of winning. This is the struggle of Benjamin, the son of Jacob born by Rachel, the son that men will love the most in life and will pay the highest price for what is important in the desire of winning. Now the servant of Joseph went to investigate who had stolen the personal cup of Joseph. Remember here that Joseph is the covenant, not the angel of technology—this cup is what creates the power of what is his to bring. The cup of the covenant contains *all* the rules and laws for the breeding of "winners" in all human value.

Now we are going to the understanding that Joseph makes himself *known* to his brothers. This is the *celebration of brotherhood.* Joseph had to make himself known to his brothers by the value of the wisdom that he had been hurt by his brothers because he could understand the dream of the Lord. Understand the pain and suffering that Joseph endured, knowing that he was betrayed by his brothers and sold into slavery. You must understand here that the wisdom of the Lord is given to those who find value in the dream of the Lord. The Lord is real in the dream of life and cannot be excluded from his value in that dream. And you must come to realize the man who is born by the wisdom of the Lord and understands the Lord's dreams with the value of the coming of all time.

You may condemn the man who dreams of a telephone, but when the dream of a telephone becomes reality, then you become the real fool. A *real fool* is one who tries to place himself in the wisdom of the wise by *condemning* the true wisdom of the wise because he cannot understand it. The power here is to understand that when you make a fool of yourself, you must have the integrity of admitting to your role, which is that you could not see the power to understand. God will always fool those who make a fool of themselves—you make a big mistake in doing so, and you have to pay with your pride, which you did not understand. You must come to the land of Egypt where the brothers recognized their brother Joseph and the foolishness that these brothers endured just because they could not understand the value of the dreamer.

Remember that common sense is to accept what you cannot understand because it was not given to you by the Lord. The big question is, *Why* did the Lord choose someone to understand and the other one cannot understand? This is because one person's loyalty is to the Lord while the other one cannot understand because he is not loyal to the Lord. I tell you, in truth, that if you try to understand the wisdom of the one who received the dream, you will be on the side of the dreamer. Keep in mind that the Lord *is* the dreamer.

Now Jacob goes to Egypt to see his son Joseph, the son he thought was dead in the land of Canaan, eaten by wild animals. Here you have common sense going to Egypt, the land of false religion, where he will be accepted by the king of Egypt and meet his son Joseph after many years. Now Jacob, who is common sense, comes together with his son, the angel of technology. This represents the wisdom of technology and common sense together in the land where false religion was practiced. Understand that even in false religion, the Lord has given the wisdom of the wise to common sense. They had the power of technology to control the life of mankind.

Those who have the best technology control those who have the lowest technology. They have created war against the ones with *no* defense. For example, the bow and arrow were *no match* for the cannon and the gun that waged war against the children of God. Even though man claimed the victory in the *physical* defeat of others, the children of God brought the victory of *spirit* over the physical battle that brought the others down to their knees. God saw the tears and the crying of these children in their defeat, but *He* gave them victory to live in the understanding that life is everlasting. The victory of the one who lives temporarily is a small victory compared to the one who will live in eternity in the wisdom of the Lord. Let this be so for the real loser, and let it be so for the real winner. The real victory is in spirit and not in this time where people destroy the life of those who are defined to have no value in the arrogant way of thinking of mankind.

Now Jacob, the common sense of intelligence, goes to meet his son, Joseph, who is the value of the *afterlife*. The famine will come to bring great abundance in the land where man must wait for his victory in the real kingdom that is to come. Jacob must be returned to the land of his ancestors, where he will be buried in the land of Canaan with his son Joseph. Know that this victory is not a victory that you can see because the human race has not been there yet. When you get there, you will understand the victory of heaven. On that day, you will understand the value of the wisdom of the Lord who preserved them. The victory in life everlasting is the real victory in the land of reality.

Understand that the children who thought they gained the victory will *lose* the victory because they will not accept the *true* victory. They will go back to the laws of old in the darkest, deepest part of the understanding. They will think that God was on their side when they did not understand the power of the Kingdom of God. Believe the lesson of Joseph and the famine. The famine will continue until the power of understanding returns to the family of man. The people did not understand the famine, and they lived in the comfort of their own false victory. They hoped to have life everlasting because they thought that good luck had saved them.

Remember well that the Kingdom of God is inside a new heart and a new understanding. If you live in your old heart and cannot fight your way out of ignorance, you will not be able to understand the Kingdom of God. You must come to believe in the world of brotherhood and the family of man, do away with what you had, and come to understand the life of brotherhood. You must cross over from living in the past to where the dignity of a new heart must be awarded to its value where the Kingdom of God will come to be.

Now we come to the two sons of Joseph, Manasseh and Ephraim, who were the two sons who came from Joseph, the angel of technology and the angel of the dream of the dreamer. The first one who was blessed by Jacob was Manasseh. Manasseh will be blessed for bringing the great technology to mankind. The second blessing will go to Ephraim, where he will have the blessing of the spiritual part of life.

Now we come to have a clear understanding of the death of Jacob. This is where a human being who lives in the common sense of intelligence died in the land where the loss of his soul is missed by mankind and to accept the power of dying with wisdom and where intelligence was given. Remember that Jacob is holy religion and holy religion died because the world could never understand the people who came with common sense. False religion has always been a fantasy world where people try to bring God to *their* way of thinking. Remember in your life that worshiping God has to be done in common sense. If you try to understand God in the way of false religion, you will get down on your knees and worship idols. You will try to replace the Lord of the spirit with the physical part because as humans, we can only understand what we see; you can only live in the human imagination where human beings try to understand something that they *cannot* see.

The world has always sought *how* to worship God, so the people who believe in the false prophet follow those who really don't know how to worship. I tell you in truth, worship God by standing up and believing that inside yourself is the dream of the understanding of life on earth. *Never* bend your knees to anyone else but the Lord. You must reach the understanding of the voices inside yourself where you can understand the God of the Creation. Try to have a clear understanding that God is the dream of the creation. A man creates a house by first dreaming about it. When he builds the house, it becomes the physical part of his dream. This is how all creation is completed. First you have the dream, then you create through that dream, and you accomplish the reason to build a house to begin with.

This is how you worship God in the value of creation that comes from your dream. This is the way God himself creates. He sets himself up first to try to understand his dream and the *value* of his dream until it is accomplished. You must worship God in the same divine fashion as you do in the human fashion. After you realize that common sense lives inside you, you must use common sense to accomplish the living spirit that lives inside your heart. You must work to worship God in the value of your dream inside yourself. If you use your common sense, which is the son of God, you will come to understand how to worship God in your life. This is where all human deeds from divine to human come from in truth. The power of your common sense is the son of God inside you, and it is created by a divine belief of the creation.

Try to live in your soul and understand the prayer of the soul, where what you must accomplish with your dream is revealed to you in order to be happy. If you cannot accomplish your dream, you will be miserable in the world of worthless value where your dream of worshiping God is not accomplished and where you cannot understand what God is. Stand up on your own two feet in the value where you understand what God is in your soul. Understand that the Lord your God *is* the truth, and when you sense that dream of reality, you will believe this feeling inside you where you will find wisdom that you never dreamed of accomplishing.

Believe that the dream of your common sense is the son of God, and through the son of God, your common sense is where you bring your life to a happy ending. Understand that *all* the religions of the world have *never* understood God or his word or his son. This is because they don't comprehend that the power of God is not in preaching and in sermons of false religion but in the understanding of the son of God, not the life of Jesus, his trials, and his death. The life of your own common sense is the son of God that is inside *every* man. Every human being on the face of this earth has the son of God inside of them. You have to understand that inside of you, the dream and the feeling that gives us intelligence has been fed by this common sense.

Understand well that the power that we accomplish in our dreams and the feelings that bring those dreams to life is our common sense. If you can bring this common sense, which is the *real* son of God, to where you feel that divine spirit inside of you, then you accomplish your dream. Don't ever let your spirit stop worshiping the Lord through His son (your common sense) and the reality of value. We are all divine because we all have common sense inside us. I am writing this book with my common sense to reach the level of the divine creature that is inside of me. I believe the divine creature tells me in my dream what to write in this book. If you find the Lord inside you, you will also find your common sense. The power of the divine spirit has placed inside your soul the common sense of the son of God so you can come to understand *how* to live your dream in the building of your life. Each person has the power of common sense because we are all created divinely in our understanding.

So many people have forgotten this value, or they have never used it because they were misinformed. If you forget the great power of yourself and you go somewhere in some "cave" that you call the church to find your common sense, you will fail in every possible way because you forgot common sense...and you let Jacob die inside you. You will *not* understand the *real* son of God.

Now we come to the death of Joseph, the angel of technology. Joseph lived to be one hundred and ten years old. This means that every one hundred and ten years, the tools that you use to create intelligence and the building of your life must improve. The hammer was replaced by the air gun, and every tool that is in your possession must be improved so you can come to make life easier in the wisdom of intelligence and the value of a new time in the history of man. You cannot use the horse and wagon to pull your load forever. This is why *new* technology was developed. Joseph must die to give *new life* every one hundred and ten years. This is the same as Jacob, who died at 147 years old.

*****

Now we come to the Book of Exodus. This is where the journey of life, in your forty lifetimes on earth, has been spent in the power where we had to learn from the deserts of human understanding to the power of the reality of the dream of life that the Lord has created inside of us. The power of the understanding of the people who gave the greatest sacrifice must always go through the worst persecution. This is because God requires sacrifice and persecution to see who has the understanding of these great deeds to be able to live in life.

Understand that the persecution which was brought upon the human race was for understanding the dream of the Lord. A human being must be able to receive the worst in life in order to receive spiritual life. If he dreams of a better life, he must endure the persecution of those who are totally ignorant and come out still believing in the Lord. The persecution is the restoration of the soul because without the persecution of the people chosen by the Lord, they cannot receive the glory of the intelligence through their sacrifice. That's the way the Lord works. Unless you're being placed in the middle of the persecution, you will never understand the kingdom of God. You have to be denied your rights in order to gain the power of life. The Lord, with all his wisdom, could never change a single thing in this creation to make life better for you.

You have to know that the kingdom of God must go through the great persecution in order to gain life everlasting. You may say that God is a cruel God because you only understand with the little mind that you have inside yourself. And you may think that God is not listening because he has not met your needs or answered your prayers right away. You still must understand his wisdom, and not the working of your little locust mind, where the Lord had to send you to endure persecution. You must suffer the hard whip of the Egyptians to come alive in the spirit of the dream of the Lord.

Understand people, you who went through the great persecution, this was meant to be for your salvation. Believe that God's judgment upon those who went through the great persecution and have received the stroke of the whip—that whip was a sacrifice that you have to endure because of the *weakness in your faith*. You were so weak that you had to be saved by the sacrifice of the dream of life, where human beings have to learn the glory of the wisdom through the persecution that the Lord has created for all of us. The rulers of the earth give you the whip to persecute you in the worst endurance of all time, but the Lord will bless you through your sacrifice of still believing in the Lord your God even though you have been whipped constantly by your oppressors. The *power of suffering* becomes your understanding in the Lord. In other words, you had to be tested throughout your life and still come up on top of your faith and still believe in the Lord your God.

If you have endured the worst in your life, it will be easy for you to receive the good (in life) and still appreciate God. When the gift of your abundant success comes, life will be appreciated. A sacrifice, in life, is not because God punishes you. It is because God rewards you in life. When you have life everlasting, that is the greatest gift that you can possibly receive as a human being. If you receive this magnificent glory of intelligence that I am talking about, life will become so much easier for you to worship the Lord your God. God's treatment of you is done outside your knowledge because you have to understand that the gift of the rewards of the Lord are *magnificent* rewards that you will come to understand when you live in the kingdom of God.

You cannot understand why people persecute you, but I tell you, in truth, that persecution is the restoration of your soul. God is so heavily persecuted by the ignorance that lives in the souls of your oppressors. The power of the wisdom of the Lord can come into the right door by the understanding of your persecution. Whoever you may be in this world that went through this great persecution, jump up in the air and be joyful that the Lord has chosen *you* to become part of his great wisdom and to bring the glory of his intelligence inside you. This is something that so many people wish to have.

Now we are going into the understanding of the birth of Moses—the great lawgiver. Understand that before Moses, there was no "spiritual" law in the human race. It is through the birth of Moses that God sent mankind the law, the power of the existence of mankind. God had saved the teaching of the law until Moses arrived and lived in the power of sacrifice to bring the law to mankind. Moses was the man chosen to bring law and order to the human race. Mankind must come to understand that the creation was made by the laws of physics as well. You must come to understand that without laws, we have *no* understanding in value and you live in the understanding and feelings of an animal.

The teaching of the law did very little to change the heart of man in the love of each other because *nobody* understood the law. God made people who look like they have no value and who are so hard to love because he wanted to "fool" the human race and our understanding of love. He made the law hard to obey because of your false faith. You have to believe in the Lord to love such people. *Nobody* enters the Kingdom of God except through the doors of the great persecution. If you enter these doors, be happy and appreciate the Lord your God.

Now we come to the sign of Moses that the Lord has chosen him to bring the law to mankind. This is a sign that you can only read in your own power to understand what is *inside yourself*. Understand well that Moses is not chosen by God because he is better than anyone else. We are all human, and God can choose anyone to bring the boundaries of his understanding to mankind. Believe that in order to choose anyone, God had to choose *someone*. If Moses came to be chosen, this means that the Lord had chosen him because of the way he felt for others inside his heart. You must make your heart "yours" in the worshiping of the Lord so you can carry the torch of freedom of the soul to others. Inside your heart, you must come to understand that there is only *one God*, and you must believe in the One God who sent this simple man who was born of a simple woman in the flesh of her womb, where she brought the one chosen by the Lord. Here, a great sin is being committed by ignorance where the man, who comes to bring the law, is condemned by those who hate him—the one "chosen" by the Lord. They try to put this man down and try to show the world that he is wrong. The Lord's choice *is* the choice of the Lord, and no one on earth, no matter how wicked he is, can change the choice of the Lord.

Try to understand the sign of the Lord to choose in all of mankind's power to bring about the writing of his Holy words. Because we are only human, no one can change the choice of the Lord. Whoever the Lord chooses is because of his divine nature, and that is the reality of truth. It is not up to a little man, with his little mind like a locust, to change the Lord's choice. This belongs to the Lord and the Lord alone. Mankind, in their little locust way of thinking, has *no* say in the choice of the Lord, so just be glad that the Lord chose someone to reveal the truth on earth. God had chosen Moses in the past time, and his choice was accurate in the justice of the past. It is also the same choice in present time.

Now we are shipwrecked on this planet, and we don't have enough water to survive. This means that we don't have enough reality to survive because we forgot to take the information of the Bible and try to worship the truth. Understand, listen to his wisdom, and worship the Lord God who created us. Everyone on earth has formed false religion and believes in all kinds of stupidity and ignorance, and they worship "false gods." This is why we are shipwrecked in the understanding of reality.

Now we have a situation where everybody worships different gods and different religions. Nobody seems to understand *how* to worship the one true God because the world has lost itself in falsehood. No one seems to make sense about the Almighty God, and the great purpose of worshiping God is gone from the world. The Christian world believes in their Jesus, and they place a man *before* the Lord. The world believes in this mortal man that they call God, and the Lord is about ready to destroy the world if we don't start worshiping the *one true God.*

Try to understand the truth about God. I have tried to find a couple of good men who understand the purpose of life and the purpose of the creation, but I cannot find anyone. The world is shipwrecked in false religion—and they don't have enough water, water meaning "reality." The disease of falsehood and arrogance lives in every man, and man cannot understand enough to create the *true* teaching of the Living God. The world finds itself out of control and is unable to fix itself. We must bring the *truth* to the light of mankind and fix the world with the little common sense that we have inside of us. This is in order to fix the shipwrecked world with the understanding of the great power of the Lord who created us and to worship God in truth because this is what *needs* to be done.

Next, we come to understand the power of Pharaoh ordering the people to make bricks without straw. In the power to understand the Scriptures, you cannot make bricks without straw. Otherwise, you break the laws of physics. Try to grasp the kingdom of God with the understanding that you can only make bricks with straw because it's a law that cannot be changed. If you go up on top of a building and throw yourself down, you can have faith that you will not get hurt, but the laws of physics don't work that way. Understand that the laws of physics are like the common sense of intelligence. You cannot have faith without common sense. You must understand the value of faith, which is important, but you also cannot break the laws of gravity. If you have faith like the false prophet, I tell you that you will *not* receive the kingdom of God. If you believe in Jesus as God, then you come to understand *nothing*. Worshipping Jesus is *not* the path to the kingdom of God. Believe me, life doesn't work that way. In every subject of life, you have to have the understanding so you can create the power of heaven inside of yourself. The Lord will take all the false teachings and throw them to Satan's door, where the false prophets will come to understand how *evil* they are by preaching falsehood in front of the Lord. When I say *Satan* here, I mean *all the lies* that they made up inside themselves to prove that they have wisdom, but their wisdom is the mouth of Satan (lies) and not the truth of God in the understating of the revelation of God.

The deliverance of the Lord comes in the salvation of man to those who have received the victory and those who also try to keep away from the false prophet. They did not go worship in the cave of the church of the false prophet. This is because first, you did not understand what they were talking about and second, you understood that they did not have the *true* word of God. All they had is the word of locusts, and they did not understand in the deliverance of the Lord. They claimed to "save" people, but they did not truly understand *how* to save people, in spirit, in the glory of the center of common sense.

They believed that Jesus was the son of God, and they talked about Jesus's life, but they mentioned almost nothing about the life of God. They just put God in a higher power but did not explain his laws. Therefore, they lost the battle of their salvation because they did not mention God in the laws of his strength and the twelve sons of Jacob; they *never* mentioned God's laws in their *entire* teaching. They did not find the sons of Jacob important enough to deliver God's word, and they did not understand the value of the *twelve verbs* inside man, where the power becomes the dream of the Lord your God.

Try to have a clear understanding that *God is the verb*. God is the *truth*, the *reality*, and the *common sense*, all in the same dream of the verb that creates mankind. Understand that the verb is just *as important* as the Lord because you must understand that we need the power to reason with reality and common sense. You have to return to the father with the truth in all verbs in the reality of what we were created for. Understand the creation and the creator for the verbs that we live inside of our understanding for ever and ever to the living people who will receive the kingdom of God.

Aaron's "staff" becomes a snake meaning that in the book of Revelation at the end of the Scriptures, you will see that when you start understanding that book, you will *know* what God is talking about. All the false prophets will come to know who created the snake, all those who practice false sorcery and magic, and all the power of those that pervert the truth in your church on Sunday morning. I want to be specific here: *in your church* means "in the cave where there is *no* knowledge of God."

The children of God will be thrown into the lake of fire that the Lord has created for them from the very foundation of the world. Close all evil religions and *listen* to the word of the Lord because you need to learn, and if you refuse to learn, you will be thrown in that lake of fire. Count all of your sins in the values of your loss because the Lord will come to the deliverance of mankind. You did not accept the truth, and you tried to prove your lies against the truth and against the value of common sense and heaven. You are trying to make other people understand what you didn't know yourself. If you did not understand the Scriptures, what made you think that you could explain it to anyone else?

You think you have lived well, yet you have accomplished *nothing* in your life because you failed to understand the power of the verbs, the power of the twelve sons of Jacob, and the deliverance of man. You thought you were so wise to preach against the truth. You thought you could make people believe that you were the chosen one that Christ honored and that you could save the soul of man in your worthless understandings. You thought you were so wise, but you didn't see the power of the Lord where the Lord will deliver your people from the sin that was fabricated in your soul.

You false prophets, ministers, rabbis, priests and religious leaders of *all* religions, I tell you to let the people of the Lord go free and close those evil churches as soon as you can. Admit to the people that you did *not* understand the Scriptures then and you don't understand them now. You will never understand the Scriptures unless the Lord opens your heart to this magnificent truth that you are so far away from.

Now we are going to "The Ten Plagues in the Land of Egypt." The ten plagues mean that the Lord will send ten plagues upon all false religions because they don't let the people go free to worship the *one true God* in *truth*. These false religions keep people enslaved by *lies*. The first plague is the turning of water into blood. Water means "reality," and blood means "understanding"; therefore, the Lord turns reality into the understanding of the truth. Anything that is a part of common sense and reality is a part of truth. Anything that is *against* common sense and reality is against the truth. And this can only happen through the Lord, *not* through any false religion of lies.

The second plague is the plague of frogs. The frogs are the false prophets. Understand that the frog speaks in riddles and cannot explain what that riddle is, so they keep talking, yet they say nothing important—just a bunch of riddles—that make no sense to the human spirit. You can listen to these people all your life, from the time of your age of reason to the age of your death, and you will still understand nothing. This is the meaning of the frogs. Know that you cannot understand the voice of the frog any more than you can understand the voice of the false prophet who tells you the same riddle week after week, after week, and never says anything. The riddle of the frog is the same in all purpose of the same voice: riddle, riddle, and riddle.

The third plague is the plague of gnats. Gnats are little bugs that swarm. This means that the lies of false religion cover everything in the land—people and animals alike. Know that the gnats came from the dust of the ground. All the dust of the land of Egypt became gnats. In spiritual terms, this means that in the entire land of false religion, the swarming of lies and false teachings confuse you and prevent you from seeing the truth.

The fourth plague in the land of Egypt is the plague of flies—the understanding of the good news of the Kingdom of God that has fooled so many people. Remember that a fly lands on the wall and tells you nothing but the same old stuff week after week where you could not find the news of the Kingdom of God, and that is exactly what a fly does. It buzzes in your ears but does not accomplish anything in understanding. You can see a little fly walking on your wall, and you see thousands of them every day, but there is nothing about these flies that is of any significance to you. It's like the media. It tells you something new, but it really tells you nothing of importance and has no purpose for what you have heard in the news. This is because the flies do not tell you anything new. You only hear the same old thing every single week. There is absolutely *nothing* about *when* the Kingdom of God will come or even *how* to get into the Kingdom—just lie after lie, hopelessness after hopelessness, and dead dreams after dead dreams, week after week—it is the same old thing. Nothing new comes in your soul to make you happy.

These are the flies in all the teachings of mankind. You cannot learn anything new from any of these old creatures of the earth. You will lose your soul entering those caves of lies and trying to worship God. This is because their teaching does not apply what you need to do to enter the Kingdom of God and understand his laws.

Now we come to the fifth plague—the plague of the livestock. Fully understand that, up to now, the spiritual teaching that comes from organized religion has been limited only to a physical teaching. They do not understand the world of the spirit, and they do not believe that the animal is only an animal and cannot be brought to the level of the Lord in spiritual terms of human understanding. The livestock are livestock of flesh and the teaching of the frogs and the flies is a physical value and not of your spiritual understanding. The plague of the livestock is what will happen to the physical part of you. If you don't understand the spiritual part, meaning if you don't worship God in the proper manner of the Laws of God, you will suffer greatly, and your sacrifice will not be counted to the Lord because you only deal with trying to save your animal being from the anger of the Lord.

Understand the significance of what this means. You worry about your physical understanding and how you are going to try to save your butt in front of everybody else. If you listen to your false religion that teaches you to save your butt in front of your spirit, then you will lose both in the intention of saving your butt. Heaven is a knowledge that you must acquire to enter the kingdom of God.

The sixth plague of Egypt is the plague of boils. Moses and Aaron, upon the Lord's command, took soot from a furnace and tossed it into the air, which fell covering both people and animals with boils. This means that it was done because it is part of the law. Remember that Moses is the lawgiver—the spiritual part of us that receives the law from God—and Aaron is love. Anything done by both Moses and Aaron was done because God commanded it, and it was also done out of love. Soot from a furnace is what is used to create the boils. The furnace is where the fire is, and the fire is what separates pure truth from lies, which is the soot. A boil is a skin disease resulting from an infection in a skin gland under the skin. Spiritual boils affect *both* the mind and spirit.

If you understand this in spirit, you can understand the plague of boils. Just replace the physical nouns with spiritual verbs like this: Pharaoh (the king of organized religion) had a hard heart (wouldn't accept the truth) and wouldn't let the Israelites (the people who were chosen by God to bring the truth into the world) worship as they wanted. The true laws of God were kept as slaves to organized religion. Moses and Aaron (the true laws of God and love) tossed the soot (the lies that go against the true Laws of God) into the air and it covered both the people and the animals (the spirit and the mind).

This caused boils (an uncleanness in both your spiritual as well as your physical understanding of life). Finally, note that the Israelite people and their animals were *not* afflicted with boils. They were "spared" because they already *accepted* the true Laws of God. Accept the truth of the Lord in your heart, reject the lies of organized religion, and you will be spared from these plagues.

The seventh plague—the great hailstorm where man was hit on the head by hail the size of a large egg. Hail has been falling from heaven for the past four thousand years and people have been hit on the head with the understanding of the false prophet. They have learned nothing to explain the hailstorm. These false prophets make up their sermons about this plague with the worst stupidity that you can ever imagine.

Ask yourself, *Where* did these people get such a belief that you must make your wife obey you? Then the woman believes it, and she is being abused because she is married to an idiot—and this has been preached by the people in church on Sunday morning. They have been hit on the head with stupid and ignorant laws that make no sense whatsoever, and these people are stupid enough to believe this because the church orders it or the preacher says so. They take a piece of bread in their hand and they call it the body of Christ. Is anything on earth as stupid in the understanding of the Scriptures as the understanding of these people that make laws without any common sense whatsoever? They are teaching people to adapt themselves to the understanding that a piece of bread will restore their soul. You must have been hit hard on the head to understand something so ignorant and believe it.

Take that stupid piece of bread that goes from your mouth into your stomach and then goes into your intestines the next day. *You call this the body of Christ?* This is among the most stupid beliefs that I have ever seen in human history. People on the battlefield fought wars and got killed by the millions and believed that they gave their lives for the purpose to make men "free." But *true freedom* comes in the hearts of those who built their lives on the glory of worshiping God and cannot be won by killing each other and destroying life and property everywhere around us.

There has *never* been a war that has made *any* common sense. There will never be a war that will make any sense for a person to defend freedom where the sole purpose of war is to kill people needlessly. *True* freedom in the land of Joshua, in spiritual terms, means living comes from peace and not from war. If you believe in the peace of the Lord, you will always be at peace with your brother, no matter what government or religion teaches you to believe.

Understand the power of the Scriptures before you understand war. What makes people free to live in peace is to accept the freedom with others. No government or religion of any kind can make you free unless you already have freedom in your heart. Understand that what did not make you free was the belief in false faith. If you believe in true peace you will remain in peace as long as you have the faith of true freedom inside you.

Do not let any religion or government get you out of your freedom because the Lord has created life through the power of freedom. Do not give in to the great hailstorm of falsehood where people must fight against their brother to preserve themselves. Your heart was born where freedom was given to you. You have to hold your head up in the wisdom of the wise and understand the great power of the Lord your God. You will be free from all the hail that falls out of the sky. It will not fall on your head—and will not make you go in the world where there is no love and nowhere to live, nor will you kill your brother in the mass grave of total stupidity.

Now we come to the eighth plague—the plague of the locusts where a human being comes to understand the Scriptures like a locust. Locusts are creatures that travel by jumping. You must come to understand, in the wisdom of the Scriptures, that locusts jump from one line of the Scriptures to another—from one book to another. They do not understand *entire* teachings—they can only explain a line here and a line there. Jumping between what little parts of the scriptures they actually do understand and not asking the Lord for the true wisdom to understand life itself is what makes them locusts.

We were warned by the Lord that there would be this great swarm of locusts that will inhabit the earth in an understanding of jumping from one single line to another. Because no one could read the Scriptures in the knowledge of life, they had to jump. They had to jump from one place to the next to understand anything in the Scriptures because they just did not have the intelligence to see the word of God in the world of reality. They said they were teachers and told the people to listen to them because they are the ones that understand the Scriptures. They also said that you must give yourself to their church because that's the only place that you can go to understand the Scriptures. This is exactly what a false prophet is—a person that does not understand anything for himself yet tries to teach other people the meaning of the Scriptures. There have been little creatures like this all over the world who try to teach above themselves what they could not understand themselves, yet they call themselves people of God. That is the plague of the locusts. The little creatures of the earth who do not have anything of value to tell anyone but they have made themselves teachers.

Mankind left the world of reality to join in with the false prophet and false religion to believe in the most ignorant things that you can ever imagine. These educated men, from all sorts of colleges, graduate as people of high learning. Then they join with the stupidity of the Catholic Church and every religion on earth to believe in the fantasy world because they have been hit on the head with the teachings of locusts and hailstones. They believe what does not and cannot make sense in all the common sense and all the reality of the world. They believe that religion must still understand something special as to take a piece of bread and call it the body of Christ. Can you see how ignorant the world has become? It did not improve; it just got worse. Try to understand that these people have to leave the form of intelligence to believe such nonsense.

Now we go to the ninth plague—the three days of darkness that God has imposed on mankind where no one could see the truth for three thousand years. Fully grasp that man was meant to live in darkness for a full three thousand years. The Lord God of Heaven brought this upon the world where no educated man that I know could penetrate and break the seven seals. The wisdom was just not given because man had to be punished. The Lord put us in darkness for the three thousand years. From the life of Jesus to the end of *this* thousand years, man had to suffer in darkness because we did not *accept* the power of true wisdom. The curtain was ripped all the way down to the ground in the temple because religion had to go through this darkness to come to the day of the Lord.

Understand well the purpose of three days of darkness. This means three thousand years of holy sacrifice, where the false prophet would lead the world in total darkness. The understanding of the seven seals would not be revealed to mankind. Only on the third day would people come to understand the role of the false prophets. The white robe represents the leaders of all religions, the red robe represents the next stage of law (the cardinals and intermediate leaders of organized religions), and the black robe represents the small people that would impose the law where no one could learn anything (priests, preachers, rabbis, etc.).

The pale-colored horse represents the marriage of the flesh. The physical belief where a woman dresses in a white dress and marries her Prince Charming on the altar of wrongdoing. People will fall in love in the deepest darkness and have a life of misery trying to live out the dream of their lost soul. Mankind was not meant to be married because like everything else, the false prophet has mixed up the lesson of the wedding feast of intelligence at Cana. You must understand the *true* marriage, which is the marriage between spirit and mind. The strong part of a person (the spirit, which is male) and the weak part of a person (the mind, which is female) must marry each other in wisdom so there can be a complete understanding between the physical and the spiritual. This teaching about strong and weak, male and female, may seem sexist but it is not. This is because male and female cannot live in truth without each other and also because both male and female (again spirit and mind) are inside every one of us. Remember, this is a spiritual teaching, not a physical teaching.

The false prophet took advantage of the situation by claiming that they were the ones who could *marry* you, and they make people believe in these lies. Clearly understand, here, that a plague is when people try to understand the Scriptures with their little minds (of locusts) that create a teaching *way outside* the truth. They make people believe these lies, and the next thing you know you have a whole world out of control and without laws in the most stupid way of life that you can imagine. It then is nearly impossible for an animal (beast) to try to find the light in all the darkness. Darkness has covered the world for three days (until the end of this thousand years) because of God's great promise that the world will be delivered by the understanding of truth, common sense, and reality. Man had to be saved from himself. The power here is for each human being to try to understand the truth for himself and turn away from all the false prophets of organized religion and all the stupidity that they have brought to mankind.

Believe that the time has come to stand up and fight for the wisdom that you have lost as a human being. The deeds of darkness that cover this world, in the deepest beliefs in falsehoods, have been brought by the false prophets of organized religion. The Lord has said that if you want to choose lies over truth, foolishness over common sense, and fantasy over reality, then He will give you the plague of the locusts for three days (three thousand years) and let you live in darkness by the will of your lost soul where the power to understand was taken away from every human being. No one could understand anything of value during that period because of the false prophet and the teaching of stupidity that you believe in as a human being. The plagues were meant for every single person in the world. It did not matter which religion you believed in. If you believed in any organized religion, you lived in darkness and could not understand for three thousand years.

Now we come to the tenth and final plague, the plague of the firstborn in the land of Egypt. Your firstborn in the land of Egypt is your salvation. You may talk about how you were saved by Jesus Christ who died on the cross, that all you have to do is to believe in Jesus and you are saved. But the false prophet of the plague of the locusts was brought on mankind for the salvation of man. If you believe that you don't have to learn a single thing in order to get into heaven, you have to understand that the word of the Lord will be taken away from you in what you believe and leave you in total darkness because the day of darkness is not over yet. The time for your salvation is not yet born in your heart even though some false prophet promised you that salvation was going to bring you to the wisdom of your salvation on the day of the Lord. They lied to you because they did not have any salvation to give you to begin with, and what they taught you to believe in was the plague of your firstborn.

People believed that they were doing good when they were actually doing the evilest thing they possibly could to another person. They thought that anybody who did not believe like they did would be the one to lose their soul. But in the end, the Lord has taken away their own salvation from them. If you still care about your own salvation, you have to come to understand and start over again in the power of the wisdom of the Lord. No one on earth should hate God because things didn't turn out in their favor. The Lord has much more power than a small human being, and He will teach you the respect of the higher authority in this plague of your firstborn. By reading this book and *truly* understanding the word of the one true God, you *will* lose your *false salvation.* You will have to start over again and try to save your firstborn because you lost your soul by believing in the lies of the false prophet.

Next, we go to the teaching of the Passover. This is the time where you must cross over to the other side of your salvation. Each person who was a part of any religion of the earth must leave the land of Egypt in the struggle of being born again in the spiritual value of truth. The children of the Lord will *have* to change their soul. This is the time where the value of heaven will be much harder to achieve because you have to cross the desert of your salvation. You must cross over to the land where it will be very hard to understand your salvation and the value of learning, and you will learn that you have to struggle to understand the kingdom of heaven.

I tell you in truth that every single human being in this world must go through this struggle to understand the power of life itself. You have to cross over a lot of rivers of life to get to the power of the reality because you were left so far in the land of the Egypt where you lost your soul believing in everything that you can imagine that was totally stupid. Now you must learn to believe in reality so you can get back where you are supposed to be in the land of the wisdom of the wise. The words of wisdom will change the mountain and the island, meaning the law, and the place of rest will change on you. You used to believe that the adultery mentioned in the scriptures was physical, but now you must understand that adultery *never* was physical—it is a *spiritual sin* where people worship human beings in front of the Lord.

Understand well that where you are going will not be easy because it is a desert in the understanding of spirit. You have to struggle very hard to come to understand the Scriptures and to live in the power that was given to you in the ten plagues of Egypt. You cannot cross this desert just by believing in some of the truth. You have to believe in *all* of the truth, and you have to learn how to worship God. That does not mean going to church on Sunday morning. It means understanding yourself and learning the wisdom of the Lord—not the wisdom of man but the wisdom that places you on the higher stages of intelligence. You *cannot* stay where you are, believing and understanding *nothing* of the truth, and expect to be saved. The truth is that Jesus saved himself by his crucifixion but his crucifixion did not save you—but what is being said by the false prophet is that Jesus saved you. That was just a big lie brought forward by the mind of the false prophet.

Now we come to the *exodus* itself. This is the trip into the land of the desert where you will receive new laws in understanding, new revelations of truth, and a new understanding of how you deal with the Lord. I must tell you here, in truth, that man's wisdom is so weak because as hard as you try to understand, your weak mind cannot understand this spiritual wisdom and just keeps holding you back in darkness. Living in the desert of human understanding is very hard because you keep on complaining about the Lord, and he gets angry and frustrated when the people do not understand and follow his words. Man falls backward every time he takes a step forward, then he takes another step forward, only to go backward again. Understand well that the desert of human intelligence keeps holding you back because the process of spiritual learning is very difficult to go through when you do not yet understand the wisdom of the wise. I warn you now from the deepest part of the Scriptures that life will be extremely difficult to understand because you were promised the false victory by the false prophet. Now you are being promised the same victory in the understanding of truth, but you fear the Lord because you did not really trust him. This is why the trip will become so difficult that many of you will die in the desert before you enter the promised land. All the generations that have sinned against the Lord will have to wait and be reborn into a new life to understand the power of their salvation. This is the promise of the Lord, and it will be lived by those who come to understand true wisdom.

Next, we come to understand the Passover restrictions where the understanding of the Lord comes inside you to give you the power to reject the false understanding of the Scriptures. You must come to understand that the blood is the understanding. To receive this understanding, you must realize that you were not given an easy victory in the kingdom of God. It is much harder now than you ever imagined because in your life, you never read the Bible much, and those who did didn't understand *true* salvation whatsoever. In the old heaven, salvation would be an easy victory—just to believe in Jesus was enough to cross over—but now, the land where you used to rest has no more ground for you to rest on.

You must come to understand that the Passover restrictions are so you can understand and take part in the sacrifice of the Lord he sends upon each one of us. Realize that you will not be going the easy way, but rather, you must struggle to understand. Common sense will come upon you and the deepest power to understand the heaven and the earth—the spiritual as well as the physical part of us—will be done in the *understanding of reality.*

Truly believe that the Lord will not be easy on you. He will enforce hardship for the power of Heaven. You will have to cross a desert where you won't understand *anything* in spirit, and you have no water, meaning no reality, to understand the truth of life. There will be all kinds of places where there is no water, which again means no reality, so you will thirst for reality to come to you. Because of your belief in falsehood, you must cross over to the other side of the mountain and "climb" that mountain to receive the laws of God. Remember when, in the Book of Revelation, it said that the mountain that you used to believe in will be moved from its place and from the island—the place of rest you used to have will no longer be there. You will have to learn to struggle inside your soul, in the battle of what is right and what is wrong, to understand truth.

Now we come to the consecration of your firstborn. Remember that your firstborn is your salvation, and consecration means "to make sacred," so the consecration of the firstborn is to make your salvation sacred. This is done by learning and believing in the truth over lies, where you will cross over from the land of Egypt where your great power of your simple life will be changed. You have to leave the world of make-believe behind and struggle in the desert of this power to consecrate your firstborn. The consecration of your firstborn is to change your heart from your sin of falsehood to truth in your heart. You must come to *live* this truth in your heart where the power of brotherhood will defeat prejudice and bigotry.

In this great power of your salvation, you will be given a new consecration of your spiritual value. This is where you will come to reflect on your understanding of brotherhood. You will learn how to live on earth without tearing down your brothers. What created wars in the past was prejudice and bigotry in the heart of mankind, but if you now want to live in peace, you have to come to understand the power of the creation. You must realize that bigotry and prejudice are *all just big lies* that you have accumulated in the false understanding of the locusts in the value where you thought that your brother was less than you. You believed you were better than they were, and you created something that made no sense in the reality of the truth. This is what created war. The evil that was created by each one of you becomes the understanding that without war the world cannot survive peace. You believed that wars are fought to win peace, but that was just a big lie like the rest of the lies of the world.

No one likes to fight wars just to kill or be killed in the value of gaining nothing of any value. Ask yourself why God places the same feelings of victory on both sides, yet He claims no value from *either* side. He has gained nothing in your winning, and He has lost nothing in your losing. To consecrate your firstborn in your heart, you must first claim the victory *inside* yourself. Before you can gain the victory against your brother, you have to understand truth first before you try to destroy your brother who does not understand as you do.

Know that in the consecration of the firstborn in your heart, you need to restore yourself to the value that the person you are shooting at believes in the same victory as you do on the opposite side. But the man who thinks straight enough to look at his brother in the same value as he views himself will win the battle of the hearts. You can kill as many brothers as you can in the physical sense of war, but you will gain the wisdom of the wise if you understand the true war of spirit. The power of all reason is to win first in the consecration of your firstborn. This is where your salvation of heaven has to be secured in value before you start judging your brother in the value where there is no winners and all losers.

Next, we come to "The Song of Moses and Miriam." Sing this song to the Lord where the victory of the heart must take over between the sister (female—meaning the mind) of Moses (male—meaning the mind) and the law. Sing a song of victory when your heart has gained the power to cross over the Red Sea. It is hard to understand God's knowledge when you live in the desert, so you must come to understand the power of yourself. You have a divine power to understand truth. That divine power is in you to reach the Lord in your heart. You don't have to climb the highest mountains to understand the truth, but you must establish the boundary between truth and lies.

As long as you understand something that makes sense, try to understand that this power is only given to those whose faith could move a mountain in the restoration of the heart and the consecration that comes in the *value of the truth*. Understand here that you have to have enemies, but try to stop understanding and believing in lies. Lies are your enemies. You must come to realize the significance of the power of living without water (meaning without reality) inside the desert of human understanding, where there is *no reality* to understand.

Most of the time, you don't have reality because life is just not there where you can see the reality of the situation and you are thirsty to drink the water of this reality of life. You must come to understand that when you travel into the desert, you sometimes cannot see, in truth, to travel any further. Life just doesn't seem to make any sense, and you cannot continue in your journey without coming to understand that you would need to have reality to survive. If you don't have the reality underneath your nose, you will break apart from being so thirsty because you cannot continue to sustain life in spiritual understanding. You cannot see in front of you to understand where you are going and what is going to be the next dream in your reality. You will try to give up your journey and return to where you came from. You will try to live in the land that you used to live in with the false religions that teach you lies and give false hope.

Understand the food you are given to eat to survive your days in the desert. Eat the manna and the meat of the quail or you will not survive in human understanding. The manna and the quail are the spiritual foods God will give you for your journey in the desert. The Lord will bring you to the promised land—the land of Canaan—where you will come to understand how to live in the land of milk and honey. *Milk* means "life," and *honey* means "love." The understanding of milk and honey is that you must come to enjoy your life with the Lord. If you do not try to understand the food you eat in the desert, you will bless your physical part because you don't understand your spiritual part. If you don't understand where you're going in spirit, then you haven't got a clue where you are going in your physical life.

You must understand the power of the spirit here. You live in *both* the physical as well as the spiritual parts of life. But if you only place your faith in the physical part of life, then you don't know where you are going. Don't worry about your physical part—try to understand that your spiritual part will be your guide in all life. Know, without a doubt, that if you *accept* and *follow* the Lord, then where you are going is to the land of milk and honey, a place of value.

Now we are entering the teaching of the law of the Ten Commandments. Understand the power by which we receive the Laws of God. The Ten Commandments of our Lord are the power to understand how to worship the Lord in the understanding of life. You must only worship one God, and under that one God, you cannot worship an image of anyone, including Jesus and all the other prophets of the Bible. God is the *only* God of the truth, common sense, and reality of life. You must worship the Creator and *only* the Creator. This is what was written to be the power of the Lord.

Understand well and worship only the one true God, for there is only one Creator. The power to understand the Creator is to understand that he is the God of truth, common sense, and reality. There is only one God that you can worship at the center of intelligence—the one who sits on the throne in front of all human beings. Remember the Lord, the one who brought you out of slavery in the land of false religion and who gave mankind his laws upon the mountain. Understand the power of the laws of God—they are spiritual laws, not physical laws—and it is not a mountain that you climb in physical strength with your physical body.

You must come to understand that the Lord is *spirit and spirit alone*, and he brings inside each one of us the spiritual value of the account of his law. You cannot worship any idols that people make inside the mind. You cannot worship *false holidays* of the earth such as Christmas, Easter, and Halloween and all the stupid lies that man believes about the Lord. This is the power that we have inside of us to reason with, and if you use it in all this fantasy of the world because you want to get together with your family and friends, this is *not* the purpose of truth. The purpose of truth is to worship *only* the Lord your God and no one or anything else. You cannot believe in any God that was produced to you by the false prophet of the world. *People think that you can worship anything you want as long as you don't hurt anybody*. But if you worship outside the truth, you are *hurting yourself* in ways that you can't even imagine. The laws are written for the purpose that you are only supposed to worship the Lord who created you in order to bring an understanding of the glory that God is unique and he tolerates no one before him.

If you worship anything like gold, silver, or things that look good such as jewelry, this is *not* the way to live your given life. You are supposed to worship the reason of intelligence that we call the reality of life; otherwise, you will be making a great mistake with your life. God is the power that we live by in the creation of the planets and the life that we live on this planet with the glory by which we were made to understand and live the truth. The truth is the Laws of God, and you cannot change them just because you feel like it. Neither you nor anyone else is allowed to worship Jesus and claim the deity that God is a human being. I tell you this in the power of the law and in the power of straight thinking where man must learn to worship the power of intelligence.

All human beings must learn from the God who brings truth, common sense, and reality. Worshiping God is worshiping in the understanding of reality. You cannot escape reality, and you cannot escape the common sense of intelligence. You cannot skip out of those boundaries and worship whoever and whatever you choose. The truth is also a boundary where you must understand the Lord your God, and if you don't understand the Lord your God, then you are commanded by heaven to learn how to worship God. The commandments of the Lord tell us that we cannot worship Jesus just because we feel that he was a good man and he performed few miracles in the eyes of men. You have no right to worship people because you think they have performed miracles. Only God can make the miracle of intelligence happen.

Worship the Lord your God in truth, and do not take the name of the Lord your God in vain. This does not mean that you shall not swear—it means that you *cannot* use the Scriptures to believe whatever you want. You are not allowed to misuse the name of the Lord—this means do not say God is here or there, this or that, when you do not know if it is true.

You have to read the Bible with *supreme* understanding. You cannot understand the Bible just by reading it. You can only understand the Bible by *living* it, and this is how you understand the events in the Scriptures that give you an understanding of God. The Scriptures *must* make total sense—if they don't make sense, then it's not true at all. For example, there are people who receive communion and they think it's righteous. This is worshipping an "idol." The *true* word of God is like bread, but it is *not* actual bread. Bread, as it is used in the scriptures, is meant in a spiritual sense. If you worship physical bread as God, you break every rule and law of God. Worshiping a piece of bread in false intelligence is the most ignorant way to worship the Lord your God—so do not take the name of the Lord in vain, and don't tell other people what to do when you don't know what to do yourself.

If you do not know the truth of life, then you have to come and understand that the Lord *is* the truth. The truth of the Lord is understanding the supreme way of wisdom, and *supreme* means to understand the scriptures in spiritual terms. God is not meant to be touched by the hand of those who are not worthy to understand. That is, until we come to the seventh day—which we are now on the road to understanding in the worshiping of the Lord your God. We are coming into the time of the great Sabbath of the Lord where you will come to know the dignity and the understanding of the Sabbath.

Man must be set free in the freedom of his soul to understand the power of the Sabbath. You were supposed to learn the Scriptures and then rest on the seventh day of the creation, the great day of Sabbath—this means that during the last thousand years, you should have learned how to worship God on your own. But the false prophets convinced people that they had to go through them to understand the Scriptures, so people didn't bother to learn the Scriptures on their own in their lifetime. They trusted the words of men to understand God. They did not work in spiritual terms to understand the Almighty God. They left it to someone else to teach them, and now the Sabbath is here and so many people are so far out from the truth. They think that they are safe and they don't want to learn anything else, but the sacred stone of the foundation was to learn and understand. You didn't need anybody from any church of any kind to understand—all you needed to do was to open your heart to the *true* meaning of the Sabbath as a resting time. The people today who understand the Scriptures in truth can rest in peace in the divine knowledge of the Lord.

Understand that the way God created mankind is divided in two parts—part physical knowledge and part spiritual knowledge. You must *not* understand the Bible with your physical side. When we talk about the commandments of the Lord given to Moses on Mount Sinai, it is not the misunderstanding that God has created a set of laws that come in your physical part. The Ten Commandments are not physical laws. They should not be understood by the mind of man, such that if you break these laws, then the court of mankind will punish you for what you have done. Spiritual laws are different. The Ten Commandments are spiritual laws for worshipping God in Spirit, not something to be understood by the mind.

Why do we go to church when the Lord is part of the spirit inside you? Your church is inside of you. Understand that you cannot worship an image before the Lord in spirit, and you cannot take the name of the Lord in vain—this also is in spirit. If you observe and do no work on the Sabbath, that is also spiritual because the seven days of the creation is the beginning of the seven thousand years that we live in now. The great Sabbath is the time of rest where you need to take a look at yourself and see where you are going in the world. Understand which way you are going in your spiritual value. This has nothing to do with the physical part of your life because the physical part belongs to people. We must respect the laws of man and live by the rule that those laws made on you, but you must also respect the laws of God, and these are the most important laws to live by. You must understand that the Ten Commandments were placed on the mountain for you to understand God's word because they are spiritual laws. You must distinguish between the reality of physical and spiritual laws. The Ten Commandments are in spirit—the physical part of them belongs to the *laws of man*. If you do wrong in the laws of man, you will be punished by man. This is the way life is set up, but if you do wrong in your spiritual laws, then the Lord himself will punish you for it. To worship the Lord is to worship one God—you cannot worship other gods. You have to worship the one God of the Creation inside your soul, but you must also not ignore the laws of man. This is your father (spirit) and mother (mind), and it is the best explanation that I can give to the world to understand the difference between spirit and physical.

Now we're going to the next law: You shall not murder. The people of this world believe that the Lord has said that you should not kill people, but this is *not* the real meaning here. The laws of man have written thousands of books. If you want to study the laws in the physical sense, then go to the books that man has made on the laws. The other law here is the law of the spirit, and you must come to understand what is means in spiritual terms—it means do not murder your spiritual part of the Scriptures.

Understand that the people who preach on Sunday make others believe that Jesus is God. *Jesus is not God.* He is the son of God but only in spirit. These false preachers offer sacrifices to Jesus. That is killing the spirit in the understanding of the Lord your God because people refer to Jesus as God. They pray to him and offer sacrifices to him, but this is killing the great power of the understanding of the Lord. This is the *real murder* here that God is talking about. Spiritual laws are not understood in the religion of the earth by the false prophets because they themselves don't understand them. They kill the spiritual understanding and man becomes lifeless in the understanding of the spirit. When you destroy a man's spirit, you destroy the man's life just like you would in the physical world. Killing in spirit is the most evil act because it makes a person change his heart and makes him believe in the false god.

There is no greater sin in human living than a person who doesn't know what they're talking about, yet they keep on preaching. All they do is make people as ignorant as they are. They have killed people, and when you kill enough people, you will have a hard time to enter the Kingdom of God because of this great sin.

Now we come to the commandment regarding adultery. You think that adultery is people who make love to women when they are already married. People believe adultery is to physically commit the fornication of your physical needs—this is *not* what the meaning of adultery is. Understand that God's laws are different from the laws of man. You are not allowed to worship any individual on earth like the "saints" that people believe in. *There is no such thing as a saint.* We are *all* both good and evil inside us. You *cannot* worship anyone above yourself on earth or in heaven and call them saints nor can you offer sacrifices to them. *This includes Jesus.*

Look at the Catholic Church. She is called the *great prostitute* in the Book of Revelation because every teaching they have is a physical teaching. God has let her survive until this day so He can *prove* that adultery is a sin inside our spirit that teaches us to worship inside the mind and *not* inside the spirit. This is the falsehood that was done by the people of the earth that they called a "miracle." You should not worship a human being, and you should not worship saints. There is no such thing in human living where any person is a saint. We *all* make our mistakes, and we all have to worship according to our lack of knowledge and lack of ability to understand the Lord. The people you call saints are people like the rest of us, and if you use your knowledge, sacrifice, and pray to saints, you are breaking the law of adultery. By committing adultery, you become a prostitute in spiritual value where you throw your spirit in different directions onto people, and this is what the Lord calls the *great prostitute*. Understand that this is a serious sin—if you believe that you are right in doing it, you definitely are *not* on the side of the Lord.

The next commandment is "You shall not steal." This is another commandment of our Lord that does not come from physical understanding. Stealing from your spiritual value is a great sin. Take, for example, if someone has a great idea and he worships God in the proper way—and you think you are smarter than this person by telling him that his idea won't work—this is stealing from his spiritual value. When you tell someone that you think it is wrong to have sex in the physical sense and you condemn them for having sex because you think in your mixed-up mind that is evil to have sex outside of marriage, this is also against God's law.

You do not have to agree with the understanding that I bring you, but you must come to understand that God is the one who sends those feelings inside of a human being. Accept the fact that in your feelings of the beauty and integrity of having holy sex because it is *not* wrong to feel what God has put inside you. False religion tells you to "override" the feelings that God sends inside us. The truth is in control of the spirit that is inside of you. This should not be overridden by anything that the false religions of the earth have told you by their worthless understanding of locusts, the little critters of the earth that do not know God at all and preach against the Great Truth in what they did not understand about God.

When two people have sex together, it is part of the feelings that the Lord has placed inside our soul for arousing our sexual feelings. If you use the religion of the earth to control your feelings, you won't be found anywhere in the truth of your feelings. Sex was created both for procreation and for the pleasure of life. Mankind must enjoy these feelings as they come inside us. You should not be concerned about being married to anyone because the "holiness" of the Lord does *not* agree with human marriage. There is nothing in the physical part of life where males and females must marry one another. When the Bible talks about the wedding feast in the land of Cana, this means the wedding feast of spirit. The mind and the spirit must understand the feelings of the physical part of a human being. If you don't understand in spirit, then you will try to understand the laws of false religion. But they do not exist in the *true* understanding of life. It was just something that man has misunderstood.

The whole world believed the *false* understanding of human sexuality because we were taught that to have sex was dirty. You must understand that the power of having sex is *totally clean* in the understanding of the Lord—sex is for procreation and also for the joyful time of your feelings. There's nothing wrong with it on either side of the understanding of male and female. I tell you the truth—do *not* listen to false religion about your sexuality because it will corrupt your heart. False religion does not understand the Scriptures to begin with, and they will not tell you to live your life according to the laws of God—the laws of feelings and to enjoy yourself.

You are not allowed to steal the values of other people's feelings. Understand that what you take from someone else will be taken from you, and this is the law of the Lord. If you take away someone's sexuality, your sexuality will be taken from you. And if you take away the pleasure of others, then the pleasures of your own self will be taken away. What you take from others because of your lack of knowledge will indeed be taken from you. Be careful of what you do not understand because the Lord will punish you greatly.

Now we go to the understanding of the *final* commandment of our Lord: "You shall not covet." This means not to be jealous of anyone else's life. Live your *own* life, and do not worry if you did not receive as good a life on earth as others did. Just make yourself comfortable with who and what you are in order to understand in the Covenant of the Lord. You must understand that the Lord has placed you in this situation of your life in the way you were created. Be happy with who you are and appreciate your life that the Lord has given you. Do not worry about any situation of your life because the Lord is *always* there to correct you and bring you to the purpose of your true existence. Respect the laws of spirit (your father) and the laws of your physical part (your mother). Respect *all* the laws that the Lord has given you. Any law that was made by God was made to help you understand the better part of yourself and to assure you of the glory that you and the Lord will have together. Understand well that these laws help you in the benefits of the spiritual power of the Lord.

Now we come to understand idols and altars. Understand well that you must not idolize anything in front of the Lord, and this includes people. No matter how smart or intelligent any person is, you must not worship them in any way. When I say *worship*, I mean do not make up anything about their intelligence—you must *not* put a human being in front of the Lord and believe that they are anything special above other people. Man is only an animal who gets his wisdom from the power of the truth of life. Wisdom comes from the Lord on the altar of your sacrifices. Wisdom should hold the respect of mankind by understanding that *all* wisdom comes from the Lord and only through mankind's sacrifice. Through his hard work and sacrifice, a human being must take this knowledge of who and what he is, in order to benefit from the gratitude of the Lord.

Come to believe that on the altar inside each of us, we must offer sacrifices where there is pain in your soul but also benefit in the gratitude of the Lord. God is a divine creature of knowledge, and his gratitude toward man will only happen because he sees actual human spiritual sacrifices that teach us the difference between truth and lies. A human being is just an animal, but he has the power to create from the wisdom of the Lord, and man must be affiliated with that wisdom. Man must accomplish the affiliation of truth over *all* lies. If you analyze what man has accomplished through the understanding of falsehood, then you cannot understand the truth of life. Man must create for himself a way of life where we can benefit from the wisdom of the Lord to accomplish great things that benefit our lives. In order to appreciate the good human living, you must transfer this gratitude to the Lord. Without his wisdom, we would be set back millions of years in our evolution where discoveries like fire and the wheel remain outside of our understanding. Do not analyze anything that man has created; instead, analyze the divine nature that brought the creation of the Lord together.

Since mankind was created on the sixth day of the creation, you must understand the last millennium where a human being was brought to life so that he could build his house in the physical and then in the spiritual value. This is where human beings will live life in the value of this prosperity in the Creation of the Lord.

Here, there is something that you must understand. The people who figured value *without* God do not really understand that whatever mankind has accomplished in their power from the beginning of the Creation until now could not have been accomplished without the Lord. So make sure that everything that was given to mankind is appreciated by the gratitude of the Lord so that human reason that comes from the Lord will benefit mankind. Understand well here that the power of intelligence comes from the Lord.

Now we come to the teaching of the law of personal injuries. Note that we are still in the value of the spiritual understanding. We must understand that what you do in the physical part of life has *nothing* to do with the spiritual value. This is a *spiritual* book, and it must be understood spiritually. A man hitting another man in this teaching means to attack someone spiritually, such as calling them stupid and telling them that they will never amount to anything. Many times, we hear this from father to son where the father does not believe in his son and will say hurtful and make demeaning remarks. This is so wrong because you must let your children learn for themselves in the power of the spirit. You are not allowed to strike them with total stupidity and claim that you are smarter than them because you think you are better than they are.

Loving people does not mean that you have to guide them into the wisdom of the Lord. You must let each person decide the value of the wisdom of the Lord in his own soul. I make a note of this because this is how you turn away from the understanding of total stupidity where you have killed another person's feelings and the value of himself. You absolutely have *no* right to hit anyone with your stupid remarks of the human mind. You may be a parent or person who thinks he is a parent. Nevertheless, there are no parents or children in the value of intelligence—we are *all equal* in the value of intelligence. You are not to take anyone away from his altar and claim your value inside them. Try to respect your children; your children will grow in value if you have value on yourself by what you say and do to others.

Most people think that their criticism of others (that has no value in reality) will benefit themselves. But when you criticize someone, you kill something inside of them and you destroy the values of others because you believe that no one is as good as you are. Do you understand that if you attack your mother or father, this is spiritual also? You must understand that God, the supreme power, is your father and the wisdom of man is your mother. Therefore, you cannot attack what you believe to be lies with your ignorant idea in your lost soul because if you attack the truth, you attack your father, and if you attack and bring your fellow man down because you can't stand the value of what your mother has created, then you attack your mother. Look above and inside yourself and find the value of true wisdom from the Lord your God.

If you do not understand and accept the truth of the Lord, then say nothing—don't try to enforce what little wisdom of the "locusts" of the earth that you have and cannot understand. Even the wisdom of your mother is just as intelligent as she can be because the rule of the wisdom of the earth also comes from the Lord. If anyone kidnaps someone and sells them into slavery of the false prophet or false religion, they are to be punished. Understand the punishment that the Lord will impose on you if you bring someone to believe in false religion. If you kidnap your brother in the falsehood of religion, where no one seems to understand the wisdom of the Lord, then you bring him into slavery in the land where he has to listen to the false prophet who knows less than he knows himself. If anyone curses his mother or father, he must be put to death. This means that if someone does not accept both the laws of God and the laws of mankind and breaks *all* the laws of everything on earth, then he must be put in that understanding of the death of the spirit; *how* you put them to death is you have to stop him from doing it.

Next, we come to the law of protection of property. Heed this law well. What you own is your property, including what you know and what you understand in your spiritual value. Realize that you own everything in your spiritual house and you must protect the true faith that's inside of your understanding. *No one* is allowed to take what you have in your knowledge, not even to try to prove what you do not know. You are aware of what you have and should know how valuable it is to understand in this value. Understand that your ox means your ignorance and your sheep means your simple humble deeds. So if someone tries to steal your simplicity by laughing at you or they try to defeat you with what you do not know, then just ignore them. If someone steals something of no value, where they try to make a fool of you, destroy and slaughter your animal being, then he or she will have to ponder to understand what they don't have. If they try to use your ignorance to steal from you, just be humble and simply admit when you don't know something; say you don't know.

Do not pretend to know what you are ignorant of. Understand that you have the right to your sheep, which is your simplicity. Be simple in everything that you are so you can come to understand the Laws of God and the reality of a simple person. *Always* be aware of what you know—the value of learning and what you have learned. Do not let anybody talk you out of doing what is right even though, sometimes, it is hard to know the difference between right and wrong. *Always* try to protect yourself and be a person of value in your knowledge.

If someone is caught trying to steal from you the value of what you already know in your own kingdom of knowledge, do not let them get away with it. Do not let anybody break in and try to make you look like a fool because they are not intelligent enough to know what is inside your soul. *Fight back* with the power of what is true. Protect yourself and keep the truth inside your heart by listening to the Lord your God. Do not listen to the people who make no sense, and don't try to compromise with what they believe. If someone breaks into your house and tries to steal what you have learned from the Lord your God, do *not* listen to him because the value of the truth will *stand* by itself in the spirit of common sense. All of this value is written in the common sense and the reality of your heart.

If you want to know whether someone is breaking in to steal from you, just listen to your common sense and reality and you will find the truth. Do not let someone else graze his animal in your field because they will try to destroy your field by making you look stupid. You must defend the truth because your field is what you know. Do not engage people in long discussions or arguments. Just tell these people the simple truth and let it go without a fight. Let them find the truth for themselves and don't let their animal destroy your feelings in the value of heaven. When it comes to any discussion about the Bible, listen to his side and make a determination to *believe only in the truth*.

Now we come to social responsibility, where you must come to understand the "keywords" in each of the Laws of the Lord. This is a spiritual teaching and is written in such a way that the mind cannot understand it. Therefore, you must come to understand the keywords in the law. Here you have the law about a man seducing a virgin—this is someone trying to mess with your mind and teach you what they think the Scriptures mean in the understanding of spiritual value. You must understand this as a human being but then "translate" it into the language of heaven. *Virgin* is the keyword—it means the virgin mind. The understanding of the virgin mind is what is written in the Scriptures. By reading each line of the Scriptures and coming to understand these keywords, you will then be able to translate each line into the spiritual understanding.

At that point, you will be able to understand *everything* that is written about the description of an animal. Mankind must translate these teachings into the human feelings of the spirit when the animal becomes a sign of what it means and makes sense to your common sense. Can you see now what the son of God is? Your common sense is the son of God that you must worship, *not* Jesus. God is the word and the spirit of the word where you look at yourself as a human being just as Jesus looked at himself to understand the Scriptures two thousand years ago. You must come to understand that as a human being, you have the power of common sense and that is the Son of God in your spirit.

If you worship Jesus, you break *all* the laws of the Creation because *no man* can replace the Lord your God and be worshipped before Him. Try to understand the spiritual power of human understanding where a human being may *not* be transformed into God. You must realize that with the power to understand your common sense, you can *know* the Scriptures. All I'm giving you here is what I have used to understand the Scriptures. If you want to understand the whole book of the Scriptures, then you *all* must be born of spirit that God wants you to live by, and these laws are the laws of justice that are inside *all* of us. You must come to understand that the "virgin" is your simple mind. If you try to understand the Lord outside simple common sense, you are breaking the laws of the Creation.

Fully understand what God has written in the power of the law where you must translate the animal into a spiritual value in order to create the power inside your soul to understand the divine spirit. Now the *true* God cannot be replaced by any human being. If any person thinks of goodness and kindness outside of common sense, he creates miracles of no value that cannot be brought up to the chair of the Throne of God. You must understand the laws of God in order to worship God properly in all manners of viewing human understanding, from the animal to the divine nature of our Creator. Grasp this power to know and fully understand the set of laws that will move the mountain and the island. This is just like the Book of Revelation, where it tells you that you have to move the mountain and the island in the spiritual power of your faith.

Do have a clear understanding that you were created to learn and understand *all* that was written in the Scriptures, but you also need to use your heart because your heart is like a parachute. Unless it opens, it will not work. In the work you do to understand the Lord your God, the power to understand is given to you, but you have to serve the Lord your God with your love and with your understanding. Those are two of the sons of Jacob: Simeon and Levi. This is where you come to use the Levi that's inside you to love the Lord your God and the Simeon that's inside you to understand. Each one of us was created with this power.

You have to open your heart like a parachute so it will work inside your soul of a simple human being. I'm writing this book in the love of the Creation because God made the Creation for man and not *against* man. Everybody must come to understand this Creation and understand the way it works inside of you. When you begin to understand things with your virgin mind, you are meant to be married in the spiritual power of the Scriptures. Nobody should seduce you with what you are to believe. Let the Lord speak to your heart, and hear him well when he speaks to you so you will marry the right way of life in who and what you are.

Here we go to the second law of social responsibility. This law states that you should not have sex with an animal. Remember that the Bible is a spiritual book—it is meant for your spirit, not your body. The laws contained in the Scriptures are spiritual laws, not physical laws. The warning against having sex with an animal means that your spirit should not have sex with an animal—the animal here means the *mind*. In other words, do not get your spiritual understanding from the mind of a man, whether it is your mind or the mind of another human. You are *only* to get your spiritual wisdom directly from the Lord and *no one else*. Jesus was an animal because he was human—you are not allowed to worship Jesus in front of God because Jesus was only human. If you offer your sacrifice to Jesus, you offer sacrifice to the animal being, and things will not go well for you in life. You will have all kinds of problems in your life, and you will pray to the same Jesus to help you—he cannot help you because he is not God.

If you pray to a different god created by the mind of mankind, you are going into the land of darkness, where you will not be able to understand a thing in the Scriptures because you worship a false god. Now if you worship by trying to understand the parables that Jesus brought instead of worshipping the man himself, then you are worshipping the true God of all Creation. Remember that Jesus himself was the servant of the Lord God. Not even those that man has called saints are saints in reality. There is no such thing as saints in the world of men because each one of us has both good and evil inside us in the choice of life, and no man can raise himself or be raised by others to be perfect in the divine nature of the Divine God. Instead, we should work (inside of ourselves) to be holy like our Father in heaven is holy by worshiping only what makes common sense. Understand that the only perfectness that we can possess is to work on believing in the Lord, which is the Truth, the True Son of God, the Angel of Common Sense, and the Holy Spirit, which is the Angel of Reality. Try to understand these things in the value of holiness inside your soul. Don't try to prove to anyone that you are a saint in spirit, and don't try to make your physical part look like a saint because sainthood does not exist in reality and, therefore, is against the Lord your God.

You can raise yourself to the value of human understanding in the teaching of the divine spirit, but you must understand that we are humans—we are *not* creators. Try to understand the lesson of the Israelites staying at the foot of the mountain to receive the mighty laws of the Lord. The people God chose in spirit (the Israelites) wait at the base of the mountain (their faith) for the laws to be brought down to them (to be explained in a way that they can understand). When you do understand these mighty laws, you will be pure in spirit. This is about *all* you can raise yourself to be in this world. Love the Lord your God with *all* your strength and *all* that you are because God is the Truth in the value of everything that makes sense in reality and common sense. This is the power of the virgin mind to understand in spirit. You start off understanding nothing until you learn, through the great sacrifice, to understand everything that you need to know about the Lord God Almighty.

If you misunderstand the Scriptures and try to teach the scriptures with the mind of an animal inside you, then you must be put to death with everything that you believe in the spiritual understanding of *no value*. Do not curse the name of the Lord your God, and do not curse the ruler that brings intelligence to a greater value. Worship the Lord your God with all your soul, and never curse the name that you don't understand because your heart and soul belongs to the Lord.

Never believe that God is evil because you did not understand his true meaning inside your heart. That would be a great sin, and you will be punished severely for that great sin where you will stumble and plant your seed in the worthless dirt among the thorns or in the sand of the desert where you will not be able to see anything and understand nothing. You will be so severely punished by losing your soul.

If you sacrifice to a false god, then the truth will be destroyed inside your soul because you placed your sacrifice to a man. Christians sacrifice their spiritual understanding to a man just like the Catholic Church does. They sacrifice themselves to a false god, and they will be destroyed in spirit for doing so. The time will come that you will not find any Christian preachers or Catholic priests because the Lord will destroy them for preaching against his word and for bringing the life of a man (Jesus) to the divine nature to mankind. You *cannot* do that. The law tells you *not* to do that, and if you do, your heart will be in shambles with the word of God.

Understand well that all your pain and sacrifice on the altar must be offered to God. Do not ever pray to Jesus or to some saint who you think is closer to God than you are. A person who ministers to people all over the world and claims to serve the Lord with their charity may have accomplished something in their *physical* struggle, but they gained nothing in spirit because they failed to understand the name of the Lord their God in the value of truth, common sense, and reality. God is the truth, and if you do not worship God in the truth, you must think again of what God is before you go and show yourself across the world to play God with people.

Do not take advantage of widows and orphans. This means do not take advantage of the poor and the helpless in human understanding to make yourself look good in front of people. Crossing the world in the ministry of falsehood does not help you to understand the Lord your God and the reward of heaven. People were meant to take care of themselves, and when you preach lies to them, you hurt their ability to take care of themselves. You prove your ignorance to them but do not help them to become intelligent and worship the Lord God. You teach them to worship Jesus and to find the love of Jesus inside them, but that is a worthless teaching. If you were to teach people to worship the Lord your God with all your soul, then you would have to teach them to plant their seed in the fertile ground to have food to eat. Instead, you try to play God and be counted among the saints so you can steal the kingdom of God with the faith of no value. Remember that *arrogance* was what you used to claim the value of heaven, but that will not help you in front of the Lord because you sacrificed yourself to Jesus and not to God. Understand the Lord well and understand the value of the law before you teach way outside the truth (that was there to begin with) and you set yourself up in the worthless value of the lost soul.

If you lend money to someone in need, do not ask to be paid back with interest like a money lender does. What this means is you *share* the value of your heart with someone. Don't expect to be paid for it like the false prophets in their churches. You think they tell you something of value, but in reality, they tell you nothing of value, and they expect payment for it because they claim that they can save your soul. Understand well, all you false prophets who build big churches that look like caves with no God in it to worship, and you bring people there every Sunday to tell them nothing that has any value for the Kingdom of God. Your claim is full of arrogance where you, the false prophets, claim above yourselves to be on the side of truth, yet you do not understand it yourselves.

You must *not* speak for God because you don't know him. How then can you teach what God is? You understand the God of the dream, not the God of truth, common sense, and reality. Yet you claim to speak on his behalf. If you did speak in common sense, the truth would come alive in the value of what God *is*. You collect your share of the profits that you did not earn in the value of claiming, in arrogance, that you are saved or by saving others in no value whatsoever. You did not teach anyone to worship the Lord and the Lord alone—you taught them to worship Jesus. This is one of the greatest sins of the human race. Because of your arrogance of raising yourself to this threshold, humanity looks at you thinking that you are higher than them. So much is to be said in arrogance where a man cannot find himself and keeps on doing wrong and yet keeps on claiming that what he's doing is right.

Heaven is a place of spiritual knowledge where a human being finds himself in the value of the new knowledge inside his heart. This is where you come to understand yourself in humility—you have to save yourself before you can save anyone else. For that matter, no one truly saves anyone else. An individual has to save himself in front of the Lord and understand the Lord your God in the value of the true words of heaven. At this point, I must ask you this question: Why would God need *you* to save mankind? God made the sin of arrogance so high that people who think of themselves to be better than everybody else will "rise" in their lost soul and try to play God on earth.

Now we come to the laws of justice and mercy—the law that the Lord is giving me to write this book. This book will be placed on tables for *all* men to read, understand, and apply his truths in the common sense and the reality of intelligence. Mankind must be brought to the laws of justice and mercy to see himself as he was created to be with the justice of the Lord. *All* human beings must look at themselves and see why they were doing what they did and understand their own arrogance where they placed themselves in the value of all that is good. Remember that the law written in this book is not my own law or my own wisdom but the wisdom of the Lord that has been given to me to write this book for the justice and the mercy of mankind. The false ministries of the Catholic church and all organized religions must be brought to the understanding of their wrongdoing. For those who are in prison or are living in the false priesthood of the Catholic Church, man must look into his *own* heart to see the damage he has brought to his brothers that made them lose faith in the Lord their God. The corrections of intelligence must be brought to the mind of those who have brought forth ministries against the Lord their God.

Do not deny justice to poor people and those who are in need. Here again you must understand the laws of justice and mercy. If a person is poor in spirit and is in need of human understanding, you must give them the fruit of your womb (your feelings), but do not give them more than they need. Just bring it to justice. If a person is low in knowledge, then give him only what he needs to eat to understand the kingdom of God. The laws of justice bring the idea of reality into a soul that has been lost for so long. In order to bring them into the Kingdom of God, you don't have to tell people everything—tell them what you feel at the present time. This would be sufficient because in my Father's house, there are many, many rooms. You have to bring the powers of justice in a way that justice is understood in the *simple way*. Be kind to the weak and love them because they also are a part of the Kingdom of the Lord. Be just with them, as the Lord was just with you when you were in the land of false religion.

You must deal fairly with your brothers who are not as smart as you are because wisdom does not come in a big package. It comes in small deeds of human understanding where you give the pleasure of human understanding to the *least* of God's children. Do not accept bribes because bribes blind the soul and keep you from speaking the truth when you're asked to speak it. Bribes confuse your brother in the lesson of the soul, and they twist the words of righteous understanding. Do not oppress the alien in your life—those who do not understand anything about the Lord. Everything you are comes from the Lord, and the power of the Lord that educated you is the center of intelligence, but not everybody knows this. In order to bring people to the same level of intelligence as you are, you must *feed* them like babies in the wombs of their mothers before you can give them solid food to eat.

Be careful not to destroy the baby who has not reached the value of adulthood and is still in infancy. *Respect* those who know less than you by not filling them with lies in your arrogant way of thinking. You think that because you know more than they do that you are more important? This is absolutely *not* true. The least of us is more important than the best of us, and the best of us must serve the least of us because justice is the deferred value of love. In order for you to be fair with others, you have to speak to others in the understanding of the small soul that lives in the least of us. Try to understand that this is the justice of the Lord.

Now we come to the Laws of Sabbath, where you must hold your understanding in the value that we are going into the land of rest. The Sabbath is the day of the Lord. It is *not* a physical day of the week as organized religion teaches. Always remember that the Bible is a spiritual book, and the laws in the Bible are spiritual. This is because your body will die off, but your spirit is "eternal"; therefore, the Sabbath is spiritual, not physical. What sense does it make to have eternal laws for the part of you that is *not* eternal? You are to work six days, but you are to rest on the day of the Lord. This means that you are to work to develop your understanding of the Lord and his laws, but you are to leave in the hands of the Lord anything that is outside your understanding. When something is outside of your knowledge, meaning you do not know it yet, you are not allowed to make up a false explanation. Just rest on that day and leave it in the hands of the Lord.

You are not supposed to think that you will be given rest when you did not work to apply your learning in the understanding of truth. The Sabbath is a time of rest after you have learned the Seven Days and the Seven Powers of the Creation where you learn to understand the Scriptures. Work six days' time and labor of your spiritual power to end on the seventh day of the creation. Understand that man was created on the sixth day, and it is on the seventh day of the creation where you *must* understand the great Sabbath. You have to understand the value of the seven days of the Lord where you reach the power to understand the seven days of the Creation of the Lord your God.

You have six days to labor and achieve your understanding of God through this spiritual value to understand the seven days of the creation. On the seventh day, you are to rest so that you can come to understand your labor of learning the power of your creation and your Creator. On the sixth day of the last millennium (AD 1001 to AD 2000), mankind was created by the Lord so we can come to this day. Understand the technology that was created by man, and you must come to understand that, on this day, it is your time of rest where people won't have to work so hard anymore. Machines and the technology of the world will make you rest, but it is also the time for *learning*. Your learning should be complete—those who are selected will be chosen and those who didn't learn anything (because of their false clothing) will not be able to enter the wedding feast of intelligence between mind and spirit. Understand well that the bride of heaven must be dressed in the white robe to enter the wedding feast of intelligence on the seventh day of the creation.

Now we come to understand the three festivals of learning in the wedding feast—those who understand and those who thought they were first, yet they find that there is no room for them. This is where the book has to be placed on the table to see who is invited to the wedding feast of God's son, common sense. Understand the Festival of Faith in the unleavened bread of life. Things were confused, and now they are revealed by the revelations of the dream that God has dreamed so long ago—that one day, the wedding hall will be open to the wedding between spirit and mind. This ceremony will be performed *inside* the wedding hall of the Word of God, where the mind and the spirit will come together in one human being to bring the understanding of life itself. This is between the spirit (male) and the mind (female). Both will come to be known in *one spirit*, where man will come to offer his sacrifice to the Lord—*not* to Jesus or the false gods of the world. The Angel of the Lord God, which means the teaching, will prepare the way for each person to understand this when the feast of intelligence will be performed in their learning.

Now we come to understand how to confirm the Covenant with the Lord. Understand the power between you and the tribe of Dan, your affiliation with the Lord. Each one of us is a part of intelligence and a part of truth. We cannot substitute ourselves to honor God because we belong to the Lord, and we have to be part of the Lord inside of ourselves. To confirm this Covenant that is within us is to make a deal because God is your Creator…and the Creator would *not* have created you if you did not belong to him. That's the way it works in common sense. You belong to the Lord your God, and you have to worship the Lord your God because God is the truth inside you. You cannot confirm the truth through lies because you are have an affiliation with the Lord.

Every time you say "Well, that's not fair" or "That's not part of justice" or "That's not good for us," look at yourself and see that your affiliation with God is real. Then you must confirm yourself with the Lord. You can refuse and say to yourself that you don't belong to any God, but that's making up your own creation, and this is where you fall to the lost souls of the lies of the world. Mankind will surely lose his soul in his own creation. Loving God does not mean creating for yourself the value of a God that does *not* exist. Your association with God is a part of you. If you go against God, then you will feel different because you're on your own. You are then going to decide to create for yourself, from the lies of the world, a different way of life.

Life is within you with the value of your intelligence, and when you try to form your intelligence with the little mind of a locust, then you live and lie against the Lord your God. You have two ways to go: with yourself or with God. If you think you can do away with God, then what's going to happen is you end up miserable, in jail, or you commit crimes because you *cannot* control yourself. You were created to be affiliated with some kind of a high-spirited side of you that tells you the understanding of life and that high-spirited side is the God of Abraham, Isaac, and Jacob. If you do away with the Lord, then you have no choice because you will not be invited to live life in the *understanding of truth*. That's what happened when people became so arrogant. They think they are so good at doing right and you're so good at doing wrong; they don't think that they need any given power so they go to prison because they made their own rules.

In the rule of life, you must consider what you have earned that is yours, but you cannot take what is not yours and claim it in the value of the laws of God. Taking from someone is wrong. Even though you may become successful in doing wrong, you still claim your own laws in front of the Lord. If you try to make your own set of laws, you *will* rob, steal, and take anything you want from others. You will claim the value after you rob others because you made your own values of who owns what in your lost soul. What you must do is come to the Lord inside of you and ask Him if you're doing right. The voice in your heart will speak to you and tell you it is not right to take the values of others and claim it for yourself.

You must come to understand the laws of your Covenant with the Lord. People you have oppressed will cry out against you to the Lord, and the Lord will hear their cries. The Lord will be against you because you took the values of others for your own. You can go on the computer or you can go to court with lies and claim any value you want, but in the end, those who suffer because of you must cry out to the Lord for justice against you. This Covenant that you make with the Lord is based on true value. You break that Covenant with the Lord by stealing from others; you have to pay the price in the laws of man *and* in the laws of God because taking what is not yours is not yours to keep. You will have to fight both the laws of God and the laws of man and you will end up in a prison somewhere where you will detest your life because you took and claimed what was not yours in some false value that your own laws you created for yourself.

Now we come to the Ark of the Covenant. This is the understanding of the tabernacle, the little box that you put in your soul to carry the laws of God with you wherever you go. When you go out in public and exercise the way of the law, you come to understand the power of these laws. These are the laws of spirit, *not* the laws of flesh. Believe me, your feelings have been torn down by Christianity, the Catholic Church, and all the laws of *all* false religion. Your feelings have really been destroyed by the false prophet. Understand well that the feelings that God has placed inside of you come first. I'm not talking about doing wrong to one another—I'm talking about the laws of feelings that make you love one another. These are the *real laws*, not the laws of stupidity that false religion teaches to the world. You must carry that box of laws with you and come to understand that God is *not* against your natural feelings. If you live by the laws of false religion, you will be miserable because you cannot live your "true" feelings in the world by loving God and loving your feelings that He sends inside you. This includes the true feelings of your sexuality, as well as the true feelings of love and your true feelings of all the things you do.

If you get angry at someone when he does something wrong to you, you don't need to get even with him. You will naturally get angry when people are evil to you, but once again, you should *never* get even with them. That is when you ask the Lord for justice from your feelings of true love. You should never think that you are evil by doing so. If you make love to another person because that's where your feelings are, do not think that this is evil. Making love to someone is one of the *holiest* of all rituals between two people. Just make sure that your feelings are holy and you have the intention of making that person feel good.

Organized religion has made you stupid in regards to your own feelings. The truth of God is for you to enjoy your life on earth and use all the benefits of life that you have. Love one another means to truly love one another inside your sexuality, inside your anger, inside your deepest thoughts of justice. To love a person in justice is to love someone outside of the world of make-believe. This is why I call the preachers of organized religion false prophets—because they teach you to live against your feelings and not in truth with one another. They tell you to live with only one woman and have sex with only one woman because of their "hocus-pocus" ideas of marriage that they call the truth.

The *truth* lives in your feelings. Everything that you *feel* comes from God, but these people tell you that these feelings come from Satan! *It doesn't matter what other people tell you.* It only matters that these feelings live inside you as a person who listens to what he feels. If you meet a beautiful woman and you feel like having sex with her (and vice versa), then make love to her. Those feelings come from the Lord because he is the Creator and he sends those feelings inside you for brotherhood. Sex is not just for procreation like the false prophet tells you—it is also for pleasure in the heart of your understating.

The laws of love should be put in your tabernacle, the box that you create for yourself, to understand and live with your feelings. The value of truth is not in the values of false religion. Those are laws that make no sense. For example, if you are with a woman and you think you should be faithful to that woman for the rest of your life, this simply is not true because your feelings for one another will change over time and that's the reality of life. Now if you are with a woman that you're satisfied with and your sexual feelings are only for her, then this is all right. Either way, you must live according to your feelings. To make love with another woman or another man will not be a sin in God's law. In God's law, you cannot deny your feelings inside you, once you come to understand them. What was created to be in the value of your own feelings is *very* holy.

You should not believe the rules of false religion that make you change your feelings because that is the "wrong over right." The right thing to do is to live out your feelings according to the laws of God, and the laws of God tell you to honor your feelings in the power and the glory of the love of God. God made us to love one another in the value of our soul in the box of our covenant law. Remember that mankind is extremely wrong to use false religious law in front of the Lord's law. This comes from the evil of false religion. The heart of the Covenant Law, in the values of feelings, is where mankind will live in the glory of his own intelligence that comes directly from the Lord, and he will be set free from ignorance.

Believe in the Lord in the understanding of truth, not in the stupid way of thinking of organized religion. God is the God of nature, as well as the God of spirit, because He created nature and nature has to be obeyed just like the spirit does. You have to obey the laws of spirit, and you have to obey the laws of the earth. You must come to understand the way things work in the world of truth. You cannot go up on top of a building and throw yourself down with the thinking that if you believe in Jesus, you are not going to get hurt. You cannot fight the laws of gravity any more than you can fight the Laws of the Creation. You must understand that God is the truth, common sense, and the reality of life. You cannot break these laws because the laws of the spirit are true, and the laws of the earth are also true.

If you wish to understand the Laws of the Lord with common sense, just think of the knowledge above you and try, with your little mind of a locust, to understand that. It may be hard for you to do, but that's because you are "stiff-necked"—meaning you always thought that you were right and what you were doing was right, but you must come to this day that the Lord has made for the human race to understand true wisdom.

Now we come to sins. What do you think a sin is? A sin is something that you cannot understand because of your ignorance, you did *not* open your heart and your mind. A sin is something that you believe in, not something physical that you do. When you sin, your spirit cannot penetrate into the truth to understand the power of truth. We have all heard the saying "Your sins will be forgiven," but what does that mean? When your sins are forgiven, this means when you change your heart and your mind. If you keep that old mind and that old spirit of worthless value, then your sins will remain and you will not be able to understand truth, and this will keep you outside of the knowledge of heaven, where the Lord cannot get through to you because you did not look at your feelings of intelligence.

You think you already know it all when you know very little. You could be a big cardinal, a big pope, or a preacher of any earthly religion...but this does not give you the wisdom of the understanding of life, and I think you should terminate your ministry until you learn the truth. Your sins are so high in your twisted mind, and this brings your soul to a great lie inside yourself where you are stiff-necked and you cannot untwist it back into reason. You have lost your soul with that stiff neck. Understand well that the Lord has all the wisdom of life because He created life. You cannot argue with the Lord or you risk going to war with him. When you encounter the truth that you never previously thought of, you must turn your head toward the Lord and ask him to forgive you of your sins because the center of your life is what you now believe. If you believe falsely before the Lord, your sins will remain in you and the Lord will not forgive you.

Now we come to understand the basin to wash yourself. The reality of common sense tries to wash off the stupidity and the ignorance of false religion. False religion made you believe in things that have no common sense and no reality. Make the basin so you can wash off your ignorance that was told to you by false religions by thinking of reality and common sense. You must not believe that Jesus was anything more than a man. Make sure to keep yourself clean in reality.

Next is the gold calf. We come to understand the purpose that man has made himself a golden calf with the understanding of Jesus. The gold calf brings your sacrifice to Jesus instead of to God. Religion made itself a God out of Jesus's life—they made this God out of their own bigotry and their own self-imagination. People thought Jesus was a good man, and according to the Scriptures, he created a lot of miracles, so they made Jesus a God in false religion. And the next thing you know, nobody worships God anymore because they replaced the Lord with a God that they can see and understand. The gold calf brings great anger in the Lord because you're worshiping a worthless idol when you bring Jesus to be equal with the Lord. This is because you only understand, in your physical self, what God is, and you do not understand the spiritual God of reality.

Now we come to understand the power of the clean and unclean food. The worst sin that you could possibly do is to belong to false religion. If you give up your soul to believe what other people tell you, you will come to eat what is not proper inside of you. This is the unclean food because you take other people's ideas as truth—you do not take the real teaching of the Lord. You must come to understand the power of eating what is unclean. To understand and believe things that are not the truth is eating what is not clean.

False religion is the *most unclean food* because it consists of all the plagues of Egypt. You must come to believe the power where human beings come in the trust of the Lord God, and you must trust the Lord your God with your information of heaven. Don't listen to anyone else but God on any spiritual matter. This is what the power of human understanding is all about in the knowledge of yourself, and this is where the Lord tells you what to believe and how to understand the Scriptures and the word of God. This is because the Lord will not tell you anything except truth; the false prophet will tell you the reality of their theology from their mind, and you cannot trust the theology of false religion. Fully understand that God has created mankind and the control of mankind in a way to make your life a happy place to live. If you don't trust in Him, you won't have the understanding that you need to have a happy life. If you listen to people who tell you nothing but lies, you cannot have a happy life. If you go to church every week to understand nothing that is clean in the value of truth, you cannot understand life because the truth is the only thing that sets you free in the value of the power of heaven.

The food that is clean is to understand the truth of reality, while the food that is unclean is to understand the falsehoods of reality. If you believe in superstitions of any kind, you go into the land of the theology of men where you believe what the priest in the church tells you. But these false preachers don't have it because God did not give his plan to anyone who believes in lies. You believed what makes no sense, and next thing you know, you are in the world of make-believe, believing in all kinds of stupid things that do not make sense. Before you know it, you are in a prison of falsehood and you can't get out of it.

We continue with the gold calf where the human race has to believe in a god they made for themselves—a golden calf in front of the altar of the Lord—and they offer stupidity and ignorance to that form of a physical God that they can see instead of worshiping the one true God of the Creation. They worship Jesus, and when they worship Jesus, this is their gold calf—the good God they believe in.

Remember that your stiff neck cannot be turned that easily to understand the value and sacrifice of the real God who has created us in the image of human intelligence inside our heart. God is the truth, but God is also reality and common sense. Jesus spoke in common sense in his parables. Love and honor the Lord your God with everything that you have. Never think that you can possibly understand the Lord through organized religion. God is the truth, and the truth is God through the power of reality and common sense that comes into his word. You must come to understand that the laws of God are written for truth, and it is the law that glorifies the name of the Lord in the power to be able to understand. You must consider the value of the truth. God's law is right and just in the value of total justice and total fairness for all mankind. It is the unity of all mankind that brings the laws of love together in the priesthood of our own heart. The truth in our own heart is the value to understand the purpose that God has made right over wrong for all purposes of the law.

*****

Now we come to the Book of Leviticus—the continuation of the Israelites' journey in the desert. Understand the power of the scriptures as a spiritual, not a physical, teaching of the mind. The Israelites are the chosen people of God. In spirit, this means that these people are the ones chosen by God to inherit the land of milk and honey; they are chosen because they have already proven themselves to be *worthy* of such a blessing. Remember that many are called, but few are chosen.

In spirit, the Land of Milk and Honey means the land of life and love. You will come to love life as it was created to be by the Lord your God even with all of what you may think are life's imperfections. If the Lord your God is perfect, then his creation would also have to be perfect, no? But that love of life can only come through the understanding of the Lord and his word. And the understanding of the scriptures is only granted through a desire to reject the lies of the mind and embrace the truth of the spirit. This means that you must be willing to reject the lies of organized religion and only worship the Lord in your heart in order to be chosen to receive the true understanding of his word and, in turn, be able to reap the rewards of living that understanding. It is a great sacrifice to endure, but it is the only way to enter the land of milk and honey. The false Christian idea of gaining salvation simply by believing in a man who died some two thousand years ago is just that—false.

The book of Leviticus starts with the offerings. Always remember that you must never approach the Lord empty handed. You must bring an offering—something you do not understand or are having trouble with, your hopes, feelings, emotions, etc. This is where the offerings come in. They are not physical offerings like most people were taught but, rather, spiritual offerings. God is a spiritual entity, and so it only makes sense that the offerings to him also be spiritual.

The first is the burnt offering. The burnt offerings have to do with animals. In spirit, the animals refer to the understanding of the mind. Each of the animals can be spiritually understood by their physical characteristics. The ox (ignorance), ass (stubbornness), sheep (humility), and ram (desire to fight) are but a few examples. When you sacrifice an animal to the Lord, you are not killing a physical animal. Instead, you are offering the characteristics of that animal for learning. For example, offering an ox to the Lord is, in essence, telling him that you are ignorant of a spiritual teaching and you wish to understand the true meaning of that teaching. This applies to all the animals you would sacrifice to God. An animal without defect is required because you must bring to the Lord your desire for true understanding, even if it means that what you have always believed was not part of truth, and the animal must be burnt because you must burn away the useless parts of the animal and bring to the Lord your pure feelings, untainted, by what others have told you to believe.

Next is the power to understand the grain offering in the Book of Life. Remember that this is a spiritual book and a spiritual book alone. You need to understand that the bread of life, or the grain offering, is the word of God. You cannot talk in the wisdom of the Lord if you live the life of worthless little locusts where you think you have to go to church to understand the power of the Lord. You have to come to understand through the parable of the Pharisees that the Lord has made the world where people cannot understand the Scriptures. You have to step in *front* of them in the understanding, and this is how you come to understand the word of God.

In the Old Testament, you have to plant and harvest the earth just like if a donkey or an ox is in front of the plow to turn over the earth into the power of the grain offering. You plant food in the earth, then after you turn the earth upside down, you begin to understand that the parable of the Pharisees of the Lord is about the twisted mind of a stubborn man. And through the plowing, your mind is turned over to the most beautiful power that you could ever imagine. Once you understand the other side of the Scriptures, you start bringing the knowledge of God into your soul, and you learn to do what you should do. You then separate the wrong from the right in the new way of eating the food of the Scriptures.

The Lord is inside of you to guide you in your harvest where a human being can begin to understand the high spirit of the value of what is written. After you have plowed the earth and turned the dirt upside down to see man's stupidity in their own lives, you will then see in the wisdom of the wise the power to bring to life the most magnificent knowledge that you have never touched before. You had to take the dirt of the earth and make it into something that you never understood before, and you had to bring this to the value of human thinking where a human being comes in the name of the Lord to bring his value to the holy place in his soul—the deal that you had made with the Lord in the power to understand true wisdom from the Lord himself and no longer yours. It's a much higher power than there is in the false Eucharist of the Catholic Church. This is the power to make bread with the wisdom of the Lord. It is a value that is so high above human understanding where no one around you can understand exactly what you're talking about, and they must think that that you are crazy. This knowledge is so high to reach that you have to understand that Christ is the chosen teaching of the Lord in spirit and not a man that lives in the physical mind.

You become a spiritual human being in the value of heaven where a human being can understand the new good grain offering to the Lord in the value of truth. The people of the earth just cannot understand you even though they twist their mind and persecute you because your knowledge is so high above them that in their heart, they wish that they would understand the power of the Lord your God. You see, the grain offering is the food that is grown by plowing the dirt of the earth and where human beings begin to understand the value of receiving the truth of life. This truth is in both your heart and your soul so you can come to the day of the Lord with a grain offering to the low value that you plowed in the dirt of the earth.

To love the Lord your God, you must take your ignorant ox, your stubborn donkey, and your stiff neck and bring it all to the knowledge where you can turn your head toward the value of heaven. If you decide to stop being stubborn and ignorant and you give your life to the Scriptures in the understanding of the Lord, then the first five books of the Old Testament will be revealed inside you because you have put your trust in the Lord. He who was in the lost soul of the false wisdom of the mind will then find himself in the wisdom of the word of God. You are like a little locust reading scriptures that don't make any sense to a human being. You have to *plow* the ground to understand the son of God himself, which is common sense, where he will reveal himself to you when you look inside your soul.

You will see the difference from what was told to you by the false religion and the false prophet of the earth, and you will understand the true religion of the Lord your God. You worship a false God in your soul and you ask yourself why you are so miserable, why you are so lost, and why have you gone so far outside the truth where a human being cannot find his soul in what makes sense. This is because you have listened to the people who do *not* have the birth of the spirit inside of them. You listened to people who went to school to learn falsehood, and that falsehood is part of you now because you listened to those who did *not* know the word of God. Because you yourself did not harvest the Scriptures on your own and try to understand for yourself, you had to go put on a nice dress and three-piece suit to go listen to a man who was just taught in a false ministry of his soul to worship Jesus in front of the Lord your God. Those false prophets were taught in school to worship the son of God, and they called him Jesus because they looked at the Scriptures with the mind and not the spirit.

The Lord your God did not give you anything of his kingdom because you have failed to understand that you should listen to the Scriptures by yourself and try to understand the *voice* of the Lord behind the Scriptures. You placed your trust in that little mind of a locust of yours that thought people were telling you the truth, but they have fooled you so they can get your money and live freely without working for a living. This is because they didn't have anything to give you in the value of the holy Scriptures.

The people who have already lost their souls are the ones teaching you their own lies so they can fool you and take your money. They thought it was right that they would save your soul when all they did was lose your soul along with their own. This is in the same value of the same church that was the cave of their soul where they went to worship Jesus as God. You must understand that the Lord is behind all this falsehood, as well as the truth, on the other side—those who did not worship God were punished by God, and he put them in the stupidity of their own souls. He made them as stupid as he can to punish them for worshiping a false God before the truth.

People who want to know true wisdom don't go to a church on Sunday morning to try to learn the truth. True wisdom is found in your own church in your own soul, where a human being understands God's word from his own mouth, *not* in the false church that is formed in the shape of a cave where there are only false gods inside. God lives inside each person, in brotherhood, with wisdom, in your own church. If you could only listen to the voice of God inside your heart instead of trying to learn the love of brotherhood in a place where God does not live.

The fellowship offering is to offer to the Lord the values of others before your own. Think of others and feel for others who have to live in a house of abuse, or think of those who live in Africa that don't have anything to eat—just don't play God and think that you have to go there in the physical form to work in the ministry that you made up in your own mind to do a good deed. Try to understand that worshiping God is to be humble before the Lord, to be humble before your fellowship offering, and to be humble before all your brothers in life. This is the ministry that you have to go to. Try to make yourself whole in the simple way of thinking that the Lord has room to exist in your soul. To love the Lord your God is to love your brother in the value of all that you have in order to feel for those who are lost. You cannot change your ways with your physical body—you can only change your ways with your spirit.

If you trust in the Lord your God for your control and understanding, then He will make you whole in the understanding of what is, and then you will be able to understand the simple laws of God. Trust in the one who comes to bring you wisdom and uses wisdom to bring yourself into a better life. Be kind to the simple people in life who live with you in the power to understand heaven and earth. Understand well the offer of brotherhood where *all* mankind is created equal to the same value. God made you who you are, and he made everybody else with the same mold and the same feeling of his design where every human being is the same as the next human being. Don't look at your wealth or your magnificent power that you try to sell to others. Just look at your own simplicity *inside your heart* where you are one who is poor in spirit. If you live in humility with others, you will live in the same feeling as others. You will be able to appreciate your life, and all that you have given to life will be equal to all your brothers on earth.

Understand that the glory of intelligence comes from the Lord. If the Lord gave you the glory to become rich, you will become rich. If God gave you the understanding to build yourself a fine house, you will build yourself a fine house. If you understand the value of a better life when the Lord gives it to you, make sure that you don't forget all your brothers anywhere on Earth who don't do so well. Just try to understand that we are all created equal. Don't go flying on your high horse like you're better than them because the Lord has given you more than what He gave to someone else. Try to consider your brother in the value that you have so you can share your good deeds with others in the value that you are equal to all others.

Now we come to understand the offering for your sin. Try to understand that the power of a human being comes in the power where you were given a judgment on others but you did not look at your own sin. This offering gives you the power to understand your own sin, not the sin of others. You must come to understand that your mind and soul are not clean, and you must make a sin offering in your love toward others and worship the Lord your God in truth.

The commandments of the Lord are based on the fact that we all must come to understand our own sin. We have a heart that is not always clean towards other people. We are animals in our feelings, and we must learn to understand the place inside each one of us where we are not allowed to feel and act like an animal. This is what the Lord is trying to put in the human spirit—the understanding of his own value as an intelligent human being *above* the animal. This is why God the son (common sense) brings the human race to the power above the animal. You must come to understand that as a person, when you do wrong, you must kill your "animal" being to understand your "spiritual" being in the sanctuary of your soul. This is why we become spiritual in our understanding that we are *above* the animal being.

You must come to understand that you are responsible for your hate toward others as well as your misunderstanding of their deeds. Know that in your own sanctuary, you need the *blood* of the animal to sprinkle around the altar. *Blood* here means "understanding." You must understand the blood of your own animal before you can judge anyone in the same value as you judge yourself.

All the laws of God are really based on two teachings: to love the Lord, your God, with all your heart and soul and to love your brother as yourself. Understand that loving your brother as yourself is to be *fair* and *just* in the teaching of the Lord regarding people who live in total arrogance. You try to save your soul, but you have forgotten about *your own sin* while you were thinking of the sin of others, and you did not perform this ritual of your sin offering. You think that religion will forgive your sin, but it is only the Lord who can forgive your sin, *not* any organized religion of human knowledge. You are only forgiven when you go through the ritual of sprinkling the false understanding of your sin around your own temple—not where you go to feel better about yourself by accusing others before you.

Going to church every week on Sunday morning is just about the *worst* of all of man's false teachings because it does nothing to save your soul. You can kneel there in front of the authors of false religion all you want, but the power to receive the true Lord is *in* your soul. It is the power to understand the real ritual of the Lord that tells you that you must understand your own sin before you judge yourself and anyone else of doing wrong in your mind and soul. The power of a human being is to understand and worship the Lord in your own soul. But if you choose to keep your animal skin and believe in an understanding of the animal in a cave of falsehood, you will never worship God there in the proper way of the laws that he gave us.

An offering is to look in your soul to see what you have done wrong using the three laws: justice, fairness, and unity. You will then begin to understand that there is only *one* God, and that one God will send you the *proper* ritual to worship Him in the most homage way to understand the *true religion of the heart*. The true religion of the heart will tell you *how* to worship God—not in some cave but in the spiritual value inside your soul. Understand that you must stand up in your own soul for the dignity of worshipping one holy God who teaches you to do right in the justice and fairness of your soul and then to unite people in your own soul where one is just as important as the other.

You must understand that by learning about God through his word, you will come to understand who you are and why God has created you. When you practice the true ritual of the Lord, you practice inside your soul the power to accept everybody. You have the power of not judging anybody in front of you—this *is* your sin offering to the Lord.

Now we come to the guilt offering where your heart must be clean to come to the table of the Lord. This is where you come across that table to understand your own guilt in what makes sense inside you. A human being sees the knowledge of his guilt offering in this ritual to understand what is right and what is wrong. This is the power to worship in your own soul where you would be seen in front of the Lord. You must *clean your own soul* before you try to clean others' souls.

Next, we come to the part of the Book of Leviticus where the idea of brotherhood comes from the Lord himself so you can come to understand the fellowship offering of the power of one human being over your own self. Understand well these three great laws. The first great law is to worship the Lord your God with *all* your soul. This means you *cannot* worship any other God created by the mind of man. I agree that Jesus was a great prophet, but I cannot worship the idea of a human being in front of the Lord.

The second great law that is equal to the first one is to love your brother outside of arrogance, where your soul must love each man whether he has done any good in this or he has done wrong. You cannot bring a man down below the earth because he has done something wrong in his life. The wrongdoer is the one that should be appreciated the most and brought in to the simple value of a man and must be kept inside the human race because there is no such thing in the human race that you can call evil. Evil is only mentioned by the Lord your God to see the difference between a lie and the truth.

The third great law is to unite *all* your brothers. If you love your brother with an evil heart or by an evil deed, you cannot determine the difference between good and evil because you don't have the understanding of the Lord to determine the power of what is true and what is evil as a human being. None of us has the power to determine the laws of good and evil. We, as children of God, are only human, and we only have our human understanding. This is why we are not allowed to bring the power of good and evil with the intention of judging anyone else because this is the person of Adam and Eve—spirit and mind—where the serpent fools your mind by making you think that you can determine good and evil.

I am speaking of a new understanding where no human being can use those words to try to understand good and evil because we are not wise enough to cross the river of life and understand the glory of the wisdom of the Lord. Only God can understand good and evil because He did not open it up to the level of human understanding.

If you claim that anyone's wrongdoing is evil, then you make a great sin, and you will have to face the Lord your God in your fellowship offering of your brother. Each man who does wrong did it for the benefit of his life, and because that person took something from someone else, he must be punished by the laws of man. You are still not allowed to judge them because of what they did, because only the soul of the wrongdoer can explain his sin to the Lord. A human being *cannot* explain his deeds just like Cain could not explain the death of his brother.

Remember that all human deeds that are done in rage or where your mind and soul are lost, they cannot explain the wrong they have done. For this reason, a man is not allowed to judge what made him do it—only the Lord knows what made him do it. This is where human beings go to become clean in the fellowship offering to the Lord. If you do not clean yourself and keep yourself clean, then your uncleanness is what makes you commit crimes of passion. And after the crime is committed, you cannot explain what was in your soul when you committed the crime because it was something that was unclean inside you that made you commit that crime.

After the crime is done, you have to face the laws of man and try to explain *why* you committed this crime. But even at this point, you wish you never committed that crime because your punishment is coming from the laws of man. This means that you, who judge him, are in the same value of he who committed the crime according to the unclean feelings in your heart or in your soul. You must come to distinguish between what is right and what is wrong in what you believe inside your own spirit.

The laws of God tell you not to kill, not to commit adultery, not to give false testimony, and not to steal from anyone. Let's take a look at these four sins in spiritual terms of the value of heaven in order to understand them. First, we look at murder and see what murder means in the value of heaven. When a false prophet brings a false understanding of murder in the power of the earth, in his little mind of a locust, he thinks that you are not allowed to kill, but the real murder of the spirit comes way before any murder of the flesh is done because a man, in his high church of false prophecy, already killed the soul of that person. His soul is already dead because of the false understanding of the Scriptures done by the hand of the false prophets who claim to know what they are talking about. They explained the laws of God in their church and in their catechism where they teach not to murder anyone, but the murder of their soul has already taken place at that point, and you can blame it on the one who introduced the false law by the mind of the weak understanding.

Next, try to understand the laws of adultery. The "adultery" of a human being is the worship of Jesus Christ, the *false* god of the human race. Understand where you are going with this small soul of the earth who cannot understand between good and evil. This ignorant soul commits evil crimes because he doesn't know who God is. You see, the false prophet is anyone who took the power to explain the Word of God, yet they have failed because they try to explain the Scriptures in the physical terms. They see Jesus as God because the New Testament—the sun—has burned them with its great heat and made them blind to the laws of the Old Testament in their physical understanding where they cannot see the laws of God in spiritual value.

True spiritual value is what has fooled the false prophet in wrongdoing. This is something they could never imagine that would happen to them because their arrogance was so high and they believed they were right in their ministry of falsehood. They thought they could teach someone to worship a false God in their Jesus because they never understood the parables of Jesus. They never understood that Jesus himself was a man and not a God. The laws of stealing are good examples. The false prophet has taken from these people and lied to them with their false values of physical understanding in the flesh. They have *stolen* from mankind the value of our spiritual understanding. These false prophets took true spiritual understanding from us and replaced God with their Jesus in the false understanding of the Almighty God. They have taken from us the value of our spiritual understanding, and they were confused by the Laws of the Old Testament.

To the false prophets I say, *Why* did you teach what you did *not understand* about the Scriptures? *The Lord is a just God.* He has teachings that you do not understand with your false ministry. You tried to teach what you didn't know, but on this day, the seventh day of the creation, you have to face the Lord your God with your sin. If you had taught the world to worship the one true God and had not introduced Jesus as God, there would be *no need* to imprison any man for their entire life for crimes that you, false prophets, have created. These false teachings bring people to where they cannot control themselves. *The sin of heaven is much deeper than you can ever imagine.* You claim that you are going to help these people by worshipping Jesus Christ *before* the Lord our God. You came to teach your own theology to the weakest part of mankind and made them criminals. If these people would worship the Lord your God, they would never commit a crime, but you recreated yourself to God by your own bigotry of trying to understand before God, and you placed the image of the servant of God in front of the Lord. Jesus was the *messenger* of God, and he brought those holy parables to the understanding of mankind.

Now we come to the sin offering of the people who call themselves men of God. All those who climb to the highest level in the name of God must be brought down. Those who proclaim the word of God and tell others that they save souls, I tell you in truth, those are the ones that put themselves *first* in life. Remember that scripture tells us, "The first will be last." Keep in mind also that God is not after the criminal or people who consider themselves humble in human living. The Kingdom of God is made for regular people who don't live in arrogance. It is made for those who live in humility and consider themselves equal to *all* mankind, which is what they are, but the false prophet, the false politician, and the people who live in arrogance in high society are the ones that the Lord is looking to destroy. These are the people who commit the worst sin because they move themselves to the highest level on the ladder of success and they find themselves facing the Lord in arrogance. These are the people who will lose their soul by the power of the arrogant human being. They climb too far up with their little mind of a locust, and they must come down to the level of humility where the Lord is.

Remember that arrogance was the first sin, and it will become the last sin. The Kingdom of God was created for humility. Arrogance is the opposite of humility where a human being must come to accept his sin. Those who think they are at the level of God and believe they are the children of God have made the *biggest mistake* of all. God does *not* need people to save others from their sins.

You must first save yourself from your own sin *before* you can save someone else's sin. The wrongdoing of others should not matter to you, but you live in arrogance, thinking that your way of life is what other people should consider as their way of life.

First, fix your *own* way of life before you attempt to fix the way of life of others. Make sure that you live in the theology of God before you teach people to live in ignorance and arrogance. If you were to teach someone to understand the Lord, you should start in humility and consider yourself one who did not climb higher than yourself. This is the kingdom of God. Learn to be humble before God and work to preserve the truth. Come on down, and worship the Lord your God in humility.

God had promised Abraham, Isaac, and Jacob the kingdom (in the power of humility) where you can cross the Jordan River into the land that gives life to you. If a man gets up in the morning and works in the dignity of all other men, he creates for himself a perfect life where he lives in the kingdom of his clean soul. This makes your heart clean and rebuilds it in the cleanness of the new Kingdom of God. Also, this is where a human being can live away from the arrogance of the world, be humble, and respect the life of all his brothers on earth, and live in the humility of his own sin in the Kingdom of God. This teaching of the new Law of God's command will work to bring mankind in humility, where he will dedicate himself to become humble in the eyes of the Lord.

The difference between the Kingdom of God and the kingdom man has made for himself is that man raised himself up in his arrogance to become popes and presidents. He created a world where each person lives in the rat race of fulfillment to accomplish their moral arrogance in front of the world. In man's kingdom, if a person climbs to the top, he has totally forgotten how to be humble in the eyes of the Lord. When the world changes in the heart of mankind, it will be a different place to live. You will see people climbing into their arrogance where they have lost their soul by trying to climb too high and make life easy on the labor of others.

God brings you to a new kingdom where you will be able to live life in the unity of one humble heart, and you can live in peace with your brothers in the new brotherhood of intelligence. No one will try to raise themselves above others to accomplish arrogance. You will come to understand the new kingdom in the value so far above where you are now in this world of prejudice and bigotry, where the miseries of living are so hard to endure. You must understand that the value of humility comes through the Lord where the soul of man will no longer be in an arrogant way of thinking. Everyone must think of their sin in the arrogance of climbing to a step above themselves and leave their brothers in darkness because it was God's plan to bring people to a perfect kingdom where all human thinking is totally clean.

Your sin offering to the Lord should bring you to think in humility. Comprehend the humility inside your sin of falsehood that was introduced to you by the hand of false religion. The book must be opened to relate with the Scriptures, and the world must come to understand the New Jerusalem, where you will come to live in brotherhood—where you won't take yourself to be more important and wiser than your brother. You will see the coming on the mountain of the Lord a new set of laws where arrogance is not accepted by the teaching of life. You will see that kingdom where a human being lives and loves his life because the Lord has condemned the worst sin of mankind and his arrogance. This is where man lives free from his sin.

I am not saying that the people who live in arrogance won't survive the day of the Lord. The Lord has chosen the sheep over the goats, so his kingdom will be built with a *new song* and a *new heart* to take with you. You will see the souls of the men becoming like sheep of humble heart where *all* people won't have to compete so much in arrogance, and the laws of the past will be gone.

We continue with the teaching that eating fat and blood is forbidden. We come to understand what the fat and the blood is. Eating the fat of an animal is the understanding of *living higher* by having wealth above your needs—that is, living high in the power where you leave all the truly good things in life to live in the lost soul of the rat race. People have jumped so deeply into this false teaching so to make their life so fat in the *value of nothing*. They believe that the more they accumulate in money and wealth of the earth, the better their life will become. It is the great American dream to own everything and gain all in the billions of worthless dollars in the land of the lost soul. You will surely lose your soul.

There is an old saying in life, "You can't take it with you," but I tell you in truth, you *will* take it with you because all your wealth is what brings you in the grave of your lost soul. Whoever tries to gain the whole world will lose his soul trying. He who tries to save his life will lose his life, and he who tries to lose his life for the sake of the Lord will gain his life. This was said in the New Testament, and it is *truth*. If a man gains the whole world and becomes a great billionaire, can that man gain the Kingdom of God? No, because the kingdom of God is not designed in the same wisdom where man calls the kingdom for himself. God made both rich man and poor man, but a rich man can become so rich that he will lose his soul, and a poor man can become so poor in spirit that he *also* will lose his soul. The wealth of the earth is the forbidden fat and blood that God has forbidden from the foundation of the world that so few men understand.

The interests of mankind are to gain this forbidden wealth, but the Lord gave this wealth for a man to feed his brother in the value where brotherhood exists. He can still gain his life, but he *cannot* use his wealth and power to separate brotherhood in rich and poor. He *has* to use his value to help the world to understand the Kingdom of God because the wealth of the world is only money. If you use it for brotherhood, you will accumulate a lot of money for doing right to your brother and to share that wealth in reality.

Now we come to the discharge causing uncleanness. Understand that what you believe is not true. If you tell someone something that is not true and they believe you, this is discharging falsehood to others. In the understanding of others, you are responsible for what you have said in the value of intelligence and the power to understand reality. If you see something out of the world of make-believe, what you see is *unclean.* And if you believe in what is unclean, then it becomes part of the value where you inspire others to believe something in total stupidity. I'll give you an example: If you think you are flying in faith and you believe that it will save you and will bring you into intelligence when it's not true, you are coming into your discharge. Discharging falsehood in the presence of others is a *great sin* and should be brought to the attention of all mankind. What you say must not only come from the thinking inside your head—verify the truth in your soul so that you won't just say something from the world of make-believe.

Understand well that the minute the world of make-believe fools the people living in the world, these people believe in all kinds of things that are not true. The world of make-believe tries to tell you what is going to happen, and next thing you know, it doesn't happen because it is *not true.* You live in a world where the fantasy of your mind tries to control the way you believe, and if you inform other people of that same power in falsehood, then this becomes the teaching of the false. You become a false prophet yourself by forming something that's not true into something that you get people to believe as truth. The reality of life is the Holy Spirit in the understanding of life. What makes sense in reality becomes common sense, and what is common sense becomes the Lord in truth. Understand these three powers of human understanding—truth, common sense, and reality—is the key to understanding the Lord your God. If it doesn't make sense, it is not true, and you are not allowed to repeat it to other people.

You will be judged by the God of heaven for an unclean discharge of arrogance and stupidity, and you will be punished for that. The punishment will be to freeze your mind and your stupidity in ignorance where you will come to live in darkness because your discharge of falsehood has been transferred to others and you are held responsible for their sins.

Next, we come to the day of atonement where you approach the holy place in the reality of the truth. This is where *all* common sense and *all* reality must come to be truth inside your soul. You cannot prophesy on any subject that you don't know anything about. You are *not allowed* to make things up just to try to prove to others that you are a smart person or to make yourself known to be a prophet in anything that doesn't make sense at all. Come to understand the holy place of worship where human beings go inside their minds and tell stories that don't make sense. At that point, you are going into the world that doesn't make sense to you.

"Atonement" with the Lord is not just a word. You must make a *deal* with the Lord that you will never believe anything that doesn't make common sense and doesn't exist in reality, and you are not allowed (by the power of your spirit) to believe anything that's crooked in human thinking. Everything that you believe *has* to be part of the truth. The reality of that truth has to make sense inside you first before all other things that you try to understand. This is the deal that you have to make with the Lord in order to understand his word.

Your spirit is the sanctuary of intelligence, and you are *not* allowed to defile your spiritual understanding with the stupidity that makes no sense. You have to make that deal with the Lord in order to understand the great power of the Lord inside you where your sanctuary of reality must live on. You cannot "defile" your sanctuary by understanding something so stupid such as the understanding of the false religion of the earth. *Truly believe* that you were created with the sanctuary of truth, yet you have been withering in falsehood all over your sanctuary by following your own false truth.

Now we are going to the law where eating blood is forbidden. You are not allowed to believe the stupidity of the Catholic Church, of Christianity, or any other religion on earth. Your sanctuary must be clean in the truth and only the truth with reality and common sense. If you leave the center of intelligence to cross over to something so untrue as a Catholic doctrine or what Christianity believes about God, you will be thrown into a deep darkness because there is *no truth* in any of these religions of the earth. The falsehood will blind your soul, where you will be like a blind person who has no spiritual eyes to see with. You remain in darkness because you have thrown your spirit to the hand of those who don't understand the Scriptures. *This* is your blood that has been forbidden by God to be eaten. You will find yourself in "hell" by understanding and eating forbidden blood.

Now we come to understand the unlawful sexual relations. Understand that Egypt and the land of Egypt means false religion, and you must *not* do what they do in the land of Egypt in the practice of your sexual responsibility. Since the scriptures are written in the understanding of spiritual value, you must come to understand what is wrong with your sexuality. This means you not allowed to have sex, meaning you are not allowed to have sexual relations with your close relatives. In spiritual understanding, this means that you are not allowed to have any relationship with other people who read the same Scriptures as you even though what they say may be related to what you think. You are not allowed to do so because they may steer you in different directions away from the truth. You are supposed to read the Bible and then make the determination for *yourself.* Don't let other people persuade you with their ignorance. You are supposed to believe only in the Lord your God because the Lord is the *only* source of truth that you should listen to in your heart in the understanding of the truth unless the person you're talking with has the same values that you have in the understanding of truth.

The power to reveal the truth inside of you is all right as long as you commit no sexual encounters outside the truth. You must speak to one another in the truth, and if a person does not understand you, then you have to walk away and believe in your soul what the Lord puts there for you to understand. The only real sexual encounter, in spirit, is to be with the Lord. If someone tells you something and it sounds like it's the truth, you must investigate it in your heart with the Lord *before* you believe it. You must look at yourself and free your mind with the encounters of others and believe only in what makes common sense and what exists in reality. Then return to the Father with the truth and really make sure that it *is* the truth in the virginity of your common sense where reality has to be brought forth in common sense. Make sure that you let *no* one mislead you or get you to believe in anything that is not true. Just because they read the same Bible you read does not mean that they understand the truth any better than you do. You must keep the Lord's laws and decrees and keep yourself holy in the spirit of your understanding.

A human being must understand the Laws of God and live by them in the understanding of life. You cannot make your own laws of the earth like a little locust. Just like a little creature in the wilderness, you have to obey the laws that were created for you in the nature of human understanding where mankind should not practice anything outside the laws of the Almighty God. No one is approved to have sexual encounters with close relatives because the Lord is the Lord in *all* wisdom. Be sure that you read the Scriptures and understand the laws of God *in truth*.

If a person does *not* understand what you tell him, just walk away from them, shake the dust from your sandals, and come to understand the power that you are with the Lord your God. Do not dishonor your father (the truth) by having sexual relations with your mother (lies of the earth). Having sexual relations with your mother means you should not practice the spiritual understanding of the past. If you do, you will defile yourself in front of your Father in heaven. Remember that religion of the past is *in the past*. Try to understand this new time and do not worship the old religion of the earth because you will be dishonoring your Father in heaven. Just because you were raised in that old religion doesn't mean that you have to follow it to get to the Kingdom of God. That old religion was full of lies from the mind and cannot be understood in the way of life that God has prepared for you. Come to understand that you have lost your soul and the only way you can regain your soul is by receiving what is *new*. You cannot patch an old piece of clothing with new material because it won't look good. The power of human understanding is in the glory of a new time for your salvation and the power to understand that God is the truth and will tolerate nothing outside the truth. Even though your parents, your brothers and sisters, and everybody else practices something in the past doesn't mean that you must practice it also in your life.

Do not have sexual relations with your father's wife. This means do not believe in something your father taught you *unless* it is the truth in the value of heaven. You are not allowed to believe what all the people that you grew up with believe or understand the same thing they do. Come to the new way of understanding the Lord your God. Do not practice the false religion of the past because that will bring you to the understanding of the devastation of your spirit, and you will destroy your life. Life is given to you by the Lord your God, and you cannot understand anything in truth if you believe in the lies of the past where the value was lost.

Do not have sexual relations with your son. This is the *next* generation. You are not allowed to tell the next generation what to believe—they must come to the understanding of truth on their own. Do not have sexual relations with your daughter or your father's daughter because you will defile yourself in front of your Father in heaven. This means you *must not believe anything* unless it comes from your relationship with your Father in heaven in the value of today, yesterday, and tomorrow. Understand that all the relationships that you have must be accomplished by the power of heaven and by the groom of heaven itself—the Lord your God.

Do not have sexual relations with your brother's wife, meaning do not believe what your brother or sister believes. Anything that comes from the mind of mankind is a relationship with *falsehood*. You must understand only the *simple truth* of the Lord. Do not listen to anyone who doesn't understand the truth from any past generations because that would be *adultery*, and adultery means that you have sexual relations with something or someone who does *not* have the truth. Make sure you love the Lord your God with all your soul. Listen to his voice inside your soul so you will not listen to anything that does not make sense. Do not have sexual relations with an animal because you will defile yourself. Understand well that we are all animals. Do not believe that having sex in the flesh is a sin because if you do, you will *defile* yourself in front of the Lord; do not believe that sex, in the physical sense, is a sin because that is *untrue* in the value of heaven.

Remember that it is your *spiritual understanding* that makes the difference in who you are. The animal and the physical part of you does *not* count in the Scriptures. The Scriptures are meant for you to understand the laws inside your spiritual value. Your spiritual value is what counts in the Scriptures, not the physical part of you. Understand that it is not your physical part that controls you but your spiritual part in charge of the animal—*this is what controls you*. Understand your feelings so the animal can be controlled. If you, as a man, have sex with a woman, this is totally normal and holy in the eyes of the Lord. No one should condemn their sexual value in the kingdom of heaven.

*****

Now we are entering the Book of Numbers, where your census will be counted in the tribe of Israel from Ruben, the firstborn son of Jacob, to Benjamin, the last son of Jacob. When the Israelites left the land of Egypt to enter into the desert, they had six hundred thousand men, not counting women and children. Understand that the words *men*, *women*, and *children*, as used here, does not mean people in the physical sense. Always remember that the Bible is a book written for the spirit, not the flesh, so the teachings are written in spiritual terms.

This cannot be stressed enough because it is one of the biggest keys to the understanding of the scriptures.

Any references to previous generations of males (father, grandfather, ancestors, etc.) means the spiritual understanding of the *past*—the way that you used to believe. The term *man* in the scriptures means "spiritual understanding of the present generation"—what you currently understand in spirit. And when you see the term *son*, that means your "future spiritual understanding"—what you have not yet learned in spirit and therefore cannot yet understand.

It is the same with females, except on the other side—the male is your spiritual side of your understanding, and the female is the physical side—your mind. Therefore, when the scriptures mention any females, this means the "wisdom of your mind."

Entering the desert is done in spiritual value, not in the physical sense. You will have inside your soul six hundred thousand feelings. This means *all* the feelings on *all* the subjects of life that you have inside you. When you first cross over to the desert, you will see very little reality and you will understand very little in spirit. This is because you are crossing into a new world that was promised to us in the Book of Revelation, where you will be given a new world to understand with.

The new world is not in the physical part of ourselves because God has already created this physical part. It is a new world in the understanding of the above, where you live in the desert for forty lifetimes and you try to understand the purpose of life and who you are in spirit. Understand well here that when you first cross into the desert, you do not see nor do you know where you going. You are going there without water, meaning without reality. You will cross the desert with Moses—the laws of God—for *forty lifetimes* on earth. This means *six thousand years* of struggling with this human understanding. The reality of the new world will be yours after you cross the Jordan into the land of Canaan.

Understand well that this is a journey in the power of the Lord who brought you to this desert of human understanding where you do not know exactly where you are going. You left false religion to go there, and believe me, *there is a lot to learn.* Try to understand that these six hundred thousand feelings are *already* inside of you. You have six hundred thousand feelings and understandings inside of you to cross over to the desert where you will travel in the sight of God to reach the land of Canaan. Try to obey the power inside you to understand that you already have six hundred thousand feelings of *value inside your soul.* You need to enter the kingdom by crossing the Jordan River into the valley and the land of Canaan.

You will have to fight your way there and gain the support of the Lord your God because you come from being a sinner. You have been struggling with the Lord in the battle of Jacob and the valley where God and man is trying to witness the *purpose of life on earth.* If one is counted in the value of the new heaven and the new earth, things will change dramatically in spiritual value where old things will be made new—what will be new will be accepted, and what is old will be destroyed.

Believe me, in this next thousand years, you will see the change of this new world and your spirit will come alive in the counted value of the six hundred thousand feelings to gain life in the spiritual value of the future. This new world will be created in the values of the God of heaven. Remember that this New World has already been created and will come to be. You must change from *where you were* to where *you will be* and from *who you were* to *who you will become.* Just understand the Scriptures where things must change to save this world from disaster—what must be destroyed must be destroyed and what must be created anew must be created anew. *The world has to change in the form of intelligence.*

The creation of God's new world will create an increase in values where humanity can find happiness of intelligence. God will come to accomplish the great value of new over old. You must accept the fact that you *cannot* bring prejudice, bigotry, and falsehood into the new world. You *cannot* bring arrogance and vanity. And you *cannot* bring physical wealth to gain everything for yourself and leave nothing for the goals of the value of living. The struggle of life will be equal in *who* we are. The value will be shared equally in what is wise and what is not wise in the same kingdom of sharing. Life will become very different in this new kingdom of the new world that is in you. You will understand Heaven through a new way to understand life itself. Life will be given in the power of love and all that we do, where all the sins of the past and all the infractions of life will be forgiven. All that was wrong will become right, and all that is created to be right will be lived in the land and the assembly of the Lord. All creation will be perfect because the Lord made it to be perfect.

Understand well here the family of brotherhood where the twelve tribes of Israel live inside your soul for the glory of intelligence. In your heart are the twelve verbs of the sons of Jacob, and you can see where you will have a different understanding that you never had before because your deeds will no longer be in the value of the world of make-believe. It will come to be a world that man did not extend their power to understand.

Organized religion does *not* have a clue what is going to happen in the new understanding of the Lord. They talk with the mind of locusts that God will kill all people and destroy all humanity on earth. But in truth, God has *no intention* of destroying humanity. However, he will separate the goats and sheep where the sheep will be on one side and the goats will be on the other. In the new kingdom, the goats will *not* push people around with their rules. You will have a new kingdom of rules where you will see the glory of justice. The people who do *not* believe in justice for all because they think they are smarter than everybody else will come to die in sin unless they repent and agree with God.

Now we come to the arrangement of the tribal camps, where the power of the spirit lives inside the camp of God's people. Be thoroughly familiar with the Creation, of the value of intelligence, through the verbs. The Lord will arrange the glory of his wisdom, where each tribe is different in the power of intelligence, where you divide the soul of the understanding of man in what we are in the wisdom of intelligence. Each tribe is a different verb. You must come to understand where this intelligence meets in the camp of God's people.

Now let's look at *faith* itself. It is close to the tent of meeting with the Lord, but it is not the most important tribe of the Scriptures. Understanding is also a very important tribe, but it *cannot* come before faith. You must understand that *love* is what decides the grief of man and the love of man. Levi is, in many ways, the *most important* son of Jacob because he represents love. In love, you must have the compassion to understand that the great gift of the Lord must be put together *with love*. Now you can understand that love has to be placed with Aaron and his son, close to the tent of meeting. Judah is the speech that brings holiness in the tent of meeting with the Lord. Then there are the four sons of the slave girls; two of them belong to the slave girl of Leah, the first wife of Jacob, and the other two sons come from the slave girl of Rachel, the second wife of Jacob.

Now understand well that these four sons are from two slave girls and the human race has become slaves to these four tribes in the value of the tent of meeting. The first one, Dan, is the affiliation with God, meaning religion. There *always* will be holy religion on earth in the tent to understand the Almighty God. Next is Naphtali, the power to form government in the hands of man. Men are allowed to set authority on the physical part of mankind, but we must respect a set of laws of justice. Then you have Asher, who brings the wealth of money to the understanding of man. You must understand that money is power in the human spirit because that power comes from the Lord. Money is really just a piece of paper, but in the faith of man's great power, you have to become a slave to it just like the other sons of the slave girls.

Lastly, you have Gad—the system of business where we have the power to deal with each other. *You have the power to deal with each other in business.* The sons born to the slave girls will also make you a slave to these ideas, and it will have to be placed around the tent of meeting, where it has to be fair and just in your dealings. Then you have the tribe of Zebulun, the fight in the souls of mankind that comes from the first wife of Jacob. This is where life becomes a fight and has to be put close to the tent of meeting like the rest of the sons of Jacob.

These are the twelve verbs that man was created by. They form the twelve tribes of Israel in_human thinking. Make sure that you understand this in human thinking where you are divided in the understanding of the human species. You may think that the

Israelites are the Jewish people on earth, but try to understand that even though they had to be given the names of man, they are still "acting verbs" inside our knowledge, where we come to understand how it works in human understanding.

We come to the tent of meeting with our understanding that comes together in *verbs*. Verbs are the words and deeds done by human hands and the human spirit where you live out the verbs in your dream of life. You must have an understanding that whatever comes from something must come from where the power exists in order to receive intelligence.

Israel became the family of man in human understanding. I'm not talking about the Jewish people here. I'm talking about people who came to be *within us* to understand. God had to use someone to describe his knowledge, and he used Israel—not as a people but as a history of the story—to describe the way intelligence works and the way the dream of God had to come true in the power of the explanation of intelligence. If you don't have the history of man to teach mankind anything, then you *cannot* explain intelligence and the way it works. Therefore, God used the story of the sons of Jacob to explain to us the way it works when you *create* human thinking and human understanding. You have to look at the past in order for you to receive the knowledge and the toleration to understand intelligence.

The meaning of the sons of Jacob is God's way to teach us how this intelligence was formed and how you begin to understand by the convergence of the Lord from the divine to human understanding. Understand that the beginning was the sons of Jacob and the end was to make man understand the events of intelligence through the story of man. This is so a human being will be able to get up in the morning and think about the way we are educated in the knowledge of life. You will find an answer in the history of man, where the power to produce what was created to be was done in the *verbs* of the truth.

Know here that the Lord is the *truth*, and he had to give us an idea on how to deal with life by understanding the "verbs" of living. The animals of the earth do not understand any verbs. This is why they can't understand anything—they just walk in the verb of walking, eat in the verb of eating, and feel in the verb of feeling. But humans can understand the feelings of *all* the verbs that we do. We can find a value in our account of what we have learned in the value of our verbs.

Understand that the sons of Jacob are the family of our intelligence. Unless you know the meaning of the sons of Jacob, you can't live by their wisdom. This is what we have as human beings—the power to understand and pursue the verbs in those twelve sons that God has used to create intelligence with. God has created great wisdom in the sons of Jacob, and we must understand the Scriptures to understand that this story gives us life in the value of building a house and making a home for us. This also helps us in the value of dealing with each other when talking and walking side by side with one another. The family of man brings mankind to an understanding with each other. We are no longer just animals but animals with a spirit in the value of the verbs where you can talk to another human being and make him understand his feelings of sadness, joy, and *all* the feelings inside of the soul, where we connect with each other with those twelve verbs.

The number of verbs must *increase* inside us to form new knowledge and to bring new ideas to the table of value. We must continue to create the values of the verbs, and the people of the earth must understand life to be more in the values of intelligence in the family of man. When I say that mankind is a family, I mean that man is in a spiritual family in the wheel of intelligence that rolls on the ground and connects all of us.

Now we come to understand the power of the people that occupy intelligence and do not even know of their occupation because they don't use it in the proper manner to understand life. Let me give you an example: If you order a man to do a certain thing and he hears you, that man is part of your family because he heard you; he is part of the *same spirit* because he knows that he can choose to obey or not obey you. He has heard the same thing in his spirit that you told him in the value of the family of man. The tribe of Judah lives in the word where he comes to transfer his ideas into yours. You are both on the same order that was given where the slave will be the master and the master will be the slave.

We cannot go through this passage of the Scriptures without understanding Levi, the third son of Jacob. Understand that Levi is "love," but in love, you must have the communication of love that is part of the human spirit that so few people have understood. You must have compassion for each other and what we are in the same flesh. Listen now to the communication of passion that comes from love. It is not just a feeling but it's a feeling that is strong enough to make a language of its own. You speak directly to the heart's passion, and if your heart doesn't heed the passion of love, it is because of your dead spirit. Love is a language that comes from the Levi priest in the passion of human understanding that you feel in your heart to give an equal share.

Everyone needs to have food to eat and a place to stay when you come to deliver the feelings of your value where we are created *equal* in your heart. When people cannot understand what they feel in their heart, it is because they are *dead* in their heart, and it no longer feels like they should live by the passion of love. If your feelings of love have died inside you, then you cannot love anyone because your dead spirit has *no compassion*. Your compassion has died and cannot be revived unless you come to the verb of your Levi and understand this language that speaks of love inside each one of us.

Love is the most tough verb that we can encounter, but the value of its knowledge in the compassion of love is the *gratitude* of the Lord that you have inside yourself. When you love the Lord your God with all your soul and you love your neighbor as yourself, you are back in the living stage of value where all the creation of the Lord is in you. Love your neighbor as yourself and you will feel a greater verb inside your soul where you come to connect in the human race and you are part of the family of man. *You cannot be in the family of man if you don't love people.*

When you take into account Levi, you come to understand that some people cannot love because their way of thinking is against love and does not work. Here I want to talk more about love. It is so unfair for a man to preach what he does not know or what he does not understand. He must come to *love* by learning the facts of love *before* he can talk about it. Levi is a feeling inside of you that reveals the common sense of intelligence. Look at common sense as the song inside the heart of every human being that has the *melody* in their heart.

A human being hears the word *love*, processes it into his feelings of common sense, and it becomes the song of the heart. The heart opens up to its wisdom and fills the soul of the person with knowledge not yet learned by the virtue of life. A human being comes in contact with the reality of truth where it fills the heart of a human being with the knowledge that never penetrated that heart before. It's like a poem that goes so deep in the heart where everything comes to life inside your feelings. Understand the power of the prophet where the truth sets you free to take what created you to feel such feelings in the value of the Almighty God. Loving God is to put him to the *highest point* and to love Him because common sense fills you with love so deeply that you have to believe in the truth to understand yourself in what you feel and the way you think. When the Lord sings the song inside you, be honest with yourself and bring God to the highest point of worship because the song is so much what you feel that you cannot help feeling it.

The power of the Lord is to *reform yourself* into the truth because you were created with the truth, and when you went out into the world in your own way, you lost what you had in common sense and you forgot to hear this song of the Lord inside your soul. Your soul was so poor in the value of the Lord that it forgot the most beautiful thing that you can ever hear—*the dream inside your soul.* There's nothing like a dream that makes sense to direct or guide you to the right way of being the soul mate in the home of your soul. Loving God and the family of man is being part of the family of the twelve sons of Jacob. From the beginning of the world until now, you must come to feel what you have missed. Feel the soul of your dream where the dream becomes reality in who you are for God's love for mankind.

Remember the family of man—the twelve sons of Jacob—and understand that God has only created *one* family in the luxury of intelligence. God's purpose of creating mankind was so that one day, the light would be known to mankind. The preachers and the false prophets of this world do *not* have that light of common sense and reality. They bypass their spirit and look in their mind to find the light (but remember that the light is a feeling and not a thought in your mind). You have to feel the light of common sense so you can come to a higher stage of value that cannot be heard by mankind unless they open their heart to see the light and to worship God into that light.

Now you must understand Levi, the priesthood of mankind, in the love of mankind that brings to light the power of existence. *You must love mankind from the lowest to the highest.* Try to understand that God created no human being to *not* be loved, and if you love, you become the light on the post on the lamp stand that brings the light to the power of human thinking where you hope to be in the happiness of your dream. But first, you must understand the light before you try to preach the light to others.

The light that's in your heart must be shared with others in the value of heaven, not in the value of your physical self. Understand well that the light of common sense is the dream of understanding. Remember that the light is not a place where you go with your physical self but a place that you go in spirit, and it is the light of life that makes common sense. Common sense lives inside your soul, where a human being can see the light on the lamp stand of common sense and live in the heart of their soul.

Now we come to understand the *Kohathites*—the descendants of Aaron, meaning the descendants of love—the power to carry the light from one spot to the next because it is the Ark of the Covenant of the Lord. The covenant the Lord made with mankind, to understand the power, is that *we are to love one another*. You must first *love* the Lord your God with all your soul because he is the Creator of this power, *not your brother*. Remember what Christianity promises: to bring people to their salvation, and they tell them they don't have to do anything to get it. It's just a great lie because the power of salvation is to worry about the feelings of your brother who lives in the agony of their defeat. You must raise, in your spirit, the power to understand the values of others in front of your old values where you come to understand the importance of your salvation.

Remember that God is the truth and the truth sets you free, but you must pay the price of brotherhood in your feelings in order to enter the Kingdom of God. The Christians tell you to love Jesus and you'll go to heaven, but the crucifixion is only the death of one man and is *not* the event that saves mankind.

Now let us look at all those who were executed in wrongdoing by the hand of their prosecutors, killed because of their mistakes or because of some crime that they supposedly committed. Understand well the Lamb of God where *all* mankind has to be judged by this curse of people who could not see the lights in their brothers' eyes and could not understand that all men make mistakes even though man had the power to punish others for their mistakes. You must have a certain degree of compassion to make your own heart a blessing in the value of the guilt of others where your own guilt of wrongdoing has not been expressed in the same courtroom. You could be prosecuted for the same crime in the spiritual value that you have forgotten, and you make the mistake of condemning your brother for the same crime that you have committed yourself. You hid in your own soul because you were caught in the same crime as your brother that you did not overlook, yet you overlooked your own crime so as not to be offensive to others.

Understand well where we are going to in the justice of us all, where crime is put on the table of reason, where you put your faith against your brother before you look in your own heart. I tell you in truth that the life of your spirit is the Lord's plan for *all* of us, but people lie to their brothers in spirit every day of their lives. They make themselves known to be the good guys when they had just killed the physical part of another human being, placed them underneath their feet, and condemned them to the injustice of the crucifixion of death in the court of our laws. See the significance here—you have been a killer of spirit that you have sustained in the court of the Lord and you *will* be judged in the same value that you have imposed on your brother because the laws of God is the "sword" that hits on both sides—spiritual and physical. Man will be judged first for his spiritual beliefs *before* he is judged by the value of the same guilt that you accuse your brother of being condemned.

Remember here that the Kohathites are the ones that carry the Ark of the Covenant of God's law. One has been accused and killed in the value of other people's law where the strike of truth has not been proven in the Valley where all crimes are equal in the court of the Lord. Humanity must stay informed in the same laws and respect the same deeds in the value of all crimes. When a person commits a crime against the flesh, he must be pronounced guilty by reason of the truth and the truth alone. But if you condemn a man for committing an evil crime on the side of mankind, and if you forget to look at the persecution that made him commit that evil crime, then you overlook the justice of society and cannot endure the power in the court of the Lord where you are meant to be judged. You don't know anything about the court of the Lord, and you are pronounced guilty of your sin, where you are guilty of understanding *nothing* about the guilt of your brother who has been accused in your court that you call justice. You did not look at the guilt of society that brought the accuser of his guilt. You forgot to bring, in your soul, your own accuser that was not brought forth in your own trial.

Understand well, you people of falsehood, you will *not* step in the arena of your own guilt that is brought forth on the other value of justice. Know that the Kohathites are the ones carrying part of the government. Their accusers stand trial for their own guilt because they failed to understand the guilt of others in front of themselves. This means that the criminal that you have accused carries the Ark of the Covenant of the Lord. This is the deal that was done between each one of us in the covenant with the Lord where a human being will be judged by his own crime before the Lord judges the crime of others. Believe that the one who carries the Ark of the Covenant of the Lord is the one that you call criminal in the court of men, so if all the education of the world exists together in a box of knowledge, then which one should be judged first and which one should be judged last?

Now we are going to have a clear understanding of the Gershonites, through the understanding of love, to carry the guilt of the guilty and the innocent in *all* crimes of passion. A man commits a crime of passion and he has to suffer a penalty in prison where he cannot escape from the power to understand the Gershonites in the clan of the descendants of Aaron. The person who was never loved by mankind, in your feelings, would be so devastated to the fact that each criminal who is in prison for committing a crime understands the passion of their deeds and comes to understand their crimes in the value of the crime they have committed to be in the prison created by man and exhibited by men or a person must reveal his soul and understand why he was in love in the world of men.

This is the power where God and man come together in the value of being punished for each crime. The trouble here is that society has committed a crime against the *soul* of the criminal and did not pay for that crime. That person is feeling inside his soul the guilt of his own sin, but the people who put them there are the Gershonites, where to them, life has given them the freedom to live as they please. The power here is the *restriction* where a man who is imprisoned has to pay a value of his own soul and the unhappiness of life. This is the time when you must understand the guilt of your physical self committing a crime, and your spirit is punishing you for that crime.

Understand well that there's a guilt inside your soul where you lost your animal being, and now you have to pay with your spirit because you allowed your animal to lose in the passion of the dream that was unclean. You can blame whatever side you want to, but at the center of intelligence, you are guilty of the physical crime and you have to fix your physical crime with some of your spiritual value. You have to stay by yourself, inside your soul, in the prison where you have to pay equally to what you have done. The person who is being punished in this world must understand his punishment is not for only this life and the sacrifice of this life but in the time to come where you will not commit crimes of the same passion. This is because the Lord has punished you here and now and took your restrictions away from you because you have let your animal live free in the wild, and now you must restrict your animal from the punishment even though society did not like or love you. Society just tried to bring you back to reality, where you would have another chance of the resurrection of the soul. This is where society is guilty here, because they take your whole life in exchange for prison time for this crime of passion. But you and that individual and the feelings that you live in are all Gershonites where your heart is full of guilt, and you cannot understand why the Lord has punished you so much.

Understand the power—that you took a life for a life, a tooth for a tooth, and a hand for a hand. Know that what you have done must be restricted to a value where you cannot do this and keep yourself clean. Now if you are in prison here in your soul, take what is evil and dirty inside your soul and get rid of it so you can live in the wisdom that God has created you to live in. Understand well here that *true* punishment in spirit is like a child who needs punishment to realize that he cannot do that again. Society has treated you unfairly and judged you according to men who have lost their souls from the loving power of Levi.

Try to understand your clans that were not loved by society because you didn't look right to them, you were not a favorite one, or because you did not have the clan to be loved. That's why the Lord made you come to the clan of Levi in the great power of the tribe of Israel. Remember that the Lord punishes those who are not loved by society for the salvation of their own soul, but do not despair. Your clan comes from Levi—the most *valuable* son of Jacob. Remember that your grandmother, Leah, was not loved by Jacob, and that is why you became the children of Leah, the wife that Jacob did not love. But you were committed to live life, and the Lord has not forgotten you because of your clan in the family of Jacob.

Now we come to understand the numbers of the Levi clans. Here, you must have a clear understanding that there are many clans in the tribe of Levi—this means many people who are not loved by mankind. You must count them in the blessing of your own love. In the clan of Levi, you have those who are not good-looking enough or they are fat and are not accepted by society. There are also those who commit crimes, and they also are not accepted by society. Then there are those who are just not good enough to be married in the false marriage of the beast. Furthermore, you have those who are crippled or disfigured at birth or through an accident, don't have the right attitude, or have decreased mental capacity, and you have those who just cannot be loved because there is something wrong with them of any kind...because of whatever misfortune befell them. You see them in society, but you *cannot* understand them with your little mind of a locust...so you ignore them. You claim it is not your fault that they cannot be loved, and so you choose to stay with the mass power of the unknown. You just don't love them because according to you, they are not lovable to your clan or to your measuring stick that is unfair.

Try to understand here that God made Levi the *most important* of his sons. A human being who is born in this world and who is not loved by society will make bad choices, and society is to be held accountable. This individual is so disregarded by others that he becomes a lost soul in the sadness of life.

Their clans were not approved in the love of mankind, and they cannot live in the society where their souls were not accepted by society and in the clan of those who are easy to love.

Now let's look down deep into our souls. See if you can exercise love in the fashion of the Lord. See if you can love those who cannot be loved, accept those who need to be accepted, and bring them forth to be loved. Understand well the clan of the Levi and understand that if you need to be loved by others, then you need to love others in the same clan of where you are. If you are good-looking and are popular with others, more will be asked of you to love those who are hard to love in the same clan that you want to be loved. This is because you come from the same recipe of those who cannot be loved. You see this in the kingdom that God has made. Try placing your trust to love others as you want to be loved and as you want to be popular in the world of men. Make sure that you love the forgotten—the people on drugs, people whom everybody hates, people who are nasty, miserable, and hard to get along with. You could be in any one of these clans with them and suffer in prisons of souls who cannot be loved because God made you beautiful and popular to test your love and see where you are going in the world. You have to be tested since you live in the vanity of your soul and you forget to love your brother.

Life in the brotherhood of the family of man must be gratified in the love of a simple heart who, for example, says hi to a person when no one else said anything to him. Or someone who talks to a person that they notice somewhere in the restaurant drinking coffee and waiting for the attention of someone else but no one else notices that they are there. If you say one kind word to them like "Have a nice day" and prove that you said it in the value of love, then the Lord will bless you. Understand well your clan in the family of man that if you give love to others, the Lord will bless you with great love, and you will be happy to be in the boundaries of other people, sitting side-by-side with the people whom you love and the people who are in love. Make sure that you love and bring love to others because you come from the same clan as them.

We come to the purity of the camp where people live. Understand well the purifying of the place where you live, in the soul of your understanding, where the living truth comes to be purified. The key word here is *camp*—the value of where you live is your camp, meaning the place where you have established yourself in the reason of your mind and soul. It is called *your camp* because you live, sleep, and stay there until you are reunited in the new place. Camping means that you move along in different spots to understand the difference between where you are and where you will be in the verbs of life.

Understand well that you live and camp in your verbs by trying to understand each deed that you commit every day in the living space in a world that you do not understand, but you still live there. Camping means the place where you stand for where you are going because if you had your house placed there, then you would live there. But since you just came there, it means that you will move along in the resurrection of your soul. Camping, in the value of your soul, is to try to understand where you will go from there and find the directions of where you are going.

Now we come to understand the test for an unfaithful wife. This is a little different than man's teaching of adultery. We are going through the land of adultery to understand the power of the unfaithful wife. This is the unfaithfulness of your mind, where wisdom comes in the power to resist what is wrong in adultery, which is when you think of your mind to be in control and where the woman goes astray. Understand that you have the battle between your soul and your mind just like it was in the time of Adam and Eve. If you let the mind win the battle, you let your wife lead you outside the words of the Lord. You must not let the weak part of you be in charge. Your mind is the weak part of you, and if you let your wife lead you on, you will commit adultery because it's your mind here that commits adultery.

If you let the feelings that come from the mind into the spirit, you have to fight against it, in your spirit, to begin to control yourself in both mind and spirit. If you let your wife be in control during the portion that makes man in the wisdom of good and evil, you will commit adultery and worship false people in front of the Lord. The groom is the Lord, and you must worship the Lord your God with all your soul and all that you have. But sometimes the mind tries to tell you what to do and what to believe because the mind is weak and if you listen to your mind, you listen to the weak part of yourself.

In order for you to bring the true love of God, you have to restrict your mind in front of the priests and form an enforcement of values from the bottom of the altar where you sacrifice your intelligence and where your feelings come in the power of your spirit over the mind. The priests and the priesthood here is how to love, but understand that if you let your mind control you, you will worship the golden calf. You will only think in the way of the mind where you can only believe what you see in your physical self because the mind has no power of feelings. The mind is just loss and gain, and that is all that the mind can understand.

You have to be very careful how you understand your feelings. Always live within the feelings of reality because these feelings have love, but your mind does not. People of the mind do not really understand love because love is in their feelings and their spirit must guide the mind to love. Otherwise, you cannot love at all, and then you'll fall into the understanding of a prostitute. Your spirit will fall with the mind and you will not be able to understand love. This is why so many people cannot understand the Bible—because they leave their mind in prostitution and they let the mind control them. When the mind controls the spirit, the mind is in charge. You fall astray in your soul and you begin to worship the Lord like a prostitute jumping from one line to the next.

Try to understand what it means when you worship false gods before the Lord, yet you still consider yourself a good person because you think you did what is right. If you live only in your understanding of the weak part of yourself, you will only grow into the curse that is written in the Scriptures. You will fall for the love of a wife who will go astray against her husband, where the value of control between mind and spirit is given to the weak side of a human being. The Bible calls this *prostitution* because the weak part is in control of the spirit, and the spirit is being cut off from the fortification of truth. You go into the land where you cannot understand anything in the truth. You fight against truth because you think you're doing right when you're actually doing wrong. You listen to the weak part of yourself just like Eve did to Adam at the beginning of the creation where the woman went astray with her husband in the land of weakness. This is where you come to understand that man and woman are equal in physical value but are different in spiritual value.

If you look at the history of mankind, you will see where women were put down by men for so many generations and women had to regain their power because of the misunderstanding that mankind made in regards to male and female. The battle, in the Scriptures, is between mind (female) and spirit (male), where the power to understand the spirit must come from the spirit and not from the mind. This threw the human race into a battle of male against female that no one really understood.

A man and a woman have exactly the same power, and they have the same spirit and mind. The way the Scriptures were written, though, everybody thought the Bible was talking about the *physical* male and female, and everybody put the woman down where she could not do what she was supposed to do as a woman. But now that we begin to understand the *spiritual* power, you must come to fight the battle with a different form of human understanding where the species of male and female are equal in God's eyes. Mankind is both male and female with the same degree of intelligence that comes from the beginning of the Creation. They have different talents, but they are just as wise as one another. They have different feelings, but that's because of the creation and the way life was created, not because women are weak and men are strong in the physical power. The strength of a man and the weakness of a woman is one together in the values of living. What is weaker is needed for being weak, and what is stronger is needed for being stronger. We must come together *as one* in the unity of power because both are needed to function in life.

Now we come to the understanding of the Nazirite—those who are willing to start over by drinking the holy wine that creates new ideas in the power to understand. The wisdom of the blood of common sense comes from the understanding of common sense. A human being must drink the perfect wine of human thinking in reality, where human beings come to understand the power that changes blood into a divine spirit that guides you in the value of truth. You change what you have failed to learn, and you bring in a new learning to the power of your spirit, where the Nazirite must be your sign of living truth. You make your vow of new love that generates from the blood of the understanding where a human being comes to be in a new way to understand love.

Love is much more than just a word, but people use this word all the time. The power of the sacrifice comes when you start understanding how painful love is in the value of the sacrifice. You have to make a vow inside your heart to bring the Nazirite value of the sacrifice so you can *truly* love people, not in the same way that you used to believe what *love* meant but in the way that it is *true love*!

Loving people, in general, is not that easy. You must come to understand that the whole world has a sacrifice in front of them. In order to love people, you believe you should look at the color of their skin and follow all the false rules of humanity before you decide who to love. But the Lord says to *love* people *as they are*. This is the *true love* behind the sacrifice of love where human beings sacrifice themselves to understand love and to see the deep part of the value of love. You see the differences between people when they come into your view. This is where the sacrifice of love almost becomes impossible, but *you have to make it possible.*

Love is not just a word that we tell each other. It is a sacrifice where the Lord comes into our soul and brings within you the knowledge of love. We must accept the dignity of being fair and just in the sacrifice of love. Make sure that you love in the sacrifice of love with the pain and suffering that you have to endure for those you love. It becomes a different feeling in the value of love. It is hard to understand the love that comes with pain because we were always taught that love comes with only joy. We were never taught that you have to pay for, sacrifice for, and give yourself to this gigantic sacrifice in the vow of love.

Now we come to the offerings at the dedication of the tabernacle. This is where you dedicate yourself to the understanding of the "little box" inside you that holds the knowledge in your feelings, not just in your mind. The dedication of your sacrifice to the Lord in your little box is your feelings. You finally earned the will to understand your tabernacle in the feelings of your soul where you dedicate to the Lord what you have learned and place it in that little box inside you. This little box of knowledge is where you take your laws one at a time and present them in value to others by the dedication that you have set yourself into a set of laws that come from God in the value of truth. God *speaks to you*, and you hear him speaking to you inside this little box that we *all* have.

Remember that we all have this box. God speaks to us and tells us what is true in the value of intelligence. If you hear it and accept it, you begin to understand that God controls your deeds by connecting with your tabernacle in the value of spirit. The Lord is teaching you through all the events of your life. He is putting together his value in salvation of the receiving of information of all the wisdom of the wise that comes to your spiritual value, such as the understanding of the future. Understand that he healed you from the infraction of the wrong that you have done in your life. He does this with the spiritual terms that we come to understand inside us—what we call the word of God. This means we understand in the value of knowledge where it comes to be so.

The box inside your soul is sacred. It contains all the understanding of what is right over what is wrong. You cannot understand the meaning of those words in the soul of injustice where a person lives. You cannot understand that little box inside you when it is filled with the lies of the world. If someone tells a Christian to love Jesus, he believes in that. But if he opened the box and saw the real laws of God that say you can only worship *one God*, he becomes confused. The truth has to be fulfilled only through wisdom. People have to work at learning through the laws of *sacrifice*. Because your soul is filled with lies, this is why you cannot understand the laws of the Scriptures. You must go by the steps of sacrifice to understand the Almighty God to get to the understanding how to get to the promised land of the wisdom of the wise. It doesn't come cheap. It is not just in the value of saying "I do," but you must actually learn and do that which you have been given to understand. The glory of the wisdom of the wise *is* inside you, in that little box of the tabernacle, where the laws of God are stored.

Here you will find the path to go through to the very center of intelligence in the reality of common sense, and you will come to realize that the corruption by those who taught you the easy way to get to the Kingdom of God is indeed false. The Lord will *not* give you the understanding unless you work for it.

Now we come to understand how to set the Levi apart from the tribes of Israel. Remember that the Levi, the children of love, have to understand the *power of love* in the understanding of life where all men are created equal in the sight of God. You have to bring the sight of God inside your knowledge where you come to understand the power of the knowledge of love. Some people are just lost without seeing any difference between the way we believe love to be and the real, natural love. These people cannot truly love, and if you cannot love, you cannot be a part of the Assembly of God. You have to learn this gift and understand those who love unconditionally by bringing the Lord to your understanding of this great gift of love.

Go out of your way to love those that are hard to love because *everyone* needs love. If your heart creates too much hate and bigotry against your brother, it is going to be very hard for you to love others, and you will *not* be a part of the Assembly of God, where God would have assembled you in life everlasting. Understand well that love is a verb that is set aside inside your temple for better or for worse, and if you understand love in human thinking, you break the power of the Assembly of God where God said, "Follow my laws."

Now we come to the understanding of Passover, where we go to the understanding of the past two thousand years of man-made religions and the true religion of the heart. We pass over from the *false* understanding of physical religion of the mind to the spiritual religion where humanity is divided between physical and spiritual. The people of the earth who believe in the false prophet in the Bible in physical terms cannot explain the Bible in truth because the power of the physical here is the power that the mind of the locust understands really well, but the spiritual part of it is not understood. When you come to pass over, it is a celebration inside your heart of the crossover power of the spirit in an understanding of spiritual truth. The Bible was *not* written for the physical part of us. It is not about physical understanding like a Christian who believes in the life of Jesus, which is *all* physical. The *real truth* about the son of God is that the son of God is the common sense of intelligence that becomes spiritual in the value of truth. Jesus is a man in physical form, and the common sense is the spiritual part of that physical form.

Understand well that you *have* to pass over. You *must* come to understand the spiritual birth of intelligence where the Bible does not meet your physical side with your spiritual side. Passover is to understand the new birth of intelligence inside your heart, where you must be born of spirit. But not like the born-again Christians believe—they believe they are born of spirit—but then they understand the Bible in a physical way, meaning they understand Adam and Eve as the first man and the first woman in the world. *This is not true*. You have to change the teachings to spiritual. For example, Adam is the spirit and Eve is the mind, and you have to understand that the two sons who were born to them were not physical but spiritual. The two sons, Cain and Abel, are right and wrong—*wrong killed right* to gain the power of the inheritance. Right was killed, which means that people could not understand right over wrong. If you translate these things from physical to spiritual understanding, it makes total sense. But if you don't translate into spiritual understanding, it makes no sense.

Now when you set apart spirit from the flesh, you come away with a different answer, a different role, and different laws that are spiritual in the value of right over wrong. But if you stay in the old understanding of false religion that the earth calls the word of God, then you will not be able to understand. And when you cannot understand something, it is *extremely frustrating*. Heaven is in the spiritual form, yet people are studying the physical part of it, and they believe that they are going to be saved by the death of a physical man.

When you pass over, you come into a world where all the laws have to be changed. All the laws have to be brought forth, from the physical understanding to the spiritual part of wisdom. The Ten Commandments change their form and become the battle of humanity on the battlefield of life over death, where you must come and fight in the battle of the spirit to understand, in spirit, over the physical part of humanity.

Passover means that you're passing from one life to the other from the land of Egypt—meaning from the land of false religion to a land of true religion where spiritual understanding will come to win the battle on that holy mountain of the Lord. No one can see God in physical form, but if you live long enough in spirit, understand the Scriptures in the spiritual way, and try to bring him closer inside your spiritual understanding, you *will* see God in the burning bush. The face of God will be at the center, and you will see him with your spiritual eyes. You will know at that point that the power of the Lord is inside your spiritual form. You will see his face, and you will see all the lies of the world in the bush. Then you will know what God is. Finally, the human spirit will come to find the face of the Lord your God at the center of intelligence. You cannot go too much on one side with anything in life, nor can you go too far on the other side with the same value where God does not exist. God is at the center, where the truth is found in the reality of common sense.

Now we come to the silver trumpets. This is the great power to raise mankind in spiritual terms. Trumpet here means that God's word is a trumpet of music that plays the word of common sense in your heart. If you listen to it closely, it plays the revelation of what is both right and what makes common sense in the truth at the center part of your understanding where God lives. Then you begin to understand the word of the Lord your God. You hear it just like the music of a trumpet that wakes you up in the morning and puts you to bed at night with the power of the value of good over evil.

The music of life lives inside you. You need to hear this music. It gives you the power to understand the gratitude of life where life becomes a home for you in the spirit of your intelligence. You can play the music anytime you want—whether you are working somewhere or just lying there in the field and feeling the love of nature. You hear the music inside your soul—the music gets inside your soul and tells you what the advancement of life is. This music reforms the human spirit to the value where you begin to understand what the spirit is and how it works.

The trumpet is the instrument that gives you the pleasure of common sense because the world of common sense rises in your soul for the value of life itself. You come and enter heaven by the door that is unlocked for you when you hear the music of the trumpet. The glory of intelligence is to be able to understand that you are *part of life everlasting*. You *feel* the need of your given right by the Lord to bring you to life everlasting in the beauty of the music of the trumpet where your pain and suffering are so little compared to the value of what you have received, *but* it will still be a fight because life is a fight. And *fight* is one of the twelve sons of Jacob. But you will understand your battle much easier when you hear the sound of the trumpet on the battlefield of pain and suffering. There will be one life for you to live and understand the pleasure of your life that was freely given to you by the Lord of heaven. Heaven is not a place to live. Rather, it's a place of understanding where you build a house in the value of your spirit. If you live in heaven, you will hear the sound of the trumpet—a beautiful silver trumpet that you hear coming from the Lord's place in your heart.

Now you will leave Sinai with the Israelites who came from slavery in Egypt where human beings left false religion behind. Organized religion of human thinking is where man becomes the precious stone in the falsehood of the human mind. But if you leave Egypt, you will start waking up in the morning sun in the value of the spirit. You will leave Mount Sinai and bring with you all the laws that you have learned there with the power of yourself. You will learn to love your brother and all the twelve tribes of Israel, where the power of your spiritual understanding will follow you to the river of life. You will cross over to the other side of the Jordan to the land that God has prepared for you in the beautiful land of wealth of all your spiritual understanding. You will get up in the morning with the pleasure of life inside your soul, and you will go to bed at night with the same pleasure. You will live in the reality of all Israel and you will not be fooled by false religion anymore because God will use this day of judgment on all false religion of the earth and bring the soul to his most heavenly knowledge.

Understand that you must leave behind what you don't need and bring forth what you do need in the spiritual value of heaven. The grace of the understanding will be of great value in what is yours in truth, common sense, and in reality. You will live for the Lord your God and still be a physical man. You will have the urge to cherish his golden pleasure forever and ever.

Next, we come to the understanding of the fire from the Lord. Grasp that the Lord has made the light of the world as a fire, which has *burned* those who listened to the lies of the world. The fire burned the world because of its bigotry, injustice and unfairness against the small people of the earth. Understanding the fire of the Lord is very simple. When you do wrong to others and you think you're doing right, the Lord gives you *lies* to believe in. This is why mankind forms false religions of the earth—to fool those that sin. False religion was formed to punish those that step out of line through believing in all kinds of superstitions.

God allowed false religion to happen in order to make you believe something that is *totally absurd* and *away* from the truth. These people still think that they are right and everybody else is wrong by believing in their false religion, that they claim by the fire of the Lord that comes from the mouths of the false prophets. The fire of hell is the word that the false prophet places inside those who believe them. It's the false teaching of Christianity, the Catholic Church, and all organized religions. They make people live in the land of the locusts, and they make you try to understand God's word when everything is a blur and nothing makes sense with what the false prophet said. *There is nothing in truth that comes from the false prophet.* This is because living life on earth is living by the nature of life, but the false prophet teaches you to live against your nature. They make you a child who forms total stupidity, and they drill in your head that they are right but they are actually wrong, just like Cain killed his brother Abel. Yet they think they are right.

Understand that the Lord sent fire to those who lie, and the false prophets are lying to you because God created it for justice. If you think you are better than anybody else, you will be burned by the *fire of lies.* And if you think that you should be above everybody else, you will also be burned by this fire. No man is to think of himself to be first, and no man must think of himself to be better than anyone else because the Lord will burn you with the fire of hell that comes out of the mouth of the false prophet. *The Lord is the Lord of justice.* He makes the arrogant think that they are innocent, yet they are actually being stupid. He lets the hailstorm fall on their heads every time they enter some church in the false cave of a false prison.

The fire that comes from the Lord into the mouth of the false prophet on Sunday morning is explained in justice. People who believe they are greater and wiser than everybody else will be burned by that fire that came from God. If you think that you will be first in the Kingdom of God, the Lord will set you in the back of the room of justice. *The fire of hell comes from the mouth of the false prophet.* You will believe in the false prophet and God will make their words look like they are coming from the Lord himself, but he will punish them because God made good and evil a part of every being human. Those who put themselves on the above will have to go to the below of it all. Understand and know well the fire of the Lord.

Let us take a look and understand the flocks of quail from the Lord. The people were moaning and complaining to the Lord God of Israel, the God of total intelligence, because they had nothing to eat and they wanted to go back to the land of Egypt where they had food. He sent food in the middle of the desert for them to eat. People look at the world and say they have no food to eat, and there is no understanding of life here...they want to go back to the land of Egypt, *which is false religion.* But the Lord will send them back to Egypt in their spiritual understanding, and he will make them eat what he gives them. He will send them some quail and manna to eat. God will also send them some flying birds that no one has ever seen before.

This is the *punishment of the Lord.* The people were not happy with the kingdom that the Lord brought to them, so he put them in the middle of the island of human reason. He sent them false religion to believe in by eating the quail and the manna. The people were fed, in their little mind of locusts, by the flying birds and the manna that was given to them at the evening dew. They ate the flying birds of false religion, and they ate the manna, week after week, after week, in the desert with *no understanding* of better food. They ate so much of it that the taste got sour in the loss of their soul.

Moses told the Lord *not* to not punish them. The Lord didn't send them back to Egypt, but he gave them false religion to believe in. This is why God formed false religion in the middle of that world. The human race would have to travel, with no common sense of reality, to *prove* their existence so they could survive in the land. They would live in the *power of wrong.* They would complain about everything *including* what the Lord tells them. If you don't believe in truth, He will send you sorrow that you will not understand and send you food to eat from *false* religion. You will go and kneel down in front of a statue and pray to the Lord. You will try to make sense out of your existence in the middle of the desert of human understanding. Now you see in this life that you guys moaned and groaned about the existence of God. You wonder if he was there with all the things that went wrong. God sent fire on the soul of mankind because they could not understand him, and they were not happy with the situation of the terms the Lord made on them.

Now let us go into the teaching of Miriam and Aaron—another example where love upholds the law because Moses is the great lawgiver. Miriam represents the mind, and Aaron represents love. A lot of people like to break the laws with their fake love. They try to make God and the law look like they should place love first before the law. But the great power of the law here comes first above everything else. You must worship the Lord your God with all your soul and mind. That is the First Law, and it can never be changed.

The laws of God are the first thing that you should believe in, above all else, because the law makes more sense than love. You can love people in different ways, but the difference between the laws and love is the understanding that without laws, love doesn't mean anything good. You have to *separate* the two from one another to understand both. In order to "Love your neighbor as yourself," you have to love the law first because the Lord God's wisdom is the understanding that the law comes first. You have to obey the law in order to love people. Otherwise, the mind will go through the deadly skin disease, like it did with Miriam. Your face will become leprous, and the lawgiver must plead with the Lord to give her cleansed face back because she became disfigured with leprosy and could not recognize love anymore. Moses, the lawgiver, pleaded with the Lord to heal her and give her back her *feelings of love.*

If you go against the laws of God, you will become disfigured by understanding love without first understanding the laws. Love becomes ugly and disfigured and cannot produce the true values of love anymore. Understand well that God is the power of the law first. *No one* is allowed to come around and make their own rules about love. The opposite of the face of love is a face disfigured by a plague that the Lord *imposed* on the mind of mankind. This is just a story of the Bible, but it actually is a strong teaching that you cannot place love above the law or you will disfigure love like some of the preachers of false religion has done. You just cannot do this in the practice of understanding true wisdom in the family of man. The laws of God come before every single thing.

The mind of man is based on loss and gain. The mind, by itself, cannot understand God's laws to the fullest capacity because the mind only understands loss and gain. The concept of loss and gain is if you win something, you gain, and if you don't win something, you lost. This is where the mind, in order to understand, makes the determination between right (gain) and wrong (loss). The mind will lose the battle between the intelligence of the mind and the spirit. Try to understand that your mind is weaker and your spirit is stronger. The weaker mind *cannot* overpower the strength of the spirit.

Next, we come to the understanding of exploring the land of Canaan. Man must send someone to explore and try to understand the land of Canaan. This is the land that the Lord has promised us to enter and possess in the value of spiritual understanding. It must be explored in the value of human intelligence where you look at the Kingdom of God in the reality of life. You are going to cross over into a new land of human understanding. The old world where we used to live in the desert of the law will come across the Jordan into the land of the *magnificent understanding*. This is the land of Canaan.

Fully grasp that there is no physical value in crossing the river because it is the river of life inside your spirit—this means crossing over into a spiritual understanding that the Lord has promised to give each one of us. You will come to the land of Canaan, and you must make sure that you are going with truth in the family of man in the valley of the spirit of humanity. You are crossing over to understand the laws in human terms and to understand the power to receive this new land in the world of a new heaven and a new earth.

The new life for you will be where the old earth and the old heaven disappears and will be seen no more. This new world has to be explored and it must make sense to you, so you send some of your feelings to explore it just like you would do if you come into a new land on earth. You feel what is right and what is wrong in your thinking where the power of the Lord brings you in this new world. The boundaries of intelligence tell us how to get to that new understanding. You will build the new Jerusalem in a new way of understanding. Life as we understand it now will be different—so different that none of the people of the earth can ever understand the *new* that is to come.

Understand that everything will be changed in human intelligence. What made sense then will *not* make sense now, and what did not make sense then *will* begin to make sense. The world will change, and people will appreciate the new world of feelings. Natural feelings will not be considered a sin anymore. They will be appreciated and not condemned. Your feelings will be more important than it was in the old world. The change of life will be given to you in the practice of life. The new will take over and make you understand that what was wrong then will be right and what was right then will be wrong. God will switch your intelligence on the circle of a dime where everything will be changed just like that, and people will accept the new change if they want to get into the new world. Some will condemn the new world, but they will not be able to fight it because they will receive the spiritual leprosy of disfigurement, just like Miriam did, and they will not be able to understand the coming of the new world. To be restored, they will have to change their hearts and be forgiven by the Lord for complaining about the new world.

Now we go to the report on the exploration of the land of Canaan. The explorers saw big, powerful giants in the land of Canaan, just as we see today in the Catholic Church, in Christianity, and in *all* organized religion—big giants of faith who studied the Scriptures over their heads. These giant men like the pope, the cardinals, and all the high priests of all the religions of the world will come in the Scriptures in the dark feelings of their understanding. *They will be defeated by the power of the laws of God.* This means that the explorers, meaning your feelings of exploring the new world, come and tell you that you cannot defeat the giants that have been in religion all their lives in the false value of intelligence. But you must pick up the sword of the Lord and bring it to the throat of those who think they are giants in the mastermind of the theology of religion. You will prove them to be wrong, and you will defeat the giants who thought they could not be defeated. The giants of false religion will come to be no more. The children of the Lord will enter the new Jerusalem and defeat the dragon of falsehood that has been ruling the world for so long in the theology of all falsehood that they brought onto the world with their superstitious false faith. These giants, meaning the great dragon of false religion, will be defeated by the hand of the Lord himself in the battlefield of right over wrong.

The Kingdom of God will come to be and what it is where feelings will become true. The emotions of false laws will become falsehoods that were made by religions in the land where you could not understand anything. The whole structure of their theology was false, and it could not sustain against the sword of the Lord that would be placed in the heart of the children of God on the battlefield of intelligence between right and wrong. The winners will be on the right side of the sword of the Lord, and no one will be able to defeat the truth. The new world is coming where people will live in the freedom of their feelings, and they will not be tempted to live against their feelings by the false religion of the world.

Now we come to the teaching of the people rebelling against the Lord—the battle that the people have with the theology of falsehood. This is where you think that the giants, because they are so big, will defeat the children of the new world. They will be slaughtered by those giants that live in Christianity, in the Catholic Church, and all the religions of the world. This is the rebellion where the people who thought they were on the side of the Lord will go to war. They will take the sword and they will fight into the new world and bring the disaster on them that the Lord said would happen.

Understand well that the children of false theology will come to be no more. The children of *true* theology will take over, and they will defeat those people of false theology with the sword of the Lord. The Kingdom of the Lord will find a way to destroy them, and the world will come to the destruction of one side and the improvement of life on the other side. This is the destruction of all the false theology of false religion that was only invented by the small mind of the locust and cannot reach the plateau of the Kingdom of God. The kingdom of false hope and false theology will come to be no more. They will be defeated because they're the ones who judge their brother. They never seem to understand that God is not on their side because of their falsehood. The kingdom of intelligence that will come to be with the Lord is plain to see and bring the value of the truth in front of all the lies that was said by the false prophet of the earth.

Understand well, false prophet, you teach the *false doctrine* against truth, reality, and the common sense of intelligence. Your false teaching must come to an end and be lost in the land of the losing power of the creation. What is false and exists in falsehood must be brought to the table where it is covered with gold and justice. You must put your book on the side of the table where the Lord will put his book against yours. The Lord will defeat you and bring you to defeat with the lost soul of your dragon. You throw fire from the mouth of your own dragon and made man believe in superstitious lies. You were all meant to be thrown into the land of the great fire where everything that you believe will be burned and then destroyed forever and ever. You can rebel against the Lord all you want, but you cannot win against the Creator of Life. You *will* be defeated because you fooled the world in your falsehood of your mind. You did not bring a single soul to the Lord even though you had the microphone in your hands for so long that you forgot to speak the truth in the value of heaven.

Now we come to understand the supplementary offerings. You need to understand these to bring about the real sacrifice of life. *You must offer your life as a most powerful offering to the Lord.* If you give up on who you are in the power of the false intelligence of mankind, you will look like a fool in front of the whole world. But the power you bring to the Word will come to soar and be accepted one day because it is the *dream* of the Lord. This sacrifice that you offer to the world makes you look foolish and stupid in the eyes of man because you cannot change things just like that. You have to work at it and experience defeat in their eyes so you can accomplish the dream of the Lord to bring reality back to the soul of mankind.

This power is to *contradict* the stupidity that mankind believes in, to bring new order to mankind, and to bring about the power of the Lord inside people, where this supreme sacrifice is to leave the interbreeding of man and to no longer carry other people on your own animal being. This creates the power to worship God in the new terms of human understanding. What you thought was true before must be destroyed to bring forth the power of the real truth over lies. The power of truth over lies means learning in the wisdom of the wise. The change of theology must be brought forth to the power to understand the Lord God. A new earth and a new heaven must come to be. What was will never be again, and what it will become will be everlasting. The old world is going to change into a *new world*, and that new world will make sense to the power of human reason.

Understand well that I bring this book on the table of righteousness, and if you disagree with the book of righteousness, you must produce a teaching of your own that will explain the coming of the new world. You must tell the world how things are going to work in this new world where feelings will take over the mind of man because feelings are what created you in love. If you think with the little mind of a locust, you *cannot* create the new world with what you believe. The world will be free from your stupidity and ignorance that you have employed in your theology of what you thought was true. *God is the truth*. This is a *backbone* of my teaching, for the teaching of the Lord will come to be. No one can ever destroy what I have written here in the sight of my sacrifice.

Now we come to understand the Sabbath breaker put to death—the false prophets who teach the Sabbath to be a place of physical rest. They fool people in theology by believing that the man, Jesus, saved the life of mankind by the sacrifice of his death. You must understand the purpose of Jesus's crucifixion. God wanted to prove the *foolishness* of mankind to those who are lazy, refuse to learn the truth, and say how easy it is to gain eternal life without ever learning about life itself through the Scriptures. Life is the most important thing that we can ever come to encounter. In order to receive life in the Kingdom of God, you will have to sacrifice yourself to learning the value of heaven, *not* to depend on your lazy bones to claim victory without the sacrifice of life. If you think for one minute that your lazy bones can save you just by existing without learning, think again. If you are going to save your life, you must save it on your own. Do not listen to the false prophet who makes life so easy for you to learn.

Why would God take the most valuable thing that he has to offer man and give him everlasting life without the sacrifice of learning? Why would God accept your lazy way of learning nothing, where a new world will be given to you on a silver platter without you learning the value of the wisdom of the wise? If you want to play the guitar or the piano, you have to *learn* how. If you want to play the harp you have to learn it. If you want to build a house, you have to learn how. Everything that you do, you have to learn. Life is not free because you think your lazy bones cannot learn. For everything that you receive in life, you have to sacrifice yourself to it in order to learn it. Why would the Kingdom of God be given to you so freely that you have to learn from someone else to enter his kingdom?

The false prophets of this world tell you that you don't have to learn because they are *false prophets*. They told you not to worry about the Kingdom of God, so you listened to them and you wait for the great Sabbath in the free ride of the crucifixion of Jesus. You have to wait inside the false learning, and your theology will not fly with your lazy bones of not learning the truth in your life. If you worship against the truth, you have *failed life* because you were too lazy to try to understand and to read the Lord on the other side of the scroll in order to understand the perfect life that comes. Understand that both the Catholic Church and Christianity give you a free salvation just by believing in the church, but you will lose your soul listening to these people and not learning for yourself. With their false theology, you will *fail* in life.

Now we come to the understanding of the tassels on the garments—the meaning of the tassels on the corners of the garments. You are not to dress yourself in a garment without a blue cord, meaning sadness in your life. You cannot wear the garment without having some disappointment and sadness where you come to understand your soul and the way you live life. The Sabbath is a time of rest where you come inside your soul to understand *why* you are sad. You claim not to understand anything, as if someone took everything away from you that made sense, and you feel all alone. Try to understand that the Sabbath is a time that the Lord does not live in your soul because it is a time of rest, and you should rest from learning because of the power where you do not travel on the Sabbath. You come to experience your sadness where your soul must rest. This is only normal where you cannot learn all the time because without rest, you cannot continue to be in the values of learning. When your time of rest comes, you must remember what I tell you here. Do not worry when you cannot feel the Lord your God in your soul because the Lord lets you rest. You feel a little sad to be by yourself, but fully understand that the Sabbath was made for rest. You cannot use the Sabbath in the time of learning—you must look at your *soul* and just be human. Say to yourself that you cannot learn right now but that you will learn when the time comes to learn.

Have faith in the Lord even though you do not feel him—understand the days of your Sabbath where the Lord is *always* with you even though you don't feel him. What I'm explaining to each of you reading this is a way out of madness and to be able to understand truth. Love all of mankind, and love the Lord your God. Observe his laws to live in the security of his great kingdom of wisdom. Understand the power that is inside each one of us to understand the Lord your God. Do not be too stubborn to understand the Lord your God. Turn your stiff neck toward the Lord, and listen when he speaks to you in your heart. Understand that the voice that speaks to you is the voice of the Lord himself.

You were separated from God by the teachings of false religion, but you have to listen and appreciate the value of his voice inside you when he tells you how to feel. And when there is a day where you don't have the feeling of the Lord, just be patient. Be sure to listen on the day that the Lord *does* speak to you, so you can come to understand his Sabbath and the garments that you wear. The sadness of your heart is just an empty space and time, but the Lord will return to inform you of the great value that heaven is inside you every day, not somewhere else after you die. You must bring yourself to the highest prestige of uniting your feelings with the feelings of the Lord.

Next, let us understand Korah, Dathan, and Abiram. Understand well that Korah is the son of Levi, meaning "love," Dathan is the son of Ruben, meaning "faith," and Abiram is the son of Elijah, meaning "the prophet of the past." Understand that these people condemned the power of the Lord and rose against Moses, the part of ourselves that receives the laws from God himself. Try to understand that without God, you always fall into great sin. You cannot let your mind be in control over the great prophet like Moses and live to win the battle of the soul. Every time you place your mind in control of your spirit, you make all kinds of excuses *not* to believe in the one true God. You feel the heart of others in charge of you with that total ignorance of stupidity that is being produced by your mind.

Even though you are a son of the great God of heaven, you go back to your mind because you are too weak to understand your spirit. You always fall in the wasteland of the mind to go against the Great Lawgiver, so you listen to the people who you think make better sense in what they tell others to believe. It may look like it's wise, but if you can see yourself producing intelligence from your mind, you can see how stupid you are to go against the laws of God. The love of God is to protect you from making great mistakes in the value of intelligence. *Separate* the mind from your spirit, but not in a way where you are totally in the spirit because it isn't separate intelligence that makes you truly wise.

The power of human thinking is your spirit, your feelings, and your mind. Your mind is just the weak part of you. If you listen to your mind, you will lose your soul. This is what happened to Adam and Eve. The mind took over and made Adam sin against the Lord and they were thrown into sin because the mind took over. And when the mind takes over, you fall into sin because you *cannot* take the weak mind and make great choices. You have to live in weakness to know what weakness means, and you must live in your spiritual feelings to know strength. Don't go into the weak mind to try to find everything. I keep on telling you that the mind only has loss and gain, and if you make decisions on what you lose, you will reverse it to what you gain. That will sometimes make you a child of weakness.

For example, you go to the casino and you bet your life savings because you feel that you can win. At that point, your mind will tell you, in your loss and gain, that you could lose it all. The mind is more powerful at that time because gambling is a game of the mind even though sometimes you have feelings to get into it. You realize that what you can lose is too much. Try to understand that even if you decide to tell your mind that you must leave the casino for the gain in your life, you will not always gain. So you have a decision to make inside of you because your spirit brings the value where you could lose something, but the mind tries to save it, not to lose it. The way it works is that sometimes your feelings could be wrong and your mind might be right. You have to understand that there is a purpose in the wedding feast of the lamb where you can lose it all, and then you won't have anything to pay your bills with.

Try to understand that the power of yourself here is to listen to the good reason of your mind because neither your spirit nor your mind knows it all. That's when the wedding of intelligence comes in where your spirit is the husband and the mind is the bride. You have to respect both so you can come to understand your spiritual power from the loss and gain of the mind.

Now we come to the budding of Aaron's staff. Understand well that the book of Revelation in the Scriptures is the staff of Aaron. This is where you have to guide yourself to understand the Scriptures in love. When you fall in love with the Scriptures, you have to get your information from somewhere, so you go to the book of Revelation to understand right and wrong. Remember that we are weak in the mind, and the book of Revelation reveals the power to understand when it tells you about the seven seals of the Lord. Now you can refer to the words of false religion on earth to understand, but this teaching is only the physical part of life—the birth of Jesus, the life of Jesus, and the crucifixion of Jesus. This really makes these words *so false* because they believe that Jesus is the man who will save their souls by his suffering and his death on the cross that happened over two thousand years ago. You must come to understand the Lord your God in the spiritual part of life.

Understand the four horsemen in the book of Revelation. The first one, the white horse, represents the pope with his white garment. He makes laws and rules for his flock to follow. The second one, the red horse, means a cardinal who also makes rules in the battle of the wisdom of the mind. The black horse represents the black garment, the robe of the priest who lives in darkness and cannot understand the spiritual part of the Scriptures. This is because the Scriptures were introduced to him in the physical meaning, and he cannot go above his mind to introduce the word of the Lord. So week after week after week, he preaches the same thing. He does not try to make sense out of his mind, and so the people only have a *portion* of what is real. Then you come to the pale-colored horse—the wedding of the mind of an animal where a woman dresses herself in the arrogance of her purity. It is just an understanding of the physical part of life and is nothing to be proud of. That "ignorant" wedding of the physical part of man is the *greatest lie*, I think, that is mentioned in the Bible. And throughout the centuries, people who had children without being physically married were condemned and told that their children were *not* children of God.

The marriage of the beast does not work inside the human spirit because it's *not true*. People tried to bless themselves in marriage, but they accomplished nothing of any value because the falsehood of this marriage is *against truth*. It cannot come true no matter how many centuries of people have been living this life of false marriage—they all came out of it miserable and unhappy because the person they married became a *different* person, and they were told they had to stay with that person even though their feelings had changed.

The idea of Prince Charming or Cinderella being in love did not come from the truth. That idea came from generations of the past because people didn't know any better. Try to understand, in your spiritual feelings, that love is not something where you "tie" two people together and make them promise to love one another for the rest of their lives—this is the pale-colored horse in the book of Revelation. It is the falsehood of all the generations who lived before us where they could not gain the value and the prestige of understanding the truth with the unity of the soul of humanity.

The trouble with the wedding feast of the beast is that it leaves too many people out. This feast is only for the people who look good to the mind, and this is what they call a "perfect marriage." People who are different in the wedding feast of the mind *cannot* be part of this wedding feast of the false memories of the flesh because they live in weakness of human thinking. But God looks at the poor who didn't have the tools to be married on the battlefield of the pale-colored horse. God remembered them. He said, "When I make my New Kingdom, I am going to take that wedding feast out where people will *no longer* get married. The false wedding that came from the mind of man will no longer be needed because all men will be treated equally, and that false wedding means people are unfair to each other and unjust in the justice of the Lord." This false wedding is *not* needed for people to make love with each other. All the people of religion, the false prophets, use the false marriage to get us to marry and make it sacred in the eyes of the Lord in the false value where God does not appreciate their stupidity.

Now we come to understand the duties of the priests and Levites. The priests represent love of the heart (not the physical priest that we know of) because they come from the tribe of Levi. The Levites must come to understand true love and the responsibility of the sanctuary. Man *cannot* do without love because it is so *sacred*. You need the sacrament of love in order to survive in the world. All crimes committed by man were committed by people who did not feel loved and accepted. When you don't feel loved and accepted by others, you fall apart and commit crimes against society. Society has let you down.

Understand well that without love, you cannot function in the world because love gives you responsibility to accept the truth. You must believe in the values of others around you and that people must treat each other with the passion of love. The simplest thing in life is to love people. It doesn't have to be much—just saying "Good morning" or "Have a nice day" to someone can go a long way to make that person's day. Try to be simple and don't try to prove that you are the wizard of all that is wise—just bring the *value of love* to the standard of others where you simply love because people need to be loved. *You* yourself need to be loved, so you should appreciate the power of the love of others.

Fully understand that you are just a simple human being who needs love from others. If you are overweight, unattractive, or for whatever reason they won't love you, you still need to be loved and appreciated by others even if you don't understand love. If you don't put love into your sanctuary by realizing you must attract loving feelings for yourself and for others, you will fail at life. Loving one another is accepting the responsibility of your sanctuary for the feelings for others—you just need to give your fellow man a little love because people *want to feel loved.* You don't have to start kissing people everywhere and make a fool of yourself. It is just that you *appreciate* the great power of the sanctuary of love. Bring yourself to the loving power of each person that you encounter every day of your life. You will live in your own sanctuary by accepting people in love. Understand that this is your *duty* that is written in the laws of God.

Now we come to the offerings for priests and the Levites. Have a clear understanding that you must offer your love to the Lord your God. Love is a *verb*, and the sons of Jacob and the value of human intelligence works by bringing this value to the Lord your God. You must come to understand that an offering is a sacrifice that hurts in pain and suffering. You must offer this pain and suffering to the Lord. Now if you meet a person who irritates you, you can still love this person. This is a sacrifice that you can offer to the Lord your God. Love this person even if you think they are so bad that you *cannot* do it. You just have to work to fix yourself in your soul in the value of your spiritual understanding. It is not this person who gives you bad feelings; rather, it is your feelings toward him.

If you don't understand love, you *cannot* love people who do not meet your idea of love. This means that you have to work harder to love these people because in truth, they are just as holy as anyone else. Maybe you set your rules too high up for them, and then you try to overrule the standard of this false value inside you. This is where your irritation comes from. You think of yourself to be better than they are, and it *irritates* you that you must love them. The words of the spirit are inside of you before the struggle of loving one another comes on the battlefield. You raise yourself to a high standard and you try to love people with an impure heart. You cannot understand the truth because you put yourself above everyone else.

The *first thing* you must do is work inside yourself and make sure you are able to deal with the situation of others so you can come to understand the value of *all* the laws of love. Loving people is a challenge that you have to face every day in a world that deals with infractions you have created in your heart. The goal is to realize that all people are of the same standard that you are. When you cannot love someone, it is because you set your standards too high, and you forgot to offer them love according to the laws of God. God created these people not to irritate you but to make you learn the value of true love. You have to search your heart where you mixed up this love with hate. You think that it is love, but actually, it is hatred.

If you *truly* love people, it should make no difference *who* they are. Be vigilant in keeping your own heart clean so that people who are different will not irritate you. Offer to the Lord the power to resist your bigotry and prejudice that you have against others because you think that you are better than them. Your prejudice could be toward someone of a different race, different skin color, or just because they annoy or irritate you. This happens because you put yourself higher than them—you *cannot* love them because they don't "measure up" to your value.

Now we come to the water of cleansing. This is where you *clean your soul* with the power that you have inside yourself to understand your own humanity. You are *not* better than anybody else, and you are not supposed to climb above them because of their skin color, character, physical, or mental limitations, etc. You *cannot* and *must not* put them underneath your feet because you feel that you are superior to them. Understand that the Lord God calls you to the priesthood of love, and He made no rules regarding people "irritating" you. If you see someone who is different from you in some way, love them in the same value of yourself where love becomes the salvation of your soul. If you don't love people, then you listen to the false prophet, and you will make people who are different from you to be lower than you—even if they don't pray to the Lord, don't worship like you do, or don't believe in your Jesus. You still must love them by the strength of the power of the Laws of God. *If you do not love them, you do not belong to the Kingdom of God.* If you wait for the world to be perfect in your eyes, you are going to wait a very, very long time.

Remember that love is also a *sacrifice*, not just a verb. Love is *not* only something beautiful to look at. When you see the face of a person you don't like, you see a different face than yours, and if you cannot love that face, you are *not* on the side of the Lord. Being in love with other people is performing great sacrifices that bring you to be *equal* with them. It doesn't matter if they are overweight or not good-looking, if they are on drugs or they are criminals, or they do not obey the laws of man or God. You must love them because that's what love is—it is to *sacrifice* yourself in front of others.

As I have said before, I am not telling you that you have to kiss and hug them. Just have something nice to say to *every* single person that you encounter. This is how to love them. Then you can come to the treasure that God has placed in your soul. You have to be kind to *both* those who love you and those who don't, even those who try to persecute you. Love is not just a word. It is one of the major sacrifices in your life as well as one of the *greatest powers* that you can receive from the Lord.

Once you have overturned all that guilt that is inside you, you will understand the water of cleansing. It is the reality of keeping a *clean* heart and the value that you step up into the heavens to love the Lord your God. Remember that it is the Law of God to love your neighbor as yourself, and you have to understand this law to go to the power and the glory of your salvation. Love is not as easy to understand as organized religion tells you—they tell you that all you have to do is believe in Jesus and you are saved. That is the biggest *lie* that was ever made up by the false prophets who cannot understand love themselves.

Now we come to understand how to produce water from the rock. This is the power to understand that water is reality in the Scriptures. When you want reality, you have to hit the rock (faith inside you) with your staff (the law). This is because life needs faith to produce reality. We live in a world where reality has been destroyed, and somebody tells you that a piece of bread is the body of Christ? Don't believe this because there is no reality. There is nothing of spiritual value in that piece of bread of false religion. This belief exists in the world of superstitions, where you believe the lies of false religion. Things that are superstitious cannot be changed into reality just because you believe in it. If you take a piece of bread in your hand, it's no more than just a piece of bread. If you believe that this is the body of Christ, then you fall into superstition that has no value in reality.

Religions form when the weak little mind of a locust seeks to believe something that's not true and makes no sense whatsoever—you must believe in those lies in order to be Catholic or Christian or whatever religion. They inform you of their superstitious faith, and they tell you that if you don't believe that the pope is infallible, you cannot believe in this religion. They believe that the pope cannot make any mistakes. This has to be the most ridiculous faith to believe that a human being who lives, thinks, and eats like an animal is infallible. It is the *disgrace* of the human race that you have a billion people who believe this falsehood in the world, even today. Other religions are just as stupid and evil as you can ever imagine. They believe in superstitions so deeply that you can't even present reality to these people.

The truth is real. It lives in the common sense of the soul. Truth does not live in some church or in some religion that tries to fool people while collecting the donation at the end of the week so they can live an easy life thinking that they were chosen by God to be part of the water of life. I tell you, in truth, that these people are way out in left field, and they *cannot* enter the Kingdom of God with such beliefs. You must come back to reality. Understand that these false religions that brought you up in this world teach a false doctrine and false theology of a world that does not exist.

You must change your heart, come to the Lord, and knock on the stone of your faith to bring reality back to your understanding. These false religions brought the human spirit to the land of the educated man. They claim to have the theologies of the Lord, but they got it all wrong. Their sin of falsehoods is the damage they caused to the human race by practicing some stupid theology where they make themselves to be called priests, cardinals, and popes in front of other men. They raise themselves so high in a religion that is so untrue in the valley of all the lies of the world. Just remember, you false prophets, that God is the truth, common sense, and reality. If you preach and try to prove that you are in front of other men, your beliefs are against the truth. If you make yourself *higher* by calling yourself priest, pope, rabbi, minister, or any such foolish title, then this is an ignorant belief. Remember that all your sins count in the value of the Lord and you have to face them one day. The Lord will judge you according to how you represented mankind in the value of your suspicious faith.

Now we come to the teaching of the king of Edom who denied passage to the Israelites. Understand well the power of the false prophet. Man must cross over into the glory of the Lord in Heaven, and the false prophet will try to keep the people from crossing over. The people here are the children of God. False religion is going to keep people from crossing over because they want to keep their little ministries and their little churches in the rules of total nonsense and keep on practicing falsehood. They will claim that the wisdom of the wise is not wise enough to overtake their faith.

It is written in the Book of Revelation that the dragon, the great Satan of the world—meaning the lies of the world—will try to intervene with the truth. But the dragon will be defeated because God is the God of truth, and He is the power of all wisdom. Whomever he gives his wisdom to that wisdom stands as one with the Lord. If the truth comes from outside organized religion, it is still the truth because the power of the glory of heaven will come to be so in the world of men. They will try to defeat the truth, but the power of mankind has no power over the truth, and it cannot be destroyed by mankind, her false ministry, and her false church.

The time will come when we will bypass them and go straight to the Kingdom of God. The people of the world are not meant to understand the truth until the Lord sends the power of the truth. The truth cannot be defeated by the little mind of the locust of the earth. Understand well that the trip in the desert to the land of Canaan will come to be accomplished by the Lord God of the Creation and the lies of the world will be defeated. He will show them how stupid they have been in the ignorance of their false faith.

Now we come to understand the death of Aaron, meaning the death of love. Understand that God created mankind with the twelve sons of Jacob and the power of Levi. Aaron was meant to die when man stopped loving his fellow man because the Lord did not give mankind the power to love one another outside of truth. This is why it is so hard in the world of falsehood to love one another. The people came and made love almost impossible. Love was destroyed, and man had to learn to live without love, just like the Lord sent the children into the desert without water, meaning without reality, and they were expected to come through anyway. It took the power of false religion to bring the human heart to death in the heart of mankind. This is to make people understand that the lesson of love had to be created through war and destruction in order to be reborn in life for the value of love.

Man was meant to kill his brother in all kinds of battles and be heard in the sacred sacrifice of war and destruction. This was meant to be until man comes to realize that all arguments made outside love are to be settled by the blood of the sacrifice. In his great power of wisdom, the Lord could not find an easier way to bring mankind through the sacrifice, so he created war and destruction, bigotry and prejudice, and all the evil things that you can imagine. Understand well that wisdom cannot be given to mankind by the snapping of fingers or by the sorcery of the magician. God creates the value of love in his own way. Man needed to go through a period of uncertainty to get to the wisdom of the Lord to find *real love*.

God is not a magician. Whatever he wants to do, he has to follow the rules of the Creation. In order to create mankind and provide the answer, according to the form of intelligence, he must go with the wisdom that He has. He cannot cross over and take a shortcut somewhere to create mankind. He had to go through six thousand years of Revelation to come to this day that we are living now so he could bring the understanding of his power to mankind.

Understand that the glory of intelligence *does not come free*—it comes from the sacrifice of the power of pain and suffering. Only then can we come to the kingdom created by God by the power of the Creation. What if God was like who the Christians say he is—a magician who can do anything he wants? People who believe this do not understand that the Lord God creates through time, through the value of his existence, and through what makes common sense.

No one, including God himself, can create outside of what exists in reality.

This is the seventh day of the creation—the great Sabbath of the Lord where you come to understand his value and his Creation in the spiritual way of being created. Love had to be created with mankind over six thousand years—the *six days of the creation.* Try to appreciate the struggle of life that brought us through forty lifetimes in the desert where we have to find ourselves and be brought to the promised land. The justice of mankind will be brought forth for those who wish to receive life. Do not believe in the superstitions of life. *Believe in the reality of life and love.*

Now we come to understand the destruction of Arad. All that is false in mankind must be destroyed to bring the kingdom in the reality of the Lord. Many great scholars have tried before now to understand the Scriptures. But no one on earth, in heaven, or below the earth could understand the scriptures in truth. Many people attempted to understand but could not because of the *seal* that God has placed on the Scriptures. Try to understand why war is so important and why so much blood had to be shed before the Lord brings the human race to understand *true wisdom.* We had to cross many lands of false religion where everybody tries to understand the glory of heaven. So many people try to understand the Scriptures and fail to do so because the time has not yet come to understand heaven and the laws of the Lord. God has *sealed* the world from the understanding of heaven, and no one anywhere could find the value of God and the value of Heaven.

Everyone has to go to the blood of the lamb to understand, meaning the blood that was shed on the ground because of all the *injustice* in the land of God. The land of God means all those people who went through the great persecution of being killed on the battlefield because of their race, the color of their skin, or rejected by society—they did not fit in and were *not accepted.* All those who lost their lives, such as the poor Indians on the prairie, were *slaughtered* by others because the destruction of mankind had to be brought to the value of all deeds that come in wrong against those that were humble to the Lord. The law of man could not do anything about all these unjust acts done by these people who placed themselves above the laws of God and on the tablets of what they thought was right for themselves.

Now we come to understand the bronze snake where you hang a snake on the pole and make it look like God. Jesus was a great prophet of the Lord and he brought us the Parables, which are true and holy because they were given to Jesus by God. But understand what the religions of the earth made out of the New Testament. These false religions were burned by the scorching heat of the sun, meaning the New Testament. They placed the Lord on a post as a man dying on the cross who is supposed to have saved the world while Christians and all the false prophets in all the religions believe in lies.

You have placed the image of Jesus on the post, and you have made yourself a *false God* believing that if you worship Jesus, you will go to heaven someday. But the Kingdom of the Lord comes to destroy the understanding that mankind has to worship Jesus in front of the Lord. I think that this is the greatest sin the world has ever seen. Worshiping Jesus in front of God is forming an image before the Lord. This *cannot* and *must not* be tolerated in the unity of God. You know very well that they placed this man on a post in the desert, and they offered sacrifices to Jesus hanging on the cross. That is the worst thing that you can possibly do in religion. Christianity, the Catholic Church, and all organized religions are very wrong in doing this. Try to understand all the wrong that the churches are doing by putting Jesus on a post in front of the church. The bronze snake is the image of a false God and the understanding of being in front of the Lord—you should put *no one* and *nothing* in front of the Lord.

Try to understand the false belief of putting a man in front of God, making him God, and offering sacrifices to him. No wonder this world is going the way it is going. The bronze snake is on the post in every church in every parish and *all* houses of worship have some sort of a cross on their rooftops as well. Man made himself a God out of the snake because man could not understand God and they were too weak to understand Him. But understand that evil is evil, and if you live with the snake, you live in evil. If you believe in the cross you missed the whole point, and if you believe the cross is going to save you, you have *still* missed the point.

God is extremely intelligent, and he makes these events come true for the purpose that He wants to separate the animals (remember, we are *all* animals) to show the human mind the weakness of what he holds in his mind. People who worship Jesus and his cross by default have missed the point. The point is *not to love Jesus*, as he was only one man on the pole who was represented by the snake that was put in the middle of the desert for you to worship. The point is to love the Lord your God and *only* God!

You are not supposed to worship the prophet that God sends to the world to bring forth the truth. Jesus was a servant of the Lord, and God sent him to the world because the mind of mankind was too weak to understand how to worship the Lord. God said, "I am going to send them a good man, and they are going to hang him on the pole. People are going to worship this man and think that he is God because of his suffering. But the world will suffer greatly by the hand that holds the cross." Understand that the slave owner in the seventeenth to nineteenth century comes from the bad blood of the cross of Jesus. They went to church and prayed to their god, but they never understood what the meaning of the cross was, and they missed the point.

The snake on the cross in the middle of the desert has a meaning in God's word. Understand that if it was placed in the Bible, it was placed there for future generations to learn the lesson in their time. You are on the wrong side of God by worshiping your cross and the snake. I am not talking about Jesus here. I am talking about the *false faith* that's inside the heart of Christianity—that is the *snake*. If you believe in that snake, then you believe in the *great Satan* because Satan was *meant to fool mankind*. Satan does not exist in the form of a man. He is the spirit inside the heart and mind of Christianity, the Catholic Church, and all organized religions because the snake of making the sign of the cross, placing the cross in front of your church, and worshipping false gods is a *great sin*.

Understand that the bronze snake on the post is the cross that is, in some form or another, outside of every man-made house of worship. The Lord purposely put that snake there *as a warning to mankind* that if you enter into and believe in these false religions, you will be bitten by the snake, and it will not go well for you.

You are not supposed to worship any man. You are supposed to worship *only God*, and you are supposed to offer your sacrifice to the Lord in heaven in spiritual value. Understand well that the mind of man was affiliated with God in the tribe of Dan, the son of Jacob, and because of that affiliation man always tried to understand the supreme God. But they could not understand God with their little mind of a locust, so they found themselves, whom they believed with their ignorant mind, was God. So God sent Jesus in the form of the man, a good man. Jesus was a great healer, a great speaker, and he brought God's parables. God also sent Jesus to fool mankind into worshipping a man because the mind was too weak to understand God.

God meant to fool the world for a period, and then bring it back to the reality of his divine nature in the wisdom of the wise. To the mind, it may look like Jesus was the son of God, but that is the way the Scriptures were written—to fool those who choose *not* to understand the truth. The false prophet tries to fool others by telling them that they came from God and how to worship the Lord. They took the power of the Scriptures away from the rest of the world and destroyed the very people they thought who understood *true wisdom.* They made themselves prophets of God in the false teaching that God had a son and his name was Jesus.

Now you have people worshiping a man as Christ in the understanding of the great crisis of the world. This is where a human being throws himself into these false teachings and worships the snake on the pole. He thinks that God will be on his side on the days of Jubilee when man will be restored to his faith in the Lord our God, but God made these people believe in the story *so deeply* that most of them will not return to the Lord, and this, eventually, forms the Lord's *power of justice* because of the weak thinking of mankind. The time has come to separate the goats and the sheep and tell them that the story is not about the physical part of a human being, but rather, it is about the spiritual part. You can hang the serpent of false teachings on the pole anywhere you want, but it will not help you to understand the Almighty God.

Now we come to the journey to Moab. This means the journeys of those who put man into the physical part of being good people or bad people in their understanding. They separate the good from the bad, the decent citizen from the criminal—they separate just about every human being on the face of the earth. This is where man separates, in his heart, every single human being who they think is evil from the ones they think are good. They think, with their little mind of a locust, that the physical part will enter the Kingdom of God—they forget about the spiritual part of the understanding of God. They are so deep in what they believe that they are willing to kill anyone who does not live like them in their physical life. They thought that the black man was not a moral human being, and they thought that the American Indians were not human. They came to the conclusion that these people were demons that the Bible talks about, and they were ready to kill them all—to destroy them and their way of life. They thought that the Lord wanted them destroyed, so they acted as good Christians to kill these people and to destroy everything that they stood for. They never understood that *both* their spirit and the spirit of any man created by God is holy. They sent the long knife to destroy and to take their freedom away from them. They called themselves Christians and thought that their morals were the morals of the Lord. They disobeyed the Lord in order to kill them.

Understand well that the Christians, Catholics, and all the organized religions that come across to fight on the battlefield of justice because they missed the point of the Scriptures are human beings who appoint themselves to the goodness of mankind by killing those whom they believe are evil. Understand well that the meaning of Moab is the people who missed the point of understanding the real brotherhood of mankind. Just like the sons of Jacob sold their brother, Joseph, to a caravan that was heading for Egypt, man was meant to deceive each other because they missed the point. Mankind sold their brothers in slavery and killed them without thinking of a single sin in the value of life. They thought they were right to take what they needed and leave nothing for everybody else.

Understand that this was done by the whole system of mankind in the beliefs of mankind because they missed the point of the Scriptures. They did so much wrong to their brothers, not knowing that the son of Jacob that the brothers had sold in the land of false religion would become second in charge to the King of Heaven in the determination of life. That will be the judgment of the Lord where the brother who was sold into slavery would bring about the judgment of the Lord to the people who have missed the point.

Understand that in the Scriptures, Jacob of the family of man and the story of his sons is what will bring the judgment of mankind in the separation of the goats and the sheep. When all is done in the proper manner, the goats must go to their side with the goats, and the sheep must go with the sheep to determine the salvation of mankind. All that was determined by the justice of mankind must come to a spiritual value. The Scriptures were written in the understanding that *all* men were created equal, and those who did not find all men to be equal will have to be taken out of the cave in their church of unfairness. They will be brought to the power of their own will in their false beliefs that they made up. Let it be so for mankind will cross into the mortality of his own guilt. Try to understand that man's brutality over his brother has brought him to the land of Egypt through the unfair religions of the mind. A human being must cross over to the other side by the will of his actions.

Remember that Christians, Catholics, and all the people of organized religion have fooled the human race so deeply that you yourself cannot understand a word of it. You made the destruction *against yourself* in the seal of your own understanding. This is the journey through the land of Moab.

Now we continue our journey with the understanding of what is the truth in the battle and defeat of Sihon and Og. The children of the desert in the land of the Scriptures wanted to cross the desert in front of the false prophet of the earth. All they wanted to do was to cross over, and they were willing to pay the price. But the false prophet of the earth did not want them to drink the water from their wells and let them go free to go to the promised land. Understand well the value of man's own selfishness. Selfishness is the king that rules over the land of the Amorites—they think these people have to bow down to the cross in their land. You must understand that *all* people have the right to walk on God's earth if they take nothing from others' kingdoms. They are free to walk through so they can come to the promised land. The Lord made the Creation for *all* men that He sends to the world, and *no one* can stop another from crossing the earth just because he claims to be the first person to have lived there.

Just look at the United States and the way its people treat foreigners who want to come to this country for the chance of a better life. Some don't want them living in their neighborhoods, don't want them as neighbors, make them feel like they *don't* belong here, and refuse to call them brothers. They forget that they also treated the Indians on the prairie or in the wilderness in the very same way—the Indians were on this land *first.* Did this stop them from taking away their land, relocating them to some forsaken land elsewhere, and even killing them? No, it did not! For the most part, the Indians were friendly people. By rejecting another human being for whatever reason, you display prejudice and bigotry. Remember that first (as man *falsely* understands it) is *not* part of the laws of God—first is because you were *born first* in the value of truth. It doesn't matter *where* you were born. You cannot take the rights from others living in the same neighborhood. But like everything else, man always claimed their own value first—they claim to be first, and that gives them the right to live there. But in heaven, nobody is first, and if you want to be first, you have to be last in the Kingdom of the Lord. Whoever claims this place to live, with the most gratitude of life, has the right to live there. Why should you claim that your brother has no right to live there because you said you were there first? Understand well that the loss of your soul is counted in your decision and in your will to deny others what you claim to be yours in the life of mortal man. Man has no claim on the value of anything on the earth. *Everyone* has the right to live where he wants to live. Whoever makes or imposes rules against others, those same rules will be made against you from the Lord in the receiving of life because the justice of the Lord works in the rule that you make to be in the same value that you will become.

You will not be able to cross into the kingdom of the Lord because you made your own rules.

Now we come to the understanding of "Balak Summons Balaam." Try to understand that the religions of the world all have differences about what they believe and what they practice, and they curse people who don't believe like they do. They think their unique faith makes a difference in the way of the Lord, but this is absolutely *not true*. God allowed every religion and their followers to believe what they wish, to make them understand the reality that no one is better than anybody else. We were all created in a world where the mind took over for the spirit and tried to control other people with religion. Everybody lived in their own little religion that was created by their own mind.

Here, you have come to the tribe of Dan, the affiliation with the Lord, where every man has a faith different from others. Every man claims to be *right* in their theology of religion. Here, I use the physical part to tell you about religion and its physical relationship with God and love. Every religion speaks of its own God as a different way to worship, and according to some people, they have the *right* to curse other religions with what they call the truth and what they think the truth should be. This is because the truth is so far away in their little mind of a locust.

Everybody thinks they have the right religion, that their religion will overtake every other religion on earth, and that everyone else will be cursed by God if others don't believe in theirs. Believe me when I say *no* religion of the earth has the right religion at this point in time. *Everybody* is off the mark with their phony little religion of the earth, and God will curse other religions, like the Catholic Church or the what the Muslim world thinks, for example. They claim that all religions people believe in will be the *curse* of God because of the arrogance and selfishness that lives in those people's mind; they think that everybody else is evil because they have the *true* religion of God! This is *not* the case because God did not produce all these false religions without a purpose. He made the false prophets of all these false religions and brought them in the arrogance of their faith to have them *think* that they were the only ones blessed by God to understand the truth. *They think the truth is on their side.* They believe they have a heart full of love for their God and that no one from other religions has what they have. So they curse them and tell them that they will *all* go to hell. They produce nothing but lies and nothing in the truth that has any value to the Lord your God.

In writing this book, I tell you in all honesty that it is through the means of *my* understanding of the Scriptures with the Lord. I don't see *one single religion* on earth that can say that they are right and everybody else is wrong. All religions are wrong because they are the religion of the physical part of humanity—they do not understand the *spiritual* part. *God is spirit*, not a man who looks and walks like a man. He is the spiritual guide in the value of a spiritual kingdom. God made sure that no religion of the earth would be right because no one raised himself in the spiritual value to understand the Almighty God. Everybody thinks that God looks like a man, and therefore, He must be a man because He speaks like a man in our hearts.

Understand fully that *God is not a man.* God is not Jesus, and the man, Jesus, is not the son of God. The Muslims and all the other religions of the earth have their own man who looks like he is the son of God or related to God, and they worship and believe that these men are godlike. This is because their mind has to create some kind of a human being that looks like God. The mind cannot understand anything in the spiritual form. The weakness of the mind makes you fall away from God just like Adam and Eve, the *first spirit* and the *first mind.*

The mind took control of the spirit and could never produce anything but loss and gain in his value, so they made religion in the form of loss and gain. Man believed in what he believed, thinking that he is better than everybody else while God was bringing him back to his loss by making him believe in this little creature of the religion that makes *no sense.* They believe in the superstition of this loss to be a gain in their value, and they think their religions of the earth have saved them in their own salvation.

Now we come to understand Balaam's donkey. Every single religion of the world has a donkey—the stubbornness and stiff neck over religion where they all believe in their faith. They refuse to take anybody else's advice about the Almighty God. Understand that the stubbornness of religion was created by God for the stiff-necked people of religion because their stiff neck cannot turn to the wisdom of the wise. Understand that the common sense of intelligence was born with the ox and the donkey. The power to understand the Scriptures is not in the value of who is right and who is wrong. Rather, it is in the value of claiming a reward for what is right and claiming a defeat for what is wrong. In their stubbornness, everyone thinks that their religion is the right one. They cannot turn their heads to the wisdom of the wise and understand what is important in the value of Balaam and his donkey.

Remember here that Jesus entered Jerusalem sitting on the white donkey. This meant that the world would try to enter the new Jerusalem sitting on the white donkey with their stubbornness. Everyone claims their value in front of the values of others, and they try to curse others because of their stubbornness. If this animal could speak in human words, it would tell you that you are wrong to think that your life has more value than theirs because you practice a different faith that in your heart cannot be broken. *You thought you knew it all when you did not.*

When Balaam was riding on his donkey and the donkey saw the angel in front of him, the donkey stopped. But Balaam wanted to push him on because he could not see the angel of the Lord in front of him. The story of Balaam and his donkey is the simple story of the false prophets. They will not give up their faith in Jesus, and the rest of the world will not give up the journey of being wrong. They believe that their image will cross them over into the salvation of mankind. The Lord has written in the second commandment, on Mount Sinai, that you are *not allowed* to place the image of a man (of any kind) in front of the Lord, but *nobody* reads that passage nor do they understand the real covenant of the Lord—to *obey his law*, not your law—to *obey his commandments*, not yours.

Now we come to the seven obstacles of Balaam, which is the power of mankind to understand the Bible. Each obstacle is part of the seven spirits of the Lord. The seven obstacles are the seven altars that make sense to the human race. The first one is to understand the obstacle of false religion. You must understand the seven spirits of God. Each one is a power inside the human spirit that God has placed there for being wise in what we consider great intelligence—the feeling that is at the bottom of common sense and reality.

To produce wisdom, you must take both the spirit and the mind and create the understanding of the four directions with the power to produce reality and common sense. The first direction is north. These are the people who think in truth and have great wisdom. The second is south—people who think in the world of make-believe. They don't read the Bible—they just believe anything that they are told. Next is east—people who believe in the illusion of the Bible. The fourth direction is west—the people who do not care either way. These four directions are where all man's beliefs and reasoning come from. This is the first altar of the Lord. To understand the altars of the Lord, you must understand the purpose of what happens in all the religions of the world.

I have *never, ever* heard any preacher on this earth try to explain the seven spirits of the Lord. If you studied theology or just attended church, you did not learn or was never taught about the seven spirits of the Lord. To understand wisdom, you must take the Creation that is set apart to bring wisdom to a situation of any kind. You must seek the purpose to receive truth in the common sense and the reality of intelligence. What happened to all the religions of the earth is that they just didn't have the wisdom to create the *true* understanding of God. They could not explain it because they didn't have it themselves.

We continue with the first obstacle of false religion where they cannot penetrate the wisdom of the Lord. Mankind could not understand and could not bring about the glory of intelligence to the generations *until now*. No matter how much they tried, in all the ministries of the world, no one could break open the seven seals and penetrate the power to understand. The false prophets tried to explain the Scriptures in what they believed, but it was not part of the wisdom of the Lord, and it did not bring true happiness for mankind. No one who lives outside the wisdom of the Lord is truly happy.

Understand that mankind did not overcome the obstacle of false religion and cannot proclaim the wisdom of the Lord. They could not understand the twelve sons of Jacob even though they were right in front of them. They just didn't overcome the obstacle of wisdom to understand. The human race argues, quarrels, and fights with each other. Both sides claim they have more wisdom than the other, and no one can penetrate the power to understand the wisdom that was created for them.

Each obstacle becomes an obstacle to the understanding of true wisdom. Everyone thought they would find it in some religion or another, but it was denied and sealed from mankind, where the wisdom of the Lord cannot be penetrated. People have been fighting for thousands of years, but they cannot find the wisdom inside them to explain it to someone else. That is the first obstacle of Balaam. Balak tried to do the job of understanding the wisdom of the Lord but he failed.

Next is the second obstacle of Balaam. The second obstacle that man cannot penetrate is wealth in the wisdom of spiritual understanding. Up until now, wealth in the physical world where mankind physically prospered was what they believed was true wisdom. Man's physical need for greed sets in where the people who use wisdom created themselves great wealth from the two obstacles of wealth and wisdom. Then the Lord created the spiritual world of intelligence of man, and no one could penetrate that wealth. Only a few people on earth became great people in wisdom, where wealth did not matter to them, but they did not really understand that wealth, so they just ignored it.

Understand that wealth and wisdom are brothers in order to secure a good life in the existence of mankind. A person with the wisdom of his mind can produce great ideas and great wealth. But when it comes to heaven, the world is different—it comes in the value where you can sell everything you have to gain the treasures of heaven. A person sees this wealth as a treasure, and he sells everything that he has in order to buy that one field where he can find the treasure of the Kingdom of God. I want to tell you here that the Kingdom of God has not been known to mankind. The Kingdom of

God comes not in the wealth of the earth but in the way of "hearing" the Lord your God, and when you do hear the Lord your God, you begin to cross over into a river of knowledge that you never thought existed. You enter into this knowledge by the door of the heavenly glory of your deeds, and nothing can produce greater wealth than to be able to hear the voice of the Lord your God and to fully understand his word.

I am writing this book with the voice of God that I hear in my soul, and I find the wisdom so powerful and full of common sense. I can see the four poles of heaven in my soul that I can understand and process into my life. Understand well that *life is everlasting*. Once you receive life everlasting in the wisdom of the Lord, it becomes a *treasure* where there is no thief who can take it away from you. You belong to the treasure of the Lord, and the treasure of wisdom belongs to you.

The third obstacle of Balaam is the glory of the Lord. No matter how wise or wealthy you become, you still don't have the glory of the Lord. The glory of the Lord is all that is true in all wisdom with the last word said by the Lord. To understand this glory, don't try to make laws of your own and try to prove to anyone that you know better than the Lord. The wisdom comes from where the Lord is, and the power of the glory of the Lord is that He already understands before anyone of us can. It's like a man who tries to own everything and, at the end of his life, has nothing because he didn't have the glory of the Lord. Understand that the Lord's glory is the last words, and the last words is the final wisdom between the Lord and men.

The fourth obstacle is honesty. To be honest, you must clean *all* of your spirit. Honor and honesty are brothers in the understanding of the spirit of God. To receive honor, you must receive honesty. To be glorified with honor means that you have to step up in the wisdom of intelligence. The seven spirits of the Lord are unique and essential. If you respect one, you must respect all seven of them. If you try to understand religion of the earth as one of the seven spirits of the Lord, that's when the obstacles became a problem. If you don't have any honor, you cannot understand the spirits of the Lord. If you practice any of the religions of the earth, you cannot enter the

Kingdom of God without honor and honesty. The reason is that a man must understand the spirit of the Lord to have the honor of entering the Kingdom of God. Balaam and Balak could not receive the blessing of the Lord unless they had honor in the wisdom of the seven spirits of God.

If you don't understand God and his seven spirits, you cannot enter into the place where God lives because life on earth must be glorified and honored by the spirits of God to bring the wealth of heaven into the wisdom of heaven. Understand the power of these spirits because God has created the world with them. And if you do *not* know them, you cannot bring the great miracle of the truth inside your heart where heaven stands to be in the glory of this intelligence that comes from God.

The next obstacle that Balaam faced was power. Understand the power of the will of man. You may have the *will* to do things but not the power because power is only given to you *if* you respect the first four spirits of God *all at the same time*. There are seven spirits in the One True God that create all that the Lord *is*. Why were the seven spirits of God left out of religion and why did nobody bother, in all their false teachings, to try to understand them? Because they didn't have the power to understand them. When you don't understand something, you cannot prove it to others because you do not have the *power of proof* since you don't know it yourself. That's what happened to false religion. False religion tried to stop the children of God from crossing over to the promised land. They tried to place a curse on them, but they were unsuccessful because they didn't have the power. These are the powers of the spirit that cannot be overlooked in order for you to receive the kingdom of God and march on to the promised land. Ask the Lord to give you the power because this is what you need to enter the Kingdom of God.

The sixth obstacle of Balaam is *strength*. Balaam wants to curse the Israelites because he is afraid of them. Strength is the sixth spirit of the Lord in the value where your strength becomes power and brother to one another. Strength is a force of the soul that makes you strong inside yourself for doing what is right—to bring *all* the other spirits of the Lord together in your strength and be part of the seven battles with the Lord to understand his spirit. The value is to gain everlasting life.

The last of the seven obstacles is praise. Praise the Lord your God with all your soul and all that you have. Praise becomes the seventh spirit of the Lord. Whoever gained praise must come to understand the praise of the Lord if they have gained the victory of a new word by the tribe of Judah. Understand that the Kingdom of God is made of the word of God. Once you understand and live the Word of God, you will be priests for the glory and power of your strength in the wealth and wisdom of Heaven. You will be glorified by the Lord, and you will be praised to understand the power of the Scriptures. Then you will receive the power to condemn what was wrong and to accept what's right into the seven spirits of God. You will ask the Lord to punish someone who does wrong to you and to bless those who have done right by you.

Come to the glory of human intelligence where you will be praised for your accomplishments. Every time you understand true wisdom in life, God will praise you. You will be praised to accomplish what the Lord is giving you in spirit. Understand well here that the seven spirits of God work inside of you, but you must use them in the power, the glory, the honor, the wisdom, and the wealth and be praised for doing right over wrong. If you work to win the battle in this world, the praise of the Lord will be there.

Now we come to understand "Moab Will Seduce Israel." Understand that *morals* have always been the downside of religion over the rights of human beings. You *know* that you live in a world where your morals and your rights will be seduced by the morals of the world that come from lies because religion always forms morals against the rights of man. We are being seduced to do what the world thinks is right instead of what you feel is right. There are times when you break the laws of the morals of the world and you are "excused" by the wrong religion. Understand what religion calls wrong is right and what they call right is wrong because their weak mind of morals *defeats* the difference between right and wrong. This is because Cain killed Abel in the same manner of destroying what he could not understand because of the weakness of the morals of the mind.

Here you must strive to understand the weakness of the human being and anyone who preaches lies over truth. For example, a Catholic priest that has been educated by the morals of mankind will protect his morals and try to defeat what he does not understand in the feelings of humanity. The problem is when this person went to his ministry to learn to understand the Lord, he was taught falsely to understand the morals on the opposite side of right over wrong. He will try to protect his morals because he was taught to produce wrong over right where he comes to destroy the principles of right. He does not know any better because that's what he was taught. You cannot blame the man for what he has learned from the source of the false religion which he comes from. If he were taught to understand the right side of the issue, then he would have believed that. But the mother church, the weakness of the mind to create religion on earth, did not know any better so he was made to believe in the value of his false education and he has to protect what he believes.

What has been lost is your soul because you live against your creation, and you are preaching against your creation. You think that you are doing right and the Lord will praise you for doing right. You think you will come to cross the door of heaven in the value of what you were taught by the Catholic Church where your morals defeat the strongholds of the truth. But you have to bring all your teaching of the locust in the land of a lost soul. In order to redeem yourself in the values of heaven, you must break down the strong wall of the Catholic faith in order to have the redemption of the Lord.

You *cannot* continue preaching falsehoods. The same goes for all the preachers of the world, especially the born-again Christians. They claim the victory of Christ is inside them, and they say that they have the birth of the spirit when they do not have it because their false morals are still part of their morality. They did not raise themselves out of their false morals to claim the victory of heaven in their new hearts of spiritual understanding. They think that they get to raise themselves to heaven by a bunch of lies in their soul. Remember that what you preach is in your soul, and if you preach wrong, that becomes your morals, and your morals are what will condemn you in the wisdom of the Lord. Do not let yourself be seduced by the morals of false religion. Stop preaching your morals to the world because they are *false*.

Now we come to the second census—the value of being counted among the believers. You must have the *true faith* of the spirit to enter the second census where the Lord will come in the value of your understanding to see if you have a stiff neck and only understand the ignorance of the false prophets of the earth. You must change the value of what you know in your mind and the values that you understand with your soul. Understand well here that you were created with the truth. If you do not return to the truth, you cannot be counted in the assembly of God. If you are going to be counted with the power of the Creation itself, you must be able to turn your stiff neck away from the lies of the world and come to the truth where your voice answers to the Lord for the power and the glory of the seven spirits of the Lord.

You must gain the victory against what you believed in the past. You must now come to change your false faith into true faith of the spirit because the spirit was created before the mind. Try to understand that what you used to believe, i.e., that Jesus was God and that God looks like the image of a man, were lies. Raise your imagination to the understanding that God is not a man but a spirit, and He does not have flesh around that spirit, so you cannot worship that image. You must worship in the understanding that God is the truth, common sense, and reality. The whole power of your faith must be structured on the fact that God is the spirit that forms intelligence that produces common sense and reality.

You must turn away from your sin to be part of the census counted by the spirit of God as a person in spiritual value. To receive the new heart that the Lord is talking about, you have to come to this spiritual value. The power to receive this spiritual value is to believe that God is spirit in the flesh of the human heart. God is not Jesus because that's an image that mankind has made to fool the human race. It is the people listening to the false prophet that brought that false teaching on the people of the mind, and it cannot be raised in value to understand the Lord their God because of the weakness that the Lord placed in their minds. When God gave mankind a spirit,

He had to give mankind a "wife," and the wife was the mind. The mind was weak and could not understand, so the snake in the tree of the garden of God influenced the mind of weakness and she gave some to her husband, Adam. Adam could not understand any better and he lost his soul against her.

Mankind became a loser because all they could understand is what came from the mind, and what comes from the mind is loss and gain. This is the weakness of the mind. Remember that the mind is so weak that it is always on the side of gain and cannot process loss. If there's a gain in anything against that loss, the mind will go for the gain, and this is how the serpent convinces you that you will gain great intelligence if you eat the forbidden fruit from the tree in the center of the garden of God's Kingdom. The tree in the center of God's garden that is forbidden to eat from is the *great dragon*—the false religion of the earth. To belong to false religion and to accomplish what the mind tells you to do comes from the serpent itself.

Fully understand that organized religion was forbidden on the tree of life. When God forbids something, He forbids what is not right for mankind. False religion has been the disgrace on human intelligence. For example, the Catholic Church bringing the spiritual understanding to a value of the physical life of Jesus. This is totally forbidden by the Lord himself. You are not supposed to form any kind of an image before God. You have to be strong enough to accomplish your understanding by yourself. You must claim the value of your spiritual understanding in the Lord your God by going through your spiritual value to regain what you have lost from eating the forbidden fruit on the tree of knowledge. You gain knowledge by turning away from falsehood and come to the power of the Creation of our Lord.

Now we come to understand Zelophehad's daughters—the daughters who come from the clan of Joseph, the Angel of Technology, the mind that *creates* in the dream of the Lord. Remember that female means the mind, not the spirit. Manasseh, son of Joseph, was blessed by Jacob himself. When Jacob blessed the two sons of Joseph, he separated the mind of technology and the spiritual value of technology. He blessed Manasseh for the mind of the technology of man.

A human being will be given the power to create and to form great miracles from the wisdom of the Lord.

Comprehend that the technology of the world comes from the son of Joseph into the mind of all of man's inventions. This is Manasseh. The great power of the Lord is to give the mind of man the ability to perform the greatest miracles of life—the technology that comes from the son of Joseph, the dreamer, where *all* technology comes from. The people of the intelligence of mankind claim that the little mind of man gives technology to us. But that is not true. The truth is that any great technologies received by the mind comes through the soul of Manasseh, son of Joseph, in the values of the product of technology. A man created by God grows up to have great ideas with great technologies in the miracle of invention where mankind has crossed over from the stupidity of the labor of the will of their mind. This brings man to change and improve life in time to come.

Manasseh is the angel that people cannot see, but he brings the value inside the spirit of mankind. He informed the scientists of the world and all the people who produce intelligence. The Lord gives man both the mind and the soul of technology as well as the science to continue improving life on earth with new ideas created in spiritual value. The life of Joseph lasted one hundred and ten years. This means that every one hundred and ten years, certain tools will have to be changed to a more perfect tool that makes life easy for mankind. Life will *significantly improve* every one hundred and ten years from value to value, from good to better, from easy to easier until we enter the Kingdom of God, where little labor will be required to live in the dignity of intelligence.

The Lord will make things much easier in a more efficient way to accomplish life where you will come to be in the divinity of your Father in heaven, bringing mankind to a better life. It takes away from the animal of mankind the harsh labor of the past and brings the easy technology of the future from age to age, from generation to generation. Labor will never disappear from the earth, but life *will* improve, from accomplishment to accomplishment, in the value where life becomes easier. The happiness of life means it will be easier to be happy in the Kingdom of your Lord.

In this book I condemn falsehood and false religion. *True* religion, which can be found only in your heart, will become easier and easier as life proceeds into the *value of spirit.* These words and this teaching will bring mankind to the value that was given to all of us by the Lord God of heaven to proceed to a better life. Mankind will still have to live a sacrifice, but we will have a great place to live in all that is new in the value of the new heart. You will also improve, and mankind will begin to believe in the spirit and destiny of Man.

Understand well that the Kingdom of God will become a reality in the soul of man. Mankind will come through this true religion of the heart to understand that he must sacrifice but he will still be happy to live life in the pain-and-suffering sacrifice of all stages of life—from birth to adolescence to adulthood to old age. You will be happy because everything will improve in time. Remember that God created mankind to be happy inside the seven spirits of the Lord. Mankind will be happy and will not have a sour heart because he will be disgusted with life in general if he cannot understand the purpose of the Creation. Mankind must live what he was and what he is until it becomes what he will be in the heart that was created for him through all the suffering that he has to endure to get to this promised land. The crossing of the Jordan River will become the reality for the human race to become what he will be in the new heart of his creation.

Next, we are going to the understanding of Joshua succeeding Moses in the kingdom that we are preparing to enter after we cross the Jordan. Moses will not go across the river because of the sin that he has, and freedom will take over where the law left off. Freedom will enter into the new land across the Jordan River, where freedom becomes the will to be free from the rules of the mind. You will cross the Jordan where the river of life, meaning the reality of life, will come to make you live without sin in the value of human understanding. You will no longer live with the ideas of the false prophet and no longer sin inside your soul. You will come to believe in the Lord your God because the Lord will *inspire* you just like He has inspired the false prophets to do wrong. You will be *inspired to do right* by the great spirit of the Lord.

Remember that you had to go through the seven days of the creation to get to this Promised Land. You had to cross the Jordan. This means you have to learn from the reality of mankind and from the reality of the Lord just what you had to do when you were living in the desert to become pure in heart and believe in the purity of holy intelligence, where there is no life, no fabrication, and nothing stupid about it. Once you beat the falsehood, the false religion in your heart, you will enter into the Kingdom of God with the value of heaven and the understanding of what you must do to receive the power to understand the Lord your God inside your soul. God will take away all the false prophets of the world, all the false prophecy that was written through books, and all that was done to make you ignorant and stupid in your great loss.

You will also come into the new land—the freedom of your soul of your feelings, where you will feel to do something real in the freedom of reality. What it means to be free is to *observe* the laws of God and live by them because you will no longer be contradicted by falsehood. Your feelings, not organized religion, will tell you what to do. You will feel the value of your soul, and you will have the freedom to think with your own mind and soul. You will live in the freedom of Joshua, the angel of freedom, who comes to you and make you feel what comes from the Lord. All your feelings of good and evil come from the Lord, and the Lord will give you the good feelings to live with. He will take away the evil feelings that come in your soul—and that's the freedom the Lord will bring you. The law will still be there in the book value, but your feelings will live to be first because the Lord made your feelings in the purity of your soul, where evil will no longer be attractive to the human heart.

Now we come to understand our daily offerings. Understand well that a daily offering is the offering of the days of the creation. The first step to understanding the creation of the intelligence of mankind is to offer the Lord our God the understanding of the New Testament and the Old Testament as days of the creation. That day was the time when there was no light. On the first day, the Lord created the light, and there was light. You must come to understand the power of the seven days of the creation. On the second day, the Lord created the earth and all the knowledge that's in it. Before that, there was no knowledge, so God created the knowledge of the earth. On the third day, the animals began to understand and create for themselves. On the fourth day, the Lord created the sun and the moon so people could understand the value that God created the Scriptures with the moon as the Old Testament and the sun as the New Testament. Then He created, on the fifth day, the values of the animals' understanding, and then on the sixth day, God created the modern man in the value from an animal to an animal that creates laws, knowledge, technology, and creation of all kinds. Mankind begins its creation to bring the value of the six days in an offering to the Lord our God where we come to be above the animal. This is where we could see the creation of the daily offering of life on earth.

We begin to understand the offerings to the Lord. We appreciate the days that were named by the time of the Lord. Each thousand years is a day in the creation, and when you live a thousand years, you come from the animal all the way up to be in the modern man. You look at the creation and find it totally amazing in the value of the animal that became man. The power of the creation is to bring intelligence deep down to the valley of the human being, where they came to grow from the little creatures of the mind of a locust to understand the Creation of the Lord.

What is amazing to mankind is where human beings can provide for himself in the value of the twelve sons of Jacob, where a man is raised from a locust in intelligence that God has made us. Understand well your offering to the Lord must be to put yourself in the creation that was created for us. Appreciate the holy value of God who has created a power inside of us to be able to create for ourselves and to make us understand the creation of your own house and what you offered to the Lord.

Now we come to understand the Sabbath—a time of rest between each understanding that comes in the value of your own creation of your own spirit. You are appointed to understand each verse of the Bible, and in between each verse of the Bible, you must save the day of rest for the understanding of the power of the next verse. For each day of rest, you must go through the labor of hard work to come to understand the next verse of the Scriptures. If you do not rest in between, you start traveling in the lies of the world.

You should honor the day of rest and think about what you have learned so it can become life inside of you in the understanding of the great Sabbath. God has made you to rest in between knowledge, where you have to find the answer, and the answer becomes part of your knowledge. You must rest on that answer before you go to the next one because your life is full of questions that need to be answered. If you don't answer yourself in the value of life, you will turn to the lies that you hear from somebody else. Then you will be full of lies, and that is why you are not allowed to travel to other understandings on the Sabbath. You must rest your soul on your knowledge and apply yourself to understand more in your inhibition where you are not to consult with others in your learning.

You must prove what you have learned from the Lord and then rest on it for the purpose that it will sink inside you in the spiritual power that you were created to be. Knowledge of the truth is the *greatest gift* that God can give a human being. To be able to understand the knowledge of life, you have to rest in between. What I mean about a rest here is that you must take your soul and bring it into common sense. You rest your soul so you can feed your mind and also so you don't make your mind wander outside what you have learned from the Lord. If you bring a teaching to your mind too fast, your mind will jump like a locust. Remember that the value of your mind is weak and you will stumble in weakness. You will forget what you have learned because the Lord has taught you something wonderful, but your mind has to rest on it before it can understand it. The Sabbath means that you rest your understanding to slow down the process of intelligence that you have taken into your soul, and you transfer it to your mind in the slow process of time gained over time lost.

Now we come to the monthly offering. This is a little different from your daily offering because a month is much longer than a day. When it takes a longer time to understand a teaching, it means more time is needed to better understand. Sometimes you learn things in a way where you must accept that extra time that is needed to understand. You begin to understand the process of your spirit where the spiritual understanding is not something that you can rush. You have to be careful that the firstborn of your soul comes first in the knowledge of the human being and is being transferred in the value of a longer time to process this understanding. You understand things differently as a child than you do as an adult. Then there is the understanding of an older person and, finally, of an old man. This is the ministry of human understanding where you progress from young to old. Each process is done in stages of learning where you need a longer time than a day to understand from new learning to old. Understand that what you do is to progress from what you have learned when you were young in this stage of value to what you have learned in your old age. The value of learning is a process of life and must be learned in sacred values of living. You must live through your learning and understanding. This is your monthly offering.

Now we come to understand the teaching of Passover in the festival of faith. When you are trying to understand and put together the Old and the New Testament in the festival of faith, you must offer two bulls—meaning that you must offer to the Lord that you do not understand the Old and the New Testaments. Bulls represent ignorance, and bulls are male, which means your spiritual side. This means that you are *spiritually ignorant* about a teaching. Make your offering in the festival of Passover that you do not understand the Old Testament or the New Testament. You are ignorant of the wisdom that you get out of it. In your offering, tell the Lord that you don't know what it means. Ask the Lord to give you some wisdom to understand it day by day, where you can come to the common sense of it because you want to celebrate the Passover of intelligence from one side of the scroll to the other.

First, let's try to understand the Parables of Jesus. The parables are stories, like the story of Jacob. You have to understand the meaning of it in order to understand the purpose of it. If you start worshipping all the people in the Bible, you will worship false gods because none of the people of the Bible are God Almighty. They tell stories to tell you the events of life. Whatever happened to the life of Jesus was part of the events of life. The Word of God and the Parables *are* God but not the man and the people that bring these teachings.

You have to understand the story and what the story means in human thinking. Once you understand the meaning of the story, you have to bring it to the human race to understand the deeds of the Scriptures. The people who brought them is the story that will happen in the creation of mankind. You cannot worship the people who brought it because that's a great sin. You have to pass by all the people who brought the Scriptures together. Even God, with his mighty wisdom, had to use stories to bring the events of life where you use the story to understand what it means in the glory of intelligence. Then you can understand what it means, and you learn to understand the law. You learn to understand mankind from past generations to the present generation and to the generations of the future. This is what you must come to understand—not going to church and obeying your minister or your priest. You have to come to understand that the Pope doesn't make any sense at all. Those false teachers who try to form intelligence with the Scriptures didn't understand any better than you did.

The understanding of true wisdom is so the children of intelligence can come to enter the Kingdom of God just like the wedding feast in the land of Canaan. They serve the worst wine at the beginning of the wedding feast, and the best wine was kept for the end. The Lord your God served you the worst wine by the hand of the false prophet so you can come to a wedding feast that didn't make sense at all. Fully grasp that wine represents the understanding of the New World. Passover is to pass over from the worst time to the best—where people will come to understand the coming of the Assembly of God in his kingdom.

Next, we come to understand the festival of weeks, where you come in the value of the wedding feast in human thinking between male and female—the human spirit and the human mind. You must come to the wedding feast where the groom (the spirit) must marry the bride (the mind). The two must fit together in one spirit and one mind. The power to come together must be married in the same flesh. They must become one in the same body of intelligence, meaning the glory where intelligence must be brought together in learning.

The mind must obey the spirit, and the spirit must also obey the mind. Common sense is brought to the wedding feast where the physical and the spiritual days of the week in learning come together in seven days of what was created in the wedding feast of intelligence. The spirit weds the mind in the value of the seven days of the creation. Man becomes involved in the past to the present to the future time. Understand well that the mind and the spirit cannot contradict each other. When the spirit tells something to the mind, their wedding vows must be honored by accepting the spiritual understanding of feelings. Do not overthrow the feelings of the Lord. Here, you must remember that the mind is weak and only understands loss and gain. You cannot separate what makes sense with the loss and gain of the mind. You must respect the intelligence and the feelings before your loss and gain in the festival of weeks.

Now we come to the festival of trumpets. Understand that the trumpets are, like I explained before, the voice of God in your soul. You hear from the Lord in your feelings, and this produces value in your mind. The way it works is that your mind receives the information from the spirit and then seeks to gain that wealth and value in human understanding. The mind is satisfied to learn from the spirit because the spirit feeds the mind in the glory of what makes sense. This becomes the wedding between the two, and that's how intelligence is formed. What makes sense to the spirit finds its way to the mind, and because of the gain in value, the mind accepts it. This is how you become more intelligent—by transferring your feelings to your mind in the wedding feast of intelligence.

The festival of the trumpets that the Lord has sent inside of you begins to make sense to the gain of the mind. For example, you go to bed one night with a problem on your mind. You try to solve that problem in your physical needs and the mind cannot find the answer. This is because the mind can only understand in the value of loss and gain. You have to claim the value of learning in your feelings. The problem will be solved in your feelings because this is where intelligence produces itself from the loss of the mind to the gain in the value of the spirit where all human thinking comes together in the entire process of problem-solving. Just sleep on it in your spirit in one night of darkness, and then tomorrow, you pick up the piece that came from your spirit and put together the wonderful miracle of intelligence—the trumpet of the Lord.

Now we come to understand the day of Atonement. Here, you offer a bull on the altar for the sacrifice of your lack of understanding. Because you have crossed over to the wisdom of the wise, you always have to offer your ignorance to the Lord, your lack of knowledge. This is because you are like a bull, in the form of an animal, because you cannot understand something. But once you receive the understanding, make sure that you put it in the salvation of your soul. Once you have learned something, you must keep it like a treasure and store it at the bottom of your heart for future need. On the day that you came with value from something that you have learned, you must bring its value in the store where your intelligence will increase in learning.

The more you learn, the more you celebrate learning until you become wise enough to make an atonement. Learning is a special message that is transferred from the Lord to you. What you have learned is yours to keep, and it keeps you away from making mistakes in sin. Most people don't know what a sin is. They keep on making the same mistakes, and they don't learn from them. The *atonement* means that you will be pulled away from sin because you have decided to learn in truth. The justice of the Lord is that when He sees you trying not to sin, He will bless you and send an atonement on you to preserve and protect you from sinning.

Now we come to understand the vows. When you speak to the Lord, speak in the wisdom of your soul. Then take a vow according to your new knowledge. Come to understand that the Lord creates in time, not like the world of religion who believes that God created things like a magician. You must understand that the Lord created man in six thousand years, and He will take another thousand years by the understanding of the Sabbath of the Lord to finish what He has started to create. This is the modern man. It was right for the Lord to create the world in seven days, and it was right for the world to be created in time and not by the snap of his fingers—the way people believe about God. If you make a vow to the Lord, you must honor it. Try to understand the purpose of the creation, and do not condemn it.

God is not a magician, and you should not believe in the false magic that people tell you the Lord will perform. Organized religions wonder why God does not fix the world he has created and why he doesn't make people do right. They believe that God has the power to change anything instantly, but this is not true. God created time, and he must go through time himself. When you try to understand the word of the Lord, you have to understand that it is not magic like people think when they believe in God. You cannot believe in a God of magic. This is against the rules of the Lord. To understand the commandments of the Lord, you have to believe that God created time by the power of the creation itself.

Now we come to understand the vengeance on the Midianites. Understand the power of the people on either side where Moses opened the Red Sea and made a path to bring the children of God through on dry ground. If you go to the right, you see the people who live in arrogance and sophistication—people who live good in the world and are not concerned about the poor and the helpless. They don't care if the poor live or die, whether they have food, or if they have a place to live. On the left side, you have the people who don't mind cheating people to bring their will in the wisdom that they believe everybody else is worthless. They treat people any which way they please. They think that they are smart in doing so and very intelligent in their dirty deeds because they think that their wisdom is the right way to live.

They have no morals against their brother, and they think they can take anything they want from others without worrying about anyone else but themselves. Understand that the vengeance of the Lord will come against them because they always lived *above* everybody else. They cannot take the wealth of the hard labor of others, place it in their bank accounts, and claim that they are smarter than others. The Lord detests such people because these are the real lawbreakers. They don't use their hard labor to make money for themselves. They use the system that was created to be perfect, and they claim the value of others for themselves even though their value comes from the hard labor and sacrifice of others. Come, and you will see the vengeance that the Lord is planning for them.

You, as a person, must bring the vengeance of the Lord in your sacrifice. Let the Lord's vengeance come upon them. The justice of the Lord must be dedicated to the Lord Himself. Call upon the Lord to bring justice where all your feelings inside your soul are *real.* When you see anger at these people, it means that the Lord's justice is working, and as long as you have these feelings of anger inside you against these people, the Lord will keep on bringing punishment on them as long as you keep your anger inside of you. But the anger inside of you must be fresh and true in the value of your account. Whatever people take from you—rich or poor—you must place the sacrifice of your own labor and pay a price for the sacrifice you will endure. Then the Lord will bless you with greater wealth than your loss.

Next, we come to understand the dividing of the spoils. If you live in a just cause and live by the commandments of the Lord, if you work hard for what you have and if you fight against the injustice of the world, you still cannot take the victory of a war between the children of wrongdoing and yourself. Just live your life accordingly. Don't worry about the victory just yet. All you have to do is keep your sacrifice burning in your heart and the Lord will take care of it. He will make you understand that when they take something from you, it means that you are going to get richer because of your sacrifice. The physical loss is your spiritual gain in the victory in the power to understand. Your hard labor and the sacrifice of your hard labor is not forgotten, and you will see the justice of the Lord live in your life.

Don't be angry at the Lord for creating this world the way it is. Just be glad that you are not the lawbreaker and that you are on the side of the law of the Lord. Don't worry about your loss. Just claim your victory after the war is over, and these people who took from you in the battle of injustice will come to be at your feet because you are going to take from them the spoils that will be restored in your value. You have sacrificed your labor, and you should be paid in full for this labor because of your sacrifice. You also will have people insult and persecute you for being poor—they will hurt you because you don't live according to what they think is right. There will be people who gossip against you, as well as those who always put you down because they just don't like you.

You need to have revenge on these people, but understand well that it is not your own revenge that you should seek. You must come to the vengeance of the Lord. The justice of the Lord must live whenever other people sin against you. They have to live that same value that you have lived in your own soul—the same persecution, the same gossip, the same being put down, plus another 30 percent to make them see how wrong they were to do wrong to others.

Now we come to the understanding of the Transjordan tribes. When you cross the Jordan and understand the Kingdom of God, you will have all these feelings inside of you to be on the right side of truth. You will not hate anyone who has mistreated you or set all kinds of calamity against you. You will not hate anyone who did anything against you or made you sad by the way that you were treated by them in the sacrifice of yourself. Understand that you are Transjordan after you cross the Jordan, where you will have inside your heart a different heart. Your heart will become holy, and you will leave behind the old world and your old heart where you could not understand anything. You thought that God showed no justice and these people got away with it because your feelings were hurt. You believed in the set of laws that they told you were supposed to be fair in the justice of the Lord.

Now that you have crossed the Jordan, you will be given a new heart to feel with. You will come to understand how the Laws of God work; however, they work in the way that you have to plead your case to the Lord. This is because if you don't bring your case to the Lord in your feelings, you cannot receive his justice. If a woman is raped, but she doesn't bring her case to the police, no one will do anything about it. In this same way, if you bring your case to the Lord and understand the power of the spirit of the Lord inside of you, then whatever people do wrong against you, they must be punished. That's the *true love of the Lord.* When someone wrongs you in any way and you don't bring your case to the Lord, then you cannot receive justice. But as I said earlier, it is very important to remember that you cannot bring vengeance on your own. You have to come to the justice of the Lord and make those individuals pay in the justice of the Lord.

In the way that you understood before, you could not penetrate the justice and understand the power of the Lord. But now, you live in a new world with a new understanding, and you must protest any evil against you to the throne of the Lord. Justice must come to be true in the value of total justice. Whatever anyone does against you, you have to bring it to the value of the throne of God, where God will be the judge, the jury, and the prosecutor of all evil. Even though you thought in the past that there was no justice, you will see great justice coming from the Lord. Anyone who has hurt you in any way because they have no faith in the Lord will be left to be punished accordingly for their sins against you. However, you *cannot* punish them yourself by taking the vengeance of the Lord on your own.

If you follow these laws like I have explained to you, then you will come to see the greatest justice when you see these men being punished by the Lord. You will claim your great victory against them in the eyes of others. Understand well here that the Lord will be on your side but *only* if your whole heart is pure in the value of the Laws of God. You cannot ask for vengeance and ask the Lord for the spoils and take in justice what is not yours to take. Remember that the Lord is holy and you must have a holy heart in your battles. Do not claim what is not yours because it will not work. The Lord knows all justice and fairness. Make sure that you are on the side of the Lord and your deeds did nothing to cause these people to do wrong to you. Only then will you receive true justice from the Lord.

Next, we come to the stages in Israel's journey. Understand well here the children of Israel. Like everybody else, there is nothing special about them above anyone else in the eyes of the Lord. Fully grasp the power of the story of being enslaved for over four hundred years in Egypt and going through the desert for forty years. The true meaning of the story is not of physical people like the Jewish people or the physical lands in Israel or the Middle East. This story is of the

Israelite journey in the desert and everything that was written for all of mankind. The Israelites lost their faith in the Lord and worshipped the gold calf and offered sacrifices to it. Even Aaron, love itself, builds the gold calf, and the Israelites worshipped it just like the people of the earth are doing now.

The entire trip in the desert and being enslaved in Egypt was the stage that marked the world for their sins. The whole world has been stiff-necked and refused to worship the Lord your God. They worship *anything* that they feel to worship. People enter into a stiff-necked religion, and they think it works for them even though they are miserable. I don't know how people can possibly be this stiff-necked and worship false gods in front of the altar of the Lord and think they are happy. As I look at the world today, I see the Christians worshipping through Jesus and all the other religions that have their image of someone to worship. Nobody seems to turn their head and worship the One Holy God who created the world. They all worship something outside truth. They worship their ridiculous god of no value in front of the Lord your God.

God gave Moses his commandments on the top of Mount Sinai. He gave them Ten Commandments that referred to worshipping God and no one who looked like a man. You *cannot* worship Jesus or any Tom, Dick, or Harry. You are supposed to worship *only* the Lord your God, and that, my friends, is the truth. God gave and set up these commandments with Moses. The people of Israel were building a gold calf, and they were already offering their sacrifices to it while the Lord was with Moses on the mountain. The people became impatient with Moses and thought that he would never come back, so the people made their own god. This is just like the people of the world today who are anxious to worship some kind of a god because they cannot wait to see the Lord God and worship Him. They made themselves a gold calf, as the story in the Scriptures tells us, so they could worship something they believed was intelligent. They have to see God in *physical form* before they can worship, so the world turned to worship Jesus through the modern gold calf and everybody offered their sacrifice to Jesus.

They try to understand their pain and suffering and offer it to Jesus, their gold calf. The people of this world with their stiff neck, their lack of knowledge, and their stupidity refuse to turn their heads to worship the Lord their God. They should offer their sacrifice to the Lord God, not Jesus, and this becomes the greatest sin of humanity. Mankind was born with intelligence and was affiliated with God. The tribe of Dan has confirmed your affiliation with God and your Creator. Yet these stiff-necked Christians and Catholics refuse to worship the Lord your God. All the rest of the religions of the world also worship their own God in their own way without paying any attention to the One True God. They look at their own interests and values and don't think for one minute to worship their *true living God* that lives in the Creation of God and that He will be there *forever and ever.*

That is why the stiff-necked people of this world *complain* about the Creation and cannot understand a god that would lead people to commit all these crimes in all the stupidity and ignorance that we live in now. The world kills each other in false values because they worship a false god in their own interests, and nobody can turn their head to the one true God because they think that their god of no value is the real God. If the world is so evil and ignorant with the stupidity that we live now, it is because people keep on worshiping against the One True God. This is where the Lord turned his head and let the world worship a false god created by their own way of evil thinking. If this does not answer your question about God, then nothing will. God turned his back on mankind not because God is evil but because mankind is evil. Mankind will not turn to the Lord their God and observe his laws and his commandments in the value of what they should have learned from wrong of the past to enter the right of today.

Next, we come to the boundaries of Canaan. This is where we come to live in the land of the laws of God, which brings sacrifice. To endure the values of learning, you must have a *strong desire* to learn. You must bring and extend the value of learning to become a better student of *true wisdom*. This will make your life perfect in the value that there is a Lord inside you, and He will teach you the way if you apply yourself to learn something from the Scriptures each and every single day of your life.

You have to learn in this value where you come in the boundaries in the land of Canaan. You cannot cross any boundaries outside the truth or draw the line into your fantasy world. You have to stay within the boundaries of common sense and reality because you were given intelligence to live with, and you are compelled to use that intelligence in the boundaries of the laws of God. You cannot cross over anywhere into the fantasy world of any kind. You have to stay within these boundaries and listen to your own heart when somebody tells you something stupid that is outside the boundaries of learning. You must learn each day, in the simple way, to understand the simple truth where you have to live within the boundaries of the Scriptures and within the boundaries of the Ten Commandments. You must learn with all your heart *never* to cross the boundaries of human thinking. If you do cross these boundaries, you will have to answer to the Lord your God, who has created you for your basic needs of intelligence. *You cannot use your intelligence in any way to do wrong to others.* You must come to worship the Lord your God with all your soul and all that you are inside you.

Now we come to understand the towns for the Levites—the understanding of love within the boundaries of love that creates a great place to live and love, where you come to understand the power of the human being. You need to be loved, and you also need the great value to love others. I mean great value because without the love of all your brothers, you will be totally miserable and you will feel left out of the world itself. Because of your ignorance against love, you become very lonely and totally miserable. Love, in the twelve sons of Jacob, becomes the greatest son in the verb that is born to mankind. Love is the power that is inside your soul to communicate in feelings with other people. Love is a verb—it is something that you do to make love happen in order to build your own place to love others in all situations of life where very few people love you back in the reality of truth. This is because the world that we live in never understood the verb of love. They learned to live without love because hate was much easier than love. Remember that Cain killed Abel, so all the verbs that become easier for you to respect come from Cain.

Understand that the Lord has created you in the intelligence that you have with the descendants of Cain. You live within the boundaries of hate much easier than love, and that is why you always have to turn to the descendants of Cain first. Your bigotry and your prejudice will come first before love, by the values that wrong always comes first because it is always easier to do wrong over right. Your feelings were set up that way, so we have to go through wrong to get to right. Since Abel was killed, it is much harder because your natural feelings will come first in life. What will happen is that you have to understand that the Creation was created that way. You have to build your own town of love so you can start loving people and not hating them. The great power of the Lord created you in the way that He wanted you to learn to be wrong *before* you find your brother Abel in the right over wrong. You really have to build your love brick by brick and stone by stone in order to learn to love. Eventually, it becomes a faith that comes with the sacrifice of love.

Try to understand here that the Lord has created you through the prescription of intelligence. This is the way that the creation works. He *cannot* simply give you the best wine in your wedding feast between mind and spirit in the value of what makes no sense to what makes good common sense unless you have *earned* it. That's the way you were created. God had to use the tools of the creation where each thousand years cannot be changed until you come to the day of the Lord. Then He can change the way you feel after you have gone through the learning and you try to understand the great power of the Creation.

Next, we come to the Cities of Refuge. This is when you tried to understand the justice of the Lord and how the justice of the Lord works inside you. Understand the way the persecution of the world works. When you are being persecuted for certain reasons outside the truth and the values of common sense, you must understand that God just could not give you his creation of whatever value in the sacrifice of your life. You had to go to that value of giving something up to gain for yourself from what the world calls their own power to persecute you. Understand the forty lifetimes that you have lived so far in the creation of intelligence. You had to suffer many, many times and sometimes give up your life for life everlasting.

The lives of the past have been the lives lived in your sacrifice. Whether you believe it or not, life is not a one-time thing and all the wrong that was done to you by the persecution of the world was imposed on you by the will of the Lord. This is because the Lord sent you great sacrifices to endure. Remember that God has created the great persecution for the sacrifice of your salvation. You were born black where you had to be slave to the white man or you were born an Indian and be persecuted because you were an Indian where your brother did not recognize you as a person. That was your refuge city. If you were born Jewish in Germany in the great time of the persecution of the Jewish people, that was your refuge city. To be born in the misery of poverty where you were starving and you had to live in the world where you could not find enough food to eat, and you were persecuted because of it. That was your refuge city. If you were born in the middle of a war and your life was taken too soon for no purpose, that was your refuge city. But the Lord did not forget you. He did not abandon your suffering because He made it happen with the tools of the creation. Persecution was the greatest tool that He had to give you—a refuge to his kingdom.

Remember that pain and suffering does *not* destroy you. Even though you are killed, it still does not destroy your spirit. Your spirit that lives the injustice of the great persecution still accounts for part of the Kingdom of God. Understand that the Kingdom of God is not free. You have to learn to understand, but it doesn't come in freedom. It comes in the great value because you need to have a great value to receive the greatest thing in life, which is life everlasting in the kingdom of intelligence. This is where people can understand the purpose of their life and can understand the persecution that they went through to understand the purpose of their life.

Your refuge is your salvation, but the Lamb of God is not just the crucifixion of Jesus. Jesus went through this great persecution himself, but it was to show you what you had to do to enter the Kingdom of God. The people who let the goat push you into the persecution with the dirty heart of wrongdoing did not go through the great persecution that they imposed on others unless they come to understand the power and the glory of the Lord. You just cannot enter the Kingdom of God unless you place the cross of your sacrifice and learn to be crucified by the hand of those who could never understand the Kingdom of God and the value of life everlasting.

Next, we go to the understanding of the inheritance of Zelophehad's daughters. Understand here the power to think and reason in the tribe of Jacob. Understand Joseph, the father of technology, and his son, Manasseh—one of the two sons of Joseph who was blessed by Jacob. Follow Manasseh into the footsteps of Joseph and technology. You must come to understand *all* the precious things that you have now—telephones, airplanes, cars, etc.—all the stuff that made the modern men different. Man thinks that these things were invented by men, with the technology of men. Understand well here that the technology that we have today all comes from the past, where a person takes one idea and perfects it to make the future better and easier to live.

You are born in this lifetime to improve the technology of mankind and to bring us closer to the kingdom of God with all the beauty of life that will come in the wisdom of the wise. Human beings will be born not knowing anything and will rise to create great inventions in the power of the new world. Life will improve mankind to the wisdom that will make life better and easier each step of the way. Each lifetime will understand the power of technology. We currently have cell phones, but we will improve again with a better way of communication in each step into the future of the glory of the Lord. Man, in the spirit of Manasseh, son of Joseph, will bring technology in each lifetime of their existence. There will be machines to do all the hard labor that we used to do. This will restore you to a longer lifetime and save you from all the agony of the past, where you will live in the luxury of your faith in the Lord your God. Understand well here where your inheritance of life will be appreciated and that we had to go through the great persecution to get there. But you are here now in the life of everlasting time in your spiritual value. The Lord has brought you here to understand this simple truth: that the

Lord God of Heaven has prepared you when things were dark, and in the darkness of your persecution, the Lord said, "I'm going to give you a great future that will be worth all the persecution of the past. It will be worth the bigotry against you and the prejudice against you that lives in the mind of the prosecutor of the past."

This means that one day, when all the persecution is finally over, you will come into this Kingdom where no one will hurt you, not persecute you, and won't make your life miserable because you have crossed over into the land that God has prepared for you in his kingdom. It will be a kingdom of brotherhood, and no one will be left out because the Lord will live in *every single heart* and will teach mankind the great power of the religion of the heart. People will not be arrogant or sophisticated anymore. Everybody will think to be equal to everyone.

The descendants of Manasseh will bring a very easy life where you will be able to afford all that is easier for you. You will live in this Kingdom that the Lord has prepared for mankind where you will not have to worry about your children being assassinated by the evil of others. You will not have to worry about starving because *all* will be given for you in the power of technology to receive the glory of the good fruits of God. You will know your needs for today and tomorrow, and they will come to be. Understand the Kingdom of the Lord where humanity will have no criminal or jail system to restrict people into a cage of prison time. People will live by the laws of nature, and they will live in this joyful understanding of what is good and what is not good for you. We will live in this Kingdom that was created by the people who went through this great persecution and gained the victory in the Lord's Kingdom.

*****

Our next chapter takes us to the Book of Deuteronomy, where we come to the command to leave Horeb. This is the beginning of the understanding of the fifth book of the Old Testament. Recognize the power of the command of the Lord and begin to understand the different value of life where you are coming into the knowledge of the spiritual value that you were never introduced to before now. You are on the east side of the Jordan waiting to cross over into the promised land, a land where you will have to fight and struggle to understand the opposite of what you have learned to believe in the past. Your old beliefs must be opposed in your understanding in order to live in truth as the children of God.

I must tell you here that the Jewish people of the world believe that *they* are the children of God, but be careful of this because you are just as much the children of God as they are. All of mankind is the children of God, and you must learn to understand the laws of the Lord, your God, just as well as anyone. You must fight against all the tribes of the world of religion and come to the kingdom where the battle will be fought on the hard ground for any human being in this world. The fight will be to the death or life where mankind will be on the battlefield of justice and will come to understand that all men are created *equal.*

If you are a human being on the face of this earth, you are promised by the Lord the victory of heaven that you can claim by the change of your heart. No matter what your sin was in the past, you are part of the salvation of mankind *if* you choose to be so in the justice of the Lord. If your stiff neck can connect with the truth and you change your heart to know the justice of the Lord, you can become a part of the salvation just by turning your head from the wrong understanding of the world to the true values of heaven and the glory of intelligence by which God has created you. You were meant to learn that the truth is the verb in the deeds of your life to change from wrong to right. No matter how selfish you were in your faith of the past, you can still come to the salvation of the Lord.

I do agree with the justice of the Lord that if you bend on the side of injustice long enough, it will be very hard to change your heart. It will be hard for the people who live in arrogance and for the sophisticated to change their state of value on the battlefield on the day of the Lord's great sabbath, when the wisdom of the Lord will come to be in the structures of the above. You must change your heart from the false beliefs that you had in the past to the truth of the treasure of the Lord's holy justice. It does not matter to the Lord if you were deep in Christianity, the Catholic Church, or *any* false religion of the earth. You can gain the victory of heaven by the command of the Lord, and you can cross the Jordan into the kingdom, where you will have to fight a strong battle to gain the justice of the Lord—where the Lord has promised you will be for life everlasting.

Next, we come to the power where spies are sent out. False religion has a strong hold on the soul of mankind. It is not easy for anyone to change his heart on the battlefield of true justice and fight on the side of common sense to gain life with the Lord. The religions of the earth are strong in the value of their faith. They are giants who believe in what they believe, and you must fight against these big religious figures. They call themselves men of God and will try to hold you back from the truth because they claim that their truth is the only real truth in their small knowledge in the land of the beast. They are going to try to prove to you that their religion is the true religion of the Lord. But the power of truth over lies will make them extremely hard to understand the real truth because they have been on the wrong side of the Lord for so long. They will try to save their false knowledge, which they believe to be the only true value, and you, as a human being, will come to *reject* their lies. You will fight these giants and destroy them in your soul in order for you to be on the side of the Lord.

Believe me, you cannot stay in their value because it is *wrong*. It is a *great sin* to believe that Jesus is the son of God and that his son is in the image of Jesus. You are *not allowed* to worship the image of any man on earth because someone tells you he is a good man and that this man brought the parables to the life of mankind. I believe in the parables of the Lord, but the parables do not belong to Jesus. The parables of the New Testament come from the Almighty God who brought the parables inside Jesus to give to you so you can understand life in what the coming of the Kingdom will be. I did say that no man is God, but a man can be given the power to understand the Lord and to bring a great teaching to mankind. However, you *cannot* worship that man. You must still worship the Lord your God above all else. This world has placed their faith inside of a physical man who was meant to bring the parables to mankind. No matter what the false prophet tells you and tries to prove to you, don't believe them because you will lose your soul believing in the superstitions that created that story. But do believe in the parables themselves because God is the Word and the Word is God. The parables are true and can be trusted, but you cannot worship the man who brought them. Don't believe those big giant people in false religion with their ridiculous teaching. Step away from the terrible sins of the past.

Now we come to wandering in the wilderness. When you hear the words of this book in your heart, don't go back to wandering in the desert if you are strong enough to try to understand the power of the words written in this book. These words don't come from me as a man. They come inside me from the Lord, my God, who stands before the glory of human intelligence. If you waste your time wandering and don't come to the value of the heavens and do not try to understand, then you will be wandering on the battlefield when it is time to fight. But this fight is not against somebody else—this fight is in your own soul, where the battle must be accomplished. You must choose the difference between the Lord and your idol of a man.

You are the children of God because you have an open soul in the value of heaven. You can understand the simple truth of life. You come to understand this simple truth in the value that comes in your common sense in the feelings of human intelligence. Just be who you are and worship the true God of the creation and no one else. Worship the Lord who brought you out of the land of Egypt, the Lord who brought you out of the false religion that has been fooling you for so long. He will bring you through the desert of falsehood and into the land of his glory, where human beings stand before the Lord, who is the reality of truth and common sense. You can listen to the false prophet and keep on wondering what will happen to you in the land of no value where you struggle to understand the truth. But if you keep wandering there, you will *never* understand the truth because truth is a value that you have to come into by yourself. The purpose of this understanding is to glorify yourself with the seven spirits of the Lord. These will bring you to the land of being one with all who believe in the truth.

Next, we come to understand the battle and the defeat of Sihon, King of Heshbon. You must come to understand the battle that is inside your soul, of the so-called pleasure of going to church with all the preaching and the singing. Try to understand that what was believed in the past was false. You must fight the battle to overcome the feelings of going to church to do nothing but sit and give thanks to the glory of nothing in reality. It makes you feel good to go to these false churches, but you haven't learned anything there. In fact, what you have learned is a *falsehood of a false God*. You may find great joy in worshipping your Jesus, which you think is good over evil, where you come and try to defeat a false king in the false value of your feelings. But remember that Satan will make you feel good because the lies of the mind are Satan, and when you feel good about something, it is *not always* because it is something good for you.

A lot of people believe in superstitions and that is not good for you, so be careful with your feelings because they can be thrown into the dirt and then you will listen only to what makes you feel good. You will go for the good feelings, and those good feelings are just as evil as any feelings you can have. For example, going to church makes you feel good, but those feelings bring you to your defeat if you don't defeat them first. Make sure that you don't live for good feelings that are against the Lord. Sometimes you think you sing and dance in the glory of the Lord when you are actually worshiping a false God, and if you don't defeat these false beliefs in your temple of feelings, the Lord God will punish you for it and He will make you lose your soul.

Now we go to the battle to defeat Og, the king of Balaam. You must defeat on your battlefield those who like to put curses on the children of the Lord. These are the people who think that your problems in life are because you do not go to church. They tell you that your suffering is made by God on you because you don't go to church on Sunday or because you don't have the same faith that they do. They believe God has placed a curse on you to live in the desert and you have no home to live in. You have to defeat that evil king who tries to put a curse on you by telling you that you will go to hell because you did not listen to them.

This is what Balaam is, in the fire in the heart of false religion. People believe in their heads that they are good and they don't want to be around you. They try to destroy you and place you on the side where God does not want you. They try to instill a great fear on you and curse you to their will and make you believe that you are the one who is wrong against right. They try to destroy you with their false fear, and then they put their goodness over yours and claim to have the victory of heaven on their side.

Don't listen to your King Balaam. You don't need to improve all religious people of the world who think that their religion is better and more efficient than the others. I tell you, in truth, that all these little false religions of the earth will come to collapse. The wrong that they brought to mankind will come to be punished by the Lord your God. If you don't straighten yourself up in the value where you claim the good news only for yourself, you better think again because your soul has already been lost in the wrong of your own self. You think of yourself to be on the right side of the Lord, but be careful that you are not on the wrong side of the Lord your God by worshipping your man-made God in your own soul.

Understand that organized religion went outside of the truth to worship who they thought was God. They introduced their false faith for the people to worship, but they did not understand what was really important to worship. They offered sacrifices to it, and they made themselves a false God. They defined themselves and their religion with false truths that they made up in their mind about God. They began to worship with their mind of physical understanding that Jesus was the Son of God. They brought Jesus as the son of God in the physical form and made him just like the father in heaven in spiritual terms without understanding that physical and spiritual are not the same in human understanding. You have to understand the difference between the physical and the spiritual parts of life. In spirit, there is no Jesus as the son of God.

Fully comprehend the instruction of the Law that Moses brings to the people of Israel. The people of Israel are all the people who read the Scriptures and try to understand in truth. It is commanded in the instruction of the law that mankind must obey the law or life will not go well for them, and they will be punished for not observing the law. The laws in the Scriptures must be obeyed by everyone. Understand that most of the laws of your mother, meaning the mind, have instructions that resemble the laws of the spirit but in the physical meaning. You have to obey the old laws and make them sacred. You cannot go on, in your physical life, killing and robbing people because *mankind will punish you*. The same goes for your spiritual laws that you have to obey for the purpose and the reality of your spiritual being. If you don't obey these laws, you will be punished by the spirit of the Lord.

The Laws of God are understood in the spiritual meaning of the law and if you break them spiritually, you will be punished. It is the same with the laws of your mother, the Earth. If you break these laws, kill someone or do some things against the laws of your mother, you will be punished. The Lord will make you pay in the mind of the police and the people in authority above you. You cannot break any law because if you do, great punishment will come on you and you will not be happy in life because you have broken the law which cannot be repaired and changed. If you kill someone, you cannot restore their life. You can be sorry about it, but that does not fix what you have destroyed. You have to go, in truth, to the penalty of an eye for an eye, a hand for a hand, a tooth for a tooth, a foot for a foot. This means that *all* laws must be obeyed in the sight of the Lord or He will bring against you the same punishment that you have imposed upon your brothers. Whether on the earth or in heaven, all violations of the law must be punished in your soul and in your mind for the wrong that you have caused on others. These laws were written before you were even born in the world. You must observe these laws or the hand of God will come against you and you will wish you were never born.

Now we come to the understanding of the Ten Commandments that you must observe in your physical as well as your spiritual life. These laws come from the power of the Lord to bring you to his justice on all sides of the scroll. Mankind must raise himself up from the animal and become a beautiful person who wishes to hurt no one and do wrong to no one. If you were treated with the injustice of the court of mankind, meaning the physical court of the earth, you will come to the teaching of the law. If someone frames you for something you did *not* do or tries to make you pay for his crime and the justice of man does not obey their own laws and the police or the court treat you unfairly, *you must come to the court of the Lord* in the appreciation of the higher court of intelligence that the Lord has set up in the great wisdom of His own justice.

When you, a small person, have been treated unjustly and unfairly by the laws of the earth or if you have been framed by the high court of mankind, you must *protest to the Lord* for all the inconvenience you have suffered. The Lord will be against your brother because he must be punished by the same sword that cuts on both sides. Whatever was done unto you, the same will be done to those who have judged you unfairly. But if their laws were fair in the court of man, you must *suffer the consequences* of your deeds where fair justice, in the love of the Lord, was brought forth and you were punished for what you have taken from another man. What must be taken from you is the same amount of punishment that you have imposed on others. Those are the laws of the Lord that comes in wrong against right.

Next, we come to the Ten Commandments of our Lord on Mount Sinai. The lawbreakers on both sides of the sword of the Lord must come to the understanding of the laws of God. If you don't understand in truth, you have done wrong in the sight of the Lord by worshipping a false god—a god of the mind of man—and you have to be punished for your sins. God tells us that you are only allowed to worship one God in the sight of the spiritual God. You cannot offer your suffering and your pain to a false god and call it the Lord. False gods cannot fix your problem because only the Lord is allowed to fix anything that is found to be unjust against you.

Let us come to the First Commandment of our Lord and hear it well. You are not allowed to worship anyone other than the one true God. This is the first law of God that was given to you on Mount Sinai. You must *observe* the reading of that law and take it personally inside your soul and worship only the Lord your God in truth. What I mean here by *worship* is being attached to the wisdom and the protection of God who will steer you to his way. You will come to understand this guidance in your life because if you worship in the sight of the one true God, you will be brought into the presence of God. If you sincerely love the Lord your God in your soul, you will succeed in the value of a happy existence because this first law is the beginning of *all* laws. It brings you to all the laws of God where you will be guided by these laws, step by step, in the understanding of the truth.

The first commandment states that you can worship only *one* God—you are not allowed to worship anything else—no saints, no image of any kind—nor can you love anyone on earth in the family of mankind in front of the Lord your God. When you replace the One God with the love of another god and offer your sacrifice to this other god, you are replacing the One God of the Creation, and you have gone *against* this commandment. Make sure that you *only* worship the One True God. Do not worship Jesus as the Lord your God no matter what the false prophets of this world have taught you to believe. To understand one God is to believe in the One True God—the one who brought us out of the land of Egypt—meaning out of the mouth of the false prophet of the earth.

Do not listen to people who teach you to worship Jesus in front of the Lord. They are false prophets because they never understood the Scriptures and cannot understand God's words. They found themselves a man-made God because their spirit is too weak to understand anything. They tried to understand the Scriptures with their little minds of the serpent that fooled them, and after they had been fooled, they turned that ignorance on other people who tried to understand God.

The second commandment of our Lord tells us that you cannot form an image of any human being or of *anyone* who thinks like a human being on earth or in heaven. You must *not* worship any human being in front of the Lord your God. Do not make any person into a god because that person was a good person or because that person had beautiful parables to tell you. The parables came from God; do *not* worship the man who brought them. Worship *only* the one who *created* them. These words were written thousands of years ago, and I don't know why the human race has wiped out that commandment out of their understanding in order to worship Jesus in front of the Lord. Where did that come from? It must have come from the *arrogance of mankind*. The Lord was angry at the world of man, and He fooled them to prosecute man for his total ignorance and stupidity.

The Ten Commandments are *very clear* in that you cannot worship the image of a man. If you do, you will be punished over and over until you realize how evil it is for people to teach other people to worship a man's image. They base their knowledge on one man's life, and they believe that this one man's life will bring salvation upon them and that they will see God in the image of that man. Remember that the image of one good man *cannot* replace the Lord, *cannot* bring the control of man from the spirit to what they made up in the shape of a golden calf, *cannot* replace God, and you are *forbidden* from offering sacrifices to it, just like the people of Israel did in the desert. Remember, that the power of their false doctrine will bring suffering in their lives for teaching false theology to the smallest people. The Laws of God tell us that if you cause anyone who believes in the One True God to stumble, it is better for you to take a millstone, tie it around your neck, and throw yourself in the middle of the ocean because you are a false prophet who taught the least of your brothers to believe in falsehood.

The third commandment tells us not to take the Lord's name in vain—meaning that you were fooled by false religion—from the school of theology that the false prophets believed in. You learned from these false prophets to believe that Jesus was the physical son of God. You did not understand that God is a spiritual being and He has *no* physical son in the understanding of the power to understand the Scriptures. If you cannot understand the Scriptures in the reality of the spirit, you should not teach from your mind what you cannot understand. Falsehood is still falsehood, and if you believe in that stupidity and ignorance, you yourself are guilty of sin against the Holy Lord of Heaven. If you teach it to the people in the name of the Lord your God, you create a great sin for yourself.

What you believe is what you instruct people also to believe, and if you teach falsehood to others in this serious matter of wrongdoing, you are guilty and must come to the throne of the Lord and be judged accordingly. If you are found guilty, after you have been told in common sense *not* to do such things to your brother and you keep doing these things in the name of the Lord, this means you are using the Lord's name in vain. You will be punished, and you will lose your life trying to save your life. Until you change your soul to be on the right side of the Lord, you cannot enter into the Kingdom of God where the justice of the Lord will prevail over you.

Now we come to the most difficult understanding of keeping the Sabbath holy. In other words, don't try to understand all of the Bible in six days. Understand that a week in the scriptures is not a week of man's thinking—it is a spiritual time of learning in the Kingdom of our Lord. You cannot learn all the Scriptures in the short period of time of seven physical days and think that you are inside the wisdom of the wise. You cannot think that you can jump over any part of the Bible that you don't understand. Try to understand that the power of the learning and teaching of the Scriptures is done in spiritual time.

Through common sense, you can understand the Lord. He lets you live through the power and rests on the day after you have gained great knowledge of something that you could not understand before. Don't concern yourself with how *little* you understand. Just be patient and thankful that you understood something in the value of truth and rest your soul for another day. To understand something great, you must be patient in the value of time and learn step by step, week by week, in the process of time. Then *rest* after you understood what you need to know in what the Scriptures mean in the understanding of learning.

The Sabbath is a span of time in between knowledge, so don't jump and travel on the Sabbath because you must rest your understanding on that day and feel wonderful about what you have learned in the understanding of the Lord. No one can understand a book in one day or one week. You have to understand it step by step in the value of each step. You must rest your knowledge and learn the sequence of time where the value of time will come to bring you great fruit in the understanding of the Scriptures. Your time of rest will come and go, and you will learn to understand the magnificent power of this great Creation that we are part of. Show respect to your Father in heaven during your time of rest. It is just as important as your time of learning.

The fifth commandment is to honor our Father in heaven and our Mother, the earth. Try to understand the power that's in between the laws of the Almighty God. The spiritual understanding of our Mother, the earth—our *natural feelings* that come from the Lord your God and also the spiritual understanding of the Laws of the Lord. Laws are made for understanding the value of yourself and the values of your brothers of the Earth. Both our father and mother come together in one big understanding of the boundary that you cannot cross over to bring yourself outside the laws of God.

You shall not murder any person in your life. This commandment comes on both sides of the scroll, both physical and spiritual. You shall not murder anyone in the physical part of life because life is precious, and if you take a life, you will have to give up your own life, in payment for the life you took. The justice of the Lord will come in the way of man's laws, in the power to understand the physical part of the human being. Know that in all the pain and suffering that you take from someone, you oppose all others of the value of your life. The Lord will bring the disaster on your own life with the laws of mankind that will oppose you and what you have done in his laws. The laws of God translate into human understanding to tell you that the values of others are important.

The murder of the spirit is much more serious than the murder of the physical body because killing people in spirit is preaching against the truth. If you do not understand the truth and you think you are within the truth, it is because you failed to understand the truth. If you impose your understanding on the life of others, you are interfering with their own understanding that comes from the Lord. You may call yourself a great preacher or a great teacher, but if you do not understand the laws of God in the values of your spiritual understanding, you are not allowed to teach something that you have no knowledge of.

If God did not teach you to worship and to be born in the value of your spirit, you should not be teaching within the boundaries of the mind of man. You should not be teaching within the boundaries of your own understanding that you made up in your mind and think that it's a great sermon to tell people to worship Jesus in the world of man. When you do that, you break the laws of the spirit because the laws have been given to you by God and God alone. No other man of flesh in the image of a person is meant to replace God, the Lord of your salvation. No man can save you because a human being is a mistake maker and does not have the intelligence and the theology to understand the Scriptures in clear thinking. *Stop killing the spirit of others* with your own theory that comes from your mind. I stand here and I think that I understand the Scriptures, but I could not make my own theory and tell you to worship the image of a man in front of the Lord God of the Creation. I can talk about the truth that I have heard from my Father in heaven, but I cannot tell you what I do not know in the spiritual power of myself and the Lord. I can only tell you about the laws of God that were written for true wisdom. I can only repeat what I have heard my Father in heaven tell me in my feelings of understanding the Scriptures in the fashion that I do, and that is the same as when Jesus spoke in parables of the values of heaven. Man is not allowed to change these laws that were written by the hand of God. You must not, by any means, worship the *image* of a man who stands before the ministry of the Lord that comes from the truth and the power to understand his laws in the value of life. You are not allowed to take the life and soul from another man by making your own laws of worshipping Jesus in front of the Lord.

Now we come to the understanding of "You shall not commit adultery." Adultery is not a sin of the physical part of what people understand. Sex between a man and a woman, man and man, and woman and woman is *never* a sin in the eyes of the Lord—it is a *natural feeling*, and it is part of our physical needs in our sexuality. These feelings that come from the Lord your God are destroyed by the mouth of the false prophet. The false prophet brings upon mankind the loss of one of the most beautiful things in life: our sexuality. You must come to understand adultery in spiritual terms. The false prophet has made people believe that adultery is a physical deed because it is such a great feeling, in the great adventure, to have sex with each other. What God meant about adultery is to not worship anyone in our life in front of the Lord our God. In other words, do not love any man more than you love God.

God has to be the *first* in the eyes and in the soul of a human being. God must be *first* inside your heart. Loving God must come to be where you place no man between yourself and God. Even if you think a person in the form of a human being is a blessing to you, your *faith in God* must be the *first* and the *only one* that you believe in before all other human understanding in front of the Lord your God. You must come to understand that God is *first* in your life—not second but first.

You must believe in your feelings and in the Scriptures before you believe any church or religion of the earth. In any subject in life that consists of knowledge, God must be *first*. Otherwise, you will commit adultery. Loving people is important. God tells you to love your brother as yourself, but religion tells you to judge people as good or evil. This is not loving your brother. This is not only replacing the Word of God but also replacing God himself. I tell you, in truth, that if you believe in any organized religion, you are in adultery. If you take a little preacher of the earth and believe him in front of your God, or if you believe your priests in front of God, you are committing spiritual adultery. Of all God's laws, adultery is the toughest one to understand because the religions of the earth just didn't understand that it is a spiritual law. So they made a teaching of their own against the flesh. That false teaching was done by the curse of God upon organized religion. Mankind was punished because the most beautiful feelings in humanity were cursed by the tongue of the false prophet. God gave them nothing to understand in the world of adultery.

They did not understand that adultery is a spiritual transgression, so like every other thing in life, mankind could not understand that they brought the curse upon themselves for believing that having sex was such a great sin in their mind. They condemned one of the greatest values in human suffering. Sex was not allowed by the falsehood of the false prophets. They condemn having sex with each other, and they condemn the people who broke these laws. They send these people to the *fires of hell* because the Lord has made it impossible for them to penetrate the most beautiful gifts the Lord has brought to mankind. For example, since the Catholic Church believes in the adultery of the flesh, the Lord sent in their little mind of locusts, they have to believe that their priests are *cursed by God* since they are not allowed to have a woman in their bed like decent men. This false church fabricated an understanding that it was a mortal sin for priests of the church, not to be consecrated as a priest if they sleep with a woman in the simple pleasure of life itself.

Now let's go to "You shall not steal." I must attack the Catholic Church with this commandment also because they put in the mind of man that they had to support this false church in the value of *money* in order to be part of the Catholic Church. The church received money that they did not earn or sacrifice themselves for. They made people believe that if they did not pay homage to the church in the value of money and if they didn't support the church, they wouldn't be able to receive the Kingdom of God. Organized religion says that they are the people who understand God and you should pay them to tell you about God and the salvation of man. These are some of the *greatest lies* that were ever told on earth. These lies were told from generation after generation to the people in the land of the locusts that could not understand the Lord their God. They could not understand because they failed to please God first in front of that evil church. People began to believe what these churches claimed was true. The value of the false sacrifice of the church is the biggest thief—stealing from one to take the values of others and claim it for himself. Everything that you take from others must be brought back to them in the values of our physical and spiritual needs that live inside of us for right over wrong.

The tenth commandment of our Lord is "You shall not covet." We must come to the point of understanding that jealousy is a feeling that we all have inside ourselves to try to be better than others. This is where people always think on the other side of the understanding of man and *undervalue* their role in life. Everyone thinks that his value is above other people's value, and that becomes sin in our society of human living. We are supposed to strive to be equal to each other. We can be satisfied just by being one in the intelligence of ourself without claiming to be more intelligent than others. Just_be satisfied with what you have and what was given to you by the Lord God of the Creation. Be satisfied that you are not more important than others in the dignity of just being a human being. Be satisfied among your brothers and be equal to all. Do not think that if a person is smarter than you, he is better than you, and don't think that if an individual is more advanced in the truth, he is better than you. Just think of yourself in the simple way of being human. That is enough for the Lord to give you life everlasting.

Love the Lord your God because these are the commandments that God has given you to *love one another*. Don't think that because you are more educated than your brother, he has less of an education, and don't think that others are better than you. Just think in your simple little soul that you love the Lord your God and work to abide by the Lord's commandments and his laws. Obey all his commandments in the value of life. Loving God is obeying his commandments because if you obey his commandments and laws, you will guide yourself within the boundaries of righteousness, where human beings hurt no one and they value everybody in the power of himself. Give to others the same intelligence that the Lord has given you, and share in everything that you know. Try to learn and understand the glory of intelligence with each other.

I must tell you here that no one person is the teacher above anybody else and you should place *no one* in front of your soul. The Lord is the one and only Savior in all the benefits of intelligence where you save yourself with the knowledge gained through the teaching of the Lord. You will come to know that what was taught to you is the truth. You guide yourself with the truth because you *love* the Lord your God in the value of the divine spirit that He placed in each one of us. Loving God is loving the truth in your soul with what makes sense in reality and common sense. I just cannot put all the knowledge that I got from the Scriptures and explain it any better than that. Because of this, we are dedicated to *love* the Lord with all our souls—the God of Abraham, Isaac, and Jacob—the god of reality and common sense.

Next, we are coming to the understanding of driving out the nations. This means driving out all false religions on the face the earth from the more sophisticated faith to the least sophisticated faith. The Lord has the intention of destroying every false religion on the face of the earth, but He will do it in time. Even though these false religions live outside the truth, it is still important to keep them until *true religion is understood* because the beast inside the human spirit would destroy the world. God will bring patience to protect the innocent and to save his flock for the truth. God cannot destroy all the religions in one day because he's not a magician. He has to take out false religion step by step until mankind begins to understand heaven and the way it works in God's Creation. He will be on the side of the innocent, and he will protect them until his plan comes in motion where there is no religion on earth that will survive the day of the Lord.

The time will come to break the yoke of the bull, the false teaching in the value of feelings inside the human heart. The truth will come to bring you home into the valley of common sense and reality, where the truth will live forever. God will come to destroy all these religions, both strong and weak, one by one, because none of those religions can enter his kingdom. Each person must look at his own soul going in the salvation of the truth that will come to be what the truth really is. He will defeat *all* that is against truth, and nothing can prevail against it. This is because truth is life, and more than that, it's life everlasting, and if you enter into life everlasting, you will come to understand that Satan and his lies will come to be no more. When the lies are destroyed, all those who live in lies will also be destroyed. All those who live in lies have made their kingdom of lies in the religion of lies and cannot enter the Kingdom of God.

Try to understand that each one of us is human and we all struggle in the faith of the Lord to understand the power of our

Father in heaven. Being human means being weak in spirit. When you are weak in spirit, you tend to forget the good life the Lord has given you. When you make any sacrifice in your life, offer it to the Lord *every time* to make that sacrifice count in the value of heaven. You forget that the Lord controls your suffering and your pain, and you must offer that pain and suffering to the Lord.

What do I mean by offering your sacrifice to the Lord? As an example, I have pain to bear and I get angry at the Lord because of it. Then I look at myself and I say, "Look at all that I have to be thankful for. Next, I'm angry because all the things that I love the most are challenged by my sacrifice." Sacrifice is just that. In the book of Deuteronomy, we are told to never appear before the Lord empty-handed. That is offering sacrifice. Whenever you appear before the Lord, which means to worship him and to ask him for knowledge and wisdom, you must bring a sacrifice. You have to give something to the Lord in order to get something from him, and just like every other subject in life, the hard work and sacrifice comes *before* the reward. That is how you prove yourself worthy of the reward. Remember that many are called but few are chosen. If you wish to be chosen, you must first prove yourself worthy of being chosen by *doing the work first.*

We sometimes forget, in our common sense, to remember that the Lord is the Lord and he's always there to make us understand the difference between a "sacrifice" and a "curse." Understand well here that a *curse* is something that happens in your life to punish you so severely that you cannot fix it, like losing a child or losing a parent—it is very painful. But understand well that a sacrifice is different from a curse because a sacrifice is something that you can fix inside yourself and change the stupidity that's in your heart in order to become wiser. A curse is something that you cannot fix, such as when somebody dies in your life whom you love very much, and you cannot change it. This is because a curse is *more severe* than just a sacrifice in the power to understand the Lord.

Understand that the Lord wants to straighten you out, and if you do not straighten out with the Lord, then He extends your sacrifice to a curse because you do not listen to the Lord your God. You live like a stiff-necked zombie, and you don't want to hear the truth. So the severity of your sacrifice becomes a curse, and next thing you know, you are in terrible pain and things don't go well for you. Try to understand that the one thing that the Lord wants of *all* of us is to be wise in the wisdom of his common sense and his reality.

If you forget the Lord your God and don't remember these things that I tell you, you will not be able to fix anything, and all your pain and suffering will be worthless. All the Lord wants to do is fix you, make you into a better person, and bring you to do what you should be doing. Learn the wisdom that you must conquer into who you are and what you're striving for. Understand well here that you should love the Lord your God and try to hear what He is telling you in your soul. Try to observe his law to the maximum power of your understanding, and try to obey His laws and decrees to gain his favor on the side of truth, where you can *live* in the freedom of the heart. Love your brother as yourself in the brotherhood of human feelings in their equal fashion. Remember, that what is pain and suffering for you is also pain and suffering for your brother who is equal to you in the family of feelings.

Now because Israel is righteousness, you must understand one thing: The children of the Lord are part of the salvation in the world of men. God is not looking for anyone to be perfect, but to be fair in true justice. Each one of us is human and weak in our physical understanding of the values of others, but understand well that God did not choose us because we are perfect and we obey the law. He chose us because of our weakness. The Lord himself created us, and each one of us is who we are and what our life has been. The Lord chose us because of the power of the one great sin that you cannot enter, and that great sin is our arrogance and our sophistication. We believe that we are better than anyone, and we act in the judgment of others. This is where a person believes in himself and takes his set of laws above the laws of God and claims his salvation in front of others.

When you believe that you are better than others, that is the greatest sin of all. That's where the separation of the goats and the sheep comes in and determines the truth and the value of what they believe just to be higher and mightier than the rest of the people of the earth. I tell you in truth that those who believe they are higher than others are equally guilty of losing their salvation to the Kingdom of the Lord your God. I tell you this so you would know whom the Lord chose and for what purpose. The humble and the people who don't think anything of themselves will be first, and all the people who believe themselves to be better than others will become last because the justice of the Lord works very mysteriously, and no one can claim a value before the Lord and say to others that the Lord has saved him in front of others. The only choices that belong to mankind comes from the Lord and brings the crop of value in the destiny of life and in the salvation of the Lord. The Lord is the truth, and He will take first those who are closest to the truth and those who claim no victory before the Lord. He who feels worthless in the sight of the Lord will come to be first and he who believed himself to be first will be last. This is *how* the Lord chooses people.

Next, we come to the understanding of the golden calf. From the beginning of time, man always tried to find an easy way to worship some kind of a higher power above themselves. People look, in goodness, to find a good man that people can call God. They look where people appear to be better than others. They need to find someone who is good enough to be God because they do not see or hear the true wisdom in their hearts, and they cannot *comprehend* what God looks like. They have no idea that God speaks in their soul, so people are always trying to find an image of someone to replace God with. People think that if you're good enough as a human being and you speak well, you must be a God figure. This is how mankind determines who God is in their mind.

Mankind, in their little mind of Eve, the wife of Adam, always seems to fabricate an image of God in their minds. This is where the false image of Jesus comes in. They made a false god out of a man because he came with great speech and great wisdom. They made a god in the shape of someone good and fair in the justice that he spoke with. The whole world started worshipping the golden calf in the image of Jesus and made him God Almighty because of the weakness of the mind. People worship the birth and the life of Jesus. They worship everything they can find on Jesus that was good in his life, and then they worship his death on the cross, which is the greatest injustice. They all felt bad for the death of this man, so they placed a cross in front of their church to worship, to make sacrifice to, and offer their life to him like he was the Almighty God. You see, this was meant to be so that people would worship Jesus as God and offer their sacrifices to him. They believe that this man will bring peace in their life because they think he is God. The gold calf is inside the imagination of the Christians, Catholics, and all organized religions. They have to make themselves some kind of a good God to pray and offer sacrifices to. Fully grasp here that those who worship the gold calf will refuse to give up this image before the Lord in order to keep worshipping Jesus, and they will enter the tomb of fiberglass because they are stiff-necked against the side of the Lord.

The earthquake will come and swallow them into a tomb of fiberglass in the generation of the technology of time, and it will remain in there forever and ever because they refused to stop worshipping the gold calf and repent of their sin. They idolize a man of physical form in front of the Lord our God, and in that tomb, they will remain in the greatest earthquake the world has ever seen, where the flesh does not disappear and will remain in the dead tomb forever because they remain stiff-necked. Worshipping a false God has brought them into that worthless tomb that they paid with their own money to be buried in. That will be the punishment of the Lord for those who live in arrogance and sophistication. They believed they were right to worship the gold calf that has no wisdom and no sacrifice to bring forth to the Lord your God.

The Lord set his tablets of the law like the first one—the original tablets that he had given to Moses in the teaching of the law. The law remains in the same value as the first set of tablets. Let me ask Christianity and the Catholic Church a few questions: On the first tablet that Moses brought to mankind, was there anything that told mankind to worship a man before the Lord our God? Those tablets tell you of the Ten Commandments of our Lord, and there is *nothing* mentioned in those commandments that man had to worship another man in order to be in the salvation of the Lord. Was there anything on these tablets that refer to the Lord and tells you that in the coming time, there would be a man who everyone will have to worship in order to receive the Kingdom of God? Was anything written on the first stone tablets that tell the people of the desert to make up a god of their own and to offer their sacrifice to that man? Is there anything in all the Scriptures that says you must worship Jesus as the son of God? The only thing that I can see is that people could not understand the spiritual part of the Scriptures to understand that you cannot worship a man before the Lord your God. The weakness of the physical part of the mind brought you to bow down on your knees and worship a man of flesh before the Lord your God.

I tell you in truth that you *cannot* worship any human being who has ever lived on this planet or anywhere else in human understanding. The life of another man is not your salvation. Understand fully that your salvation comes from the Lord and the Lord alone. The salvation of man does not belong to Jesus or to any other man. A human being has the hardest time to save himself from falsehood and, therefore, cannot save anyone else because the salvation of the Lord only comes from the Lord Himself. It cannot be transferred to anyone who claims the power of the Lord and tells you that they are the one who saves souls in front of the Lord.

The false prophets of this world claim the value of saving souls in front of the Lord, and that is a *big lie* that come out of their mouths. Only the Lord can save your soul, not a man with the little wisdom of the locust of the earth. Locusts are just little critters that stumble onto the ground of the dirt of the earth, like we all are, yet they claim to save other people's souls. No one on earth can stop people from physically dying because the Lord decides when it is your time to die. The same goes with the spirit. No one on earth is allowed to save other people's souls. You, false prophets, will have a hell of a time to save your own soul and enter the Kingdom of God because of your pride in claiming that God gave you the power to save souls. This false power that you claim was only ordained into a ministry of the earth in the value of a little locust. And remember that a locust is a little critter of the earth where you have to jump from one verse of the Scriptures to the next because you are just too weak to understand anything in full. You have to jump around and try to find yourself in your own soul.

Love and obey the Lord. Come to the power to understand how to love the Lord your God. Work to obey the Lord your God with all that you are and all that you have, and love the Lord in the power of what makes a man holy as your Father in heaven is holy. You must come and worship the God whom you don't even know and obey his rules that you haven't got a clue of what they mean. In order to love God, you must first learn to understand God. Next, you have to understand His laws, and in order to obey them, hear and listen to His laws in your spirit, in your soul, and in your heart. If you do not read the laws of God in your own soul and think about it, in the wedding feast of your mind and spirit, how can you understand the laws of God?

You have to marry the mind with the spirit in order to receive the laws of God in the brotherhood of life on earth with other people. And you have to *obey* the laws in your *spiritual understanding*, where all laws are first in the calculation of your intelligence. You must come to make the laws of God *first* before you make any laws of your own, and you have to obey them first and for all time. You just don't read them, ignore them, and say, "Well, they don't make any sense to me." You have to learn to make sense with the laws in order to obey them. You cannot learn the law and say, "I live my life according to my law, where I can cheat people as long as I get away with it. I can use people and steal from them as long as I'm not punished for it." Or "I can kill and fool people as long as no one knows about it and I can get away with it."

You cannot believe in these things because the laws that you made for yourself are *not* the Laws of God that you're supposed to obey in the value of *right over wrong*. If you believe that you can get away with anything that is not part of the truth, just think again. Understand that what you believe to be your laws are *not* the laws of God, and if you break the laws of God and replace them with your own laws, things will not go well for you. You will be buried in the tomb six feet underneath the ground where there is no way out because you have broken the laws of the Lord your God and believed in your own laws. Every time you break the laws of God, you offend your brothers and take something away from them in spirit that you don't deserve to have. To obey the Lord is try to understand what is fair in the justice of love. You must break your own set of laws and stop claiming the value of these laws in front of the Lord your God. Understand well what comes from the value of your own laws versus the power of the Almighty God.

Next, we come to the one place of worship. Understand that the one place of worship is not in any church. That's the worst place to go to gain the understanding of the Lord because this is where you feel the presence of the false god. You believe that the Lord lives in that church, which is a belief that you made up on your own. You feel good, and you believe that you're in the house of the Lord because you went to church. But I tell you in truth that the people who go to church to find the Lord there will be the last to be able to find the Lord because the House of the Lord is *inside your soul*, where reality lives.

The common sense of human intelligence is *not* in some building of stone made by the hand of man. No church of such magnificent power to understand can possibly be built by the hand of a human being because the House of the Lord is something precious. It contains the tabernacle of your soul in the spiritual value that comes to form common sense and reality in the presence of human thinking. So much can be known inside the heart of a human being that *no* church and *no* earthly building can be built to house the spirit of a human being.

The House of the Lord, inside of a human being, is the greatest foundation where the luxury of the spirit can be understood and where you draw knowledge to come to the wisdom of such power in your growing need to understand life itself. Don't try to worship in a man-made church—a cave of worthless value where the truth cannot be found and that people call the house of God. God does not live there and does not produce anything in the value of intelligence by the hands of the false prophet. Just ask God, and what He will tell you is exactly where you should *not* go to find your answer. A liar is a liar and does not know where to go. So how can you find out where to go when you cannot question a man who doesn't know the truth? Question him all you want. Even if he tries to tell you where to go to worship God, he will not tell you the truth because he claims he knows how to save souls. Do not trust the liars of the world in the *false* house of worship. Trust in the Lord your God and ask Him in your own house of your own soul where to go and how to get there into the reason that makes sense to your spirit. If you go somewhere and enter the wrong house and question the wrong people, you will learn the *wrong* answer. You will think you are right because you went to the wrong house, and those are the wrong people who told you where you are going.

Next, we come to understand that worshiping God can bring you to the wrong house and to the wrong answer by worshipping people in front of the Lord. If you want to know the truth, ask the *one* who has the truth and you will benefit from the truth. But if you ask a false prophet to tell you about the truth, he will send you in a direction away from the truth. You will not be able to understand the truth because you just did not go to the right source of information and you asked the wrong person. If you think that Catholic priests can tell you where to go in truth, try to understand that they will tell you to go where you should not go, and you will be in the wrong house at the wrong time to understand the wrong things.

This is what happens when you worship other gods. To the wrong person, you ask a question and understand that this is the reason you will get the wrong answer. The ideas of the false prophet are as many as the grains of sand on the seashore because they claim to be the ones sent from God who will *inform* you of the truth. But you are asking the wrong questions of the wrong god—they cannot tell you where the truth is because they did not find the truth themselves. They will lead you to believe in the wrong god in their physical value because their common sense is the same common sense of the locust that they picked up themselves to make lies with, and they will tell you to go the wrong way. When you worship the wrong god and you obey the wrong set of laws, how can you give the right advice or the right answer to those in need? *What is false is false*, and you cannot restore falsehood with more falsehood.

Next, we come to clean and unclean food. What you spiritually eat must be clean in the reality and the common sense of intelligence. You cannot eat anything that makes no sense or try to understand what makes no sense because your spirit was created in the in the valley of truth. Your spiritual understanding is created for the truth and common sense. If you *swallow lies* that live outside common sense and reality, you will become sick in the weakness of your mind because these lies are *not clean*. If somebody tells you that God sent a man to the earth to be God, I tell you that it doesn't make any sense because inside of you, you are a human being and you know a human being cannot think for the whole world. Mankind only has the power to understand common sense and reality, one thought at a time. If you try to use a human being and make mankind believe that he can possibly be God, this is unclean because each one of us as a human being does *not* have the power of God.

You *cannot* and *must not* believe that Jesus had the power of God, even though they tell you this totally *ignorant* statement and try to prove it to you with their fancy little Christian teaching that Jesus is the son of God and is equal to the father. Jesus spoke one sentence at a time, had one thought at a time, and spoke one parable at a time, and that makes him human. If you're human, it would be unclean to call yourself a god before God. I don't think that Jesus called himself a god, but I think the false prophet of the world who could not understand made him a god with their unclean souls and made him equal with God. If they only understood God, which they did not, they probably would have tried to destroy the ideas that Jesus is God, and they would not call him the son of God manifest.

Jesus, in the parables, calls himself the *son of man*, and the son of man is the history of mankind. Jesus was part of the history of man, and that is why he calls himself the son of man. This means that he would be part of the story of man because God gave us the son of man. Jesus was born from a man and a woman in a simple understanding that he was the son of man.

Where the story comes from is that Jesus was designated the son of God in AD 325. Jesus was designated the son of God by the false religions at the time of the first council of Nicaea, when all the religions of the time got together and, with their lack of knowledge, made Jesus the designated son of God. This was the biggest lie that was ever told, because they did not have the authority to make a statement like that and call a man before God the designated son of God. *Organized religion has always been wrong*. They always make statements with huge lies in the arrogance and their sophistication of thinking that they know better. They are the ones that designate the big lies. That food is *unclean* and has been swallowed by the human race, time and time again. This unclean food first fools those that have fooled themselves and then passed that the ignorance of lies to the poor and the helpless who don't know any better.

Mankind has been eating this unclean food for almost 1,700 years, and it has repeatedly said that Jesus was the son of God by each generation that came after. It was fed to the world, time and time again, until the time comes that we have all these diseases of the spirit of humanity for worshipping a false god. Mankind has been eating unclean food generation after generation until it comes to this day where the world is lost and poisoned by the false food of the spiritual value of a false god. They have lost the human spirit, and now the human spirit is shipwrecked on the desert island with no water to drink, meaning no reality to extinguish the fire that burns in their souls.

People make careers out of this false ministry without knowing and understanding the one true God. They are feeding this poisonous food to the children of God, generation after generation. They have replaced the Almighty God with the falsehood that Jesus was the designated son of God. So now, the majority of the world is worshipping falsely because they believe that Jesus is the son of God. if every one of us, good or bad, small and great, would understand the divine form of intelligence, we would hold the son of God as the way of speaking the truth. Always remember that *no man* is God above any other man.

Now we will understand tithes. Make sure that you put aside your tithes of the value of where you are in the animal that is inside you. Try to understand here that you were created from an animal. After the Lord placed the spirit inside you, you had millions of years of being an animal first. When the Lord placed the spirit inside of you, that became the human spirit. You still felt your animal being, and that's why we have so much crime and disorder in the world.

God created mankind and gave a small spiritual understanding to manifest intelligence to a higher point, where you can create for yourself a place to live in human understanding. But you have to destroy and always put aside the part of you that came from the animal being to understand the full measure of human thinking. You have to go deep and set aside that there will always be 10 percent of your feelings that come from the animal being into the human being. That is how crimes are committed (by your animal instinct), and if you do not educate yourself to understand the power to go above the animal, you will have those feelings inside you that you cannot put aside. Say to yourself that you are no longer an animal, but there is still 10 percent of you that remains part of the feelings of the animal.

When you get angry at someone, you feel like killing him. That is the animal inside of you, and if you don't try to control that animal inside of you, you will do the most stupid thing that you can ever imagine. To save yourself from this stupidity, you must *feel* the animal inside you and *correct* that instinct that lives inside of us. You still feel like an animal, so you must consider yourself to be 10 percent animal and 90 percent human to complete a human being. Understand the feeling that gets inside of you when you get angry or hungry or when your needs are not fulfilled in the full value of your feelings. When no one wants to hear what you have to say to make things right for yourself, you still feel the instinct of the animal that's inside you, and you must set it apart from your spirit in order to control yourself as a human being.

Try to understand that the Bible was written for you to understand these things that the Lord made in the accomplishment of his Creation. That's why *none* of us are perfect. The Lord left inside of us 10 percent of the animal to accomplish his Creation. He did not make us completely human because then we would not go out of control and we would not understand the full circle of our creation. The part of the animal that's inside each one of us grows in wrong inside us where wrong was meant to destroy right *until* we fully understand our animal. Here, I'm going back to Cain and Abel to explain to you that all your feelings come from the Almighty God, but God used an animal and turned them into human beings.

For that purpose, God left 10 percent that is still a part of the animal inside of us to bring together *falsehood.* The wisdom of the Lord could not find a way to create justice without keeping part of the animal; otherwise, justice would have no balance to *be* justice. By keeping 10 percent of the animal inside a person, when a person feels neglected or mistreated, anger must show up to prove your side of the animal. Even the Lord could not find wisdom that made us perfect because if we were perfect, we would need no one to worship. So in that little 10 percent comes a new learning to be better and to accomplish greatness and still be part of the animal that gave the victory to that 10 percent of the animal.

Animals do not need God to control themselves—it is their *instinct* that controls them. The 10 percent of the animal that's inside you is part of the wisdom of the Lord to keep the animal of the human being in control. Worship God in the wisdom of the wise to understand how to treat each other in the glory of intelligence. When you *touch* the animal that's inside us, you have feelings such as hunger, pain, and the need for a place to stay. Use that part of the animal to accomplish the creation of mankind where you come to feel all the things that you need to physically survive. God gave mankind all the tools of preserving our lives in the luxury of our needs, and we must strive to accomplish all our spiritual needs inside our soul.

Now we come to understand the year for cancelling debts—your debt to others that you must cancel in the justice of the Lord, where you live and gain value for yourself. Since you are born into a world of value, you must consider that value to be of the things that we need and a few creative values above yourself. You think that all you have is yours because you placed your name on it, but you have to share the values of the human mind.

Remember that, in the last chapter, we learned that we were lifted above the animal to became humans but you still have 10 percent of that animal inside you. This comes to a value of 100 percent of all that you owe. But in the legality of the Lord, you don't need all that you can take even though you claim to have earned everything. Here, you must understand your needs and also the needs of others, who are equal to you. If you need a bed to sleep in, others also need a bed to sleep in. If you need a house to live in, then others also need a house to live in. And if you need food to eat, others also need food to eat. Understand that it's your talent (prosperity) that comes from the Lord who has given *equal share to all.* If you have more talent than others to pursue the gain of your needs, and if there is some of your needs left over from your crop, you need to share your talent in the values of all mankind that is equal to each other.

The 10 percent of your animal being will help you to gain for yourself all that you can eat. You are allowed to control what is underneath your feet in the value of the beast that's inside you in your attempt to keep everything for yourself. But you must *cancel the debt of others* to the value of what you do not need for yourself to survive. Just let others claim their values that are equal to you, and the Lord will always bless you and give you great talents to accomplish great dreams of success where value is given for value. What you give is of equal value for you to accomplish what you are willing to take for yourself. What was freely given to you by the Lord is what you should freely give to others and do not claim back from others what you do not need.

Now we come to the understanding of how to free your servant and the power that the Lord is giving you—great wisdom. If you have been wrong about something, you must come to admit that you are wrong in front of other people that you have inflamed in the mind and the spirit of others as they realized it wasn't really true. You must admit to them that what you told them was wrong so you can free those who listen to you and bring them closer to the understanding of the law. If you made a mistake about anything, make sure you are telling them that you have learned to understand the Lord's words in better terms. You must admit that you were wrong about what you said. Remind them that you are human and you did not really understand what you said and that you were wrong to tell them something that is not true.

Many people who come out of the land of Egypt, meaning the land of false religion, did not really understand the Bible that well. If you talk about the Bible to anyone, they trust in you to understand the Scriptures in truth. They know that the Scriptures all have a special meaning, and it is your responsibility to not tell them anything that is untrue. So as a human being, you have to learn from the beginning where you are at the center of the desert like everybody else. Try to understand the word of the Almighty God and make yourself a *true teacher* in the word of God. Neither you nor anyone else can read the Scriptures and understand everything in them because the Lord has put a seal on the heart of all naive people, and they cannot penetrate the seal and gain the understanding of the Almighty God.

Understand that your firstborn means your *first notion* of what truth is. The idea comes into your mind, then it comes into your spirit. Next, you have to verify these ideas with the Lord. If you tell someone where you made a mistake, you must reopen the case and tell them what it means. Remember that we and everybody else are, in human terms here, *human*. To understand the power of what the Lord means here, He had to take both mind and spirit in the wedding feast of intelligence and marry the mind with the spirit, where both mind and spirit can agree with it so you can come to understand what is the *true meaning* of the Almighty God.

Your servant is the one who listens to you, so you must make sure that you fool no one with the Scriptures, not even yourself. The truth of the Scriptures sets you free, but if you happen to make a mistake because you are human, make sure that you admit that your mistake has hurt you because you have to be human to be part of the Kingdom of God. There is 10 percent of you that is in the animal, and sometimes, you understand in the way of the animal, and you must correct yourself at all times. Always make sure that you speak the truth to all who hear you because they will become your servants in spirit. They will listen to and believe what you say in the truth of the Creation. Your servant listens to you because they think you're wiser than them. Make sure you don't bring any arrogance or sophistication to prove your feelings to be higher than theirs. You should strive to be equal in the value of what your feelings are. *Make sure that you are a man of truth and reality*. What you have received from the Lord did *not* come from your mind, yet you start thinking that you are higher than others.

Make sure that you keep your soul to the level of human understanding. Don't go too high to make people believe that you are better than what you are. Just tell the world the simple truth and correct yourself when you think you are wrong. Understand the power of the Lord that's inside you where corrections are most important. Try to feel that the Lord has blessed you greatly by giving you the little truth that you understand, and make sure you are humble enough to take care of yourself. Correct yourself in front of other people when you are wrong.

Next, we are going to the teaching of Passover. Understand well that Passover is a festival inside you. Every time you learn something in the Scriptures, you should celebrate inside yourself. This is not a celebration like the celebration of the earth where mankind dances and plays music, but the dancing and the music take place inside your heart. Understand that Passover comes once a year on the physical Earth, but every time you bring truth to a better understanding of the Scriptures in your soul, you should be dancing with the music of the intelligence of humanity that plays inside yourself.

The music and the celebration of the soul inside of you will make you very happy to be alive because it opens a door to heaven and unlocks something that you could not figure out before now. You come to this marvelous knowledge that rings great music inside your soul to *understand truth*. Like everything else, you must endure the *sacrifice* of learning. You should be happy that the Lord sends it inside of you. Now you see where the crossing of the Red Sea is. This is the power to understand what it means to cross over and understand something that all the people around you did not understand. You can bring the part that you understand to your friends and family and introduce them to your new festival of Passover, where you can now open the Red Sea and see where people believe in falsehood. This is where you were in the land of the lost soul before you understood the music inside of you. Understanding God's value is when you are able to understand the music and the dancing of the soul. To cross over any Scriptures is your Passover—to understand things that you could not understand before—and that is your great power to unlock the door and see what is written in heaven. This is the value that heaven is a great knowledge to see what has been written by the hand of the Almighty God.

You are *not* being saved by the understanding of Christianity, the Catholic Church, or any other religion on Earth. You are being saved in your soul by receiving the key to the door of heaven, opening the door and seeing what is going on there with what was made to be and what God has planned for the human race to understand life everlasting. The plan of God is to bring life everlasting to our little knowledge of the earth that will bring you to the understanding of truth. This is the music and the power to dance on the floor of heaven, where you have established a strong floor to walk upon and to dance about to the music that makes the human heart, in such happiness, *grow* and *understand*. Heaven is *not* a place that you go to after you die but a place where you live in knowledge and learn the things that were so hard for humanity to win the glory of understanding…where you can look into heaven with your little soul and understand what God is and what heaven is.

Now we come to understand your firstborn animals. I have told you before that you have ten of your spirit that is still in animal form inside of you, and when you pass over from the animal form to a spiritual form, what was physical then becomes spiritual. Offer the debt of your animal where you have a firstborn animal that just came as spiritual value in your soul. Offer what you didn't know before so you can become a spiritual power to live in heaven and understand the spiritual creatures of God that are created for you. This is the value of being raised to a level where you can understand the same God who created you inside the form of his own spirit. You can cross over to the physical power and to the spiritual power of what you are and keep on learning every single day of your life. You can come to live in and understand heaven and earth. Follow the laws of your mother the earth and your father in heaven and you will understand the true purpose of your life and your happiness where you cross into a land that you never thought even existed.

Now you live in the value of heaven because you crossed over into the land where your wisdom has risen to the point where you can understand this marvelous glory of heaven that so many preachers and false prophets have tried to understand before you but never could understand because they did not worship the Lord their God. They worshipped the image of men and forgot to worship the Lord their God. It is not your spirit that makes mistakes with your animal being because you believe that we are an animal. *Believe in truth*, and your faith comes out of you. Then the animal power to understand becomes easier. That is why you keep your spirit on top of your animal so you can understand the value of the spirit.

Now we come to the *festival of weeks*. Learning is *both* short-term learning and longer-term learning. Understand that you won't learn everything in one day, but you are learning the process of time into it. You learn by the day, the week, the month, or the year, and every week you are going to learn something new in the Kingdom of God. Learning comes in the sequence of time, so you learn it in any of these time frames. What you learn in the festival of weeks is the power that each week will have something new on the table of reality and common sense. If you become familiar with the Scriptures and you're an honest person who does not believe in all the lies of the false prophet, you will learn every single week something that will increase your knowledge. You will learn more and more so you can come to live in the Kingdom of God. The Kingdom of God comes in the way of learning, and when you open your spirit to learning the truth, you *cannot* belong to these false religions of the earth. If you believe what the false prophet tells you, at that point, you will be under God's curse and the Lord will stop you from learning anything. The Lord will destroy your spirit outside the truth because you failed to trust in Him for all of your learning. If you go to the false prophets and listen to them in their church of false value, then the Lord will put a curse on you and you will receive no food from heaven in your spiritual understanding.

You have to trust in the Lord your God every single day of your life without putting yourself in the hands of false religion that does not know anything of truth. They cannot bring you to a place that they have never been to themselves because they don't know where it is. False religion will bring you in the ignorance of falsehood to a place you don't want to be. If you bring your spiritual learning to the Lord inside your heart, the Lord will lead you on to understand marvelous things in the Scriptures that you will learn every single day and week of your life. There is only *one* Teacher and only *one* Holy God. If you put your faith in the false prophet of the earth, and if you believe in their false preaching, you will be a *lost soul* because of the curse that the Lord will place on you.

When you cannot learn anything in the Scriptures on your own, that is because the Lord has placed a curse on you because you go to someone else who doesn't really know what the truth is and you believe in them. This is how you lose your soul—by trying to understand what doesn't make sense and rejecting what does make sense in the values of the common sense of heaven. Understand that only the truth sets you free, and the truth comes from the King of Heaven with common sense and reality. This is where you get your information from, not from other people who think they know better than you and teach you nothing week after week after week and cannot penetrate the Lord's *true knowledge* because they themselves do not trust in the Lord. Instead, they placed their trust in the church or the ministry that never taught anything in the value of heaven.

Understand well here the journey in the desert after you cross the Red Sea on dry ground as the children of God's Word. That journey will bring you into the promised land and make you understand the crossing of the Jordan in the values of truth and the reality of common sense. This is where you must gain all your information in common sense and reality and from the truth itself, which is the *Lord our God*, who brought you out of the land of Egypt—meaning *out of false religion*. You must come to understand the Holy and Mighty God of Heaven inside your soul where truth is truly heard.

Now we come to understand the festival of Tabernacles—that little spiritual box for storing knowledge that comes to you from the Lord. This is where you store your knowledge and holy understanding of the Lord your God. You store in your tabernacle all your information that comes from the Lord your God in common sense and reality. Each spirit of understanding that comes inside of you is for protecting you in the value of the sword of heaven. I take everything that I have learned in truth, common sense, and reality, and I place it in my little container inside my heart. This gives me the freedom to *love* the One True God inside the truth and to place all information of truth in my tabernacle.

Here, you must come to understand the power of the curse of God when you worship other gods. If you make your preacher into the Assembly of God and believe him in front of the Lord your God, the Lord will curse you greatly and make you understand nothing in the value of heaven. You will be in darkness because you hear nothing and learn nothing of truth. The Lord will give you the fantasy world as a curse because you listen to the voice of the false prophet and you believe in their physical power of understanding the image of a man before the Lord your God. You are supposed to worship and to believe what comes out of your spirit.

If you do not understand what comes out of your spirit, you are under God's curse because you trust in the voice of the good speech maker who doesn't make any sense. You are supposed to believe what comes from the Lord *inside your temple* and not from what other people tell you. Open your spiritual understanding with your feelings and only agree with what you have heard from the Lord that comes through in your heart. Believe in the power of human understanding to the value of your soul, *not* from the soul of others. It's all right to hear something true coming out of every human being, but you will not fully agree with that truth until it comes alive inside your soul. This is because the truth is made to be born in your spirit, and only in your spirit can you learn the great value of heaven.

Fully understand that other people who do not speak the truth, common sense, and reality are not speaking the true word of God. Their teaching does not come from the Lord your God. If you worship with them and the stupidity that they impose on you to worship Jesus or any other gods, you will lose your soul. Try to understand that God has already put a curse on you and that you will not be able to see what is a false God and what is a true God. The difference between the teacher of falsehood and the teacher of truth is the former talks about the physical part of God that they made up in the assumption of their false value, and the latter is one who speaks the truth in the reality of truth. In the real Kingdom of God, you will come to the reality of the Almighty God—the One True God who gives you the common sense to understand the difference between lies and truth. If you fall into the lies of falsehood, you will worship a false God by believing that you are simply worshipping God, and there will be a very hard-fought battle inside you to understand the Lord your God.

Do not believe that God is physical like Jesus was physical. I do not believe that a man like Jesus is equal to God. He was not a son of God, but you must understand what God is. God lives in the spirits of all seven billion people on the Earth. You have the spirit of God—to control more than seven billion human beings, to understand everybody's problems, and to answer everybody's prayers and sacrifices. Jesus was a simple man of the earth whom God used to send his holy parables to mankind. He was just a simple man who brought to mankind an understanding of God's law in the way of common sense. The people of the world could not understand the Lord's laws because they didn't use common sense. This is where Jesus came, as a 100 percent human being, to teach us this common sense.

No man on earth, including Jesus, has the power of God over the Creation. God alone is God, and He cannot be replaced by any animal. There is no man of the earth that could possibly be called God. Even the Catholic Church calls the Pope *Holy Father* and thinks that he replaces God on earth. That is the most foolish belief in all of human history that people can come to that total stupidity of ignorance. It is the deceptive values of poor judgment to say to each other that this man has been raised to that power and can be praised in such an unlawful fashion.

No human being is allowed to be called God or the son of God in any human knowledge. The power of truth must live on to be the truth over all that man believes. This is because God is *mightier* and *greater* in human knowledge that can ever be understood by mankind, and you shall not make any statement that any human being could possibly have the might of the holy God of heaven. To claim that value by any human being is to have *no respect* for the might of the Lord your God. There is nothing on earth or anything above the earth, that can replace the might of God. How can a little locust of the earth that cannot even understand the simple Scriptures bring a man to the value and the might of God? We are all little creatures of the Earth inside a locust, understanding that counts for nothing in front of the mighty power of the spirit of the Lord.

Now let us go to the courtroom of the Lord. Come and understand the throne of the Lord and how it works. You will be judged according to your beliefs and what you have learned in the understanding and the justice of the Lord. You will be prosecuted if you did not learn anything or if you try not to learn anything and leave it to other people in some false religion to teach you how to worship God. These people of organized religion are people who have no value in the throne of the Lord.

Understand that you will be judged according to what you have learned. You will be judged by the Lord sitting on the throne. He will judge each man according to his value. You either try to understand the way of the Lord in your heart or you bury yourself, learn nothing, and expect others to teach you. You will be judged according to the justice of the Lord. Let's say you have someone who tried to learn but just didn't have the way to understand the Scriptures. Even though they tried, the Lord will have some kind of mercy on them and then will invite them to the great supper of the wedding feast. But if you hide or bury your talents, you will be judged accordingly. Those who try to fool others with their little understanding of the Scriptures will be judged accordingly.

The scroll of the Lord will be opened. It will be set up in a way that the revelation of God will judge mankind, and I can tell you that it will be done in justice and fairness to all divine knowledge. The wisdom of the Lord will take place, and no excuse made by people who were too lazy to try to understand for himself will be accepted. The power of the scroll of justice will be understood in human thinking and human understanding. This brings a value of justice where no human being, and no human thinking could possibly penetrate human understanding to understand the court of the Lord. You will be judged according to what you have learned or failed to learn. You will be judged by a justice so righteous that a human being will be surprised how the Lord kept records of all wrong that he has done to others, either in bigotry, judgment, or ignorance. You failed to improve yourself because of your laziness of not learning the truth.

The throne will be set up in the way of human beings' value of what you have conquered in love with all your brothers in the brotherhood of all human beings on the face of this earth. *God will judge you on your hate and on your love.* The standards by which you love or hate others will be the greatest value of all the judgment against you. All the blessings will be on your side if you try to love others and you did everything you could to love your fellow man. But if you did everything in your feelings to hate others, then you will be under the curse of the Lord because love, the priests of the Levi inside you, will be the greatest determination of your salvation that you can possibly understand.

Understand well that the court of the Lord will come to be where you fail in your evil feelings because you have failed to learn the consequences of what you believe. You have failed in the value of learning because learning is life, and in learning, you understand the power to do what is right. You will not become a human being that the Lord will choose because the throne of the Lord will judge you accordingly, in all of the power to understand and the power not to understand. Remember that you cannot hide because the Lord will cause you to think that you were right doing wrong, and there is no court and no judge in the world that can judge you fairly in such justice. Everything that you did according to what you have learned will be brought forth to bring you to the destiny of your dream in the values of justice.

Next, we come to understand the king. Understand well that we were created in intelligence with the power to understand. When the Lord chooses a king, He chooses the most powerful genius who brings all the truth to the light of mankind. A king is a genius in any field of human understanding. When you become king, you become a genius in the events of your life. The king is to reveal the power of the wisdom and to understand the greatest part of the wisdom of intelligence. To be king is to be a mastermind of intelligence and say the right thing at the right time. To become king is where you find the wisdom inside yourself. To be king in the land of your spiritual value is where you can break any stone, big and small, in the faith of the Lord your God in the huge mountain that comes to you in the teaching of the Scriptures.

Any one of you reading this book could be king and break the biggest stone by opening the Word of the Scriptures because that is the Word of God. And the Word of God should be opened in the book of spiritual value where you understand the power of the Scriptures inside yourself that can be translated into your little heart and spirit of the value of heaven. You must come to understand the King of Heaven, which is God. The power to receive the crown of all knowledge comes from the King of Heaven.

Now let us go and try to understand those detestable practices that people made up by the power of their own minds where they sit and worship idols and false gods in front of the Lord your God. This is when you do not fear the Lord and you think you are right when you can be so totally wrong by worshipping idols and idolizing men in front of the Lord your God. I want to tell you here that I bring the great Babylon to this—the mother of all prostitutes, the Catholic Church itself. I tell you that these people worship the life, the birth, and the death of Jesus. They idolize that man and made him God because they misunderstood the teachings from the New Testament. They worship his manhood from his birth to his death. They analyze everything in Jesus's life to be of value to them and call themselves Christians and children of God in front of the Lord.

Understand well that the value of their faith is against what the Bible tells you *not* to do. They take those detestable practices, and they bring it to the throne of God Almighty. They claim that if you don't practice this doctrine, you will go to hell, and they say that is a sin against the Almighty God. They also call the pope "Holy Father" and claim that he works on the side of the Lord. Understand fully that all these false practices and idol worshipping is what has been condemned by the Bible itself in the Old Testament. You cannot raise any human being, including Jesus, to the throne of God and worship a false god before the Lord your God. They also claim that their pope is infallible in front of the Lord. This is one of the greatest sins on the face of this earth where a little man in the land of locusts makes for himself a teaching from his little mind in the value of total darkness. This falsehood has been raised to such an evil practice where their teaching is in total pain of Satan, which is *all the lies of the world*!

Organized religion teaches people a practice that is *totally detestable* to the Lord. This is a practice that can no longer be tolerated by the Lord. I tell you all to come out to the beach that sits on the seven hills and fear no false god. Fear nothing in the values of her falsehood. If you do not practice what false religion tells you, then according to them, you will burn in hell—flesh and spirit in the fire that will consume you day and night forever and ever. This is a lie that will surely bring mankind into the very fire of hell that they have been preaching and scaring people with for the past two thousand years through fear, false teaching, and lies.

I tell you, in truth, to let the people who belong to the Lord our God alone. Set them free from that unworldly practice where men were made slaves in your church only because they were trying to gain the value of the Lord on their side. You evil men must stop that evil practice and restore the people to the soul of the Lord. You must admit how wrong you have been when you make people worship idols in the image of a man and your so-called saints that you all worship in front of the Lord your God. You have great sin to answer for. Call upon the Lord and change your teaching to the worship of the Lord your God by taking all those idols and all those images that you have introduced to people for so long and *destroy all those idols.*

Ask the Lord for forgiveness, all you popes, cardinals, and black robe priests in your false prophecy of misguiding the children of our God. Come to the Lord your God and turn away from that false practice by being humble in front of the Lord your God. Ask for the forgiveness of the Lord for all the great crimes that you have done in the value of lies. You are shipwrecked in your teaching and cannot go on believing in falsehood against all the Scriptures. I tell you, in truth, to keep away from that awful practice that you are ordained by the false prophet to practice.

Now we go to the *false prophet*. Understand well that if you are a false prophet, you will *never* understand the words of true religion. Whether you belong to the Catholic Church, the Christian teachings, or any organized religion of false value, the Lord has continued to condemn you because you worship idols, and you idolize people and men before the Lord your God. You must stop this practice and admit to the Lord and to your people how wrong it was for you to tell people to worship Jesus in front of the Lord and call him the son of God. God has a son, but his son is the common sense and the reality of common sense. Common sense is a spirit that lives inside mankind just like the truth lives inside mankind. But there is only one truth, one common sense, and one reality, and that is God Almighty.

You cannot jump like a locust and try to prove your case on the jump of the locust. You cannot believe that you have the truth and that you should be worshipped in front of the Lord. Your arrogance has brought you to the point where you made your soul sophisticated in front of the Lord your God, and you claim that you were ordained by the Lord your God. You are saying to the people that you represent God in this lie and you require yourself to believe it and to bring the side of the Lord to your own value that places you into the image of a man to be the one who replaces God on earth. What you said must be believed by all those who heard you, who came to your false practice, and listened to your word that you have made up to worship Jesus in front of the Lord.

God sent the Scriptures into the world, gave Moses the law on Mount Sinai, and told you *not* to worship the image of anyone, including Jesus. So *why* do you worship the Lord your God and tell everybody that you worship God but then turn your attention to Jesus in front of your assembly, where you feed falsehood to them and then claim that you speak in place of God Himself? Do you really think that God will give us the Scriptures so that you could ignore anything you want and worship to the satisfaction of your mind and get away with it?

Understand well that the Lord has a set of laws that have a *great value* in the justice of his throne, and the value of his laws and his decrees should have been honored by you in front of the world, but you made yourself a false prophet against the Lord your God by teaching with your mind and not in the feelings of your soul that told you, time and time again, to worship the Lord your God. You could not bear the idea of being wrong because all your feelings in your heart have been burned by your arrogance and your sophistication that made you believe that you were right. Time and time again, the Lord had told you in the Scriptures that it was wrong, but you cannot believe that it was *you* who taught falsehood. You made yourself believe that you will worship one true God, but you turn all your feelings and all your mind to worship Jesus in front of the Lord. Wrong is wrong and right is right, and right will overturn your own feelings when the laws of God come and hit you in the face of wrong over right. This will bring you in front of the Lord to be judged by the throne of the Lord your God.

Now we go to the cities of refuge. This is where your soul goes when you have been so wrong for so long in such a false practice and you told the whole world that you are from the Lord. This is where the justice of the Lord comes to *humble* those who claim the high ground in the Kingdom of God, and to prove to them that they are *last and not first* in the Kingdom of God. The cities of refuge are where you go to ask for forgiveness because you claim you did not know better. You thought you were doing what the Lord expects of you, but you did not really know how wrong you were. The cities of refuge are where you find refuge in the arms of the Lord even though you are so wrong because you failed to understand the words of the Lord your God in the value that you were created with.

But now you have to ask the Lord for forgiveness. You claim that you thought it was right to do what you did, but if you cannot admit that you were wrong for preaching falsehood, you cannot enter the Kingdom of God. To enter the Kingdom of God, you must humble yourselves before the Lord and thank Him for sending word to you that you are wrong by worshiping the image of a man before the Lord your God. Seek refuge in the Hand of God, be humble when you appear in front of the throne of the Almighty God, and claim that you need time to think about what you have been preaching. You must come to read the Old Testament, and you must make it count in your spiritual value, where you have lost yourself in the land of the image of Jesus. Destroy that old teaching in the ministries of your own soul, repent in humble deeds, and tell those around you that you have been wrong. This is your receipt for the wrong of your sin where you find refuge in the cities of refuge. Understand well that you can't be forgiven for your sins, and you cannot enter the Kingdom of our Lord with great success unless you humble yourself before the Lord and tell the people that you were not speaking on the Lord's holy side. You must tell them that you were wrong and that you had no idea that you were not on the Lord's side. You must live in the cities of refuge, and every day of your life, you must admit to others how wrong you were. Then you will come to find the Lord your God. The true God of Israel and the God of Abraham, Isaac, and Jacob, where you will learn the truth and the truth will set you free from all that nonsense that you used to believe.

Now we come to understand the witnesses in the soul of mankind. Someone is accused of having done wrong in the sight of the Lord, and you are a witness to what you saw in your own heart. You must bring the witness against someone who has done wrong in the sight of the Lord. You must bring the case of what you have witnessed against the truth of the Lord your God. You must bring a case against those who have preached falsely and who have made people believe in falsehood. Understand well here that you have to go to the teaching of the Lord and understand the value of the truth in front of the children of the Lord. You must bring the proof of wrongdoing in front of their own minds so they can see where they have been wrong when they taught falsehood that was not with the permission of the Lord to do so.

The witness must aim for truth in the reality of the Kingdom of God in front of the throne of the Lord. In the full value of wrong over right, the one who is the witness must prove his case by bringing to reality *the truth* of what he saw against the word of God. He must express the wrong that he has seen done against the throne of the Lord and bring this case to the Lord. I stand here, in my soul, and I bring witness of what I have seen done by the false prophet who claims a false value above themselves to teach without the authority of heaven and tries to replace the laws of God with their own laws. They claim to be righteous to the Lord by doing so, but they believe the values of heaven to be on the other side, away from the truth.

As a witness, I want to name these false prophets in the trial of the Lord. *What is wrong is wrong*. You thought you were ordained by Almighty God, but you were *not* ordained by God. You were ordained by men. I have witnessed in my life on earth that *none* of you priests, ministers of Christianity, and all the religions of the world were ordained by God. You were ordained by a little man of the earth. They didn't have the power of the theology to ordain anyone because they themselves did not understand the Scriptures. You don't understand the Scriptures today, and if you keep preaching that falsehood, you'll *never* understand the Scriptures and the salvation of life.

Now we are entering into the understanding of going to war. I must tell you now that this war on the battlefield will not be pleasant and people will fight to save their spiritual value. You will see the children of the real God become victorious at the end of the battle because the truth, common sense, and reality is God. In the end, you false prophets of the earth with your satanic lies will not be victorious. You will be defeated because it is written in the Book of Revelation that Satan and his angels who have been preaching false truth in the heart of the great dragon will come to be *defeated* and *destroyed* forever and ever.

It may take a thousand years to defeat Satan and the big dragon of false religion, but all false religions will surely crumble and fall over because the God who brings the truth is the One True God. No one can defeat the Lord because truth, common sense, and reality will end up being victorious at the end of the battle. And those who believe in truth, common sense, and reality will also be victorious in the end. Whoever wants to keep up with his falsehood can go on to where he will lose his soul. Anyone who lives outside the truth will be left to give up their life on the battlefield of right against wrong.

Next, we come to the atonement for an unsolved murder. The wisdom of the Lord will hide the truth about the murders of the world in the middle of the burning bush for justice. Those who have done wrong must continue doing wrong by killing the spiritual understanding and destroying the human spirit. They will continue to believe that they are right to do wrong, and that it was their ordination of falsehood that tells them they were doing right by killing the soul of their brother in the false teaching of their faith.

Those that raise themselves above the truth of the Lord will be ordained by the hand of the arrogant human being in the value of falsehood. I call it arrogance because of what was in their thoughts and motives in the sight of what they believe was a truth for them. They believe that they can replace God by making a group of human beings come to their church, and then they destroy and kill them in the false spirit of their faith. Understand well that those who don't accept any teaching outside the New Testament have been *burned* by the sun's scorching heat. Their minds became dull and useless because they failed to hear their spirit talking to them. They thought that voice was the voice of Satan inside them. They confused the voice of God with the voice of Satan. They created themselves a satanic religion of the mind, and they were happy to go against the Lord because they thought it was the voice of Satan inside their soul. They told themselves that it was the voice of Satan because they did not understand the voice of the Lord that lives inside man's spirit.

These people think that Satan is real, but the real Satan in the Scriptures is all the lies of the burning bush, where God is at the center and who makes lies look like the truth. They have been lying to themselves for so long that when they hear the truth, they think that Satan is talking to them. They will not turn from their sin because they believe that the truth is a lie. They are so weak in what they understand that they turned themselves into liars and claim that the Lord is on their side. What is not true in their lies of their lost soul becomes their truth. They believe lies to be truth in their little human understanding, but the Lord will come to destroy their lies because these false prophets murdered people by the millions. They claim the false victory of their soul, and they claim that they are right when they are so wrong. The Lord will make it impossible to repent because of their stiff neck that will not turn to the truth of Abraham, Isaac, and Jacob. They will lose their soul because the Lord does not need anyone who believes they are right even when they are so wrong and cannot see the divine knowledge of the Lord.

Now we come to the teaching of marrying a captive woman. If you become captured into the world of superstitious belief, your spirit will accept that superstitious belief just like Adam accepted Eve and went on to eat from the forbidden tree in the wedding feast of intelligence. They were fooled by those who think they are in authority over these people, and these people in authority will claim the false value of authority. They will not think about others, but they will make themselves known to be the authority over others. They will take the power of others to think for themselves and steal that power in the value of what God has created them to be in claiming that they were authorities and should be respected because of their claim.

But they are just liars who make such claims in front of others because it is *not* God that placed them in authority. They placed themselves in that false authority, and they think with their injustice that they are the head of authority. They made themselves to be important in front of the simple and the humble people. It makes them feel good because they filled themselves with lies over the authority of others. They married the selfish mind thinking and believing that they should be worshipped by others. They bring a curse on others by their own will.

I want to tell you here that if I am wrong and all the prophets of false religion are right by worshipping Jesus before the Lord your God, then the Bible would be wrong because I step on every stone to understand the Scriptures, and all the Scriptures that I encounter tell me that the Bible is right. The Bible tells me that the false prophets are the ones who are wrong because you are told in the Old and New Testaments to worship the Lord your God with all your soul and all that you are. Now you don't have to believe me, but I have spent forty years in the Scriptures trying to learn the power of the understanding of the Lord my God with all my soul and all that I have for myself. I came to this conclusion after reading the Bible for so long and making my heart central in the understanding of the Scriptures. I also came to the conclusion that the false prophets of the earth just don't have the *true teaching* of God because they worship Jesus in front of the Lord God and they claim a false deity as their god, and that is wrong. I'm sorry, but all Catholics, Christians, and all the other religions of the world who worship men before God *do not understand the truth about the Almighty God.* You are married to a slave girl that you captured with falsehood in your soul. Just keep on believing in your false gods, keep praying, offer your sacrifices to Jesus, and *you will lose your life.* Remember what the Lord has given me to reveal to you so you can understand the Kingdom of God and how it works.

Next, we come to the right of the firstborn. What is your firstborn? It is the first spirit that comes inside your soul that makes you understand the Lord your God. Your firstborn is the feeling that is inside you that tells you what to do, just before Satan and the lies of the world confuse your mind with what is not real. Your firstborn is what is real, and you have a right to believe in your first feelings. But someone comes and destroys your first feelings, which is to keep the Laws of God on your side. They do this by trying to make you look ridiculous in your feelings. But the right of the firstborn is to hold on to yourself. Hold on to your first feelings even though the stupidity and ignorance of others try to make you look foolish. This is because they cannot understand the value of what you have first felt inside the birth of your intelligence. Your first feeling is to understand what is true.

Understand well here that the feeling of God comes first inside you before somebody poisons your mind with something as stupid as the education of the world in the false understanding of God's value. First, you must listen to your own heart, and I promise you that *the Lord will not lie to you.* You will be set free from the stupidity and the ignorance that false religions strive to impose on you. They try to make you look foolish in what the Lord has truly given you. They make you fall into their own teaching of sin, and they try to take your soul from you. Understand that your feelings should be *first* before all the introductions of the mind.

You are not supposed to fall out of your spirit even though the mind of man has tried to make you an idiot because of your feelings.

Remember that the Lord your God is the one true teacher, and he will not forget you in your feelings, but you have to put your trust in the Lord your God and understand the value of that one perfect God who has given you life and who brought mankind out of the land of Egypt, meaning false religion. Just give the right to your firstborn to be accepted inside you by all that is good and true in the true religion of the Lord that teaches you to worship one God and one God only. Idolize no man of any kind or do anything to let your mind be disturbed by the mind of others and trust in your feelings to hear the truth from the Lord.

Now we come to the rebellious son. Understand that the rebellious son is a son in your soul and in your mind who rebels against the truth. You have feelings that keep rebelling against your mind and soul. They make you feel foolish to believe in the Lord your God and to have the true faith of the Lord. You cannot feel or understand God because that feeling is always in rebellion against your soul and your mind. You cannot believe in God because that feeling inside of you keeps popping up and it makes you feel foolish.

There is a deity above us that we call God, and whoever does away with that one holy God becomes a fool himself by listening to false teachings. This brings you to war against yourself, and that is a war you cannot win because of that foolish rebellious son inside yourself. The war begins at sun up and never ends at sundown—you never have peace of mind and spirit because you fooled yourself to believe that there is no Lord, no creator, and nothing that is above you. I'm talking about the people who cannot believe in anything. Those are the people who say, "Well, I have no faith and I cannot believe in faith." This is because the foolish false prophet that lives inside you is the one that has climbed to arrogance, believes in his own God, and makes a fool out of himself. Don't be a fool and think that the planet just created itself. Don't think God didn't have anything to do with it because without God, there would be no intelligence and nothing of the natural world.

If you rebel against yourself or against God, understand the power of the creation in intelligence. Without a creator, you have to come up with the facts and figures of your own existence. The human mind and the human spirit must be given life at some point over the other creatures, and the Lord makes life possible. Of course, you cannot believe in what the false religions of the world teach about God and who they claim to be God. These are the lies and the stupidity of false religion.

I can see where a person who claims to rebel against God cannot believe what the false prophet made out to be God. This is because the Lord is *not* in what religion teaches. God is more than what the power of man can possibly explain to the human mind and the human spirit. So few men in the world have ever been able to understand the deity of the Lord. No human being on the face of the earth has ever been able to explain the true deity of the Lord. With all the facts and figures, they cannot prove beyond any reasonable doubt the power of the Lord your God. We can only understand a small part of the Lord our God within life everlasting. Maybe the human race will come to understand the full power of the Creator of the world and be able to explain what the mind and soul of a human being cannot comprehend in the power and the full value of the deity of God. So to all you rebellious sons of the spirit of man, do not fool yourself by believing that there is no eternal God above us.

Next, we go to the understanding of various laws. If you see someone who has been found guilty and exposed on a pole, take them down and bury them on the same day in your heart. This means that if someone has been found guilty of violating the spiritual laws of the Lord and they have been put to death in spirit, then do not leave the body hanging on the pole. Take it down and bury it the same day, meaning "Do not leave this false spiritual belief exposed." Bury the body in the Earth with the false teachings of the Earth, and do it on the same day, which means at the same time you discover that it is a false belief.

If you see your brother's donkey straying way out of contact with reality, do not just ignore it. Make sure you bring the animal idea back to him and tell him what it means. This means that you see your brother making no sense at all in the value of the Lord, and he humbles himself before you by telling you that he is not educated and he does not understand something in spirit. Well, you must bring back to him the spiritual understanding. Even if he makes no sense at all, give him a few words of truth, something that he can remember and start practicing with. Don't make a big fuss about it. Just tell him the simple truth, and make sure that you lead him on right track, and if it doesn't work, that's not your problem anymore. You did your duty in the Kingdom of your Father. Be satisfied with the result because you were once in false religion and the Lord took you out of the land of Egypt, meaning false religion.

Understand well the power of the Lord here: "What you do to the least of my brothers, you do it to me." Follow the simple words of this parable, but do not make yourself look like a God in front of anyone. Do not disrespect the laws of the Lord. Instead, try to be a simple man in who you are by just simply loving the Lord your God with all your soul. Just be another person, as simple as you can possibly be, in the laws of the Lord. Do not try to walk with all the false saints and try to make yourself look better than anyone else. Just be simple in who you are and don't cross over the line of being unjust. Try to show everybody that you are on the side of the Lord. Just be simple as your Father in Heaven is simple. God has all the wisdom, but He still remains simple. Just make sure that you are like your Father in heaven, simple in deeds and knowledge, and don't try to make yourself more than you are. If your brother does not live near you and you do not know him, just take him home with you and feed him in the simplicity of the Lord. Tell him how simple it is to understand the Lord your God by being *simple* and *humble* before Him, and make sure that you live in the same house of being humble and simple.

Do not make anybody think that you know it all because it is not important for you to know more than anyone else. What is important is that you love the Lord inside humble deeds and be simple in the way of the Lord, then you will be part of the Assembly of God. Many people came before you and made themselves known as a person of great knowledge. They considered themselves to be greater than anyone else because they forgot their humble Father in heaven, who will always be a humble God because *humble* is the way of the Lord.

If you see your brother's donkey or his ox fallen on the side of the road, do not ignore it but get it back on its feet. Understand here that we are talking about the wealth of the earth. For example, you see a person fall behind on his rent, cannot pay his bills, and you see him fall to the wrong side and try to steal or take something that doesn't belong to him. Or he does something that is wrong in the value of the earth. Do not ignore him because of his lack of knowledge or the poor education that he has. Make sure that you help him. You think that you have a thousand reasons to judge him and you have a thousand pieces of advice of your own to make him look stupid and ignorant, but don't leave him there to rot in the dirt of the earth. Help him with what you have. Be kind and good to the poorest among you who does not have the proper way to live. Teach him in a simple way how to take care of himself by *worshipping* the Lord your God, and God will make him prosper because of the simple and holy deeds that you have done in a humble way to understand life.

A woman must not wear man's clothing nor a man wear woman's clothing. In other words, you must not try to understand with your mind what you should understand with your spirit, and you must not try to use your mind to understand your feelings. Remember that your mind was created by the Lord to understand what you gain and what you lose. Your mind is too weak to understand the spiritual value because your mind is the weak part of you. Don't let your mind lead you with your loss and gain. If you want to do good deeds for others, your mind will tell you not to do it because that would be a loss for you. And if there is no gain in value, the mind will tell you not to do it because there is no value in it for the mind.

Understand that you have to *let your spirit lead you* to understand the values of heaven. This is the real value in deeds that will cost you greatly in the loss and gain of the mind, but you will regain it in the values of heaven if you obey your soul. Fully grasp that it will be a fight with your wife, meaning your mind. The spirit must take control of the mind in the wedding feast of heaven. This means you must come to understand the value of heaven before the value of the earth. Understand well here that the value of heaven does not come from being weak in your decisions—it comes from the *strong value of the spirit.*

If you come across a bird's nest, either in a tree or on the ground, and the mother is sitting on her eggs or sitting on her young, do not take the mother with the eggs. This means that if you see great new knowledge flying inside the form of intelligence, do not destroy the mother (meaning where the knowledge comes from). Just agree to it and do not disturb it, but you can take the new birth of knowledge that flies well in the understanding of your mind and spirit. Truth will rule wisely within you from the information that was given to you. But leave the mother of the knowledge to keep on producing your ideas. Do not disturb the mother, but take what was born to be yours in your knowledge so you can become wiser.

When you build a new house in the understanding of your spirit, make sure to make a parapet around your roof. This means that when you build a new understanding in your spiritual value, make sure that you build the reality in your soul as well as in your mind. Try to control yourself in everything that you learn, and make sure that *everything is understood in both reality and common sense.* That means that you should put a parapet, which is an overhang, around your roof where the water will not fall on you and drown you in reality because *water* in the Scriptures means "reality." So stay in reality and common sense, but do not let too much reality drown you.

Do not jump into all kinds of superstitions like the Christians and the Catholics do. Stay within the boundaries of reality and common sense. Do not plant two kinds of seeds in your vineyard, meaning "Do not plant both good and evil in your vineyard." Try to understand good on the side that good lives, and understand evil where evil lives. If you do evil and you think it is good, and if you do good and think it is evil, that's because you have planted two kinds of seed in your vineyard. You must refresh your mind to understand good and evil, which is spiritual understanding. Good is good, which makes sense. Evil is evil, and it doesn't make sense.

If you bring, in your church or religion, that Jesus is God or the son of God, you better check your vineyard because you have done evil in the sight of the Lord. Even if you think that you have made a good deed on behalf of yourself, you have done an evil act by breaking the commandments of our Lord that was given to us on Mount Sinai. The second commandment of our Lord tells you *not* to worship an image before the Lord your God, yet you have done so in an evil deed against the truth. You claim good in your soul when you have done evil.

Do not plow your field with an ox and a donkey yoked together. This means, do not try to understand the Scriptures with both ignorance and stubbornness because those two animals, that are inside each one of us, give us the *value of nothing*. Just close the book if you are going to be ignorant and stubborn about it by thinking that you're always right and you cannot be wrong.

Make tassels on the four corners of the cloak you wear, meaning make sure that all that you believe in, on the side of the four corners of intelligence, makes common sense and reality. Whether you go north, south, east, or west, *make sure it makes sense.*

Next, we come to marriage violations. A man takes a wife, dislikes her, slanders her, and gives her a bad name. This means the spirit (man) cannot get along with the mind (woman). The man is not happy with himself because he does not like life the way it is. He wants to change for a better life and a better way of thinking because he cannot understand the power of the spirit. He curses life for what it is, and he brings himself to slander what he has married, which came from his mind. He is in a bad marriage and cannot find proof of the virginity of what he believes. Or he cannot cross over to understand the virgin part of his creations with his mind, and there are no feelings in the spirit to understand a better marriage between mind and spirit. The soul is just not happy being married to this woman, and even if the mother and father of the girl prove the woman's virginity, he is not happy with this woman, meaning with that idea of the mind.

An example of this is someone telling you that Jesus is the son of God. This is an idea of the mind. Let's say you try to believe this idea. That means you have married this idea because you have tried to bring this idea of the mind into your spirit. The mind is female, and the spirit is male. Therefore, bringing the mind and the spirit together is the "marriage" the Scriptures are referring to. Now if you cannot find evidence of the female's virginity, meaning if you cannot prove that the idea of the mind is pure and true, she shall be stoned to death. *Stoned to death* here is killing the untrue idea with your faith. This is how you understand the scriptures, by changing the nouns to verbs.

If you do not find the mind of Christianity, Catholicism, or any religion of the earth to be a virgin, and if you do not understand the purpose of the creation and the value that you have been created to understand things in the true and perfect order of the truth, then you have to "divorce" this idea of the mind and bring your spirit to marry a life in the spirit of the virginity of what you are. Make yourself happy by divorcing what is not true. Marry what is true in the wedding feast of intelligence where both mind and spirit live as one in the values of truth. This is where both mind and spirit become satisfied with the glory that is at the center of intelligence. The virginity of common sense comes to be the real purpose for any wedding in the value of human intelligence, and the laws of God work in the power of spirit and mind.

But if the woman's virginity, meaning the mind's way of thinking, is not acceptable in the pure marriage of the spirit and the mind, then the mind must be stoned to death by the power of all spiritual understanding. You should go on to find a better way of thinking and cross over to the feelings of your soul. Try to understand the *pure heart* of the *pure soul* in understanding the truth.

If a man is found sleeping with another man's wife, both the man and the woman must be stoned to death. This means if the spirit sleeps with the ideas of others and uses the ideas of the false prophet to worship Jesus as the Lord, both him and the idea must be destroyed by being stoned. This means to use your faith in the truth to stone them to death because it is evil. You must not believe in this evil, and you must not pass it on to the poor children of the earth.

If a man meets a virgin in town who is pledged to be married and he sleeps with her, take both of them to the gate of the town and stone them to death. The meaning of this is not killing people for sex acts of the flesh. This is a spiritual teaching. It means when you see a virgin mind that did not make up her mind of marriage with the groom of common sense and you mix her up with the stupidity of worshipping Jesus as God, then you must kill *both* the false spiritual teaching and the virgin mind who accepted it. You don't kill in the physical sense here. You must *condemn*, with your faith and your mortal mind, that it is wrong to have spiritual sex with a virgin, meaning a simple mind that doesn't know the truth and the reality of the spirit. Make sure that if you do not know the Scriptures, just mind your own business and keep the stupidity for yourself. Don't try to poison the minds of others with ignorance and lies. Just worry about your own soul before you correct anyone else's beliefs. Don't try to influence the mind of anyone else by the *falsehood of the earth.*

If you find a virgin mind and you try to rape her, meaning the spirit tries to influence the mind with a false faith by getting her to believe in any false spiritual teaching, then only the man shall die. The false spiritual teaching that raped the mind must be put to death, but the mind has committed no sin. The mind is a virgin and is only trying to find spiritual truth to believe in. But the spiritual teaching that tries to corrupt that virgin mind is *guilty* of a serious sin that is punishable by death, meaning you should take all the life out of that false teaching by stoning it to death with your faith. If you try to prove that you know better than anyone else and you try to destroy the poor mind of the person using false intelligence, you have committed a rape of false value and you have thrown your soul into the destruction of the souls that you bring upon others. *You have lost your soul yourself because you tried to rape others of their souls.*

If you meet a virgin who is not pledged to be married, meaning that person doesn't care to be informed, and if you tried to rape her with the falsehood of believing in your Jesus as God, you shall pay to your Father in heaven fifty shekels of silver in the restoration of your own soul because you are guilty of the sin of doing wrong to others. Fifty shekels of silver was a large amount back in those days, so that means you have to pay a great value. You won't be able to divorce her, and with all the falsehood that you brought upon another person, even though you don't understand the value of the price that you have to pay, the Lord will make it extremely hard on you. None of your kind deeds will be able to bring mercy on you because you have shown no mercy on anyone else by bringing false hope on others. You refused to mind your own business, and you will never be able to divorce your own falsehood in the justice of the Lord as long as you believe in those lies.

A man is not to marry his father's wife, meaning you should not put yourself in the generation of the past and worship what your parents worshipped. You must come to worship in your own soul that the Lord has given you. Worship the Lord your God in your own way. Do not listen to the religions of the past that are full of falsehood.

Next, we come to exclusion from the assembly of the Lord. No one who has been emasculated by crushing or cutting may enter into the Assembly of the Lord. This means those who have no courage to defend the truth must be cut off from the Assembly of the Lord. No one who is born of a forbidden marriage or any descendants down to the tenth generation may be part of the Assembly of the Lord. If you are not part of the *true* marriage of spirit and soul in the wedding feast of intelligence, where the mind is married to the spirit in the wedding feast in the land of Canaan, you cannot be part of the Assembly of God because you live outside the truth.

This is a spiritual understanding that you must respect with *both* your mind and soul so you can enter into the Assembly of the Lord and be part of the greatest knowledge that life can possibly bring to you in the value of that assembly. No one from the Ammonites or the Moabites may enter into the Assembly of the Lord, meaning that none of your animal instinct or any animal understanding of the Bible or any of your animals' morality will enter into the Assembly of the Lord. In other words, you cannot bring your animal being of the mind into the understanding of the Bible. You have to separate the physical and the spiritual in order to understand the physical part of yourself, and none of what you believe in your animal self can enter the Assembly of what the Bible is talking about. You cannot bring anything physical to the understanding of the Scriptures. *This is forbidden by the Lord.*

If you try to understand the Bible with the physical side of yourself, you just won't understand the meaning of the Word of God. Everybody else has tried to understand the Bible with their physical mind, and they have all failed to do so because it is *not* a book about your physical part—it is a spiritual book, and you cannot bring the physical into the spiritual. Ninety-nine percent of the teaching of the catholic church is about the physical part of a man because they falsely understood the physical part of Jesus to be the Lord. It is a *disgrace* on the human race to have a billion people in the world at one time with no knowledge whatsoever of the spiritual part of the Scriptures. They understand everything in the physical part for generation upon generation. They married their own mother, and that desecrates the Father's bed in heaven.

Understand well that if you fall in love with any religion of the earth and you worship any of these religions, you sleep with your mother in a sexual encounter with your Mother Earth. And therefore, you dishonor your Father's bed in heaven in the spiritual sexual encounter of falsehood because you took your spiritual understanding and replaced it with your physical understanding. You try to understand the Bible with the mind when the Bible was written in spiritual value. You have twisted things around in your mind because you could not understand in spirit. You made yourself a set of false laws, from a false theology, to understand with and that is your sin, my friend, because you failed to understand the Lord as a spiritual, divine creature in the value of spiritual understanding above physical understanding. Just remember that God is *not* a physical being, so when you talk to the Lord in the physical value, you won't hear Him because He exists only in the spiritual value. Understand that these laws are written for your spiritual value and are not meant for the physical part. These laws will make *no sense* to your physical part.

Next, we come to the miscellaneous laws. If a slave has taken refuge with you, do not turn him over to his master. Let him live among you wherever he likes in whatever town he chooses, and do not *oppress* this person. For example, if you encounter a poor Christian or Catholic who has been a slave to the master of these false religions, don't return him back to the master of falsehood. Protect him with your life, and do not oppress him by trying to tell him that you are better than he is. Just tell him the simple truth about worshipping the Lord your God in simple truth. Let him believe what he wants, and don't try to guide him on your turf. Give him an example of what it's like to be in the understanding of the One True God without saying a single word—just let your actions speak for themselves so you will restore his heart and show him what to do in the simple power of worshipping the One True God. Just tell him to simplify himself for truth in the value of the One Holy Spirit where the Lord lives. Let him believe what he wants until he has learned what he must do to be part of the Kingdom of God.

No man or woman must become a *shrine prostitute*. Understand well that prostitution, in the spiritual understanding, comes in the way people worship other men and women. When you listen to someone who does not tell you the truth, that is the false wedding in a sexual encounter of the spirit. When two people agree with each other in the belief of something false, that is the adultery of spiritual understanding of people who translated the Scriptures into something untrue. To be in adultery, the prostitutes of both parties will convince each other to believe that the man was a good preacher and a good person. They think that this person can't make any mistakes because they believe that he is so smart.

God is God, and He's a loving God of truth. If you believe anything outside the truth that doesn't make any sense (like when you believe God is a magician and Jesus is his physical son), you bring falsehood *against* the Lord your God. When two people have a sexual encounter of believing something about God or Jesus that is not true, then they commit adultery.

If a man kidnaps his fellow Israelite and makes him a slave, the kidnapper must die. You must understand here that the power of the spirit is *much different* from the physical meaning. A fellow Israelite means a person who reads the Scriptures and tries to understand just as you are trying to understand. If you trap him into believing in your fabrications of the Scriptures, then you have made him a slave to your false fabrication of the Scriptures. This becomes a great sin because you kidnapped this person into your way of thinking, and he has to go through *you* to worship God. He becomes your slave and every time he needs to know something he has to go to you to understand the Scriptures. That is slavery because, in reality, you have kidnapped him.

And if you are wrong with your fabrication, then you live in sin because you have destroyed your brother's will and the ability to understand for himself. This is a great sin in the eyes of the Lord. In the eyes of mankind, you think that you are doing good, but you are really doing evil because each person was given the ability to understand for themselves without your control and without you kidnapping him to believe in your false god. You brought him in the Scriptures to believe in the deity of Jesus, and then he becomes the child of total ignorance by believing in your arrogant way of thinking. You believe you are serving the Lord your God when you should just mind your own business and learn the Scriptures for yourself before you start teaching to others what you yourself do not even understand or practice in your own life.

You missed the point of something that is not supposed to be your business to begin with. You believe that you are doing good, but you are actually doing evil. You may lose your life if you don't stop that detestable practice because of your arrogant way of thinking. If you don't change and stop fabricating your own truth and kidnapping people, *you will lose your soul.* And that, my friend, is the faith of the false prophets who believed they knew something in the Scriptures when they have really learned nothing. You are supposed to let other people go free in their own thoughts and the Lord will bless you greatly in the understanding of the Scriptures. You don't have to prove your genius in front of others to receive the Kingdom of God. Just *be humble* in front of others with what little you can really understand. Don't kidnap anyone, but try to learn the Scriptures for yourself before you try to teach it to others.

When you make a loan of any kind to your neighbor, do not go into their house to get what is offered to you as a pledge. Understand well here what you have offered to the Lord in the pledge of your own sacrifice to the Lord. You must not steal from your brother what he has already sacrificed himself in what he made up of the Scriptures through the sacrifice of his weakness. You must not take away from him that which he has received after his sacrifice was given to the Lord. If you believe in Jesus as a god and you try to convince someone that you are right in making Jesus as a god before the Lord your God because of your weakness and your arrogance, your soul will be a lost soul. You have tried to convince others in your own fabrication of what God looks like. You made the image of Jesus and put it in front of God Almighty, and if you teach that to others, their souls will become lost like your soul is lost. This is the evil that comes from the heart of your arrogance. You believe that you are right, but you are destroying your brother.

All human beings on the face of the earth are affiliated with God from the tribe of Dan, the son of Jacob, born from the slave girl of Rachel. All men are affiliated with God because we all have faith in God. We do not all understand God in the same form, but everyone who has received the spirit, from Adam until now, lives in the form of a divine god. This idea shall not be destroyed because someone thinks that you are not right but that *they* are right. They try to trap you in their thievery of what's right and what's wrong. They try to steal from you what you have pledged to the Lord to believe in. Your faith that comes from your own affiliation with God is just as good, if not better, than any belief that comes from the false preacher. Why do you false prophets go out of your way to preach what you call God's word and what you believe to be the truth when you know your fabrication didn't come from God? You have no right to enslave the mind of any man who has his own thinking. You have no right to capture him in your wrong deeds by thinking that you are better than him and that he should listen to you. Is it not written in the Book of Revelation that the mountains could not be found and the islands fled away? What used to be called good deeds will come to be called the great evil of the world. Here you have the *arrogant notion* of the false prophets thinking that they are right by preaching to people who have less education than them. Remember your *own punishment* that the Lord has *imposed* on you—first, by making you believe that you are right when you are so wrong, and second, by making you understand that you have to admit to people of the earth how wrong you are. You will have to look into your own heart and see your own evil in the arrogance of your lost soul. Understand well here the punishment of the Lord on you. Just look into your own feelings and find the courage and the value of admitting to the whole world that you were preaching about a *false* god. This is the *justice of the Lord.*

If a man is poor and does not understand what is right, no one has the right to bring salvation to him because the *Lord only* is the one that he should pray to. If he doesn't pray to the Lord his God to understand the right way to live, that will be his problem. *Everyone* is affiliated with God, and everyone should have their own thoughts and feelings about Him. Every person is just as important as the one who lives in arrogance and thinks he is better than you because God has changed the value of intelligence from the rich to the poor in the value of the Kingdom of God. God has given both the rich and the poor man his knowledge. Whoever thinks and believes that he is better than you is actually much lower than you because of his arrogance. Anyone who thinks and believes that he is better than you has much more to learn than you in the values of heaven.

If a poor man in spirit would pour out his knowledge and claim what he cannot understand, this would be greater than all the understanding of the rich one in spirit. When a man admits, in his humble deeds, that he doesn't understand, this is *much more* than a rich man who admits about what he knows *in arrogance.* Because the truth stands far above the value of what is in the person who says yes to God but doesn't do his will is not closer to God. Those who say "I do not understand" will be blessed by the Lord in their own heart. He will understand the life of himself to be better because he will have to think about it and ask the Lord to forgive him for what he did wrong. This is much greater than the one who claims to know everything when he's the one who has brought the false truth of worshipping the image of a man.

Do not take advantage of a hired worker who is poor and needy, whether he is a fellow Israelite or a foreigner—this means someone who reads the Bible or someone who does not read the Bible. If a man reads the Bible regularly or if he is poor in spirit and never reads the Bible, do not take advantage of either man because both men still have the truth to conquer, and both must be set free to understand for themselves. What you understand as a person in the false prophecy and what the truth is are two very different things. A person is always poor in spirit because he didn't understand truth. He did not read the Scriptures, and if he did, he probably did not understand them. But if you tried to tell them what you know, you are only going to confuse them. They may turn from the truth and pick up your falsehood and be like the rest of the Christians, Catholics, and all the other religions of the world because none of us are God. Only God is God, and if a person is meant to be in the Salvation of the Lord, He will send him some kind of persecution of his own. *True wisdom* will come to us through that persecution sent by the Lord.

It is not up to any one of us to save the world. God brought the great persecution of mankind for our salvation and to bring mankind to his great Kingdom of Peace through the noble deeds of trying to understand the spiritual truth that they do not know. Understand that you are not going to be saved in the Salvation of the Lord by going to church or going to any organized religion of the mind. The children of God have to cross the Red Sea on dry ground by being persecuted on both sides. A human being will have to go through this persecution if he wishes to come to the marvelous Kingdom of Peace and Brotherhood. You will go through this persecution because the world did not think that you were fit for the Kingdom of God. *Understand these words well* so you will save your own self by accepting the great persecution against you. You did not know what to do to enter the Kingdom of God, but your salvation will come out of the great persecution where the pain and suffering of being put down, time and time again, by those who hold the law over you and made you suffer for being poor and helpless in the great Kingdom of the Lord.

Make sure that you pay hired workers fairly and with justice in the eyes of the Lord. If you want to be a great prophet, try to understand true justice and the power of the value of heaven. You suffered greatly in your life by being away from the basic needs of life where you had to do without and live in a kingdom where fair justice was nonexistent because you were poor in spirit. You did not understand all the faculties of life the way you should have.

The Kingdom of the Lord is at hand for those who suffer in poverty, those who are misguided by false religion, judged for all their poor crimes, and put in prison because they could not understand the true value of what is right. The world made you pay for it and placed you into a cage of falsehood. You had to do without all the means of *true* brotherhood. You were persecuted by everything that man believed against you. Understand well here that the mountain and the islands are moved from their place, meaning the laws of God have been moved because the time is here for man to see the true justice of the Lord. Fully comprehend that the justice of the Lord is like the justice of man, and whoever tries to bring their own justice into what is the Lord's, they will be in their own justice. The true justice of the Lord will truly be imposed on the human race.

When you are harvesting your field and you overlook the sheaf on the side of the field, just leave it there for the poor and helpless so they may have something to eat. Leave it for the foreigner, the fatherless, and the widow. Completely understand that the power of the Lord lives in the *charity of free learning* where you are not to impose your own learning upon the learning of others. Leave some food behind in this glory of learning for those who need to eat from what is left to understand.

Everyone can learn for himself after his sacrifice is given to the Lord to receive the beauty of life in spirit. The spirit is the only thing that lasts forever. Your physical body will die a thousand deaths, over and over, but your spirit will last forever. You will live, in each lifetime, the spiritual value that you have gained from the great persecution you have endured. If your human understanding only understood the laws of man compared to those who understood the Laws of God, then who will be punished worse? When the Lord comes and separates the truth from the lies in the value of his justice, you will be judged according to what you have learned in truth.

When people have a dispute, they are to bring it to court. Understand that what this means is a *spiritual* dispute in the spiritual court of the Lord. The guilty will be condemned, and the innocent will be acquitted. Understand the power here where the Lord has created the world to be proven innocent or guilty of the great crimes against nature. The guilty becomes the innocent, and the innocent becomes the guilty in the court of mankind. That will be the first value in the court of mankind. The great persecution of the innocent is what this court is all about.

God did not just create all these religions and the court of the justice of mankind for nothing. All those who judge others will be brought to the Throne of the Lord to be judged according to the values of the justice of the Lord. Whoever sins in his mind and soul over what people call justice and fairness in the unity of mankind must be brought to the priests for determination to see just what is the truth in the revelation of the heart.

You see, mankind has a strange evaluation of the limitations of right and wrong. They believe with this certain limitation of human understanding. They twist the facts to figure wrong over right because of the death of Abel by the hand of Cain. Right was killed by wrong, and that created a human mind and the human spirit of being wrong over right in the limitation of human understanding where what you think is right with your little mind of the locust can make a man so wrong because of this limitation to understand the power of right over wrong.

If the glory of the truth is not there to determine wrong over right, what will be left is the understanding of the locust, this little critter of the earth that lives in mankind's mind and will not be able to understand the power of the true justice of mankind. The mind of a man is not meant to understand spiritual truth. That is the job of the *spirit*.

If a man is innocent in the court of the Lord, but has been proven by the court of man to be guilty, the one who is truly guilty must pay with his life in the prison of their own ignorance. These are the limitations that they have in the value of the court of man. But if a man is guilty of the great sin of his own wrong, he must still pay but not by the wisdom of the court of man. He must pay by the higher value in order to understand in the court of the Lord. He has to be persecuted for the wrong that he has done and there is punishment in the justice of mankind. But remember that his persecution is already the judgment of the Lord, and if he was judged according to the laws of man, he will not be judged in the heart toward the high court of the justice of the Lord because he just paid for his crime against humanity and the Lord will not judge him in his court.

Remember that the throne of the Lord is set up for those who have never been judged and did not sacrifice themselves in the great persecution. These people, above all, must be judged for their mistakes in understanding their brothers by their own justice. They will be brought to the Lord's justice because most of these people never offered a single sacrifice to the Lord. They always thought they were right in their deeds taught by the mind of their little critter of the earth, but if they make a mistake, now will come the justice of the Lord who will punish the guilty and free the innocent in the court of the Lord. God will set up a throne in front of the whole wrong against right in all human deeds where true justice will be served in the spiritual value of life everlasting. This was God's plan from the *very beginning of the world.*

Do not have two different weights in your bag, one of them heavy and one of them light. Make sure that you carry the weight of true value and place it in your bag so you will not cheat anyone or take anything that was given from the Lord to those who work hard for what they have. For example, stealing is like those of organized religion who preach falsehood and get money and wealth, yet they bring nothing back to the community. Week after week, they steal from others and they offer nothing of value to the community. If you do not understand the Scriptures yourselves, why do you teach what you don't understand? You do not understand the first five books of the Old Testament, and you cannot explain anything that is written in them. You cannot explain the Book of Revelation because you don't understand it, yet you preach every week and bring great disaster on your brother by misleading them into darkness.

You take no account of what you take from your brother. You live a comfortable life doing no good by bringing your people deep into the world of the unknown, and you take wealth from your brothers without teaching anything of any real value. You claim that you are doing God's work while you hide the truth deeper in darkness because you did not find the truth in the first five books of the Old Testament. You do not understand any of the Parables of Jesus, and you don't understand anything in the Book of Revelation that should be known to you as a walking stick of the Scriptures.

You claim that your teachings are true and honest, but I tell all you false prophets that you have had your day. You will protect yourself by trying to make yourself look good after the Book of Revelation comes alive, and the power of the Lord will come to defeat you little locusts of the earth. You will be upset because you will hate the dream of the dreamer (just like Joseph in the book of Genesis) where you will sell your brother into slavery and try to say that you are doing good. You will blame somebody else, and you will attack the Lord your God and risk going to a holy war against the Lord Almighty because you always thought yourself to be smarter than the Lord. But you will lose that battle with the Lord.

Remember what the Amalekites did to you along the way. These are the kind of people around you that believe they are wonderful and they try to help you. Try to understand that they don't know that they have to be great and kind in the knowledge of the Lord as long as they are kind and good in the knowledge of the mind and they try to comfort you on your journey. The Amalekites are kind and good in the heart of goodness even though they don't really understand the Scriptures. They live their lives by a set of morals that are not always part of the Kingdom of the Lord. The morals of the mind of man are not always just and fair, yet the Amalekites believe strongly in these morals, and they will try to destroy you with them.

You as the children of God are simple, and equal to you are all those that are simple in the value of each other and bow down to the power that we are all children of God in the love of God. If a person wants to be your friend, *be his friend.* If someone is merciful and kind to you, *be merciful and kind to them* because we are all children of God. We are children of God because God created us with his own image in the reality of love. Where we are, in love, is because of who has received this love by living in the heart of the Lord. Remember that love is the verb of the lover. If you love others as the Lord loves you, you begin to have the effect of love that comes from the Lord Himself. People don't have to agree with your faith or try to understand the way you think. But make sure you love them if they love you and are kind to you. Do not be judgmental in your religious value and claim that you are better than them.

Make sure that you *love everybody equally* no matter what they think or what they feel. Love their animal as if it was your animal. Protect them and never forget that inside their heart, they are the same as you. The Lord loves them as well as he loves you. Be a friend and be kind to everyone wherever you go and whoever you meet. Be kind and friendly with everyone from the bum on the street to the highest president of all nations. People don't have to agree with you and believe the way you do—just make sure you *love* them.

Next, we come to firstfruits and tithes. When you enter into the land that the Lord has given you to possess, take some of your *firstfruits* and give them as an offering to the Lord. Your firstfruits are to be kind and good to others in spiritual value and to love others. When you meet a person, don't expect him to know what you know about the Lord, and don't expect their learning to be like yours. Just be kind and try to love them as they are. Do not try to possess them or dominate them into a new way of thinking. Don't even try to bring them into your faith. They don't have to have the same faith as you. There's no way that you can bring faith in them. That's the Lord's job.

Understand that love is not faith. Love is love, and all mankind doesn't have to think or feel alike. Your firstfruits are to love and be kind to them. Loving them is what is first. Remember that love is a verb that cannot be changed for another verb. Love is the first verb of your firstfruits where you come to understand the Lord your God. Love is the priest inside your humanity of a great soul where you cannot determine life without it. If you need to be loved, this means that other people need to be loved as well. You don't have to be a genius to be loved, and people don't have to be a good soul in the way that you think for you to love them. You must love them without any conditions whatsoever in the holy land of Canaan after you have crossed the river of the Jordan into your new world. Love is part of crossing the Jordan, where you will find peace on earth. Do not add or subtract anything from love. This is the command of the Lord.

Now we come to understand the altar on Mount Ebal. Make sure that after you cross the Jordan, the river of life, you change the value of your heart after forty lifetimes in the desert, and you come to understand the Laws of God. Come across the Jordan and listen to your heart. Now you are part of the new world where you come to live in peace with your brothers and sisters in what we are in our feelings. The old kingdom was sophisticated with lies and the destruction of the spirit. Once you come across the Jordan, you will find your new life to be in the values of your spirit. In the old world, all the value was in your physical needs and your physical desires.

You wanted to be rich and powerful in the old world, but now you must change and come to understand the value of your spiritual self. You must live in happiness where your spirit is not always in turmoil with your brother, and you must call upon peace in your heart to be your best friend. Find the *real* treasure of love to be the most valuable of your firstfruits in the Kingdom of Intelligence, where good feelings make you rich in your spiritual value. You should find physical wealth to be of little value, and you should find your spiritual self to be of great value in love, kindness, and peace with everyone around you.

In your soul, the holy value of the Laws of God is not like the laws of man that can turn on you. They can always be trusted because the Laws of the Lord give you a way in and a way out. But the laws of man give you a way in where you *cannot* get out or a way out where you cannot get in. The Laws of God are simple and humble, where you can find your way in and get out where you want to. It's just that simple on the altar on Mount Ebal.

Now we come to understand the curses from Mount Ebal. Then Moses (the great lawgiver) and the priests, meaning the feelings of love, said, "Be quiet and listen. Make sure that you have love in your heart before you tell people that you love them. Do not be a hypocrite about love. Make sure that you understand the great laws of love to reveal for you the purpose of love." *What is the purpose of love?* You have it in the twelve sons of Jacob. Levi is the purpose where love becomes the most important thing in the salvation of the Lord. The Lord will save love because love is the greatest challenge of humanity to the soul and the mind of humanity. Love is a verb that the human heart rejects, and it is the *most difficult* verb to explain to the human heart. Love is also the greatest drag on the human race, and that is why the verb of love is so hard to explain to the human race. It is a verb that's very hard to enter the human mind because you have in your mind your loss and gain where love almost becomes impossible to understand.

The way God has created the human mind is to be *partners with the heart of humanity*. He put loss and gain in the mind for this purpose. The mind *contradicts* the spirit, and there is a battle between the spirit and the mind. *The mind has no feelings* and only understands when it gains something in value. If you have a loss in the value of giving freely for love, this is the battle inside yourself. The heart must bring back love without gain, and this is when you must fight in that battle between heart and spirit. Your gain is important to the mind because it has no feelings like the heart has, but some of these feelings are not there for the mind to see.

Your mind will always favor a gain over a loss, so understand well here that it is the battle of the wedding feast. You need the mind to gain the power of restoration in your spirit where you take on a gain in feelings that gave compassion to your feelings but not to your mind. Try to understand the difference when you give something of value to someone but the mind finds no value in it. In the state of the mind, you have a contradiction between mind and spirit. This is where the battle is between the weakness of the mind and the compassion of the spirit, and it's the battle that you must win to cross the Jordan into the land of Canaan that the Lord gives you to possess.

When the Lord created the mind, the wife of the spirit, He knew that there would be a *great* battle between the two, just like in your physical life. A man and a woman are the *contradiction* of weak against strong, and this will *always* be a strong battle. But this is where your victory belongs to the salvation of the soul. Your strong feelings must fight in strength against weakness because even God, with all his might and glory, cannot find a better way to bring the value of intelligence to mankind.

Next, we come to understand the curse of the man who worships a graven image or casts an idol. Fully understand that these Laws are *real* and can be *trusted*. Whoever carves an image or casts an idol worships *against* the Lord God. The Catholic Church, Christianity, and *all* houses of worship are *full* of idols and the image of Jesus that they worship in front of God. Do not *ever* place an image before the Lord and claim salvation through this detestable practice of falsehood that the Lord hates the most in the world of men. The Lord tells you in the Scriptures *not* to believe in this detestable practice of humanity by false religion on earth. This is where a human being goes to church on Sunday morning to worship the image of Jesus and all the idols that they hang on the walls all around them. They bend their knees to worship a false god, but they think they are worshipping the real God. God has led them, in their free will, to create such a poor value of God Almighty where they place saints and idols before the Lord our God. They brought their *physical* value instead of their spiritual value to the salvation of their soul, and this is why they have failed.

Remember that God is spirit, and He will bring a curse on anyone in false religion who worships in the physical body where he refused to understand his true spiritual value. God will place a curse on anyone who worships in these false practices where they don't consider the spirit to be of value over the mind. If you try to save your soul but in the physical way of the image of God, you will be under the Lord's curse in the restriction of not understanding a single thing about your spirit. You will come to know so little because you do not understand the Scriptures. You have placed your false faith in an image of a false god, and you idolize saints of false value in a false religion that *makes no sense* whatsoever. Just look at your faith, and when you don't understand anything and you have to depend on somebody else to explain it to you, that means that you been *cursed* by the Lord Almighty.

Cursed is anyone who moves his neighbor's boundary stone. This is the boundary of what a person believes. If you move anyone's boundary stone, you are telling them what to believe, and this is forbidden by the Lord. Cursed is anyone who thinks he is better than his neighbor and believes them to be evil in the boundaries of his understanding. He makes it look like his neighbor is evil in his heart and thinks that his neighbor is going to go to hell because he has disagreed with you in what is right. Cursed is the man who leads the blind astray on the road.

A false prophet or false Catholic priest uses the image of Jesus to lead others into worshipping idols and saints. They make rules on people to go to their church, and if they don't go to that church, then they will go to hell. This is leading a man into darkness. The darkness that Jesus talked about in the New Testament is when a human being tries to see what is right in the truth and just cannot see what makes sense in the reality of the creation. This is the three days of darkness that was mentioned in the plagues of Egypt. Three days of darkness would cover the land for *three millennia of time*. From the death of Jesus until now, the world and the preachers of the world and all the governors of the governments of the world would live in total darkness where they just cannot see reality by the limitation of the sight of God. They cannot see what is real and true and they cannot understand *how* to worship the Lord God.

God Himself put the seal on religion because religion was so evil. They kept on preaching the evilest things they can muster against the reality of truth. From the bum on the street, to the highest learner of theology, all Scriptures and the Word of God, *everyone will be blind*. It looks like everyone has been cursed and sealed off from the truth where no one can see or feel anything that makes sense. Yet in technology, we came with a great value of common sense by the lost tribe of Judah. This means that all those who took the microphone could not penetrate the darkness of the earth. You just cannot see past your nose, and you cannot understand the meaning of life meant to receive life ever after.

The Lord has closed their eyes because some of them are really trying to understand the Scriptures, but they could not penetrate and break the seal that the Almighty God has placed on the human race. They just could not understand no matter how hard they try. They missed the point of God being *first* in the worshipping of heaven.

They could not penetrate that little spot on their face, and they could not see the wisdom of the Lord because they were in the value of the false heaven. Darkness fell on Egypt means that no false religions of the world, whether it is the Muslims, Buddhists, Christians, or anyone on earth who preaches religion could understand God without placing some kind of an image or idol in front of them.

The human mind cannot accept what it did not understand in the value of their loss and gain and what they could not understand with their spirit and soul. Just remember the explanation of the battle between mind and spirit. That's where the battle was lost by religion because the people of the earth just couldn't understand the battle and the curse that was placed on them by the seal of the Lord. Only God knows how much some of these people try to penetrate and understand the Scriptures because He has *sealed* it from all of mankind because no one in heaven or on earth could break the seal. No one could break the seal of the four horsemen of the Book of Revelation. Everyone on earth thought they were good and proper to go to church and marry a woman in the sight of God. No one could break these seals and open the door of the Kingdom of God to understand what is really wrong and what is really right. The whole power of human understanding was just sealed by the Lord.

Cursed is the man who sleeps with his father's wife, for he has dishonored his father's bed. If you sleep with the religion of the past, you are misplacing the truth because the truth is not in the religion of the past. Truth is in the Scriptures, but you have to keep on digging in the Old Testament to understand the Scriptures. Only then will you come to feel the Lord of the Creation and understand the Bible by understanding the journey that the Israelites went through in the lost ground of the desert. Understand well here that even though the children of the earth tried to understand, they worshipped a God of make-believe by the hand of all the false religions of the earth.

Man formed himself the world of make-believe about the existence of God because he lives in darkness. The people tried to pull them out of the world into salvation, but they do not have a clue of *how* the Kingdom of God will come to be, so they slept with their Father's wife and dishonored their Father's bed. The three days of darkness covered their eyes where the plague, in the land of Egypt, made their eyes blind where no one could see or hear anything that the Lord planned for mankind. People just slept with their mother of the religion of the past and failed to understand the way of the Lord and the modern man.

Cursed is the man who has sexual relations with any animal. He will be under God's curse. All human beings on the face of earth are animals, including Jesus. And so are all the false prophets and all the so-called saints. Remember Adam and Eve? They believed in the idea that came from the serpent, one of the animals of the earth, and look what happened to them. Having sexual relations with an animal means that you believe in Satan with all his lies. Satan is *alive* in the world. It is not that you are having sexual relations with a person, but Satan is an animal in the mind of men. And if you listen to anything of the mind of man, you are having a spiritual sexual encounter with an animal. Do not think of Satan as a creature with horns on top of his head because that comes from the world of make-believe. There is no such thing as a Satan or the devil in hell like you were taught by false religion. That's all from the world of make-believe. Even the dragon did not exist in reality then. It is just a word to describe what evil and liars look like.

The truth is that the animal that cannot understand the Word of God is the *real liar* of the world that forms in the mind of man. This is the devil, the Satan of man's own truth. People believe that there is a Satan that looks like a man with horns. The people of false religion just could not translate all that was said in the spiritual understanding, so they made up this false image of Satan from the world of make-believe against the Lord our God. The false prophet did not realize that when the scriptures were talking about a Satan or a devil, they were talking about all the liars in the world of make-believe that we live in now. Nobody had the power to understand the Scriptures, so they formed the world of make-believe by having sexual relations with an animal.

Cursed is anyone who sleeps with his sister, the daughter of his father, or the daughter of his mother. This means a man who is sleeping with the religion of the mind of either the present time, the time of yesterday, or the time of tomorrow. You are *not allowed* to have any sexual encounter with any religion of the mind by going to anyone's church that is old, that is new, or that will be tomorrow. You are supposed to *sleep in your own soul* and try to determine the value of all time where the understanding of all time becomes valuable to you without throwing your spirit to where it was, where it is now, or where it will be tomorrow. You are only allowed to be in the sexual encounter with the Groom of Heaven, who is the Lord your God with all your soul and with everything that you are in the boundaries of the justice of the Lord. Understand that all religions of the mind are always the same *false truth*. The false truth that was yesterday is the same false truth that is today, and it will be the same false truth tomorrow. Do not sleep outside the truth where the Lord is nowhere to be found.

Cursed is anyone who sleeps with his mother-in-law—this means to sleep with the laws of man. Mankind made laws to punish the guilty and to set free the innocent, but you cannot always believe in these laws because they are not totally clean. They cannot always be trusted in the truth. Anything that comes from man's way of thinking is not always clean. You must understand that man makes mistakes with what they think is the right thing to do. Remember that man's way of thinking is not within the boundaries of the Lord because man is a mistake maker who does not understand the power of the intelligence of the Lord. Man thinks he can be just as fair as God, but that is not possible because the mind of man was not created to be as wise as the Lord. If we were as wise as God, we wouldn't need Him above us. And that's obviously not the case.

Cursed is anyone who killed his neighbor secretly, which means if you kill a man in his spiritual understanding. Remember that the Bible is 90 percent spiritual and 10 percent physical, so there's very little of the Bible that talks about the physical part of life. You must understand these laws in the spiritual part of life. A human being is killed spiritually by the world of make-believe, and then he makes great mistakes by trying to teach the Scriptures to others in a physical understanding. If someone comes and explains to you physically what the spiritual scriptures mean and you believe them, they will totally destroy your spirit. You will go home confused and still not understand anything. The Bible is not made for your *physical* life—it is made for your *spiritual* understanding. If you cannot explain a law like this one here in spiritual understanding, you should close your church and try to learn how to understand the Scriptures before you go and destroy the life of other people secretly.

Do not preach to your neighbor because you do not understand the spirit yourself. You do not have a clue of what is real and what is not real. I would tell all the priests of the Catholic Church and Christianity to put tape on their mouths and say nothing that you cannot understand for yourself because lying to people is a great sin in the mistakes of mankind. You are bringing people to the wrong side of the truth where the power of your lost soul becomes the power of those who listen to you. That is unfair, and you will be prosecuted for your sin if you do not turn away from your lies.

Cursed is anyone who accepts a bribe for killing an innocent person—this means what you said regarding the law of God, "You shall not kill." The meaning of this law in the physical sense is that you will be punished by mankind in the court of man for physically killing another person. But when you commit the spiritual crime of killing the spirit of people, the Lord is waiting for his day to punish people. The greatest punishment of all is to *lose your spiritual life*. Life is precious, and you only have one life that repeats itself seven times in each millennium. This is where you come back to life in life everlasting.

Living on this planet is a gift from the Lord, and you have to respect your life by trying to understand the precious gift of life that is given to you in each of your lifetimes on this planet. God has made spiritual to be spiritual and physical to be physical. The physical part of you dies out, but your spiritual life is everlasting. The physical part of you just goes to sleep in the flesh for a short period and then wakes up and lives on as long as the existence of God lives.

Fully understand that your physical life is short and sweet but your spiritual life is everlasting. You must pay the price in your spiritual life and go through the great persecution of life. Understand that you must be strong when people persecute you. This is the great persecution against the goat that pushes you around with man-made laws that are created with no compassion of the spirit. You must come to understand and be glad that the Lord has chosen you even though you feel bad about it and you think it's unfair. But the justice of the Lord is fair for everyone.

Make sure that you accept your tears and your sorrow *with joy* in the spirit that you were created with. Don't be afraid of the unfair justice of mankind. Just love the Lord your God with all your soul no matter the consequences of any action against you. Be glad and jump up in the air. Enjoy your salvation because it is not the one who went to church and listened to all the preachers and tried to make good Christians of you that will receive life everlasting in the salvation of the Lord. It is the one who went through the great persecution and suffered a great deal in poverty and injustice, time and time again.

Cursed is anyone who does not uphold the words of these laws by carrying them out. These laws were written for justice for all mankind to follow, but some people think of themselves to be *above* everybody else. They claim, inside their spirit, to be better than anybody else, so they take the position of being some kind of a judge in the court of mankind, and they make their rules stick on the life of others. They push people around like the goat pushes the sheep, and they make other people's lives miserable while claiming to do the work of the Lord.

Understand well that if you take the job of being in an office of some kind and you lead people with injustice by judging others, you are *against* the Lord your God. If you are the top dog and you lead people into injustice with these laws and if you treat people unfairly because you sit in a powerful chair of injustice, you must look at yourself and come to the Lord your God and repent. The Lord will send you into the same persecution that you have persecuted others with. Understand well the laws of God. No matter how good a Christian you may be, if you sit on any seat of power and you treat people with injustice, you will not be able to enter into the salvation of life everlasting. Justice, fairness, and unity, are the keys to "unlock" the door to the Kingdom of God!

Now we go to the blessings for obedience. You have to understand here that the justice of the Lord is not like the justice of mankind. In heaven, you are judged fairly inside your soul by the throne of spiritual value that judges you accordingly and sits in the same chair that you yourself used to judge others. If you judge others unfairly, you must be judged unfairly by the same throne that you opposed. The same unfairness that you used against others will be used against you in the justice of the Lord. Whatever you made up and claimed to be the rule will be used against you, just as you used the same rule against others. Be fair inside yourself and treat others the way you want to be treated because you will be judged accordingly in the same value that you have judged the life of others.

If you judge the values of others, you will be judged by the same value. Things will not go well for you if you have treated others unfairly because the laws of God will overrule everything in the theology of religions and bring a fair process where all mankind will be treated equally, even the smallest person in your life who has been proven guilty. If he is not guilty, then you will be truly condemned by the Lord with his own justice. Now let's look at the justice of the Lord. If you do everything that your obedience to the Lord calls for, then you will receive in your favor the calves of your herds and the lambs of your flock.

Understand well here that you were first created as an animal and then the Lord gave you a spirit to live inside the animal. You are only 10 percent animal and 90 percent spiritual, so this means that your animal on this earth suffers 10 percent of the injustice of the world; 10 percent of your life suffers when the physical part of you is being punished by mankind. They cannot touch the 90 percent of you that is spirit. Your spirit is still free to enjoy life no matter what evil and unfairness was done against you.

Your spirit is freer than theirs, so just offer your 90 percent and obey the Lord your God with all your soul. Understand that if you live in the true value of yourself, the Lord will bless you greatly. Even though you have been treated by the seat of mankind that was unfair in the justice of the Lord, you still have your value in your livestock and in your spiritual partner in your soul. Just be thankful, jump up, and clap your hands in the joyful feeling of your existence. They can take everything from you in your physical part of life, but they cannot take your spirit.

No one on earth, in any unfair deed of mankind, can take your soul in the value of the 90 percent of your spiritual self. Stay faithful to the Lord and your basket will be blessed with the good fruit of the Kingdom of God, and you will see that your enemy, in the value of their throne, will soon be out of your sight. They will soon be punished because of their unjust laws. This is not a question of revenge or getting even with someone. It is a question of justice, and that justice is what you were created for in the love of God.

Next, we go to the curses for disobedience. If you do not obey the Lord your God, you will be punished just like a child is punished by the love of his parents. You won't be able to understand anything, and you will be in darkness by always thinking that you are right when you are so wrong. You will think in your mind that you are on the side of the Lord, doing what you are supposed to do. You believe God gives you the power to punish other people, and you will not have the feelings of wrongdoing. You will think that you are right in prosecuting others, and your heart will be hard like the king of Egypt, always thinking that you are right because you believe you are the king and you make yourself wealthy in the world. Then you will sit on your chair of injustice, claiming that you are better than anybody else, and next thing you know, you will judge the life of many people as doing wrong without realizing that *you* are the one doing wrong.

You will lose your life because you tried to save your life by being powerful in the 10 percent of your physical life. The Lord has fooled you in religion, so He will fool you on the seat of your own justice, just like a wise parent disciplines their child. But if you do not repent of your role against others, you will lose your life in what you have believed to be the facts in your soul of lost life. Think of others in the least and the smallest of mankind to be your brother. Change your value from wrong to right in the change of heart and you will be safe from losing your soul. I want you to remember here that your physical understanding *does not count* in the salvation of your soul, but your spiritual understanding will save you from God's curse *if* you do change wrong to right.

Next, we come to prosperity after turning to the Lord. When all these blessings and curses come upon you and you take them to heart by turning to the Lord, He will disperse you among all the nations of the earth. This means you will not call yourself Catholic, Christian, or any name of any religion on earth. You will call yourself by your own given name that your parents gave you, and nothing else will be added in the value of any false religion. You will be a *simple* human being, and you will live in the simplicity of the humility of your simple name. You won't have a cross on your neck of any kind, and you will live in freedom from all the rules of false religion that used to scare you. You will lose the rules of the world of make-believe, and you will *finally be free* in the land that the Lord is giving you for life everlasting.

You will bless and worship the One True God under the stars of heaven. You will offer all your sacrifices to the Lord your God, and you will no longer choose a man of the earth to offer your sacrifices to. The Lord will make your descendants as wise as you are, and you will be just as free as all your descendants to love and serve the Lord your God with all your soul in the reality of life. You will live with people all around you who have the same understanding of the real pleasure of human living in the value of worshipping One True God. You will never place the image of any man in front of the Lord your God, and you will prosper in the value of heaven.

You will understand every living word of the Lord's value, and you will understand the purpose of your own life, where you will live forever and ever, lifetime after lifetime, in the pursuit of true happiness in the Kingdom of our Lord. Life will be different in your new prosperity because you will be introduced to the new earth and the new heaven, meaning to understand life in the new fashion of the new earth where all your physical sins will disappear and where your spiritual sins will be of the value of a new understanding. Heaven will be brought forth with a new idea that will come to live inside you. The Lord's great wisdom will enter you, and the pleasure of the true happiness of human living will come to be so.

Remember that you will cross the Jordan River on dry ground. This means that in your spirit, you will believe *none* of the understanding of any religion of the earth. You will reject the false beliefs of the mind, such as the sex of the flesh being impure. And when you do cross the Jordan River on dry ground, your heart will live in reality, where you do not think of anything outside reality. You must learn to understand that every single thing that you think or feel inside of you has to be pure in reality. You cannot believe something outside reality.

Your heart must be as pure as the day you were born. This is what it means to be pure when reality hits you. The purpose of what is real and not real will hit you inside your pure heart of the Holy Spirit Himself. You will bring the twelve sons of Jacob, the leaders of the twelve tribes of Israel, inside you, and you will think of others to be equal to yourself. When you look at someone else's problems, you will feel for them because what they are going through is *real.* You just don't ignore them because it is not your problem. You feel for other people in every sorrow and every pleasure that they go through. If things have been going well or if things have been going wrong for them, just keep your heart pure in the understanding of *true spiritual power.*

You must feel for others just as you feel for yourself in the value of holy thinking and in the value of love, the Levi (the third son of Jacob) who lives inside you and who makes you live in the spirit of the Lord Himself. When you do good to others, do good as reality presents itself so you can love the Lord your God with all your soul. This is what the Lord calls for. To love the Lord is to love reality and common sense. When you love the truth, common sense, and reality, you love God. But when you ignore reality and other people's feelings, that is not love.

To understand love, you must understand the *purpose* of reality. When another person hurts you and you are in a sad situation, you must take the one who rejoiced over your sadness and you must hold it against them in the justice of the Lord. It's important that the love for your brother must be brought to the court of the Lord. Whatever your brother has done to you, he has to pay for his stupidity so he can come to the throne of the Lord like everybody else. He has *no right* to hurt you in reality because it is impure, and when you are impure, you act with vengeance or some other stupidity that you're playing on others. Once people *break* the laws of the Lord our God, you have to bring them back to the throne of the Lord and make sure that this person pays for his infraction against you in equal share of what he has imposed on you. This is what the purity of common sense and reality means in the supreme power of the Lord your God and his holy throne.

Next, we come to the offer of life or death. God is making the Israelites this offer. You need to remember that this is an eternal spiritual teaching, that is, for *all time.* This has been repeated time and time again in this book, but it is the *very foundation* of being able to understand the Lord your God and his laws. So it bears repeating. The Israelites live inside the human heart as the chosen people of God—this means the part of you that has been chosen to receive the inheritance of the promised land of milk and honey. The Lord is making you the offer of life or death. This means that you can choose to either accept the truth of life in the understanding of the spirit which leads to eternal life, or you can go on believing the lies of the mind, which lead to the death of the spirit. Always remember that it is the Lord himself who will grant you life or death, not a man and certainly not some false devil creature with horns that man has made up in their minds. *God created both good and evil.* There are *not* two gods. Good and evil *both* come from the Lord, where good means living according to his holy word and evil is living against it. God will judge what you believe in as being good or evil, but remember that such judgment is a result of what you have freely chosen to believe. So if you live in lies outside the truth, it is your own fault. The Lord must offer you this option so you can understand that it is *your* free will of choice and that the results of your life come from that choice.

Now we are going to the understanding of Joshua succeeding Moses. Moses represents the law, while Joshua represents freedom. The law will point you in the right direction, but it won't get you across the Jordan into the promised land. Freedom is what completes the journey. Let's understand this. With any laws or rules, physical or spiritual, there obviously are outcomes for either going along with or going against these laws. Everyone knows this. But there is no value in simply following any law out of fear of punishment. The value comes from the knowledge of *how* the law works, which gives you the freedom to choose for yourself what you are going to do.

People go to churches, temples, and mosques. They avoid eating meat on Fridays during Lent, they get married, and they believe in about a million and a half other superstitious practices because they are told that they must do these things or suffer the consequences. But when you *educate* yourself to understand what these laws *truly mean*, you are free from the false understanding that holds you back, and it is exactly this freedom that is required to enter the promised land. The law alone is not enough. You need the *understanding of the law* to make the free choice to follow it or not. This is something that organized religion does *not* give you, and it is why *no* man-made religion will ever be on the side of the Lord.

*****

THE NEW TESTAMENT

We are going to understand the Parables of the New Testament, beginning with the Book of Matthew. The New Testament is the power of God to send a man to bring the understanding of God's word to mankind. He sent Jesus to bring us the New Testament. Understand that God did not send anyone to replace Him as God. Jesus, the man that people call the son of God, is not the physical son of the spiritual God. A spiritual understanding cannot possibly have a physical son. Jesus was a man who came into the world to do the work of the Almighty God, which is to bring the parables to mankind. He was a man like any other man, *not* God in the physical form. He was just a man that God had chosen to bring us the parables. God speaks through us in our spiritual form, and we have to translate that teaching to our physical form. For example, your voice tells you things in the physical form, and you must bring these things to the *spiritual part of yourself*, which is your feelings.

God is a spiritual being that always was and always will be, but man is born and then dies because he is *mortal*. You cannot raise a man to the level of power of the Lord. This is not so and can never be so inside any man because we are born in flesh and we are flesh in physical form. We can only have one thought at a time inside of our mind, and we can only have one feeling at a time in our spirit. When we speak to one another it is with one word at a time, and the Lord who lives inside us gives us these feelings and these thoughts where we are one in the feeling of the covenant of the Lord. He sends us to feel the power and the understanding of our human form. How can any mortal man possibly be God or the son of God? What the son of God means is the common sense needed to understand life itself.

Common sense is the son of God, and Jesus's teaching represents common sense. So the common sense of Jesus's teaching is what is to be worshipped as the son of God, not the mortal man who died some two thousand years ago.

Understand that God is *supreme*. He brings truth through the power of his own spirit in who we are so we can come to understand the glory of human intelligence where God is in the mind and soul of every man on earth. God gave us the power of wisdom, and each one of us has to return to that power to understand the Almighty God. The birth of a man in the world does not mean the birth of a new God, but the explanation of the old God. God sent Jesus to explain the old God who had no beginning and no end to it. You cannot make a God out of the birth of a man because he is just a man that God has created like the rest of us. Worship God for creating life, both here on earth and in the understanding of heaven that He is God with all the supreme power. The result is the supreme word in all the theology of all faith.

This is the power to understand the Almighty God. God had to *judge* the world, so He placed Jesus in front of Him to fool those who have always fooled themselves and those who tried to fool others with their own false idea of what God looks like in the physical form. Understand that God is not flesh in the physical form of any kind and you cannot replace Him. If you worship Jesus in the form of a physical God, you have missed the whole point of placing an image before the Lord your God. Worshipping an image before the Lord your God is *breaking all the laws* that God has given us on Mount Sinai. People have desecrated the first set of stone tablets by worshipping a golden calf before the Lord, the supreme God of all.

By worshipping Jesus, you have failed to understand the *true* laws of the Almighty God. I say to you, all the false prophets of the world, that worshipping any man before the Lord, the Supreme God of the Creation, is a *great sin*, and each one of you who has broken his commandments and his laws must turn your stiff neck toward the Lord your God. You false prophets have preached day and night to worship Jesus, and your false foolish notions have trapped the rest of the world in the false hope, false understanding, and false value in the image of a simple man of the earth.

Presently, I wish to talk about the *salvation of the Lord*. You have fooled yourself by worshipping a false God. Now God has sent the truth by the hand of His prophet. This will tell you how wrong you were in your own sin of worshipping Jesus before the Lord your God in the image that you, false prophets, have made up on your own. On the seventh day of the Creation, meaning here, in this next one thousand years, you have to redeem yourself on this great day of Sabbath that the Lord has brought upon us.

Next, we go to the escape to Egypt and return when it's safe in the land. The whole human race, meaning the family of man, had to go to the land of Egypt. The prophet of the Lord—and here I mean Jesus—had to return to Egypt. This means that all of mankind has to go to false religion. True religion was not safe because the evil of the lies of the world would destroy the great prophet of the Lord. Why we had to go to the land of Egypt is because everyone in the whole world had to go to the falsehood of false religion to *understand the true religion* of those who are blessed by God in order to receive the blessings of the Father of Heaven.

I must try to explain to you, from the book of Genesis, that you have to go through Esau, the firstborn of Isaac, to understand why Jacob receives the blessing of Isaac, his father. Understand that from the very beginning of the Creation, God planned this event to bring the explanation and understanding of the creation of intelligence, as well as the knowledge of how you are going to be blessed in the values of heaven by the God who has created you in intelligence. You must understand that the weakness of the mind is that the mind has to be introduced to your spiritual understanding in order to understand what God is so you will understand the Angel of Reality.

As a baby who does not know the difference between right and wrong, you had to learn from wrong—you had to go through wrong in order to be able to understand right. So the new baby in the new teaching must go into wrong (into the land of Egypt) to learn false religion before he can enter the Kingdom of God with true religion.

This is the way it works. If you do not go through the worst in life, you just cannot understand where the best in life is. Understand the power here where Cain killed Abel to receive all the land for himself. This means that wrong has to kill right because you have to go through wrong to understand right. Just like a baby who does not believe that fire will hurt him until he tests it and he finds out that it does burn. It is the same thing with wrong. You have to touch wrong to find that wrong hurt you and you do not want to do it again. Wrong is a fire, and right becomes the water that kills a fire. Then right becomes the wisdom of the wise, and this is why the Lord sent the whole human race through the falsehood of false religion where the children of wrong were burned by the fire. Drink the water of right and you will come to understand right over wrong.

Blessed are those who have been persecuted and when people falsely say all kinds of evil things against them. Rejoice and be glad because great is your reward in heaven, for in the same way, they persecuted the prophets who were before you. Come and understand the power of the Lord for those who went through the great persecution. The Lord planned this on the human race for those who think they are perfect, and God placed an evil "king" in their heart to make them appear so wonderfully beautiful. He gave them a heart of such evil deeds, and He made them so perfect in man's human thinking.

Next, we come to understand the fulfillment of the law. Try to understand that the teaching of the world did not change from the Old Testament to the New Testament. Understand well that the Laws of God cannot change. But the false prophets of all the religions of the earth changed the law from spiritual to physical understanding where no one understood the way of the Scriptures. This put the human race in *total darkness*, and the world of religious understanding became the verdict of the life and the death of Jesus, and they worship in the lies of the world which are against the laws of God.

To fulfill the laws of God you must come to understand the power of the First Law of God, which is to only worship the *One True God of the Creation*. You are *not allowed* to worship the image of anyone, including Jesus, because the New Testament can bring you to the scorching heat, where you will burn your butt and jump like a locust. You will jump to the second Commandment of our Lord and start worshipping a man *before* the Lord your God. With the false understanding of the New Testament, you will think that Jesus is God or the son of God...but *we are all sons of God* because we come from the Spirit of God. We do also come from an *animal*—this makes us half-animal and half-spirit between our mind and spirit. You must understand yourself and the purpose of life and continue to worship with your spiritual understanding that comes from God.

However, if you start letting the *mind* lead the spirit (and since the mind of an animal can only understand the physical part of our understanding), we fall, with our mind, to the physical understanding of the earth. And the next thing you know, the whole world has the same disease because they are all worshipping a false god like the world is doing now. That is a great sin because the whole world fell deep into darkness in the teaching of the beast.

Now the world worships the birth of a man as a little baby. Then they worship the life of Jesus, going deep into the beast and worshipping the body of a man of the animal. They worship the death of that man and make the *proud claim* of worshipping the death of a man. They call the death of that man their *salvation*. They claim in error that the suffering of that man is their salvation, and they don't have to do anything in the control of their life but to worship the suffering and death of that man. They say that the suffering of Jesus is enough to save their soul and that there is *nothing they can do wrong* that will make them lose their soul because the death of Jesus has already paid for their soul.

The idea that by the death of that man, they are safe from the Lord's anger is the *biggest lie* ever told. They really think that Jesus is the son of God, but every one of us is a son of God because we were born from his spirit and spiritual value. You may believe in the Lord your God, but to be on the side of truth, you must also believe in common sense and reality. You cannot change the laws of God because you do not believe in the one true God. You *cannot* make yourself a God of your own by worshipping the golden calf in front of the altar of the Lord. If you are offering your sacrifice to the gold calf, you are not worshipping the one true God of the Creation.

Next, we go to adultery—the sin that has corrupted the world. If you think that adultery is a sexual relationship between people, you are wrong because the sexual relationship between people is the holiest of all rituals that the Lord has given us to make another human being feel as good and satisfied as a person could possibly be. You may call it what you want, but loving people is part of the truth. Making love to your fellow human is holy and proper in the power within ourselves, which is the glory of human intelligence where you come to understand what feels good in the glory of the Lord. God made man to love one another with all that is holy in the Creation of his holiness in the values of our feelings. This is where a human being can have the great feelings of others and be happy in this faith of holiness that we can love one another in who we are.

Let's look at adultery in the proper manner of what God calls adultery. Understand that adultery is a spiritual sin that happens *when you place your faith in another God* in the wedding feast of the groom, which is God Himself. Understand the power of offering your sacrifice to someone other than God. Why do you think they call the Catholic Church the "great prostitute" in the Book of Revelation? It is because the Catholic Church makes "saints" out of people, and people worship those saints—they offer sacrifices and believe that these so-called saints will hear their prayers and will pass them on to the Lord as a favor.

I tell you, in truth, that these are the *biggest lies* that you can possibly teach people. There is no greater sin in the world than the sin of the Catholic Church and organized religion. That is the sin that brings the people to the lowest of all points in human thinking where they worship a man who is nothing more than an animal. Worshipping people in front of the Lord is what the Lord despises and arouses his anger against mankind. You are *not* supposed to worship any man or anything with an image of any kind. What's wrong with the Scriptures that tell us not to worship these images, and what's wrong with the Ten Commandments that tell us not to worship the image of a man?

The Scriptures tell us not to worship the image, so why does organized religion put mortal men before God and destroy his laws and his commandments to worship in falsehood? I tell all of you popes, cardinals, priests, and ministers that you ate the apple on the forbidden tree in the garden of Adam and Eve and that Adam, the spirit *you made your own choice in false religion.* Eve, which is the mind, ate the apple and gave it to. They both thought they were wiser than God and ate the apple on the forbidden tree of good and evil in what you thought was the proper way to worship your Jesus in the flesh—in birth and in death. But you made so many mistakes that you became the "great prostitute" and you worshipped in the practice of falsehood with your adulterous mind. You listened to the serpent on the tree that gave you the forbidden fruit and you thought you knew better. You broke every law of the Scriptures of our Lord, the True God of all.

Now we go to the law of divorce. You have to come to the understanding of the law of divorce where Eve (the mind), makes you sin in adultery, teaches you to worship false gods, and makes you eat the forbidden fruit in the paradise of total intelligence. You have to divorce that mind and make your spirit control the mind. You must *reject* all insufficient deviations of the mind because the wine that the mind drinks is weak and has no flavor. It is only based on your loss and gain. The mind has no feelings of intelligence except for loss and gain, so it is right for you to divorce the mind. The Lord makes sure that you bring nothing of spiritual value because the mind does not understand anything in feelings.

Love your enemies. Who are your enemies, and why should you love them? Your enemies are the opposite of the power of love. When you say "I love my enemies," it does not mean that you should love wrong over right. It means to love those who do not understand in the way of the Lord. Try to bring to them to the truth in the good example and in the value of heaven so you can heal their infractions against you. You must love them because they are *equal* to you. Love them as human beings and try to understand that in the Kingdom of God, *no one* was created to understand everything in perfect form unless he received the birth of the spirit.

Teach them the value of the Kingdom of God through your humble deeds. Don't make yourself better than they are. Use what you have learned in the faith of the Lord your God by understanding the power of the door that you came through in the value of heaven. Remember that you also lived in false religion before now. You went through the narrow entrance yourself. You had to go and crawl to the Lord your God to receive the wisdom of the wise so you could understand your Heavenly Father. Now that you understand, you should bring the power to understand to others as well as increasing your own wisdom by showing the narrow entrance to those who did not find it. Use the Key of Heaven to love them with. This is loving both your neighbor and your enemy.

Next, we go to the understanding of giving to the needy. Make sure that you humble yourself within the law of giving to the needy. I tell you here that nothing could be a worse sin than stealing from others. If you give to others, don't make yourself look like a good person that comes in the value of a god toward them. Make sure that you give in terms of justice and fairness so people will see justice and fairness in your deeds. Do not give what you do not need just to look good in front of others. Make sure that what you give is within the boundaries of justice, fairness, and unity.

What you give in spiritual value to your brother should be the truth. Make sure that you have within you the ability to give to your brother in humble deeds in the value of Heaven. Use your wisdom and the glory of intelligence as proof that you don't show off in front of anybody else to show that you are better than them. What you give inside your spirit is valuable—not just in the way of the wealth of the earth but in the way of the *spirit* also. You should pronounce good over evil so the power of the Lord will live in your deeds and keep you humble. *Love your brother as yourself.* If a person does not have enough intelligence to do for himself in the values of heaven, you must open the door of heaven for them as well as for you. You should help those who cannot take care of themselves. Remember that the Lord made you intelligent enough to take care of yourself. He gave you enough for you to be holy, which you are, so make holiness live in their sight. This way, both of you can see the truth in which you have given others by the spirit of the Lord your God. Giving to others is as holy as you possibly can be. Be kind to others as the Lord is kind to you, and love all your brothers in the justice of fairness and unity.

Following along, we go to the understanding of prayer. Do not pray so that everyone will see you and think of you as a good man who prays for others. Learn what praying is so you can understand what it means to pray for others. First of all, do not be like a hypocrite who tells people what you pray about. Do not pray in the church of false religion to show all your friends how good you are in the heart of your soul. That is not true prayer. True praying is in the church of your soul where no one can see you. When you do pray, do not speak repetitious words of no value. Pray inside your feelings for the justice of the Lord to come upon those who you pray for.

Make sure that what you ask of the Lord is part of his justice and fairness. Pray with a heart full of love and unity so everyone can benefit from your prayers. Do not pray to heal whatever is wrong with your physical self. You have to make sure that your prayer is in the best interests of the spirit and not in the physical way. If the Lord sends some physical ailments to your brother, make sure you pray that your brother will use that physical pain and suffering to make himself better in spiritual terms so he can see the *light* from his suffering. Don't just pray for someone to get better in his physical needs.

Remember that God is the *teacher* of all who suffer. If God would have mercy on mankind in the way that man thinks, He would never send any physical infractions to anyone. He sends those infractions to show that person his mistakes in spiritual value so he can straighten out his sins in the value of heaven. It is not a man's physical disease but rather his spiritual disease that kills him. Praying for the wrong things by trying to rehabilitate mankind in physical needs will not help them in spiritual value. So make sure that what you pray for another person is to help them with spiritual life because the Lord did not waste his time sending him a physical disease for no reason. The Lord sends these things to make him see the light and worship the one true God.

Next, we are going to understand fasting. This is a ritual in your spiritual value, and it is not about your physical needs whatsoever. Fasting in spirit is to understand the value of what you should eat and what you should not eat in the value of your spiritual needs that come from the Lord your God. We come in the shape of an animal, and we think that what we should sacrifice to the Lord is on the physical side of life. But to fast in the way of your spiritual value means that you shall not enter false religion of any kind. You are *not* supposed to be Christian, Catholic, or any religion on the face of the earth. Religion has to be *obsolete* in the value of falsehood. You should not eat what comes out of the mouth of the false prophet, and do not eat what comes out of false organized religions. They trick you into believing in their church, and they get you to sell your soul to them for no value whatsoever.

These people do wrong, but they think they are doing good by inflaming your mind with falsehood. They do not understand the Old Testament—that the New Testament is nothing more than a blur for them. They try to teach what they believe from their false religion, but you should stay away from it and learn to eat what comes out of the mouth of God. Don't eat what comes out of the mouth of the false prophet because if you do, you'll believe in something that has *no value* whatsoever, and you will leave your true feelings that God sent to you.

You must come to understand that a blind man cannot teach you the way of truth by making false intelligence look good. If you believe these false prophets, you believe the lies of the world and you are stuck in falsehood because you have eaten the forbidden fruit in the Kingdom of God. The Lord has forbidden you to eat the apple. But false religion comes in the center of intelligence, where Eve (the mind) ate the forbidden apple from the forbidden tree at the center of the garden of God's word. She then gave it to Adam (the spirit), and your spiritual understanding ate the fruit of spiritual falsehood.

Now we come to understand the value of the treasures in heaven. Learn what is valuable in this world and who is the one that gives you life in the values of heaven. You didn't think to understand and worship God even though you had your Bible next to you on your nightstand. The Bible tells you that you are supposed to worship only *one* God and to not place any image of anyone on earth or in heaven before the Lord. False religion changed the laws of God by worshipping Jesus in front of the Lord and made him god.

What happened to the teaching of the law? Why did the false prophet move the boundaries of all the laws of heaven? Why did he make himself a new set of laws by worshipping what was forbidden in the Old Testament? You are supposed to worship only one God so you will have the treasures in heaven. But what happened to this world is that people used the story of Jesus and changed the whole system of law so they could understand it with their little locust minds. People must come to understand that the treasures of heaven *did not change*, but the people of this world listened to the false prophet who tells them that they have a new covenant with the Lord. God established a new covenant with mankind, but He never changed any laws. He made a new deal with the people of the world because we decided to worship Jesus, but the false prophet told us that God changed his laws.

Next, we go to the understanding of do not worry. Do not worry about your physical self—just worry about your spiritual self. Understand the power of your spirit because your spirit is what *controls* your physical self. If you lose control of yourself, you will not be able to understand the power of the law and that's exactly what happened to the world. If a person does not believe in the one true God of the Creation, he makes his own law and does not respect the laws of the universe. Understand well here that the laws of the universe *are* the laws of the Almighty God. If you don't believe in the Creator and if you worship the image of a man before the Lord your God, you *break* the laws of the Creation and you cannot enter the kingdom that the Lord has planned for mankind.

You may believe that the laws in your belief system work just as well as a loving God, but they don't. When you deal with man's laws over God's laws that live inside your soul, the next thing you know, you make all kinds of mistakes because your feelings will be *falsely* understood. You will make the greatest mistake of your life, and you will be in the man-made prisons for breaking the laws of the Almighty God and the laws of mankind. You will find no way out of that evil place that you created with your own sins. This is where you have chosen to live your life because you refuse to know the Lord your God.

You made your own god in the understanding of the mind because you worried about what you would eat and what clothes you would wear, but your worry will do nothing for you. You will just try to live on stolen money or kill people in violence because you think you should have that which is not yours to have. You think you can trick the insurance company or the government by killing your wife or your husband, and you think that no one will know. But what you don't know is that there are laws that you do not believe in, and in these laws is a spirit that controls all human deeds.

What you thought would never come out will come out. The Lord made those laws. He put them in the Creation, and He called them the laws of justice, fairness, and unity. After you have broken these laws, you realize that you are not allowed to eat the apple that came from the forbidden tree at the center of the garden of the Lord's justice. You thought you were so smart that you could break the laws and get away with it. But now, you sit in a jail cell thinking of how to find new laws of your own to get you out of there and free you from the prison sentence. However, you will only try trick the world again if you find your way out with your own law.

The Laws of Truth are not on your side, and no matter how much you try to lie and cheat, you are condemned of the violence of your crimes. You worry about what you are going to eat and how you are going to dress yourself with stolen money. You are thinking that the perfect murder has brought you to the justice of the Lord. You didn't think that there was a set of laws above you, and now the prison term you are serving is justly imposed on you in the values of the justice of the Lord.

Next, we go to the understanding of judging others. Understand the purpose of this law because you are not allowed to call them evil in your soul. You can say that they committed evil deeds if they committed a stupid crime like killing, raping someone, robbing a bank, or doing anything wrong that they have committed. But you are not allowed to go into your spirit and call them evil. We know that these are evil deeds, but we are still not allowed to call them evil because these deeds are deeds of passion that come from an evil idea. They thought they could get away with it, and they tried to live their evil dream and protect themselves with lies. But the truth of it is that their heart is as holy as yours and you are not allowed to judge them and call them evil. You are not allowed to use these words against anyone because if you judge these people with these types of words and you think of yourself to be better than them, you *break* the laws of God because God did not create them to be unclean. The Lord has created them in his own image just like he created you, and you are not allowed to judge them. That's for the Lord to do.

Now let us come to understand, ask, seek, and knock. If you knock on the door of the Lord and He hears you, He will answer you. Understand that these things are done in spiritual value. You should not ask the Lord for anything in physical value. The things that you ask for must be done in the spiritual understanding where you come to understand that the way of the Lord is intelligence. The physical things that you ask of the Lord are not important to Him. What is important to the Lord is that you are a spiritual learner in the value of the spirit. You should not ask for things in your physical life because your physical life can only be improved by your spiritual understanding. So again, I repeat, if you ask the Lord to fix your physical life, this is *not* very important to Him. If your physical life doesn't work, it is because you need to understand things in your spiritual way of thinking.

The reason that God sends you all the problems that you can handle in your physical life, is to straighten out your spiritual way of understanding of what is the truth, common sense, and reality. And if something is wrong with the truth, the common sense, or the reality that lives inside you, then God sends you physical punishment of your physical way of life because God is trying to help you understand the value of your spirit so things will go right for you in your soul and you can make things better in your physical self.

To follow, we come to understand the narrow and the wide gate. Entering through the wide gate is when a man wants to be powerful and wealthy, and he thinks that his money and his power will be approved by the Lord. It's all right to be wealthy, but make sure you are *fair* with your wealth. How can a rich man be fair with his wealth when he claims everything for himself and he leaves nothing for others? The wealth of the earth is not like the wealth of heaven. On earth, it is physical things that count, but in heaven, it is the wisdom of caring for each other.

The understanding of caring for each other is to *share* with each other. The power of being poor, in front of being rich, is almost impossible to understand with the human feelings because the mind tells you that being rich means being happy. The mind tells you that you can do what you want because you have the power to decide for yourself what your needs are, but when you're poor, you just don't have that same power. It's confusing for mankind to realize that you must come to understand the power of these feelings.

If the Lord made you rich, it is harder for you to enter the Kingdom of God. But the justice of the Lord made *both* gates open to all men—one is a little wider, and the other gate is made much smaller. It doesn't mean that only poor people will enter the Kingdom of God and the rich will be not be able to get in. Being rich or poor *both* have their own rewards as well as their own sacrifices.

Now we are going to understand the tree and its fruit. A good tree produces good fruit and a bad tree produces bad fruit. But understand that you can produce good or bad fruit whether you are rich or poor. If you are rich in value, you still can produce good fruit, or you can be very poor and produce the worst fruit that you can ever imagine. Understand that evil is in the heart and in the spirit of your dreams. Mankind tries to find a shortcut to the laws of God, and if he does, he loses his soul. Whether you are rich or poor, if you have no respect for the laws of man and the laws of God, you can lose your soul by the bad fruit that you produce.

Jesus heals a man with leprosy. If you understand leprosy in spiritual terms, you will come to understand the power that exists in spirit as well is in flesh. Mankind uses leprosy in terms of a physical disease, but you just have to look in the spirit to find the same disease. In physical understanding, leprosy is a disease that destroys the flesh and makes a person look like their skin is all deteriorating and awful looking. Now let's look at it in the way of the spirit so you can understand what was written in terms of a physical disease that also comes to be known as a spiritual disease, like hate. The leprosy of the spirit becomes hate in your heart. The more you begin to hate, the more you look awful to the human spirit. If you hate someone and you continue hating them, your spirit is unclean. And when your spirit is unclean, it is just like the physical part—you have a disease just like the disease of the flesh. You continue hating until hate destroys you and brings you down to your knees. Then you come to a point where you are full of hate, and it causes your spirit to deteriorate because hate is a disease of the spirit. Eventually, your hate will come to a point beyond your control, and it will keep on destroying your spirit because hate is unclean. Hate will destroy you completely.

Next, we come to the faith of the centurion—the faith of a Roman soldier telling Jesus that his servant is dying, and he needs help. Jesus saw the faith of that man and said to his followers that he had not met anyone in Israel with faith like this. The power to understand faith is to understand reality. Mankind really needs to understand faith to see this great power. The Lord has placed us into a situation where the people who believe in miracles and healing of the flesh must come to understand the power within ourselves. God has placed inside of us Ruben, who is the firstborn of Jacob, in the understanding that faith is part of our beliefs in the power of the Creation.

Faith is one of the twelve sons of Jacob because it was created inside of us for the power of the *unknown*. To have faith is to understand the power of the Almighty God. It is the power to know that there is a God to help us understand life inside our soul and to understand that life *is* within us. Faith helps us to believe in one God, where the Lord can free any doubt that we may have so that we can understand what the Lord looks like *inside us*. This becomes our spiritual "eye" in that we see what the Lord looks like and to understand his power in human thinking.

Faith gives us the understanding of the power of the Lord who heals us in time with the natural power of the Creation. When the Lord sees that you have the power to understand faith itself, then you will come to the glory of the seven spirits of God. Remember that

God is *not* a miracle worker. All these miracles are done in time and in the value of the understanding of life itself. God can change the situation of your physical life into a blessed way in the time of his value. The way Christianity looks at faith in the superstitious mind gives them nothing more than false faith. If you have a strong faith inside you, God will change your physical value to the spiritual value. You must come to understand the power of the Lord so you can see within yourself the reason to have faith in something. You know that there is a God who can change things, but all faith must be spiritual inside the heart of a human being. What you have lost in the physical part of life will be gained by your spiritual faith. It is the true faith in the Lord that will accomplish your dreams in time to bring to life the reality of the heart so the physical part of you will become blessed by the spirit. The people who go to church have faith in superstitious teachings, but they do not have faith in the Lord God in their time of need.

Now we come to understand the healing of many where a human being is sealed by the power of his faith. If your faith is superstitious and you put your physical needs *before* your spiritual needs, then you will find yourself sucked in by your physical needs. That will deceive you, and your faith will just be superstitious. It will not be the true faith that the Lord has placed inside the heart of mankind. You must remember here that the Lord did not create mankind to live and suffer in pain. Understand the outcome of faith where you must first be healed in spirit before you can be healed physically. If you are full of spiritual diseases like hate, prejudice, jealousy, and bigotry, then you are *not clean*. You will spread all kinds of evil to others because your heart is impure. False religion taught you to believe in all kinds of evil ideas of judging others. How can you be healed in your physical needs when your spiritual power is full of dead bones? Try to understand that Jesus healed the people who were simple and humble in the wisdom of the Lord God.

Next is the cost of following Jesus. You must come to understand the power of following *common sense*. The real son of God is common sense, and this is why the New Testament refers to Jesus as the son of God. You cannot worship the man Jesus and call him the physical son of God. The Word is God and the Parables are God but not the servant of God who came to bring the Parables for he was just a man like the rest of us. Jesus was the servant of God who brought forth the Parables from the Lord our God. You *cannot* change who God is on the altar of the Throne of Heaven. This is *not* a man-made story like a man who owns a big company, a big bank, or a large business, and he leaves his son (of flesh) to take over for his father. The son *cannot* replace the father any more than Jesus can replace his father in heaven because flesh is flesh and spirit is spirit. You *cannot* find a man who lived before us or who will come after us on earth, who has or will ever replace God.

God institutes intelligence in the values of learning and teaching, and He will send the servant to bring common sense in the Parables. There is *nothing* in the New Testament that tells us that the man, Jesus, is God. Jesus *did* call himself the Son of Man, but the Son of Man means the history of man in the way that the Lord sends the Parables from the past to the present and to the coming time. These three parts of time will be understood in the way of the Son of Man. The Son of Man is in the power of history and intelligent thinking.

Do *not* mix up the son of man with the son of God. You must understand in the power of the Lord and think intelligently when you refer to the Scriptures. Try to make sense of the spiritual way of the Scriptures. Understand that the Lord is spiritual, and you cannot change Him to the physical value of flesh. When you were a child, you talked like a child. Now that you are a human being, in an adult body, you must understand like an adult and leave the ideas of a child in the past.

Now we go to Jesus calming the storm. The real son of God, common sense itself, will calm the big storm of false religion. The power of the hand of God will calm the big storm of falsehood that we live in today in false religion. God made people believe in Jesus because they falsely understood that Jesus was the son of God. They made Jesus God in the weakness of their mind, just like Eve ate the forbidden fruit from the forbidden tree of false religion. What made the world so ignorant was the worshipping of Jesus as god in the worst storm of ignorance the world has ever seen.

Common sense will come to calm the storm of the false prophet that we are experiencing now in the world. Common sense will be known to all mankind by the teaching of the son of God Himself. Man will come to know who God is, and they will start understanding that common sense is the truth and the truth is common sense. The two are in One God in the values of the intelligence of the Creation. Common sense was the son of the father from the foundation of the world. It is the same truth now and for all time to come.

If you come and live with common sense in the power of God, then you live with the Father, the Son, and the Holy Spirit in the reality of the One God of the Creation. It should be understood, for all generations to come, that He is the One Unique God of all and that this One Unique God has *all* the power to calm any storm of any false religion of the earth that steps outside of the boundary and into falsehood by worshipping One True God of the Creation. People of the earth have placed the man Jesus as the Almighty God, and they offer their sacrifices to Jesus in the greatest falsehood the world has ever seen. Christianity created the greatest storm of falsehood where people use the name of Jesus in front of the Lord your God.

Understand that it was meant to be that Eve, the mind, would deceive Adam, the spirit, into listening to the serpent on the tree of the knowledge of good and evil. It was also meant to be that people would worship a false god and offer their sacrifices to this false god, just like the people in the desert made themselves a golden calf and offered their sacrifices to it. The death of Jesus on the cross was a great tragedy inside of everyone who thinks and feels that he was the physical son of God and everyone who worships him in front of the Almighty God.

But you must realize that it was the plan of God to make the false prophet believe that Jesus was God. And it was *also the plan of God* that mankind would take the advice of the great serpent on the tree in the form of the forbidden fruit that came from the forbidden tree in the garden of human intelligence. People believe the falsehood of a false religion by the false prophet, and they worship the golden calf that was made up by false religion from the forbidden fruit of organized religion. That is the big storm that lives across the centuries of time where the world would be fooled in the mind of men, and Satan, the falsehood, would *win the battle* on the battlefield of the world.

Next, we come to the healing of two demon-possessed men. You must understand who they are and what they are. You have to realize that the first demon here is the Catholic Church and the rest of Christianity. First, let's look at the Catholic Church. This is the first demon, and this demon produces a false mass in front of the offerings of the Lord. Understand well here that the Lord sent many dreams in the heart of mankind to tell us to *abolish that stupid mass* they claim is an offering to the Lord. They were told, time and time again, to get rid of that daily mass that the human race believes in so deeply where the people receive a worthless piece of bread as an offering to the Lord. This, also, is one of the greatest falsehoods the world has ever seen.

The daily mass became the daily sacrifice for many people. The church made the people eat the forbidden bread and drink the forbidden blood that made *no common sense whatsoever*. Because of false religion, people worship the golden calf on the altar where they offer their sacrifice of daily living. Fully understand that this false daily sacrifice of believing that the blood of Jesus, the physical man, was offered on the altars by the teachers of false religion. There's nothing in this world that can be more in falsehood than the Catholic and the Christian mass over the bread and blood that is supposed to be the body and blood of Jesus. There cannot be any falsehood higher than that in the spirit of mankind where no one in the world could pass by without being attacked by those two evil spirits. Now common sense is coming to the world by the Hand of God. He is condemning those two evil spirits that have been in the soul of mankind, where they build big, evil churches all over the world to manifest such evil spirits and offer all of the daily sacrifices to a false god.

Now that we are deep in the evil spirit of the world, try to understand the power that made people miserable by worshipping false gods. When you worship the two evil spirits, you make your life totally miserable and unacceptable where people commit all kinds of crimes. No one could point out where all that evil came from because the power of worshipping evil gods, evil objects, and idols is the *evil-est thing* you can do in the decisions of your life.

People make great mistakes in the values of their life, for example, when priests *deny* themselves the satisfaction of sex in their lives or when they choose to offer their sacrifices to Jesus with their stupid mass. The most stupid act that a human being can possibly do is to bless a piece of bread and a cup of wine with their human hands and make people *believe* that that bread and wine is the body and blood of Jesus. Try to understand that there is *no reality* in any of these deeds and there is *no common sense* at all in the false thinking and understanding of mankind. If you teach what is *not real* and tell people it is common sense and if you teach people in the power of total superstition, you *cannot* be on the side of the Lord. If you do such evil things against the Lord by worshipping against the truth, common sense, and reality, you are teaching against the Lord your God.

Next, we go to Jesus and John the Baptist. Understand mankind's false belief of baptism where you pour water over a person's head and call it *baptism of the soul.* When you do this, you are doing a physical deed. People look at the Scriptures in their physical understanding because they have not developed their spirit, so their mind told them that they had to go get physically baptized. They committed this and other great sins, in the belief of falsehoods, where you pour water over a person and make that simple mind believe that they are pure in heart. All the false rituals that these people call sacraments are all physical deeds. In order to purify your soul, you need to do this through a spiritual process, not a physical one.

Now let us look at the *real baptism* that brings the birth of intelligence with the purification of your heart in what is true and untrue in the values of common sense and reality. You must live in truth, common sense, and reality in the simple truth of life, and that is how you must baptize other people. Don't make anything up in your soul and tell other people all kinds of false things against common sense and reality. The truth has the power to flourish inside the soul of another man, so you must add reality to the purpose of common sense where the blessing of your dialogue will baptize them in the understanding of common sense and reality. Understand well here that you don't have to prove the whole Bible to anyone. Just baptize them in the simple truth, and that will be enough for you to baptize them in the Holy Spirit. When you teach religion on the physical part of the Scriptures, you make a lot of mistakes and the baptizing of the physical body is an *insult* to the Lord your God. Remember that the Bible is a *spiritual book*, and no one is allowed to teach the Scriptures in the physical understanding. If you don't understand the Bible in the spiritual way, you should not be teaching the Bible at all. If you do, you are a great sinner in front of the Lord your God. And if you do not eat these words, things will *not* go well for you. Just repent of your falsehood and from all the false teaching that you have brought upon mankind in the physical way to understand the Scriptures.

Next, we go to the Sabbath. If you have read the Scriptures every day for six days in a row, you should try to rest on the seventh day and rejoice in what you have learned in the previous six days. By resting your mind and soul, you can better understand what you have learned within the six working days of the Scriptures. Understand well that the Sabbath is a day of rest for the Lord, and the seventh day of the Creation comes after six thousand years of sending Scriptures to the world. The seventh day of the Creation is the seventh day, where the Lord will see what you did with what you have learned.

We are currently living in the time of the seventh day of the Creation, where a human being learns from the six days of labor that are spent serving the Lord your God. Remember here that man was created on the sixth day in the full value of education. Every man has the privilege of going to school and learning to understand the Scriptures in intelligence, and each man was given an education to understand with. Also, we were given a Bible on our nightstand to read and to understand the Word of God. If you do not learn anything in spiritual value, that's your own fault. And if you do not learn anything about loving your neighbor as yourself, that's your fault as well. Use the priesthood of Levi, the son of Jacob, to love your brother. You must bring the priests of love inside all your dealings with others.

Now we go to the woe on unrepentant towns. Woe to you, Catholicism and Christianity. Woe to those of you who do not change the false religion that you brought upon the earth to lie to people and make money with it. You made yourself an easy life out of doing nothing of value in the world. You made yourself a priest of the church so you could escape the production of the world and have people worship you. You took the way of easy living, where you live in the sin of falsehood, and you fooled many people into believing things against the Lord your God.

The time is coming when you will have to understand the New Jerusalem, but you will be too proud and arrogant with your stiff neck to change your teaching because you already think that you have the right teaching in your soul. You will not change because you don't believe you need to change. However, the Lord did not approve of your false teaching. In the Scriptures, the Lord tells us that a man will come in his name and bring a false teaching. You will refuse to change your mind and your stiff neck because you have been worshipping a false god before the Lord.

You must *change* your worshipping of Jesus that was so wrong to begin with. Understand the power of the creation and why God made you a false prophet. Now understand well, you false prophets of the earth. Understand, all you Catholic priests, archbishops, cardinals, and popes. Understand, all you Christian preachers, rabbis, and all false prophets of false religion. You made a *big mistake* by worshipping the physical part of the Scriptures and accusing people of physical sins that should have never been understood as sins. You have failed to understand the truth because you have read the Scriptures with your weak locust mind that God has given you to understand with. You have fooled many people for generation after generation, and now you must pay for the stupidity and the ignorance that you have preached on earth. Now you will be left holding the falsehood that you have brought to the world.

You will say to yourself and to others, "Do not believe this man who wrote this book," and you will tell people, "This man does *not* understand anything of Scriptures." But I tell you that I have the Bible behind me, along with the teaching of all the prophets.

Everything the Scriptures said is that you have misled the world by worshipping the physical part of Jesus and by making a man equal to God Almighty in the teaching of your soul. Remember that you have to pay for all your sins in front of the Lord and in front of the fires of hell. Woe to you, false prophets and stiff-necked Christians. You have deceived many, many people in your lifetime. Now let's see how fast you can turn that stiff neck around and start worshipping the Lord your God in heaven with all your soul and with all your mind.

Try to observe the laws of God inside you spiritually. The first commandment of the Lord our God, given to Moses on Mount Sinai, was written for you who took the name of the Lord in vain and preached outside of human understanding. Unless you change your heart real fast in front of the Lord, accept your sin, and repent all your sins against the Lord God of heaven, you are in violation of this commandment. Learn the Bible, page for page, from the Book of Genesis with Adam and Eve through to the great flood that fooled the world of falsehood. Then start believing in the God of Abraham, Isaac, and Jacob, and try to understand the twelve sons of Jacob.

Repent of your past mistakes when you made the Lord *forgotten by mankind*. You have brought the *false image* of Jesus in front of the Lord and made him the god of the world. Understand well, you unrepentant city of falsehood, you have led mankind to break all the laws of God by the hand that *betrayed* the Almighty God. Woe to you, false prophets of false religion—you turned the heart of mankind into the *worshipping of idols*, and you made idols look like they were part of the spirit of the Lord.

Next, we go to the understanding of the rest for the weary. Come to the Lord, all you sheep that tried to follow the teaching of the false prophet because you will worry about your soul in the New World. Come to the new world, and experience the truth about the Lord. You have been lied to for so many, many years in the value of false religion. Repent of your weakness where the false prophet has taught you to believe in the false understanding that you never really understood inside your heart. Repent and you will be forgiven. Don't let your stiff neck of Christianity make you lose your soul.

Understand well that God has *planned* this falsehood on mankind from the very beginning of the Creation to make the false prophet live in arrogance and superstition. This is so the Lord can bring justice upon the world and to punish those who live in the arrogance of Eve (the mind), who has eaten the forbidden fruit and transferred it to Adam (the spirit). It is a sin against the Lord to eat the forbidden fruit of the tree of life of good and evil. The Lord has forbidden the mind of weak men from determining good and evil until the day of the Lord where good and evil will be explained in reality and common sense for all mankind to hear. Practice the holy religion of the heart by standing up and worshipping God in your life—but *not* in those worthless caves that people call churches where the Word of the Lord God of Heaven is not being taught.

Let us proceed to Beelzebub. You have to understand the healing of demons inside the soul of people by the common sense of intelligence. Understand that every time the scriptures refer to Jesus, you have to go to the spirit to understand the meaning where Jesus represents common sense. Anyone who goes into common sense to understand the Lord your God will understand the common sense of the son of God. This is because your common sense *is* the son of God. If you claim that Jesus is the son of God, then you claim an image before the Lord, and this is a great sin. God is the truth, common sense, and reality where the power of truth and reality stand in the spirit of the Lord.

When you refer to God, you cannot refer to Him through the animal of a human being. If you do, then you start believing that the animal human being is the image of God, and that becomes a great sin. Replacing God in spiritual value with an animal is *unforgivable.* Whoever commits that sin has to be restored in the value of the truth itself. You must repent of your stupidity of worshipping false gods before the Lord. The false prophets are blinding you, and Satan sends his advocate to bless the image of men before God. This is a great sin that needs forgiveness by the Lord Himself. When you're trying to understand God with the image of a man, you create a great sin because the image has nothing that can help you with all your spiritual sacrifice.

Next, we go to the sign of Jonah. Jonah was in the big fish for three days. Understand that the three days mean three millennia of human living time. Two thousand years ago, the prophecy and the Parable of the New Testament were born. Now we have another thousand years to live in human living time where all false religions must be defeated—only then will our seven lifetimes of human living be accomplished for the seven days of the creation. The power of the spirit of humanity will be restored as we enter through this millennium of human time living. The soul of humanity will be restored where the goat will be separated from the sheep. The sheep will be restored as sheep in the beautiful pasture of the Lord, and the goat will be placed in the same evil that they have brought on the life of others.

Remember that the three days are the three last days of life living time that will be completed with this last millennium, which is the seven days of the creation where the Lord must rest and bring you through into the heart of mankind. All that was hidden will be known, and the truth will be spoken for all mankind to hear, and whoever decides against the truth of God and his law will lose their life, but whoever tries to gain life and tries to hear the truth in his soul will *gain his life*.

Now we are going to understand the parable of the Sower. Understand fully the parable of the good seed, which is understanding the Scriptures by yourself, and to live a good life on earth by being the person who listens to the wisdom of human intelligence. When you fall asleep in false religion, your enemy plants some bad seeds in your intelligence—this means your garden of human intelligence or human understanding. When this happens, you come to understand the power of what looks good to the mind where you cannot see the evil seed that was planted in your garden of worshipping Jesus in front of the Lord. You will forget to worship the Lord your God because the false prophet put you to sleep with what they taught you to believe in falsehood. And these lies cannot be understood as part of the truth. If you do not worship the Lord your God in truth, somebody will trick you by preaching lies. They will make you worship the image of a man before the Lord your God. If you worship the image of Jesus, you are worshipping a false god. And the one who planted that seed inside you is the false prophet of the Earth, the evil spirit that brings lies inside your garden of human understanding. They planted these seeds of lies, and you will come to believe them. You will start worshipping Jesus, the image of a man, before the Lord your God, and when you do, you are breaking the commandments of the Lord God.

It is very critical that you only worship *one* God. You cannot worship an image before the Lord your God, and you must offer all your sacrifices to Him alone. You have to set your prayers in front of the Lord your God. Do not worship Jesus like the world of false religion does, where everybody's offerings are sacrifices to Jesus. I think the Bible explains all that, but Christians and Catholics don't read the Old Testament. Do not take the seed of the false prophet by believing in Jesus in front of the Lord. Understand well that these false prophets try very hard to teach people to worship Jesus. They pound their seed of falsehood inside the heart of mankind so deep and they make stiff-necked people out of the world where *no one* can understand how to worship the one true God.

Try to understand the evil seeds of the lies of the false prophet. Worship only the truth with the power to receive the Almighty God inside your heart by *following his laws*. Live in the protection of his laws by turning away from the false prophet and worshipping the Lord your God with all your soul and all that you have in human understanding that the Lord has given you. Now let's see what it is to worship God. Worshipping God is not going to church on Sunday or any other day of the week. That is where you pick up the evil seed and you think you are on the side of the Lord. Worshipping God is standing up on your own two feet, using your own two hands to read the Scriptures with your own heart, and claiming the value of only one God in your life by rejecting all the lies of the false prophet.

Stand on your own two feet to learn everything without asking anyone but the Lord your God for answers about the Scriptures and the way life works between men. Make sure that you get all your information in your heart from the Lord. Sometimes, you may be wrong and you may understand something backward. But *trust in yourself* to understand the Almighty Word of the Lord your God, and the Lord will feed you with his mighty knowledge. You will be restored to your good seeds, and no one will trick you to believe falsely. And if you do make a mistake with your own thinking and your own feelings, then just trust in the Lord, and He will restore you to proper health and feelings in the understanding of truth.

Next, we go to the parables of the hidden treasure and the pearl. In the Kingdom of our Lord, we have the hidden treasure of love. It is a hidden treasure because there are so few men that understand this parable of *true love*. Love hides itself in the burning bushes of the Lord where you can only see the Lord in the *center* of the bush. Understand what true love is. The burning bush is the hate of the world, and at the center of it is the face of the Lord your God, love itself. True love is Levi, the son of Jacob, where God displays in your heart the holy feelings that have existed from the beginning of the Creation. Love becomes the power to understand the Almighty God where you can see the face of God, just like Moses saw the face of God through the burning bush.

The burning bush is *all* the lies that create hate and in the center of the burning bush, where you see the face of love, which is the face of God. So few people on earth have understood love because the burning bush around the face of God is all the lies of the world that make you hate people and destroy your love. Love comes from goodness, and if you do good to others, you will love them. But if you use evil dialogue against other people, you will hate them. Love is not produced by hate—it is produced by goodness, fairness, justice, and unity with others. Love is only produced when you talk well of others. If you use the wrong of others to explain your heart, you will say the wrong thing at the wrong time and you will hate. But if you try to protect others with your dialogue, then you will love them. It all depends what you do with your dialogue and how you express yourself.

Remember that it is your dialogue that will decide which side you're on when it comes to love. If you are on the side of love, you can only see the beautiful treasure and the pearl that has been hidden for so long. You will go and spend everything that you have for love. Love is a treasure that has been hidden, and you cannot find it unless you find that wonderful pearl of being *holy* in love. If you say all kinds of evil things against your neighbor, you cannot love them because love can only be found in the priesthood of your heart. Love exists in the most powerful way of human thinking where you love your brothers as you love yourself. You will never find love in evil dialogue because love does not come from evil dialogue against your brother. It only comes when you speak in the dialogue of truth, where everyone is counted for in the justice, fairness, and the unity of the Lord.

Now we go to the parable of the net in the understanding of the Lord your God. First, you must understand love because love is the key to understanding the Lord your God. Then you go to Reuben, faith in the Lord your God, and Simeon is the understanding of that faith. Ruben and Simeon mean the first and second understanding of the sons of Jacob. Levi, which is love, is the third son of Jacob and Judah, which is dialogue, completes the understanding of the first four sons of Leah and Jacob.

You must understand the Kingdom of God to understand the sons of Jacob inside your soul and to create faith, understanding, love, and dialogue. This is where the treasures of heaven are hidden, and if you haven't found these treasures, it means that you don't understand how the Lord works inside your spiritual life. You find the hidden treasure by *understanding the twelve sons of Jacob*. If you do not understand the twelve sons of Jacob, it is because of all the lies you have heard from all the religions of the world. There is nothing more valuable than to understand the twelve sons of Jacob and to live with your natural feelings in the practice of understanding the great power of the family of man. The treasure of the family of man was hidden in the Old Testament, but few people have tried to understand *anything* that came from the Old Testament. They went to the New Testament and failed to understand the power of the treasure of God.

Loving God is loving his Creation within the family of man. If you missed that great treasure that came out of the family of Jacob, you then created war instead of creating peace, and instead of creating love, you have created hate. You have not created the good values of the Kingdom of God, but rather, you have created all the *misery* of the earth and brought upon mankind the *superstitions* of your dream and the falsehood of your heart.

Understand well that the family of mankind comes from the family of Jacob and his twelve sons, who became the twelve verbs of the Creation where we come to find all the hidden treasures and the pearl called love. Don't mix up love with hate. The love that I'm talking about must be for all mankind, not just for your friends and those who are like you. Your faith in others must be with the family of all mankind that comes and loves each other in the greatest gift of all time. The hidden treasure of the family of mankind lives in the twelve verbs inside mankind.

I will leave nobody out here. There is *no one* on earth that you are allowed to hate and call your enemy just because you don't like them and you think they are more evil than you. Just look at your *own soul* before you find anything wrong with your brother.

Next, we go to understand the power of a prophet without honor. Understand that a false prophet teaches from his mind and fools others. He takes no account of his sins, and his false faith is within himself to be uplifted by other people in the grace of his own soul. He finds pleasure in praising the god of his choice where the image of a man has become his god. This is because the image of a man is much easier to understand than a God that he could not see or hear. God does not live in the image of a man. He is not an image of anyone, and there is *no one* that can stand for God.

The false prophet has produced no value of truth and is guided by his little mind of Eve that makes him bite the apple on the forbidden tree of Satan at the center of the garden of intelligence. God placed the forbidden tree right at the *center* of the garden, where organized religion would bite that false apple and eat the forbidden fruit that killed the spirit of Adam. Mankind bites into the fruit in spirit, and both mind and spirit become the loss of his soul. Man had to suffer because of the falsehood of the forbidden fruit of organized religion that made the fruits sour. Everybody bit into the forbidden fruit of good and evil and made themselves, in their own mind, good over the evil of others. They thought of themselves to be God's chosen ones in front of others.

Now we go to John the Baptist. You must come to understand the power of the physical part of John the Baptist having his head cut off by King Herod at the request of Salome, the dancing girl. Understand well here that the sacrament of baptism in the physical part of religion is false. Man has *no power* to baptize people with physical water from their fake river of life in their false religion. People pretend to use the falsehood of washing people in these sacraments of total ignorance and stupidity in the superstition of a faith that makes no sense at all in the form of intelligence that God has created us with. Understand that the superstition of physically baptizing people with water is a great sin because you are trying to change the spiritual understanding into physical understating. Whoever performs such false deeds will have their head cut off.

You can jump in the water with your whole body and it will *not* make you a better person. Being baptized by someone in the *true meaning of faith* is for them to tell you the simple truth without any superstitions outside of truth. You are not supposed to perform anything outside the truth that is outside your natural feelings. These false prophets do things in the superstitions of their physical deeds, and they tell you that you going to hell if you don't believe in these lies like they do.

Now let's talk about the fire of hell and what it means to be burned by the fire of hell. Fire means lies, and lies mean hell. The fire of lies is when a person cannot understand the Scriptures and has to go to the false prophet to get his understanding. Those lies that organized religion tell you only serve stupidity and the superstitions of false faith. They are what make your life totally miserable in what you can do or you cannot do in the reality of life. The false prophet makes sure that they drive you into the superstitions that make no sense in reality.

Understand here that the fire of hell that we are talking about is the incorrect understanding of the seven sacraments they made up to institute a religion of their own convenience of making money_with total lies and superstitions. People lie to you and charge you for it.

They take money from you that you have worked so hard to earn. If this is not the fire of hell that the Bible is taking about, then I don't know what it is. They make you believe that you have done a good deed in the name of the Lord in the fabrication of all the lies and stupidity that you can ever dream of. They make poor people believe in the superstitions of those seven sacraments that made no sense at all to the form of intelligence. And if these people don't get their heads cut off for doing so, then I have to wonder where the justice of the Lord is.

Next, we go to understand the power of Jesus walking on water. Understand the superstitious part of it, and understand the reality of it. Let's understand the spiritual part first, and then I'll tell you about the physical part of it. Water means reality, and the parables represent common sense. The parables of common sense are walking on reality with *no* superstitions of any kind. Common sense can walk on reality without sinking or falling. Understand well that the seven false sacraments of the Catholic Church and Christianity have almost totally destroyed the world. The world of superstitions has destroyed reality to the point where reality does not make any sense anymore in the way of organized religions. If you do not believe in these superstitions, they tell you that you will go to hell.

Truth, common sense, and reality died on the cross. That means that these three things have not been alive in the heart of mankind since that time. The people of this world must wake up and smell the truth because their superstitions have blinded them. If you make a person who is poor in spirit happy to believe in those superstitions, then they will believe they must be purified with physical water. They will believe they can be forgiven by the hand of a physical man and that a person has to sell his soul to the Catholic Church or Christianity by being confirmed to the church. They will tell you that people are tied together by the hand blessing of a human being and they must live together according to these rules until the day they die. They believe they have to eat a piece of bread to purify their heart and then receive the last rites of the church, and then they will be blessed into heaven in the superstitious faith of total ignorance and stupidity that is so far outside the form of intelligence that God has blessed us to have by giving us life.

These seven sacraments were made up and fabricated by the minds of those who could not understand the Scriptures in spiritual value. Therefore, false religion is based on superstitions and the fabrication of total stupidity. They claim that these things came from God, but they are the *seven biggest lies* the world has ever seen where their fabrication is stuck in the minds of man for two millennia until the Lord takes over and destroys these evildoers along with their fabrications.

Now we come to the yeast of the Pharisees and Sadducees. Just how many superstitions from the mind will people call true faith? The belief in the superstitions of Satan is what rules the world by the fabrication of ignorance and stupidity in the world of men who could never understand or believe in the truth. In all of organized religion, everything they teach and believe in is part of superstition, and human thinking becomes the fabrication of total ignorance by the hand of the people who claim they know the truth of what was written in the Scriptures.

You must understand here that it was God's plan to fool the world with the teaching of those who bring the fabrication of lies by telling people that their leader cannot make mistakes in the name of God. That's *another big fabrication* they made up along the way. They tried to fool the world in order to create a life of easy living for themselves where they did not have to work. Instead, they lied to others and fooled them into doing all the hard labor. On this day, the Lord has made them look so ridiculously stupid.

For the past two thousand years, the Catholic Church and Christianity have fooled the world. It will be another thousand years before these evil religions will be destroyed by the hand of God. These religions of lies will come to be no more. It tells us in the book of Revelation that this big, evil church, the woman sitting on the dragon with all her falsehood, will finally be destroyed by the hand of God because she was born without glory or honor. People will not listen to her lies anymore. God will also destroy all the rest of the organized religions of the world. God will *not stand* for anyone who comes between Him and mankind. We will enter into the freedom of Joshua, and each one of us will remain in this value of freedom.

God has planned for each man to have the freedom of his faith and to believe in the association with God by himself. No man will have to answer to any man-made religion anymore, and no man will come and spread lies like the stupidity of the past. We will *all* believe in One God and associate ourselves with the Almighty God with no lies whatsoever. What is done in the name of God will not be done by men who claim to speak for the Lord. Mankind will know the One True God who controls the world, and every single person on the face of the earth will come to be affiliated with the Lord God. I tell you, in truth, that there will not be any intervention between religion and God anymore because all organized religions in the world will be destroyed.

Next, we go to where Jesus predicts his death. It was meant to be that common sense would be destroyed by the hand of false religion, just like it happened in the time that Jesus lived. Understand well that common sense was meant to be destroyed by all of the false faith of the world. All the religions of the world would kill the son of God, which is common sense, and every religion will only have their falsehood to present as a sacrifice to the Lord. Since the Catholic Church is mentioned in the Book of Revelation, the faith of the great prostitute will be destroyed first by the plan of God. As the great prostitute falls to earth and closes their doors forever, you will see the faith of all these false religions destroyed, just like it was in the time that the Egyptians crossed the Red Sea. You will see all the soldiers with their horses and chariots drown in the Red Sea, the sea of blood, which means man's false faith.

The Bible tells us that the resurrection of common sense will occur in *three days,* which is three thousand years after the death of Jesus. In spiritual terms, this means three thousand years after the death of common sense. After three thousand years of human living, we will come to the *rebirth,* where common sense will be alive again. The world will come to understand the value of truth and intelligence. Mankind will no longer be fooled by the lies of the false prophet of organized religion, which is the evil Satan.

To follow, let us proceed to the Transfiguration. Comprehend fully what the Transfiguration means in the prophecy of life. After six days of the Creation, common sense will take the Catholic Church and all the other Christian religions of the world and lead them up onto a high mountain in the way of the Lord. On this high mountain is where common sense is proven to be holy and righteous. Let's try to understand the *power* of the Transfiguration of the Lord. The Transfiguration opens us to a new understanding where we begin to understand the Scriptures in spiritual terms. In the past, in understanding the Scriptures, everything was physical because all we could see was the physical side of us. Now we begin to see in spirit. Jesus's clothes turning white means that common sense is riding the white horse, and on the shoulder of the white horse, you begin to see how misled your brother has been in false religion. The white horse is the true human understanding that makes sense where your heart becomes pure as snow, and you begin to feel different about everybody in the world. You begin to understand the power of being kind to the needs of others, and you will know the power of the great laws of the justice of the New Testament. By that power, you come to understand how it works in the Kingdom of the Lord your God.

Before now, when you heard slander against your brothers, you just ignored it and went on with yourself because your heart was not pure and white in the justice of the Lord. You could not understand it because your heart was full of bigotry and hate and could not be overturned. Now, after six days of the Creation (meaning six thousand years and forty lifetimes of your humanity), you find yourself on the white horse, and you ride him in purity. You come to understand the values of others, and in your soul, you begin to understand who the Lord is and what He will always be in the love of others. Fully grasp that love is not just feelings in vain but a whole set of laws where you must be fair to others.

When you say things about other people, what you say is supposed to be true in the understanding of justice in the unity of all mankind. God is *inside* every man, and he does the same things *inside every man* in his justice and fairness. You must reunite mankind together in justice, fairness, and unity. This is the spiritual power to receive the white face and to ride on the white horse in the Transfiguration of the Lord.

Now we come to understand the power where the common sense of intelligence heals the soul of a boy who has an evil spirit or a demon inside him. Jesus represents common sense because the real son of God is common sense, not a man. When you come to understand common sense as the real son of God, you begin to understand the spiritual power that's inside of us. This is how we function in truth in the wisdom of the Lord. When we solve a physical problem, we use our own common sense. And when we do not understand something in spirit, we should also use common sense. That makes us all sons of the Almighty God in the spirit of common sense. Can you now see that you cannot worship the image of a man in front of the Lord?

The spirit of common sense is what makes us part of God, and in order to believe in the One God of truth, you cannot worship the image of Jesus any more than you can worship the image of any other man. If you are going to heal anyone with a demon inside them, you must use common sense to come to the resurrection of the soul of another person so you can free the demon from inside them. But first, you must understand what a demon is. A demon inside a human being is when they understand something *backward* from the truth itself. Understand that Satan does not really exist in the way that the mind of false religion believes. *Satan is the opposite of truth* in the human spirit. You are not supposed to even make an image of the man that looks like Satan.

There is *both* an evil spirit as well as a good spirit inside every human being, and you should understand that what makes sense in the truth does not look like the image of an evil man. You break the laws of God by believing that Satan is a man, just as much as you break these laws when you believe that Jesus is God. The same goes when you *create* an image of anyone. When you do this, you *create a demon inside your soul.* If you do not want to create a demon inside your soul, you cannot think of Satan as a man. You are *forbidden* from making an image of Jesus, Satan, or anyone else in all the Scriptures because the Scriptures were written for the understanding of *both* the good as well as the evil spirit. You must understand this in spiritual value.

I am trying to explain to you how the spiritual world works and how you should *conduct yourself* in the values of truth. If you go outside the truth and worship what your mind tells you to worship, you are *breaking* the Laws of the Lord your God. You will not be able to receive the Transfiguration of the Lord and enter his kingdom, where the values of spiritual understanding are so important. God did not place that second commandment for no reason. When God says there is to be *no image* of any kind under the earth or in heaven anywhere, you must *respect* that law with the gratitude of human understanding. You must respect the laws of God and each of his commandments. You must learn to live by and respect the common sense of the real son of God with all the power that you have. If you understand this story of the demon-possessed boy with your mind, you will understand in the physical way. You will come to the superstitious physical way of understanding what should be understood in spiritual value. Understand that the spirit of common sense can cure anything.

Next, we go to the temple tax. What is the fee of the tax of heaven inside of spiritual understanding? You must pay a tax to heaven in the temple. If you leave that to the false prophet of the earth, they will tell you to give them the money and support their worthless church of no value. The only thing that giving money to the false prophet will do is enrich their church that has *no value* to the Kingdom of God. You give them your money because they tell you that it is written in the Bible to pay tax to their church. They are collecting money for preaching lies to the people, and if you give them money, you are helping them make a living without the daily sacrifice of hard labor in the understanding of truth.

These false prophets condemn everybody else into hell except themselves. They think they are *perfect* in the way of the Lord and that the Lord will definitely make them first in his kingdom. They are promising their followers that they will all go to heaven because of the money they gave to this false church and that they will be rewarded by the Lord Himself in Heaven one day. They also say that anyone who gives money will receive the peace of the Lord. Such lies are repeatedly said daily in *all* religions of the mind.

Every false religion claims the temple tax for themselves to support their lazy life of no value in truth, yet they claim it is for the Kingdom of God. Remember the commandment of the Lord that says "You shall not steal" and learn the concept of value for value. You use your own worthless value to collect the fruit of your labor that brought you to do nothing for your daily sacrifice. You thought you were so wise to be a false prophet and collect the value that you did not earn or even work for in your daily sacrifice. You believed you were doing God's work, but you were actually working *against* the Lord. What you took from others will indeed be taken from you. This is what *value for value* means. Come to understand that it is the *justice* of the Lord to bring you down in the coming time to be.

The heart of the real value will be taken from those who have earned nothing but claimed to teach true value in the purpose of wrongdoing to your brother. Remember that those who have followed you have respected you for what you have said. If you told them lies, then you are responsible for these lies. You are also responsible for the money that you took from them as a gift in front of the Lord. Maybe you do not understand the Lord your God and how He works, but the day must come where the Lord will ask you to account for your wrongdoing in his court of justice. You were happy to receive it, and now you will be miserable to lose it according to the justice of the Lord.

Next, we come to understand divorce. Think about it. A man and a woman are *both individuals*, and there is nothing in the words of any man that can bind them together for life. All these sacraments that the false prophets claim that they have the power to perform are *not true*. These false sacraments make no sense whatsoever to the form of intelligence. There is nothing in the power of human words that can marry people together. It's just a bunch of superstitions of no spiritual value that people fabricated to make money with to make people feel important on the day of the wedding. *The truth is that males and females are not meant to be wed in matrimony.* And as for adultery, there is no such thing as the fornication of the flesh.

The people who believe in the scriptures in physical terms are those who cannot understand the spiritual part of their life. They tried to make sense out of matrimony, but the power of physically uniting two people together does not make them pure, no matter what the false prophet told them. The flesh is pure when we live by our natural feelings, but the flesh will be impure by living in falsehood. The physical part of you was created with nature, and your spiritual value was created with feelings. Your physical value must be married to your spiritual feelings. Both of them must become one, united by the Creation. That is the *real wedding feast* in the land of Canaan. The spirit must unite itself with the mind to become one understanding.

Understand well that the husband, which is the spirit, must have control over his wife, which is the mind. This means that while there is both a physical as well as a spiritual part of life, the spirit must be placed higher than the mind. You must first develop your spiritual understanding and then follow it with the understanding of the mind because you were created first in spirit before you were created in flesh. Also, the flesh is mortal, while the spirit is eternal. If you develop your common sense, it is not difficult to see why the spirit is above the mind. But the human race has misunderstood this law since it was written. People believe that God is telling us that the physical man is above the physical woman. This is where the false prophet has made a big mistake in life and has fabricated a big lie. They made people totally miserable in this fabrication of stupidity that they imposed on the human race.

Remember and fully comprehend that God created man for the holy value of the Creation. He created male and female in the physical meaning of life, and he created male and female in the spiritual sense. This is where the false prophet made up the idea of a false matrimony in the physical sense of life. The Creation of the Lord was made to be understood in spiritual value first, and it *cannot* be undermined by falsehood. *Nothing* in the Scriptures should be changed into physical understanding. If you cannot understand the Scriptures with your physical mind, you have to use your spirit. Only then will the male mind and the female spirit be able to come together in the true wedding feast of intelligence.

Next, we go to "Jesus comes to Jerusalem as king." The new Jerusalem is the power of human understanding where mankind will be able to understand the Scriptures in a crystal-clear vision of truth. You will enter Jerusalem riding on the white donkey, where the common sense of intelligence will enter the new Jerusalem in the glory and honor of your new faith. The old body must be crucified for reason, and the new body of common sense must ride back in three days with the spiritual understanding that will give you life everlasting.

Each man must sacrifice his crucifixion of the past to enter the new kingdom. At this point, you will be glorified with great honor in the new matrimony of mind and spirit. You will come to visit the Lord in your spirit, and you will be able to understand the true victory of the soul in this wedding feast where spirit and mind will be on the same page. You will be able to understand both the mind and the spirit that was created by the Lord. Understand well the *triumphant entry* where you have crossed the river of life, meaning the Jordan, to the land of Canaan, where you will be able to enter life itself and understand the purpose of all that happened in the old Jerusalem of physical value of the past. You will be able to understand the new Jerusalem of the spirit and live in the understanding of your Creator with all his laws.

Presently, we go to understand Jesus at the temple. Understand that common sense will *drive out* all the moneymakers of religion in the world. People used to charge others to teach them because they were supposed to be the authority on learning. But these so-called teachers could not understand the message of the Scriptures to begin with, so they charged people money to learn all the lines that they fabricated. Common sense will come to destroy these false teachers and all the lies that they made up with the Scriptures. All the people who have made money with the false understanding of the scriptures—all the false prophets of *all* the religions of the world—will be sent away like flying doves and flying pigeons with the dust of the earth.

God is angry with them for all the falsehoods that they made up in the mind of man. That falsehood will *finally* be destroyed from the world where the human spirit will have to be told the truth that can only come from God Himself. God does not need little locusts that jump from one teaching to the other in the understanding of nothing. The truth will be spoken by the mouth of all men in the *temple of intelligent understanding*. Religion was the only subject in the old world of teaching value where a human being was allowed by all the laws of man to lie in public and get away with it.

Just imagine now if the teachers in school were allowed to teach falsehood in arithmetic, science, or any other subject with their imaginations. But religion was allowed by law to teach *against* all truth with the fabrication of the image, and they used the Scriptures as proof of their imagination. *The Scriptures are the truth*, not a fabrication of what happened in the past history of mankind, and must be proven with the reality of the divine power above us. If you enter into the temple of mankind, you must not sell your own imagination with the mind that corrupts the spirit. Understand well here that the Scriptures must be learned in reality.

Next, we go to the parable of the unmerciful servant. Again, fully comprehend that the thinking of God is different from our own. When you are thinking about celebrating the life and death of Jesus the man, you are doing something evil because you are worshipping an image before the Lord your God. You think that you are doing good in the name of God, but you are going against the Scriptures by worshipping a man. That is *not* worshipping God in the way that you should worship God in truth. This is why I call you a *false* prophet. If you were a *true prophet* of the Lord, you would learn the Old Testament before you teach the New Testament, and you would believe in the Lord your God with all your heart and with all your soul. But you made the mistake of worshipping the *image* of a man by replacing God with Jesus. You claim to understand the laws of God, yet you call the man Jesus the Lord. That is a *great sin*. You taught only from the New Testament because it was much easier with your little locust mind to believe in the image of a man than to teach the *truth* of the Lord your God.

Let us go back to the forbidden tree in the garden of Eden where Eve, the mind, bit the apple and then gave it to her husband, the spirit. They both went for the easy way to understand good and evil by worshipping the image of a man before the Lord God. You must understand here that when you worship the image of a man, you are worshipping the image of Satan, who tells you it is easier to worship. That is a great sin of worshipping the image of a man before the Lord your God. You must come to an understanding that human beings do evil in their hearts when they believe against the truth of the Lord.

Let's proceed with divorce. This does not mean the divorce of the flesh that mankind believes in—it is the power of the spirit. God created both male and female in the physical form, and on the other side, He created both spirit and mind. The spirit is more important than the flesh because the flesh dies out, but the spirit does not die. Your body will die and the flesh will deteriorate, but the spirit will rise again and live in the body of a new baby in the value of the same spirit in the birth of intelligence.

In the beginning, you were given your spirit that would live forever. God created a spirit inside us that is everlasting. A human being will receive the death of the spirit if he does not believe in the One True God of the Creation. *This is the justice of the Lord.* We were created to believe in the One Holy God, and if you step out of that boundary of human intelligence, *you can lose your soul* by the value of your own arrogance of superstitious faith. You think you know better than God, so you divorce yourself from the truth. You are not allowed to divorce your spirit with your mind, and that is the power of the divorce between spirit and mind. If you do that, you will lose your soul. That is the *real divorce* that the Bible is talking about.

Next, we come to "Two blind men receive sight." Jesus gave sight to two blind men sitting by the side of the road. The power of the spirit can be totally blind when it comes to the understanding of the One True God. Giving sight to these two blind men is a physical prophecy of the *true spiritual understanding*. Common sense has the *power to restore sight* to the spiritually blind people. The meaning of the two men here are the Catholics and the Christians. They believe in the life, death, and resurrection of Jesus in the physical sense. They believe with all their heart that Jesus is God, and this makes them totally blind where they live in the ignorance they created. They live in blindness and stupidity where they were burned by the scorching heat of the sun, meaning the New Testament, because they cannot understand the meaning of the New Testament. You must understand that the New Testament was for explaining to the world the coming of the Kingdom of God. Each man had to learn, through the parable, the understanding of the coming of the Kingdom of God.

You were supposed to continue worshipping God in the heart and soul of mankind, but the Lord knew that these two blind men would come with their teaching of superstitious value and fool the world. The power of the Son of Man, meaning the *history* of man, has fooled the world with two blind men that are Christianity and Catholicism. The world fell into the deep darkness of worshipping the image of a man before the Lord God.

Understand the parables that God has given us through the power of his eternal spirit. The Lord sent to mankind the parables that were not known. He sent the life of Jesus to us in the New Testament to make man believe that they had to worship him in front of the Lord as an image. So man worshipped the image before the Lord God. That is what separates the goats from the sheep and brings those who understand with their mind into the kingdom of intelligence that we were created with. They fabricate themselves a false god before the Lord of Heaven, and they worship the beast of the flesh of Jesus in front of the Lord God.

This was the plan of the Almighty from the very beginning to see who would worship the Lord and who would fabricate a god of their own with the image of Jesus. It was meant to be so the false prophet would find a way to worship a false god of their own with their mind and believe it is logical to worship a human being before the Lord our God. And the next thing you know, the human race was worshipping in their worthless churches, in caves built by stone of false faith, against the Old Testament. Everybody bowed down to the image of Jesus, and the whole world made an image of their own in their own religions. *They worshipped a man before the Lord God.*

Next, we come to Jesus in the temple. In this parable, there is all kinds of buying and selling in the temple. Jesus got very angry and drove them out because they were making business in the temple of the Lord. They took the spirit of man and turned it into a business of making money, where they would sell the Word of God for profit. People preached in the name of God inside the temples of mankind, and they turned it into a business deal where they could build themselves big churches, be admired by man, and make themselves look like men of God.

The false prophets made themselves an easy life, and they believed that they were doing good by turning the Word of God into a business deal. No preacher or false prophet on earth ever figured out that they were doing wrong by turning the Word of God into a business deal. They made the poor buy and sell in the temple, and they made themselves children of God by the money system of the world. But I tell you in truth that when you enter into the temple of man and do business with their soul where you sell the Word of God for money, then at that point the Lord gives you no wisdom, and your teachings become false teachings. You are not true to the Lord because you collect your rewards here on earth. Therefore, you will have no reward to receive when you enter heaven.

Moving along, we go to "Jesus curses a fig tree." Understand the times when you're hungry and you're looking for food but you cannot find anything to eat. You search and you get irritated at the tree because it gives you no food. You become frustrated at the tree that produced no food. It is the same thing in spiritual understanding when you listen to someone who has no spiritual food to give you, and you have nothing to eat in the spiritual power of the Lord your God. I am talking about people who go to church every week or even every day, and they hear the same words over and over.

Whether it's yesterday, today, or tomorrow, people become very frustrated because they think that they are saved, yet they have nothing to eat. The false prophets of the world are making big money preaching and exchanging words that make no sense in the big promise of working so hard to see the coming of the Kingdom of God. But nobody seems to understand this value. They tell you there is another world above the earth that they cannot even understand themselves. They have no fruit of heaven to give you even though you are very hungry to understand what they're talking about.

It is always the *same promise*, the *same salvation*, and the *same big lies* that make no sense to anyone. They charge a lot of money for these lies to pay for their churches, where these people build a big life and a big house for themselves with the money that you received for your hard labor by the sweat of your brow to make money to feed your family. They take your money that came from your hard labor, and they use that money to parade themselves around with big white robes where everybody thinks they are so honest and dedicated to the Lord. But they are the *biggest liars of all.*

Next, we go to the "Authority of Jesus questioned." Every time that a prophet comes into the world, there is always a big question on the mind of the people who live by their stupid superstitions. They always try to find some kind of a of Satan or a demon with the truth because it is too high for them to understand. So in order to make sense with the situations in their stupid, superstitious mind, they make something up like it's evil because they cannot understand truth. They question the authority of the truth because they believe that if the truth doesn't make sense to them, it can't make sense to others either. They make themselves look foolish by questioning the truth, and they bring their Satan into it by bringing the power of their own darkness into the situation of what they don't really understand. Comprehend fully here that the question of the false prophet comes from his own darkness and confusion because the truth is above his comprehension. This is because the mind can only understand loss and gain. The false prophet does not know that the truth must be understood with the *spirit.*

Now we come to the parable of the two sons. Understand well that when the Bible talks about two sons, this means two different kinds of people. There are two different kinds of people because everybody believes in God, but the way you understand the Lord your God is the difference. You have one that says yes to God, but he does not do his will. This is because saying yes to God is not merely believing in God. This is like saying to a person that you are

Catholic, Christian, or part of any other organized religion. You may call yourself Catholic, Christian, or any new denomination of the world, but that does not mean that you believe in God.

In the family of man, in the tribe of Dan, you have the affiliations of understanding that there is a God because God made you in the divine nature of his spirit. If you claim that you are on the Lord's side and that you believe in the Lord your God with all your soul and with all your being, you must first understand his rules and laws, and you have to *practice* those laws. If you claim to believe in God and say you understand "You shall not steal" or "You shall not kill," you have to practice those laws in *truth*.

You cannot go around stealing from people and think you're wiser than them. You cannot take the life of another person or *claim* to believe in one God then jump to the image of Jesus and believe Jesus is God. You also cannot believe in what people call saints. The truth is that you have to believe that there is only *one* God. That is a law straight from the Lord. You cannot change the laws and then think that you can ask the Lord to forgive you after you broke those laws.

First, you must understand and believe in the laws of God with all your heart and soul, and you must practice them *every single day* of your life. Only then you can say you believe in God. If you say yes to God, you must practice his laws. And if you say *no* to God, it means that you haven't thought about it yet. The angel inside you tells you to be honest and not to steal from others. That's what it is to believe in God. Every time you do right in the face of the laws of God, it means you said yes to God. Every time you say no to God, you have *ignored* his laws and you have chosen to do as you please.

Now we go to understand the parable of the tenants. The tenants are the ones who were put in charge of a vineyard in the name of God. These tenants opened a big ministry and started preaching to people. They built a church so everyone can go there to learn the Word of God. These are the people that, at first, said yes to God… and the ones who are the first to say yes to God do not always do his will. If you build a church that becomes a trap for the poor people to pay you money, you are *not* doing God's will. And if you use the money from the hard labors of others to make your life successful, you still are not doing the will of God because what you take (in the little mind of a locust that lives inside you) is to *save your own life.* You live a life of luxury where you use the labors of your fellow man, and you think that you have the right to do so. But you are actually working for yourself and the Lord gives you nothing of any value to tell others when you preach to them on Sunday morning.

Understand that when you preach falsehood and turn people's necks towards the image of Jesus, you are not working for the Lord. You are worshipping who you think God is, but you are not doing the *will* of the Lord because you twist the story of the Scriptures for your own benefit. This means you do not worship the Lord your God in truth. You are *performing evil deeds*, and you have no mercy on anyone else but yourself. You can fool the world and all the people on earth, but *you cannot fool the Lord your God* because the wisdom of the Lord is *above* your false wisdom. You are false prophets on earth. The way you think is the way of mankind's little locust's understanding, and the way God thinks is totally above your own. You think with your little mind of the locusts that going to church is so important because you want people to *admire* you on your high pedestal. That means that you are working for yourself and for your own ambition in life when you say yes to God, but you don't do his will.

Most important here, all you who read the Scriptures for yourself but refuse to do God's will. The power that you bring to others is your own ambition to be mounted on the high balcony of heaven, have people look up to you, and listen to what you say. What you think is what you believe is good for everybody else. Understand well that God's thinking and man's thinking are not the same.

When you tell people that they must go to church on Sunday, it means that you want them in your trap of wrongdoing because you think like a man, with the little mind of a locust. You try to bring people into your trap where they give you money so you can become richer by stealing their money. In the eyes of mankind, that is considered doing good by building beautiful churches for man to enjoy. But in God's eyes, that is just an *evil plan* of your own ambitions to reap in the money of others for yourself. You think the world is like a marketplace where you come to gain the business of others. That is not what the Lord explained to mankind in the Scriptures. Remember that *God doesn't think like man does.* You may believe that you can take other people's money for yourself, but you have to answer to the Lord after you have stolen what does not belong to you.

Next, we go to the Parable of the Wedding Banquet. Remember that you are living inside of an animal as a human being because your physical part is an animal with the physical needs of an animal. Unless you place your spirit in control of that animal, you will only have the feelings of an animal. When God created the mind, He added to the physical part of that animal, the power of loss and gain inside that animal. You must come to the wedding feast, where the spirit must marry the mind and become husband and wife inside you, from the Book of Genesis to the New Testament inside the value of human understanding.

Now we come to "Paying the imperial tax to Caesar." Clearly understand that Caesar was the governor—the authority—of the time. You must come to comprehend that the power of government was established by the Lord through Issachar, the son of Jacob and the slave girl of Rachel. Understand the *slavery* in it. *Every man* has to be some kind of a slave to government because we cannot live without government. There must be a higher authority over the human race where you must establish laws in order to have peace on earth. Government makes laws that you must abide by. You must come to understand that it is fair to pay tax to a government that provides roads to travel on and water to drink.

When you are poor, you resist the idea of paying taxes because you don't have much money. When you are rich, you do the same thing. You try to hide the money that you made so you do not have to pay so much in taxes. Everybody hates the tax collector who charges them for something that they don't believe they should be accountable for. The spirit is just like the mind that hates to pay the tax. So it's a contradiction between your mind and your soul, where both mind and spirit do not want to do it because they believe it's fair to avoid paying taxes. But the taxes of this world are more than fair because we live in a system where you can function even though government uses your money to wage war on the world among other things you may not agree with.

Religion has always been kind of jealous of government because the mind can be jealous, just like the wife of Jacob. When the mind turns to jealousy inside you, the next thing you know, your mind has twisted your spirit in jealousy and you become a *hypocrite*. You become filled with hate because *jealousy is not clean*. Jealousy is part of the loss and gain of the mind. When you become jealous, you claim a value that you don't deserve. That's the way it works inside your mind, where your jealousy can make you lose control of yourself. Then you will become a hypocrite and blame all your jealousy on *everybody else*. Your heart will become impure, and before you know it, you will do evil deeds, thinking that you are doing good and everybody else is doing evil. This is because your mind has tricked your heart into jealousy. Understand that jealousy is a feeling that is born in your mind by self-centered thinking. It turns you into a hypocrite where you lose your soul, thinking that you're right and everybody else is wrong. Jealousy makes your heart impure and evil.

Next, we come to understand the seven woes that Jesus talked about. Woe to you Catholic priests and Christian ministers who sit in Moses's seat and claim to be speaking for God. Stop being hypocrites and look inside your own heart to see all the wrong that you have done to others with your bigotry and your prejudice against everyone else, yet you go to church every week and claim to be a good Christian.

Woe to all who claim to be God's servants but choose to run the crooked business. You are on the take for all that you can get so long as the laws of man allow you to call yourself honest preachers. Woe to you who look like you help others in front of your little religion of the earth, yet you do wrong and you never understand and realize how wrong you are. Woe to you who pray in public and gossip about everybody else, but you don't realize what is inside your own heart. Woe to you who does not think that your sin matters to anybody else, but everybody else's sin matters to you in your own gossip.

Woe to you who practice that evil Christian religion that makes you think you're better than others. Remember that the Lord planted that religion inside of you to fool you. Woe to you who believe that you are going straight to heaven after you die—you have already lost your soul in the religion of bigotry and superstition. Woe to you who make that worthless sign of the cross to prove that you are a God-loving person but you don't do His will. Understand well that the time is coming for you to account for all you have done.

Understand that we are coming to the age of the end of time. I want to talk to you about the end of time. We are living in the seventh day of the creation, meaning the beginning of the seven thousandth year. Remember the word of the Lord when He created mankind six thousand years ago. He said that on the sixth day, He created man. That means that mankind was just created in the last thousand years. Now let's understand this. When I say mankind was created in the last thousand years, I don't mean physically. We already know that modern man evolved about two hundred thousand years ago. But up until six thousand years ago, man was just like any other animal. Then, on the first day, which are the first thousand years, God created the heavens and the earth. This is the separation of physical and spiritual understanding.

Man has been given what all other animals were not given, and that is the ability to gain spiritual knowledge and wisdom. This is why God put us in charge of all the animals. All other species just go about their lives eating, sleeping, etc., but they never understand why life is as it is because the Lord did not give them the ability to question their purpose. Man was given this ability, and there are great rewards from our Father in Heaven for those who understand life on the side of truth and not on the side of lies. But there are also great punishments for those who choose to believe against truth.

Before now, man was not educated. During this last thousand years, man has started to become educated with both the mind and spirit. That's why you must come to understand the Lord God. Every human being could educate himself if he wanted to except for a few people in third world countries where they didn't have much of a chance for an education. The Lord has created modern man with the gift of technology, but everything will be judged on the spiritual part and very little will be judged according to your physical part because in the justice of the Lord, all your physical deeds have proven that you have done it wrong in your understanding.

Everything that you did to improve your physical side does not count. It's what you have done to improve your spiritual side that will count in the justice of the Lord. The justice of the Lord is perfect in his gigantic computer of intelligence. I call it a computer, but it's the great memory of the Lord where what will be counted for in this justice is not the little sins of your physical self. What will be counted is your *spiritual value*, where you have thoroughly failed to learn where you could have been a better person. If you learn the truth so you can live a better life, you will be judged on what you have learned and what you have failed to learn.

Understand well that no matter where you live in the world, all this education was available. Yet you have learned nothing from your spiritual self. You have failed to learn because you thought that the false prophet would teach you what you should know about your spiritual value for the benefit of life everlasting. Everything will depend on what you know and what you don't know in your spiritual understanding of God. If you did not think that spiritual life was important and you ignored the value of your spiritual life and life everlasting and if your lazy bones did not want to learn anything because it didn't mean anything to you, it will be remembered on your records of knowledge. God has given you six thousand years in the value of learning and forty-two lives of the learning process, yet you have failed to learn the truth about the Lord your God. Just what are you waiting for to understand and believe in the Lord your God? You expected the false religion of the earth to teach you, and some of you have paid big money to learn from them, but you still have failed to learn anything of value from the Lord your God.

The four sons of Jacob born from the two slave girls are Gad, Asher, Dan, and Naphtali. This means that you are a slave to these four subjects: your affiliation with God, government, money, and business. Being a slave to these four subjects means that you cannot exist without your affiliation with God. Even if you claim to be an atheist or whatever false god you choose to believe in, the Lord God of Abraham, Jacob, and Isaac has created you, and you are affiliated with Him whether you choose to believe it or not. It's the same with government. Man needs to have a form of government. Otherwise, there would be chaos. We also need to have a form of money and a way of doing business with each other. We are slaves to these four subjects because there is no getting around the necessity of them.

Most of you out there have learned *nothing* about the Kingdom of God. You listen to the false prophet who was telling you that you are free in the Kingdom of God, and you believed them. They told you that all you have to do is believe in Jesus and you would be saved. But now, you will be asked by the Lord to give account of what you have learned on this very powerful seventh day of the creation that God has planned on the world from the beginning.

Next, we come to understand the day and hour unknown. We are coming to the power of the Scriptures to understand the end of time, where the sun will not give its light anymore and the moon will disappear. You must first give your heart to the Lord, then He will give you spiritual understanding by the wisdom of your feelings. It is this understanding that tells you what everything means in the Bible. You must understand these spiritual feelings. It is a great gift from God to be able to understand, and you really have to understand the power of where He comes from. To know the day and the hour, you have to understand the truth, common sense, and reality of intelligence. Your common sense will verify the Scriptures in the way God thinks and the way God talks in the power of his mighty spirit. This is how mankind will come to understand exactly what God means.

No one knows the day or the hour except the one who lives in spiritual value. God is a total mystery to the people of the mind. They cannot understand anything that comes from the spirit because it doesn't make sense to them. So they go down to their loss and gain, and they try to understand with the weak loss and gain of their minds. If you come to understand that this is the way it works, you begin to understand and believe in the Lord your God. I have written this book so everybody will come to understand the power of the spirit. You could be the most educated person in the world, but if you don't have the *common sense* to understand, you are just as blind as anyone in spirit.

If you think you know it all, then the Lord will take away from you whatever you have because God's truth is not a teaching of the mind. It is for those who are born in spirit to receive common sense and reality to understand the glory of human intelligence. All time is one time in the Creation, so it is whatever you do as part of the creation that gives you the power to understand. You *must believe* that God is a spiritual being inside you to understand the day and the hour of the end. You must understand that in spirit, there is *no physical time*. All days are one day in the same creation of all time, and if you don't restrict yourself to the physical understanding of the Scriptures, you will be informed of what's going to happen. Understand the time that you live in when you transfer your spiritual understanding from physical to spiritual value.

I told you earlier that you are 90 percent spirit and 10 percent physical. Therefore, if you do not understand your spiritual value, you are not blessed with that 90 percent of the spirit, and you will not understand life. If you don't understand life, you are miserable because you don't understand the events of life. You think life just goes on and on without human understanding, but that is not the way it works inside you. Your *spirit* controls your animal being, and if you do not control that animal being, you are just like an animal out of control. You must come to understand that you cannot control yourself unless you have your spirit in control of your animal. If you live only like an animal, then you will fail like an animal because you are meant to have both mind and spirit to control yourself. The part that controls you is *very important* because without the spirit to control the mind, you become a person without feelings. And when you have no feelings, you lose your value in the power of yourself because you don't understand anything that life brings to you. You will be like an animal without value because all value comes from the spirit.

If you do not take life seriously and if you do not believe in the truth, you will not be able to understand life_in everything that you do. Your spiritual value must claim your happiness in who you are and what you want to be in the time of your life. Your life will become *everlasting* if you believe in the Lord your God and not in Jesus. Jesus was a great prophet but he is not God. God is the truth, but you must understand that *no one on earth* can understand what God truly is because He is the form of intelligence that controls the human race, which is over seven billion people. No human being could do this, and that is why you have to worship the Lord your God and live by the value of your spiritual understanding by receiving the birth of the spirit inside your soul. Everything that is written down in spirit is spiritual, and everything that's written down in flesh that tells you about your physical side is physical. The Bible is a spiritual book in the understanding of what you feel.

Next, we go to the Parable of the Ten Virgins. You must understand the Ten Commandments in the spirit of intelligence. You must come to understand the power that lives at the center of intelligence. On one side is the physical side, and the other side is the spiritual side. The virgin means your mind in human understanding. You have to train your mind to understand the Scriptures in your spiritual part. Do not waste your life trying to understand spiritual teachings on your physical side. If you worry about your physical side and you take all the precautions that you can take to make sure that you're in the right place physically, you are *wasting your life*. If you believe that you're going to go to heaven when you die because you are a good Christian or whatever false religion you belong to, you are also wasting your life.

There are *two different versions* of the understanding of the Kingdom of God. You have the lazy one, and you have the ambitious one. Organized religions preach that it is extremely easy to go to heaven—all you have to do is believe in Jesus Christ and you are going to heaven. They tell you that you don't have to learn or do anything. They have preached over and over again that if you believe in Jesus, you *will* go to heaven, and that's all there is to it.

But the Kingdom of God is not made for lazy people. The Kingdom of God is made for those who work hard to understand the power of the spirit of the Lord. This is the Parable of the Ten Virgins. In this parable, there are ten virgins, which are physical teachings that do not understand much about the word of the Lord. They all went out to meet the bridegroom, which is the spiritual truth that your mind must marry to have a complete understanding. Five of the virgins were *foolish* and didn't bring extra oil for their lamps. This means they did not prepare for this journey to take a long time. The other five virgins did bring extra oil because they prepared for a long journey to understand truth.

The five foolish virgins are the religions that teach that your salvation is easy to achieve, and the five ambitious virgins are the religions that start in the heart of mankind, and they *learn* the way it really works. On one side are those who think that entering the Kingdom of Heaven is easy, but the wise ones think it is a hard job to do. *They believe you should work on it with all that you have and all that you can possibly do.* You should keep working on it with all your soul and everything that you have inside you until you can hear the Lord your God in your heart. The false prophets of Christianity and the Catholic Church tell you it is easy to get to heaven because they picked a shortcut. They say to just believe in Jesus and that's all there is to it.

On the seventh day of the creation when all is revealed, they will not be able to understand what is happening. The sun will no longer give its light—this means that *not a word* of the New Testament will give any light to those lazy people who think it's so easy to understand the Kingdom of God. The *true* Kingdom of God deals with learning in reality. You have to acquire the power to understand *from the Lord Himself,* not from Jesus. This is what will happen to the power of understanding that is within you. The children of the mind became lazy when the false prophet told them they didn't have to do anything except believe in Jesus. When all is revealed on the seventh day, those who did not learn anything will not be able to understand. They were always secure in the understanding that it was easy to enter the Kingdom of God. But it is *not* easy. It is the most powerful thing that you could ever imagine.

You enter the Kingdom of God by working hard to understand his laws. You have to be in the glory of human intelligence, and you have to be *reborn in spirit.* What you believed in the past with your mind is *worthless. The more you learn about truth, the more you want to learn*. That's what the parables of Jesus teach. You have to *work hard to understand.* No matter what anyone else tells you, you still have to *learn for yourself.* The people who learn the Scriptures for themselves will not have a hard time understanding. They know the Kingdom of God and how it works through the hard work of their life by doing all the things that they should do to follow the laws of God.

To receive the Kingdom of God, you have to come to an understanding that it is not free by any means. You need to learn every day. Read *both* the Old and the New Testaments, and understand the power of both. Don't confuse yourself with what the false prophet tells you. Don't listen to people who do not care about your soul. Listen to the people who tell you how hard it is. Listen to the side that tells you that you have to be ambitious enough to understand the power of the five virgins that chose ambition for the value of their soul.

If you want to enter the Kingdom of Heaven, you just don't get it for free. That would not be fair to those who work hard to understand the Scriptures by themselves. You should *never listen* to anyone who tells you they already know the Kingdom of God because there is so much to learn that you will spend your *entire lifetime* learning the Scriptures and you will not even be halfway there. Just keep on learning, but make sure that you have oil for your lamp on the day of the great earthquake. All those who took the teaching of the Kingdom of God seriously will be able to understand the coming of the Kingdom.

Next, we go to understand who will inherit the Kingdom of God. As we saw in the last parable, the people who work hard and are serious about the understanding of life will be the ones to receive *true wisdom* from the Lord. You have to give everything you have to understand the Kingdom of God. You must also understand that if you have been given more, then more will be asked from you. Let us look at education here in the way it works in the truth so you can come to the Kingdom of God. God is the truth, and you have to understand truth, common sense, and reality to enter the Kingdom of God.

How do you come to understand truth? By working as hard as you can to understand for yourself. You don't get this from anybody else. You have to learn the truth for yourself because that is the road to your own success. You cannot learn from the church because they cannot teach you anything of spiritual value. The Lord has given them *nothing* to tell you that is important in the Kingdom of God. Use your talents that the Lord has given you. If you have a great education that *understands truth*, then more will be asked of you. But if you are less educated and you give up by listening to other people because you are afraid that you will make a mistake in believing something wrong, then the Lord will give you nothing. You will be left out because the Kingdom of God comes from your talents in human intelligence. That's the way it works with the Lord. You have to work and learn for yourself the power to understand the Kingdom of the Lord your God.

The Kingdom of God is not free. Great power in yourself and in your talents is *required* to understand this value. If you show no value in yourself and you always look for free handouts, then you look at yourself in the mirror of stupidity. And if you accept your stupidity and you believe you are not smart enough to understand, you will let other people explain things to you. But true spiritual wisdom doesn't work like that. You must understand that there is a God in heaven because you are affiliated with God from the sons of Jacob that are inside you.

Dan is your affiliation with God. *Every man* has some kind of faith that there is a higher spirit. But the false prophet teaches you that if you don't listen to them, you will burn in the fire of hell for all of eternity. This is the part that comes from *fear*—some people truly believe that if they don't listen to these people, they will burn in the fires of hell. They will come to understand, by these false prophets, what is true and what are lies. They will listen to them in fear, and they will continue the fear of not learning. They will listen to these false prophets from the beginning to the end of their life and still learn nothing because learning is not free. *You have to work at it!* The more talents you have, the harder you work—and the fewer talents that you have, the Lord will bless you less. You must work for what you get.

If you want to receive all of these talents that the Lord has given you, then you must understand that these parables were written for those who stand for true wisdom that makes sense. Everything will be *done in accuracy* in the justice of the Lord, but you must also work at it to understand for yourself. Don't listen to other people who don't know any more than you do.

Next, we go to the Parable of the Sheep and the Goats. This is about the pusher and the receiver. Understand this parable well because it tells you what you must do to enter the Kingdom of God. The goats are the people who push their ideas inside you, and the sheep are the ones that try to serve these people by believing them. There are two kinds of people in this parable—the master and the student. The master is the pusher, and the student is the follower.

If you go to church on Sunday and you listen to what they tell you, it becomes their teaching, not yours. If you are the pusher, you push your understanding on others. If you are wrong with your understanding of the Scriptures, then your student becomes just as wrong as you are. If you are the student, whatever you learned from the masters of the earth will be wrong because God did not give these people permission to be master over you. The goat is the teacher who tells others what to believe, and he claims that he knows what he's talking about. The sheep is the student who listens to the goat even though it makes no sense. If you believe in these false prophets, you are worshipping a false god before the Lord. You are a student, and you listen to your master. If the master is wrong, you will be wrong also. You are supposed to take your information only from the Lord your God, not from any mortal man who thinks that he is above you and understands better than you. God has given nothing to these people to understand.

Understand well here and now that God speaks to every single human being on the face of this earth inside your heart. You can be the most inefficient person of the Scriptures, but your understanding could be much better than that of those whom you call *master*. The power of intelligence is given by God and only those with a *humble heart* can understand the Word of the Lord. Sometimes the truth doesn't seem to make sense. This is because God doesn't think like man thinks. These people who call themselves teachers are fake because they don't understand anything that comes from the Lord. He has a higher power of understanding than they do.

God does not give them anything because of their claim to be master over their followers. This is *not* the way it works in the Scriptures. God will give them very little to understand because of their superstitious way of understanding. If a man thinks he has the power to lead other people in spirit, the Lord will take everything that he has and give them nothing in return. These so-called masters have no true knowledge of the Scriptures. They just pretend to know better than you with fancy words, but they do not understand a single thing about the Lord God.

There will be a *big war* between these self-proclaimed masters and the followers. People will leave false religions by the millions to come to the table of the Lord God. Then they will understand the way God believes in the faith of the reasonable, the common sense, and the reality of intelligence. These false preachers will be left behind because they did not feed those who were hungry, they did not visit those who were in prison of a false faith, and they did not give you rest when you asked for rest. All they did was put a big burden on you in falsehood. They did not feed you any truth when you were a stranger, and they did not give you any of the understanding that they should have had if they actually listened to the Lord his God as they claimed.

You false prophets have pushed people around with the horns of the goat. You have taken something that you have no knowledge of and made your followers strangers in prison outside the Lord's Kingdom. You did not feed them or give them anything that they needed to know about the Kingdom of God. You pushed them into hell with fear and told them that if they did not listen to you, they would go to hell. What you did was to give them a scorpion, not a fish or a viper and not an understanding of truth. You disgraced their spirit with lies, and now the Lord will not know who you are. All the work that you claimed to have done in the favor of teaching has no real value in truth. You will not be able to understand the Kingdom of God because the Kingdom is locked for you unless you unlock it by being simple in the eyes of the Lord.

You must ask the Lord to forgive you for what you have done, but your sophistication and your superstitions will come to have a toll on you. You will not be able to understand *unless* you take the advice of the truth and come to understand the Scriptures in the way of life. Tell your followers that you have inflamed them with stupidity and lies and that you were wrong because you *did not really understand the Scriptures*. It's going to take some courage to enter the Kingdom of God, but this is where the "key" of the Kingdom of God will lie for you because you claimed to know what you didn't know. You claimed to be good when you were doing evil to them, and now you must face the Lord your God.

Next, we go to the Last Supper. Fully understand that what is called the Last Supper is not the supper of Jesus and his apostles in Jerusalem two thousand years ago. It is the supper of *the power to understand the bread and the blood of life*. The Lord lives in the value of spiritual understanding, so you have to *translate* the Last Supper to a spiritual value that you must understand in order to enter the Kingdom of God. You must come to understand the unleavened bread of the Old Testament to understand the Last Supper. You must also understand that the disciples of Jesus are not physical men but spiritual understanding. You must come to accept this in your new spiritual power to understand.

The Last Supper is the power to be able to eat the bread and drink the blood of life. To eat the bread of life is to read the Scriptures. The unleavened bread is anything you don't understand in the Scriptures. You must take what you do not understand and translate that from physical to spiritual value. To drink the blood is to understand the meaning of the Scriptures in spiritual value, where mankind can no longer use his little mind to understand the Scriptures. Try to understand the *keywords* of the Scriptures so you can reveal to yourself what it means in your drinking of the blood—which means the understanding of the bread of life.

You must use your feelings to understand certain words, and they will become the keywords to understand the prophecy of the Lord. For example, if the Scriptures mention water, you have to translate that word into the word *reality*, because water means reality in spiritual terms. Then you will understand what it means that to wash yourself with the water of life is to wash yourself with reality. You must *turn away* from the superstitions in the lies of the false prophet and start understanding the Bible in these new keywords inside of yourself, or you will not be able to understand the way God thinks and the way God lives inside of our hearts. The bread of life is the Word of God. You must translate the Word of God to the side of your human understanding—you must come to understand the power of your physical being inside your mind and the spiritual person inside your feelings. You must also translate everything that was said in physical terms into a spiritual understanding.

If you listen to anyone who is not part of the Kingdom of God, they will teach you to believe in the Scriptures with your physical mind. This is why I call them *false prophets* of the earth. They only understand the Scriptures with their minds. This is the way man thinks, which is the *opposite* of the way God thinks. To understand God in spirit, you must travel to the world of the spirit to understand the spirit and to live with the Lord your God. You must learn to understand the way God thinks and the way God understands things so you can worship Him in truth.

The power to understand the Lord your God is to be able to understand that He is the Lord of justice first. Then you can understand his justice and the way it works. But God's justice is not like man's justice. If you don't think like God, then you don't know that. This is what it means to say you believe in God but you don't do his will. You must understand that before you say you believe in God, you must understand that God is perfect in all justice. If you think that it's all right to steal, kill, rape, and destroy all the values of the laws of God and hate people with bigotry and superstitions, then you do *not* understand the Lord your God. If you say you love God yet, you do not understand Him; that means you love a false god that does not condemn all these things because you ignore the real laws of the real God and all that his laws stand for.

Understand well that God lives in the spiritual values of justice. If you do something wrong to someone, that same justice will rise against you. Don't think that the Lord will not punish you if you say you love God and then turn around and do wrong to others. You may think you have a good heart and the faith that you believe is in God, but if you do not understand his laws in truth, you have *no faith* in God. Most people on earth don't believe in God because they try to understand his laws with their mind instead of their spirit. They think with their little mind of a locust that justice only belongs to other people and that justice stands against them just as well as it stands against their brother. Come to understand that whatever you do to others in wrong is wrong even if you think that the Lord will not see. But his justice sees all.

Let us now go to Gethsemane. Understand well the power of the death of Jesus. The people of Christianity keep worshipping Jesus as the Lord of Heaven. Pray that this will not happen to you and that the Lord will pull you out of the mess of Christianity that makes no sense at all to the spirit of the value of the Kingdom of God. Mankind looks at the life of Jesus and they claim that he saved the world, but I tell you *in truth* that the death of Jesus is what will bring death upon your soul if you believe that a dead man can save you and if you try to understand the power of heaven through the death of Jesus.

Be fully aware here that whoever gives his life to the belief in the death of Jesus will lose his life because he believes in the wrong way to understand the Scriptures. Jesus will not give you life everlasting because it's not a dead man who gives life. *It is life itself that gives life.* The false prophet took the teaching of the death of Jesus and tries to say that this is what will save the whole world, but that is *not true.* The only way you can enter into the Kingdom of God is to go through the great persecution and then change your heart from being the one to bring persecution on others. Repent of your sins, and ask the Lord to forgive you. Then you will be saved. But you have to be *saved by your own deeds*—that's the way it is.

You cannot depend on another man's sacrifice to earn the power of the Kingdom of God. That is not the way it works. You have to go through the true misery of your own sacrifice to enter the Kingdom of God. The Kingdom of God is much more important than using the sacrifice of another man to enter it. If you were not persecuted in life, you didn't suffer, so you don't know what suffering is. If you are a perfect-looking person with a great education, then the door to heaven is much harder for you to reach. The power to enter heaven in the glory of human intelligence and civil truth is impossible to reach if you believe in the mind over the spirit.

If you have an easy life in which you live with a good job and a great education but you are poor in spirit, the door to heaven is much narrower for you. But if you were blessed in life by being persecuted for the way you look and the little education that you have, the door to heaven is wider for you. No one gets into heaven freely like the false prophet told you. That is a big lie that has fooled many, many people. If you believe that lie, then the glory of intelligence did not bless you—it has *cursed* you. You have received everything and never sacrificed anything. This is why you do not know the truth.

Next, we go to the arrest of Jesus. Jesus was arrested for bringing the Word of God to mankind. He came into the world to bear witness to the truth, and if you come in the world and bear witness to the truth, then the people who cannot understand the truth believe you are doing wrong—you are going against their false beliefs. This is the same way that it is today where the truth angers those who cannot believe in common sense because their feelings are so twisted inside them with what they have called the truth. Their lies cannot comprehend the wisdom of the truth, and they always fight against truth so they can make sense of living in the sin of lies like a dead man in the tomb.

If you were to awaken someone in the middle of their sleep, they would be mad at you because their sleep is comfortable and they do not want to be disturbed. The dead man that I am talking about here is the *dead man in spirit* that only lives in the physical part of himself. If someone is dead in spirit, which is the way that false prophets are, and you wake them up, they will retaliate against you because they don't want to be disturbed. For them, the sleep of ignorance is much more comfortable than trying to understand the heavenly knowledge of the Lord. They really believe that the Kingdom of God is free; they don't want to be disturbed. For them, the *sleep of ignorance* is much more comfortable than trying to understand the heavenly knowledge of the Lord. They really believe that the Kingdom of God is free and they shouldn't have to work for it. So if you go into the grave of falsehood and disturb the beliefs that they cherish so much and if you come with the teaching that the Kingdom of God is not free and should be earned like everything else, then these false prophets will be against you.

For every subject in life that you want to learn, you have to go through the process of learning. If you want to learn to play the guitar, build a house, or learn another language or any other subject, you must *work at it* and make it happen for yourself or you won't learn anything. No matter what it is, learning does not happen for free. And receiving the Kingdom of Heaven is especially not free. You must work at it to understand because if you do not understand, you *cannot* enter the Kingdom of God. Remember that the door to the Kingdom of God is a narrow gate and you cannot have it for free. So the arrest of Jesus means that everybody who wants to enter the Kingdom of God has to go through this narrow gate and enter with great sacrifice.

Now we come to understand "Jesus before the Sanhedrin." This is where the common sense inside you stands before the false religion that has been taught in the understanding of mankind. In these false religions, they teach you to not think for yourself and to just believe what they tell you. These people did not receive the gift of the Lord to understand the Scriptures. They teach people according to their minds, but what comes out of the mind of a man is far from the spiritual truth. They all believe it, and they try to punish people who don't believe it. Believing in this falsehood makes your heart hard and leads you *away* from the Kingdom of God. If you believe in any of the fantasy world that they believe in, you will perish in false religion.

The false prophet believes that if the true understanding of the laws of God were known, nobody would believe them. Therefore, they have to prove to the people that the truth does not exist and that *they* have the truth. They tell you that you should listen to them, not to someone who brings common sense like Jesus did. The *common sense* of Jesus looks worthless to them. It looks like a troublemaker because it disturbs their little grave of falsehood that they have been buried in for so long. They attack anyone who tries to disturb that little fantasy world of theirs. It is the same thing now in the world where religion has made a little fantasy world of stupidity and they try to destroy anything that would make them look foolish in the eyes of the people.

They think God is with them and not with anyone who they consider to be a troublemaker. But what these so-called troublemakers bring to them is the *reality of truth*. This truth will make them look so foolish in front of mankind, but they have to go through being proven wrong in the Kingdom of intelligence in order to be on the side of truth. If any proof of their religions being part of falsehood ever gets known to the people and mankind comes to believe that they are wrong, that would destroy all that they tried to build with their easy way of life. The pope, the cardinals, and the priests as well as the leaders of all organized religions are living in the easy way to teach their fantasy world. They don't want anyone on earth to believe in anything other than what they are preaching because worshipping the image of a man before the Lord is easier than trying to explain a god that you cannot see or understand.

That is why these people like to hurt anyone whom they call the *troublemaker*. They try to turn their stupidity into the logic of truth and trick others into believing it. They had such a hard time understanding the fantasy of their false religion, and they didn't want to start over again. They taught people the wrong way to worship the Lord, and they mislead people with their fantasy world. Wrong has always been evil and will always be evil. The wrong of organized religion is *worse than evil* because it *destroys the soul* of the simple children of God. It makes them believe in the fantasy world that these false prophets have made up as a "free" Kingdom of God where you don't have to work to learn anything. Everything is handed down to you just like it was handed down to them. They never realized that there is no such thing as receiving something free in the Kingdom of God. You have to enter through the door of your sacrifice that God has made. What was taken away from you by the laws of man will be *restored* to you in heaven through the sacrifice of learning. Do not listen to anyone who says your spiritual sacrifice has already been done for you by a man who died some two thousand years ago. Nothing could be *further* from the truth.

Next, we go to "Judas hangs himself." Understand well that those who betrayed the truth are those who only understand with their little locust minds. They believe in the lesson of the life of Judas in the physical understanding instead of as a spiritual lesson, which is the true meaning of all the Scriptures. Mankind falsely believes that *physical wrong* is the sin of humanity. Understand that Judas did *not* want to see Jesus die on the cross. He thought that what he was doing was in the best interests of Jesus's teaching. He thought that Jesus would talk to the Sanhedrin, they would hear his great teaching of common sense, and that would change their understanding of the value of the Kingdom of God from physical to spiritual. But when he saw that the Sanhedrin had turned Jesus over to the Romans to be crucified, he could not live with himself because he had *betrayed* his master. He *rejected* the thirty pieces of silver he was paid, and he hung himself.

This is a *very powerful teaching*. Judas's life represents the false prophets. Just like in this lesson, the false prophets really do want to help mankind. But the money that they make from their false understanding of the Scriptures has corrupted them. They figured out that they were preaching against the Word of the Lord, but they couldn't bring themselves to abandon their lifestyle of living off the hard work of others. The sacrifice that man must endure to enter the Kingdom of Heaven is a spiritual sacrifice, not physical. But these false prophets made all kinds of *physical sacrifices*. They denied themselves the pleasures of sex, they denied themselves material possessions, and they took vows of poverty and silence. They have learned just about nothing of truth because they took the wrong path of physical sacrifice. The Lord has given them nothing of real value because their sacrifice contained no real value.

When these false prophets realize what they have been preaching with their little minds of a locust, they will try to turn it around and understand the wisdom of the common sense of Jesus. They will try to understand true spirituality, but they will *refuse* to sacrifice their high place in the minds of their followers, and that will lead them to sell the common sense of Jesus to be crucified. Remember that the high priests at the time were just like today's religions. They didn't want anybody to touch their little fantasy world, so their intention was to send Jesus to the Romans to be crucified. That is not what Judas thought would happen. He was acting in the best interests of what he believed, but he did not understand the way it works in heaven. The power to understand truth works in the heart of mankind. You will see the same thing happening in the world today. Many, many Judases will try to protect their sanity in their little minds of locusts, and they will *destroy* the common sense of the Lord to do so. They like what Jesus said in the parables, but they do not understand the *true meaning* of the parables. That will lead to them sacrificing the teaching of Jesus to protect what is more important to them.

Now let us go to Jesus before Pilate. Jesus was sent into the world to bear witness to the truth, but that does *not* make him God by any means. Nobody else at that time understood the truth, so Pilate asked him what the truth is. Jesus didn't have to answer because the truth can always be seen by anyone who understands in spirit instead of with the mind. The truth is inside each one of us and has to be understood so the world can come to believe that God Himself is the truth, common sense, and reality. The truth is simple, and that is why the children of the old world full of lies cannot understand it. If you live in the sin of these lies, you live in darkness and you cannot understand the light of heaven because the truth is not made to be understood by the *mind.*

The mind is too weak to understand the truth. Therefore, the mind cannot understand the *wisdom* of the Lord. And if the mind cannot understand the wisdom of the Lord, then Pilate, who is the representation of government, is not strong enough to understand the truth. That is why we still live in a government of spiritual darkness. The people of government today are just like Pilate. They wash their hands of the truth because they don't want to hear it in their soul. They believe that the truth confuses a person between the low authority of government and the high authority of God. They cannot understand the difference between the two, so they wash their hands of anything spiritual.

Pilate represents government, which is of the mind. And the mind cannot understand in spirit. He could not understand what the high priests had against Jesus because it was a question of *religion*. He could not make any sense out of the high priests, so he went with his mind, which can only understand loss and gain. Remember that the weak human mind cannot understand spiritual things. The mind favors gain over loss because it does not understand how to lose anything. Pilate didn't want to offend the high priests because he was afraid they might revolt against the Romans. The politicians always go with the people who have more value. That is why all governments on earth do not really understand anything in the way of the values of heaven. They just take the weak part out, and they try to control the country with something that people gain. They don't consider a single man to be of any value in their belief of gain over loss.

Pilate took the easy way out, and that proves that it will always be done like this in government. The majority will rule whether it's right or wrong. Pilate represents government because he was the governor of Judea. He ordered the crucifixion of Jesus, and then he washed his hands of the responsibility, just like the government that we have now with the priests' molestation of children. They washed their hands of it and didn't punish them, but other people were punished for doing the same things. This is because the police and the high officials of government did not consider the priests' crimes and did not hold the Catholic Church responsible for what they did. Government holds coaches, doctors, scout leaders, politicians, and all others responsible for molesting children, but they refuse to do anything when it comes to *religious leaders* committing these same awful acts.

But understand well that molestation is not the sin of the priest himself. It is a sin of the church that took from the priests their feelings of sexuality and forbade them from having sex with anyone. This brought these priests into situations where their sexual feelings had to come out in this way. The children came to have no value to the church because it was a sin of the church. *No man has any right to forbid man to have a woman in his bed like a decent man.*

Human sexuality is a very important teaching in the understanding of life. Man was created by the Lord with feelings of sexuality. These feelings are holy, and there is *nothing unclean about them.* They grow inside all of us, and we need to act upon them. You can deny your natural sexual feelings, but sooner or later, those feelings will come to a head. They will be released. If you give your sexuality a positive outlet by understanding what it means, you will not hurt anyone because you will properly honor these feelings in truth. But if you fail to understand your sexuality, you will deny your natural feelings. And when everything comes to a head, that is when things like molestation and rape happen. You cannot deny your own sexuality or that of others. That is against the way the Lord created us to be. If you do, you will have great sorrow in your life.

If you take away the sexuality of a man, you destroy the *feelings* of that man. No religion of any kind has the right to take the natural feelings away from any man. That is the *greatest sin of all.* Organized religion has taken the feelings of man and woman and made them suffer for no reason whatsoever because of their arrogance and pride. If you take something away from the *nature* of mankind, you are going to have problems. And they did have problems for many, many years before now, but they just swept these problems under the rug.

They knew there was something wrong with what was happening, but they would not change the situation because they are just children of the mind who do not really consider the value of all natural human feelings. They think that people's natural feelings should be a sacrifice, but that is the biggest lie that has ever been told on earth. Organized religion took the natural feelings of humanity and turned them into a source of false practice. They considered the feelings of these people to be of *no value.* No human being who claims to be on the side of God Almighty should consider such evil deeds to be righteous.

Now we go to "The soldiers mock Jesus." The representation of this event is what people do to someone who was defeated by man's backward understanding of good and evil. If a person thinks that he has the right to make a human being feel like a clown in the battle of good and evil, he will take the position of what he believes is evil, and he mocks that so-called evil. They make a fool out of people who were condemned by society. That mockery of evil deeds is done in our world every day of the week by the people who think they are perfect. They hold a position on earth where society doesn't think that anything they do is wrong. These people cannot see themselves as doing anything wrong, and they think of themselves to be right over these people. That's where the common sense of intelligence will come to destroy these people and to show them how evil they are in what they think and believe.

Whenever a person mocks someone for being stupid, that same stupidity will fall on the one who mocks others. You must understand that the power of this prophecy is to understand that whatever you do to others will be done unto you. Before now, *nobody* understood the New Testament. They just look at Jesus as a good man and they did not like the injustice of his death, but they never understood the purpose of why God brought this upon earth. Mankind didn't understand all the stupidity and ignorance that was foretold in the book of the living. They didn't understand what made sense and what made no sense. Everything that happened to Jesus was because he came to bear witness to the truth.

Next, we go to the crucifixion of Jesus. Everything that happened in the Scriptures was meant to happen to mankind. Jesus was a *messenger* of God, just like Jacob, Moses, and all the other prophets. This means that what was going to happen to mankind was that common sense would be crucified by the hand of religion and also by Pontius Pilate when he washed his hands in total falsehood. What happened in physical form back then will happen to the world in the spiritual form. Look at it and you will see it is just like John the Baptist when his head was cut off in the physical form. That means that within you, those who believe that being baptized with water will have *no head* to think with.

Look at all the priests, the cardinals, and the popes of the Catholic Church. They baptize people with water, and these people become totally against all reality. The next thing you know, they think that physically baptizing people with water is essential to the truth. They take a piece of bread that has no meaning in spiritual value, and they believe that it is the *body of Christ*. They use a hand motion to marry people, and they think that it is *legal* in heaven. They also take that same hand motion to give the people the last rites, and they believe that it is proper because their mind is so weak in superstition and ignorance. Just like John the Baptist had his head cut off, they also had their heads cut off.

The false prophet cannot reason like intelligent human beings because God has placed a curse on them. They teach people that they have to be physically baptized with water because they have lost their heads. King Herod had John the Baptist's head cut off by the request of a dancing girl that Herod was lusting after. In the value of heaven, the false preacher is the dancing girl. And mankind lusts after the false preacher who promises the reward of heaven to them. Mankind believes that they are going to heaven because these preachers falsely promised it to them. This is what the priests are doing with their dance against reality.

The Kingdom of God was created by truth, common sense, and reality. The people who believe in lies think that it is proper to bring someone to a lake or river and physically baptize them. But if you want to truly baptize someone, you have to baptize them with the Holy Spirit, which is the angel of reality. You baptize a person by telling them the simple truth and by helping them believe in something that makes sense. Water means reality, and when you baptize someone with a teaching that is not real, then you turn to the world of make-believe, and you teach people to believe in *ignorant* things. Remember here that the God of heaven is the God of truth, common sense, and reality. If you want to believe in God, you must believe in truth, common sense, and reality. If it doesn't make sense to the form of intelligence that you were created with, then it is not true.

Any time you believe in something that is not true, it becomes a hoax against all truth. You live in that falsehood believing that you are on the side of the Lord because that's what the false prophet told you. The preachers of organized religion are the masters of falsehood, and if you believe in them, you are a student of falsehood. They tell people to do things because it's been written in the Scriptures, but they have interpreted_the scriptures in physical understanding, not spiritual understanding. That is the crucifixion of common sense.

You can throw yourself in the river if you want to. You can try to understand the Lord in your physical mind, but you will not understand the Lord God because He is not a physical God, but a spiritual God. You have to understand the Lord your God in spirit and not in physical form. Jesus appeared in the court of Pontius Pilate in the physical form, but if you think that Pontius Pilate understood anything of the spiritual form, then you believe in the physical crucifixion of Jesus that was ordered by a man who did not answer to anything spiritual.

Next, we come to understand the death of Jesus, where we will come to understand the power of life. Life in the truth means the real life of the spirit and not the physical life. If you understand only the physical part of the life of Jesus, then you're out of touch with reality and you cannot understand the spiritual side of life. You are living outside the boundaries of spiritual understanding where you cannot cross over to understand the Scriptures in spiritual understanding unless you turn away from the evils of organized religion.

When Jesus said he would send his disciples into the world, he meant that he would send *common sense* throughout the world to preach the Word of God. God has punished the world because the world has always been stiff-necked and they won't consider anything other than their little locust teaching that makes no sense in reality. Pontius Pilate and the high priests took the physical life of Jesus, but the spiritual life of Jesus lives on because the spiritual teaching is what is written in the parables. The understanding of those parables became the power of God in these words, and the Word is God. The spiritual understanding of the parables is what God *is*, not the physical man.

The glory of intelligence is when the person understands God's will with his spirit. You cannot understand God in the physical form like the Christians do by worshipping the physical form of Jesus and by believing that Jesus is God Almighty. That is wrong because there is nothing in the Bible that is written for the understanding of the physical form. Jacob was called Israel, and Moses was the great law-giver, but that still does not make either of them God. All these people in the Bible *served* the Lord—they were *not* God. Understand the Scriptures on the spiritual side, and then you begin to see what God is.

God is the spiritual power of a human being in our understanding. No physical part of a human being can replace God. If you worship the physical part of the Scriptures, you worship the beast and the image of the beast. That is where you make a big mistake because *God is not flesh* and will never be flesh. God is the spiritual form of intelligence that is in the Scriptures, but you cannot understand it physically. If you understand it physically, you worship the beast, and that is not the intention of God—to give you a beast in the physical form to worship. Remember that God uses people to bring the truth to the light of mankind, but He uses people in human thinking as servants and you have to understand them as servants.

Jesus was a man like the rest of us. He was God's servant. He said what the Lord wanted him to say, and he did the deeds that the Lord wanted him to do. What God sent on the world was a curse on the life of Jesus because He knew people would worship the physical man and not his spiritual teaching. God knew that whoever was not true to his spiritual value would throw themselves in the belly of the big fish. People two thousand years later, still believe this lie because it was God's plan to separate the goats and the sheep to bring upon the world great justice. The people who sold themselves into slavery by making a god out of a man would suffer greatly by believing in that man with all their hearts and they would call him the Lord. Try to see the death of Jesus not as the death of a man but as the death of common sense. You should try to understand that the Lord is totally spirit, and you must believe in what is spirit and reject what is not spirit in the physical form. Love the Lord your God.

Now we go to the burial of Jesus. Understand that the flesh of Jesus was buried in a cave. And the people of false religion follow the death of Jesus in caves that they call churches on Sunday morning. Everybody went into the cave of falsehood to worship Jesus, but they worship the body of a dead man. This is because the *flesh* of that man was all that remained from the life of a beautiful man who brought the parables to light. The people did not understand the spiritual part of it, so for the last two thousand years, they worshipped the body of Jesus in the cave where he was placed. *Nobody* could break and open that great seal in the value of intelligence. All they worshipped was the *flesh* of that man. They did not worship the Lord God with all their soul.

The Lord planned all this because He wanted to know who would be loyal to the true teaching of the spiritual God and who would be loyal to the physical part of Jesus and worship that man in the cave every Sunday morning. People cannot understand God because they placed Him in the cave inside their thinking. They buried Jesus in that cave where they would see only the death of the man who was buried there. They thought they were worshipping the spiritual God of the Creation, but it was a great sin that they did not understand the Lord God in the spiritual sense. That's the way men will be judged. If you turn your head away from the falsehood of the cave to the life of God forever and ever in the understanding of the spiritual God, you will receive life everlasting. But you have to believe in the Lord in the spiritual form, not in the physical form.

Next, we go to "the guard at the tomb." Understand well here that whoever guards the tomb of Jesus represents the false prophets of the earth. They are the priests of the Catholic Church and the ministers over the Christians. These are the people who guard the cave—meaning the church of those Catholic and Christian people that worship a man in front of the Lord. The church is the cave that they guard. They keep on claiming that the death of the man Jesus is their salvation because they are men of physical value and they refuse to answer to the spiritual side of their understanding. You have to bring to the altar of the Lord the understanding that God is the truth in the spiritual form. You have to understand God in a spiritual way. Do not understand that a human being in flesh is God. The Bible was written in a way that God would hide Himself from mankind so people have to *work* to understand the One True God through the Scriptures. It is the lazy people who take the shortcut and worship the flesh of Jesus in front of the Lord their God.

This was planned by God from the very beginning in his beautiful and perfect justice. People could not understand the spirit, so the Lord sent the great wisdom of his spiritual salvation. Mankind will have to make a choice between Jesus and God—between that body in the cave or the real spiritual God. Now the truth has turned to the side of spiritual value. Who among you will turn your stiff neck to the value of the spiritual God of heaven and stop worshipping Jesus in front of the Lord? All these things were meant to be in the God's plan. I write this book so *everyone* can understand who will turn against the falsehood of the earth and follow the Lord your God in the spiritual way of understanding.

Now we go to the resurrection of Jesus, the common sense of the world. The resurrection of Jesus means that after three days, meaning three millennia, the common sense of intelligence will return to the world and mankind will come to understand the purpose of the Scriptures. The life, death, and burial of Jesus two thousand years ago meant the life, death, and burial of common sense,_where humanity worships Jesus as the Lord and pretends that Jesus was the Lord in the physical form. In other words, the false prophet believed that God sent Himself into the world in physical form. They believe in the physical form because it is easier to believe in than the spiritual form. The false prophet did *not* understand the spiritual side. They just used the parables to prove that God was physical as well as spiritual. But that is not the truth because God is not a physical form that you can see. God is a spiritual power that you can only see through the *true understanding* of the Scriptures and that you can only understand with your heart.

The people who live and preach in darkness only understood the physical part of it. They brought the life of Jesus to the understanding of the Lord by believing that the son of God is God in physical form. But God has never existed in physical form. He used the physical form to make people understand falsely because it was his plan to fool those who have fooled both themselves and others. God wanted to trap them with all their lies, stupidity, and superstitions. That is the way God wanted things to be because he wanted to know who worshipped him with all their soul and all that they are in their heart. *In your heart is the only place where the truth can be found.*

When you worship God in spirit, you worship the seven spirits of the Lord: wealth and wisdom, glory and honor, power and strength, and praise. The seven spirits of God are meant to be worshipped and understood in the way of living. You must have wealth and wisdom in the spiritual terms of intelligence to understand them. You must have glory and honor to understand them, and you must understand power and strength to believe in them. Finally, you must praise the Lord your God in truth. That is how you believe in the faith of the seven spirits of the Lord your God. You have to find all seven angels in the spiritual terms of the value of heaven.

Understand that the whole teaching has to be part of the spiritual value of heaven where you must come to understand that these seven spirits are *inside you*. They are living inside you every day of your life, and you must understand them in truth. You must have wisdom and wealth to live a good life, and you must have glory and honor to be honest. You must have power and strength to be complete in human understanding, where you don't change your mind about everything that comes your way, and then you must have praise for the Lord who created you with intelligence. If you praise the Lord your God in truth, you will receive that intelligence inside you.

Next, we go to the Guards' Report. The high priests gave the guards a large sum of money and told them to lie about what happened by saying the disciples *stole* Jesus's body while they were asleep. This is where the people who understand the Bible in falsehood will lie by pretending that the truth will never come back to the world and that the common sense of intelligence is dead forever. But the common sense of intelligence comes to us through the seven spirits of God inside of us. True life is *not* in the physical form of Jesus like the false religions claim. The life that God is talking about here is the individual life of each man on the face of earth. True life is in the spirit where a man gets up in the morning and keeps his spirit and his mind in the perfect form of reality. This is the real life in the spirit of the Lord.

You must come to understand that those seven spirits inside you are where a human being is *loyal* to the Lord. God is where those seven spirits come from, and he brings the holiness of intelligence to the value that will make you *perfect in spirit.* You will understand his true justice in the same value because it is *true justice*—not the justice of mankind or the justice of the false prophet but the *real justice* where there is no one favored above another in the eyes of the Lord. Only truth, common sense, and reality are favored in the eyes of the Lord. Bad justice, false justice, or no justice at all are the *enemies* of the Lord and cannot be accepted in the clean spirit of true value. This is what you must do to be in spiritual value. Understand how these seven spirits work inside of you and *practice them every single day of your life.*

Now we go to the Great Commission. This is where you are commissioned by heaven to understand the truth, common sense, and the reality of the Lord. All authority has been given to common sense. This means that you must use common sense to understand exactly what the truth is. And it is that understanding of truth that will lead you to the reality of life. Do not worship an image before the Lord here in this teaching. It is not the physical man Jesus that you are to tell people to worship. It is the common-sense understanding of God's laws that you must tell people to worship. Do not believe and preach on the physical side or you will be against the Lord God and you will be under his curse.

*****

Now we come to the understanding of Mark, the prophet who learned the story of Jesus from others. Understand that Mark was too young to be there for himself. He talked to people who were there, and he came to understand that Jesus was the son of God, but the truth is that God has no physical son. Jesus is the *messenger* of God because the meaning of the son of God is to understand that in the physical form, people have sons to take after them, and in the spiritual form, God sent a messenger to the world to bring *his truth* to the light. This messenger carried a message to the mind of man by the spirit of the Lord that lives inside them. That was Jesus.

You cannot put any man as the son of God—that is *not true*, and you should not believe that. Man is a physical being, and there is *no such thing* as a physical son of the spiritual God. It doesn't work that way. When you look at the way it works, it is different from the understanding of your physical needs. You have to have a son to take after you, and all the prophets are the sons of God because they took after God to introduce the Father in heaven inside each one of their prophecies and inside each one of their parables of human understanding.

Remember that the One True God means that in God, you have the truth that comes on the gold and silver platter that makes sense all the time and never turns away from truth for one moment. God is also the God of Heaven who lives in human understanding inside over seven billion people. *No one* could possibly be equal to God in any way because God is the spirit of revelation. He is also the spirit of the truth that brings reality through the common sense that makes sense to all human beings. No man can carry that burden inside himself. Mankind is wrong to raise Jesus so high that no one can understand God except in the physical way—the physical way is *not* the proper way to understand the Lord your God. Try to understand God inside your soul as the power to understand the deity that lives inside you and that cannot be replaced by anything else but the Lord himself. God sent his servants to the world to bring his spirit out of the value of what people think. God's servants bring the truth to the light of mankind, but if you worship these servants, you will be destroying yourself by worshipping men before God. That's not a good thing that happens to a human being because at that point, you start offering your sacrifice to a man, and next thing you know, you believe that that man is God who can fix all your problems that comes through your sacrifice. You start to believe that that man is the image of a god, and that's not what the Scriptures tell us that God really is.

Understand the power of the disciples of Jesus. Understand why Simon Peter is called the first disciple of Jesus. This means that the catholic church will be formed by that name in all the religions as part of the disciples of the Lord. You must come to understand that people would come to worship Jesus in front of the Lord and make him the son of God. That was all part of the same plan where the people would become Christians and form all kinds of false religions. This is because God wanted to set his plan into motion where the people of the world would worship *outside* the truth, and they would worship the image of Jesus because of his miracles and his teaching of the parables. It is all organized religions, and especially the Catholic Church, that will become the great Babylon, the great prostitute sitting on the beast.

The world never understood the plan of the Lord. Mankind never understood how important it is to believe in One God. So the Lord (out of the blue) gave them another god of religion to worship and admire. That is what was meant to be for all men who would fall for the teaching of the *image* of a man. It is nice to say that a physical man becomes God, and it's easy for people to understand that God exists in the image of a man. It's much easier to understand these lies than it is to try to understand the Scriptures and God Almighty in truth. The worshipping of Jesus was explained by God to make people worship the man Jesus.

When the day of the Lord comes, people will have to change and turn their stiff necks in the direction of the Lord and understand that Jesus was *not* God. That is what was written in the Scriptures. It will be *almost impossible* for the people of the earth to change their minds and turn their stiff necks toward the Lord God of Heaven because God did not want to make it too easy for people to enter the Kingdom of Heaven. He gave them lies to believe in, and *they believed in those lies.* The Lord wanted to see who was worthy to understand his laws and worship him in human intelligence. God made Jesus and his disciples so all these false religions would worship a false god. The time is coming when the Lord will turn it around for all mankind to understand that God is not a human being and that they have falsely worshipped the image of a man.

Next, we go to understand "Jesus drives out an impure spirit." You must understand that impure spirits are already inside people. It is not something that comes inside of you just to make your life miserable. An impure spirit is something that you believe in inside you, like killing a person. If you believe in killing someone, then you will go ahead and do it because you believed it was all right to do so. That evil spirit that was inside you becomes your *obsession*. In order for you to be free of that evil spirit, you have to work at it inside yourself and understand that it is not good in the way the laws of God work. If you don't understand the laws of God in your soul, then your soul is free to believe all this garbage and you can kill someone and still think that it was the right thing to do.

If you want to be on the side of the Lord, you must believe in the set of laws that the Lord put inside of you. If you leave your spirit unprotected by these laws, then you will think it's all right to do things like stealing. Some people think that stealing is all right as long as they don't get caught, and when they do get caught, they fight to protect themselves because they have evil spirits inside of them that make them feel important. They believe they can steal or kill without remorse, and the more they go, the worse they get.

If there was no understanding of true wisdom inside you and the people taught you to steal and kill, then you *accepted* their evil spirits. These evil spirits came inside your soul in a conference of evil that you accepted because you were part of the family that has accepted those things. You let those feelings come inside you because you had no protection from the true laws of God. You just think like the animal that you were born as, and you continue believing as an animal in the loss of your soul. The next thing you know, you become just like the people who kill and steal without remorse.

You believe you can hurt people without remorse because that evil spirit lives inside you, and every time somebody tries to straighten that out inside you, you get very angry at them and you try to protect yourself in that false belief. You continue to dominate your soul and your mind with lies when you can understand the *true set of laws* inside you that tells you that you're not better or worse than anyone if you live according to the laws of God. If you don't accept the true laws of God, then these evil spirits will enter you. *Only common sense* can drive out those evil spirits and free you from doing wrong to others.

Now let us go to understand "Jesus prays in a solitary place." Understand well the prayer of common sense because the prayer of common sense is not like how most people pray. When you pray in common sense, you have to be alone in your soul where no one can see you praying. If you want to pray properly, you must pray in the common sense of intelligence. You should *never* pray for good things to happen to you. You should pray to *understand* and to *bring about a better world*. That is a *prayer of intelligence*.

What I mean about a prayer of intelligence is to pray for the *understanding of how the world works*. Pray for the *knowledge* of what is evil and what is good. When you pray, don't pray for people in particular. Pray for *all mankind*. Ask the Lord to help you say the right things at the right time to bring the truth to the light of the world. Pray for the truth to come in your voice and tell people how to understand the Kingdom of God. You must come to understand that these prayers are not for individual people but for the *masses* of the world. You must come to understand that the power that is inside you in prayer is so that you will say the right thing at the right time to help someone who comes in the name of the Lord your God to understand truth. A human being is weak, and he needs to improve his weakness into strength. He will find your words refreshing if they come from the great mountain of the laws of God that were created for the benefit of all men. Pray in your heart for this glory of human intelligence to come inside you. Try to bring the spirit of God into everything that you pray for.

In your prayers, make sure that you build no one up and/or bring no one down. Just bring the power that you were created for in the feelings of human thinking where the power of heaven is inside your soul. Understand well here that prayer is not something that you do in public in a church in front of other people. *True prayer* is done *within the solace of your heart*, where only you and the Lord are present. Pray in the magnificent value of common sense. Call upon the Lord to bless you in what you say and do in front of your brother for right overall. Don't pray for God to give you a car or a house to live in because those are physical things. Don't pray for physical good to happen to you in life because the main point is your spiritual part. A *strong understanding of truth* will lead you out of the shadow of the evil spirit that can enter you and make your life miserable.

Next, we go to the understanding of "Jesus forgives and heals a paralyzed man." Being physically paralyzed means you can't move some or all of your muscles. So if you look at someone who is paralyzed, you might see someone who can't function normally and may have a hard time getting around. Inside yourself, you might be disturbed to see someone in that condition that it makes you feel sorry for them, and you would try to help them if you could. You would like to heal them from being paralyzed and make them better so they can function normally. It is the same way with people who are *spiritually paralyzed.* They understand everything backward, and you would like to heal them so they can understand right over wrong. But they are paralyzed with an evil spirit inside them.

Understand the evil spirit that is inside you. You are paralyzed inside your soul, and you cannot understand the spiritual part of yourself, so you live in the agony and the defeat of a person who is paralyzed in spiritual value. The great power that can *heal* a paralyzed spirit is to say words and blessings that will take that evil disease out of someone's soul to make them understand that they have been paralyzed and to bring upon them the restoration of their soul. These evil spirits stop you from living a normal life. You do things that are not normal and you commit crimes, but you cannot understand why.

If you are *spiritually paralyzed*, you are not a bad person. It's just that you are possessed in your evil dreams and you can't get out of it. The people around you make it nearly impossible for you to recognize the truth inside your soul that you were created with. They leave you in the situation of worthlessness where you can end up in prison or in any place that you do not want to be in. You need to cure yourself from that worthless disease that comes inside you, makes you do wrong, and totally takes control of you. You try to explain it to someone else by saying the devil made you do it, but it's not the devil. Actually, *there is no such thing as a devil.* There are only the *lies* inside you that are a result of the very miserable life of your past. You must change everything inside of your soul from the_understanding of lies to the understanding of truth. Only *this* will bring you to the restoration of your faith in the Lord your God. You were stepped on, beaten, and left for dead. That is why these feelings are inside you and you can't get rid of them.

Next, we go to the calling of Levi. Understand well that the tax collector was not popular at the time of Jesus because the Roman empire was collecting taxes from the people of Judea. They couldn't figure out why Jesus, who claimed to be a man of God, was eating with tax collectors. Mankind is always persecuting those whom they do not like because they do some government work or they physically commit crimes. But that's not the persecution that you should be aware of. What the Scriptures are talking about here is when you *persecute the helpless for being simple and poor.* That's the persecution that is against all the glory of the intelligence of the Lord. Man needs to have a form of government to bring order, and the idea of government should be respected by all. But also, it should be respected if it is a system where everyone is treated fairly in justice.

Truly understand that you cannot condemn something that works well and gives us the power to live in peace with each other. Money is *not* the root of all evil. It is the worship of money in front of the Lord that is evil. Money is one of the sons of Jacob that was born from the slave girl. That means we are all slaves to money, meaning that mankind cannot exist without it. Money is a good tool for dealing with each other, but it is just that—a tool. You cannot condemn people who work for money because that is how it is supposed to be. If you are fair with money, it is a fine tool and it settles a lot of good things. Take the truth about money and bring it into good deeds, then you will know that it was created by God like the rest of true intelligence. Money is the purpose to deal with each other in fair trade. It is part of what makes your life just and fair in the Lord's wisdom. Try to understand that money itself is not evil. It is just as good or evil as the people who use it.

Remember that God created all these things. He created government, money, business, and religion. All these things can be understood on the side of truth or on the side of lies. For example, let us look at religion. We can try to understand the true religion of the heart which unites us, or we can understand it as the false teachers do, which divides us. Religion is just as good as everything else as long as you use it in your heart to do good and make life easy for yourself and others. The organized religions of the world do more evil than good. That's the way it is when you believe you are better than others who do not believe as you do. Remember that in life, nothing is evil unless you make it evil, and nothing is good unless you make it good. That's the common sense of intelligence.

Now we go to "Jesus questioned about fasting." Understand Jesus as common sense here—not in the way that man thinks but in the way it was written in the Scriptures. Jesus is *not* the son of God—common sense is the son of God. The Bible was written for your soul, and you have to come to understand it. Man put his mind above his spirit, and since his spirit was not developed enough to understand the word of God, the Lord had to use physical words to make people understand. He sent Jesus, as a man, to the world to bring a new understanding so people could understand in spirit that no one can replace the Lord your God.

The purpose of life and the teaching of Jesus is so we can understand the Scriptures in our minds. Then we can bring it through from the far left to the far right so the human spirit can understand these teachings. The word of God is not meant to be twisted in the way that Christianity teaches with the idea that Jesus is the physical son of God. *Common sense is the real son of God.* You must understand that God used the life of Jesus to show his common sense to the world. Writing the Scriptures is not easy. God had to use different words to describe his teaching, and the people understood his teaching backward. That's what happened to Jesus.

God had the descriptions of his teachings written down in the form of the parables, and to the mind, it looks like Jesus is the son of God in the physical form, but the truth actually exists in the spiritual form. The Lord used words that could confuse people, so Christianity worships the man Jesus as the son of God because they just didn't have the spiritual education to understand it on the side of truth. It is also the *will of God* to use these words so He can trap those who fool themselves and others and those who live in arrogance. Mankind must learn to separate the physical part from the spiritual part because that's the way that God treats people. If you desire to be on the side of the Lord, you must understand the Scriptures in the way that He has written them.

Next, we go to Jesus and the question about fasting. What is physical should be put on the side of physical, and what is spiritual should be put on the side of spiritual. The fasting that is referenced here is not the fasting of the flesh. This fasting is in the spirit and should be understood in spirit. You should not take the whole Bible as one giant teaching. You must read the Bible law by law, page by page, and line by line. Do not feed yourself with too much from the Scriptures. You must understand what you read before you move on to the next teaching. If you read the Bible and you don't fast, you will confuse yourself by overeating the spiritual teachings of the Scriptures, and that will not benefit you.

You must *graduate* from one verse before you jump to another verse. This is the way the Scriptures are meant to be understood. And don't jump like a locust all over the place when you try to understand the Bible. People of organized religion are jumpers—that is why the Bible calls them *locusts*. They jump around from teaching to teaching, but they cannot understand much of what is the truth. They can jump, but they cannot fly—that's why they are called locusts.

In order to graduate from a certain paragraph in the Scriptures, you must learn to understand the keywords in every single phrase of that paragraph. Understand what it means, not just the words you read. The *real power* of the Scriptures is to be able to eat the "fruit of life" in the value of your spiritual understanding. If you place *too much information* inside your soul, you will not be able to understand. There are people who read the Bible time and time again, yet they know practically nothing because they use their mind to understand instead of their spirit. The spirit does not work by feeding yourself with all kinds of garbage that doesn't make any sense whatsoever.

If you cannot bring the Levi, the angel of love, the third son of Jacob, into your spiritual value, you cannot understand the truth about the Bible because you have to open your heart and do away with false religion to understand the Scriptures. If you don't listen to the Lord your God and instead, you listen to some false prophet, you cannot understand the Scriptures because the Bible is a very technical book that will give you life. But you must understand that the Scriptures are written in spiritual value.

Next, we go to understand the huge crowd following Jesus. Don't follow Jesus because you think he is the son of God. You should follow Jesus to understand common sense. Do not think of a man to be the son of God or even God himself. That is forming an image before the Lord, and that's against the commandments of our Lord. You should look at Jesus not as a man but as the common sense of intelligence, and it is that common sense that brings you to the reality of the truth. If you follow that teaching, you are in common sense with the Lord. In common sense, you have the understanding of God inside you. This gives you the power to understand the way God understands in the common sense of intelligence. You will be able to understand and think like God because the common sense of intelligence is the real son of God. The real son of God is not in flesh but in the value of spirit, where you come to understand the power of the feelings in spiritual terms before you understand them in your physical value. You must leave your feelings to the spiritual God, where your feelings come true for you. There is a *difference* between God's thinking and man's thinking.

For example, if you have feelings to make love to someone, those are *spiritual feelings*, and they come from the Lord. But if you say you cannot make love to that person unless you are married to them, that is physical and it comes from the mind. If you reject your spiritual feelings in favor of physical value, you *break the laws of feelings*. God did not send the feelings inside you for nothing. There is a feeling between you and this person, and that feeling should be lived accordingly. The laws of man tell you that it is a sin, but in the laws of God, it's *holy*.

In life, it is the value of feelings that *come first*, so try to understand the way God thinks and the way man thinks in feelings and physical value. You must come to understand that your feelings are part of the understanding of life itself. When you feel something, it is important to understand those feelings. If you have feelings to make love to someone, those are *holy feelings* that come from truth. But if you have feelings to steal from somebody or to kill them, you must understand that those are feelings that come from a *false* understanding. You must determine the power of your own feelings so you can come to the understanding that God will send inside of you. You are not supposed to get into those feelings of stealing and killing anyone, but the feelings of your sexuality that people call adultery are honored in heaven and should be honored on earth.

Condemning any holy feelings leads to the destruction of your spiritual understanding. You will become a human being out of touch with reality because your feelings are very powerful. All the molestation of children by priests happened because they denied their sexual feelings, and that led them to turn toward evil. There is great power in your sexuality. If you reject your sexual feelings, you will end up much worse than you are now. What would be more proper than for a man to call himself a priest before his fellow man and to make love to a woman? They tell him he cannot honor his sexual feelings, and if he does not honor these feelings, he is going to live the *consequences* of it because those feelings are powerful inside a person.

Failure to honor these feelings makes a person look like he's out of touch with reality. The reality is that you must come to understand and live your feelings according to the laws of the master, who is the intelligence above all intelligence and the power to control your feelings. If you get angry and you want to kill someone, you probably won't do it because you know in your heart that you cannot take a life because life is precious. But life is also precious in your sexuality, and it has to be lived accordingly. The feelings of the animal are extremely important, and the feelings of your sexuality must be counted for because God sent these feelings inside you and you have to live those feelings in truth. It's holy to make love to someone because you *give* value to them, but it's wrong to kill or to steal from someone because you take value *away* from them.

Next, we go to the appointment of the twelve disciples of the Lamb of God. Let me explain what the Lamb of God means. Jesus went through the great persecution, and he went through the crucifixion as the Lamb of God. But the Lamb of God is not just Jesus. Everyone who was executed and had to give their life for lies is the Lamb of God. Everyone who had to struggle in life because they were not pretty, were too fat, were unintelligent, had the wrong skin color, etc., is part of the Lamb of God. Whatever the Lord has given you that was not acceptable to mankind is the Lamb of God.

Now that you understand the Lamb of God, try to understand the twelve apostles of the Lamb and why God called Jesus and his disciples the Lamb of God. The twelve apostles became part of the Lamb of God because Jesus taught them to be simple in the value that a simple man can be crucified for being who they are. God called people by their proper name, and He made people who came in the name of the Lamb of God to be the first ones chosen by the Lord.

If a person is fat or ugly in the eyes of mankind, you must understand that God made it that way for their *salvation*. If a person does not live by the rules of other men, God made him that way so we can choose him for the Lamb, meaning the simple people of the world. Understand that it is *almost impossible* for a person to follow *all* of God's laws perfectly, every time, in the knowledge of wrong and right. People break laws for what they think and the way they believe. You must understand that laws are laws and we have to live by a system of laws that was created to be followed by all men. The exception is the way people feel about some of these laws.

The laws of man are not always fair. The laws of God are always fair but not always understood as being fair. Some people think that it is fair to kill anyone who makes them miserable and are evil to them, even though the laws of God tell you that you shall not kill. In that person's heart is a certain justice that tells them to destroy these people. They develop these feelings of killing others because they *do not respect* the Laws of God. You must understand that if you are a disciple of the Lord, you must obey the laws that come in your heart. You must live by the power of right over wrong.

If you kill people for no purpose and no value, that is definitely wrong. If you steal from anyone for no purpose and you just do it because you want to get ahead, that is wrong. *There is a wrong and right in everything*, and you must understand what wrong is and what right is. You cannot continue using the Laws of the Creation to destroy people because they will retaliate through the power that is inside them to destroy what makes them so miserable on earth. We were not created to be in the same situation. Man was created to defend himself and to protect himself against what is evil in others as well as what is evil in ourselves.

Now we go to understand Jesus and Beelzebub. Understand that good is good and evil is evil. You cannot put a patch of an old fabric on a new fabric and make it work. The patch will always be part of an old fabric. *Understand the power here.* To understand intelligence, you must understand the power that you are, within yourself, on one side or the other. The Lord is the Lord, and He created intelligence to be *both* right and wrong. He could've made it all on the side of right or all on the side of wrong, but it would not work that way. Wrong is wrong and right is right. Intelligence has to be separated between the two to create a value of right and the defeat of wrong. You must come to understand that this was the Creation from the very beginning. Realize that every one of us could be wrong or right. True wisdom is understanding the *difference* between the two.

If you acquire an evil spirit inside you, you will do wrong. The same goes for right. You have to acquire right over wrong and then you will achieve right. Cain, who represents wrong, thought he had destroyed his brother Abel, who represents right. But he made a mistake thinking that he can destroy one side and be by himself as one and only. This is a mistake because when you are wrong, you stay in wrong by yourself and you have no more brothers to help you out. And when you are right, if you destroy wrong, the same thing will happen. You will be by yourself without any help from your brothers.

The truth is that we come from *both right and wrong*, and unless you have one, you cannot have the other. You can kill right over wrong and live only in wrong, but you have failed to understand that right is just as important. You need your brother, right, to be complete in the value of the situation that God has created us. Everybody thinks that if they take all the wrong out of the world, there will only be peace on earth. But that's not true because God did not create one without creating the other. There is *nothing* in this world that can be created *without both sides.*

If you build a house, you must build the front as well as the back because a house with no back has no value. If you build the right side, you have to build the left side also. And if you put a foundation to support the house, you better create a roof so the triumph of intelligence can live and have both sides of everything that makes sense. This house is where you will put everything in place that you need to complete intelligence. The understanding has to be of right and wrong, good and evil, and bottom and top to have complete wisdom.

The world never figured this out, so they tried to kill one of the parts that they didn't understand to complete the part that they did understand. They tried to do the same thing that Cain did to Abel, and they never built a complete house of understanding. That is why intelligence is so *poorly understood* in the world. Everybody thinks they are right and everyone else is wrong, but if they were to come to complete intelligence, they would have to understand that a human being was made to be both right and wrong to complete his house and to make the completion of what he is and to learn to live in peace with others. People can be both right and wrong because your words and deeds are all the sides to complete your house. That is where you need the understanding of Beelzebub and Jesus together at the same time to understand the true Creation that God has Created. You cannot go too far on one side and destroy the other side because you need both sides of yourself and everything that you are to complete the house the Lord is giving you to build.

Next, we go to the understanding of Jesus's mother and his brothers. Who is the mother of Jesus, and who are his brothers? According to the Scriptures, my mother is what I believe inside of my soul that came down to me from the generation before, and my brother is what lives within me. This is what I am in the values of my human thinking. This is what comes to me from my ancestors in the feelings of human intelligence that comes in the value of the way I should respect other people.

The question of who my mother and brothers are is answered by what we are inside ourselves and how we learn the value of each other in spiritual understanding. If my mother and my brothers are waiting for me, that means that my past generation of knowledge and my immediate learning is here waiting for me to learn what is in the Scriptures. This is where the Lord your God gives you a knowledge that belongs to you—a knowledge of how to treat the past generations into the existing generation for the laws of the Almighty God.

Every person on earth is your *spiritual brother*, even though they may not be in the same spirit as you are or they cannot really understand what a brother is. You must understand your spiritual brother in the understanding of spirit where you have to love your neighbor as yourself. That is the spiritual way to understand who your brother is. You must come to understand your brother in the *true value of brotherhood*. If you see someone that no one respects, he becomes your brother. If you see someone that is not important to anyone else, he also is your brother. If you see somebody older than you that no one respects, that is your mother because they come from an older generation. The simple part of being someone is to understand that we are all created with the same feelings that you have.

All people on earth are just as holy as you are, and everybody has the right to eat at the same table as you in spiritual needs. *We all have the right to be considered a spiritual brother.* If you see an Indian with warpaint and feathers on his head, he should be recognized as your brother even though you always thought of your brother to be from the same family, race, culture, or people who have the same religious beliefs as you. Any man created by the same Creator is your brother in spirit because we all share the same Father in heaven. You cannot value people as better or worse than you because of the place that they come from, the religion that they practice, or the values that they consider important in life. *You must come and love your neighbor as yourself.*

Now we go to the Parable of the Sower. This is the farmer who spreads his seeds in the value of living. Understand well that the seeds do not always fall where you want them to. The meaning of spreading the seeds of the Kingdom of God is that you go through the sacrifice of living, and you spread what you have learned in the value of yourself. You spread your seeds, and they fall where they fall. You must understand that you are a human being who lives the life of a human being. You cannot choose where your seed falls because you have to live in the same creation as all of mankind in the values of order.

Just like the physical seed falls in the farmer's garden, the spiritual seed falls on the earth. Some people pick up your example, and other people cannot accept it. This is the difference between what you understand and what others come to understand in life. We cannot sow the seeds and expect the same result for everyone because we all must come to the understanding of life on our own. You may have the will to understand inside yourself, but you cannot share it with others in the way they understand because they're probably not there yet to understand. You must strive to make your seed grow wise so you will have a good harvest.

Never claim the salvation of others for yourself because each person receives a different message from the Lord. You cannot expect other people to understand what you understand. Just leave your understanding according to the will of God. If your seed fell on the fertile ground and other people did not get it, it is not your fault because people went on their way to believe whatever they wanted.

Next, we go to the lamp on the lampstand. Understand life in the heavenly glory of God. God does not think like mankind. In his kingdom, suffering is what leads to the *restoration of truth* inside each one of us. Your sacrifice is to understand God as a shepherd who leads us back into the value of his understanding. The glory of intelligence becomes a lampstand and gives you the purpose of bringing the truth to the light where everybody can see the light through you. But if you do not have the right things to say, just say nothing.

The light from the lamp that we are talking about here is the *light of heaven*. It is when you can see the difference between the truth and the lies of the world. The light of heaven is the wisdom of the wise where you come to see things in the higher level of human understanding, and you see the difference between the corruption of lies and the high level of the truth in heaven. When I see people believing that Jesus, the physical man, is equal to God, I see no light there because that is a lie. Seeing the light is to believe in the One True God. You must believe in the truth even though much of the world believes that Jesus is the physical son of God. It is not part of the light to understand it that way, and that's why people live in darkness. They cannot see the light of heaven because the light of heaven is a knowledge that cannot be substituted with lies.

The light of heaven is a tool we use to understand the coming times and to see the dream of the dreamer and the reality of that dream. The events of the future will come to your understanding in the prophecy of time where the world will change its course, but the light will still be there.

Next, we go to "The Parable of the Growing Seed." Understand well that a human being is just a man, and as men, we have to learn *how* to understand the Kingdom of God. The Kingdom of God has not changed anything about our physical life on earth except that we can now understand a clearer way to think and we have a new heart to feel and understand the thinking of God inside our souls. Life on earth is the same as before, but now man can make himself a new understanding from the growing seed of true wisdom that's inside him.

God has made this learning possible for you to understand. Before now, learning was almost impossible. Now, in the new way of understanding, if you want the power to be able to understand heaven, you cannot think of it as a place where angels fly around. Angels are ideas, and you must understand that these ideas become feelings inside you. These feelings make you happy in the way to understand the Lord your God because you are now living in truth, common sense, and reality. Back in the time when you lived in darkness, all you had was misery. You will still have your sacrifices, but now you will have the power to understand the future in spiritual ways. You will understand that people are not God and that He is the only God that there is. You will no longer worship any human before the Lord your God.

When you worship the Lord in the understanding of truth, you will be in heaven because everything that you need will be added to your name with what you receive from the Lord, and life will become much easier. There will be times that you don't understand something, but *just ask the Lord for the wisdom.* You will come to understand it, and you will come to live it in your soul and in your mind in the understanding that heaven is a *place of knowledge.* What you have gained in the knowledge of true spiritual value will make you a happy person in the land of common sense and reality, where the Lord has made you to understand the power of all the Scriptures.

Before now, everything in the Scriptures was hidden from mankind. That is why the world is in such a state of darkness. Now the Lord wants to open it for everyone to understand and to feel the time of the coming of the Lord. Everybody thought, with their little locust minds, that God would appear to the world and everybody would see God. You will *indeed* see God, but you will see Him in *spiritual understanding*—not in the way that you think with your *physical* mind. You will see God in your spiritual wisdom, and you will be able to *live* with God. All of mankind will be able to do this same thing, but only those who *reject* the lies of false religion will *truly understand.* You will come to understand that the earth is a beautiful place to live, and you will never want to leave the earth. Heaven is a place of knowledge, and knowledge is what is going to make you happy because God created you with knowledge.

The only reason that you were so miserable in the old world of the old truth is because you could not understand. But now, with the heavenly knowledge coming inside you, you will be perfect in everything that you do. You will know when you do right and when you do wrong. You will receive a way to understand the power of right and wrong and what is right to worship the Lord your God with the common sense and the reality that is inside you.

Now we go to the Parable of the Mustard Seed. God has placed inside you a little mustard seed. The meaning of this in spirit is that the mustard seed is the smallest of all seeds. If you grow into the spirit of the Lord, you will come to understand this small seed, and you will bring the small seed to the great power that we have within ourselves to understand. The *smallest of all teachings* can grow to be *giant wisdom* inside you. God has the Kingdom that we call heaven, which is the beautiful power of human understanding. It is a Kingdom that is much different than the earth and the heaven that we know now. It will be in the understanding that the laws will change to where they make more sense. You will come to understand these laws in your *feelings*, not in your mind. What you understood before was the teaching of the mind. The mind went all over the place to condemn what was good and made people do what was wrong. Now what will come to be within you will be the power to understand and the glory to be able to live in the great power of truth.

The truth will become much easier to live than it was in the old world where you could not understand true power. In the past, you could only have sex with one woman. You could not understand that you had different feelings than what was taught by false religion. Now false religion will be gone. God will destroy them forever, and they will not come back on the earth to fool anyone anymore. You will be able to understand your feelings, how they work, and how you come to live with them in the values of truth.

In the old world, you were taught that every physical need that you had was wrong. Every feeling that was inside you was a sin. In the new world, things will be much different because the new heaven and the new earth will teach you to love and to live your feelings. Nobody is going to tell you that your *natural feelings* are wrong because you feel them in reality. True wisdom will be given to you so you can live in the reality of your feelings. Sexuality was totally destroyed in the old world, but now you will be able to have sex with any person that God chooses for you to have sex with.

You will always have the understanding of how life works in power. The spirit will live on, lifetime after lifetime, forever and ever. You will live seven lifetimes every thousand years, and you will understand how to live life in the Kingdom of this great spirit. That *little mustard seed* that God has planted inside your heart will grow in the feelings of humanity. You will be happy in the Kingdom that, before now, did not make any sense. In the past, you had to be a good person where your feelings were not counted for. But the truth is that your feelings come from God, not from man.

You will come to understand that people will not kill each other like they do now because the beast will be killed inside them. You will be a part of the Kingdom where people will not hurt you or destroy you anymore. You will live with people, and everybody will be happy to see you in the way life is supposed to be. Everything in life was created for *life*. Try to start living life the way it was meant to be, not the way it is right now. You will come to find *true happiness* with that little mustard seed that the Lord has placed inside you so long ago. Mankind had to go through the time of turmoil in stupidity and superstition that we lived before now where man-made religions would forbid you to live life according to your feelings. Now you can live in your feelings, and you will be able to make love to anyone you want. You will live life without having anything to distract your feelings in the reality of truth and common sense.

Next, we come to "Jesus calms the storm." The meaning of this is that you have to go to common sense to get the information you need to calm the storm. There has been a big storm in the world for so many thousands of years where people kill each other in all kinds of different battles, and make life miserable. People just destroy each other's lives in the *great storm of stupidity* that has made the world a terrible place to live in. They cannot understand why God sent this great storm on us and made it almost impossible to be happy in life. But you must understand that *you cannot be truly happy* unless you have some disappointment in the power of learning. It is only through the sacrifice of disappointment that you will learn what *not* to do, and this will help you figure out what you *should do*. You have to learn from the mustard seed, and you have to also learn from the great storm. Unless you endured the storm and saw the violent wind and waves, you will not understand what was going on. You must see the *worst* in life to *appreciate the best.*

You must understand the power of the Kingdom of God. The farmer cannot plant the seed and expect it to grow overnight. He has to wait for it to grow. That's the way the Creation of wisdom was formed. Everything had to be lived in the certain time of the Creation in order to have the seed planted and the storm calmed inside you so you can learn from that little mustard seed that was created for you. Then one day, you will understand. God cannot give it to you all at once because life is not made that way. That little seed that He has given you had to grow in time. That's the way it is, and that's the way it always will be. You have to live through the sacrifice in order to understand the pleasure of life.

If you live through all these sacrifices for six thousand years and you come to understand the power of those six thousand miserable years, then you will come to understand how life works inside you. You will understand that everything that you are created for is in all your feelings. The Lord is the Lord, and whoever believes in the Lord must believe that everything has to be done in the process of time. Do not believe that God could jump over everything and make your life perfect from the very beginning. Try to understand the past, the present, and the future of your life. You had to live according to the misery of the world first. Then you had to be taught to live and worship the Lord your God *in truth*.

Most people don't worship God properly because they think that they don't need to, but that's not the truth. The truth is that if that little seed doesn't grow inside you, you will not be able to be happy. That is the way happiness comes inside of you—you have to *suffer and sacrifice* for your learning. That's the way life is and always will be in the Kingdom of human understanding. If you make a mistake in the new Kingdom, it will be the same as before, but you won't be as vulnerable to make mistakes because you will know the difference between right and wrong. You will not create wrong over right just to please yourself. You will know that everything that God is giving you is part of the truth.

In the old world, you lived according to the way you thought with your mind. In the new world, you will be able to live according to the feelings that are in your heart. That will make a big difference because Adam is going to finally have the upper hand over Eve. You will be able to understand that you have to have your Adam be in charge of your Eve. You must come to understand that the loss and gain of the mind is very little compared to the power of the Lord God in your soul. That is why the Lord sent the great storm, to teach you the value of what is wrong. You must live in wrong for so many years before you can receive right.

Remember that Cain killed Abel because he wanted to know what it was like to kill his brother. This is what happened to mankind. The Cain inside of us, which represents wrong, killed Abel, which is the right inside of us. Real life is a place where we live within the boundaries of justice. In the old world, justice was not even considered to be anything more than words. But in the new world, justice and fairness will be appreciated and lived through every event of life to execute your love for one another. You will come to understand the power between what is wrong and what is right. This is the greatest gift that you will receive from the Lord.

In the old world, you live in the misery of wrong, and you think that you are right. But in the new world, life will be understood in a better way. You will come to completely understand right and wrong, and you will not believe what you do now. To explain the Kingdom of God, you have to understand the mustard seed and the great storm. Just like the Israelites had to go to through the forty lifetimes of living in the desert, every single life must be lived in the time of the Creation. You have to come to understand *why* God made war, the destruction of your physical body, and all the things that do not make sense in the old world. You thought you understood life, but you could not touch good over evil. That's why the Lord made you come to the benefit of truth. He created you with the power to understand truth. This brings you to the teaching of life on earth.

Now we go to "Jesus restores a demon-possessed man." God allowed all these demons to possess your soul because in the teaching of truth, demons are like angels in heaven. Demons and angels are both teachings—one on the side of right, the other on the side of wrong. Demons live inside the human spirit. A demon is not a big devil with horns on his head like you think or were taught it is. Understand well that a demon is a *feeling* that you have inside you to do wrong. Every time you see right, you have to try to counteract that and make it wrong. That's what a demon is, and if you have a demon that wants to kill someone, rape someone, or wants to do some other wrong, you just want to prove that these demons are on the side of right. It is not easy to understand what is right and what is wrong by the power of the spirit. If you are possessed by an evil way of understanding life, you cannot change yourself just like that.

You have to learn to be on the right side and to do what is right for everyone around you. But if you are possessed by an evil spirit, you cannot enter the Kingdom of God. Understand well here that your spirit becomes possessed by a demon when you do wrong. You cannot change the wrong to the right side in your soul that easily. You have to bring the situation to the truth where wrong must be punished for being wrong. For example, if you are consumed with feelings inside of you to commit murder and kill someone, those feelings don't go away because you have placed that feeling inside your soul and you are possessed. That is why you do it without even thinking of the circumstances of what will happen.

It is very hard for a man who has feelings to do wrong inside himself to admit they are not right because he is possessed by these wrong feelings. When you are possessed by something, you think it is right to do so because you believe the other person probably deserves what you are giving them. You think it's right for you to hurt that person and kill them. But you are not just killing that person—you're actually killing yourself as well. Then the laws of man will come against you. You will see that great demon of the laws of men come after you, and they will not stop until they put you in prison for the rest of your life. You will say to yourself that you hate to be in that prison, and then you will realize that you are possessed.

If you are possessed by a demon, you have to live it through in order to prove to yourself that it was wrong. You cannot just look at yourself and say that it's wrong to kill people. You have to actually believe it in your heart. To be possessed is to have your soul taken from you. And when your soul is taken from you, you cannot determine anything because you are confused between right and wrong. You have no reason to live on the side of right when you are possessed by wrong because your feelings are twisted inside your heart. You think that you are going to escape wrong, and you think you will get away with it. That's part of the possession of the feelings that you have inside you. To be possessed, you have to think that you are right by doing wrong, just like when Cain killed his brother Abel.

Now you can see how hate possesses your soul. Hate is an evil spirit that grows inside you. It makes a hole inside your soul, and your house becomes divided. When your house is divided, you as the master of the house exhibit what you feel the most inside your soul. Then you fall for what is wrong, and you cannot control it because you think it's right to do so. This is the confusion that comes from inside of you, and it gives you no pleasure in right because all the pleasure is for doing wrong. Wrong has made a home inside you, and you think it is right to destroy other people's lives because the world has not treated you in the way you wanted to be treated. The next thing you know, you find yourself searching your soul and asking yourself why you did these evil things. It is because you *let* evil live inside of you and you made your house comfortable in evil. That made you an evil spirit possessed by what is wrong, and that is why it comes to you and makes you think that you have lost your sense of goodness. You ask yourself why you did these things that did not give me any true pleasure whatsoever.

Now we come to "Jesus raises a dead girl and heals a sick woman." Understand the power of the dead girl and the sick woman so you can come to know what is evil and what is good. In spiritual terms, evil means that your spirit is dead and cannot understand anything in true spiritual value. When the Bible talks about a girl, it means a young mind inside a human being. Life becomes a dead zone where the mind is sick and cannot come to understand anything about the Lord and anything else in truth. The mind only understands in the way of the *struggle* of the world. If you let your mind lead your spirit, you think you can kill people and take what they have. You think you can rape a woman and do anything you want because there's no life inside your soul. You buried your spirit in the physical part of your understanding, and nothing can raise it because your soul is lost. The sick woman is a sick mind that you have from believing in falsehood.

To heal the sick woman and to bring the dead girl back to life, you have to come and fix the mind, the mother of that young spirit, inside you. In order to do that, you have to destroy the old king that possesses you and *fix your mind with common sense.* You must *understand the Old Testament* in order to re-enter the Kingdom of God. You have to bring Levi, the priest, which means love, inside your soul in order to begin the healing process of that which possesses you to be who you are. With common sense you can heal almost anything, and you will come to understand that common sense is the real son of God inside your soul. You will come to understand that your soul is a process of intelligence that operates in both good and evil to bring the determination of healing.

Next, we go to "a prophet without honor." A prophet without honor is a false prophet. It is very important to understand that a false prophet is anyone who believes in the understanding of their mind in front of their spirit, and yet they claim to be on the side of the Lord. If a man wants to be a prophet on his own without the Lord, he brings nothing but lies to others. He thinks he's doing the word of God by reading the Scriptures for himself like a locust jumping from one place to another. He tries to understand the Scriptures with his mind, and he writes speeches according to the *physical* part of the Scriptures. People listen to him, and the next thing you know, you have a whole congregation of human beings who believe that this man has the power to explain God.

The false prophet *uses his own interpretations of the Scriptures,* and because of this, he does not think like the Lord God of Heaven. He preaches like a man, thinking that he's doing God's work, but he does not understand enough because the Lord did not give him the wisdom to explain the Scriptures. With the power of his false teaching, the false prophet brings people to the cave on Sunday morning so he can tell them nothing about the reality of the Lord God because God didn't give him anything. He gives his flocks nothing in the understanding of the power of life on earth.

Every one of us has the power to understand the dream of heaven. But in order to receive this power, you must allow the wisdom of the Lord to come inside you. You cannot preach about it or explain it to other people when you yourself know nothing about it. The true word of the Lord cannot be understood with your mind.

You must come to understand the Scriptures for yourself in your spirit. You must *feel* that it came from the Lord before you understand it for yourself in your heart. Make sure that what you believe and teach to others comes from the Lord and not from man's way of thinking. If a teaching comes from man's way of thinking, it doesn't come from the Lord.

The false prophets teach what they know and what they have seen with their mind, but the truth, above all, comes from the dream of heaven in the spirit. Try to understand this and you will become a prophet of the Lord. Until then, you are a *false prophet* who believes that you know what you are saying and that other people appreciate what you are saying. Everybody thinks that the false prophet is a great preacher, but he does not understand the way God thinks because he thinks in the mind of man. People believe in these false prophets, and they think that they are going to heaven. They think that Heaven is another world somewhere else, and they preach about that world without knowing what it is. Next thing you know, you have been seduced by the false prophet into stupidity, superstition, and ignorance because you have no honor to understand the Lord your God. You think man's justice is just like God's justice, but you cannot begin to understand the power of the way the Lord thinks because you live in the false prophecy of your soul. You have used your mind to complete the understanding of heaven. Therefore, you are a prophet without honor.

Now we come to "John the Baptist beheaded." When a man of the earth preaches, he preaches from his mind. He sees the word *water*, as used in the Scriptures, as physical water and not as reality, which is what it means in spirit. He looks at heaven as another place separate from earth and not as the concept of living in the Creation of the Lord God. He thinks with his mind, which is not how God thinks, and he baptizes people with water, not with reality. The penalty for that is to be *beheaded*. And by beheaded, I mean that every belief inside your soul makes no sense about the Lord God of heaven because you believe that God is like the understanding of the earth. You believe that your *physical body* is going to travel to another world that you think is heaven, and you believe inside your soul that if you are a good person, you will be called to the Lord and brought to that place of rest. Even the American Indians understood that the flesh was not as important as the spirit. They believed that the Lord will bring them to a better hunting ground. This made more sense to the Lord than the beliefs of all the Catholics and Christians of the world.

Mankind lives on earth, but the Kingdom of God is also here on earth. You should be happy to understand that this kingdom is the life that is everlasting in the spiritual value of a happy hunting ground where there will be plenty of grass for your horse and your animals, and there will be plenty of water. That makes more sense than all the teachings of Christianity and all the other religions of the world because the Indians had the right idea. There is no more beautiful creation than the Creation of this world. Why would you want to leave this world to go somewhere else to practice the love of God inside your soul?

This is the place that the Lord has chosen to be his kingdom, and if you believe in the Great Spirit like Indians did, you will one day be able to understand the value of both heaven and earth. You must understand that the law will not be changed by the *word* of it but by the *spirit* of it, and the power of all truth will be here, forever and ever. You will live life generation after generation and believe in the Holy Lord your God, and there won't be false prophets to make you believe against true wisdom.

John the Baptist was beheaded because he baptized people with water. He took water from the river and tried to wash their souls. And every man who came after him, who made people believe in the same things, will have to be beheaded by the great power of the King of Israel and the pleasure of the dancing girl who wanted his head on a platter. John the Baptist preached what he did not understand, and he offered a kingdom that is not part of the Kingdom of God. Whoever came in his name was not the chosen one. There was *only one* who came after him with the common sense of truth, and you must come to understand that common sense is the son of God. The Lord is the one that controls the situation of what man says and what man does, and no one else can replace the Lord your God in the teaching of intelligence. God is God, and no one can replace God on earth or in heaven.

Next, we go to "Jesus feeds the five thousand." Understand well that this is a spiritual prophecy. There is a *meaning* behind the physical story, and you must understand this meaning so you can come to understand the power of the Scriptures. In this prophecy, there were five loaves of bread and two fish. The five loaves of bread represent the first five books of the Old Testament, which are the main books of the Scriptures, and the two fish represent the Old and the New Testaments. Jesus took the five first books of the Old Testament, which is the bread of life, and he feeds you from the first five books of the Old Testament. Then he turned the two fish into a *prophecy*, which means that both the Old and the New Testament will give you life everlasting and you will never be hungry again.

If you read the Old Testament and you understand what you read, you will have more than enough to eat and you will be fed well. The same goes for the New Testament. The two fish are fish stories because they don't always make sense to the human mind, so the Lord called them the two fish. *Understand the power of the prophecy*. If you cannot translate the two fish into an understanding that make sense, then you will not eat and you will not be part of the five thousand who were fed. But if you want to enter the Kingdom of God, you must *translate everything* in the Scriptures that doesn't make sense to where it starts to make sense. You must start bringing the truth to the light and eat the plentiful value of the bread of life.

You will come to eat this bread, and your brother next to you will also eat the bread. Next thing you know, the bread of life will come to feed the whole world because there's no end to the teachings of both the Old and the New Testaments. You have to understand the prophecy that is in all the parables of the New Testament as well as everything that's in the Old Testament so you can feed yourself with the reality of human reason and still come to understand the Kingdom of God.

The trouble with the world right now is the way people are acting. People have been fed for some two thousand years by the false prophets who stop them from believing the truth. Now we have come to a situation where the Scriptures don't mean anything to people. That is why the world is in such disarray and mankind cannot understand anything. They act like animals that have no guidance, and they do not feed themselves in the value of heaven and earth to understand that what they were taught was *not* really the truth.

Not one of these false prophets can extend your knowledge to understand the simple feeling of the Scriptures. To feed people in spiritual value is to bring out the background of the prophecy so they can look on the other side of the scroll and understand that the scroll is written on *both* sides. When you see the other side of the scroll, it makes *much more sense* than to understand only one side of it. When you believe only on one side, you don't see the wisdom of the wise. You must come to understand that heaven is knowledge above all knowledge that gives you the scroll written on both sides.

Now we come to understand "Jesus walks on water." This is the power of walking on water in *spiritual understanding*. It's not physically walking on water but walking on water in *spiritual* terms. Walking on water means walking on *reality* because water represents reality in the Scriptures. And walking on reality means crossing over from one side of the understanding of reality to the other. It is important to understand that Jesus and no one else is the one who walks on water. We know that Jesus represents common sense, so it is common sense that walks on water where human beings should use common sense to understand the reality of life.

But the people of the earth just cannot walk on reality because they put their minds above their spirit. They cannot understand that reality is on the other side of the scroll. The scroll of life has two sides—the side that understands life on the opposite side of common sense, which is what organized religion teaches, and the other side, which is the side of common sense. It is common sense that walks on water. You baptize people with the water of reality, and you walk on the water of reality after you understand the other side of the scroll. What I'm doing here is walking on water because I'm writing this prophecy in the understanding of the other side of the scroll. That is walking on water.

You just don't walk out to the middle of the lake and start walking toward the shore. The same goes with your spiritual value. If you don't try to understand the other side of the scroll, which is the reality of life, then you will sink under the water. You will not be able to get out of the water, and you will drown against all reality. But for two thousand years, mankind could not walk on reality because God made it impossible for people to read the Scriptures and truly understand what these teachings mean. He did this because mankind had to learn to understand *both sides* of the scroll. The Lord brought us to the side *opposite* common sense so we could know the difference and so we could work our way back to being on the side of common sense.

To understand the prophecy of Jesus walking on water, all you have to do is translate this prophecy into spiritual value so you can come to understand that this teaching is all about using common sense to understand the truth. All the superstitious value has to be eliminated because if you believe that a man physically walks on water, then you will find yourself to be a fool in what you believe. But if you see the reality of the Scriptures on the other side of the scroll, you will come to understand that it *is* possible for any human being, including yourself, to walk on reality every single day of your life.

It is the mind of the fool that thinks Jesus was such a miracle maker that he could physically walk on water. He was actually walking on reality. There is *absolutely no way* that a human being can physically walk on water. Everything that is written in the Bible is the truth, but it is the truth in the reality of life that makes sense. The problem is that most people believe that superstitions make more sense. If you try to understand the Scriptures by putting yourself above others, then you are going to return to the same principles that make no sense. You won't be able to restore your intelligence on the side of reality and common sense.

Understand the Holy Spirit here. Isaac is the Angel of Reality from the Old Testament. Abraham is the truth, Jacob is common sense, and Isaac is reality. You have the power to understand and have faith in Abraham, Isaac, and Jacob. But it's not these physical men you should worship. It is what they represent in spirit that should be heralded. The reason that these teachings have physical names is that God uses the understanding of man to teach the mind of a human being. And if you cannot translate these minds into spiritual understanding, then you will lose your soul. That's what happened to religion on earth. They tried to understand the Scriptures in the way of the mind, and they made the *biggest mistake of all time in faith.* They'll never be able to understand the Scriptures because they read them with the mind first. After you come to understand the truth with common sense and reality, you must try to understand everything in that same reality. Then you will be a man of God, and you will be able to preach with the wisdom of the Lord.

Next, we go to "Jesus honors a Syrophoenician woman's faith." As he entered into the house of that woman, Jesus wanted to keep it a secret that he was there. But the woman understood who he was. She had a daughter who was possessed by an evil spirit, and the woman begged Jesus to make the evil spirit go away. Understand that an evil spirit lives inside you, and there's nothing you can do to change your mind. Evil enters into your spirit and takes possession of all your value. You think that you are right by doing wrong, when you are actually wrong in doing right.

The power of the evil spirit is to *contradict* one side from the other and to take the side of wrong in the benefit of your life. The evil spirit exercises that wrong even though it knows that it makes no sense. You have to bring common sense to the reality of that evil spirit, and you must come to understand that the power of evil is *against* the side of intelligence. The Lord your God has created both sides when it comes to the spirit. On one side, He created good, and on the other side, He created evil—both sides are part of the Creation of the Lord. You have to come to common sense to determine the difference between what is right and what is wrong. If you can prove wrong to be wrong, you will destroy the evil spirit and you will make sense out of what is right.

The battle between right and wrong is like a war. The fight has to be fair, and when it's not fair, the weak part takes over the strong part of yourself. Hate and the destruction of one another becomes involved, and the next thing you know, you have two evil spirits fighting against the truth. If you do not put right over wrong in the great battle of intelligence, your spirit will be defeated inside you, and you will not be able to understand the glory of this mighty intelligence that the Lord has created for us. Find the center between right and wrong, and the center will set you free.

Now we come to Jesus feeding the four thousand who gathered on the side of the lake to listen to him. They had been there for three days, and they were hungry. So the Lord fed them with seven loaves of bread, which are his seven spirits. The seven spirits of the Lord are wealth and wisdom, glory and honor, power and strength, and also praise. These are the seven loaves of the bread of life that will feed the spirit of as many people as can gather together. No matter how large a group of people who come to hear common sense, you must give them something to eat. And if you only have seven loaves of bread, you must extend the amount of bread to make it enough for everyone to receive and to listen to the bread of life. Everyone will be fed spiritually and will come to understand the value of the bread of life, which is the Word of God. Then they will receive the blood, which is the understanding of God's Word. The people will be fed, and they can then prosper in all that they have learned because the Word of God feeds the world internally as the bread of life that will never die in the understanding of its value.

If you teach yourself to understand the bread of life, you are forever in the pleasure of human understanding. Understanding the bread of life is to feed yourself with the events of the reality of the truth, and that brings you to the kingdom that makes common sense to your intelligence. This is what feeds you forever. You will never be hungry again because every time you think of the reality of truth, you will be able to understand the kingdom of reality for yourself. God will always be there with the angels of common sense and truth to teach you the value of his bread and what you should eat for life. The trouble with the world is that mankind has gone too long without the meal of the Lamb of God. Man cannot understand the power to reverse stupidity into intelligence and what makes sense in the common sense of intelligence. The spirit that comes inside you to tell you the truth is the *real son of God*, which is common sense itself.

Next, we go to "Jesus heals a blind man at Bethsaida." When you are blind in spiritual value, come to understand that when the common sense of the truth spits in your eyes, you begin to see differently and your feelings change. To be blind is to not see anything in the spiritual understanding of life itself. It is very important to understand the power that is created inside you when you hear the common sense of intelligence. It is like a man that cannot see through his mind and soul, and then things are revealed to him that have always been there. He feels that these feelings are coming alive inside him.

Some people are blind in spiritual value for their entire lives. They just cannot understand anything because they made up their mind to believe against the Word of the Lord. They try to see and understand, but they cannot see anything of truth because God has sealed their minds. They cannot see that the spirit should lead the mind in the understanding of life because their mind has tricked their spirit, and they see things in the way of the evil spirit. They believe in something that they found in their mind, and they like that feeling because they think that it makes them wise. This is just like when Eve ate the forbidden fruit. She thought that she would become wise and have the wisdom that the serpent told her about and that she would be able to understand. But what happened was that she became *blind*. Then she gave the forbidden fruit to Adam, the spirit, and he ate that forbidden fruit.

False religion is the forbidden fruit on the tree of the knowledge of good and evil. You are not supposed to claim that you are good, nor are you supposed to claim that you are evil. Just be what you are created to be, which is a simple human being in the understanding of both good and evil. But don't try to understand good or evil because you're blind to it. You will see evil, yet you won't condemn it, and you will see good, but you won't appreciate it because you're blind. You don't understand that the blindness that you have is because you cannot decide for yourself what is really good and what is really evil. So you try to touch the side of evil more than you will touch the side of good because you are in between good and evil, and you cannot cross over to one side or the other because of your blindness.

You seek to have peace, but you cannot see either the truth or the lies because inside you, there is no understanding between the two. Therefore, you become frustrated and you tell yourself that the Kingdom of God is impossible to understand. The key to understanding the Kingdom of God is that it is important for you to feel that there's something good when it comes to you. And it is also good to feel evil when it comes to you. I'm not saying you should live these evil feelings as if they are good feelings. You should *feel all your feelings*, both good as well as evil, for understanding the difference and how it affects you. You should appreciate good over evil, but if you don't understand this, it is going to be very hard for you to differentiate between the two. That is what makes a man blind in spiritual value.

I am not here to tell you to be prejudiced against evil or against good. You must split the difference inside you. You should never call another person evil. You can understand what is evil for yourself, but you cannot say that other people are evil. You may understand that they have evil spirits inside of them that make them create evil, but it doesn't make it totally evil because every human being was created by the God of Heaven, and if they fell into the understanding of an evil spirit, then they have to take that evil spirit out in order to understand good and evil. It's quite simple. You cannot judge another person, but you must judge yourself. Then when you find what is wrong inside you, you have to straighten it out and bring it to the side of good. Work to understand truth inside yourself. Don't work inside other people because you cannot straighten anybody else out. You can control yourself in common sense, which is the son of God, but you cannot control anyone else.

Now we go to understand the death of Jesus, why he predicted it, and why God allowed him to die on the cross. Christians claim that Jesus died for our sins, but that's not true because Jesus was a man like the rest of us, and no man can save another man. Therefore, it is *not* possible that he died to save other men. The death of Jesus and the way he predicted it was that he was sacrificing himself for the world. I believe that what he meant was that we have to go through great persecution and be killed in the justice of the way man thinks. The Lord made his death so horrible because God wanted to show us how to sacrifice our life in the name of justice to receive the Kingdom of God. The wisdom of the Lord was trying to teach us to give up our physical life for life everlasting in the spirit.

Understand that because Jesus was just a man, it was not worse when he died on the cross than it was for some poor black man in Africa who was killed for no reason. Remember that every injustice in the world is part of the Lamb of God. But man does not like the way life is, so he tries to get away from what is wrong to sacrifice himself for the wrong that was done to him. These people have no choice but to go through their own crucifixion. Jesus died on the cross because he had no choice but to show the world that you must die like a seed in the ground. Your flesh will rot away because your flesh is not as important as your spirit is. Jesus died on the cross to show mankind what we must do to enter the Kingdom of God.

Accept the injustice of others, and accept the power to suffer on earth so you can receive the Kingdom of God. People who believe in lies will judge you and make you suffer because you believe in the truth of the Lord your God. You try to live by the Scriptures, and people hate you and try to destroy you because you bring the truth to the light of the lamp of the wisdom of the Lord. God made us vulnerable to be crucified and to live in prejudice and injustice, and the people of organized religion have the power over us to do as they please. The benefit of this is to receive life everlasting in the spirit.

When you lay down your life for the truth, you have already gained life everlasting. And when you gain life everlasting, you don't have to worry about if you're right or wrong or if you were good or evil. You already know where you stand because you gave up what you had for good over all the injustice of the world. Do not think that a person who lived his entire life in prison is a lost soul. His suffering and his sacrifice stand before him in the value of heaven. Heaven is not a question of being good or better than everybody else because at the end, good and evil don't count. It's what you have sacrificed to the Lord that counts.

Sacrifice yourself and follow the teaching of the parables. The parables tell you that you must sacrifice yourself before the Lord and before mankind. If you make this holy sacrifice, you will look like you were the one in the wrong, and you will be brutally destroyed by the hand of mankind. You think that the world will appreciate you for your desire to understand the Word of God in truth, but they don't. They only see you as an evil person who deserves what he gets.

Don't think for one minute that the people who are behind bars are not going to enter the Kingdom of God. If you see a man who does something wrong like killing or raping someone, that's just an act that takes place in an instant. He will suffer and pay for his crime for the rest of his life on earth when people condemn him, put him away in prison, or kill him because they think he is evil. But the real truth is that you are not supposed to judge people. You can take these people away from society so they do not hurt anybody else, but you are not allowed to judge them as good or evil. *That judgment belongs to God alone.*

Another thing, don't think that if you have unfairly judged others and you were never punished for it that you got away with it. There is a big difference between good and evil as man sees it and the real good and evil in the eyes of the Lord. Whoever brought injustice upon others, claimed to be good, and said that they didn't need justice for themselves are the ones who need more justice than the criminals. You must understand the lesson of God and his justice. God doesn't think like you. His justice is *not* like your justice. Whatever you take from another person by taking his life must be restored to his life and, in turn, taken from your life. That is the *true justice* of the Lord God of Heaven.

Next, we go to "Peter declares that Jesus is the Messiah." People worship Jesus in front of the Lord, but there is something wrong with that. *No man is God*, and you cannot worship any human being before the Lord. There is no prophet who can be placed in front of the Lord and be called the Lord because God is the Lord of all. *He is the one and only God.* No one is allowed to worship outside the truth by worshipping a human being before the Lord. *This is very important!*

Jesus asked his disciples, "Who do people say that I am?" and they replied that people believed he was one of the prophets.

Then he asked them, "Who do you say I am?"

Peter answered, "You are the Messiah." The *Messiah* means "the chosen one to bring the parables." Jesus brought the *parables*, but that does not make him God. I will now explain this perfectly so that no one makes that mistake in generations to come. No man has the mentality to be God because we are just men, and men should not be worshipped before the Lord. If you do worship the man, Jesus, as the son of God or as God himself, you are practicing the stupidity of the ignorance of mankind. You will become a very superstitious person who believes in false miracles, and you will not understand true spiritual value.

To understand God, you must understand the power of the Scriptures. The Scriptures were written in a way that for generations, no human being could figure them out. If you make a man into God, you cannot have true wisdom in your soul because you don't understand who God is. When you don't know God, you think He is like a man. Jesus was created to be a man like the rest of us. Yes, you should admire that he was the one who brought the parables, but you cannot worship Jesus nor should you offer any sacrifice to him because the time is coming when you will be destroyed for doing so.

Try to understand God in the highest knowledge that you can have. God could not be a man because he is so huge and so intelligent. No man can reach that level of power within himself, and that includes Jesus. People always try to find a God that they can see because they cannot understand a God that they cannot see. So they make Jesus into God, and they call him the son of God. God has a lot of sons, not just one, because people before God and the common sense of intelligence are part of the son of God.

Now we go to the Transfiguration on the mountain where a human being can be transformed into the spirit to understand the Lord your God. There is a way to bring that Transfiguration inside the heart of a human being, but that does not mean that this human being will become God. People who don't understand the Scriptures look at these lines in the physical meaning. But there is only *one God*, and you are not allowed to go into the understanding that Jesus is the son of God because we are all sons of God in the common sense of intelligence.

When you speak in common sense, then you are speaking the true word in the name of God. In the Transfiguration, the clothes of common sense became dazzling white. Your clothing, in spiritual terms, is what you wear in your wisdom and the value of spiritual understanding. Everything you say and do is what covers you with the truth. Your clothes will become dazzling white in clear thinking, and things will become crystal clear in the truth.

If you are Catholic or Christian, you *cannot be dazzling white* because to be dazzling white in clear thinking, you cannot think that there is another god in front of God. You cannot call the Lord by his name because you have darkness in your heart and you do not understand the Scriptures in the reality of truth. That makes you *unclean*. Being unclean is taking something that's not true and believing it. It's simply *not true* that Jesus is the son of God, that he is equal to the Father, and all that other garbage that Christianity and the Catholic Church teaches. People who are not clean must come to understand that they are dirty because they have a filthy understanding. God does not appreciate you believing in another god. He will not accept your offering of what you believe, and you won't be able to enter the Kingdom of God with your understanding against the truth.

Just remember that God is the truth, and you must believe in the truth in order to believe in God. If you say to yourself that you believe in God, then you must make sure that your spirit comes in the ownership of the truth. The Transfiguration is that you have to change your soul from the lies you believed in the past to the white, crystal-clear truth of all that makes common sense of true intelligence because you believe in One God.

Next, we go to "Jesus heals a boy possessed by an impure spirit." If you have an impure spirit inside your soul, it will *control* you. Your spirit controls the physical part of your life. So if you let an impure spirit inside your heart, it will control your physical life as well. For example, if you get an idea to kill someone, that's an evil spirit. If you let it control you, you will end up *killing* that person because you feel that that man did not treat you with justice. That evil spirit inside you controls you, and the next thing you know, you commit an evil crime and kill this person.

You must learn to control yourself and not let this evil spirit control you. If you let the evil spirit inside you, it will control you. Next thing you know, you have destroyed your life because you thought you were right to kill them. And self-defense is no excuse, either. If a person attacks you and you kill them in the process of defending yourself, it is still a crime because it is the evil spirit inside you that was relieved to get back at him. If you want to be free from that evil spirit, you must pray inside your_soul that you don't kill anyone because you will also destroy yourself if you become a killer.

Both good and evil live inside you, but if you don't see that, then you live in darkness and you cannot control yourself. Remember that your spirit should control your mind. If you let your mind control your spirit, you will destroy both your mind as well as your soul. Next thing you know, the world around you is all corrupt and you cannot understand anything except violence. Try to understand that common sense is the son of God—and common sense will overrule evil in any form. If you wish to understand and live by the common sense of the Lord, you must reject the evil spirits by making your spirit the leader of your mind.

Now we come to understand who is the greatest. If you want to be great in the world of God, you must consider yourself to be last in human understanding. When I say this, I'm not telling you to be physically ignorant. What this means is if you wish to be spiritually wise, your spirit must lead your mind. When you do this, you will not concern yourself with physically trying to get ahead of others. You will be satisfied having enough to get by and maybe a little extra. You will no longer feel the need to be the smartest, the best-looking, the wealthiest, and so on. Also, you will consider yourself to be a servant of mankind. You will do whatever you can to help others, and you will put your own needs second. This is how to consider yourself to be less in human understanding.

For the people of arrogant understanding, it is almost impossible to consider themselves last in the wealth of the earth. The people who are in great positions in the way of the earth always foolishly believe that being first is the most important thing that there is. If you live with the understanding of your mind leading your spirit, you try to build yourself up in the way of the earth. You call yourself a big, important person in your church or in any part of life with what you have accomplished. You try to make yourself to be the one in the first seat of the glory of man, and you believe you will have a high place in the false heaven that you believe in.

The purpose of being last is not very attractive to the human mind. Everybody likes to claim a value above others in the situation that they are in. They say things like "I'm a big lawyer and I cannot be last" or "I'm a priest so I'll be first to enter the kingdom of God." But they don't understand that this is not the way it is in heaven in spiritual value. To understand this heavenly knowledge, you must accept being last. Let everybody else try to make themselves first and try to be important people in the world. You must come to understand that the *true winner* is the one who takes the last seat. All those who always had the best seat on earth are the ones who have the worst seat to see the Kingdom of God.

God has prepared his kingdom for those who are not important to the world. Those who put themselves first—from the pope down to the presidents of countries and all the big shots—will all be powerless to understand the kingdom of God because the power of the kingdom is to be able to understand it in a very *simple* way. For those who think that they are great, what they have is not good enough for them—they have to be the *greatest.* Whoever is the greatest on earth is *not important* to the Kingdom of God. If a man was born with a silver spoon in his mouth and always had the best in life, he cannot understand how important it is to be *humble.* And when he gets to the top position on earth, he has nowhere to go because he has received everything that was valuable from the honors of others.

Humbling yourself before the Lord is not an easy thing to do. Remember that the Kingdom of God is not a place that you go to with your mind. God has made intelligence possible for all men, but He has created the human heart backward from the understanding of the Kingdom of Heaven. The reverse of this situation will come to be where a poor peasant who did not really dedicate his life to understand will be *first* in the Kingdom of Heaven. The poorest of the poor in human intelligence who was not considered important in the world will say and do the greatest things because the Lord will give them the wisdom in their heart. He will give these simple people the new heart first. They have accepted being put last for so long in the learning of life, and when they become first, the joy will be complete for them. Those that were first in the old world will not appreciate this marvelous kingdom of intelligence because they always thought that they knew better than these poor people who didn't know anything in the old world.

Next, we come to "Whoever is not against us is for us." If you come across someone who understands the same way that you do, you would say that this person is on your side. "You are with us because you are not against us" does not mean that your brother, who is equal to you in knowledge, gets the knowledge from another god. That is not true. He got his knowledge in the same way that everyone does. There is only one God, and He gives *everyone* the same truth that He gives to you. It belongs to your brother as well as to you. You cannot use jealousy and say God is only on your side.

Understand that the Kingdom of God does not belong to anyone, but it does belong to *everyone*. Rich or poor, great or small, it doesn't matter who you are. If you go through the sacrifice of learning, you are just as important as anyone. No matter how much you have learned, do not put yourself to be first above others. Instead, you should be thankful that the Lord chose you to understand his great glory of human understanding that we live in. There is no jealousy that can cross the border into *true spiritual life*. The ones who will be let into the Kingdom of God will be those who understand that all of mankind is one on the same page of humanity.

If you see someone who has more intelligence than you and speaks better than you, that doesn't make him a better person than you. Remember that the Lord has given them and you his wisdom. Understand well that God has placed the book of the righteous on the table for all men. Everyone who opens his heart to understand the coming time will be part of the same faith in the same God, and you won't have to look for God anywhere else outside your own heart. In the old world, there were priests, ministers, rabbis, and all kinds of other false prophets that all the people worshipped in front of the Lord because they were told they had spiritual wisdom. But that's not going to be the way it is in the Kingdom of God. There will not be any false prophets who will try to trick people into giving them money by claiming that they know better than anyone else.

Now we go to "causing to stumble." The little ones that Jesus is talking about here are the people of the earth who do not understand very much in true spiritual wisdom. Anyone who causes them to sin by telling them to worship idols before God, and anyone who tells people to believe that a human being can possibly be God is *against* the Lord God. They are trying to bring their followers to that same side of wrong. These false prophets preach on the side of worshipping idols and on the side of worshipping men before the Lord your God. This will bring people to their downfall and away from the Kingdom of God.

Organized religion taught mankind that life after death was a place in heaven, and the whole world believed that when you die, you go to this place called heaven. But they never understood that heaven is right here on earth. So people were waiting to die so they could go there. This is one of the *biggest lies* that has ever been told by religion. Heaven is not a place where you go after you die. Heaven is knowledge given by God inside your soul that feeds you with the wisdom of intelligence.

If you humble yourself and ask the Lord to show you the true meaning of heaven, you will be given all that you need to understand it. You will be able to understand heaven because you will have a *new heart* to understand it with. But that heart will be given only to those who are humble and have turned away from their arrogance to be simple like the children of God should be simple. Your heart will feel wonderful because heaven is a place put aside by God in your heart where you can understand the power and the glory of intelligence.

Next, we go to understand *divorce*. This is not the divorce of the flesh like mankind believes it to be. The *real marriage* that mankind is supposed to practice is the wedding feast of intelligence between spirit and mind. This is where the two (mind and spirit) become one flesh and one physical power to learn the spiritual understanding of life together. In spiritual terms, both male and female are *inside* each human being. Many people do not understand that the Bible is a spiritual book, not a book about the physical part of life. So they made it look like the Bible was talking about the male and female of the flesh. False religion could not understand life in spirit, so they formed falsehoods by using a *physical* interpretation of the Scriptures. They tried to make this work in the spiritual part of life. The grace of heaven let it happen because man had to be punished for their infidelity to the Lord.

The divorce mentioned here is the divorce of the mind and spirit. The wedding feast of intelligence is the *only* marriage that the Bible is talking about. What this means is that you must have an agreement between the male (your spirit) and the female (your mind) to *join together* to achieve the knowledge of the Word of God. God has given every one of us both a mind and a spirit. He has joined them together as one inside us for achieving the *understanding of life* in the Kingdom of Heaven. This means that *both* the mind and the spirit must be on the *same page* in order for a complete understanding of the Word of the Lord in order for this to be possible.

The mind only deals with loss and gain, whereas the spirit only works in feelings. Since they are often on opposite sides of understanding, they will not always agree. When you have a split between what you feel in your spirit and what you think with your mind, that becomes a divorce. Divorce is adultery in the eyes of the Lord because He joined both your mind and your spirit together inside of you for wisdom when you were born, and you will not learn anything about the Word of God by deciding on your own that your mind and spirit will not work together.

Now we go to "The Little Children and Jesus." We are all little children in the name of God, and we should learn the power of the Scriptures in the simple way of a little child. Being simple is what God meant with this parable. To gain the wisdom contained in these parables, you must return to the *feelings of a child* in the simple manner of thinking where you rate yourself not above others but equal to others in the knowledge of being simple. If you try to only understand good in the world, then you become an adult on the seat of judgment of your fellow man. But the Lord tells you to return to your mind of being simple like a child and look at yourself to be one of many in the world.

Good and evil are two sides of the same teaching. You learn the Scriptures on the side of good or on the side of evil. If you think you're better than anyone else, you will also think that everybody else is evil. That's when you become an adult in the evil ways of thinking because you raise yourself up to a false value where you think you are on the side of right in the judgment of the Lord. In other words, you try to play God. And when you start playing God in your adult feelings, you rate yourself too high to be content among the sheep. When you do that, you begin to believe that you are more important than others. You *raise* yourself above the animal that you were created to be, and you think that your spiritual feelings inside of you are better than most people around you. Then you will judge those who you think are lower than you. This is where man's judgment is unclean.

You must keep yourself clean from the values of arrogance because arrogance was the first sin that God hated, and more than likely, it will be the sin that will make you lose your life because you rate yourself too high to be part of the Kingdom of God. Return to being a little child in the understanding of life where you try to see nothing wrong with anyone else and you try to do no wrong to others. That's what the feelings of a child are.

Next, we go to "Jesus Predicts His Death a Second Time." The death of Jesus means the death of common sense. What you understood with your mind in the old world must be brought into a spiritual understanding in the new world. This is where the power of common sense is destroyed and crucified by the false prophets of the earth and brought down to the low point of value. Organized religion says that the death of Jesus is your salvation. But how can the death of a man_be your salvation? You will see the wounds of Jesus, meaning the wounds of those who went through the great persecution of the Lamb of God. You will see, in the great power of common sense, that God made a plan to catch those who fooled themselves and fooled others because they did not understand the Scriptures.

The same thing will happen to the false preachers promising people life everlasting when they didn't have anything in the understanding of the prophecy of Jesus or anyone else. The death of Jesus meant that common sense would die in a brutal way by the voice of the false prophet. Remember that it was a false prophet who turned Jesus over to Pontius Pilate—and the people that had him crucified were the *people of religion* of the time that Jesus lived. That was a prophecy to be understood that Jesus would die on the cross in a brutal way.

The children of the same God will be spiritually brutalized, and a crown of thorns would be put on their heads. This means that the false prophet will fill them with the most stupid beliefs that you can ever imagine and make them believe that the cross is their salvation. The death of Jesus meant that the false prophets of all the false religions of the earth will *crucify* the human race. They will build churches that represent the tomb and bury people in that tomb. Then after three days, the great power of common sense will return to the human race, and you will live again in the common sense of intelligence.

This is *far* from what the preachers of the earth have promised people. They promise you salvation, but the salvation they offer you is based on all the stupidity that you can ever imagine of what they made out of the Scriptures. So much was said in the ignorance of the death of Jesus that people believe that this was their true salvation. They went on believing this because they thought the false prophet *knew* the meaning of the death of Jesus—they never thought that same death could come and fool them in their arrogance. This is because arrogance is the greatest sin of all and it will always be the greatest of all. If you leave the childhood behind and become an adult in the judgment of others, you will lose your soul and you will not be able to enter the Kingdom of God because these false prophets are so false that it cannot be explained in human words.

Now we come to "The Last Supper." This was not the physical meal eaten by Jesus and his disciples. That was just a *prophecy* of what the *real* Last Supper is. That prophecy was that mankind would not eat the fruit of the common sense of the world for the next two thousand years. People would not be able to understand what happened in Jerusalem two thousand years ago, and they would not be able to penetrate the teaching of God's Word. This is because God put a seal on it, and the true meaning of this teaching was sealed off from the false prophets of the earth where no one could understand the truth.

Common sense was going to be turned over to the high priests, meaning the religions of the time, and then it would be turned over to Pontius Pilate, the governor. Since the high priests worshipped with their minds and not their spirits, *common sense became corrupted into ignorance*. Then this ignorance was transferred to the King of Israel, where the meaning was to be placed in the hands of religion and then placed in the hands of government. The government would force the hand of this false teaching of ignorance, and even though they knew there was something wrong with religion, they would just wash their hands from it. Ignorance was then transferred to King Herod, the King of Israel, meaning that it would be prophesied that in time, the world would turn to believe these events in the most imaginable way possible.

Understand that it was the hand of God that caused man-made religions to go against intelligence and believe something way outside the doctrine of truth. God made people step *outside* the form of intelligence to believe the most false things to be true, yet it was practiced by every generation for the past two thousand years. It was God's plan to make people stupid and vulnerable and to make them believe in stupidity and total ignorance. The false prophet went on and on and preaching things that were not part of the form of intelligence. They preached that God was like a magician and that he could make almost anything happen. They believed that this magic which, in reality, is part of the world of make-believe, would be brought forth to the day of the Lord. And the world will look at it and see that life on earth would be ruled by the false priests of the Catholic Church, the false ministers of the Christian world, and all the other religions of the world.

Religion became the subject that did not fit the center of the form of intelligence. The Scriptures did not make sense to man-made religion, so they just called it a *miracle* because it was something they could not understand. And you had to believe it because otherwise, they told you that you didn't have any faith in God. It did not make any sense that Mary, the mother of Jesus, had a baby without the sperm of a man. But the false prophets made people believe that. The Lord in heaven saw all these things happen and let it be for the destruction of those who preach in falsehoods. *Mankind must come back to the center of intelligence to believe in what is true and reject what is not true.* Understand that this was brought forth to fool the human race and to bring upon mankind the justice of those who said they knew God's will but did not do His will—and those who said they would not do His will but thought about it later and then did it.

You can now see how the false prophet has been fooling mankind with their false understanding of the *plan of God*. God wanted to see *who* had enough common sense to say *no* to falsehood. The triumphal entry of common sense into the world happens through the door of the backside of human understanding. It did not reach the *heart* of all mankind. God said that those who look stupid in the eyes of mankind and don't believe the garbage of organized religion will be His children. That's the way you came to be, and that reality must live on and be in God's Word forever and ever.

Next, we come to "The Greatest Commandment." The greatest commandment is the *first commandment*, which is "Believe in One God and One God Alone." You should love the Lord your God with all your soul and everything that you think in your mind and feel the understanding of the Lord your God. The next one is to love your neighbor as yourself. This commandment is hard to follow because it brings an understanding of the people that are distant from the side of goodness in the way they live their lives and the way God created them to be.

For example, God has created homosexuality for fooling those who think are so perfect because they only make love to the opposite sex and only after practicing the wedding feast of the beast. Another example is that God made the Indians look different where you could not recognize them as your brother, and He made the black people and the white people different skin colors so each side could not recognize the other one as their brother. God has created different things in different people, such as different attitudes and different values. But we are all brothers, and if you do wrong to the least of these little children that God has created, you are doing wrong to the Lord your God. If you cannot love what you see in other cultures, and if you cannot love your fellow man with all the differences between one and the other, you *cannot enter* the Kingdom of God because there is no greater commandment in the way of life. You may go to your church and pray day and night, but you cannot enter the Kingdom of God unless you see no wrong in your fellow man. In order to enter the Kingdom of God, you have to see wrong in yourself. Understand that the narrow door that leads to the Kingdom of Heaven is narrow because your nose does not fit in there. This is because you have lifted your nose too high in arrogance to enter the Kingdom of God. You will not be able to enter because you are part of the arrogant thinking that you are better than anyone else.

God made loving Him with all your soul and all your mind and loving one another as the *two greatest commandments*, but the false prophet changed this commandment into loving Jesus in front of the Lord and worshipping the *image* of the man before the Lord. The false prophet has no respect for their brothers who are lower than them. If these false religions believe in the Lord our God with all their soul and all their mind, then why did they have to go and *worship the image of a man in front of the Lord*? If they worship one God and one God alone, then *why did they change the commandments*? They changed them because they live in darkness and they cannot understand the Scriptures in spiritual terms because in their little locust minds, they think they want to worship a god of their own choosing. And since Jesus was, in their minds, the son of God, they worshipped the animal before the Lord God.

Now we go to "The Destruction of the Temple and Signs of the End Times." Of all the great buildings, not one single stone will be left on another. The meaning of this is that not one single *faith* will be left on another. When the Bible talks about stones, that means faith. These buildings are spiritual buildings, and they are built with stones, which is faith. This means that all man-made religions, which are built from false faith, will be *torn down*. Therefore, your faith must be changed in order to enter the Kingdom of God. Whatever was an island in the old world will collapse into the bottom of the sea, and the cave in the old world was a church where you had to go through the cave to worship God, and all the laws of God fall on you. In other words, you believe you are right in believing in Christianity, in the Catholic Church, or in any organized religion, and you open the laws of God on your side, but the laws are not there where you are because you *worship in a cave* where there is *no God*. You must go to worship in your spirit where the Church of God exists. You must understand that the Lord will change these laws that you were taught to believe by the false prophet, and you must come to understand that *the world must change*.

The new world must be born along with the new heaven. What the old heaven and the old earth brought to you was not the truth. Your spiritual teaching will no longer be a promise that comes out of the mouth of the false prophet, but instead it will be the Word of God Himself that will change your attitude and make you understand the *real laws of God*. Come to the *reality* of the law, and understand what is real and what is not real. You must understand that you have lived in the fantasy world for so long that you cannot understand the true meaning of the law. And you will see the island, the place of rest that you used to believe in, and you will see that it is a falsehood. Then you will be able to understand that the laws of God will change from its place.

The *adulteries* that were great sins in the old world will become great virtues and great rituals of sacrifice in your life so you can understand the pleasure of life that God has created. When you cross over the Jordan into the land of freedom with Joshua, you will come to understand that the laws will be different and everything that you were told was a sin in the old world will be a *ritual of holiness*. You will come to understand that the people who preach the truth and tell you not to worship falsehood will be the *real prophets* of the new time, and everything will be turned upside down. The truth did not live in the world because of the death of common sense. What made sense then will not make sense in the new world, and what didn't make sense in the old world will make sense in the New World.

What you were taught to believe will no longer be there for you to believe, and your understanding will be born in the rebirth of the truth. The truth will look like it's evil, but you will come to understand that the truth is simple when it comes to you in the new birth of intelligence. Some of you will crawl to the earth, and others will rise to the heavens. The one who lived before on the island of rest in the old world will be disturbed, and whoever was disturbed in the old world will go to their rest. What was persecuted in the old world will be admired in the Kingdom of God. What was left behind and called no good in the old world will be the stone to build your house in the new world.

The world will change in human understanding, and the value will be so different from what it is now and what it will be in the new world. You cannot expect people to understand the new heaven all at once, but the change will take place generation by generation until mankind comes to understand the Kingdom of God. And of course, the false prophet will try to save their whole world. But the Lord is more powerful than any false prophet, and at the end, the Lord will win the battle of the change of the world where people will no longer be persecuted for being simple and humble before the Lord.

Next, we come to the "Day and Hour Unknown." One day, the world will open its eyes. This will be a day where the book of true wisdom will be put on the table for the value of intelligence, and the old religion of lies will be condemned. No one knows when that time will come. Everybody worships the God that false religion introduced them to, and everybody thinks they're safe in the wedding feast that they believe is the truth. They believe they are already saved by Jesus's death, but the day will come where the book of what God thinks of religion and the false prophet has to be put on the table. That book will cause many people to lose their faith, and there will be terror inside the heart of mankind.

I tell you, in truth, that there will be a day where every single person will have to look at his soul_and see where he stands in the value of the Kingdom of God. So many people have stood in wrong against right, and this will continue until the day comes when the book on the table will be in front of every human being on the face of the earth. You will see the glory and the power of human intelligence where common sense will open up all the values of heaven to mankind. This will be a revelation like you have never seen before, and to the false prophet will come a revelation that will destroy their false faith.

Understand well that you were married to your faith, and you thought it was the greatest faith of all. But your faith will not be accepted in the new world because you worship the image before the Lord your God. The day will come where the image will not look so great, and the power to receive what you had in the old world will be gone. Nothing will be able to change that stiff neck of yours, so you can look in the direction of God and receive life in the spiritual value of truth. But if you are too high in your false belief, then the truth will not matter to you, and you will continue to fall in the loss of your soul. Whoever is loyal to the Lord will stay loyal to the Lord. Whoever is loyal to the beasts will stay loyal to the beasts because they are stiff-necked and do not turn their heads when the truth speaks to them.

Now we go to "Jesus Anointed at Bethany." When the power to change the human heart is given to you from the Lord your God, you become *one with the Lord*, and the power that is inside yourself cannot be changed back. God gave you the power to understand the truth, but it is not the same as the education of mankind. You must come to understand the higher power of the Creation, and you don't need the education of the world to do it either. The new understanding is in spiritual value, where before you thought in physical value, but now you step up to the spiritual understanding. This is totally different from the way you used to believe because in your spirit, you think like God—while in the old world, you thought like the human race thought. When you reach a *higher* spiritual level, you climb inside your soul to the value that makes sense to the power of the *spirit*. This changes the course of human thinking to a way that you cannot really understand when you are person of the *mind*.

God gave you a wife, meaning a mind, and that mind is weak. If you live by the weakness of that mind and you don't ask the spirit to take control of you, then you live in the weak wisdom of your mind—you live within the boundaries of your physical understanding, and you think in the physical way of life. But once you enter the spiritual way of human understanding, you climb to the level that Jesus was at two thousand years ago. You begin to understand things in different ways where you feel it inside yourself, and then you accept where the spiritual value is high in the physical way of the mind.

This is why the people of the mind cannot understand someone who speaks in spirit. They think that this person is a foolish man because they don't understand the above. They think that what is foolish is evil, and they condemn people for thinking in such a way. They believe that their faith is higher in human understanding, but they are not born in spirit. And when a person does not have the birth of the spirit inside them, they will understand things in a different way. The people of the earth will condemn the true word of the Lord God because to them, wrong is what they cannot understand, and they think it is right to persecute someone who thinks like God. The people who worship with the mind have not been anointed by the Lord to understand the higher meaning of intelligence.

Jesus understood things that no one else did. Everybody thought he was crazy, but that was because they couldn't figure out his common sense because he was talking in the higher language. The Kingdom of God comes in a different way of life, where the heart becomes healed in the opposite direction from the beast. You don't think of hurting people anymore because you find the values of others to be just as equal to your own. But in the way of the beast, you think you have to destroy and kill everyone around you in order to receive the glory of God. It's actually the other way around. In order to worship in the way of the Lord, you have to destroy the beast that's inside you and heal your heart to the truth so you can come to understand heaven. But to a person who only understands with his little mind of a locust, he thinks that everybody else will to go to hell except him. That's the way it is in the beasts. However, that is *not* the way it is in the precious power of the Lord our God.

Next, we go to "Jesus Predicts Peter's Denial." In the Bible, Peter represents the Catholic Church, where these people will *deny* the common sense of intelligence three times before the rooster crows twice. You yourself will disown common sense three times. Now let's try to understand this. The rooster is the hour of the judgment. Before the hour of the judgment comes, you will denounce common sense three times in three thousand years. Christians and Catholics will deny the Lord God *three times* just like Peter did because the meaning of Peter denying Christ did not happen two thousand years ago, but it has been happening in spirit this whole time.

When I talk about Christ here, I mean the Chosen One. You must come to understand that the Chosen One is not Jesus, but it is the right way to live. Come to understand, in spiritual terms, that there is no name or image before the Lord your God. Everything is done inside the *spirit* of a human being. You claim that you will never turn your back on the chosen parables of the Lord, but you will indeed deny the Lord your God three times before the rooster crows twice, when you hear the common sense of intelligence. The real Christ of the world, in spirit, is the *true way* to live life on earth. This is the chosen way where you have to live your life by the Commandments of the voice of common sense that speaks inside your soul.

Christ is the chosen way to receive the Lord your God and to practice the way of the Lord. Organized religions have been practicing for two thousand years, and they will still deny common sense, the son of the Lord God, because they put an image of a man in front of God. *God is not a man.* He lives in spiritual understanding, and you have to address Him in the way of the spirit. Until you learn to address God in spiritual terms, you do not believe in the One True God of the Creation. You believe in the *image* that you have created for yourself, and you have placed that image between you and God. What a terrible sin this is!

Now we go to "Jesus Arrested." You must come to understand that Jesus was arrested by the high priests of religion. These are the people who put themselves in front of God and claim they are the *masterminds* of religion. They are the ones who arrested Jesus because they didn't like their little fantasy world being troubled by anyone who challenged their way of thinking. They use their little locust minds, and they think it's the right thing to do, to *destroy the man that denies their faith* and messes around with their little fantasy world of believing in their false god. This is the same way that the false prophets of today will come and try to destroy the truth about the Kingdom of God because they cannot understand it.

The Lord did not give the gift of wisdom to the false prophets of yesterday or today. The false prophets will never be able to understand the Kingdom of God because they continue to do wrong in the name of the Lord. If you don't understand the laws of God, why then have you no spiritual knowledge? Why are you trying to teach people to understand something that you yourself do not understand? I pose that question *to your heart* to try to make you understand that your heart is in trouble of being destroyed because you have done wrong. It would have been better for you to tie a millstone to your head and go throw yourself into the sea. Peter, I tell you, in truth, that you have denied Christ in three different millennia, and you are still not willing to repent and learn to love the Lord your God in your soul.

Next, we go to "Peter Disowns Jesus." Peter became the continuation of the teaching of Christ, meaning the chosen way to live. After the death of Jesus, Peter became the symbol of Christianity. They continued this teaching in the way of the mind because Peter was not born in spirit, so he could_not understand with his mind what he was meant to understand in spirit. And the people who came after him—all the popes and leaders of organized religion—did the same as he did. They tried to understand the teaching of Christ (meaning knowing how to live in the way of the Lord) with their minds.

All these popes, cardinals, bishops and priests never understood the life that was chosen for mankind. They didn't have the new heart to live with, and they did not have the real knowledge of the Scriptures in spirit, so they continued teaching from their minds. They became very evil doing so because they thought from their minds what they did not understand from their spirit. Their teaching became the denying of Christ, and they did disown Christ because they just did not understand the message that Christ is the way to live life in spiritual value.

When you are born of spirit and you understand spirit, life becomes different for you. The value of another human being is so important to you that you value them more than you value yourself. You think of others to be the key to open the door of heaven. (But when you live with your loss and gain of the mind, you think that you are the most valuable thing that you want to save. You work to save yourself and you don't think about the values of others. You don't think that they are valuable enough because you live in the way of the loss and gain of the mind.)

To receive the key and open the door of heaven, you have to *put all souls into heaven* and *condemn no one*. You must bring the value of the Lord inside your soul, love your brother as yourself, and value your brother no matter who they may be in any form of life. It doesn't matter what color their skin is or their sexuality or even if they are worthless people. You have to make them brothers and open the door of heaven—not just for yourself but for *every single person on earth*. I want you to think about the values of the people whom you think the least of.

You must think of those who call themselves first and put them down as the last in your book so you can come to understand that *all people are equal* in the Kingdom of God. All people, rich and poor, winners and losers, those who have the power in government and those who don't, those in jail who have no one to pray for them, and even those who are left in some homeless situation. You have to look in the Kingdom of God and bring all people whom you think should be in this kingdom. Make yourself the *servant* of all people, and then you will be able to open the door to the Kingdom of God because denying Christ means that you denied all the others the right to the Kingdom of God and you placed yourself first. That's what denying Christ is all about.

Now we come to "Jesus Before Pilate." Pontius Pilate was governor of Judea. In spiritual terms, that means the government. When we talk about government, we talk about one of the *four kings* of the Scriptures that we are slaves to. The four kings that we are slaves to are God, government, money, and business. When I say we are a slave to these kings, I mean that we cannot exist without these four kings that are inside of us. Being a slave to God means there must be a Creator above us. There also must be a *set of physical laws* to live by. That's *government*. And finally, there must be a system of both money and business as a way of dealing with each other. We must have these four subjects, or we could not exist. There is no getting around these four kings. That's why we are slaves to them. But you must understand that these four kings exist on the side of truth as well as on the side of lies. This means that you can understand these subjects in a way that helps you or in a way that hurts you. It's up to you to learn which side is which.

Now let's talk about government by understanding Pontius Pilate in the Scriptures. Government washed its hands of all the crimes of religion because religion became part of human understanding where they can believe whatever they want as long as they don't cause any trouble. We just leave them alone where they can step out of the form of intelligence and do anything that they want with faith. There is nothing we can do with what people preach as long as they call it *religion*. That's the way the world has turned out to be where religions could molest children and commit the most evil crimes that you can imagine.

Throughout the centuries, all the crimes of religion were forgiven by man because it was religion. But it was not forgiven in heaven because *religion was the greatest criminal of all*. They were respected by the people of the mind for the power that they supposedly brought to all mankind, and so the hand of government didn't do anything about religion until the twenty-first century when they finally figured out that these people were molesting children. Now they are trying to arrest them and bring them to justice, but there's still more control by the high hand of religion to let them get away with it. The stupidity of humans thought that religion provided for mankind because government thought that religion was affiliated with God. They thought that if they did anything about religion, it was a crime for them and the Lord would destroy them.

So this fear of religion came to be in both the spirit and the mind of mankind, and religion continued to produce stupidity and superstition. It was religion that allowed man to teach outside the form of intelligence as long as they called it *faith in God.* No one did anything about it as long as it was sacred to the people who believe in it. A Catholic priest was supposed to be a man of God, and mankind let the church get away with telling Pilate to crucify Jesus. They let religion make their own judgment upon the world. Even though they knew that religion was not always right, they turned their heads away from the truth when the church decided to have the "forbidden act of marriage" to increase that which was *immoral and wrong.* The people let them get away with it, and nobody in charge of government did anything about it.

A priest was *not allowed* to marry a woman. That was a great sin because if you destroy the sexuality of a natural human being and call it a sin, that is way outside the form of intelligence. But the government did nothing about it even though they understood sexuality was very powerful inside every human being. The government didn't do anything about it. They just turned their heads and looked the other way just like Pontius Pilate did. Don't think that for one minute, government could stop them from being so stupid. The common sense of intelligence told everybody that it was wrong for a man to be forbidden by religion to have sex with a woman, but it was swept under the rug like everything else. *No one* could contradict religion because God has placed a seal on things, and no one could prosecute religion in the court of law and punish them for their crimes. This is because God wanted mankind to see the evil of religion in the downfall of ignorance and superstition. The Lord kept organized religion from prosecution because He is going to punish them in His own time. In the punishment of the Lord, mankind will come to see the great Babylon, the mother of all prostitutes, destroyed from the face of the earth where all lies and liars will suffer in the lake of fire. The face of government will also be severely punished for letting these people get away with their crimes of false faith for century after century and millennium after millennium.

Next, we go to "The Soldiers Mock Jesus." This is where a human being is being persecuted for what he knows in the understanding of Heaven. Jesus represents common sense, and common sense lives inside us. The soldiers represent those who have the power to persecute and condemn others. This story must be understood in spiritual terms if the power of its meaning is to be unlocked. You must take this physical story and raise it to the spiritual level in order for it to have meaning here in the twenty-first century. Otherwise, it will only be a story that happened thousands of years ago, and it will have no meaning in your life today. The soldiers of evil and wrong, who are in charge, meaning in the majority, think that it's right to mock the people who understand heaven. They cannot understand the crimes and the sins that they committed when they mocked the man who brought the Word of God to others.

You must separate what is false and what is true in order to understand the difference between the two. On one side is the man who understands in the way of the mind with no evidence of truth that comes from the Scriptures. Everybody agrees with what he is saying, and they think he's a good man because he thinks like they do. Remember that the man who speaks in the voice of the serpent speaks in the way that the heart of the serpent will understand. And on the other side is the man who understands in the way of the spirit. That man will be persecuted because he has the higher knowledge of heaven that goes against the false beliefs of the religion of the mind. Almost no one seems to understand the true meaning of the parables of Jesus. The parables make a lot of sense to those who do understand, but they also attack the people who were sitting on the throne, meaning those who believed they were in charge of wisdom. The high priests were nervous about it because they only understood with their minds of locusts. They could not understand anything higher in the common sense of intelligence that God has given to mankind that raises your heart to understand something greater than what the high priests believed. It is the same in the world that we live in today. The people who speak against the lies of false religion are looked upon as people with no understanding. The people of the mind appreciate the people who speak in *parables of fantasy* that the people of the world who don't have a clean heart can understand.

When you hear something that you cannot understand, it is because it is above your level of understanding. Then you will complain because your mind, which is the only thing you understand with, will fool you and make those with the higher knowledge of heaven look ridiculous. People of these false religions put themselves on the high pedestal of learning. And if you knock them down a little bit, it looks ridiculous to the mind. This is because God's Word does not match religion and common sense. If someone comes with common sense against religion, it becomes ridiculous for the children of the mind because they believe in their religion in the *fantasy world* and they don't want you to mess around with their little fantasy world that they live in. They think that they are in the salvation of the Lord your God and they became soldiers in the fight on the side of evil by trying to protect their little fantasy world. They will kill you in any way they can just to shut you up and make you go away, up to the point that they will commit murder by destroying anything they cannot understand. This is because the Lord God has given them nothing to understand but murder itself.

Next, we go to the crucifixion. Understand well the background of the crucifixion of Jesus and see what was the purpose of God to make it happen in human living where a man had to be crucified for the Kingdom of God. God explained the crucifixion of Jesus from the very foundation of the world that it will happen for right or wrong. This is so you can see wrong in the power of what is wrong and know what is wrong in your soul so that when you come to understand right, you will understand the purpose of God. Adam and Eve, which represent the spirit and the mind, had two sons. Cain, who represents wrong, and the other son was Abel, who represents right. The story of Cain and Abel is that wrong went and killed right. And just like it happened then, it also happened in Jerusalem when Jesus was crucified. The battle of right and wrong is part of the plan of God, and in that battle, wrong always has to defeat right in order to bring the Kingdom of God to a value of truth. It was supposed to be that wrong would have power over right for the first six thousand years because of the weakness of the human mind that God created us with.

God is not a magician who can create anything He wants, like the Christians claim He is. Even God Himself cannot step outside of the guidelines of intelligence. For example, if a man wants to build a house, he cannot just snap his fingers and then, like magic, the house is built. That is not the way it works and that's not the way it will ever work. First, you have to have a plan. Then you have to build the house with your labor. And you cannot live in the house until it is built. That's the way it works, and it works the same way in heaven. The Lord your God is not a magician. He creates by the *value of time*. His Kingdom had to be built step by step in the value of His hard labor. Us little men of intelligence were so weak at the beginning that we had to go by this guideline of building a perfect house. When the house is completely built, there will be a lot of scrap left over that has to be burned and destroyed. If you didn't cut anything off, you will not have a proper house—you had to cut off what you did not need to be used for the house. And the Lord has cut the evil out of the house. This is the little piece that didn't fit in, and you could not do anything with it except burn it after the house had been built.

So you must understand the way it works with the Lord your God. He is a spiritual Creator just like man is a physical creator. The Lord had to build His own house by using the guidelines of the Scriptures to build His house with a perfect heart, a perfect soul, and a perfect heaven for all men. The crucifixion of Jesus was part of the plan to build a perfect house in a perfect earth, the perfect heaven in order to create the perfect world, and the crucifixion of Jesus because it was in the center of the earth to be understood by all generations that you had to be monitored, ridiculed, and persecuted by all the stupid people of the world in order to receive this perfect world.

Now we go to the death of Jesus. You have to understand with your perfect spirit to understand the death of a man who was brutally killed by wrong over right so mankind could come to understand the sacrifice for the Creation. If you don't thank the Lord your God for your sacrifice every time something happens to you, how can you build the Kingdom of Justice if you refuse the sacrifice that was awarded to you by the Almighty God? Those who only understand inside the loss and gain of the mind will never be able to understand the value of heaven because heaven is a place created for those who suffer and die for new life in the value of a new wisdom.

Understand well that everything that happened to Jesus is what was meant to happen to the human race. All the things that happened to him must be changed to mankind. You cannot worship Jesus because he is not God. The death of Jesus is the death of the human spirit in common sense. Through the death of Jesus, mankind was meant to understand that common sense will be killed by the hand of religion and government will do nothing to stop it. The Lord's plan was to destroy common sense in the world and crucify it by the hand of religion so you would know that it was the false organized religions of the mind that destroyed the common sense of intelligence.

After common sense was crucified, the world was in *total ignorance*. People started believing in all the false sacraments like being physically baptized, confessing your sins to a man, receiving communion, confirmation, being married together by the hand motion of a man, being ordained as a priest, and receiving the last rites. Those seven false sacraments created by the church are just as worthless as anything you can possibly come up with in this world. They understood the Word of God by making physical sacraments over the authority of man, and these false sacraments destroyed the human heart even though they thought they were acting on God's Holy Word. Common sense was crucified by the hand of religion, and government washed their hands of it because they didn't want to get involved against religion. This is because politicians who were elected to office thought that the church had the power to keep them in their high office of politics. So everybody was working for himself, and nobody was working for the Lord your God. No one understood that the real son of God was common sense and that the Holy Spirit is the Angel of Reality, so they did things outside common sense and outside reality and they claimed to be working for God.

The Lord *punished* the world for being stiff-necked and believing in evil spirits. Mankind was created with intelligence, but they could not understand the basis of intelligence and common sense. The Lord punished them for their stupidity and ignorance because they broke the laws that He had given to them on Mount Sinai. The Lord said, "Do not worship anyone except the one and only God." But the people ignored that, and they turned to a false god, and they worshipped the man, Jesus, as God when Jesus was *just a servant* of the Lord.

Let us continue with the death of Jesus and what it was in the world of men. Mankind was meant to be placed in the tomb underneath the earth. I'm not talking about the physical tomb here. I'm talking about the *spiritual tomb* where man believed they had to go to church and worship God in the big cave that they call a church. They really thought that God was there in that church. That is the tomb that I'm talking about. People went into these caves built with stone and mortar, and they prayed there for the mountains, which were the laws of God, to fall on them. You were worshipping the Lord in that cave and praying to a god that doesn't exist, and you believed Jesus was the physical son of God.

The false prophet didn't have a clue what the death of Jesus meant and what the Bible was talking about, so the people worship in total ignorance and superstition. They claim to know God, but they worship Jesus as God. They could not understand the Scriptures, so they developed a false understanding that they made up with their little minds of locusts. They fooled the whole world, and this is terribly wrong in the eyes of the Lord. They bring people into their tomb on Sunday morning, in the cave where no one understands the power of the Scriptures. They preach according to whatever little knowledge they have about their false religions that they organized themselves, and they make it look like it was the will of God. That is the real meaning of the death of Jesus. No one can understand this unless you repent and ask the Lord to forgive you. Only then will you be able to enter the Kingdom of God.

Now we go to "Jesus Has Risen." This is where common sense comes to be resurrected. Common sense must come and reunite with the human spirit. Those who want life everlasting must come to understand the Scriptures in common sense and accept the truth as written in the Scriptures. God had to go through the system of the terrible and brutal death of a man who was cruelly crucified by the hands of evil men. God didn't have any other way to do it except with the common sense of intelligence, so you can see in your heart that the Lord uses a little bit of suffering for the benefit of making His common sense the way to understand the truth. Jesus, meaning common sense, has been crucified and will come back to life early in the morning of the third day. The third day here means after the third thousand years where God sends His own common sense to the world for a new resurrection of true common sense.

*****

Next, we come to the Book of Luke. Understand well here the power of the Lord to give His servant to foretell the coming of the birth of John the Baptist, who then foretold the birth of Jesus. This is the account of Luke, who lived in Greece during the time of Jesus and wrote what he heard from those who actually witnessed the ministry of Jesus. Luke was a physician, and he *loved* the story of Jesus so much that he wrote down the account of what he heard from various people who were there. Luke is the man who heard these things and wrote about them so the world could understand.

Now we go to "The Birth of John the Baptist Foretold." The story of John the Baptist was to understand that those who baptize with the physical water of the earth would have their heads cut off. Every prophecy in the Scriptures is a prophecy of what was going to happen to mankind. The life of John the Baptist was where people would get baptized by water in the false understanding of the mind. What this means is, like all the other parables, a physical example is used to teach a spiritual lesson. The lesson of John the Baptist is that we should be baptized in spirit with the water of reality, not physical water. He may have used physical water but only so the mind could understand the concept. We are then supposed to take what the mind learns and raise this teaching of baptism up to the spiritual level where we know that the true baptism is in spirit. But mankind stayed in the physical understanding of the locust on this, just as they did with all the parables.

Man continues to believe in the physical baptism, and that is actually keeping them from the knowledge of the meaning of the parables, and the next thing you know, you have a whole bunch of prophecies that don't make sense. But God created the world that way because He wanted the false prophet, who believed in the theory of the mind and brought religion on earth according to the mind, to learn from the mistake of believing in their false religions. Mankind continues to hold on to these falsehoods, but I tell you, there will come a time when the baptism of the mind will indeed be proven as a horrible lie.

Next, we go to the "Birth of Jesus Foretold." Jesus was born from a virgin who was foretold that she would become pregnant and give birth to a son. The story of the events of the birth of Jesus does not refer to a physical virgin, meaning a woman who has not had sex. You have to remember here that a woman *cannot* have a baby without having sex with a man. So the birth of Jesus was indeed a *physical birth* that happened through *physical sex* between a man and a woman, but the birth of common sense is the spiritual birth that the life of Jesus represents in the Scriptures. Common sense was what was born from the virgin. This means that the spirit, which is female, is not corrupted by the false teaching of the religion of the mind and is therefore a virgin, who will give birth to the common sense understanding of the Scriptures. It is this common sense that will save mankind, not a man who died some two thousand years ago. Now you can see how Mary was a virgin who gave birth to a son. You can see it if you understand that this story, like all stories of the Scriptures, is a spiritual teaching, not a physical teaching.

Now we go to the "Understanding of What the Mind Means in the Scriptures." When the Scriptures talks about a woman, this is *not a physical woman*—it means the understanding of the Scriptures by the *mind*. Inside a human being, the mind and spirit together give birth to intelligence. When you begin to understand the Scriptures as a spiritual teaching, everything changes. You will see that it is not the physical flesh that is important in the Scriptures. The entire teaching of the Scriptures is in the spiritual understanding where the power becomes spirit, and the physical part must be taken out to understand the prophecy of the birth of Jesus, which is common sense born from the virgin mind that is uncorrupted by false beliefs.

Unless you change all the physical references in the Bible and try to understand them spiritually, you will never understand the Bible. This is because the Bible contradicts itself if you try to understand it with your mind. Organized religions have been trying to understand with their minds for thousands of years, and when they discover these contradictions, they just skip over them or they say it's a mystery and that we're not supposed to know the answer. Now I ask you, What kind of a God would give us an entire book full of His laws and teachings in the understanding of life itself and then tell us that there are lessons in this same book that we are not supposed to know the answer to? The answer is that there is no part of the Scriptures that will not be revealed to mankind in time. False, man-made religions that tell you that any part of the Bible is a mystery is really saying that these things are mysteries to them. But always remember that, as the Bible says, with man, it is impossible; however, with God, it is possible.

You must understand the Bible in spirit, and it is the same thing with the birth of Jesus. It is a virgin mind that gives a spiritual son to mankind. Don't think for a moment that the Christian world will understand this because it's too deep for them to understand. They twisted their mind with the physical part, and they cannot understand in spirit because they are just not born of spirit to understand in truth. Their minds will trouble them, and they will reject the truth just as they rejected Christ two thousand years ago.

Jesus gave birth to a new teaching_that was the prophecy of common sense of the spirit, but the people of the mind made their own teaching so they could celebrate Christmas, Easter, and all the false holidays of the mind. They never learned that if you are not born in spirit, you just cannot understand the Scriptures as they were meant to be understood. And when you don't receive the birth of the spirit, you just don't have it. The birth of the spirit is to understand the Scriptures in spiritual terms. Christians call themselves *born again*, and that is a lie because they don't understand anything in spirit. Everything that they teach is in the physical way of understanding. The power that they have to understand with is in the physical teaching and not in the spiritual teaching, where the truth is. And you cannot enter the Kingdom of God unless you understand in the spiritual way of life. You should not claim to understand what you cannot understand. You must first receive the birth of the spirit. Then you can go out and teach God's word in spiritual terms, where you will not teach falsehoods to people.

Next, we go to "Mary Visits Elizabeth." Grasp fully that all references to women in the Bible represent the human mind. Mary is called the Queen of Heaven because Mary is a mind who understands the spiritual laws of the Scriptures very well. In the Bible, a woman is what you try to understand with your mind. The womb of Mary is the womb of the mind, where you must change what you understand in the Scriptures from the spiritual wisdom to the wisdom of the mind so you can explain it to the mind of another person. Then that person should translate it back into spiritual value.

Jesus used plenty of real physical examples to explain the parables, which are spiritual teachings. When he talked about things such as the fig tree or the man who sold all his possessions to buy a field, he was explaining things in a way that anyone who has developed their mind but not their spirit could understand. And once people understood the physical example, Jesus said that it was the same way with the Kingdom of Heaven. This meant that you should use the same common sense that you use to figure out the physical world but use it to figure out the spiritual lessons of the Bible. That's the way it works, but it doesn't work if you don't change the understanding from your mind to your spirit. If you don't, you will not understand. And if you don't understand, you won't be able to explain the Scriptures to yourself or to anyone else.

So the womb of Mary had a baby. Let's translate that into spiritual value. The mind was pregnant to give birth to a new understanding. In the womb, meaning in the heart of humanity, there is something growing that will teach the world to understand in the value of heaven. With this new teaching, mankind will be able to understand the Scriptures in the spiritual terms. You will understand the difference between the teachings of the mind and the teachings of the spirit. The Bible was created by God to be a spiritual book. It is not a book about the physical part of life. It's a book about the spiritual way that we think, feel, and understand. If you do not understand the birth of the spirit, try to keep your mouth shut and do not try to explain what you don't understand because you will be known as a *false prophet*. This is because you are *not born of the spirit* and you cannot understand in spirit. It is like a language that you never heard of, and you cannot translate it unless you have learned it. When you come to understand and separate the mind from the spirit, you will come to understand that in God the spirit must be separated and understood according to the way that it was written. Do not change the Scriptures to make the physical meaning look like a king. The real honor is in your spiritual understanding. Without spiritual wisdom, you cannot be part of the Kingdom of God.

Now we go to "Mary's Song." This is a real song of the mind. Mary's song means that your mind is pleased with the Lord because He gives you salvation in the common sense of intelligence. To give birth to intelligence, you have to go through the power of yourself to understand with your mind and also with you spirit. But you must realize that the mind understands differently than the spirit. You must make sure that what you learn with your mind is *verified* by your spirit. The spirit has all the power of intelligence, so when you come to learn something with your mind, this can be a contradiction.

Remember that your mind only understands in loss and gain. When you gain something, the mind loves it and agrees with the spirit, but the compassionate part of you that deals with loving others and being part of mankind comes from the spirit. To understand anything with both your mind and your spirit, you must have a *wedding feast of intelligence*. Unless you have the wedding feast of intelligence, you cannot understand for yourself and you will not know why you do stupid things most of the time.

Next, let's learn the meaning of the "Wedding Feast in the Land of Canaan." This means that you marry your mind with your spirit to make your mind agree to the feelings that you have inside your spirit. Human understanding is very strange because there's two different parts inside you—the mind and the spirit, and the spirit does not always have the control over the mind. For example, if you see a poor person on the side of the road who needs your help, your spirit has compassion for that person. But when it gets to your mind, you will start to think about loss and gain, and you will lose your compassion because the mind is stronger than your spirit. That's where your heart does not work properly in being compassionate with your fellow man. You have to look at these things with the control of the spirit that makes more sense than the mind. The mind is the side of you that will get you to defeat your compassion. That's where the song of Mary that lives inside you is grateful for the spirit. Marry your mind and your spirit together so you can have *complete wisdom.*

Let us proceed with "The Birth of John the Baptist." The birth of John the Baptist meant that religion and falsehood would come to be born. You cannot follow the physical man John the Baptist. You have to follow the common sense of intelligence. John the Baptist accomplished *nothing* in spirit, and that's what happened to Christianity. These false prophets baptize people with water in the physical world, but they did not baptize people with the Holy Spirit. This meant that false religion was born from that evil idea that did not make sense to the soul. You can see all the false prophets coming who misunderstood the parables and who taught people to do wrong in the eyes of the Lord. They taught people to worship Jesus in front of the Lord because they did not understand the parables and they did not understand the Old Testament.

Worshipping Jesus made sense for the false prophet, but they didn't realize that false religion was born with the birth of John the Baptist. They believed in the physical baptism, and the rest of the false sacraments of religion were all born from that *false truth.* They preach falsehood on the balcony of sacraments of religion, which were all born from that false truth. They preach falsehood on the balcony of *wrong.* This is how you enter into the fantasy world and believe in God like a fantasy god and do things in your physical life that makes you look stupid and ignorant. Now the time is here to join the mind to the spirit, where you will begin to feel inside yourself what is right and what is wrong. But those stiff-necked false prophets of organized religion have no wisdom to change wrong into right, so the time is coming for them to be cast into the great lake of fire and sulfur because they have *perverted the truth* and made people believe something that is not true.

Now we go to "Zechariah's Song." Be careful with worshipping Jesus in front of the Lord when you learn about this song because it refers to Jesus being God. To understand Zechariah's song, you have to turn your spirit to the Lord. The Lord of Heaven is the real God of the Creation. The false understanding of these prophecies and these parables was what tricked the world into understanding that Jesus was God in front of God the Father. This song is the *song of the spirit* and not the mind. God had to send someone to bring His teaching to the understanding of the mind, and so He chose Jesus. But that does not mean that Jesus is to be worshipped. It is only the common sense teaching that Jesus brought that is to be worshipped. When you are full with the Holy Spirit inside you, you will come to understand the truth because the Holy Spirit is the angel of reality.

Make sure you don't enter into the fantasy world here and start worshipping Jesus. The worshipping of Jesus comes *from the mind* because it's a gain for the mind to understand God in a physical form. But the mind that worships Jesus in front of God enters into the fantasy world, and the next thing you know, the whole mess of society is worshipping Jesus in front of God. That brings great stupidity and total ignorance to mankind, and this makes mankind miserable because they are unable to learn the meaning of life.

This song was sung by a man who was full of the Holy Spirit, but it was twisted by the mind of people of no wisdom, and eventually, the whole world is worshipping Jesus as the savior of the world. God said, "You will not know everything until I reveal it to you on this day of the Creation. You will *continue doing wrong* until this time comes." Mankind will worship a false God, and they will continue to do wrong because they think that wrong is when they do what is right. They don't understand right over wrong so they will continue to do wrong. Until the Lord reveals His truth, there's nothing that can be said by the Lord your God that can change your heart. The false prophet will continue to believe in lies, but the revelation of the truth will destroy them.

Next, we go to the "Birth of Jesus." Let's translate the birth of Jesus into common sense. Jesus represents common sense in the spiritual meaning of the Scriptures, just like Moses was a great lawgiver, and Jacob was Israel. These people were not any more than men like you or me, but God had to use the name of a man to explain His spiritual value. The spirit does not learn like the mind does, and you have to explain the spiritual teaching to the mind. This means that you have to use explanations that the mind can understand, and that leads us to the birth of Jesus.

The birth of Jesus means the *birth of common sense*. If you don't learn the word of the Lord through common sense, you are going to miss something very important here. It seems that the whole world worships Jesus, but the true Son of God is common sense. Therefore, you should translate the words of Jesus into *common sense*. Only then can you begin to understand God's word in spiritual terms. If you still think of Jesus as the *physical* son of God, you worship an image before the Lord—and when you worship anyone before the Lord, you break the very value of the Ten Commandments.

You *cannot change* the commandments of the Lord by twisting your mind in a different direction from the truth. When you have twisted the truth and you begin to worship Jesus, you will find yourself on the *wrong side of wisdom*. The Lord *punishes* people for doing so, and that is why the world has been so evil. Everybody is worshipping a false god before the Lord, and they offer their sacrifices to that false god. That becomes the golden calf of the children of Israel in the desert. The Bible was written for spiritual understanding, and when you mix up the spiritual teaching and twist it in the way of the mind, you lose the common sense of intelligence. The next thing you know, you condemn people who understand on the side of truth.

You think you are right by worshipping Jesus because the Lord twisted your faith into an understanding where you have lost your soul. You condemn other people in front of you who you think are not as good as you, and you come to understand the power of wrong over right. This is just like when Cain killed Abel some six thousand years ago. Cain could not understand his brother Abel. He began to hate him, and then he killed him. The word of God tells you that those who judge their brother falsely will try to destroy them. Just like the people of today who think that anyone who doesn't believe in Jesus will go to hell, so they kill them *in spirit*, and they claim to be the one that will keep on living on the earth forever and ever with the truth. But the *real truth* is that the people who didn't believe in the physical Jesus on the cross and, instead, understood that the common sense of the Scriptures that was not twisted by the mind was the truth, will be the ones to inherit the earth. And that is the meaning of the birth of Jesus.

Now we go to "The Shepherds and the Angels." Let's see the meaning of that. Remember that Luke got his information from other people, so the stories from Luke come from what he has *heard*, not what he has seen. Here, the power of the Lord talks about shepherds that are tending to their flocks, and the angel of the Lord appeared to them. Now what is the angel of the Lord? This is a very important part. The angel of the Lord is a feeling that you have *inside* you, and the shepherd is what the mind that tends the flock *understands*. When the angel of the Lord comes inside you, it is like a *revelation of truth*. The Lord wanted these people to know that something was going to happen in the world that no one has ever heard before.

A new way to understand the Scriptures in spiritual terms is coming to the world. The people of the earth, right now, are tending their flocks, meaning the physical animal or, more correctly, the physical understanding of the mind. They are waiting for the new coming of the angel of the Lord inside them so they can come to understand the Scriptures. But if they listen to the false prophet, they will not learn anything of the truth because there is no false prophet that has ever been able to explain the parables in truth. So if you are part of the simple people of the world, meaning the shepherds who are doing the work to try to survive in the world, you are doing what you're supposed to do when the angel of the Lord comes inside you. The angel of the Lord is your common sense that will give you a new birth of intelligence so your heart will not be troubled with all the lies that were taught before now. You will see the difference in the new understanding of common sense coming into the world. This is the new way to understand the Lord God, the Creator of the world.

You must understand the Lord in the new spiritual way that was never really taught on earth by anyone before now, and he will come to refine the spirit of mankind and save the world from the stupidity that was taught before. If you have read the Scriptures before now, you may not think much of God because you never understood His teaching. But a new time is coming where mankind will come to learn that God's word is written for all of mankind. The truth will be raised up, and the falsehood of the false prophet will be destroyed because it is the weak part of mankind that twisted the human mind into understanding nothing. The time has come to reveal the power of the Scriptures for all men to hear and hold in their heart the value of the intelligence of common sense.

Next, we go to "The Boy Jesus at the Temple." Jesus was just a man like the rest of us. He was born physically from a mother and father. He grew up as a child, and he received the Holy Spirit of the Lord inside his common sense. Jesus was born in common sense, and so the Lord gave him a great understanding to bring to mankind. It is also the same with every human being. If you are born in common sense, your spirit will come to be lived in the great gift of common sense. Then you can talk from your spirit because common sense is the real son of God. You can do great things with this great gift. You can *heal almost anything* in spiritual value because when something makes sense, it replaces what doesn't make sense. This is the value that all people have inside them, but they don't know they have it. If you go to the understanding of the simple way of thinking, which is common sense, you can figure out almost anything.

You can heal your soul and your body with common sense because the power of what makes sense is the power to understand everything in both the physical as well as the spiritual side of life. God gave people the common sense of understanding in the center of intelligence where you are born from the Holy Spirit in reality. Then you go to adulthood and you can be anything you want to be because common sense really is the son of God. It is given to everybody, but some people in this world will never make any sense because they don't think for themselves—so their common sense is of no value. This is the power of common sense that lives inside you that we call the son of God.

The Son of God makes sense at all times. You cannot destroy common sense because it is upright thinking that makes you intelligent, and it makes sense inside of you. This is not like the Christians tell you to believe in Jesus because worshipping Jesus before the Lord is the *opposite* of common sense. If you believe in the truth, you are *saluting* the Lord your God with all your soul because you are on the same page as God in the truth and the reality of the Holy Spirit, and common sense is the Son of God, and if you don't live by the value of common sense inside your spirit, you have to go to others to get it, and you will never work for yourself. You will always work for somebody else trying to make other people's common sense work for you. And you will end up learning nothing in true spiritual value.

Now we go to "John the Baptist Prepares the Way." This represents people who baptize others with physical water even though it's wrong to believe spiritually in the physical part of you. The real baptism comes from the water of the river of knowledge in the preparation of the way for mankind. The life of John the Baptist means that the people who believe in Christianity by worshipping Jesus in front of the Lord still have to *prepare the way* for the Scriptures to be understood. For example, I was born in a Catholic family, and as a Catholic, I read the Bible, albeit in the false Catholic understanding of the mind. But even though I read the Bible as a catholic, it still prepared me to understand the Bible because reading the Bible, even if you are doing so as part of a false religion, is your *exposure to the Scriptures*. And when you are exposed to the Scriptures, you are given the choice to understand this book for yourself. But as long as you practice the Catholic religion or Christianity or any other organized religion, you have to understand what they tell you. And if you don't practice what they tell you, they say that you're going to hell. But that's not true at all. The truth is that whatever you do for yourself is where you find the way to understand.

Don't think that God favors false religion. He brought John the Baptist and false religion to prepare the way for the true religion of the heart. When you start understanding the purpose of the Scriptures and what they were written for, then you *begin* to understand the Word of the Lord. Because of Christianity, the Catholic Church, and other false organized religions, God made it possible for us to take the Bible into our hands and read it for ourselves—we didn't need the guidance of these organized religions. All we needed was the *understanding that there is a God*, and that was given to you by organized religion. You must first know that there is a God in order to understand what is *good*, what is *evil*, and to practice the religion of the heart.

No one was born knowing everything at once. This has to be done *through learning*. The learning that mankind made out of the Bible was over many periods, and this gives you the way to understand the Scriptures. You were baptized with water by false organized religion because we all needed the understanding of falsehood first so we can come to learn in truth. Even Jesus was baptized with *physical water*. John the Baptist said, "I baptize you with water but one who is more powerful than I will come. And he will baptize you with the Holy Spirit." This means that the salvation of man comes inside you with an understanding that comes from the past into the present and then into the future. You have to learn from the past, accept it in the present, and learn from it in the future. That's the way the Creation was made, and that is why you have to go through common sense and reality before you can get to the truth.

Next, we go to "The Baptism and Genealogy of John the Baptist." This was written by Luke, and it was written in a way that Luke was the investigator of what happened. Try to understand the descendants of John the Baptist in spiritual value. The generations of your physical self are not what makes any sense to your spiritual power. Any man can get the spiritual power inside himself, and you have to understand that it doesn't come from your ancestors. It comes from what you made of life by yourself and the generations of what you are now. I don't know how many generations can make a difference in what you personally know because your knowledge is not mine to understand.

Now let's look at it in the way of the spirit. I understand the Scriptures in spirit because spirit is what's important to me. It's all part of a spiritual understanding where you have to *translate* from the teaching of the mind into the teaching of the spirit. You must come and understand this translation, and if you understand in spiritual terms the way it was written, then you will be able to find truth. For example, Moses and Aaron were both descendants of Levi. Those are the physical generations, but you also have to understand in spirit with the glory of intelligence to see where you spiritually come from. Spiritual generations come from the power of your soul in what you have accomplished in spiritual learning.

You cannot think that the spiritual descendants of the father come to the son in the physical sense. That is not true spiritual power. If you come from God, then you can make up your own mind. You don't have to listen to what your parents have told you about spirituality because that's the past generation. The present and the future generations is what you believe yourself. The power to understand in spirit is that Jesus, the man himself, did not get the spiritual value from John the Baptist. He got it from the *Lord God*. The Lord saw a man who tried to make sense with his life, and that's the spiritual generation right there. It comes from the Lord your God, and it cannot be translated to the image of a man who lived before you. It has to be something that you have understood in your own soul so you can come to understand that you don't come from your ancestors in spirit but you come from the Lord your God. You cannot place the image of a human being in front of you to understand where your spiritual value come from. It comes from the Lord your God, and He sends them to you because the Lord sees in your heart what is important to you.

Now we go to "Jesus Heals Many." That's where the spiritual understanding comes in the value that common sense can heal both physically and spiritually. But you must first be healed spiritually before you can be healed physically. The feelings of healing are *inside you*. If you know that a certain disease can affect your physical body, then you must do whatever you can to keep away from that disease. The feelings of the great power that we have within ourselves comes to the understanding that the Lord your God in spiritual terms comes from that power.

I told you before that you are 10 percent physical and 90 percent spiritual. This means that you must heal yourself in spirit first. When your spirit is healed, *only then* can you become pure in your thinking. That means you can heal the power of where you are and what you are physically and spiritually. But first, you have to come to a *new spiritual understanding* that is in spirit, not in the way people understand the Scriptures with their minds because that doesn't work. You have to be in spirit inside you and translate anything that's in the Scriptures into a *spiritual* value. If you cannot do that, you cannot heal yourself in flesh or in spirit. If you *hate people*, you have to *heal that* before you can understand. The power of healing comes from the Lord, but it also comes from your spirit. You have to make the decision to translate everything to spiritual terms when a parable is in front of you—you must understand that parable in spiritual terms. You think you cannot do that, but you actually can. You just have to practice because like everything else, *practice makes perfect.* That's the way life goes in the understating of all your spiritual deeds in the power of the Lord your God.

Next, we go to "Jesus Heals a Man with Leprosy." This is how to translate what is said in physical suffering into spiritual suffering. I will use the word *suffering* here so you can understand how to translate these things. Leprosy is a physical disease, but it is also a spiritual disease called *hate*. This is because hate grows on you like leprosy. The reason that God uses these terms is to make you understand that you have to *translate the Scriptures* from the physical understanding into the spiritual understanding. When you start understanding the *leprosy of the spirit*, then you understand that it is *inside* every human being, and if it is allowed to grow, it will come to destroy your human needs. And before long, every part of your body comes to be destroyed. The next thing you know, you hate the whole world because you do not understand the leprosy of the spirit.

Hate is the leprosy of the spirit. The more you hate, the more it takes from your spirit to hate. And you will lose more in spiritual value after you start hating people. You will come to a point that hate is such a disease inside you that you can *no longer function*. You kill people because of hate. You rape women because of hate. You destroy your spirit, thought by thought, spirit by spirit, until you are *totally destroyed*, and you die with that hate in your soul because you didn't have the strength and the understanding inside you to know that you were caught into a bad disease that grew on you until it totally destroyed you.

If you hate anyone in your life and you continue hating to the point where you cannot heal yourself from that terrible disease that lives inside you, that's when you need the Lord your God to come in His common sense and heal what makes you feel so disparate in everything that you feel. The leprosy of hate is a disease that doesn't go away unless you try to understand common sense, which is the *real son of God*, to heal your spirit and to make you a better person. The Lord sends these diseases inside you because when you cannot love someone, you live in the fantasy of a lost soul, and you have to go to common sense, the real son of God, and ask Him to come inside of you with a refreshing understanding against all hate. Only then will you be able to be healed of hate.

I hope you can now see the difference between believing that Jesus is the son of God and believing that common sense is the real son of God. Common sense is the spiritual power that lives inside you and *heals* you. If you do hate someone, you have to work at it and repent of your sin because hate is a great sin in the Kingdom of God, and you *cannot enter* the Kingdom of God with the evil thinking of hate inside yourself. You have to correct yourself of that hate to enter the Kingdom of God. The Lord did all these things to make you understand His Kingdom. You had to go through your forty lifetimes of living in the desert so you could understand what made you miserable. Now the trip across the desert is over, and you must come to understand the Kingdom of God and how it works so you can inherit this Kingdom. You have to do away with hating anyone for no good purpose whatsoever.

Now we go to "Jesus Heals the Paralyzed and the Lepers." A paralyzed person is someone who cannot change himself. When you're paralyzed, it means you cannot move to change what's *inside* you. It is a disease that restricts your body to a bed where you cannot move. In spirit, a paralyzed person is someone with a stiff neck who cannot change his way of believing. And when you are paralyzed in spiritual understanding, you think that you already know the truth of life and you don't want to change for anybody. This means that you cannot move around and open your heart for the new teaching to come to you. You are so paralyzed that you cannot come up with the healing of your spirit, and you will not try to change the understanding of your soul with common sense.

Once an evil spirit enters into your soul, it is very hard to get it out of there. In Christianity, they worship Jesus in front of the Lord. That is one of the *worst sins* that you could ever imagine. If you are paralyzed with the understanding that Jesus is the physical son of God, you cannot move. And if you cannot move, then how can you enter the Kingdom of God? You are not allowed to worship a man before the Lord your God and expect to enter the Kingdom of God. The false prophet has paralyzed you with stupidity, ignorance, and the superstition of the image of a man. But now you have to be *healed* from that and come to understand the power of the common sense of intelligence that lives inside you. You have to listen to the voice that speaks to you so you can come to understand the true word of God.

When you are paralyzed, you cannot move. You cannot change anything because the Kingdom of God is made for you to grow, not to lie on the bed for the rest of your life where you cannot move or change anything in your heart. You have to grow up in your own heart and change what is not right in order to learn what you need to introduce the kingdom of intelligence into your heart. God is the *only* God, and you must worship the Lord your God in truth in order to enter into His Kingdom. Truth and common sense are together, and if you cannot change the truth and common sense in your heart with the angel of reality, how can you enter the Kingdom of Heaven?

God is the true reality and common sense. God is not the flesh of a man or the image of a man that was taught to you by the older generations before you. Changing what you believe and asking the Lord to give you a new heart is a tough thing to do. But the Kingdom of God is so beautiful, and if you inherit this kingdom, you will enter into a world where people will finally be human again, not like the children of hate and stupidity of the world as it is now. If you *refuse* to change from the lies of organized religion, the common sense of intelligence cannot help you. This is what the Kingdom of God is—*take it or leave it.*

Next, we are going to "Love for Enemies." This is the truth of what love means in the Kingdom of God. I'm not talking about the love of all the people that surround you. I'm talking about the *whole world.* Who is your enemy in the Kingdom of God? Your *real enemies* are the people who don't believe the way you do—they don't *live* the way you do, and they don't accept the way you live because it *contradicts* what they believe. They become your enemy who is not on your side. The people who are not on your side in religion, in government, in our money system, or in the business world become enemies of yours because you only love the people who think and live like you do.

Back in the old days when the long knife used to fight the Indians, the white man called the Indians their enemies. They were children of God like the rest of us, but the Christians could not love the Indians because they believed they were savages. The white man decided to take these people and destroy them from the earth and kill them unfairly. But this isn't only on the white man here. The Indians felt that the white man was their enemy, so they wanted to kill them as well. On both sides, the enemy was someone who didn't fit in with their way of life. There was *great hate* between the Indians and the white man because the Indians thought that they were there first and they felt that this was their land. However, the government felt that they wanted the land for the white man, and they sent an army to destroy the Indians.

This is the way to the Kingdom of God. He made events like this happen for the purpose that you could clearly see the hate of your enemies and you could understand who your enemy is. God gave us all the pages of history to make us understand what hate was. This is so the whole world could see the mistakes made in the history of mankind. You have to change your heart and come to love your neighbor as yourself because those are your enemies. The black man living in America was *not accepted.* He was persecuted for just being there, with his black skin, in the world of the white man, and that's the way it still is today. The black man did not feel any different about the white man, and they grew to hate the white man because of the way they were treated.

The white man thought he was more sophisticated, and they brought the black people to their land to make them *slaves.* Of course, there was hate and prejudice on *both* sides. The white man hated the black man because they did not obey the white man's laws. They felt that they brought them out of Africa and they taught them to live in the modern world. But the white man was unfair with them, and there was a lot of prejudice, especially in the old South of America where people hated the blacks to the extent of killing them.

History tells us how the white man became cruel human beings who tried to destroy their brothers, but they could not make their brothers disappear because the Lord remembers the blacks as well as the Indians. He brought them to his kingdom along with the whites, and today, they are here to learn and to be part of this kingdom just like the rest of us.

Being in the Kingdom of God means that *you are part of the Lord's truth.* The truth cannot be eliminated and must be respected by all men. You may think that your brother is not as good as you because he doesn't look like you—for example, the blacks or the Indians or any other people in the world like the Middle East. They don't think or act like others do, and ignorant people who believe in falsehoods are prejudiced against them. Understand that the world was created by God, not to be white, black, or any other color but to be human. Loving your brother means to love *all* humans. You only come to the understanding of love by loving the whole world, not just loving the people around you who are good to you. You must love the people that *don't* like you as well. You must love those people because in the Old Testament, love means the Levi, the priest inside you that determines the value of life itself.

Love is inside you, where there is *no prejudice whatsoever.* When you love someone, you must love them without an exception of any kind. You have to love with an open heart and treat everybody that you meet every day of your life *with respect*. You must come to love those who are far from the way you understand because their way of thinking is just as good as yours. Loving people means loving those who are both physically and spiritually far away from you, like the people in Africa, the Middle East, or even South America. Love the people who have a hard time surviving because life is hard for them. I'm not telling you here that you have to send all kinds of money to them or start a mission and all that because that's a *big fraud*. What I am saying is try to understand that their feelings matter, and if you have feelings for these people, you should help them. You don't have to go there in some kind of ministry to help them physically. Just ask the Lord to help them once in a while. This will make life much better for them as well as for you, and you will come to understand that love is not in the human deeds of bringing physical things to others. True love comes from the spirit, and it is treating all others the way you would want them to treat you.

Now we go to "Judging Others." The Lord said that you are not allowed to judge others. In the Old Testament, Levi the priest, which means love, is where you determine the values of others and where you come to understand the power to bring about the love that other people need in order to function. When you judge a person according to your standards and not the Lord's standards, what you are doing is bringing him lower than you, and you think that you are better than him. That is one of the two greatest sins that there is in love. To judge a person according to the false standards of the mind is to figure inside your heart the evil of others, and whoever lives in that evil understanding *cannot* be part of the Kingdom of God.

Do not judge your fellow man because your fellow man is just as good as you. He was created just like you, but you think that his spirit is more evil than yours. Then you put it on the scale and you think that your balance is more accurate than your brother's balance. If you judge a person's deeds with your mind, i.e., if he doesn't go to church or if he is in all kinds of trouble with the law, then you think that this person is evil. But the common sense of intelligence tells you that these people are not evil. They just failed to learn and understand the truth of the matter. If we never did anything wrong, we would never learn the truth. Think about a person who has killed someone and was sent to prison for the rest of his life. Think for a minute about the feelings that are inside this person and the understanding of that person that you have unfairly judged as evil inside yourself. Only *God* can judge people, so it's unfair for you to judge him because you think you are better than him.

To understand love, you must understand the power that you are half-wrong as well as half-right. And your brother is also half-wrong and half-right. Maybe not in the exact same way in their physical or spiritual needs, but that person has tried to be as good as he can be, and that is the same thing that you have tried to do. Sometimes when you try, there is no success, so you keep trying, and you keep making mistakes which add to your misery. But that misery is what will come to save you in the end. Maybe that misery is the choice of the Lord that He gives to you in your life to come out of that stupidity that you believe by judging others. The Lord will turn your judgment of others *against you* to make you understand the values of others. Judging people means you put no value on others, and you put all the values on your own soul when you really don't understand what the other person is trying to do.

If a person steals something from someone, it is usually because he is just trying to find a way to feed himself. And if you destroy the life of others by killing them to try to make a better passage for yourself, it means that your deeds are all wrong. But you must come to understand that it is only through wrong that you can find right. Sometimes you have to go through these wrongdoings for your own justice. No one can see what's inside your soul, and when they judge you, they hurt you deeply. You are only trying to survive in an unfair world. And even though you fail and you are, at times, proven to be wrong, you have tried to improve your learning. The reason that these people have done these crimes is they have judged others as well as you have judged them.

Now we go to "A Tree and Its Fruit." A tree in the wilderness is a man in this parable. A human being is born into a world that he does not really understand because he cannot understand wrong and he cannot see right. You live in the wilderness, and sometimes, you cannot determine between wrong and right because the power of the Creation created you in a way that is hard to understand. Remember that Cain killed his brother Abel. This meant that wrong killed right inside the human spirit. Sometimes, the spirit of wrongdoing that is inside you kills your brother right, and next thing you know, you do wrong because you think wrong is the only way out just like Cain did to his brother Abel.

Try to understand that these stories of the Bible represent the way people are going to turn out to be until the day of the Lord arrives. These are the Seven Days of the Creation that we are living now. You must come to understand that the power of the Lord gives you the wisdom to do right, but right doesn't seem to be very interesting, so you killed your brother right to do wrong. That's what the story of Cain and Abel means, and that's the way people live. You saw others doing wrong, and you believed that it was correct to do wrong. You kept doing wrong, and no one can teach you anything because you have a stiff neck. And with that stiff neck, you cannot change wrong into right.

You can become like all the rest of the trees in the forest and bear good fruit, but you have to learn to bear the good fruit. And if there's no one there to teach you *how* to bear this good fruit, then it's hard for you to learn. That's what happened with the people in the middle of the spiritual wilderness—they had no one to teach them the difference between right and wrong, so they could not learn. In order to receive new life, you have to abandon wrong and try right. It's not easy, but you have to relearn the Scriptures in the way they were written instead of the way you were taught by the false prophet of organized religion. Then you will learn with the common sense of intelligence, and you will be able to live in right over wrong. This is what the Kingdom of God will be where people will learn in truth. The Lord will teach you the new way of understanding life in His Kingdom.

Next, we go to "The Wise and Foolish Builders." If you hear the voice of common sense and begin to understand the wisdom of life on earth, you will build your house on the foundation of the values of truth. The common sense of that truth and the stone of your faith will hold your house up in the middle of this great storm. Understand the great storm that's coming to the world. The power of the great earthquake will come to be where people will fall deep into the bottom of the earth by trying to understand the old ways of false religion instead of the new way of common sense. That will be the greatest storm ever known to mankind. You must leave behind all the false religions of the past and come to understand common sense in the time that God has prepared for you. Unless you build your house on the solid foundation of truth over lies, you will have a hard time understanding the coming time of the Seven Days of the Creation of the Lord. Those who want to enter the Kingdom of God must come to understand in *total common sense.*

The foundations of truth must be brought for justice for all human beings so mankind can come out of the desert and come to the promised land after they cross the Jordan River into the understanding that the Lord has prepared for them. If you come to understand the truth, you will bear good fruit. But if you do the opposite and believe against the common sense of intelligence, you will *not* bear good fruit. Build your foundation on the truth so that your trees will bear good fruit.

Now we go to "The Faith of the Centurion." The meaning of this story is that the faith of other people is just as good as yours. The reason that this story was placed into the Bible is because it was meant to be understood that even the Centurion guard from the Romans can have faith in common sense. Remember that truth, common sense, and reality are inside every single person on the face of the earth. No matter how good or bad you may be and no matter what your situation is, you must understand the faith of others as well as your own. You must come to understand the faith of the people that society doesn't like.

If you believe that the Russians or the people of the Middle East are the ones who are all wrong and evil, you will eventually come to the conclusion that everybody else is wrong and your beliefs are the only ones that are right. But you must understand that all these other religions in the world have the same ability to understand and to love God in truth. You don't think that anybody has true wisdom except those who believe like you. If you are Catholic or a Christian, you don't think that anyone has any truth except for your church. But I would say that the vast majority of mankind lives in darkness. Very few people have the light of heaven. When you do have the light of heaven, you know that you are not allowed to believe that your goodness is above everybody else's. We are all just animals, and your spirit can rise up in knowledge, but it does not make you better than anyone else. Being better than anyone is something that you are not allowed to believe inside of yourself. If you do, your belief is *against* the Lord God. You cannot live in justice with people who you think are not like you because we always make an opposite of ourselves on the other side of the issue of good and evil. We think we are good, and no one else can match that. Try to understand that all of mankind, even though they may appear to be different, are just like you. If you unite yourself with mankind instead of dividing people, you can come to understand true wisdom.

Just because a human being thinks he is a good Christian and does everything that Christianity asks of him, that doesn't mean that he actually is good. If you are Jewish and you think that the only true religion on earth is your Jewish faith, that's not the way it is. If you're Catholic and you think that your religion is the most righteous one, think again. *God has made those religions to fool people.* Believing in them doesn't make you better than anyone else, just like America is not better than all the other countries of the world. Try to understand the goodness that lives in the *heart* of a man, not the goodness that lives in your mind where you think you are better than anybody else. You cannot fairly judge what you have seen with your physical eyes. But you can accurately judge with your *spiritual eyes.* Goodness does not come from your mind but from your *spirit.*

Next, we go to "Jesus Raises a Widow's Son." This is where your spiritual wisdom must be used. If you think of the widow as a woman who lost her husband, you are still in the physical part of yourself and you don't understand the spirit here. In spiritual terms, a widow is a mind that does not have the spirit to control her. The son of the widow is a child who gets his information from his mother (the mind), and the son of the widow really does not understand the reality of the truth. You have to come to understand this lesson in spiritual terms.

The Bible was written like this so that the people who thought within the physical form and claimed they knew the Bible actually knew nothing about the Scriptures. That's why the false prophets are called *false prophets*—because they are the *false authority* on the Scriptures. They believe the key to the Bible is a physical understanding, when the real way of the Scriptures is in *spirit*. When they look at a widow, they see a woman who lost her husband, but when *I* see a widow mentioned in the Bible, I see a mind that lost its spiritual understanding and just cannot understand anything in spirit. The son of such a mind is a person who, like his mother, does not understand the spiritual value of the Scriptures.

When you see people who judge other people according to the understanding that was not translated into spiritual terms, then you see a lost soul as a widow. They don't have the spiritual value of the male spirit to understand that we are spirit first before we are physical. You must come to understand the spiritual meaning of all the Scriptures before you can walk freely into the new Kingdom of God. The world is in darkness when they use the mind of a widow to understand the Scriptures. And to try to understand the Bible with the son of the widow will be an even bigger disaster on all who think they know the Scriptures. That is why God has written the Bible this way—to make sure that the people of the world don't come to provide something physical in exchange for something spiritual. Now you can see what the widow means and how she will not be able to understand the Scriptures. And if you cannot understand the Scriptures, you cannot enter the Kingdom of God. You must repent of your ignorance and your stupidity so God will bless you greatly.

Now we go to "Jesus Anointed by the Sinful Woman." Try to understand the power of the world and the way people are being judged by those who live in the fantasy world and think that people who sin in the physical part of mankind are the real sinners. You must come to learn that a sin is spiritual, not physical. Man will persecute you for doing things that they believe is wrong according to their false understanding of the Word of God. They don't understand any better, so they live in the fantasy world of sin. They think of right and wrong according to their own way of thinking instead of what the Lord has taught us. But their understanding is no higher than that of a little locust, so they think that a great sin is in *physical deeds.*

The truth is that your physical side is the animal, and the animal can make mistakes. But it's not the animal that will be punished by the Lord for doing wrong. The laws of mankind will punish you for all your physical sins that people think are so evil. Your spiritual sins are what you will answer to the Lord for. Your learning of what sins really are must come through your spiritual understanding. Many things that people believe are sins are actually holy. Ask the Lord to give you wisdom so you can learn what is really a sin. Mankind has tried to impose justice on the physical part of the human race, so people will get punished by man's laws for their physical sins.

The Lord will appoint the mind of man to punish you according to your physical sins. But the high priest of man-made religion thinks that a sinful person is a person who physically lives against the law that they made from the Bible. The false prophets don't understand the Bible, so they make any physical law they want with the laws of God. But the *real* laws of God are not made in physical terms—they are made in *spiritual terms.* Something that is physically wrong may be spiritually right. God made the religion of the earth and the false prophet always think about sins in physical terms. They do not understand truth because God has put a block on both their mind and soul and they cannot understand the power that makes sense in the truth. This is what people think today in the world of organized religion. The power of organized religion is what makes people sin in their physical deeds. Then these false religions hold that against them. This is the justice of the Lord because what you condemn other people for doing is what you will do yourself. You *will* get caught doing it because you yourself have the same feeling inside your physical needs.

The physical mind is the center of understanding according to false religion because they didn't learn the true meaning of the laws of God. They did not understand that your physical needs are your natural feelings that you feel every day of your life. They feel the same thing inside of themselves, but they hide that and become hypocrites. They make sure that no one knows their feelings because they hide them so well. They made laws against what they believed was the wrong part of life, but they don't look at their own feelings. They cannot penetrate the understanding of the Lord, so they condemn others for what they think they did wrong. But the truth is that people do more wrong by judging others than anyone can possibly do by having sex with different people. That is part of the judgment of the Lord.

Next, we go to "The Parable of the Sower." When we come to this teaching of the Lord's power, you must realize that what is written in the Scriptures is the Word of God. The parables were given from Jesus, the servant of the Lord, to mankind. When you give people new food to eat, it doesn't mean that they will eat it. It doesn't mean that the people will understand these parables. It just means that you have food to eat and you can translate these parables into spiritual understanding. Eating this fruit will restore your faith away from the fantasy world and into the blessing of God's holy word.

When a parable such as this one is given to you, it is spiritual food to tell you how to handle yourself in spiritual matters and how to translate them into food inside your spirit. Remember that the parable of the bread of life is not a piece of physical bread that somebody blessed in front of you. The *real* bread of the parables is what you eat with your spirit in the understanding of life. You must understand the way it was written. Just as the farmer plants his seed in the ground, the Lord plants His seed inside you, and that seed must grow. Your understanding is the fertile ground. The purpose of fertile ground is to make the seed grow, which gives you an understanding of the parables. You can't just ignore these parables or try to understand them with your mind. That's not what they were meant for. They were meant for you to recognize and eat the spiritual bread of life that will give you life outside the fantasy world that you now believe in.

You have to look at the parables of Jesus and eat the body of his teaching, *not* the body of flesh the way that the Catholic Church preaches it and Christianity understands it. You can eat all the bread you want, but unless you transfer the parables into *spiritual understanding*, then you did not receive the body of Christ—meaning the chosen Word of God. I tell you in truth that unless you translate the Word of God with your spirit, you will not receive the Kingdom of God. It's time for mankind to understand God's Word. The reason that you did not understand His words before now is you go to church every week, and the false prophet placed an evil spirit in your soul when they told you to understand the Scriptures on the physical side.

If you are not on the spiritual side, you will miss the greatest part of the meaning of the parables. Learn this parable in your heart and see how the devil, meaning the lies of the world, makes you understand things upside down and backward. This backward teaching is what you learn by going to church every week. You are supposed to learn on your own in your heart. The Lord gives you all the tools you need inside you to understand, and if you can understand on your own, you will be far better than all the teachings of all the false religions of the past two thousand years.

Now, we go to "A Lamp on a Stand." The lamp is the light of heaven. If you ask the Lord to give you that light, you will be able to see the *true meaning* of the parables. I asked God for that light some forty years ago in order to understand the parables, and I believe the Lord has given this light to me. I did not put myself above any other human being, nor did I ask Him for anything more special than He would give to anybody else. I simply asked for and have received the power to understand the Scriptures.

You can think whatever you want about my teaching, but you should at least try to understand the power that I have to be able to translate this. The Lord has given it to me for understanding the power that is inside me. I believe that I have the lamp on a stand through the light of heaven to understand the Scriptures. I feel inside myself the power of that light to be able to *understand* and to *visualize the truth* and all that is written in the Scriptures. Remember that I am not any more special than any other person. This is a gift that anyone can get from the Lord. But if you never ask for it, you'll never get it. Now you just don't ask to get this gift from the Lord because you want to be a big preacher who gets to inform the people. When you receive this gift, very few people will listen to you. But it is part of the will of the Lord that nobody realizes where the light comes from unless they ask Him directly. Just about no one knows *how* to ask Him directly. This is why this teaching needs to be understood in truth.

The light of heaven is in the parables, not in any church where the priest consecrates a piece of physical bread. What they practice in those churches is a bunch of baloney that the people of religion made up because they could not understand the parables of Jesus. They could not understand the Old Testament either, so they burned themselves with the scorching heat of the sun—meaning the New Testament—that was too hard for them to understand. They made up what they thought it meant with their minds instead of with the wisdom of the Lord in their spirit.

The false prophet preaches in the name of the Lord but not with the *understanding* of the Lord. Because of this, they have misled many, many souls as well as their own. They thought they were doing good when they were actually doing so much wrong because they could not understand the parables of the Lord. They don't know what it means to translate the parables of the Lord with the *spirit* even though Jesus himself told them that you have to be born of spirit to enter the Kingdom of God. You are supposed to go through the birth of the spirit before you start teaching the book in the physical understanding. These false preachers only made sense to the people who don't understand *common sense*. They translated the physical part of the Scriptures into another physical part that also made no sense. But to them, it made sense, so they believed it and tried to understand it. They only received false hope because the Lord did not give His light to their fantasy world.

Next, we come to "Jesus's Mother and Brothers." Who is your mother and who are your brothers that are outside? You must understand the keywords in every prophecy and every parable, or you will not be able to grasp the meaning. "Your mother and brothers are outside" means they are outside, as in *not in the spirit*. Your brother is the one who stands in front of you and tells you that he doesn't understand anything that you tell him in truth. Make sure that you don't try to confuse him or try to make him think that he is stupid. And don't try to make believe that he can understand what you say to him. Just try to teach him like a little baby. Try to feed him slowly into the field of truth.

Your mother is your mind. You must understand that we are all children of the mind because we are all born from the mother in spiritual understanding as well as in our physical understanding. When you start learning "stuff" in the world, you develop it into a knowledge of the mind. You have to be nursed by your mother in the mind *before* you can be nursed by your spirit in the values of spiritual understanding. Your mother, the mind, is outside, and your brothers are outside waiting for you to understand this parable.

Once you have been nursed by your mother, you start being the child of an understanding of your Father in heaven, who is spiritual, and you begin to understand the spiritual part of life. You have to look at your brother who is outside you and try to understand the value of your brother. Try to learn how important it is to dedicate yourself to your mother because this is where you come from. Your brother is here to show you the way to serve both him as well as your mother in great value. But the mind has placed a very tight hold on you, so you have to forget being in the womb of your mother because now you are inside the spirit of your Father, who really is the one to give you life in spiritual value. The mind is your mother, which is the mind of the past and present time. And your brother comes to you with the difficulties of understanding life. If you did not learn anything, you can't help them because you are useless in the way of the spirit. But if you learn and dedicate yourself to the spirit, you can then tell people the simple facts of truth that will heal them from all stupidity.

The son of God is common sense, and common sense will heal all those who need to be healed. But if you don't study the parables with common sense, you will not have the knowledge to deal with people around you. It doesn't matter if you were born to be a prophet or not in the reality of truth. Whatever you learn in truth, no matter how much or how little you learn, it is still a value that you bring to others. You can heal your brother with the little that you have by just simply speaking the simple truth to his simple soul. Then he will understand that you are his brother and the mind is your mother.

Now, we go to "Jesus Calms the Storm." There is a huge storm of religion in the world today. The four corners of the world preach different things about different gods. Nobody seems to understand the center of intelligence of the One True God of the Creation, and they do not understand the way God is in spiritual value. The storm is so severe right now, and people are dancing with the music of false religion in their heads and in their souls. They think that they have the right God, but they do not worship anything that is affiliated with God because their teachers are not affiliated with God. They do not understand the Lord God, and they don't preach about the understanding of the Lord God. The storm is so severe that only common sense, which is the real son of God, can calm the storm.

You must understand that the severity of the storm has totally inflamed the minds of the followers of false religion. You can see in all their churches the great storm of falsehood that entices the people to believe in a false god just like it was in the story of the gold calf. When you worship the gold calf, you break all the Laws and Commandments of our Lord in the worst storm ever endured by humanity. You can see in the four corners of the world many different false teachings, and nobody seems to understand what God is. Nobody can really bring it down to the value of the true spiritual God. All they do is understand what was written in the way of the physical part of the Scriptures, and nobody seems to understand the spiritual God at the center of all human intelligence.

Next, we go to "Jesus Restores a Demon-Possessed Man." The world definitely does not really understand the meaning of a person who is possessed by an evil spirit. Mankind cannot understand the way it works because they read all kinds of different things and they watch shows on television about how people are evil. They think that a person with an evil spirit is evil because they don't understand what an evil spirit is. *No one is totally evil*, and you are not allowed to call any man an evil person. You can only look at what a person says and does as the result of an evil spirit that lives inside them. *Every single human being is a 100 percent holy creation of the Lord.* But if anyone believes in an evil spirit, which is a spiritual idea that goes against truth, common sense, and reality, that is why they say evil things and perform evil deeds. It is the *false idea* that is evil, not the person. And since we were created by God, if you call another human being evil, you are calling His creation evil. That is a great insult to the Lord your God.

You cannot call the temple of a man evil because it's a great sin. Things like killing, raping, or stealing from someone are evil spirits. If you have evil spirits inside you, it does not make your entire spirit evil. It means that you have to learn to understand what is evil in your soul and try to get rid of it. But if you listen to these evil spirits, you will be possessed by them. An evil spirit is something that enters your soul and lives there. For example, if you think about killing someone and you do it, then that deed becomes evil. It doesn't mean that you're not sorry afterward. You will regret your evil deeds because your spirit is not totally evil. And you will have to answer to the Lord your God for what you believe in what makes you say and do these evil things.

You cannot call your brother evil because his spirit is part of truth, common sense, and reality just like yours. But if you accept false teachings inside you, you are possessed by an evil spirit. An evil spirit makes you do wrong—it's not the devil that made you do it. It is the lie that you accepted as truth that made you commit such an evil act. If you commit an evil act, your spirit is impure and must go through the sacrifice of learning inside your soul to destroy these lies.

You have to worship in truth, common sense, and reality inside your soul in order to *truly* understand the Word of God. Remember that reality is the Holy Spirit, and you must go to reality to clean your heart of wrongdoing. You cannot do it any other way. You have to look at reality in a way that if you kill a person, *reality will come after you.* The people of the earth, such as the police and the court system, will come after you. But it also applies in your spiritual side. *A lie is an evil spirit that lives inside you.* If you get caught in that lie, you will try to cover yourself with other lies. This goes on and on until your spirit does not hear the truth and you are not in reality anymore. You must believe that the truth is what will set you free, but you have to go to the reality of the truth to make it happen. That's where reality comes in and teaches you the outcome of your deeds to straighten you out and get rid of these evil spirits that entice you.

Now let us go to "Jesus Raises a Dead Girl." This is *not* a physical girl who physically died. The meaning of this is that it is a *dead mind* inside you that cannot understand anything in the Scriptures. Remember that, in the teaching of the Scriptures, a woman is the mind, and a male represents the spirit. "Everybody thinks she is dead" means that mankind thinks that the mind's ability to understand true wisdom is dead. But the spirit is still alive inside her. All you have to do is have faith in the spirit and life will come back to the girl in the spiritual sense. When you begin to understand the power of the mind and the spirit, you begin to understand life itself. The life and death of the spirit is just like the life and death of the flesh, but it is on the spiritual side. You can use common sense to revive the spirit and bring it to life again inside the mind. This is part of the understanding between mind and spirit, where you come to learn the Scriptures in spiritual terms.

Next, we go to "Jesus Sends out the Twelve." Remember that when men are mentioned in the Bible, it means the spiritual side of mankind. The Bible is written for the spirit, not the mind. So the teachings in the Bible are not physical lessons but spiritual lessons. This means that the disciples of Jesus are the disciples of common sense. Try to learn in spiritual terms so you can learn the Scriptures. Jesus gave his disciples the power and authority to drive out demons and cure diseases and sent them out to proclaim the Kingdom of God. This means the followers of the teachings of common sense are to go among mankind and use that common sense to drive out the demons of lies and to cure mankind of spiritual diseases such as stupidity and ignorance.

Remember that this is a spiritual lesson. All this happens inside each one of us. We can choose to worship the Lord God in truth or we can ignore this powerful teaching and choose to believe in the lies of organized religion instead. Jesus also told them to take nothing for this journey. This means that we do not need anything but faith—

faith that the understanding of the truth we gained through common sense is real and that it will defeat the lies of the mind and teach us the spiritual truth. The last part of this teaching tells us that people say all kinds of things about common sense and who its disciples really are. This is because people do not really know common sense in spiritual terms, so the mind believes all kinds of things that aren't true and it tries to understand the Scriptures. But the mind will fail terribly because the spirit has not been put first.

Now we will come to understand "Jesus Feeds the Five Thousand." The five loaves of bread are the first five books of the Old Testament, and the two fish are the Old and the New Testament. This is the *real* bread of life. The first five books of the Old Testament teach us to live life in spiritual wisdom, where you will eat all that you can eat and you will never be able to eat it all. There will always be spiritual food in the Old Testament for any man who is hungry and wants to hear the truth inside their soul. You have to read the Old Testament by yourself and not through any organized religion because that will throw you into darkness and you won't be able to understand anything. You have to work inside yourself and translate the physical teaching into the value of the spirit. Then you will come to understand the most magnificent book that mankind has ever seen on Earth.

If you do translate these teachings into spiritual wisdom, you will be able to understand the parting of and the crossing of the Red Sea and the trip in the desert with the children of God. You will be able to understand Abraham, Isaac, and Jacob as well as Jacob's twelve sons. You will come to understand all these things in spiritual terms. You will not be blind, and you will not be crippled anymore. You will not be left in the middle of the desert by yourself because the Lord will take care of you if you trust in him. He created you, he gave you life, and he will also bless you with all the knowledge that you can ever understand inside your spirit.

The two fish, the Old and the New Testament, will set you free from all the stupidity of the world and will make you so wise because the Lord created you to be wise. Mankind will be able to understand the true power of the Scriptures as long as they open their hearts to the way of the Lord. I tell you from experience that I have placed my trust in the Lord, and the Lord gave me everything that I need to understand the Kingdom of Heaven. Since then, I have never been given more than my spirit could possibly eat.

Next, we go to understand "Peter Denies Christ." The time is coming to realize that false religions, such as Christianity and the Catholic Church, have been denying Christ for the past two thousand years. Unless you repent of the sin of believing in these man-made religions, it will be in the hundreds of thousands of years of believing in falsehoods before you know it. You think that you are saved by Jesus, but you must come to understand that *no one* can replace God. You cannot be saved by the image of a man in front of the Lord. Jesus is the *servant* of the Lord, and you cannot be on the side of truth unless you believe in the Lord your God with all your soul and everything that you have.

If you wish to be on the side of truth instead of the side of the lies of organized religion, you must admit to the Lord your God that you have been worshipping a false path. Ask the Lord to help you to worship the One True God of the Creation so you can receive life everlasting. What you did in the past is because you didn't know too much in true wisdom, so you went for what you heard from the false prophet and you followed the wrong advice of those who don't know what they're talking about. But do not use the excuse that somebody else told you to believe in these lies. Make sure you admit inside your soul that you went for these lies because you thought it was the truth.

Now we go to "The Transfiguration." We must try to understand the power of the transfiguration of the soul inside ourselves. You have believed in the fantasy world of man-made religions for so long now that you must go through this transfiguration in order to receive the understanding of the Scriptures. This is where the Lord comes into your soul and brings inside you a *new value of truth* where your soul comes to be part of the new knowledge and the new thinking. Common sense inside of you will become as bright as a flash of lightning in the doctrine of reality. This is the transfiguration of knowledge, where common sense changes inside of you and you can no longer see anything true coming out of the mouth of the false prophet. And no matter how much you try to understand the old world, it just will not make any sense anymore.

The old religions of the past that you believed in will be part of the past. You cannot return to that day because the transfiguration of your beliefs from fantasy to reality comes to be inside you. When you begin to understand and see the face of the Lord in your life, your spirit becomes bright white in the understanding of truth. Everything that you believe in has to make sense in the common sense of intelligence. You *cannot* believe in anything that any false religion has ever taught you. The transfiguration is real, not some fantasy story but the truth itself, by the power of the Lord God who exists inside your soul. Bring your beliefs from the side of lies to the side of truth so you can have everlasting life in the Kingdom of Heaven.

Next, we go to "Jesus Heals a Demon-Possessed Boy." Try to bring yourself to believe that we are created with spirit first. The reality of life is that your spirit controls your physical part. So whatever your spirit believes in, whether it is truth or lies, that is what controls you. An evil spirit inside you is like a serpent that crawls on the earth. If you believe in an evil spirit, it is because you stepped out of the spiritual side of human understanding and you are controlled by your animal being, which means your mind. The trouble is that when you come to understand life with your mind instead of your spirit, there is no common sense to understand anything with and you do not know how to free yourself from that beast that lives inside you.

At this point, you can do almost anything in wrongdoing because your anger is a feeling that is very hard to control. And if you live within the understanding of the mind, you cannot control and reason with your anger because it is evil. Evil is not just a word. It's a *feeling* that you have inside you that is the difference between what makes sense and what doesn't make sense. This feeling just overpowers you, and the next thing you know, you have destroyed your life by committing crimes that you would not have committed if you were still in common sense.

The feelings of common sense that tell you not to believe in lies as well as the feelings that come from believing in lies both live inside your soul in human understanding. God is your control, and if you want to leave that control and go on your own, that is an evil spirit that wants to be free from the wisdom of the wise and the wisdom of common sense. If you let that evil spirit have control, then before you know it, your life is out of control because you have accepted that evil spirit inside of you, and you will find yourself in the situation where you have done something way out of common sense. You have destroyed yourself with that feeling that you have inside yourself, and you will lie to protect yourself. But at the end, you have to admit to what you have done because you were out of control. You ask yourself why you did that, and the only answer is because you believe in lies above the truth. You can believe whatever you want, but you will not be able to accomplish anything true with lies.

Now we go to "Who Will Be the Greatest?" In order to be great in the Kingdom of God, you must bear your sacrifices and live according to the Scriptures in the power of simplicity where a human being lives as simple as a man can live and fears no evil inside him. You don't have to conquer the world to be great among mankind, and you don't have to be noticed by everybody. You can be great just by being a simple human being walking the paths of learning and admitting to the wrong that you have done. This will bring you to the understanding of yourself.

To be great is to understand what you are in the simplicity of good and evil and to choose goodness over all that is wrong. But most people think great people are those who stand in front of an altar in a church and tell the whole world how to live their lives in what human beings think. But the truth is that the greatest among men are the people who live life in simplicity with what they have received from the Lord. They are thankful to understand life in the simplicity of their soul. A *simple man* is greater than all the high, important people of the world. No one knows who he is, but the Lord in heaven knows who he is.

Try to be simple in the greatest form of humanity that you could ever imagine where you live in the simplicity of your soul, like a simple carpenter who works every day and builds houses for other people. Every day, he gets up in the service of others to help construct the world into a better place to live with the tools of his hands and the wisdom of his mind and soul. No one can be greater than that because to be great in the Kingdom of God, you have to help establish a better way for mankind to live. God wants people to be simple and practical and to offer their labor to the Lord for the values of others. If this is not a great man, then I don't know what a great man is because being simple is the *real value of heaven*. All the rich and powerful people of the mind have lost their soul trying to gain the world with what they thought was so magnificent in wrongdoing. Be simple because life is given to the one who freely gives to others and takes only what he needs in the world.

Next, we come to "Samaritan Opposition." When you go toward the great glory of the understanding of heaven, you are going toward Jerusalem in the Scriptures. This is the teaching that God has sent upon the world for understanding good and evil. In the history of mankind, many people came and lived a great life and became kings and leaders in the wisdom of the mind of mankind. But simple people are not appreciated in the world of the mind. Take a man who packs up his lunch box in the morning and goes to work every day to feed his family and makes very little wealth. There's not a greater man that can stand on the side of God because the simple man is the one who does all the work to make life easier for other people.

The simple man brings his lunch box underneath his arm, goes to work every day, and creates real value for himself and for everybody around him. This is someone who made the sacrifice to get up in the morning to work for mankind. If you do simple work in simple deeds, you are being a good Samaritan by working to accomplish the dream of putting bread on the table and living by the values that are not important to the people of the mind. Understand that nobody praises or glorifies him, but he has the power to feed his family and the strength to go on every day. That simplicity is greater than anyone in the world who lives above himself and speaks the word in the crowd but does not do the Lord's will.

Now we go to "The Cost of Following Jesus." I just told you in the last part what you must do to follow this road that the Lord has given you. There is a big cost to pay for living in the value of simplicity. No one wants to admit that you have much value at all because you are just simple and humble. But the simple man is going to be the most important man of all because whom God loves the most is any man who lives a simple life and hurts no one. He may accomplish little in the value of the mind, but he can accomplish everything in the triumph of good over evil, where he lives in the simple heart of a simple man.

If that's not the greatest power to be part of the Kingdom of God, then I don't know what it is. This is the glory that I've seen from the life that I have lived in my sacrifice for justice. The greatest challenge in life is for a man to love and take care of his own as long as he obeys the laws of God. And believe me when I tell you that the laws of God are *very different* from the laws of man.

Next, we go to "At the Home of Martha and Mary." The meaning of this is something in your physical understanding because in the Bible, a woman represents the mind. And you have to understand the great power of spirit to truly understand the mind. I'm just trying to teach people how to read the Bible and understand the power that comes from how you read it and how you understand it. Most people live in such darkness that they only understand the Scriptures with their mind. They don't change it into a spiritual understanding, so the fruit in the Bible that the Lord has meant for people to understand is not understood.

In this lesson, common sense made friends with two people of the mind. This is the way you translate the Bible in the understanding of spirit after you have received your transfiguration. You have inside you the power to understand the Scriptures, but you have to first understand the Scriptures in physical terms and then translate them into spiritual terms. This creates verbs out of the nouns, and that is important because a verb is a living thing. When the verb is understood, that means the prophecy or the parable is understood. But you have to first go through the transfiguration, where the Lord sets you free by the understanding of the Scriptures.

You cannot learn the Scriptures without the *understanding of the verbs*. This is the most important thing because the verbs are the part of human thinking where you come to understand the deeds and the actions of the Bible. And when you understand that, you are in the transfiguration of true wisdom between the mind and the spirit. At that point, you'll be able to talk to the Lord your God in your spirit, and you won't feel foolish about it because you know that's the path to true wisdom.

When you can translate the teaching of the Lord inside yourself, you have the power to speak to God. And when you speak to God, you will understand the great things in life that the Lord has written for mankind. God has written the Scriptures for mankind, and they are based on true wisdom, not on foolishness. When you first start to read the Scriptures in truth, you may feel like a fool. But then the Lord will give you the understanding that you have asked him for. God is the verb, and once you understand the verbs, you understand how to live your life in true wisdom. Then you are free from believing in the evil spirit.

If you cannot understand what I'm trying to tell you here, it is because you are a person of the *mind*, and the mind will fail you every time you try to understand anything practical. If you let your mind lead your spirit, you will think it's foolish to understand with the Holy Spirit inside you, which is the angel of reality. But when you cross over into the land of the spirit, you are in a new way to understand life in spiritual terms, and you won't have to go see the false prophet on Sunday morning to find out how little they know about the Kingdom of God.

If you think you are foolish by understanding the Word of the Lord that's inside your soul, you *cannot* enter the Kingdom of God. The power of true spiritual wisdom is to be able to change the nouns into verbs because God exists in the verbs of the truth. So you must translate what is false into what is true. And when you cross over from the understanding of the mind to the wisdom of the spirit, you can free yourself from the stupidity of man-made religion. Then you can start understanding something valuable and great inside yourself, which is to receive the transfiguration of the Lord—and you will know what is good and what is evil. You will come to find out that organized religion is the great Satan in front of the Lord because they tried to tell you something that simple is not true. If you want the Lord to pull you out of false religion, make sure that your soul is open in the reality of truth so you can cross over inside your spiritual deeds. Only then will you come to understand the *freedom* of life. Until that time, you are just an animal—thinking like an animal—and you cannot rise to the spiritual understanding of the Lord.

Now we go to "Jesus's Teaching on Prayer." This is common sense teaching you how to pray. You must change the nouns into verbs, and you must change the parables of Jesus into common sense. Everything will begin to make sense after that because God is not a man but a spirit. You have to learn in spirit when you read the Scriptures because they were written so you can free yourself from the weakness of your mind into a spiritual understanding. This is the proof that Jesus is not God, because Jesus tells you to pray to the Father of heaven and not to him. You can pray to common sense because that's part of God, but you are forbidden to form an image of anyone or anything in front of the Lord inside of your spirit.

Try to come to a conclusion of reality where you begin to believe in the power of the spirit when you pray to the Father of intelligence. And make sure that when you understand the Lord your God, you understand it and believe it in spiritual terms. I use the word *understanding* a lot here because understanding is Simeon, the second son of Jacob. I use the sons of Jacob a lot because if you change the nouns, which in this case are the names of people, into verbs, Jacob becomes common sense and the sons of Jacob become the sons of common sense. You must change these things in the understanding that God is a spiritual God, not a God of flesh, and definitely not an image in front of the Lord your God.

People go to church for their entire life from birth until death, and yet they fail to understand the *true power* of the Scriptures. The Scriptures are written for humanity—not for the mind but for the simple understanding of the simple soul of humanity. If you believe that God is the God of spirit and you pray to this God and call him Father, that means that the first seeds of true wisdom inside you have been planted. When you pray to the Holy Spirit, which is the angel of reality, you increase your knowledge in reality. And when you pray to your common sense, you realize that faith exists in the simple truth where a human being comes to understand that he is in the real life and was given the spirit of reality as well as the spirit of common sense to live with.

The true power of wisdom comes from understanding and believing who God really is inside your soul even though you are created in flesh. But you cannot forget your animal, the mind, and leave that behind. You need your animal to carry you across the burdens and the sacrifices of life so you can worship the Lord your God in the desert and understand and truly believe that what you are doing is proper and good. Try to believe in the truth and receive the power to set yourself free from the lies of false religion. Believe me, this power is certainly not easy to get. First, you have to go through the transfiguration from the understanding of the mind to learning in spirit.

Now, I want to mention here some things that are not real. First, let's look at a few of the seven sacraments of the Catholic Church. Look at them with both your mind and your spirit and see what is real and what is not real. First is baptism. It is not real that you can take physical water and purify your soul—you have to use reality to purify your soul. Next is the forgiveness of sins. You must understand that if you have committed sins against the Lord, you must ask *him* for forgiveness. You're not supposed to go talk to a priest, rabbi, minister, or any other false preacher. They cannot forgive your sins—they were *never* given this power in the first place. *Only the Lord himself* can forgive sins, and it happens *directly in your spirit*, not through another man in the practice of stupidity and ignorance. And the Confirmation is for you to confirm yourself with the Lord and the Lord only. It is not a false ceremony like the Catholics teach. These sacraments can be understood on the side of truth (as the Lord has instructed us) or on the side of lies (as false religion believes). It's up to you which side you choose to believe on, and you will have to answer for this choice.

Next, we go to "Jesus and Beelzebub." This is the power to understand Jesus, which is common sense, and Beelzebub, which is ignorance. To understand *both* common sense and ignorance, you must understand one side in order to understand the other side. On one side of wisdom, you have common sense, and on the other side, you have ignorance. There is a *war* between these two sides of wisdom. Don't think for one minute that ignorance is not powerful because ignorance causes you to become lost in a kingdom that is imperfect in the false teaching of the word of God. This is how common sense was crucified by false religion. Understand well here that religion and the face of government led the crucifixion of Jesus. Organized religion was the most involved in the crucifixion of Jesus, and government washed their hands of enforcing their laws on religion, so religion took the power to the point of Jesus being crucified.

Jesus is common sense, the servant of the Lord. Whatever you did to Jesus, you did to the Lord. Organized religion wanted to crucify Jesus because they were afraid of him. This means that in order to establish religion, fear would become the number one king to crucify people and to make people do wrong to the servant of God. Remember that organized religion has killed the common sense of the Lord and had to be punished for doing so. Until now, mankind didn't realize that their religion is what crucified Jesus. These false religions made people believe that Jesus was the physical son of God, and they raised him above the throne of the Father without even understanding any of his parables.

These man-made religions are the *key of wrongdoing*, where they took religion to a standard of value above themselves to make a man look like he is God. They made people all over the world believe in their lies for over two thousand years by thinking of themselves to be the only ones that understood the Bible. But the plan of the Lord is to bring justice on mankind, and it will happen just as it is written in the Scriptures. Align yourself with the side of truth, not with the side of lies, so the Lord will count you among His people.

Now let us go to "The Death of Jesus." It was God's plan to *bring the world to a halt* by the death of common sense. Common sense could not be understood because it was sealed from mankind upon the death of Jesus. This was not the death of a man but the death of common sense. Jesus was a man, and he did physically die, but it is the spiritual meaning of his life that the Lord wants us to understand—and that is common sense. It was taken from the human race for the three days of darkness where mankind could not penetrate the son of God, which is common sense, the spirit of intelligence that lives inside us. People went to church on the side of wrong, thinking they were doing right, by condemning those who didn't believe the same as them. If you didn't go to church, you were persecuted, attacked, and almost destroyed by the people of false religion. You were brought to the trial of falsehood and skinned alive by the people who went to church. Going to church was their faith in God, and if you didn't have the same faith in God as they did, you were persecuted for it.

God made these false religions in order to fool the world during the Seven Days of the Creation. God sent the three days of darkness over the world just as it was told in the time of the Egyptians and Moses. What happened during those plagues of Egypt is what happened to mankind in spiritual terms. The plan of God is perfect, and the world has to be dealt with and convicted by the power of the Holy Spirit itself where the reason of common sense is not going to be around for three thousand years. The world will fall into darkness, and nobody will know the time of day.

Jesus died and was buried for three days. Then he came back alive in the common sense of intelligence. But man worshipped Jesus instead of his teaching, and that was the penalty of the Lord upon mankind. You think that only one man was good and the rest of the children of God were not good. Nobody, including the false preachers of organized religion, could understand the Scriptures in truth or explain the three days of darkness. They didn't think they were in darkness, but God has given them nothing to understand. The Bible was there sitting on the table, and nobody could figure it out because God has sealed it for three thousand years, which are the three days of darkness.

I have written this book for mankind. People will read it, but very few people will believe it because it was not meant to be believed in these three days of darkness. Only the *humble* will be able to understand it and come to the Lord on the day that the Lord has chosen for the defeat of mankind. All that was written in the Scriptures is according to God's plan in the way of life for those who want true life as well as those who continue with their stiff necks and think that Jesus has saved them. They tell you that Jesus was a good man and that he was the servant of the Lord, but he was not God. So be careful what you believe because the time is coming for the judgment of mankind. There will be a throne set in place, and that throne will judge each one of you by your deeds of what you will take from this book. You can be on the side of common sense, or you can stay with the false prophet. Worship the Lord your God with all your soul and you will be safe on the day of the Lord. But if you reject the teaching of truth and common sense, you will *not* make it into the Kingdom of God. That's the way the Lord will separate the goats from the sheep. Be humble in common sense, and you will see the Lord your God.

Next, we go to "The Burial of Jesus." You must understand the plan of God. You must take the death, the burial, and the resurrection of Jesus seriously. Common sense was buried in darkness for three days. The Book of Revelation tells us that there will be a thousand years where the serpent, the great Satan of all the lies of the world, will attack you and it will try to confuse you by making you think that what is false is true and what is true is false. Be careful because *the false prophet is coming*. He will fight against the truth and try to destroy the truth. Whoever holds out in the way of the Lord will be safe, but whoever continues to worship idols in the stupidity and ignorance of the darkness of the world will be lost. This is the plan of the Lord. The truth of life is within the boundaries of common sense. If you go to the false common sense of the false prophet, you will lose your soul.

I tell you this ahead of time so you can come to understand the power and the glory of intelligence that God planned for the world in the value of His extreme wisdom. It was meant to be so you would come to understand the burial of common sense. To understand the power of the common sense of intelligence, you must go deep inside your heart and see that what was written is what was meant to be. It was written two thousand years ago that this day would be here. If you live in false religion, leave those lies behind and come to the Lord where you can learn the truth. Nobody can change the mind of the Lord. The Lord is everlasting and does not change His mind or His plan. It's up to you to say, "I'm coming to you, Lord. Forgive me for what I have believed in the past. Come to me and give me life in the spiritual values of human intelligence." I know that I will not be popular and I will be crucified for whatever I write down in this book, but I'm a man and only a man. The Lord has given me the Scriptures to give to you. You can have them, or you can reject them. It's up to you.

Now we go to "The Resurrection of Jesus." After three days of darkness, the resurrection will happen where common sense comes back into the world. This is not a man that is coming. It is the common sense of intelligence that comes back from the dead where the people will see the plan of the Lord and they will try to understand it. But it's going to be hard because God's plan is perfect in the way of life. There is no free ride into heaven in human intelligence. You must understand the resurrection of the spirit of common sense because that is the truth. Whoever denies it will be denied before the Father of heaven, but whoever accepts it will be accepted in heaven.

If you follow the false prophet, the time will come that you will deny Christ three times just like Peter did. You will make a fool of yourself because you were the one who worshipped Jesus with your mind, but you could not understand the power of the plan of God. Now you must pay the great price because you were part of false religion. You must go through the persecution of the Lord for learning what you do not know. Try to understand the value of the Kingdom of God. It does not come for free like the false prophets told us. The understanding of heaven comes through sacrifice. The Lord made the sacrifice of the change of heart inside each one of you that whoever changes his heart and comes to the Lord God will be safe, but whoever stays with the false prophet and believes in their lies will be lost forever.

You have to make a big decision inside yourself of *which side* you are going to be on. Worship the Lord your God with all your soul and reject the lies of the false prophet, and you will come to see the Kingdom of God. If you think that the Scriptures were written for no reason and whatever is in the Bible is just a teaching of the fantasy world, then you will not be able to understand the true plan of God. The plan of God is for you to go through the greatest sacrifice of all, which is to change your heart. Those who refuse to turn their stiff necks away from false, man-made religion will not receive the Kingdom of God, and that's the way it will be. Come to worship the Lord your God.

The resurrection of Christ is the resurrection of common sense. The great power of the Lord will come into the hearts of those who receive the new birth of common sense into their hearts. If you do not believe that, you will not be in the understanding of the Scriptures. Remember that truth, common sense, and reality are all part of the Lord. To cross over into the new world requires a sacrifice that most people will not be able to endure. The coming time is not going to be the easiest thing in the world. You have to change your heart piece by piece, bit by bit, into a new heart that exists in true wisdom.

Those who thought they had the victory in the old teaching of falsehood will know that they do not have the victory in the new understanding of truth. Remember that this is the Lord's plan. Everyone, from the highest one in the highest learning of the world to the lowest one, will have to go through the decision of either being part of His kingdom or rejecting it. Before now, no one could have figured out the plan of the Lord because His plans were sealed from mankind and no one could come to the value of His understanding. You either accept or reject the true meaning of the Scriptures. Each one of us has to make a decision inside our soul to love the Lord God with all our soul and to love our brother as ourselves. If this commandment is not observed on this day, you will not be able to understand because the Lord will not send wisdom inside your heart to understand and to come to His Kingdom.

Next, we go to "The Ascension into the Kingdom of God." The soul that turns toward the Lord will be brought into heaven safely away from the serpent's attack. The world will come to change this power of human understanding into a new way of thinking that will become different. The Old Jerusalem will come to be the New Jerusalem in the creation of right over wrong. Everything that is done through the Lord is right and true in the judgment of mankind. Everything is perfect because the Lord is perfect. The ascension of mankind is to come to the great power of those who were persecuted for just believing in the One True God and rejecting the lies of organized religion. These are God's chosen people from the very foundation of the creation. If you were not part of that and you could not change your heart, then God will not accept you in the kingdom of the greatest power ever known to mankind. God is the truth, and if you don't believe in the truth, you cannot enter the Kingdom of God because He will not give you the sensibility to understand His Word.

If you don't believe in the Lord, you will say any curse you want against the Lord your God but it will not bring you to Heaven. If you are full of jealousy, it is because you never understood the Kingdom of the Lord. You had to be separated from the sheep and placed on the side of the goats because you were not part of the Kingdom of God. You must change from the Old Jerusalem to the New Jerusalem. Only then can you be on the side of the Lord. If you did not love the Lord your God with all your soul and with all your mind, the value of the Lord will not be in your soul and you will not be able to enter in the ascension of the Lord your God. God is the truth and the truth will set you free but only if you reject the lies of false religion and believe on the side of truth, common sense, and reality.

*****

This is the beginning of the Book of John, and first we go to "The Word Became Flesh." We're talking about the Word of God becoming flesh. People believe that the Bible was written for the flesh and the physical part of the human being, so they put Jesus, a man of flesh, in *front* of the Lord. The problem with this is that we are *not allowed* to worship any physical man. No man is good except God. Why would you call a man good when a man is just a little locust in the understanding of true wisdom? How can you take a man and compare him to God Almighty by putting any man of flesh between yourself and the God of the Creation? No one has the right to do that on earth, in heaven, or anywhere else.

In spiritual terms, Jesus represents common sense, and it is common sense that is good, not any man of flesh. The Scriptures are meant to be understood in spiritual terms, not by the mind. When you learn the Scriptures in the way of truth, you will know that it is common sense that heals the sick, raises the dead, turns water into wine, etc. These things are possible because the Lord created them on the side of spirit. They are possible, but they will not happen unless they are understood and lived as they were created to be. I don't care whom the person is that you might mention. It is simply not possible for any man, past or present, to physically raise the dead or turn water into wine. If you understand things in this way of true wisdom, you will know that no person, including Jesus, is meant to be worshipped above any other person.

That's the way it is, and you cannot change anything the Lord has created. When an ignorant person calls himself or anyone else good, he creates an evil spirit inside himself. And when that spirit is created inside him, he has to live it through and get rid of that evil spirit or else he will suffer greatly from his ignorance. We are created in spirit, and we must try to understand and live by the spirit of the Lord because we are men, not God. The Lord can give you the benefit of understanding His Creation, but neither you nor any man can be God, and that includes Jesus.

You can understand Jesus in the way of spirit, but that does not turn flesh into the divine spirit. No one can be part of the divine spirit that God gave to mankind *unless you understand the truth*. You have to be chosen by God to understand it. God can choose anyone He wants to receive His message, but He must choose someone. And when He chooses someone, that person becomes a servant and he speaks in the way of the Father because the Father gives it to him. But that does not make him above any other man in his mind or his soul.

The Bible tells us that the Word was God, *not* the man that brought the word. He is only a servant of the Lord and *should not be worshipped as God*. You should not offer your sacrifice to Jesus because if you do, you are a *sinner*. You become a fool in the spirit of evil where you think you are so wise, but remember that the wisdom of God is not the wisdom of man. God will give you the wisdom to understand that everything you have comes from God. God has given the understanding of His Word to me, and He will give it to you if you worship Him in truth. True wisdom starts with the understanding that no man is God, and that includes Jesus. All men are 100 percent flesh, and you cannot change the physical part of anyone into a spiritual part just because you want it to be so.

Next, we go to "John the Baptist Denies Being the Messiah." John the Baptist was the one who was baptizing people with water because he could not understand the Holy Spirit. This means that the people who were baptized by water are the same people that will betray us to the light. They destroy all the good that's inside people, and they become false prophets in the land of the lost soul. They do everything they can to make us understand life in the way of flesh because they have been baptized with water. And if you are baptized with water, *you have not been baptized with the Holy Spirit*, which is the angel of reality. This means that you live against all the knowledge of reality and against the truth because you were baptized with water in a false way to understand God.

Being baptized with the Holy Spirit is *not* the same as being baptized with water because you are baptized with the angel of reality. And when you're baptized with the angel of reality, you think in reality, but when you do not think in reality, you think like the people of the earth who believe that their religion is good and that their false preachers are good, holy people. If you do not live in the way of the spirit, you live in the way of sin, and you think you're better than your brother.

People of false religion do not understand true wisdom because they were not baptized with the Holy Spirit to understand the glory of heaven in the understanding of God. When I grew up, it was a sin to not be baptized. If you were not baptized with water, people believed that you were a child of wrong and you would do wrong. The truth is that you cannot be baptized with water because water has no power. Reality has power, and that's why the real baptism is the baptism of the Holy Spirit, the angel of reality.

Telling people the *truth* is the real baptism of the Spirit. A child who is baptized with reality will grow up to be kind and good. But if you baptize with water, that is not the Holy Spirit. Baptizing people with water is *fake* and should not ever be done on earth. If you cannot baptize people with reality, don't baptize them at all because you have an evil spirit inside yourself who thinks they have power to baptize people. Believe in the Lord your God and only baptize in the way of truth, reality, and common sense.

Now we go to Jesus and the Lamb of God. Who is the Lamb of God? It means Jesus was the *preferred servant* of God. But understand well that there has been many Lambs of God. *Anyone* who was crucified on earth by the evildoers of the world and went through the great persecution is a Lamb of God. Anyone who was killed for false religion is a Lamb of God. If a black person was made a slave, their children sold into slavery, and they were used like animals and given no value for their hard labor, they are part of the Lamb of God.

The crucifixion of Jesus was an *injustice*, but it is *not* the only injustice that was done on earth. An Indian who was killed on the battlefield by the long knife for no good reason other than because of his race is the Lamb of God. You can say they were evil people, that they were not civilized, and all the things that you want to say about them. But they were only fighting to save their land and their families. The Indian and the black man believe that they are just as good as a white man. *It is the same feeling and the same purpose that every human has.* We love our children just as much as they do, and everybody on earth is the same, but the twisted mind that the false religion of the mind gives us is what makes us think differently. With that twisted mind, they persecuted many people. This persecution is what the Lord does not allow in the way of the spirit, but the people who were baptized with water did everything they could do to hurt their brothers and to look at them as children of evil.

They did not respect their way of life, and they did not respect them as people. They called them all kinds of names that made them look like they were stupid, but they were part of the Lamb of God. The Lamb of God is a person who says something intelligent because they have learned the understanding of life in intelligence. The Lamb of God has been disrespected, beaten, and killed for saying something intelligent. That's what happened to Jesus two thousand years ago, when people thought it was right to destroy everything that another man believes. They took his life and destroyed it in the land of the loser.

Understand well that God has created people who are *both good and evil.* There have been people from all races who have done terrible things because of their ignorance and stupidity, but no matter what anyone from any race has ever done, they were not more evil than the white man who killed people for their own well-being, and were glorified by other white men for doing so. They did not understand that God created man to be *equal,* so they made an insulting statement to everybody who didn't think like they do. They *never* understood the truth itself—to understand the values of others.

The Lamb of God is every single person in the world who went through the great persecution, was crucified, had his physical and spiritual life taken, and was made to obey someone else's will. *Anyone* who has gone through this is the Lamb of God. Mankind has never understood the *true* Lamb of God. We always think of the great injustice of the crucifixion of Jesus, but that's not the only injustice that was ever done on earth. There were so many great injustices, but I have only mentioned a few here. The Lamb of God is anyone who has suffered physically and spiritually by the hand of mankind for his beliefs in the true teaching of the Lord.

Next, we go to the First Disciple. Understand that the first disciple of common sense is that the man, Jesus, was *not* the son of God—he represents common sense as a servant of the Lord, but he is not God. A disciple in common sense is a man who comes forward and tries to understand the way of the Lord. A disciple tries to create an understanding inside of himself that makes sense. He tries to understand the way God thinks in the spiritual value of heaven. I will tell you again that heaven is not a place that you go after you die—Heaven is a place in knowledge where you can understand the Lord. He has created us with enough intelligence to understand the power of the spirit. And if we can understand that, we can climb inside the great chamber of knowledge, where a human being becomes the child of a learning process with the understanding that life is created in spirit inside of us for understanding spirit before flesh.

The value of spirit is *above* the value of flesh. This cannot be understood by people of the mind. The mind only knows loss and gain and *cannot* understand the spiritual value of heaven because it is not made to understand the spiritual value of heaven. Letting your spirit lead your mind will help you become a better man in the power of what you are in your spiritual value of what you understand. After you have received the birth of the spirit, you will start understanding things in different ways.

In the old world, you believed that a person was good enough to go to heaven based on what you believed with your mind. He may have been the most spiritually evil person on the face of the earth, but you could not see that. You could only see the deeds that he physically did. For example, a catholic priest who looks good to people is not really good because he inflamed the mind of many to believe in the wrong things. You believe that these people are good in spirit, but if you could see the other side of their soul where they hurt the children of God, you would say, "Boy, these people are ready for hell." But heaven and hell do not exist like you think they do.

Hell exists in human thinking, and you can be so twisted in the false wisdom of the mind that you never know what to do to get out of it. Hell is a place on earth that lives in stupidity and ignorance. If you traveled there to understand what it is, you will come to understand that hell is not a nice place to live. When God sends you to hell, He sends you to a place where you cannot understand or believe in anything that makes sense, so you fall apart and become a broken man in the loss of your soul. You live against the truth, and you think you are right doing so because your faith in lies has twisted you to the devious power of your own spirit that's full of garbage.

You live like a demon, and you practice stupidity because you live according to the rules of your mind over your spirit. You try to hurt people when they hurt you…and you try to destroy people when they have tried to destroy you. You try to get even with everyone in the world because you don't understand that your twisted, devious spirit is inflamed with the fire of an understanding that makes you stupid and totally ignorant of the value of common sense. If you want to be a *disciple* of the Lord, you have to come to a new way of thinking and turn away from the devious power that made you so miserable in the land of falsehood. You must become one in the spirit of truth, common sense, and reality where the glory of intelligence lives inside you for being a decent human being in the wisdom of heaven. Try to gain the power of the highest knowledge in *spirit*, not the highest knowledge of the *mind*. Then you will no longer live in stupidity, but you will *believe* in the Lord your God.

Now we go to "Jesus Calls Philip and Nathanael." The twelve apostles of the lamb are the twelve religions of the Earth. There's Catholicism, Christianity, Islam, and all the other religions of the world. This is the way it works: A disciple is a religion formed by the mind of man and understood by the mind of man. To understand the great power of what is in the Scriptures in the intelligence of mankind, you have to come to understand that you cannot take your religion in vain by thinking that your religion is better than any other one. God placed the same value on all man-made religions to fool mankind so the world would come to understand that He's the boss. And if you *don't* believe in the Lord your God, then you are going to believe in the false religions of the earth.

You have to do away with all organized religion of any kind in order to understand and enter the Kingdom of God. You must leave those disciples to go down to your crucifixion and be counted as one who is outside of false religion. When you come to that point, the people of false religion will *crucify* you. They won't respect your faith because your faith is not part of their religion. When you come to understand the disciples of Jesus, which are the religions of the earth, you will learn that these people are not practicing true religion with their beliefs that do not make any sense. You will come to be persecuted because you don't agree with them and you're not part of them. Remember that Jesus was the only one crucified while the twelve apostles got away. That is why you must keep yourself out of all religions and understand for yourself with all the feelings that come from the Lord your God. If you stay away from religion and don't practice in falsehood, you will be a perfect man in the eyes of your Father in heaven because you will listen to only him and your feelings to understand the truth.

Next, we go to "Jesus Changes Water into Wine." Let's translate this into common sense—water means reality, and wine means understanding. So common sense changes *reality* into *understanding.* The two words, *reality* and *common sense,* are the sons of God where you come to understand that God is the truth and reality is part of the truth. Common sense is also part of the truth, so try to understand that every time you see these words in the Scriptures, you have to translate them into spiritual value. That's the way you believe in the Lord your God. It is very important to understand that the wedding feast mentioned in this teaching is *not* a physical wedding. You have to translate these words into spirit. When you do, it becomes the wedding feast of mind and spirit, where you come to understand that your mind and spirit must be joined together as one. You must make your mind obey your spirit in order to enter the Kingdom of God. The mind is only the loss and gain of human understanding. You have to train your mind to obey your spirit in order to marry the spirit and the mind together into complete intelligence. So in order to join your mind and your spirit together so you can understand the word of God, you must let common sense change reality into understanding. Use common sense to understand these teachings, and you will be on the side of the Lord.

Next go to the understanding of "Jesus Clears the Temple Courts." This is where we understand false religion in the way of *wrongdoing.* Everyone who sits in those churches on Sunday morning are there for buying something for themselves so they can be safe in the justice of the Lord. They think that they are good people, but they still need to be forgiven for their sins. And they have *no knowledge* of what their sins are. That's the problem with people who think they are better than everybody else and they don't do any wrong according to what they believe the Bible tells them to do. But the Bible is not a book of clarification. It's a spiritual book that you have to translate from physical teachings into spiritual wisdom.

If you worship only in the physical part of the Scriptures, then you are far from being good because goodness does not come from your physical understanding. The *biggest sin* is to ignore the truth and to live and go to church outside the truth and believe that you are better than everybody else. You must learn to understand that the Kingdom of God is for looking at your soul and seeing what you are doing wrong in your spirit. If you are persecuting people because you think they have done wrong but you don't think *you* have done anything wrong, then you have to go back to the purpose of the truth itself and look inside your soul and see what you have said or done against someone else.

Only the Lord can judge what is right and what is wrong. Don't think for a second that any human being, with their little locust understanding, can judge what is right and what is wrong and preach against what is wrong. You have to understand that you are not God and you cannot replace God on earth.

The sin of the false prophet is just as great as the worst murderer or the worst criminal. Preachers of false religion made the people think that they are better than those they believe to be sinners, but that is simply not true. It is just like the lesson of the Good Samaritan where you see a person who has been beaten by all the evil people of the world and left him there to die because of the stupidity of their sin, and you do not try to correct his wrong. You believe that you are better than him, and that's why you won't help. But the Lord will not let you get away with that belief.

You see criminals who have been condemned by society, and you claim it's their fault. But it is *not* their fault—it is the fault of all of society that made these criminals. Man doesn't understand this with their tongue—they persecute and destroy the heart of mankind. The next thing you know, you have society against them. You don't try to help them or give them the fruit of life inside their souls. You only tell them how evil they are. You never tell them that their sins can be forgiven if they listen to their own heart and ask the Lord to forgive them because you did not believe this yourself. *Common sense cleared the temple.* This means that all the people who go to church and claim their goodness in front of the Lord are the ones who are against the Lord. He will clear them out of the temple because they do not humble themselves before the Lord and ask for forgiveness for believing in and preaching lies to their brother.

Now we go to "Jesus Teaches Nicodemus." *No one* can claim the understanding of the Kingdom of God unless he is born again. Those are the words that were said two thousand years ago in the Bible, and those are the same words that are being said today. Unless you are born of spirit and receive the birth of the spirit inside your soul, you *cannot* understand the Scriptures of yesterday, today, and tomorrow because the birth of the spirit is the birth of intelligence that teaches you the truth in the common sense of reality. You cannot understand the truth with the mind because the mind just cannot recognize the reality of truth in spirit. Remember that the mind only understands loss and gain. The mind is happy to gain something, but when it loses something, the mind becomes stressed about losing. That's why God gave to the spirit, the mind, a wife to guide the spirit in the goodness of life. But the mind does not have the same feelings as the spirit. That is why you have to receive the birth of the spirit inside the mind in order to *unite your mind and spirit* in the wedding feast of intelligence. Only then will you be able to *cooperate* with the difference between mind and spirit.

Jesus told the high priests that a man has to be born again, and the high priests asked Jesus, "How can a man enter his mother's womb for the second time?" This tells us that they are trying to understand a spiritual teaching with their minds, and that is *impossible*. But Jesus said what is impossible in the way of man is possible in the way of God. When you become born again in spirit, your mind becomes the *wife* of the spirit. And when the mind becomes the wife of the spirit, it *obeys* the spirit. If you are not born again in spirit, your mind is like a bad wife inside of you that always tells you how wrong you are.

You have a feeling for the truth inside your spirit, and if you listen to your mind, the great power of loss that comes from the mind will destroy the spirit because remember that your mind cannot understand feelings. And if you cannot understand feelings, how can you see the difference between what is supposed to be and what is? If you are not born in spirit, where the agreement between the mind and spirit becomes one flesh, you will not be able to understand the power that is inside you. Sometimes the spirit must listen to the mind, and sometimes the mind has to listen to the spirit. In order to become one married to the other, you cannot always be right with your feelings, and you cannot always be right with the loss and gain of the mind. Come to the Kingdom of God with a new heart and a new mind, where you will worship the Lord your God in the *new truth*, not the old lies.

Next, we go to "John Testifies Again About Jesus." Understand well here that Salome, the little dancing girl, had a lot to do with John the Baptist being put into prison and having his head cut off. Try to translate the meaning of the little dancing girl in front of King Herod and in front of the people in order to understand the purpose of the testimony of John the Baptist. People go to church and see the dancing, singing, and the jubilee of these false religions, and it attracts them like a dancing girl. Remember the soul of mankind and see why John the Baptist's head was cut off. This is the same as the people who call themselves Christians because they have been baptized with water. The whole world of the people who were baptized with water, meaning those who understood the scriptures with the mind instead of with the spirit, had their heads cut off. This is the teaching of the Scriptures.

Everything that happened in the Scriptures has happened in the reality of mankind. Both sides of the Scriptures must be understood, both in spirit and in physical terms. Whatever happens on the physical side must be part of what happens on the spiritual side. You must come to understand that the Scriptures are spiritual lessons, which are told through stories of physical understanding. You may understand the Scriptures on the physical side, but you will *never* be able to understand the spiritual side unless you are born again in the spirit of human understanding.

Everything that was written in the Scriptures is the duplicate of what would happen to the human race to bring about the power of human understanding in the glory of human intelligence. You must transfer the physical story of John the Baptist into a spiritual teaching where whoever destroys the spirit must come to have their spiritual head cut off. This great teaching of life on earth was done by the God of heaven to regulate the physical into the spiritual part of what was, what is, and what will always be. The people of false religion will have their faith destroyed inside of them because they have understood everything backward. In order to understand life in truth, you must *first* love the Lord your God with all your soul.

Now we go to "The Disciples Rejoin Jesus." The meaning of the disciples here is all the religions of the world. The rejoining of Jesus means that these religions are rejoining Jesus, the man, in the *physical* part of the Scriptures, and they cannot understand the *spiritual* side of it. Here we are crossing over to the other side of the understanding of the Scriptures to understand the power of the physical side. Try to understand the physical side of the history of mankind so you can come to understand that the Son of Man is the history of man, meaning where man came from and where he's going. The Scriptures were meant to determine the value of all that exists in the value of human intelligence. God is the truth, and the truth is God. When you take all the religions of the world and place them in one big catastrophe of wrongdoing, you begin to understand that religion was forbidden from the very beginning of the Creation.

Organized religions are *not* what the Lord meant for the world to worship because organized religion comes from the mind of man, not the spirit of God. It does not match the Scriptures, and neither does the physical and the spiritual parts of the understanding of the Lord your God. Mankind has been reading the Bible since it was created by God. We know there's a God in heaven, and we try to respect God by trying to understand the Scriptures. But if you don't study the Scriptures with your heart, you cannot understand wrong and right. That is why all the religions of the world cannot understand the teaching of the Lord. They don't know what life everlasting means—they think it is where you go after you die. This is *not* what life everlasting is.

The children of the mind and the apostles, meaning all the religions of the mind, believe that they will go to a better place after they die, and they call that heaven. But that is just a big lie made up by the mind in front of the spirit. This is something they cannot understand. They believe that if they don't physically do good, they will have to go sit in a lake of fire and suffer for the rest of eternity. They believe this because the mind is so weak and only understands in loss and gain. They cannot understand the Scriptures because God didn't give it to them to be understood with the mind.

We are supposed to *receive the birth of the spirit* in order to understand the Scriptures, but people are so weak in their understanding because they let their mind lead their spirit. They cannot understand their feelings, so they do not try to understand the Scriptures with their *feelings*. They live within the loss and gain of the mind where they believe heaven is a place of gain and hell is a place of loss—so they all went for whatever they could gain out of it to preserve their life and go to heaven after they die. They believe that God will give them the gratitude of receiving heaven if they are good people. This was a story of heaven with the gain of heaven.

But mankind did not truly understand what was really evil and what was really good. They claimed a false value in front of their good deeds, but their actual good deeds were few and far between because they were *mixed up in mind and spirit*. They thought the world belonged to them just like when the white man took the land from the Indians. They did not consider them to be of any value. That was a prophecy lived by both the Indians and the white man. It tells you that you must consider your brother to be equal to you even though they don't look like you, don't think like you, and don't pray like you.

Mankind looked at anyone whom they considered to be different and thought they must be the bad people that God is talking about. They considered them to be the bad people, and they considered themselves to be the good people who follows the laws of God. The white man did not consider the Indians to be their brothers. This is just like the black man who they put into slavery. They could not understand that these people were equal to them, so they treated them like they are insignificant and that God doesn't care for them. And man still treats those they view as different this way.

The Kingdom of God is the Kingdom of Brotherhood where you must love your brother as yourself. You are supposed to love God with all your soul and everything that you have, and you are supposed to love your brother as yourself. This is the highest commandment of the Lord. You must bless the Lord for His magnificent power, and you must look at your brother to be equal to you. Most people cannot understand that because they put their little locust mind in front of their spirit. That is why you have prejudice and injustice committed by the people who cannot understand the difference between what is right and what is wrong. They think that the Lord must have chosen them to be right and the neglected people were chosen to be wrong.

That's why the white man could not recognize his brother on the battlefield of justice. They took their land because they were more powerful and had more weapons, but you must come to understand that all the sins of the human race must be understood in the value of *justice* in front of the throne of the Lord to be judged accordingly. The one that the Lord gave more power to destroy the other one became the one who destroyed himself, and the one that the Lord gave less power to defend himself became the victim. Which one is truly guilty of sin between the thinking of man and the thinking of God? The reality of truth comes in the value of justice where the side of the weak becomes the most powerful of all, and the side who thought they were strong loses power and becomes the value of none.

Next, we go to "Many Samaritans Believe." Here you must understand the Samaritans to be *outside* the land of Canaan. They believe in the man, Jesus, because they listen to the woman that brought great testimony on the side of Jesus. Understand the *power of the mind* here so you can understand the prophecy. When you have transferred the physical teaching into spiritual wisdom, then you and your heart can begin to understand the Scriptures in the way it was written so you can come to understand the way God thinks in the magnificent power of the truth. Once you transfer the understanding into a spiritual value, you can understand where you come from and who you are.

If you were Muslim in the land of the Muslim, you will understand the faith of the Muslim, and if you understand Christianity in the land of the Christians, you will understand everything in Christianity. The same thing goes with Buddhists. They will understand everything in the teaching of Buddhism. That's the way people understand and accept religion. Even though there are so many organized religions of the world, it means that you understand from where you come from, where the glory of the Lord lives inside of us to give us the *truth*.

The door is always open to understand the other side of the Scriptures, but when you look at yourself and think you are right in what you believe, you cannot see the other person's beliefs and you cannot understand why they believe like that. You are compelled to understand the way you were brought up, and that is exactly the way it is now. So who is right? The Lord is right, and whoever does not believe in the way of the laws of the Lord *cannot enter* the Kingdom of Heaven. If you want to have life everlasting in the wisdom of truth, you must understand the way people are and bring one unique teaching to the faith of mankind.

The Lord will send *one* holy religion that *all* people will come to believe in. No matter which region of the world you come from, mankind will come to understand that worshipping the Lord your God with all your soul and all your heart is the first commandment, and the second one is to treat your brother how you want to be treated by believing that any man born in this world should be respected as a person—not by the will of religion and not by the will of the people who think that they are better than them. You must love your brother as yourself according to the understanding that we are all equal in the sight of the Almighty God.

Understand the power of the one unique religion, the holy religion of the Lord, that brings us to the power of true wisdom. We are all created with the power to understand the truth and to love your brother as yourself. Love the Lord your God with all your power to understand the wedding feast of intelligence between the glory of right and wrong. Then the Lord will make you see right over wrong with His great wisdom and the greatest power of all to understand the glory of human intelligence.

There is no religion anywhere on Earth, including Catholicism, Christianity, Muslim, or any other man-made religion, that can be more powerful than you when you understand the true God in your heart of loving one another in all that we are. Inside each one of us lives the soul of His understanding so we can learn the truth on the side of the Almighty God in order to *love* and *serve* the children of all nations. This is where we come to understand that the teaching of the Lord is *unique* from all the religions of the earth.

Now we go to "Jesus Heals an Official's Son." You must translate this into *spiritual wisdom* so you can come to understand the Scriptures. Then you will know the Supreme God of Heaven in your soul in the feelings of human intelligence. When you love the Lord your God with all your soul, you will receive the birth on the spiritual side of wisdom. You will come to understand that there is no man in any religion that can look down at anybody anywhere like he's more evil than they are.

Do not look at *any* other people to be more evil than you. Do not destroy the soul of others by thinking that you are good and everybody else is evil. Everyone is created just like you—a little weak in the mind and a little weak in the spirit. *No man can control himself perfectly.* When they try to control themselves perfectly, they make more of a mess in reality than you can ever imagine because man was not meant to be perfect in the way that the mind thinks is perfect. Try to be perfect in the way of the spirit and understand how common sense can heal the son of a Roman soldier. You must understand that in common sense, there is no one who is better than another. We are all in the same value because we have all been born as men in the same value.

You are *forbidden* to destroy another person because you think he's worse than you, and you are not allowed to hurt him by telling him that he is a piece of garbage. You're not allowed to say anything like that to another person because they were created by the Lord just like you were, and the Lord did not create anyone from garbage. All people have inside them the *soul that was created by God.* He created man according to the spirit of His own value, and He sent them into the world as His children. All the children of God are the children of intelligence. If a person skips some part of the truth and commits something evil, it is because society created them to be twisted by what society thought to be true.

God is the truth, and He has placed the truth in every human being's *heart*. Each one of us is a son of the truth. Even though we may have failed with the truth many, many times, we are still a child of the truth. Every one of us was created with the truth, and we all hope to live in the truth. No man ever asks from the day of his birth to be a criminal, and no man ever asks to be on the side of evil in front of others. We all grew up to understand what evil was, and even though you see evil in others, you cannot judge them based on the understanding of your own law. Try to love your brother as yourself because sometimes you will be on the opposite side of the truth as well.

We were all sold into slavery and became slaves to the way society thinks. Try to understand that society could be very wrong. Try to live by your own power *inside* of yourself. Worship the common sense of the Lord, and you will be judged by the Lord and not by society. If you listen to society, they will judge you and make you imperfect, but if you listen to the Lord, He will be the one to judge you based upon *truth*.

Next, we go to "The Healing at the Pool." When you see someone with physical problems, you feel bad for them because it's only natural to feel bad for those who don't have all that they need to live a good life on earth and to be free from all the diseases of the earth. But it is very important to understand the purpose of the common sense of intelligence once you translate that common sense into a spiritual value. When you do translate things into spiritual value, you learn that there are people who are blind in spirit—their spirit doesn't see anything in truth, common sense, or reality. You also have the people who are paralyzed in spirit. Come to understand the healing pool of the water of life that comes into your soul to form what is real and what is not real.

Understand the power of reality so you can understand this parable, not in the physical way but in the spiritual way. When a person is blind in spirit, he cannot see and understand things like the parables in the New Testament or the Pharisee of the Old Testament. If you let your mind lead your spirit, your mind will blind you from the truth, where you cannot see spiritual understanding in the way of truth. And when you're paralyzed, you cannot move in spirit inside yourself. Come to the pool that contains the water of life, where you can make yourself a better person by transferring all that exists in physical needs into spiritual needs. Then you will come to understand the power of common sense inside you, where the road of life will come to be your salvation.

When you see someone without wisdom, you have to give it to them if you have it. If you don't understand true wisdom, you don't have it, and you cannot give it to them. *None* of the false prophets of organized religion understand true wisdom, yet they give their false understanding of the Word of God to people every day. Spiritual value is *so important* in the understanding of the heavens and the earth. When a person tells you something that is true in spirit, you think that they are stupid and they do not understand the power of spiritual value. But when somebody tells you something that is against the Word of the Lord, you believe it right away. You don't want to hear the truth because you don't understand it. You just choose to believe what makes sense to your little locust mind, but you don't realize that putting your mind in front of your spirit will paralyze you. If you are paralyzed, it means your nerves and your muscles don't work in spiritual value, and you cannot do anything that is truly good for yourself or for another person.

I have written this book to bring the power to understand and the power to feel inside the human spirit to mankind. This is the same understanding that I have inside me, and the purpose of my book is to make the spiritual power inside mankind work to heal them from their blindness, deafness, and from being paralyzed in spirit. To bring healing to mankind is to explain the way life truly works, and the way the human spirit works inside of a human being. To bring the light of God into a human being is to give him life.

Now we come to understand life through the son of God—this means life through *common sense.* The transformation of the Scriptures is to understand how God works. God is a spiritual God, not a *god of flesh* by any means. But He created the flesh in the understanding of the value of your physical side. The laws that Moses brought to mankind are not the same laws that you have learned to understand from man-made religion. Loving God means loving only *one* God and *not* Jesus in front of Him. God is not the shape and the value of a man, and He does not exist in the image of a man.

Everything changes when you come to spiritual value. You do not live in the same place that you used to live in the old heaven. The New Jerusalem comes with the new way of understanding life, which is written to understand life itself in spiritual value. Mankind has changed the son of God away from common sense. But true common sense must be without an image of anyone. I write this book with the wisdom of common sense because I want you to understand the son of God with the power that God is spirit and spirit alone. Then, you have to understand the angel of reality, the Holy Spirit, so you can come to understand that in God, there are three powers: truth, common sense, and reality. In the new understanding of spirit, we understand that the father is the truth, the son of God is common sense, and the Holy Spirit is reality.

You must practice the understanding of true wisdom through the birth of the son, which is common sense. If you are born of common sense, you are born of the reality that God is the power of truth that has to come to reality to make sense in the value of the spirit. If you take the image of a man and you try to fit that image in front of God, you are going to make a lot of mistakes because God is not flesh. You won't be able to understand anything in the Scriptures. There are so few people that have understood the Scriptures in full spiritual value. The ones who have know that God is the truth, common sense, and reality. And none of these are physical teachings. They are spiritual teachings.

In real spiritual value, truth, common sense, and reality are *verbs*, not *nouns*. You can only understand these in the value of spiritual intelligence. You cannot change the Lord into some kind of a physical God, you cannot understand common sense outside the verbs of your own feelings, and you cannot change spiritual reality into some kind of physical reality. You have to understand these with your spirit. That is where they have always lived, and that is where they will remain forever and ever in the teaching of life in real value.

Next, we go to "Testimonies About Jesus." Jesus came into the world to bring the true teaching of common sense. He spoke about true spiritual wisdom, but almost nobody has understood what he said because they twisted everything around in their little locust minds. Try to understand that the Lord has hidden the truth in the parables. This is so the people who work for the evil spirit could not understand, for example, if a blind man tells you that he can see, or a deaf man tells you he can hear, or a paralyzed man tells you that he can walk. They tell you that they can do everything that anyone else can do, but when you see them try to do it, you realize that they do not know what they are talking about. They think God can be seen with their physical eyes and can be heard with their physical ears. Because they have placed their mind above their spirit, they have failed to walk in the way of the Lord.

What I am doing here is trying to explain to you how life works in spiritual wisdom as well as in the physical world. The false prophets of organized religion have a false knowledge of the Scriptures and cannot see on the other side where the truth lives. For the past two thousand years, they have been proving their ignorance because the whole world is crippled by these false teachings. Mankind never will be able to understand the spiritual part of the Scriptures until they turn away from these people and learn to understand from the Almighty God the great power of His words and deeds. Understand that you have been crippled just like the Good Samaritan was beaten down to the ground by robbers.

When you come to the common sense of intelligence, see the way the Scriptures have been written, and see all the predictions of the Old Testament coming true in the understanding of the New Testament, you *will* see the way the world works. You will begin to understand the way life is and the way that it will always be. Whatever was written in the Scriptures will come to be the *truth* that God has planned for the world. You will come to understand the glory and the power of intelligence.

Now we go to "Jesus Feeds the Five Thousand"—this is the understanding of the five loaves of bread and the two fish. The five loaves of bread are the first five books of the Old Testament. You can spiritually teach and spiritually feed as many people as you want with the first five loaves of bread from the Old Testament. And you'll never run out of bread because the teaching of the Lord is to understand the Scriptures. The two fish represent the Old and the New Testaments. You can feed the whole world over and over, and you will never run out of food. There will always be food for you to understand the true word of the Lord.

Understand the way you eat in spirit, and understand well the food of the spirit. Your body needs physical food, and you need the food of the spirit to survive in the understanding of the word of God. The whole world is hungry and starving for the truth because no truth has been spoken for the last two thousand years. Man has lived in the desert for these two thousand years and still doesn't understand how to worship God. The whole world has fallen into stupidity and ignorance where they believe that they can worship any god they feel like and call any man *God* in front of the Lord your God. The Catholic Church is one of the leaders in the world of stupidity because they worship saints in front of the Lord, and they have forgotten the laws of the Lord our God. The first law is to worship God with all your heart and with all your soul. The next law is to love your brother as yourself. People have forgotten to love the Lord first. You love God first because God created us. Second, you love your brother as yourself. This means treating people the way you would want them to treat you.

You must come to love *everything* that God has created. Loving people who don't like you is also the creation of the Lord. People are so mean and cruel to each other. They honestly believe that a person who doesn't think and do the same things like they do are a piece of garbage. But God did not create garbage. *Society* creates garbage. Understand that God did not create the criminal. Society created the criminal because the *heart* of society is so cruel and so quick to condemn people. Next thing you know, society creates criminals with their tongue. They put people down, and they cannot understand why these people are not as good as they are.

God created you to be who you are, and He created others to be who they are. A crime in the way of mankind and a crime in the way of heaven are two different things. God punishes society by sending criminals inside their little locust minds, and they deserve every bit of those criminals. These people are no worse than anyone, but the heart of mankind persecutes them and makes them unhappy. Before you know it, you have a whole bunch of criminals in society because *society* has created them. And then you wonder why people are so evil, and you wonder why God let it happen. You think that God is not doing his job, but God has already done his job by creating people in his own image. It is society that is to blame for all the stupidity that the world is living in now.

You are supposed to be a *person of love*. You are supposed to love your brother as yourself and understand that people are not all the same. If you don't treat people decently, they will be affected by that. You have to learn to respect people in the same way that you worship the Lord your God with respect. Try to love people. If you don't do this, you are part of the creation of evil. And if you don't respect your brother as you respect yourself, you have created the world against you. The world was meant to be a *good world*, but you have messed that up because you didn't bother to understand the people who has not been respected by society.

You have to learn to respect your fellow man. You cannot call a man a piece of garbage. You cannot call a man evil or stupid. You are *not allowed* to do that. You must respect people even though that person may have dirty clothes or faults or they are just being themselves. You must respect all human beings because every one of us was created with a *holy heart*. At the end, the Lord will create a new world of a new heart where people will come to understand the purpose of that new heart. And those with a new heart will come to be fed with what is written in both the Old Testament and the New Testament. God will create a new *religion of the heart* that is not part of any organized religion. This will be a new religion that will confirm the values of all mankind in a new understanding where people will be respected for all that they do.

Next, we go to "Jesus Walks on the Water." Change the meaning of this parable from physical words into common sense. Water means reality in spiritual terms, and as we already discussed, Jesus represents common sense. Therefore, in this parable, common sense walks on reality in spiritual understanding. You must come to understand that the Lord your God has created reality, and reality was with the Father from the very beginning, just like common sense. God created everything in common sense and reality. That is something that the animal does not understand. He did not give reality and common sense to the other species of the world, but he gave it to mankind, where a human being can create for himself true wisdom in common sense and reality.

God gave you reality, and you must understand things in reality. Otherwise, you will be fooled by the way man thinks and believes. Next thing you know, you will want to start believing in the same false beliefs as organized religion. The world does not believe in reality when they read the New Testament. They think that a man really physically walked on water, and they believe in this false miracle as a way to escape reality. But if you try to escape reality into the world of make-believe, then you will understand everything in the world of make-believe. The Lord can make you believe anything you want to believe when you step outside of the truth, common sense, and reality.

The truth of life is meant to be in reality, but if you try to understand miracles as God's way of doing things, then you don't understand God at all because you are walking in the world of make-believe. The false prophet tried to prove to you that they can do anything that Jesus did because in order for you to believe them, you have to jump outside common sense and reality. These false prophets tried to prove to you that they have the power of God inside of themselves. That is a big lie that tries to fool the human race. And the human race is very easy to fool because they come from thousands of years of believing in the world of make-believe. So be careful what you believe in.

Do not believe in these people who try to tell you that they have special powers because the only special power that these people actually have is the power to fool you into believing in falsehood. Try to go to the human spirit here, and try to understand that it was meant to be that people will turn to the world of make-believe. *Believe in the real world and accept the real world.* You will be much better off if you believe in the Lord your God and observe his laws. Then you can travel in the *real* world. You may think that you can be Superman, but that is just not true no matter how much you try to believe in these false miracles. Believe in the *real miracle,* which is that *common sense walks on reality.*

Now we go to "Jesus, the Bread of Life." Many people will fall for the world of make-believe, but the Kingdom of God is *not* for people who believe in the world of make-believe. It is made for the people who believe in the reality of common sense because common sense is His son. Understand that the world was created for people to think straight and have a pure heart. In order to have a pure heart, you must come to understand that God did not create you to be physically perfect. You will fall for the sins of mankind if you don't listen to your spiritual self to understand the Lord your God in your heart. You will be introduced by the false prophet to believe in the world of make-believe.

The man Jesus is *not* the bread of life. You must translate this teaching where common sense is the bread of life, not a physical man. This is because common sense is where you get your information from the Lord who lives inside you. Common sense is a living spirit inside of you that gives you the information you need to enter the real world so you can believe only in the Lord that belongs to the real world of common sense and reality. If you believe that in worshipping a physical man as common sense, then it's impossible for you to enter the Kingdom of God because the Kingdom of God was not made for people who believe in false teachings.

The bread of life is the body of common sense, and the truth is God, the father of intelligence. Try to get that straight so you can understand the Kingdom of God and the way it works so you will not be fooled by the false prophet. The false prophet has a goal to make a lot of money, and they will do anything to get you to follow them into their world of fantasy. And if you believe in the fantasy world and all these false miracles, then they got you coming and going. Next thing you know, you believe that and you act according to what they say. You are fed by the lies of stupidity and total ignorance so they can make a lot of money. You will feed them with your money, and that's all they want. They have no true spiritual power or wisdom, neither has God given them any real honor or glory. They cannot save your soul because they have no power to do so. And you're stupid enough to praise them. Remember that *the truth is God.* And truth, along with the body of common sense and reality, is the bread of life.

Next, we come to "Many Disciples Desert Jesus." The truth is not meant for everybody to believe. That is why on one side, we have heavenly knowledge, and on the other side, we have the fire of hell. The fire of hell is not a fire that you going to sit in for the rest of eternity. That is the ignorant understanding of hell. The fire of hell is something that you understand that is not true. And when you understand what is not true, you live in some kind of fire where you get burned by the stupidity and the ignorance of falsehood. On the other hand, heaven is a knowledge of reality and common sense. We have to choose in our own soul which side we want to understand. If you are going to go and fool yourself with the false prophet, think they are Superman, and that they have something that comes from heaven, then think again.

Both truth and lies exist inside your heart. You have to choose between truth and lies so you can come to understand what makes sense to you. If the lies of the world make sense to you, then you go with those lies. But if you want to learn the real way that life was created to be, then go toward the truth. You must come to understand that the disciple of common sense is a person who lives within the reality of common sense and truth and cannot be fooled by the false prophet. Many people become disciples of common sense because they like what they initially hear. But most of these people will desert that same common sense when it becomes clear that sacrifices and hard work must be done to understand the truth of life. This is exactly why many are called but few are chosen, and this is also why no one can come to common sense unless the truth has enabled them to do so.

Next, we come to "Jesus Goes to the Festival of Tabernacles." This is the understanding that the laws were written by the Lord and given to Moses on Mount Sinai. Understand that the tabernacle is how you carry these laws inside you. First, you have to understand the laws that God gave to Moses. There are so few people in the world who understand these laws because everybody has twisted those laws into something physical. The physical understanding of these laws has no real power in truth. The spiritual part of yourself is the law that Moses brought down from Mount Sinai to the heart of mankind. These laws have to be observed in spiritual value. So when the law says "Do not worship any god of any kind before the Lord your God," He means that in spirit. When you go to church and you bow down to saints, popes, statues, etc., you are thinking of an image of someone and creating for yourself your own god. *The true laws of God do not work like that.* You must observe the laws of God in spirit, inside you where no one sees it. It's a little box inside your soul that has a lid on it and is covered in the understanding of the Lord's Word. *You must practice the Laws of God in spirit.*

If somebody tells you to come and worship their god in their church, don't do it because you carry the laws of the Covenant of the Lord *inside* your soul. You don't have to prove to anyone that you're right or that you're better than anybody else. Just believe in the one true God of the Creation. Follow the law in your own heart and only worship *one God.* You are not supposed to change whom you worship every time you turn around. You are supposed to worship *one God only.* Do not worship any other man, including Jesus of Nazareth. You cannot change gods in the middle of the stream, and you cannot change the law to your liking. You have to learn to love the Lord your God, the one who *created* you.

The other laws are just as important. You must love your brother as yourself, and you must learn and follow all the other commandments that tell you how to worship the Lord your God. When the Lord tells you to worship the laws of the Sabbath or when He tells you not to take the name of the Lord in vain, He means just that. Don't use the Scriptures for your own benefit. Don't steal anything in spiritual value from anyone. Don't let people believe what they want to believe, and do not commit adultery. This means don't have a spiritual relationship with any teaching outside of the true laws of

God. The Lord will punish you for all these things. Don't lie when it comes to the Scriptures. You have to understand that the Scriptures are very important, and you must respect the Covenant of the Lord. The worst thing you could possibly do is to teach people to worship a false god because you're responsible for that great sin.

Whoever teaches something in the image of a man breaks all the commandments of the Lord because all the commandments are affiliated with the Lord. Take all these laws, understand them in truth, and place them inside your soul. Hold them there, in your heart, until you die and your flesh goes into the ground, and the Lord will provide for your life everlasting, just like he promised. I'm not asking you here to go crazy with your mind and soul. Just believe in the Laws of the Almighty God. You don't have to prove it to anyone. Just live by the laws of the Lord and practice them in your spirit. It is as simple as that. But if you want to be sophisticated and say you love Jesus and you love this false teaching and you love that false god, that is entirely up to you. What I give you here is *exactly* what is written in the scriptures: the truth about how to worship the one true God.

Now we go to "Jesus Teaches at the Festival." To understand the teaching of Jesus, you must understand that worshipping God is simple. It's not something that religion has made up where you have to go to church every week or you have to recite the rosary like the Catholics believe. You don't have to say and do all the dumb things that are part of organized religion that make no sense whatsoever. Just walk on the earth as a simple person, and try to understand the Kingdom of God in your soul. Make the Kingdom of God your kingdom, and understand that the Kingdom of God is the value of your soul. Don't try to make yourself to be better than what you are in front of everyone. *Never* use any title of any kind to prove that you are better than anyone else.

The Kingdom of God is inside you. Do not try to show that you are better than others by wearing a big cross around your neck to prove that you love God because *that is not the way to do it.* Don't even let anybody think that you love the spirit that is inside you. Just love that spirit that gives you all the information you need about *both* your physical part and your spiritual part, and you will live in the freedom of your own soul. No one will be able to tell you this is a sin or that is a sin—you will know inside your soul what is wrong, and you will know what is right. You will be as simple as you can be, and you will come to the Lord with the simplicity to understand the Lord God of Heaven.

Live by the wisdom of your *tabernacle*—the little box of laws that is within you. Then if somebody tells you to worship the pope, a rabbi, a minister, or any other human, you will tell them that the Lord forbids us from worshipping any mortal man. When you find the wisdom of truth inside your soul, you will be the happiest person on earth. The great power of the Lord's true understanding is Simeon, the son of Jacob, in your heart. When you understand the power of Simeon, you will know what it means to understand and be true to the Lord. Once you understand the Scriptures, there's nothing in this world that can ever replace that. There is no money, no value, no business, or anything that your physical body can bring that can penetrate the power of happiness in your soul any better than *having the understanding of the Word of God.*

Why is it called a *festival*? Because it is a *celebration*. In this case, it is a *spiritual celebration*. The power to understand the Word of God is a festival because that's the thing that brings you *happiness*. It is a *festival of knowledge* that the world calls *heaven*. Everything is knowledge that you bring inside yourself to prepare you for the feast of the great power of *true wisdom*. You have to clear your soul and your mind of all that you have learned in the past, and you have to start reading the Bible like it is the first time you ever read it. The power of starting over again is where the truth will come. Once you bring your heart to be pure and stop believing in anything that you have heard that is false, you will be part of the kingdom of intelligence that lives inside you in the festival of value that you never had before.

Heaven is *not* a place like organized religion believes in. When you come to the festival, the food is so good that you try to fill yourself up with the Creation of the Lord in your natural feelings. Your natural feelings do not condemn you from having sex or doing any of the things that religion has condemned you for. You have to follow the laws of the Lord. Don't take anything from anyone; don't try to hurt anyone. Worship the Lord, and He will bless you greatly. You will come to be part of the festival of intelligence where you can eat all that you want in the truth, and the truth will set you free from all the stupidity and the ignorance that was preached to you before. Listen to the Word of the Lord, and he will bless you greatly. Turn yourself toward the Lord, and you will have great value. When Jesus is talking, it is your own soul talking, and if you understand this, you will be in the festival with all the food you can eat in spiritual understanding. That's what heaven is. It is not a place that you go after you die. It's a place of knowledge inside you where you will be able to understand everything that was written in the Scriptures. It will not be somebody that tells you what to believe. It is going to be your own soul that is going to teach you how to handle yourself. You will learn to pray to the Lord—not in the fashion of organized religion, but it will be a new way to pray to the Lord your God, and you will be able to understand the great power of the religion of the Lord.

Next, we go to the "Validity of Jesus's Testimony." Understand that common sense is the son of God. Come to understand the glory of intelligence that was meant to be for all men. When you speak in the name of common sense, you have to speak with the understanding that God is the truth, and no one can replace the Lord your God. Understanding the word of the Lord means understanding *everything* that comes out of the mouth of the Lord. When you begin to understand the Word of the Lord, you do not understand anything that comes out of the mouth of man anymore. You only believe every word that the Lord gives you inside your sanctuary, and you place it there by trying to understand what is valid in the truth through common sense.

Your intelligence was transferred into you from the soul of Adam and from the mind of Eve when your mind and spirit become part of the truth. To be on the side of the Lord, everything that you say must be part of the truth. Loving God is *loving His Creation*, and if you cannot love the Creation of the Lord, you cannot be in His Kingdom. If you think you're better than everyone else, then you don't believe in the Lord your God. Believing in the Lord means you are not allowed to worship gods that do not exist in reality. God created the universe so you would need to understand life for it to have any real value. You also need to come to understand the Lord on the basis of the power of reason. You can see evil, but you don't have to believe in it. When a man speaks in common sense, he has to bring all of common sense out, not just part of it. And you have to believe that God created all life. Even the most evil things that man can ever imagine comes from the Lord. From the death of Abel through the death of Jesus on the cross, every single part of all evil comes from the Lord your God. This may be hard to believe, but once you understand what God is, you will see exactly how life works.

Everybody puts God on one side, and they put Satan on the other side. Then they put a wall in between them. But to understand God, you have to understand that he created the entire world that *includes* both good and evil. If the Lord did not create evil, He could not bring good. Unless you have *both* sides of human understanding, you don't have a complete understanding. You must have the other side in order to understand the first side. For example, think about who killed Jesus. Who put the idea in the high priests' heart to destroy and crucify Jesus? It was done by the *hand of God.* When you speak in the name of common sense, you have to bring *all sides* to the table of value. This means that you must understand both truth and lies, both good and evil. If you take one thing out, you have to take the opposite out. You *cannot* have good without having evil. The Lord created both sides, and you must learn both sides in order to have a *complete understanding.*

Now we come to understand "The Children of Abraham." The children of Abraham are *not* the children of Israel. That is a lie. The truth is that *all people* who are trying to understand the Lord God are the children of Abraham. Remember that the Scriptures are a spiritual teaching, and in order to understand correctly, it has to be in spiritual terms. Abraham is the truth, Isaac is reality, and Jacob is common sense. So when you speak of Abraham, you must look at the power of truth in the understanding of the spirit. Truth will come inside the soul of a person who tries to understand the truth. It may seem complicated, but it really is not complicated at all.

You have to understand that what is true is what makes sense to you. If you cannot find common sense in the truth, you cannot find God and that's all there is to it. If evil makes sense to you, then you believe in something other than the truth. When you look at the truth and you don't understand it, it means that your understanding is not on the side of the Lord. That's why God made an opposite to the truth, which are the lies of the world. When you believe in the lies of the world, you cannot believe in the truth. If you believe in the lies of the false prophet, you believe in something different than the truth and you do not believe in God.

The children of Abraham are the children who believe in the truth that comes from the Father. They know that for any teaching to be true, it has to make common sense and *exist in reality*. But if you go and try to understand outside the common sense of the truth and reality, you just don't believe in God. To be the children of Abraham, you must come to understand that Abraham represents truth like a servant of the Lord. Try to understand that Isaac represents reality, and Jacob is common sense. All three represent the Lord your God to make the language of intelligence.

If you understand this way, then you begin to understand what God is. But many people don't believe in *one* God. That's why you have all these religions that believe in all kinds of false gods. They say they believe in God, then they don't do his will. If you cannot understand truth in the value of common sense and reality, then you do not understand the Lord your God. I don't know how else I can explain it, but that's the way it is. You must come to understand the One True God.

Next, we go to the children of the devil or Satan or whatever you call him—these are people who believe in the lies of the world. This is the way it works: A lie comes out of the mouth of humanity and it travels from one spirit to the next. If you say something that's not true and it makes sense to someone next to you, this creates a belief that has no value in truth. A lie does not really exist because there is nothing in common sense or reality to back it up. The truth exists in common sense and reality. In intelligence, you have reality that tells you that something is real. You can see it and you can feel it and you have common sense to understand the reality of the truth. On the other side, you have a lie that tells you something that doesn't exist. If you believe in the lie, that lie becomes a Satan that is created by the mind, and it does not stand with any common sense or reality.

The people of false religion tell you that you have to believe things that are *totally ridiculous*. Religion is the only subject in the world that can make no sense, but if you don't believe in it, they tell you that you have no faith. This is an example of stupidity. They tell you something that is not true, and you have to believe it. But how can you believe something that doesn't exist in reality? They think that Satan exists as a devil creature that is separate from the Lord, but the truth is that there is no devil. This is a *lie* created by the imagination of the mind, and when you accept a lie, you believe in nothing because a lie is nothing in reality. If you believe in the lie, then you believe in a false god because you are in opposition to the truth.

If you cannot determine between the truth and lies, then you become a person who believes in *nothing* because what you believe is part of the dust of the earth. And you will keep on believing in lies until you lose your own life in spirit. That's why organized religion was forbidden in the Kingdom of Adam and Eve in the Garden of Intelligence. The serpent on the tree tells you to believe in the falsehood of the earth that does not exist in reality. And if you fall for the lies of the world that come from the false prophet, you believe in something that is not part of the truth and does not exist in reality.

If you believe that there is place where you go after you die that you call heaven, or if you believe there is a place called hell where you sit in the lake of fire for all of eternity, those are lies because they don't exist in the way you believe they do. The Bible does mention fire, but fire is the lies of the world. If you believe in the lies of the world, you will be burned by these lies, and you will live forever in these lies. You will believe in them like they were the truth, and you will be fooled by the false prophet who will tell you what is stupid and what makes no sense and you *will* believe it. If you believe Jesus is the physical son of God, then you will not understand the one true God. Understand that Jesus is just a physical man who was sent to the world to bear witness to the truth, but the false prophet made Jesus into a god.

Now we go to *spiritual blindness.* Spiritual blindness is something that no one has been able to understand. The Lord comes in a way that no one sees and no one has ever understood. A blind person is someone who cannot see in spiritual value. A blind person claims to be a good person and looks at everybody else as evil. That is what being blind in the scriptures is. Spiritual blindness makes a man think that what is evil is actually *good.* He does good deeds and tries to follow what he thinks the Scriptures mean. He thinks that heaven is only for him, but he is a blind man because a blind man comes in the value that he thinks of himself before anyone else. He thinks he will enter heaven before anyone else. *That's what blindness really is.*

If a man never claimed to be saved or he never claimed to be on the side of the Lord, you are probably a lot closer to heaven than the one who does not understand God but claims he is saved. When you are blind in spirit, you always place yourself first before anybody else. And when you try to read the Scriptures, you think that the Lord will choose you first. You go to your false church every week trying to understand that the laws of God are on your side, and you cannot understand how people who don't believe like you do can be so evil. When you look at other people's hearts, all you see is evil, but you never stopped to consider that it may be that what you believe is the real evil.

You think that everybody else is evil because you don't see anything in your heart to be evil. When you see evil inside the heart of others but you cannot see evil inside your own heart, that is what makes you blind—you see what is not good in others, but you cannot see the evil in your own heart. If you believe you are a good preacher and you tell people to love Jesus, you have committed an evil crime that you cannot possibly understand because you are blind in your spiritual way of thinking. You see yourself as a good person, and you believe everybody who doesn't think like you should be wiped out of the Kingdom of God. Then you place yourself at the foot of the mountain of God on the side of evil over good.

What you see in another person is what you judge them by, but you do not judge them according to the laws of the one true God. You judge them according to the laws of man, and this is where you have lost your sight in the false understanding of wrong over right. You go to your church on Sunday morning thinking that you have obeyed the laws of God, but the reality is that anyone who believes in any false religion is *against* the laws of God.

Next, we go to "The Good Shepherd and His Sheep." As we come to understand the Kingdom of God, you must understand the suffering and pain of others that you yourself did not go through. Some people will endure the worst of life, while other people never endure the worst that life brings to them. Understand well that whatever life has brought to any one of us must be recognized in the justice of the Lord to bring mankind together in the understanding of *true wisdom*. Some of us are happy in life, while other people endure the worst in life. Try to be *conscious* of other people's suffering because if you have an easy life, you do not know what the rest of the world has endured.

Understand that not everybody has had a good life, and that is why the Lord tells you not to judge others. This is because you have no idea what they went through. You call people criminals, but if you could understand the truth of life, you would know what made them that way. And you will also understand why these people went crazy with the idea that the world was against them. They tried to defend themselves against the world, but the world just did not like them. The world *labeled* them and made them suffer even more. You don't know what makes these people the way they are because you haven't got the book of their life to see what they have gone through in the stupidity of others against them. You look at them, and you call these people evil.

For example, take a man who has raped a woman then brutally killed her. Try to understand what he has gone through to get to that point; understand that you should try to bring them to the values of a good life and try to make them a better person. But instead, you put them in the prison where he will hate to be there, and he will be abused even more without justice that comes from the understanding of what he has done. If you are against these people, they will come against you. And when you stand in front of the tribunal of the Lord, you will see their faces, and you will know that you will be judged accordingly. They will be on the other side of the tribunal, and you will see what you have done. You believed you were a smart man, and your job was to condemn and convict people, so you did your best to convict them.

Now the tribunal of the Lord will come against you and will ask you for an account of what you have done. You have to understand there will be *no one* on your side to help you. Whatever you brought against other people will be brought against you because this was the flock that was supposed to be saved from disaster that the world has imposed on them. You were supposed to protect them, but since you are blind in spirit, you could not see that they were part of your flock and you thought of them as animals. You cannot understand why these people were so evil in your measure of thinking. But the same punishment that you imposed upon them will come to be imposed upon you because the justice of the Lord does not work with the false justice you made up in your mind to be against them. When you saw a man that you believed needed to be persecuted, you thought it was your job to persecute them. But the Lord will bring the same case against you in the court of the Lord your God in the understanding of life.

Now we go to "Dispute Over Whose Children Jesus's Opponents Are." The meaning of the *Jews* mentioned here is *organized religion*. Believe me, there are no more unbelieving people than the people of organized religion. These are the *real unbelievers* because they only believe what saves their butts. They try to preach to the people thinking that if they believe in Jesus, they will be safe. But these people who believe in the false religion of the mind believe only in themselves, and as long as their name is written in their book of the salvation of the Lord, that's all they care about.

There is *no worse thing* for anyone to believe than to think that they're better than everybody else. When you think that you are better than anybody, you don't consider anyone else's feelings, and you don't know why people commit evil crimes of all kinds. They commit these crimes because they live in the house of desolation, but you cannot understand that because you believe in organized religion and you think you are saved. Christians think you should do some kind of a ministry to try to save the world, but if you think you have to waste your life going across the ocean to somewhere in Africa or South America and try to save people from themselves, you got another think coming.

Life is given to each one of us in the same value in our heart. You think because they don't know God, and you believe that you do know God then you're better than they are. But let me tell you that when you're Christian, Catholic, or you belong to any other religion of the earth, that's when you don't know God. You have no idea who God is because you worship outside of true wisdom. You think that anyone who doesn't believe like you do is in danger, but those who are actually in danger of losing their life are the people of organized religion because those are the people that have judged others.

Remember that he who tries to save his life will lose it, and he who tries to lose his life will save it. This is something that most people do not understand. This means that if you try to save your life in the old world of the mind being in charge of the spirit, you will lose because that old world is coming to an end and those who don't change to the new understanding will be left behind. But if you try to reject that old world in favor of the new understanding of truth where your spirit is in charge, you will not be left behind. You will be welcomed into the new heaven. Don't think for one minute that the chosen people of God will be the ones who have the best life on earth. The good life is coming for those who are a part of the Kingdom of God, but who will be part of it—the people who always had a spoonful of soup in their mouth, or the people who went hungry and were persecuted?

Organized religions of all kinds want to tell you that you are *saved* after you sell your soul to them and give them money, but how can you become saved just like that? In order to be saved, you have to go through the great crucifixion of the persecution of the world. If you were persecuted by mankind, the Lord will give you plenty to eat. But if you were not persecuted, you will have to find your own fruit in the justice of the Lord. If you do not understand the Scriptures in truth and you don't do anything to help others who are being persecuted, you cannot enter the Kingdom of God. This is because you never understood this Kingdom, and you don't understand what you need to do to be part of it.

Next, we go to "The Death of Lazarus." We currently have the highest learners that we have ever had in this world, but we have learned almost nothing from the truth. Understand well here the power of the death of a man and how common sense brings you back to life when you begin to understand truth, common sense, and reality. Before now, everybody had lived in darkness for the past two thousand years. Now we are coming to the third day of darkness to understand the power of God in the land of Egypt. The land of Egypt means *organized religion.* Try to understand that Lazarus, the man who died in this story, represents someone who is spiritually dead because he believed outside of the *true* Word of the Lord. The women placed him in the tomb, which means the mind, and through organized religion, they have attempted to seal the spirit off from being able to understand true wisdom. Remember that the mind only understands through loss and gain. That is where it operates. So, if you put your mind *first* in front of your spirit and then you try to understand the Scriptures, you will come up with a spiritual understanding that is based on loss and gain instead of truth, common sense, and reality. And spiritual teachings based on the loss and gain of the mind are the foundation of all organized religions. Can you now see *why* these false man-made religions actually lead you away from the Lord?

But a man who is trapped in the tomb of organized religion is not dead. He still has his common sense, and common sense will bring him back to life. A man who comes back to life can understand that Jesus is common sense and he will now look at life in a different version from what the false prophet has told him. Understand that if you have common sense to lead you, you cannot die because the death of the spirit would be the end of life, and life is everlasting. Jesus is not the son of God—he is just a man who lived two thousand years ago. But in spiritual terms, he represents common sense.

This means that you have to *change* his teachings from the physical understanding of the mind to the common-sense knowledge of truth. Otherwise, you will *never* understand the Scriptures.

The Scriptures were meant to be understood by your common sense and what it means in the power of spiritual wisdom. Jesus raised Lazarus, the man who lived two thousand years ago, from the dead. But this is not the meaning of it. The meaning of it is that a spirit comes back to life on the third day where you come to understand your common sense. You must understand that common sense is inside you. It is not a man outside yourself. It is the reality of your feelings and how it works when you explain something in common sense to another person. The Scriptures were written in a way that people cannot understand them with their mind, but the power is to understand the Scriptures in your own common sense.

Jesus doesn't save you—common sense saves you and brings you back to life in the creation of the Lord. If you believe that Jesus is the physical son of God, then you believe in something that is not true because the real son of God, the common sense of intelligence, is inside you. Lazarus was dead for four days when Jesus brought him back to life and he walked out of the tomb. This means that if you understand the power of common sense, you will come back to life in the understanding of the spirit, and you will have life everlasting. You cannot bring the value of a man of flesh in front of the Lord because if you do, you are breaking the First Commandment of the Lord God.

God created intelligence and placed it inside the human spirit. Mankind must follow the teachings of common sense in order to understand his laws. The New Testament is so powerful, but mankind has not understood it for the past two thousand years. If you do not understand the parables of Jesus, you will be burned by the fierce heat of the sun which, in spiritual terms, means the New Testament. Anyone who has an open mind will come to understand the truth, but the people who come with a stiff neck and do not turn their heads toward the spiritual value of common sense will not be able to enter the Kingdom of God.

A human being who was dead inside the tomb for three days comes back to life. This means that if you worship the Lord in truth and reject the lies of man-made religion, spiritual life will be given to you in intelligence. But if you accept the lies of organized religion, you will be put into the tomb where you will be sealed off from life. You will be placed in the cement vault at the bottom of the earth where there is no life and no little critters to eat your flesh so you can come back to life. Try to understand that this is how life works. At the end of your physical life, your flesh is worthless. It's only food for the little critters to eat. And it is supposed to be this way. The spirit goes to sleep for a time, and then the spirit comes back to life in a new body. But if you trap the spirit inside the dead body in the tomb, life will be taken away from you because the little critters will not be able to eat your flesh. Then your spirit will not be able to leave that body, and your intelligence will be buried with that body where it *cannot* come back to life. That's the understanding of the death of Lazarus, meaning the death of common sense. If you are sealed off from life inside the tomb, you will need an earthquake of some kind that will open the tomb for you. This seems impossible, but what is impossible for man is possible for God.

Let us now go to "Jesus Comforts the Sisters of Lazarus." Understand here that Martha and Mary are two sisters who love Jesus. You have to translate Jesus into common sense in order to understand. The power of the mind is what fools you in the fantasy world. When you come to the two sisters in the Scriptures, you come to two religions in the battle of learning. The two sisters are two different teachings of the mind—they are Catholicism and Christianity. For years, Christianity said that Catholicism is wrong, and the Catholics claimed that Christianity is not perfect enough. But the truth is that everybody who worships a man before the Lord is wrong because you are not allowed to worship a man before the Lord.

You must understand the parables with your spirit in order to bypass Jesus in the flesh and understand the spiritual part of the Scriptures. The Scriptures were written in a way where the truth was hidden, and you have to discover that truth *inside* your soul. That is the *treasure of heaven* that is sitting in the field. You will find the treasure where you find common sense in the reality of common sense come alive inside of you. You could not understand before, but if you believe in this common sense and the reality of truth, you will come to understand. But you have to look for it. It is not something that is given for free like the Christians and the Catholics say. The truth of the matter is that you have to cross over into spiritual understanding in order to understand what was written in the Scriptures.

If you cannot change Martha and Mary into spiritual value, you cannot understand the true religion of the Lord where your mind and spirit must be married in order to understand life in true spiritual value. You have to cross over and open your heart. Your heart is like a parachute—it does not work unless it's *open*. The power to understand is to transfer the religion of the flesh into the religion of the soul. Only then will you come to understand the meaning of the Word of God. If you don't transfer Martha and Mary into the wisdom of common sense, you cannot enter the Kingdom of God.

If you have been a criminal in the past, if you were part of the stupidity of man-made religion, or if you were part of all the worst things in life, *your soul can still be restored*. If you were a person who believed that you were right and everybody else was wrong because you were too proud to be wrong, then you too can enter the Kingdom of God. Understand that this teaching has come into the world, in this book, to give you life. If you don't understand this teaching, you will try to judge the one who brings it. Remember that if you *condemn* the one who brings true wisdom, you will not be able to understand that life is only given to you by the power of the Holy Spirit and the power of common sense. The Lord is the truth, and he controls all power inside you. And if you worship the Lord your God in truth, you must come to understand the Scriptures in common sense and reality and come to be one with the truth in the Kingdom of the Almighty God.

Next, we go to "The Plot to Kill Jesus." Just as it was written two thousand years ago, it will come to be. There will be a plot by the false prophet to destroy the teaching of true wisdom and to bring the teaching of common sense *away* from man's heart. The false prophet claimed that they had the teaching of the Lord, but what was physically done then will be done on this very day when the wood is dry. What happened on earth two thousand years ago will come to happen in spirit. Scripture tells us that there will come to be a battle for the end, and *nothing* will be able to change the work of common sense in the world.

Mankind will come to understand the power of what is evil and what is good, and people will not go into caves to try to find the Lord. This means that people will stop going to church because the new human intelligence will be created inside the heart of mankind, and the stiff-necked people of false, man-made religions of the world will come to understand true intelligence. Anyone who remains on the side of the false prophet will die because of their stiff-necks, and they will not be able to understand the Kingdom of God. Those who refuse to answer to the common sense of intelligence will not be part of the coming of time because the future is meant for common sense to live forever in reality.

If you deny the truth, you will be condemned to death because you *cannot* continue worshipping idols and physical men in front of the Lord. If you cannot turn your head because it's stiff on your shoulders and will not return to the truth, you will *lose your soul.* Many people will lose their souls because they think they already have the meaning of life figured out, but they don't. Whatever happens will be for the reality of the Almighty God and His plan. *No one* who believes in the lies of false religion will enter the Kingdom of God.

God is the eternal light, and this eternal light will come to be inside your soul. You will come to know that it is true because it makes common sense. The only thing the false prophet can think of is how to destroy common sense. But at the end, the *serpent,* meaning the false religion created by the mind of man, will be defeated, and all the followers of that serpent will come to lose their soul. The Lord made this change in life for all men to understand the coming of the Kingdom of Intelligence that comes from common sense where all reality will come to be so, and the prophecy of the Lord will come to be true.

Now we go to "Jesus Anointed at Bethany." This is the place where Lazarus was brought back to life. Everybody thinks this is about the physical resurrection of a man, but you must try to understand the spiritual power of a man dead in the tomb who comes back to life after three days. Lazarus was a man, and he died in flesh. Try to understand that the flesh dies but the *spirit does not die*. You can *revive* the spirit inside a man back to life, but most people don't understand that because of what the false prophet told them to believe in the stupidity and ignorance of the teaching of false religion. We are human, and we only understand as humans. We only understand the physical part of death. What we don't understand is the *spiritual* part of death. We cannot see any further than the physical death of a man.

The spirit can return to life. If you have faith and believe in the Lord your God, then life will be everlasting for you. But you cannot worship God as the image of a man like the people of false religion do. You have to believe in the *real* God of spirit. If you change your heart to a different kind of god, then you believe in the god of your physical mind of flesh. This is a false god. When you believe in something that is not spiritual about the Lord, you don't understand what God is. God is the spirit that gives you life in the understanding of intelligence. If you live only like an animal, you live only for the pleasure of living. You will feel all the pain and the sacrifice with no value. But understanding the spiritual part of life will bring you back to life.

When you understand the *one true God* that has created you, you come up a step from the animal being to the value of common sense that is part of the reality of the creation of the Almighty God. In God's word, you have the value to place yourself above the animal in common sense and reality. This is something that the animal does not have. There is no common sense to know reality inside the head of an ox or a donkey in the value of their understanding. They live only with what they have learned in their instincts, and they are too stubborn to change what they're looking for. Common sense and reality *is* the way to understand the true Word of God.

Next, we go to "Jesus Comes to Jerusalem as King." He was sitting on the white donkey, and he entered Jerusalem to transfer the land from the physical to the spiritual value. All the stiff-necked people of Christianity, Catholicism, and all organized religions will try to enter the New Jerusalem sitting on their white donkey. When you talk about a white donkey, you talk about people who think they are good and also people that are very stubborn with their beliefs. They believe in their Jesus with all their soul and all that they understand, and they don't want to change. These are just like the people who lived in the time of Jesus two thousand years ago. They can praise a physical man all they want and put palms on the road to Jerusalem without thinking for one minute that they are worshipping a false god with their stiff neck belief in the falsehood of worshipping Jesus.

Jesus was chosen by God as a servant, and he was also chosen to *fool* the human race. Mankind always fools themselves with what they think with their little minds, and they never really understand that they can read the scroll on both sides—one side being the *physical* understanding of the mind, and the other side being the *spiritual* understanding. One side of the scroll of the Scriptures tells people to worship Jesus, and the other side tells them not to worship a false god in front of the Lord God. But most people only read the Scriptures from the side of the mind. Unless you read the laws of God in the spiritual power, you cannot understand what they mean. Many people are called, but so few are elected to understand the power of the Lord.

God has made it *impossible* for the people who do not have a pure heart to understand his Kingdom. When you don't have a pure heart, you live in *total ignorance and stupidity* because your mind is not flexible to understand both sides of the Scriptures—you only can understand one side. To them, Jesus is a man whom they can see and understand with their minds, but they cannot understand his spiritual teachings of common sense. They did not understand that he came to separate the goats and the sheep by putting the sheep on one side and the goats on the other side.

There are always going to be people who cannot understand because they have stiff necks and they don't turn their heads to understand the coming of time where the Lord has placed his value into humanity. God said let there be light, and there was light. The light that he was talking about was not the light that the false prophet brought into it. *It is the light of the truth of the Scriptures.* But the false prophet could not understand what that means *in truth* for the power of the elimination of wrong. There will be a coming of right that stands on one side of the scroll, but this side cannot be understood because the people with stiff necks cannot turn their heads to understand the great power of the New Jerusalem, where everything will be revealed in the power of reality for all mankind to see.

Where does this value come from, and why would God trick the people who trick themselves? The ones who claim to be first are part of the Seven Days of the Creation when God must come to judge mankind on the great Sabbath where all of mankind has to make a choice and decide for themselves which side of the Scriptures they are going to be on. The Lord will bless the sheep and curse the goats for being against the truth itself. The truth stands in common sense and reality for human understanding.

Now we come to "Jesus Predicts His Death." Remember that this is the *death of common sense*. When you understand the Scriptures by putting your spirit in *front* of your mind, you come to know the meaning of the first being last and the last being first. If you live your life trying to be worshipped by other people, or you put yourself above others in importance in the physical world of loss and gain, you cannot understand the true spiritual teaching of the Lord. This is because you have put the importance of the physical world ahead of your spirit. And when you dedicate your life to only improving yourself in the world of the mind, you will be last in the world of the spirit because your spirit cannot understand much of anything. The same goes for those who dedicate their life to spiritual wisdom. They start to abandon the things that the mind considers important such as fashion, being popular or important, physical wealth, etc. Thus, they are last in the kingdom of man.

The Scriptures are a spiritual teaching, meant to be understood and lived by the spirit. Mankind has not developed their spiritual understanding, so men do not recognize any spiritual teaching when it comes to them. They have only developed their wisdom in life based on the loss and gain of the mind, and that is why the *true spir-*

itual teaching must come first through the mind, as it is the only side that mankind currently uses to understand anything in life. This was true in the time of Jesus, and it is just as true today. Once we understand the physical teaching, we are supposed to then raise that teaching up to the level of the spirit. That happens by first recognizing that spiritual understanding is more important and, therefore, above the understanding of the mind. Once you have done that, now you can develop the power of your spirit. Then you can learn the laws of God in spiritual terms as it was meant to be.

For example, let's use the parable of the fig tree. Jesus, who represents common sense, is telling us here that when we see the leaves start to form on the fig tree, we know that summer is coming. The common sense of the mind is reminding us of how the process works in our minds. We physically see something, and we logically can predict what is likely to come after. This is something we are no strangers to. But then Jesus says it is the same way with the Kingdom of Heaven. This is the part that we are strangers to. For two thousand years, we have not developed our spiritual common sense. We did not realize that we are supposed to take the same common sense that we use to understand things with the mind and use it to understand spiritual teachings as well. Therefore, when we see things in spiritual terms, we can predict what is likely to spiritually happen next.

The death of Jesus is the death of common sense. We know that common sense has died, just as Jesus predicted it would, because we can see that man does not use common sense to understand spirituality. They form all kinds of organized religions from the wisdom of the *mind*. Each one is somehow different from the rest, but *absolutely none* of these man-made religions have been built on a foundation of spiritual common sense.

The Lord has caused spiritual common sense to die so that mankind can experience life in which it doesn't exist. And this was foretold to us by Jesus. But again, it wasn't only a man predicting his physical death. Remember, we have to raise these physical teachings to the level of the spirit. The lesson here is that spiritual common sense was going to *purposely be taken away* from mankind by the Lord. But we are told that common sense would return from being dead on the third day. And when it does, we will finally know the *true power* of using common sense to understand the Scriptures. Mankind had to go without it because that is the only way the stubborn and ignorant people of the mind would come to appreciate it.

Now we go to "Jesus Predicts His Betrayal." This is common sense telling us that someone is going to spiritually betray him. How is common sense spiritually betrayed? By helping it become captured by the enemy, and the enemy of common sense is *ignorance*. Judas betrayed Jesus for thirty pieces of silver. When you try to figure out who got paid to betray common sense into getting captured by ignorance, the only answer is *the false prophet of organized religion*. Many, many people pay these false prophets every week when they go to these false churches and what they get in return is a bunch of *lies*. They are told by these preachers to worship Jesus, to pray to him, to eat the communion wafer so you can have him inside you, and all sorts of lies about Jesus. Now the understanding of Jesus is in the hands of the enemy, which is ignorance, because religion is the first place people go to find him. And false religion has *killed* the true understanding of common sense. To anyone who looks for the reason why mankind seems to be so screwed up, I say look no further than *organized religion*.

Next, we come to "Jesus Predicts Peter's Denial." Understand well the prediction of Jesus. This means common sense predicts that he will be betrayed by the people who say yes to him. Understand that common sense is the son of God. You can use common sense to understand the Laws of God, but you absolutely cannot worship Jesus in front of the Lord. I keep on saying that because *it's so important*. You must understand that there's nothing in this world more important than *not* to worship the image of a man because worshipping the image is the *denial* of those who say yes to God.

Just saying yes to God is *not* worshipping him. Worshipping God is understanding how to worship Him. If you take the advice of the false prophet and worship Jesus, you are going to deny the Lord God Himself. Do you *see* where the denial is now? It is when you're supposed to work for the Lord, and then you commit adultery by worshipping Jesus in front of him. Neither you nor anyone in the world is allowed to worship anyone but the Lord God. Worshipping the Lord means something much more important than just bowing down to him. When you worship God, you have to understand that you must learn his laws *first*. Only then can you *truly* worship him because that's the way it is with the spirit.

Try to understand and love people because people are a Creation of the Lord. Worshipping God is really worshipping His Creation. That means all the people who are around you who are not good-looking, are fat, or have physical and mental problems. Disrespecting people who don't look like you is not worshipping God. Accepting the Lord's Creation is how you worship God. You must love all human beings no matter how ignorant they may be. You have to love them as they are, and you cannot consider yourself to be better than them because if you do, you're not in the truth. Everybody has faults, and if you cannot accept people with their faults, how can you love the Lord's Creation?

The Lord has created mankind according to his ability. He did not create all human beings to be perfect. In any crop, you have some rotten fruit. Don't think of God as a big magician who can make everything perfect for you. If you think that you are made perfect and that everybody should be perfect like you, that's *arrogance*, and that will set you *apart* from the Lord's chosen people. Then you become a goat in the war of wisdom and you fight against the sheep, but you will not win the Kingdom of God *unless* you turn your heart to the Creation of the Lord and love life the way he has created it to be.

You cannot judge anyone, because that is not allowed by heaven. You have to make inside yourself a picture of true justice that is *fair for all mankind*. If you don't put yourself in the situation of the Creation as it was created to be, you *cannot understand* the Kingdom of God because you have placed yourself too high above everybody else. The Kingdom of God will *not* accept you because you are not part of the Creation of the Lord. The crucifixion of Jesus is to show you that even the best man on earth can be crucified and reestablished in the land of the *spiritually perfect*. If you are going to be perfect in spirit, you must be physically imperfect in order to enter the Kingdom of God.

The Lord is asking you to love your neighbor as yourself and to love Him and His Creation as is. You cannot create a new creation on your own, and you cannot do better than what the Lord has done. So accept the truth and the truth will set you free. But if you do not accept the truth and you place God too high for you to understand, then you will think of yourself as being above the Lord, and that arrogance will take you out of the Kingdom of God. Remember that the serpent was arrogant, and he fed the apple to Adam. If you do that, you will have no place in the paradise of intelligence because you will think the crop is too imperfect for you. And if you are perfect in the way that man thinks is perfect, you cannot live in the paradise of intelligence because you made yourself too high for everybody else. The paradise of the Lord is to be simple and to love everyone in the same way you love yourself in the values of justice, fairness, and unity.

Now let us go to "Jesus Comforts His Disciples." Remember that the Scriptures are a spiritual teaching. So while there were *actual physical followers* of Jesus some two thousand years ago, the disciples of Jesus whom you need to learn about in order to gain true wisdom are not physical men but spiritual followers of common sense. Just like all the teachings in the Bible, this one must also be raised up from a physical story that is understood by the mind to a spiritual lesson understood by the spirit. It is of little value to us today that there were twelve men who physically followed Jesus some two thousand years ago. Like all other people on earth during this or any time in history, they are just humans who lived and then died. They are no better or worse than any other person who has ever lived. No human being, including Jesus or anyone else that has ever lived or ever will live that you may believe to be a great person, is in reality any better than the least one of us. And the least one of us is no worse than those we call great people. Physically, we are all equal—different, yes, but *equal.* And because we are all equal, the Lord has forbidden us from worshipping any other human. If you do worship people, you are going *against* the laws of God, and you will be held accountable to the court of the Lord for this and all your spiritual offenses.

It is only when you understand this lesson in spiritual terms that the lives of these disciples contain any meaning that can benefit you. And since Jesus represents common sense, they are, in spirit, the disciples of common sense. Try to understand that all spirits are one spirit. Even though each of us has a spirit inside us, all spirits are part of the great spirit, which is *God.* This means that the lessons we learn from the disciples of common sense are spiritual lessons that each of us can use to understand the Scriptures, for example, when Peter, who was closest to Jesus, denies that he knows him or when Judas betrays him into the hands of those who killed him.

These are not merely physical stories from years ago. These are *real events* that can and do happen inside the spirit of mankind. The only way to avoid falling into these traps is to understand how they work and make it your goal to not deny common sense, or betray it into the hands of the enemy. This is why it is *very, very important* to learn the meaning of the Scriptures in your heart so you can follow them. Don't just blindly believe what false organized religion tells you. Ask the Lord for true wisdom, and you will surely receive it.

Next, we come to "Jesus, the Way to the Father." Let's translate that. Common sense is the son of God, and the Father is the truth. That means common sense is the way to the truth. And, in common sense, you are free from all the stupidity of mankind's false ideas about religion. Once you start listening to the Lord God inside your soul, you begin to understand that God is not so high that you cannot reach Him. God is the Father who has created us *with intelligence* so we can reach the standard of common sense. And it is common sense that brings you to the Father. If you don't go through the son of God, which is common sense, you cannot understand the Father. This is because your little mind of a locust keeps you too low to the ground to understand the height of heaven and the knowledge of true common sense that makes sense in the reality of life.

Be simple as the Father is simple, and get out of that arrogance that makes you think that you stand higher on a pedestal of stupidity where you think way ahead of yourself to be the one who was chosen for the Kingdom of God. The Kingdom of God is created to be simple and honest in our heart by the understanding of the height of heaven. It is a knowledge so simple that even the smallest of God's children who are simple and honest with themselves can understand the Kingdom of God. But religion came and raised the human mind to believe that in order to get to heaven, you have to be in ignorance and sophistication.

Many souls have lost themselves by trying to be perfect in the way the mind thinks, when it is the *simplicity of the heart* that brings you to the Father. God has created you to be simple in His justice and to make you a child of the reality that the Lord has created to put inside mankind for the rest of eternity. To be *simple* is to be in the Kingdom of God. To be perfect in the way man thinks is perfect is what makes you so imperfect in the way of the simplicity of the Lord. Be simple, and love the Lord your God with all your soul. If you were not a good-looking person in the way man thinks, the Lord will make you perfect in his kingdom. If you're fat in the way man thinks, you will be skinny in the Kingdom of God, and people will love you as you are.

Love the Lord your God when people persecute you and do all kinds of evil against you, because the time is coming for the Kingdom of God to unroll his holy carpet and welcome you in. When you live in common sense, you begin to understand that all your faults are created by God to make you happy in his kingdom. Take all the faults that you have by the Creation of what you are and bless them. Thank the Lord for sending them to you because now you know exactly where you are going and how you want to get there. The Lord has *blessed* you and didn't make you perfectly beautiful in the way that men think, but *he made you perfect in his way*.

The day is coming when the imperfect people will become *perfect* in the way of the Lord. True holiness lives inside the soul of the greatest glory of human intelligence ever known to mankind. Thank the Lord your God *every day*, and let those who persecute you keep going to the degradation of their own disgrace. They created this disgrace for themselves by being inside the serpent of wrongdoing and they are going to be condemned by the spirit of holiness. The tragedy of their soul is sure to be lived. Understand that your common sense is the son, which is the way to the Father. When you live in the son, you live in the Father, and the Father of common sense will treat you to the way of everlasting life of the purity of the heart.

Now we go to "Jesus Promises the Holy Spirit." I want to tell you here that no one has ever understood the Holy Spirit, the angel of reality, that comes inside of you and brings reality to your common sense. *Reality is part of truth, and the truth is God.* You have truth and reality on your side, and then you must go on the side of common sense that makes these things happen inside your soul. To love the Lord your God is to love the truth, common sense, and reality. Loving God is to love the *simple* things in life. Understand that the simple things are what makes you happy. Being simple is thinking simple. It is loving being simple because simplicity taught you what to do to understand the simple God of the Creation. He created you as an animal, and then he poured his beautiful spirit inside of you.

The *great power of wisdom* is to be able to understand the glory of the seven spirits that were placed inside of you by the Lord. The seven spirits of God are: wealth, wisdom, glory, honor, power, strength and praise. Understand well that these seven spirits inside of you, come from the Lord your God. Don't think for one minute that you can come to understand true wisdom by being arrogant in the sophistication of human thinking. These seven spirits belong to those who live in humble and simple deeds, and they can only be accessed by those who are chosen to be part of the Lord's Kingdom. If you want to be part of the Lord's Kingdom, you have to change your heart to a *simple heart* in the understanding of the Scriptures.

You will be simple and humble if you choose to be. But if you choose to keep up the sophistication and arrogance that put you into slavery at the hands of organized religion, you will lose your soul because the crop of the Lord is to be simple and humble. These are the souls that He calls to be part of His Kingdom. Love the Lord God with all your soul so you can receive the Holy Spirit, the angel of reality, and become part of His Kingdom.

Next, we go to "The Vine and the Branches." The Word comes from the Lord. Every branch of truth in your heart is part of the vineyard that bears good fruit. But if you find a branch that doesn't bear good fruit, then you must cut it off. If you don't, the Lord will send something in your life where you will know that it's wrong to not cut off that barren branch. If you do prune that dead branch, you will be able to be perfect like your Father in heaven is perfect in the understanding of the reality of what you are and who you are.

Your soul was created to be a *perfect vine*, but there are always things inside of you that do not work right. You can always find the understanding of the loss and gain of your mind that tricks you into understanding outside the truth. Truth is the feeling you have inside your soul to *bear good fruit*. But you don't always see it that way because of the weakness of the mind—and loss and gain come into your soul from the mind. When you find a loss inside of you that you cannot explain, more than likely you will go with the mind. That is why you have to *separate* the mind and the feelings so you can bear good fruit. Try to understand that true fruit is from the spirit of intelligence given to mankind by the Lord, and the mind is loss and gain. That's the way God has created you. And you have to have the Lord your God, the Father of Heaven, prune your branches so the world will see you as someone that bears good fruit, and you will not fall for the loss and gain of the mind.

Unless your Father in Heaven prunes the branches inside you and gives you feelings to understand *how* to bear good fruit, you will get mixed up between your mind and your spirit. That's why the wedding feast of intelligence does not work and your mind and your spirit do not get along in the glory of intelligence. The Kingdom of the Lord comes in the value that all things are created in reality so you can come and prune your vineyard with the hand of your Father in your holy feelings. Your feelings must come first. When you feel for someone and you look at that person in your feelings, you come to understand your vineyard.

Your vineyard is your understanding, and that is the way you bear good fruit. But if you don't listen to your spirit, you will bear awful fruit, and you will fall for the terrible wine that tastes like vinegar inside your soul. You will feel terrible because you failed to understand the feelings from your vineyard and the grapes that bear good fruit. *Try to understand the way your soul works.* It is like a tree and it has good feelings and also terrible feelings. This is where you come and separate the mind and the spirit. Once you have defeated your loss, you will come to understand the tree that bears good fruit because the tree that bears good fruit is the understanding of the reality of truth, and the truth is God. When you understand that the truth is God, you will not be able to continue your unclean heart where there is no value to claim good fruit.

Now we go to "The World Hates the Disciples." To be a disciple of common sense, you have to be firm in the faith of your feelings because your feelings are what makes you different from the people who don't feel for others. Your feelings make you a disciple of both the truth and common sense because if you don't feel for others, you do not have what it takes to be a person of the Lord. When you are a disciple of the Lord, you have to *understand* your feelings. The animals of the Earth don't have the feelings of intelligence like humans have. When you have no feelings of intelligence, you are just like an animal. Feelings are the *difference* between a disciple of the Lord and an animal.

The world doesn't like people who live by feelings of intelligence because the world is selfish like an animal and cannot change themselves. That makes them the animals of the earth, and that's the way they live. Understand the *great power* to be a disciple of the Lord. Being a disciple of the Lord means that you are *affiliated* with the Lord. He sends feelings that live inside you, and he makes you understand the *values of others.* Doing good to others is part of the true feelings that come from the Lord. In order to love the Lord your God, you have to *listen* to your feelings inside you. If you have no feelings, you are dead just like an animal.

When I say that you are dead like an animal, this means that you have *no feelings* to understand the values of anything else but yourself. God created all humans *equal to each other.* But those who feel they are only equal to themselves have no knowledge of what other people feel in the process of intelligence. If you want to be a disciple of the Lord, you must learn *how* to understand your feelings in the way you are and the way the Lord has created you to be. That's what the glory of intelligence can do for you.

The world of feelings is a different world than the world of the mind because when you enter into the world of feelings, you *gain value* in the understanding and the thinking above that of the animal. Then you cross over to the value of intelligence where you are one with the truth. That means one with the Father, who is truth. Then you can try to do what is right over what is wrong. That's the way it is with all the feelings of a disciple. *Mankind must learn to love inside their feelings.*

Next, we are going to "Understand the Holy Spirit." I talked about the Holy Spirit in a previous part of this book, but you must understand that the Holy Spirit is the spirit of reality. When you enter the spirit of reality, you are going into a different world. You see, the world that you live in now is the *fantasy world* where everything comes through as a fantasy because you don't understand the *truth* about reality. Reality is something that comes from common sense, and both of them come from the truth. The difference is that reality has a purpose to say things that are real and to understand what is real.

To understand the Holy Spirit, you have to understand the value of what is real and what is not real. We live in a world where religion has brought you outside the world of reality with all those false miracles, and so you think that God is a miracle worker because you were told that He is. But that's not what the Lord is in reality. You can pray to the Lord to give you your fantasy world, but that's not what the Lord is about. Part of the Lord is reality, and another part is common sense. So, reality is something that is real against what is fantasy. You must understand the words of the Lord in reality. Understand that reality is the spirit that brings the truth that is not revealed by organized religion. That's why I condemn religion so much. It's the *only subject* out of all human subjects that lead people to create a belief in fantasy, and they tell you it is the *truth*.

If you believe in the false god that is outside reality, then you cannot understand the one true God that lives in reality. The great power of the Lord is that you cannot believe that He will heal you in some magical form. You must understand that you are *not allowed* to step outside of reality because every time you do so, your soul is being destroyed and it becomes harder to *return* to reality. When you start worshipping Jesus like the Christians do, you lose your sense of reality. You begin to think that the magical world that you believe in is real, and you think that this is the faith you must have in God. But it is really the other way around. Once you leave the center of reality to believe in all the superstitions of organized religion, you lose yourself from trying to understand these lies. And the next thing you know, you are so far outside reality that you cannot cross over to the understanding of true wisdom.

Reality gives you the purpose of understanding what is right side up and what is upside down. If you leave the world of reality and believe in the fantasy world of religion where Jesus has saved you and you don't need to know anything to go to heaven, you will not be anywhere near the Kingdom of Heaven. That is a fantasy world, and the false preachers who live in the fantasy world are preaching this to you. You have to look at yourself and ask yourself what is real. Is God real? Yes, it is part of reality to believe in a God of true spiritual value who exists in reality. Try to understand the difference between the fantasy of the mind and the reality of the spirit. Your feelings are real, and when you're talking to God with your feelings, you are *talking directly to him*. But when you're talking to your fantasy god and you try to pray to someone that is not God because you made Jesus a god in front of the Lord, that is a *fantasy* that organized religions have made up.

Now we come to "The Disciples' Grief Will Turn to Joy." We must come to understand the value that comes from the truth. As I told you before, the disciples in the Scriptures are not the disciples of Jesus but the disciples of common sense. When you are a disciple of common sense, you live by common sense and you think for yourself. God does not count people of organized religion among his children because these people don't think for themselves. When you think of what somebody else tells you to think, you are not using your own spirit and your own feelings. That's why the Lord said the world won't like his disciples, and they'll probably do everything they can to make their lives miserable.

You must understand, however, that your pain is *only temporary* and it will change the false value into the value of right over wrong. All the pain that you have now will disappear from your life and the Lord will place great happiness and great joy inside your soul in the value of learning the truth. Once you understand the value of learning the truth itself, you will be full of joy. You will be able to understand the proper way to worship the Lord your God. The joy that the Lord is talking about here is a *joy of feelings* that comes inside you. You will look at life everlasting for yourself and you will know that you have endured the worst of life because of the pain and suffering that the people who didn't receive life have imposed on you. That suffering will turn into joy once you have received the joy of being *who* you are in your natural feelings.

God is the truth, and when you begin to understand that truth, you will realize that everything that was done in the persecution of the children of God was done for *total justice*. You were meant to have your time in the persecution of the world. This means we had to be poor, helpless, made a fool of, and disgraced by humanity. But the Lord will take the people who persecute others out of the world, and the world will become a better place to live in because we can come and understand the glory of human intelligence. *Grief will turn into joy*. That's the key word to understand. You were persecuted in the old world, but you will be welcomed in the new world with open arms. You will come to understand *why* you were persecuted in the old world, and you will have joy in your heart. When you start understanding that, you will have *earned* the victory of heaven, and you will see all the people who persecuted you to be *away* from that victory. You will know, at that point, what joy is inside you, and you will learn to love the Lord.

Next, we come to "Jesus Prays to Be Glorified." The hour has come to glorify your son, common sense. You must come to understand the meaning of the crucifixion that happened two thousand years ago. The crucifixion was meant to be an understanding of the value of heaven, where you have to pay a heavy price to receive the

Kingdom of God. It is not free like the Christians claim. You don't just believe in Jesus and that automatically saves you. The truth is that you have to go through the great persecution yourself in order to enter the Kingdom of God. You cannot enter the Kingdom of God without being crucified in the persecution of the world. The crucifixion of Jesus represents the suffering and the pain of the salvation of heaven. You have to go through that salvation with your own crucifixion by the hand of those who don't understand the Scriptures. You must be crucified in a way that each one of us has to go through this crucifixion of our own for salvation.

No man can enter heaven unless he has been crucified by those who don't understand the Scriptures. This is just like it was two thousand years ago. Each person was meant to go through this great persecution, which is the *stupidity* that the world has imposed upon the helpless. Jesus was a hopeless case according to the high priests of Israel. They could not change his mind or destroy his teaching, and they could not prove that his teaching was false. So Jesus was crucified by Herod and Pontius Pilate for *trying to wipe away the truth*. They could find *nothing wrong* with him, but they crucified him anyway.

Pontius Pilate washed his hands of the event. This means that *government* would wash its hands of all the wrong that religion does, and they will just brush it underneath the carpet. This is just like the little boys and girls who were molested by the priests. They just put it underneath the rug because government didn't care about the crimes of Catholic priests or any other religion that did wrong against another man or against the laws of God. They just brushed it away and let it go on until the twenty-first century when they had to do something about the evil of molesting children by religion.

No one was supposed to brush it away and make it look like it never happened and to let religion continue preaching stupidity and ignorance. That is the *real rape* of the children of God. They had a *false understanding* that was way outside the form of intelligence. They have *lied*, and they continue lying without any common sense of intelligence whatsoever by practicing seven sacraments that are way outside the form of intelligence. This is the real molestation and government has let them get away with it. You can take a man and baptize him in water all you want, but that is *stupidity*, not intelligence. You can take a man and say that this man has the power to forgive sins, but that also is not part of intelligence.

The human race believed that they were forgiven by the hand motion of a man and that is what lets them out of their sin. But the truth is that if you made a sin against someone, you have to go to that person and ask that person for forgiveness, *not* the priest. Then you have the *false confirmation*, where you confirm yourself as part of that evil religion of the physical part of nothing with laws that make no sense whatsoever. False religion makes people eat a piece of bread and tells them that this piece of bread is God. This makes *no sense* because a man-made hand motion over a piece of bread *cannot* turn it into God.

Then you have the *false marriage* of a man and a woman in front of the *false priest*. This is another falsehood that is just as worthless as the dust of the earth. Many people falsely believe that if you are not married, you are not supposed to have sex. Where is the common sense of intelligence here? Man believes that he has to be led by a priest (who is no better than he is), and be blessed into a wedding feast that doesn't make sense. Then you have the false priest himself. He is *supposed to be holy* in the sacraments of the order of priests. This is the most stupid thing that a man could ever imagine. A physical man who becomes a priest has no more power to understand the Scriptures than the common soul of the most ignorant man on earth.

Then you have *extreme unction*, or the last rites. The false preacher promises life after death if you receive this sacrament. But I tell you these false sacraments actually destroy intelligence. What made a human being so stupid as to teach and process such lies? The glory of the power of intelligence tells you that you cannot leave the center of intelligence to believe things that do not exist in reality and make them the truth. How can you make a religion out of all the falsehoods of the world and claim it's the truth? They made up the whole mess of nonsense and created false religion. They organized it with lies and made people step outside the form of intelligence by telling them that if they didn't believe this, they would all go to hell when they die. *This has to be the greatest sin on earth.* If there's a greater sin, I would like to see it.

What gave the right for any human being to step way outside the center of intelligence and call these falsehoods sacraments? The word *sacraments* means that it is *sacred* and cannot be changed. What does sacred mean to a liar who keeps lying to protect his ignorance and then fills the world with the most stupid things that you could ever imagine? The false preacher fooled you because you were ignorant and without the common sense of intelligence. If you believed in these lies, you tragically destroyed your soul with such lies that cannot and will not be forgiven that easily. The Scriptures tells us that for any man who spreads such lies in the world, it would be better off for them to tie a millstone around their neck and throw themselves in the deepest part of the sea.

There will never be another Babylon to take the place of the Catholic Church. You will see all false religion disappear from the face of the earth with your own eyes. They will be gone forever and ever, never to show up on earth ever again. The world will see the end of false religion because these lies were so huge, and mankind must learn to turn their stiff necks, bow down to the Lord, and ask Him to forgive them because they didn't know any better. They were taught by the people who claimed to know better than them, but these false preachers actually knew very little, if anything, of truth. If you wish to inherit the Kingdom of Heaven, find a resting place in what makes sense before it's too late.

Try to understand the *huge sin of religion*. This is the *forbidden tree* in the center of the Garden of Eden—the serpent on the tree that made Eve eat the apple and then give it to Adam. Ask the Lord your God to forgive you for being so stupid and so ignorant because you did not know any better. You did what you did because you *thought* you were serving God. But you were really serving the serpent on the tree of right and wrong. You were actually in between what was meant to be right and what was meant to be wrong. The justice of the Lord must come to be, and whoever worships falsely must be exposed through the power of right over wrong for the Lord's justice.

Now we go "Jesus Prays for his Disciples." Understand that the disciples of Jesus are your own disciples. The people who see the way you live, the way you talk, and the way you bring the truth to the light of mankind are your disciples. If you have bad disciples, it is because you have taught them badly and you're responsible for them. When we think of the twelve disciples of Jesus, we think that these are the only disciples. But you have your own disciples. These are the people that use your words and your information to guide their lives.

You must have a good teacher inside you to teach you what is good and *not* what is false. You must come to understand that what you teach to others around you must be within the teaching of truth. The words that you speak to other people must be understood in the truth itself. If you do not have this truth inside your spirit, you will just *repeat* what you heard from the priests, the pope, or any of the false prophets of the earth. Your disciples will come to understand in the same false way, and you are responsible for what your disciples come to believe. If you tell people to worship Jesus, your disciples will become *false prophets* like you are. Remember that this is your flock around you that you either inform with the truth or you lie to. And if what you tell your disciples is not the truth, then you are responsible for lying to them. These lies will come to trick you in your own understanding.

The Kingdom of God is the Kingdom of Intelligence where you believe in only one God. You *cannot* place the image of a man before the Lord and tell people to worship something that's not true. Love the Lord your God with all your soul, so He will give you the right words to say in your time of need. Your time of need will come for you to understand the truth and live with the truth itself. So do not inform your disciples to do wrong. If you don't value your words to be from the truth, you must come to understand that this will result in the loss of your soul.

Next, we go to "Jesus Prays for all Believers." The believers are your flocks. Your flocks are the people who live around you in the understanding of common sense. You cannot give all the power to Jesus. You have to give it to yourself because you have common sense inside of you. Use that common sense to understand the Word of

God. You are part of the flock that the Lord has placed around you. When you pray for your flock, you make the world around you a better place to live. If you believe in common sense as the real son of God, you are entering into the spirit of human understanding. But if you pray to Jesus, he is not God and he doesn't have the power of the Lord.

The power of the Lord is inside the Word, and the Word is God. The common sense that is inside of you is the understanding that you are in the spirit of the Lord. You have to learn to think differently than you do now. I have explained it to you in the best way that I can, but you have to work on it to understand it yourself. Praying to common sense is the *real son of God*. Reality and common sense is where the truth comes from, and if you pray to the image of a man, you will gain nothing. This does *not* help your brothers on earth. But when you pray to common sense and you pray to the value of all the understanding of common sense, you are praying into the Word of God. And when you pray to the word of God, you will be blessed with the power of the Lord your God. You cannot change that and say that the false prophet told me to believe in Jesus. Forget about the false prophet and believe in the Lord your God in the spirit of your human understanding.

Try to understand that the false prophet cannot tell you anything that is true because the Lord did not bless them with the truth and common sense. They don't understand how the spirit of the Lord works above them because God gave them nothing in true wisdom. They think they know, but they do not know. They are the people who preach the Word of God, but they don't know what the Lord is saying to them because they don't hear the Lord inside them. So how can they tell you what to believe in?

The false prophet has a notion of heaven but does not understand a word of what heaven really is. This is because the false prophet himself lives in darkness. All *false preachers* of all man-made organized religions *live in darkness*. They don't understand the Lord their God. God has given them nothing because they keep on worshipping the *image* of a man before the Lord. That is why God gave them nothing. The Word of God is to be *true* to the Lord. You cannot jump to another god anytime or anywhere you feel like it and worship the image of a man who lived two thousand years ago. Jesus was a good man, and I appreciate that he brought the Parables. But he was a *servant* of the Lord, *not* the son of God. The son of God is something in *spirit*, not something in the *physical* part of us. So how can he be the physical man that you make an image of and worship in front of the Lord your God? This is the best explanation that I can give you.

Now let us go to "Jesus Arrested." Try to understand the verb of the arrest of a human being. People judge others according to what they believe, but that doesn't mean they have judged others by the *facts* of life. How many people got arrested because they *looked* like someone who could have committed the crime even if they didn't? Or how many law enforcement officers arrest someone just for arresting *anybody* because they're searching for someone that they cannot find, so they just pick somebody and arrest them? This is the way it is in the world because people jump to conclusions and try to judge everybody.

If you see a man who doesn't look right to society, they will try to put him in jail and make him look bad. They will bring him in front of a court and accuse him of doing something that he never did. All of these are part of the lamb of God. These accused people feel so bad inside because they *know* they haven't committed this crime even though they have been accused of it. And the police are working extremely hard to make sure that they are convicted for that crime. In the past, forensics was not part of the system of arresting people. Today, with things like DNA evidence, it's a little different. But mankind is still quick to judge others without understanding the facts of the case.

Try to understand the person who everybody is judging to be a criminal even if they did not commit that crime. This is the power of the common sense of intelligence. Don't jump to conclusions inside your soul before you prove that they did the crime. These people are part of the lamb of God, and if you accuse them without knowing if they did the crime or not, you are accusing the lamb of God. This is the worst crime that you could ever commit in the eyes of God. Use common sense here to understand what I'm trying to tell you. The lamb of God is the people who have been accused of something that they did *not* do.

Try to understand the feelings of such a man and then you will understand the feelings of Jesus. He came to *bear witness to the truth*, and he was accused of sedition and messing up their phony little Jewish religion. The Lord let them get away with it, but He viciously punished them by making them practice false religion for two thousand years. What they imposed on Jesus was not true and whoever imposes such a crime on another man, the Lord will have no mercy on you. You will go to your tomb just for that one big crime in your life of being the police officer who misjudges a person and tries to keep him in contempt for your own feelings. This is where you must come to understand that the Lord is the truth. And it is *you* who will have to answer to God because you have falsely treated your brother and arrested him falsely.

You must come to understand that they took Jesus and judged him with their foolish little religion of their fantasy world. But they didn't know that they were bringing common sense to be judged falsely. They thought they were working for a good cause. People think they're working for the good side when they are actually working for Satan himself by doing the work that Satan (the lies of the world) likes to do. They fill themselves with evil in their heart by accusing someone of doing evil when they cannot find a single thing that is wrong. But they make up stuff that is not true so they can convince others of this false belief. That's the way it is with mankind. If someone thinks they have a case against another person, they bring all kinds of foolish lies against them to make them look evil. They are ready to punish this man for doing wrong, and they think that they're doing good in the eyes of the Lord. If you want to avoid being on the wrong side of the Lord's justice, make sure that everything you believe in your soul is within the boundaries of truth, common sense, and reality so you can cross over and live on the side of the Lord on the side of true justice for all of mankind.

Next, we go to "Peter's First Denial." Here, we are talking about false religion and what they did to bring their little fantasy religion in front of the tribunal of the court of the Lord. Peter represents the

Catholic Church and the rest of Christianity. It is man-made religion on earth that thinks it is okay to judge people. Religion is always telling mankind how righteous it is for them to judge people. But they are the *first ones to commit crimes* against the common sense of intelligence because they do not understand the Word of the Lord. The Lord thinks differently from mankind. Religion has tried to do God's thinking, and so they gave people like the pope the false power of being absolutely right in all of the decisions that he makes. According to this infallibility, anything he says is the truth that comes from the Lord. False religion makes people swallow this evil statement, and mankind believes that the pope has that false power. They make mankind believe that stupidity. In reality, the pope has less power than any homeless person living on the street.

The homeless have more power with their faith and their prayers than the pope, all the cardinals, archbishops, and priests have because the homeless deal *directly with God.* Anyone who is homeless on the street is part of the Lamb of God. When you come to understand the power of that truth, you live in reality. Understand that the pope and all the false preachers of organized religion are not living in reality. If you're homeless and living on the street, you only eat when somebody gives you something to eat. You have to be kind to people to get anything of any value. When you are a high person in the high place of religion, you have people who *serve* you, and you have everything that you need. These people, in their high places, have judged those who have nothing, but those who have nothing came to be higher than them.

The truth is within the power of reality, not where people raise themselves to be high above others. People who put their minds in front of their spirits think they are ahead of everybody when the reality is that they are so far behind with no way to restore themselves to the truth, common sense, and the reality of intelligence. They think they are big people in their big church, and they believe that they will be the first in line for heaven. They look at the homeless person on the street and they think that these people are so far behind from the Kingdom of God. But they will see the reality of truth come to life.

Those who put themselves first in the glory of heaven will find themselves placed at the end because there's no way that the Lord will accept you the way you are in a *false religion* preaching falsehoods with people and being honored by everyone around you. This is your flock—you and your flock have been deceived because you have deceived them. People thought you were great when you were actually so small. The poor person on the street whom you thought was so useless became the one in front of you. You have to step back and take your place behind every single one who comes and speaks for the flock. That is the justice of the Lord. What you claim to be in front will come to be so far behind, and the one you claim to be so far behind will be first at the finish line by the verity of truth.

Now we go to "The High Priest Questions Jesus." The Word of the Lord comes to us in a different way when we come to understand the power of the Scriptures and the way they are written. Try to understand that *the first will become last and the last will become first.* Understand well that in this teaching, the high priest stands for organized religion. This is just as true today as it was then. What was written then is what is going to happen *now* in the world. A human being was born to be poor, and another human was born to be rich. The values of both are counted for the reverse of the power of true wisdom. Those who claimed the position of high learner will become the poor instructor, and what they placed in great value becomes the value of nothing. Those who brought nothing into the world will become the ones who will be raised to the highest point.

Which one of them really understood the Lord—the one who had to pray for every scrap of food that came into his mouth, or the one that was served in front of everyone? Which one will be served the best food in the Kingdom of God—the one who had to pray for everything in life, or the one who never prayed for a single thing because everything was handed to him? Which one is going to be admitted to the kingdom of true intelligence? Which one will the Lord have compassion for, and which one will be put in charge of the treasure of the Kingdom of God—the one who had to sacrifice for everything that he has, or the one who condemned the poor in favor of the wealthy?

God set the sacrifice, but the wealthy one on earth didn't accept the sacrifice because he did not want to suffer. He wanted to have everything for himself. How hard it will be for those who have claimed the value for himself, and how easy it will be to enter the Kingdom of God for those who had to beg for every sacrifice that they ever received from the Lord. Now which one is which? I will leave it up to you to figure out the answer because the time has come for the common sense of intelligence to live inside each one of us.

Which one has been chosen by the Lord? The Lord asks each one of us this question, and the answer comes from *your own common sense*. This is why it is *so important* to develop your common sense instead of relying on some false preacher who has placed himself above you to give you the answer. *The Lord will prove the truth to you*, and you will see where both wrong and right stands to be. This is just like it was in the time of Cain and Abel where wrong killed right for creating the kingdom of common sense. You must answer the question in this parable so you can come to understand the way of the Lord.

Next, we come to "Jesus Before Pilate." The four kings of the world are the four subjects that mankind believes in the most. These four kings are religion, government, money, and business. Pontius Pilate represents *government*, which is the understanding of the laws of man. Understand that the crimes of yesterday by Pontius Pilate are the same as the crimes of today by the government of today. Pilate washed his hands of the crucifixion of Jesus. He could not find anything that Jesus did that violated any laws, but by washing his hands, he stayed out of it and allowed religion to crucify Jesus. That means that mankind would always wash their hands of the crucifixion of the Lamb of God and send someone to their death unfairly. They washed their hands and claimed that whoever was responsible, whether it was the police, the judge, or the jury, they did not do anything wrong. They were only sending a criminal to the justice of their mind, and they refused to take responsibility for it. This is just as it was in the time that Jesus lived. Everybody from Pontius Pilate, down the line to the soldiers and the people who condemned Jesus had something to do with the crucifixion. But all the people just washed their hands of it and refused to take the blame for their part.

To be condemned of a crime that you didn't commit has to bring *the most sadness of all* in the understanding of life. If a man spends twenty years in prison paying for a crime that he didn't do, the Lord's mercy will be upon that man. If he kept telling them that he did not commit this crime and nobody believes him, he becomes part of the Lamb of God. The man who was crucified by the laws of man and by the laws of religion is the Lamb of God. It is not only Jesus who is the Lamb of God but everyone who survives such crucifixions. The Lamb of God is looked at by mankind to be a lost soul, but their suffering is part of their salvation. No matter what they did in life, *they will be brought up to heaven* in the case of value against all wrongdoers for the justice of the Lord.

Understand well that *the tribunal of man is not accurate*. They cannot determine what is truly a crime and what is not. What if the policeman or the prosecutor did not like the person and planted evidence that would make an otherwise innocent person appear to be guilty? Each of these people must be prosecuted according to the laws of God and be placed outside of his kingdom because the Kingdom of God is *too important* for such people to be easily forgiven. The crime of their passion against their brother is so huge that even the Lord will have a hard time forgiving them.

The man who is not guilty of a crime must come in front of the Lord, kneel down in front of him, and state that he did not know what he was doing. He must ask the Lord for forgiveness, and that's the way it works. But if you are not sorry for what you have done—for example if you had the desire to kill someone and you did kill that person—you are just as bad as any criminal who has committed the worst crime in the kingdom of man. You are not allowed to wash your hands like Pontius Pilate and claim that you did it in the service of mankind to protect the life of others.

You wanted to be known as a good police officer, a good prosecutor, or a good judge, but you have performed an injustice above all. Do not wash your hands of what is wrong. If it's wrong, then you must use your office and your power to *uphold the truth*. If you don't uphold the truth, you will be very heavily punished. Things will not go right in your life, and you'll never be able to understand the truth because you have used your badge and your seat for condemning someone who has no power to fight you. Life will not be pleasant for you because you made people worship your own stupidity and ignorance. For that reason, you will have a hard time entering the Kingdom of God.

Now we go to "Jesus Sentenced to Be Crucified." This is the next part of the justice of the Lord. If you sentence someone to be punished for a crime he didn't commit, you are responsible for every part of it because the worst crime in life is to punish someone who didn't do anything wrong. It is horrible to take a man that you have never seen before and condemn him to death because you think it is your job. You try to enforce the law accordingly, but if you cut anything out of the truth, you are so guilty of sin that you cannot imagine the huge charge placed against you in the court of the Lord. What you did to your brother is what's going to happen to you in the *spiritual way* of being in prison in your own soul.

What you have done to others in flesh is the same justice that will happen to you in the spiritual value of the loss of your life. You have committed a crime, and you cannot be forgiven for it unless you repent. *Repent* means you have to go to this man that you have disliked in your heart of hate and you must do all that you can to make sure that he is *restored* to what his life was before your crime was committed. And anyone else that you hurt in the same manner, that hurt must be *imposed upon you* in the equal share in the justice of the Lord. No matter how hard you try to understand the Kingdom of God, you will not be able to understand because, remember, you were *blind* when you condemned your brother, and you still will not be able to see when the Lord condemns you.

Remember that whatever you have imposed on your brother, the same will be imposed on you for the forgiveness of your sins. If you think for one minute that the Lord will let you get away with it, you are *wrong* again, and you have understood the situation wrongly just as you did on your brother. The Lord is like a big computer, and everything that you do wrong to others must come back upon you.

The Lord must judge all of mankind according to what is done in the same value of the same crime.

Next, we go to "The Crucifixion of Jesus." This is the *great sin of religion.* Religion was guilty then, and every religion that came after was just as guilty. The Lord has proclaimed religion to be guilty because of the crucifixion of Jesus. The Lamb of God was crucified by religion and religion will be, themselves, crucified for the wrong that they have done in the crucifixion of common sense. If you were in any kind of a religion practicing the doctrine of the New Testament, and if you believe that you were saved by the crucifixion of Jesus in the Kingdom of God, what you believe is the *opposite of true intelligence.*

If you believe that you were saved by the death of Jesus, this means that you are actually lost by the same death of Jesus. *You placed your salvation on the death of a man on the cross.* How evil it is for you to believe such a claim. You see a man who has been sentenced to death for a cruel act, and you jump up in the air and claim the value of that victory, yet you see Jesus being condemned for a cruel act and you claim that this saves you? How ignorant can a human being be to proclaim such cruelty for himself at the expense of such pain on your brother? This means that you *agree* with the cruelty of the crucifixion of Jesus.

Understand the *purpose* of this where common sense had to be crucified. The Lord has planned this from the very beginning of the creation in order to make His Word become reality in the world of mankind. The crucifixion of common sense was needed for the prophecy of the Old Testament to be fulfilled. The Old Testament states that there was going to be a man who would be crucified by the hand of the evil mind of mankind for justice. *What is the purpose of justice?* It is to be able to understand why God created man to kill one another. There were so many wars and so many injustices that had to be lived so mankind would learn to live in the peace of His Kingdom for the reality of mankind.

Showing mankind the cruelty of the heart of humanity is how the Lord teaches the world to understand the power of the Creation and to live within that power to receive the glory of intelligence. Man will come to learn to be kind to one another because of the lessons of the past. The human race will see where the old understanding of wrong over right has led us. What happened there, at the beginning of the Creation, when Cain killed Abel, was the *purpose of the Lord* from the very beginning. The verb *wrong* would kill the verb *right*, and wrong would be first to the understanding of the Creation. This means that we would have to live out all the wrong so people would learn from wrong to become part of the Kingdom of doing right for each other.

It took some six thousand years to come to this point to bring man to the understanding of *how* to do what is right for each other. Man had to be introduced to wrong in order to understand right. To understand what is right, you must understand that any verb has two sides. And since wrong killed right at the beginning of the Creation, the human race was just cruel and wrong and could not understand anything right. This is why the crucifixion of Jesus was so important to understand what wrong is. Wrong is what happens when the human spirit loses its grip on reality and every single person becomes wrong and there is no right to understand in order to enter the Kingdom of God.

Now we go to "The Death of Jesus." As we come to understand the death of Jesus, we must understand the power of the three days of darkness. Common sense was meant to be crucified by religion on the face of the Earth because religion was the one to condemn Jesus. The same crime that they accused Jesus of is what was imposed on the false prophets of religion. Whatever was done by the hand of false religion will be done to false religion in the understanding of the power of the Lord your God. The same punishment had to be put on their heads for the purpose of this very day that we are coming to.

After three days of darkness, the world will come to find out that religion was *wrong* in stupidity and ignorance. They condemned Jesus of a crime, and they claimed he was lying, but they didn't understand the truth. The same thing happens with the religion of today. Jesus was the *servant* of God, and when you accuse a servant of God of doing wrong, *the same plague falls on you*. That's why all the people of false religion, from the preachers to the priests and everyone from the pulpit down to the lowest, they all practice falsehoods because it was the *high priest* who falsely accused and crucified Jesus. When the death of Jesus came to be so and he was crucified for a crime that he didn't commit, this means that the power of Jesus fell upon them. They were meant to worship Jesus in front of the Lord God.

Whatever was done two thousand years ago was meant to be for the three days of darkness. People would come to worship the *image* of a man before the Lord their God, and they would come to falsely accuse common sense by believing that Jesus was the one who was not telling the truth. If you do wrong, you do wrong, and it is this belief in wrong that cannot be changed that easily. Right now, the world of false preachers and all the people of false religion are preaching something that doesn't make sense and is *not part of true intelligence*. It does *not* make any sense, whatsoever, for a piece of bread to be the body of Christ. Nor does it make sense for a glass of water to baptize a child or that a man can forgive your sins with the motion of his hand. And it does *not* make any sense that a male and a female are married in front of the false prophet or that people go through the false confirmation. All they did was confirm themselves into the understanding of a false church.

The great power here is to understand that whatever religion accused Jesus of is what religion became the teacher of. What happened is that they live in the world of make-believe, and they try to offer seven sacraments that do not make sense, yet they think that they are on the side of the Lord. This is what Caiaphas believed two thousand years ago. He believed that he was working for the Lord, but he crucified a man because of his jealousy and stupidity.

In the last two thousand years, many false prophets have come and have tried to understand the Scriptures, but they cannot understand the Scriptures in truth because they don't stop worshipping Jesus and start worshipping God. Worshipping anyone in front of the Lord, including Jesus, will corrupt your mind where you could never understand the Scriptures. This started with the accusation against common sense by Caiaphas the high priest. Every generation would be in darkness, meaning without the true understanding of the Scriptures, for three days. This means two thousand years from the death of Jesus plus another thousand years of darkness will cover the world. Satan will be let loose to put the world in total darkness for another thousand years. Understand the prophecy of this. The death of Jesus tells us of the of the coming of the power that man would be crucified for worshipping Jesus in front of the Lord. When this day arrives, it will be *great pain and great suffering* for those who *impose* their teaching on the poor and the helpless. They are *responsible* for putting a false god before the eyes of mankind by teaching the fantasy of false religion.

Next, we go to "The Burial of Jesus." Understand well here that the world was buried in false religion, and they could not get out of it. This was done by the *hand of God* to punish the world of religion for the crucifixion of Jesus, who represents common sense. They did not understand the Parables of common sense in the New Testament, so they preached against it and crucified it. But the power of the Scriptures had to be proven by the revelation of time where mankind would come to learn the value of the truth.

What happened in the time of Jesus was *meant to be.* God made it happen exactly the way it did happen. And since Jesus was buried in the tomb, it was meant to be that people would go in the tomb in their churches, made with bricks, thinking that they are praising the Lord and receiving a blessing from Him. They worship the image of a dead man in the tomb that they call a *church*, give money to their false church, and bring themselves to believe in this false god *because the Lord has punished mankind for the wrong of religion.* It was said from the very beginning of the Creation, in the Garden of Adam and Eve, *not* to touch the reason of right and wrong. But religion did not listen to a single word, and they became the children of worshipping false gods because of the crucifixion and burial of Jesus.

Those who believed in falsehoods and thought they were on the side of the Lord had to be punished for what they believed against the Lord. Those who thought they would be first to enter the Kingdom of God *will be the last* because the teaching tells you that whatever happens to the people of this world was meant to happen for the stupidity and ignorance of mankind. The Lord took Adam and Eve and He put them into a *paradise of intelligence*, but there was one tree at the center of the garden that they were not allowed to eat its fruit. That tree was *religion*. Religion was not allowed to be tampered with.

The people who turn away and do not accept religion because it is a fantasy world, are the ones who will receive the Kingdom of God. Be careful to do no wrong, judge no one, and you will not be judged. If you judge others, think that you are a good person in front of everybody else and you have the right to persecute others, you will be tricked by the Lord and brought to a place where you don't want to be. But if you *repent* of your sin and try to change your ignorance of religion into an understanding of truth, the Lord will give you the true wisdom of the Scriptures. Religion is not holy and will *never* be holy. You are not supposed to organize religion and make a teaching of your own in front of the Word of the Lord. You have to come and understand the Scriptures *in truth* before you can preach anything on the Scriptures. And if you understand the Scriptures in truth, you will come to know how false organized religion is. Anyone who preaches the Scriptures from inside organized religion has proven how little they actually know of the Scriptures.

Now we go to "The Empty Tomb." This will happen as it was meant to be. People will go to the cave on Sunday morning to find if the Lord is there, but the tomb will be *empty*. Try to understand the glory of intelligence here. The Laws of God will be lived exactly as they were written. People would keep on believing in the false church by worshipping false gods. What you are supposed to do is to worship God inside the sanctuary inside your spirit. You are supposed to worship the Lord your God with the understanding that there is only one God and you cannot worship the image of a man before the Lord.

If you worship Jesus, you are worshipping a false god, and that is a terrible thing to do. The tomb is *empty* because of your sin. The body is not there because you did not understand that Christ is common sense. If you want to believe in the *real* Christ, you have to believe in the real son of God, which is common sense. If you believe in the stupidity and the ignorance of religion, you will be in that cave every Sunday morning and you will try to pray to save your soul. But you will not be able to understand the Lord your God in the spirit of intelligence that you were created with.

The tomb is *empty*, yet people go there to worship *every* Sunday morning. Some go almost every day to try to find the Lord so they would be the first one to enter heaven by praying to their Jesus. But you did not understand that you buried him two thousand years ago, and that tomb is empty because the power of the Lord took Jesus out of the tomb. If you worship Jesus, you worship and offer your sacrifice to a *false god*. That's not going to work in the kingdom of the Lord your God.

Next, we go to "Jesus Appears to Mary Magdalene." Understand the part of the prostitute. What is a *prostitute* in spiritual understanding? It is a person who sells their soul to someone other than the One True God of Abraham, Isaac, and Jacob. The church that believes in the image of a man has prostituted themselves to understand the image of that man. They have turned their heads *against* God, and they became prostitutes. Every single organized religion of the world has prostituted themselves by believing in man instead of believing in the God of truth, common sense, and reality. If you worship in the tomb on Sunday morning and offer your sacrifice to a man, you prostitute yourself in the understanding of your spiritual value.

I don't know if I explained it right, but what I do know is that if you prostitute yourself, it means that you bow down to the understanding of the image of a man before the Lord your God. And to worship that image is forbidden by the Commandments of our Lord is to prostitute yourself by the power of falsehood. Understand the glory of intelligence here. God has planned this whole disaster on the world, and if you want to repent of your sin, you must start worshipping the Lord your God. If you want to repent of your sin, you must start worshipping the Lord your God. If you want to continue to turn away from the Lord, that's up to you. But if you do, you will not be part of the Kingdom of the Lord your God. If you are angry that the Lord has brought these things to pass, then you don't really understand the teaching of the Scriptures. That is why you cannot understand and live in the power of the Scriptures and the understanding of reality.

Jesus appeared to the prostitute—I'm not talking about Mary Magdalene here. I'm talking about_*the church*. To understand this story of Jesus and the prostitute, you have to learn to sin no more. You cannot prostitute yourself by worshipping false gods because that's *adultery*. You have condemned people for having sex with each other, but adultery is the sin of the prostitute who worships someone who is *not* God. You offer your sacrifices to that false god, and that is a great sin in the eyes of the Lord. You cannot do that because the Lord is inside you as part of the great glory of the understanding of reality.

Where is the Lord your God in the understanding of the great prostitute? If you believe that God is in the *tabernacle* in your false church, you are worshipping the prostitute, and you will be heavily punished by the Lord. Learn the truth and start worshipping the Lord your God. Jesus came into the world to make sure that people worship God and God alone. But religion twisted things to understand that Jesus is God, and that is absolutely false in the great power of the Lord your God. When you judge people who do not believe in your religion, you are judging yourself. Try to worship one God above all, and worship him as the Lord of all Creation in the common sense of intelligence.

Now we go to "Jesus Appears to His Disciples." The meaning of this is that the power of the Scriptures is inside us to understand the glory of intelligence. Like I told you before, the disciples of Jesus are your disciples in your own life. Your family and your friends are your disciples. Everybody that surrounds you are your disciples. When you appear to them, make sure that you tell them that there is no other God but God and that you cannot worship Jesus in front of the Father of intelligence because it's a great sin. Make sure you tell them the truth. You cannot fabricate anything, and you cannot say that you went to church last week and you prayed to Jesus.

If you pray to Jesus, you are praying to a false god, and what will happen is *backward* from what you want to happen. Try to understand that when God blesses you with a blessing it is actually a curse on you. When you think you have been blessed by the Lord for worshipping a false god (i.e., Jesus), you are really under the Lord's curse.

God is the power of the truth, common sense, and reality inside of you for the great power of the spirit of the Lord your God. Those who worship in the truth and refuse to go to church on Sunday because they think man-made religion is a lot of nonsense and hogwash that makes no sense, those are *prophets* of the Lord. Those are the people who tell you they don't believe in what you preach because you're not speaking with the voice of the Lord, and you're not obeying the power of the Scriptures of the Lord. They don't go to your church because you're not doing what you are supposed to do, which is to bless the Lord your God with all your soul.

When you are in front of your friends and families, just tell the *truth*. Be simple like a simple person and just say "I believe in God" and that's it. All you need to do is to believe in the Lord your God. The Christians will tell you that you have to believe in Jesus in order to enter the Kingdom of God, but that's a *falsehood*. You cannot trust the words of the false prophet because their words are not the truth. The truth is the simple power of the reality of mankind. God fooled the world by making Jesus look like he was God, and mankind tricked himself by believing what they want to believe. The Lord makes you believe what your intention is to believe.

If your intention is to believe in a false god, then the Lord will make you start worshipping false gods and false things. That is a great sin in front of the Lord. You cannot imagine what you are doing to yourself when you go to church on Sunday and worship a man before the Lord your God. If you only understood that all your misery, pain, and suffering in your life happens because you are guilty of sin. You have to turn away from your sin and meet your disciples in the new understanding of the truth.

Next, we go to "Jesus Appears to Thomas." Now we are coming to an understanding of the *non-believer*. These are the people who have to see in order to believe. You may think of Thomas as a hard-headed man, but understand that he had to see and feel to understand. After he saw and felt, he understood. Thomas is a disciple of the Lord, but he had a *different faith* from the other disciples. Understand that you cannot worship the image of a man before the Lord your God, and you cannot offer sacrifices to anyone but the

Lord because it tells you in the Old Testament that if you worship a false god, then things will not go right for you and you will come to understand the emptiness of your feelings.

Thomas was *empty of feelings* and could not understand, so he said, "Unless I see it, I cannot believe." Then he saw it, and he believed. This is how the false prophet works. If you don't believe in their Jesus, they make it appear to you in the value of what is not the truth. They make up an understanding for themselves so people believe in what the false prophet tells them to believe. They throw their entire spirit into that false faith. Try to understand how important it is for them to believe in Jesus just like Thomas had to see to believe.

People go to church and see all these false miracles from the false prophet, but now, the relief is coming in the form of a crackdown on stupidity and ignorance like there's never been in the history of mankind. Putting your faith in a man in front of the Lord is the *worst faith* you can ever have. They worship Jesus, and they have inflamed their minds even worse because of the false prophets.

Remember that Jesus said many false prophets will appear and they will fool many people. The false prophet fooled people so they could make money because all their big huge churches are beautiful buildings, built with stones and precious metals from the earth. Everything is *physical*, and it comes from the physical understanding of the words of God, which is on the side of *falsehood*. When a man worships another man, it creates a beautiful church of human understanding where Jesus looks like he is god. They're the first ones to worship Jesus, and you will become one of them by worshipping in the falsehoods of religion. Worshipping any man in front of the Lord is what the Lord tells you *not* to do.

Now we go to "Jesus and the Miraculous Catch of Fish." Understand that Peter represents the Catholic Church and Christianity. The heads of these religions would have a big catch of fish that would fall for their stories. When the catch of fish comes to be, you will see the glory of the Lord your God in that beautiful catch of fish that comes from the understanding of reality. There are over two billion people who believe in Christianity and the Catholic

Church. Both churches worship Jesus in front of the Lord your God, and they all perform the practice of the prostitute in the understanding of a false god, the image of a man who lived two thousand years ago.

They put the serpent on all kinds of posts in front of their churches. Everybody has a cross in their house that represents the bronze serpent in the desert with Moses and the understanding of the Old Testament. Try to understand the *power of the serpent* on the post in every single religion in the world of Christianity. Every church has a cross in front of it, and if you believe in that cross, you believe in the serpent because it's a lie. There is no devil the way mankind believes a man with horns and a pitchfork. But there is the devil in the form of the lies of the world, and these people spend billions of dollars to worship this cross in *front* of the Lord. They think they are worshipping the One True God, but they are actually worshipping the *image* of a man inside of the physical part of themselves. I don't know why these people are so stupid and arrogant, but the Lord made them that way. It is his plan to destroy those who speak differently from the truth and make images appear in front of man and call those images the Lord God.

So many fish are born to be fish and float in the oceans with no purpose. What is a fish in the ocean? It's a fish that swims around and has no purpose of human understanding. These fish will come to the destruction of themselves at the end of their life, only to produce another fish, and life goes on where no one has any understanding of the Lord's Creation and the value of intelligence. *God is the truth* and you must worship him in the sanctuary of the Lord, not in the sanctuary of a man.

Next, we go to "Jesus Reinstates Peter." The teaching of the Lord tells us that the Catholic Church and Christianity will be reinstated. This is the last part of the book of John. The great power of the truth that has come inside of me to bring this book to the reality and the salvation of mankind is to understand that only common sense can save mankind in the reality of truth. The common sense of intelligence was brought forth to the understanding of the great power that God is the truth and the truth is God by the understanding of common sense and reality.

All that is true must be real, and all that is true must be in common sense. Therefore, you must understand the power that I have brought to you to understand this great teaching that will bless you into the Kingdom of the Lord. In this book, I did not attack anyone directly. I have only attacked the falsehood of mankind and the wrong that mankind is doing in *organized religion*. I have only brought to the light of mankind the reality of the great miracle of what God is in the situation of right over wrong. I have tried to help you understand what to do to enter the Kingdom of God that is upcoming and to read these words in the truth so the power of the truth can come inside of you and make you ritually clean.

Cleanse your soul of all the infractions against reality and common sense, and make yourself holy in the eyes of the Lord so you can come to understand life itself inside your spirit. I wrote this book for the value of all of mankind, and I did it for life on earth for all mankind to come in the blessing of common sense and the power of reality to understand the truth of the Father of heaven that is inside of you. Come to understand the *glory* of that intelligence. Thank you, and God bless you all.

*****

ABOUT THE AUTHOR

I am Roger Akerley. I was born the last of seven children in 1947 in St. Leonard, New Brunswick, Canada. I grew up as a member of the Catholic church, and due to the circumstances of my family, I left school after the fifth grade and went to work. I came to the United States at 17 years old in 1964. I have read the Bible for my entire life, and I have always had the feeling that anyone, regardless of their level of education or ability, could learn the true meaning of the scriptures for themselves. In my lifelong struggles of learning, I have had to learn the English language as well as adapting to a new country as I became a US citizen. I believe that the Lord has revealed the true meaning of the scriptures to me, and he has asked me to inform mankind of this understanding. I have accepted this responsibility for the purpose of increasing the knowledge of humanity. The sacrifices of both learning this great wisdom as well as passing it along to the human race are what I have humbly endured as my gift to my fellow man for posterity.